TRADE DISPUTES AND THE DISPUTE SETTLEMENT UNDERSTANDING OF THE WTO: AN INTERDISCIPLINARY ASSESSMENT

FRONTIERS OF ECONOMICS AND GLOBALIZATION

6

Series Editors:

HAMID BELADI
University of Texas at San Antonio, USA

E. KWAN CHOI
Iowa State University, USA

FRONTIERS OF ECONOMICS AND GLOBALIZATION VOLUME 6

TRADE DISPUTES AND THE DISPUTE SETTLEMENT UNDERSTANDING OF THE WTO: AN INTERDISCIPLINARY ASSESSMENT

Edited by

James C. Hartigan

Department of Economics, University of Oklahoma, Norman, OK, USA

Emerald

United Kingdom – North America – Japan
India – Malaysia – China

Emerald Group Publishing Limited
Howard House, Wagon Lane, Bingley BD16 1WA, UK

First edition 2009

British Library Cataloguing in Publication Data
A catalogue record for this book is available from the British Library

ISBN: 978-1-84855-206-7
ISSN: 1574-8715

LIST OF CONTRIBUTORS

Andrew G. Brown	P.O. Box 1763, Wellfleet, MA 02667, USA
James H. Cassing	Department of Economics, University of Pittsburgh, Pittsburgh, PA 15260, USA
Indranil Chakraborty	Department of Economics, National University of Singapore, Singapore 117570
Pao-Li Chang	School of Economics, Singapore Management University, 90 Stamford Road, Singapore 178903
David Epstein	Department of Political Science, Columbia University, New York, NY 10027, USA
Wilfred J. Ethier	Department of Economics, University of Pennsylvania, Philadelphia, PA 19104-6297, USA
James C. Hartigan	Department of Economics, University of Oklahoma, Norman, OK 73019-2103, USA
Henrik Horn	Research Institute for Industrial Economics, Box 55665, SE-102, 15 Stockholm, Sweden
Leslie Johns	Department of Political Science, UCLA, Los Angeles, CA 90095, USA
Tim Josling	Freeman Spogli Institute, Encina Hall, Stanford University, Stanford, CA 94305, USA
Mitsuo Matsushita	Nagashima, Ohno, Tsunematsu, Kioicho Building 3-12, Kioicho, Chiyoda-Ku, Tokyo 102-0094, Japan
Petros C. Mavroidis	Parker Professor, School of Law, Columbia University, 435 W 116th Street, New York, NY 10027, USA
Bryan Mercurio	Faculty of Law, Professor, The Chinese University of Hong Kong, Sha Tin, NT, Hong Kong SAR

Sharyn O'Halloran George Blumenthal Professor and Professor of International and Public Affairs, Columbia University, New York, NY 10027, USA

Joseph Pelzman Department of Economics, The Elliott School of International Affairs, George Washington University, 2115 G Street NW, Washington, DC 20052, USA

Kara M. Reynolds Department of Economics, American University, 4400 Massachusetts Avenue NW, Washington, DC 20016, USA

B. Peter Rosendorff Department of Politics, New York University, New York, NY 10012, USA

Gregory Shaffer Melvin C. Steen Professor of Law, University of Minnesota Law School, Minneapolis, MN 55455, USA

Amir Shoham School of Business Administration, College of Management, Rishon LeZion 75190, Israel

Robert M. Stern Department of Economics and Gerald R. Ford School of Public Policy, University of Michigan, 735 S. State Street, Ann Arbor, MI 48109-3091, USA

Naboth van den Broek Wilmerhale, 1875 Pennsylvania Avenue NW, Washington, DC 20006, USA

Amy L. Widsten Department of Political Science, Columbia University, New York, NY 10027, USA

Sebastian Wilckens Department of Economics, University of Kiel, Wilhelm-Seelig Platz 1, 24098 Kiel, Germany

CONTENTS

INTRODUCTION

James C. Hartigan

Department of Economics, University of Oklahoma, Norman, OK 73019–2103, USA
E-mail address: hartigan@ou.edu

A principle reason for the inability of the General Agreements on Tariffs and Trade (GATT) to serve as the vehicle for international trade liberalization was that it was the protocol for the establishment of the International Trade Organization. It was never intended to become a functioning institution. As such, it did not have a well-designed system for the settlement of trade disputes. At least partially because the GATT was not intended to function as an institution, an arguably excessive reliance on consensus emerged as the vehicle for the resolution of trade disputes. A consensus to accept the recommendations of a dispute panel became the standard for resolution under the GATT. Because the defendant could always object to implementation of the panel's recommendation, thus denying consensus, successful resolution of disputes were relatively infrequent. In the 47 years, during which the GATT was the principle international trade forum, 101 panel reports were adopted. Given that it is possible to file disputes on the basis of nullification and impairment of expected benefits, which is a considerably weaker standard than the allegation of a legal breach, it is apparent that the ineffectiveness of the dispute resolution mechanism was a deterrent to the filing of complaints. As the GATT increased in membership and pressures to address increasingly complex trade issues (intellectual property rights and agricultural subsidies, for example) emerged, it became apparent that the GATT could be undermined by an inability to resolve disputes.

The negotiation of a unified Dispute Settlement Understanding (DSU) for the World Trade Organization (WTO) was a primary achievement of the Uruguay Round of the GATT, which concluded in 1994. Foremost amongst the changes to dispute resolution attained through the DSU was the adoption of reverse consensus, or a consensus against the adoption of a panel report. This precluded the blocking of a panel report by the defendant in a complaint. As an indicator of the success of the DSU, consider that 378 disputes were filed from January of 1995 through June 20 of 2008. With an increase in the number of disputes, comes an increase in interest in the analysis of dispute resolution. In fact, it can be argued that serving as a referee for disputes is becoming as important as the negotiation of trade liberalization in the current and future roles of the WTO.

Despite the achievements of the DSU, there remain many disagreements, and many opportunities for academic investigation. First, the preference on the part of the DSU for consultation and resolution through negotiation. This creates a tension between settlement and compliance, as the outcome of settlement may not be consistent with obligations under the negotiating rounds of the WTO. Second, the continued allowance for disputes on the basis of nullification and impairment, as a signatory cannot be required to reform a policy that is not a violation. Third, the priority for settlement, rather than the passing of legal judgement may leave important questions of international law unaddressed. An increasingly important realization is that of the failure of the DSU to serve the interests of less developed countries, particularly the poorest amongst them. This has attracted proposals for reform, as well as, scholarly evaluation of their efficiency, rationality, and fairness. The various subagreements underpinning the WTO, such as, the antidumping, sanitary and phytosanitary, and subsidies and countervailing duties have attracted their own analysis pertaining to disputes. The interface of the DSU with dispute settlement (DS) under preferential trading areas is a topic of recent interest. In addition, there is the provision for the losing member to have a reasonable period to bring its offending policy into conformity with the ruling of a panel, and to interpret the ruling in the context of its public policy. That is, to choose how to bring its policy into compliance.

When this is not possible, the disputants enter negotiations to determine mutually acceptable compensation. If agreement cannot be reached, permission from the WTO to impose sanctions is requested. When an agreement is reached or sanctions are authorized, the WTO monitors compliance. Compliance and remedies are fertile material for scholarship.

As the DSU of the WTO is only in its fifteenth year, there is much to learn as to its functioning and achievements. Nonetheless, there is a richness of material to be analyzed. What's more, the analysis of disagreement is a natural purview of legal scholarship, and as mentioned earlier, there were 101 panel reports adopted under the GATT. In addition, the deficiencies of the dispute resolution mechanism under the GATT have received considerable discussion. Thus, there is a corpus of legal scholarship of reasonable size on trade disputes in existence. This is much less the case in the profession of economics. There was little peer-reviewed scholarship appearing in economics journals before 2000. (I am aware of three papers in the 1990s, two of which were published at the end of that decade.) However, dispute resolution is now beginning to attract the attention of economists. As there are substantial numbers of scholars in international trade and international trade law, the two professions share an interface. What's more, this interface is shared with political science. The emerging interest in disputes on the part of economists, and the ongoing interest on the part of legal scholars and political scientists, has the potential to provide an interesting interplay among the professions. An objective of this proposed volume is to stimulate cross-fertilization of these professions. This approach was successful in the *Handbook of International Trade, vol. II: Economic and Legal Analyses of Trade Policy and Institutions*, which I coedited with E. Kwan Choi and was published by Blackwell in 2005. That volume was more general than this volume, and contained contributions by scholars from economics and law.

The volume is partitioned into five subareas. The first pertains to the process of dispute resolution and appeal under the DSU of the WTO. The initial chapter by Henrik Horn and Petros Mavroidis provides a thorough descriptive discussion of member's participation as complainants and respondents in the DS system. Participants are classified into four income groups, with their activity and success compared and contrasted. Additional discussion pertains to disputes transpiring under the various subagreements of the treaty establishing the WTO. The second chapter, by Andrew Brown and Robert Stern, addresses the issue of fairness in the resolution of trade disputes, an increasingly important issue in the criticism of globalization. They begin with a consideration of what constitutes fairness in trade relations. In particular, they evaluate the major disputes from the perspective of equity arising in the context of three primary categories: fair competition, contingent measures, and the nexus of regulation and trade. They conclude by considering fairness in remedies for noncompliance. The establishment of the possibility for appeal is considered one of the most important achievements of the DSU. In the third chapter, Petros Mavroidis addresses the Appellate Body of the DSU, beginning with a discussion of its role. He then evaluates its record, concluding that its panels have been generally risk averse and textualist in approach. He concludes with proposals for reform. Pao-Li Chang develops a two-sided (complainant and respondent) asymmetric information model of the dispute process in the fourth chapter. She contrasts the incentives to block and to appeal panel reports under the GATT with that of the DSU, and compares the resulting equilibria of the two regimes.

As disputes are amongst and between sovereign nations and are embellished by politics, the second section will address politics and disputes. The section begins with the interface of domestic politics and trade disputes in a chapter authored by David Epstein, Sharyn O'Halloran, and Amy Widsten. Motivating their empirics by a model of incomplete information regarding costs of evasion of a judgment, they invoke a Heckman selection estimator to address three hypotheses. These are (1) the probability of winning a dispute is higher for a liberal government, (2) early settlement is more probable with a conservative government, and (3) adverse decisions are implemented less frequently by a liberal government. The sixth chapter continues with a discussion of domestic politics and trade disputes. Leslie Johns and B. Peter Rosendorff begin with a critique of the application to this topic of the infinitely repeated prisoners' dilemma, demonstrating that it does not replicate the historical record. They contend that the state should not be viewed as a unitary actor, and that domestic politics creates a demand for trade violations, and a punishment mechanism for violations of agreements.

The third section considers power inequities in access to the DSU. Gregory Shaffer authored the initial chapter with a compelling argument that legal capacity is as important as market power in successful participation in the DSB. He contends that participation matters particularly where jurisprudence affects interpretation and social perception of the law, creating a systemic effect. This effect imbues domestic political bargaining over a potential case. In Chapter 8, Kara Reynolds observes that a third of registered trade disputes are classified as pending or inactive. She estimates a binary choice probit of the complainant's decision not to pursue a filing. Her primary result underscores the allegation of power imbalances in the WTO: less developed countries are less able to resolve disputes successfully. In the final chapter of this section, Sebastian Wilckens motivates a model of power considerations in dispute resolution by a sequential game. He then estimates a probit model, with a novel sample selection criterion, of the decision as whether or not to litigate. He finds support for the hypothesis that size, including retaliatory capacity, matters.

The fourth section considers specific categories of disputes, such as in agriculture and antidumping. The initial chapter is by Tim Josling, considering agricultural disputes in international trade. He observes that agriculture accounts for a disproportionate share of trade disputes, and expresses pessimism regarding prospects for this changing. The basis for litigation is broad, encompassing market access, subsidies, safeguards, and health and safety. He conducts a detailed analysis of the salient cases under the Uruguay Round Agreement on Agriculture (URAA). The ensuing chapter in the section is written by Mitsuo Matsushita, and it addresses disputes pertaining to the safety of food products. He engages in legal analysis of all articles and agreements that have an impact on food safety. Particular emphasis is given to Article XX, the Sanitary and Phytosanitary Agreement (SPS), and the Technical Barriers to Trade Agreement (TBT). James Cassing, in the 12th chapter, explores the conflicts that arise from "forum shopping" when regional trade agreements include DS procedures. He explains that advanced economies can exploit power asymmetries more readily in RTAs than in the more diffused WTO. So as to deter less developed members from utilizing the more equitable DSU of the WTO, Cassing discloses that advanced economies have an incentive to weaken DS procedures under the WTO. This, in turn, limits commitments that members are willing to make. The final chapter in this section is authored by James Hartigan, discussing disputes arising under the Antidumping Agreement (ADA) of the WTO. He contends that the purpose of the ADA is to address adverse shocks in import competing industries. He contends that protection consistent with the ADA should be regarded as weakly cooperative, rather than as a defection from free trade in an infinitely repeated prisoners' dilemma. The purpose of the DSU, in his framework, is to ensure that members adhere to proper procedure in the investigation of shocks, and to preclude countries from abusing the consensus of what constitutes a shock.

The fifth partition considers compliance, enforcement, and remedies. The initial chapter is authored by Wilfred Ethier, which provides a bridge between this section and the second grouping. He presents a formal general equilibrium model of trade. He then imbeds lobbying and derives a noncooperative equilibrium. In view of the recent empirical literature addressing the proliferation of antidumping laws, he establishes that countervailing duty laws arise endogenously, and are not a result of trade agreements. He portrays trade agreements as an exchange of market access, and recommends that signatories permit breach if there is no retreat from reciprocity. He notes that this provides justification for an underpinning of the GATT, that of the withdrawal of equivalent concessions. The subsequent chapter is authored by Joseph Pelzman and Amir Shoham. As a means of improving compliance, they suggest interpretation of WTO agreements as binding contracts with a liability rule, the breach of which should be evaluated as efficient or inefficient. Their remedy is a (monetary) fine. In reviewing several recent cases in which eliciting compliance was problematic, they establish that the current system of emphasizing negotiated settlement with authorized retaliation in the absence of adherence to a DSB judgment underscores a conflict between settlement and compliance. Bryan Mercurio contributes the following chapter, in which he considers alternatives to retaliation by the complainant as enforcement mechanisms. In his thorough critique, he raises the important question of what are the objectives of the DSU? He notes that any proposal to introduce retrospective compensation must solve the problem of it being voluntary. As such, retaliation remains an essential component of compliance instruments. Although monetary compensation would not be distorting of trade, Mercurio contends that it would be likely to reduce compliance. Naboth van den Broek focuses on eliciting compliance for disputes that are or may be filed by the least developed of the WTO signatories. In doing so, he identifies a fundamental contradiction: the DSU system of compliance enforcement attempts to overcome power-based international relations, while relying on the economic power of the complainant state to enforce panel judgments. He contends that the failure of the DSU to achieve equity for the least developed undermines their liberalization of trade. His novel proposal is for limited direct effect for LDCs. Direct effect refers to the application of the rights and obligations of an international agreement to the domestic legal order, and whether or not these rights can be invoked before domestic courts by aggrieved parties. The volume and section concludes with a chapter by Indranil Chakraborty and James C. Hartigan, devising a model of compliance in which members form interpretations of their obligations. A dispute arises when these interpretations differ. The DSB determines the correct interpretation. The authors contrast retrospective punishment, prospective punishment, and retrospective penalties reinforced by retaliation. They conclude that compliance as well as the willingness to make and accept concessions is likely to be strongest with a simple retaliatory mechanism.

In addition to the interdisciplinary focus, I have sought two other dimensions of balance. One is to include established and emerging scholars. The other is to include perspectives from many different countries and regions.

I anticipate that such a volume will be purchased by both law libraries and general interest academic libraries. It should also be purchased by research institutions, as well as, the libraries of government and international organizations to which it is germane. Finally, individual scholars in dispute resolution or those wishing to enter this avenue of research are potential purchasers. It may serve as a supplemental text for some courses.

PART I

A Critical Discussion of the Process of Dispute Resolution and Appeal at the WTO

CHAPTER 1

The WTO Dispute Settlement System 1995–2006: Some Descriptive Statistics

Henrik Horn[a] and Petros C. Mavroidis[b]

[a]*Research Institute for Industrial Economics, Box 55665, SE-102, 15 Stockholm, Sweden*
E-mail address: henrik.horn@ifn.se
[b]*Parker Professor, School of Law, Columbia University, 435 W 116th Street, New York, NY 10027, USA*
E-mail address: pmavro@law.columbia.edu

Abstract

The purpose of this chapter is to report some initial findings based on the WTO Dispute Settlement Data Set (Ver. 2.0) that the authors have compiled for the World Bank. The data set contains approximately 28 000 observations on the workings of the Dispute Settlement system. It covers all 351 WTO disputes initiated through the official filing of a *Request for Consultations* from January 1, 1995, until October 25, 2006; and for these disputes it includes events occurring until December 31, 2006. Each dispute is followed through its legal life via the panel stage, the Appellate Body stage, to the implementation stage.

The descriptive statistics in the chapter points to three observations. The first and obvious observation is the almost complete absence of least developed countries. Second, less poor and developing countries are much more active and successful than the authors would have expected. Third, the EU and the United States dominate less than expected, being much more often the subject of complaints, than a complaining party, and they have a very low share of all panelists.

Keywords: WTO, dispute settlement, developing countries

JEL classifications: F13, F53, O19

1. Introduction

The purpose of this chapter is to report some initial findings based on the WTO Dispute Settlement Data Set (Ver. 2.0) that we have compiled for

Frontiers of Economics and Globalization
Volume 6 ISSN: 1574-8715
DOI: 10.1108/S1574-8715(2009)0000006004

the World Bank.[1] The data set contains approximately 28 000 observations on the workings of the Dispute Settlement (DS) system. It covers 351 WTO disputes initiated through the official filing of a *Request for Consultations* from January 1, 1995, until October 25, 2006, and for these disputes it includes events occurring until December 31, 2006.[2] We have used exclusively official WTO documents. The data have been collected for the purpose of promoting research on various aspects of the WTO.

To shed some light on differences across WTO Members as far as their participation in the DS system is concerned, we will group the Members into four groups (Table 1):

- G2: the European Community (EC) and the United States;
- IND: other industrialized countries;
- DEV: developing countries other than least developed countries;
- LDC: least developed countries.

The group G2 needs no further explanation, except that we counted EC-15 as one of its two constituent members.[3] The LDC group corresponds largely to the list of LDCs according to the United Nations. A more discretionary line is drawn between IND and DEV. We have here classified Organization for Economic Cooperation and Development (OECD) Member under IND; we have also classified under IND, non-OECD Members who have become members of the EC, or are at an advanced stage of their accession negotiations. Finally, under IND we have also classified countries that are not OECD members but have a very high per capita income, for example, countries such as Singapore. The DEV group consists of all countries that do not fit into either of the categories mentioned earlier.

The chapter is structured as follows: Section 2 discusses some aspects of participation of the groups defined earlier in dispute proceedings, when acting as complainants or respondents. Section 3 deals with the subject matter of disputes. Section 4 highlights a few aspects of countries' success with regard to the legal claims they made before panels. Section 5 provides information as to the nationality and the appointment process of WTO panelists. Section 6 focuses on the duration of DS procedures at different stages of the adjudication process. Section 7 deals with a brief conclusion.

In what follows, we reflect some *very* preliminary and partial observations stemming from a first look at the data. We neither claim to

[1] The data can be downloaded from www.worldbank.org/trade/wtodisputes.

[2] These correspond to disputes DS1–DS351, according to the number given to the dispute by the WTO Secretariat when a *Request for Consultation* is filed.

[3] Twelve additional countries acceded the EU up until 2006, but at such a late stage that they have not been included in our definition of "EC".

Table 1. Country classification

G2	*LDC*	*DEV*		
EC	Angola	Albania	India	Tanzania
US	Bangladesh	Antigua and Barbuda	Indonesia	Thailand
	Benin	Argentina	Jamaica	Trinidad and Tobago
	Burkina Faso	Armenia	Jordan	Tunisia
IND	Burundi	Bahrain	Kenya	United Arab Emirates
Australia	Cambodia	Barbados	Kuwait	Uruguay
Bulgaria	Central Afr. Rep	Belize	Kyrgyz Republic	Venezuela
Canada	Chad	Bolivia	Macao-China	Zimbabwe
Croatia	Dem. Rep. Congo	Botswana	Malaysia	
Cyprus	Djibouti	Brazil	Mauritius	
Czech Republic	Gambia	Brunei Darussalam	Moldova	
Estonia	Guinea	Cameroon	Mongolia	
Hong Kong-Ch.	Guinea-Bissau	Chile	Morocco	
Hungary	Haiti	China	Namibia	
Iceland	Lesotho	Colombia	Nicaragua	
Israel	Madagascar	Congo	Nigeria	
Japan	Malawi	Costa Rica	Oman	
Korea	Maldives	Côte d'Ivoire	Pakistan	
Latvia	Mali	Cuba	Panama	
Liechtenstein	Mauritania	Dominica	Papua New Guinea	
Lithuania	Mozambique	Dominican Republic	Paraguay	
Malta	Myanmar	Ecuador	Peru	
Mexico	Nepal	Egypt	The Philippines	
New Zealand	Niger	El Salvador	Qatar	
Norway	Rwanda	Fiji	St Kitts and Nevis	
Poland	Senegal	F. Yug. Rep Maced.	St Lucia	
Romania	Sierra Leone	Gabon	St Vincent & the Gr.	
Singapore	Solomon Islands	Georgia	Saudi Arabia	
Slovak Republic	Togo	Ghana	South Africa	
Slovenia	Uganda	Grenada	Sri Lanka	
Switzerland	Zambia	Guatemala	Suriname	
Turkey		Guyana	Swaziland	
		Honduras	Chinese Taipei	

highlight the most interesting aspects of the data, nor do we undertake any statistical analysis of the material. We only display a small fraction of the data, and point to certain features. It is indeed our hope that researchers using this data set will offer more penetrating analyses.

2. *Who are the complainants and respondents?*

A natural first question is to ask who participates in the DS proceedings? This research area has attracted a lot of attention in literature. It is impossible to address this issue, absent a definition of "a dispute", a dispute is the *unit of account* in this endeavour. There are various ways in which this could be done, and the particular method chosen may importantly affect the outcome of the investigation. Unfortunately, there is no single correct method applicable across research interests. Instead, the correct procedure depends on the question at stake.

The basic idea behind the approach adopted here, as in some of the literature, is to view disputes between WTO Members at a bilateral level. That is, if two Members are complaining against a third Member, we count each one of them having a dispute with the third Member, that is, there are two "bilateral" disputes in this example. Naturally, all original complainants are involved in such bilateral disputes. In many disputes there are also countries that file a Request to Join in Consultations. They clearly have some form of interest in the dispute, but as a general matter, it is not clear whether they are on the side of the original complainant. If they are, it is natural to include them among the countries that have a bilateral dispute with the respondent. But, it is also possible that they are on the side of the respondent. For instance, they may pursue policies that are similar to the challenged one. In the latter case, one would not want to include these countries among those having a dispute with the respondent. In practice, it normally seems more common that countries that request to join in consultations are on the complaining side.[4] We will therefore in Table 2 include these countries among those having a bilateral dispute. This will increase the number of bilateral disputes by almost 300%, making the total number of disputes equal to 965. But we want to emphasize that by doing this, we will no doubt erroneously include some instances where countries joining in did not do so because of a conflict with the respondent.[5] We will also in Table 3 examine whether there is any systematic difference with regard to the propensity to join in consultations across country groups.

A natural starting point is to examine the number of times the Members of the WTO have participated in a dispute. The G2 countries have complained 266 times, that is, 27.6% of all the 965 bilateral disputes, making it the third most active group. IND leads with 369 bilateral complaints, that is, 38.2% of all disputes, followed by DEV with 322 bilateral disputes, or 33.3%. LDC has complained only eight times, that is, in 0.8% of all bilateral disputes (and as emphasized earlier, even this low number may exaggerate their participation.

G2 is the most active group as respondent. Its practices have been challenged 541 times, which accounts for 56.1% of all bilateral disputes. DEV follows with 256, that is, 26.8%. IND countries finally have acted as respondents on 165 occasions, that is, in 17.1% of all bilateral disputes. LDC countries have never acted as respondents.

---

[4] A look into their pleadings is the best possible way to classify them as complainants or respondents. With a very few exceptions indeed, countries that join in consultations have sided with the complainant's claims.

[5] We are grateful to Greg Shaffer for alerting us to the likelihood that we exaggerate the extent to which LDCs are represented on the complaining side through this procedure.

We can note that, when comparing participation as complainant and respondent, the G2 group is appearing as a respondent roughly twice as often (541/266). IND countries, however, have been twice as often a complainant (369/165). In DEV's case, the discrepancy is not so pronounced, although DEV countries are still more active complainants than respondents (322/259).

Let us now turn to the question of who targets who? Table 2a shows the distribution of complainants over the individual Members of the WTO, and Table 2b provides a summary view of this pattern. It is evident from these tables that G2 targets almost evenly G2, IND, and DEV: G2 complaints against G2 constitute 33.8% of its total complaints (90/266); against IND 29.3% (78/266); and against DEV 38.4% of its total complaints (98/266).

The other three groups target G2 much more often than they target any other group: 58.0% of all IND complaints are directed against G2 (214/369); 71.4% of all DEV complaints concern G2 practices (230/322); and finally, 87.5% of all LDC complaints (few as they are) aim at the G2 countries (7/8). We can thus conclude that the majority of bilateral disputes involve a G2 country as either a complainant or respondent.

Table 3a provides information about the extent to which the different groups have become complainants (using the definition of bilateral disputes discussed earlier) by participating in the original Request for Consultations, or by joining in at a later stage. We observe an asymmetry between G2 and the other groups. In complaints against G2 or IND, G2 will more often act as original complainant; only 31.1% of all G2 complaints against G2 and 37.2% against IND, are cases where G2 joined in consultations. However, in the case of complaints against DEV, G2 has joined in 53.1% of its total cases against this group. Hence, G2 seems more proactive in trade disputes against developed economies, and it rarely takes the initiative to launch a dispute as original complainant against a DEV country.

DEV countries, however, have a high propensity to join in when the target is the G2 (in 70.4% of all their complaints against G2, DEV joined in consultations). But, DEV countries act more often as original complainants when targeting practices of either IND countries or other DEV countries. IND countries consistently join in consultations more frequently than they act as original complainants, no matter what the target group is. Hence, in conclusion, we might say that IND and DEV countries prefer to join in, whereas G2 act as original complainants.

Table 3b gives data on individual WTO Members' participation as third parties in panel proceedings. DEV emerges as the highest represented group, with 398/831, or 47.9% of all appearances as third parties in all disputes. IND is second, with 308 appearances (37.8%), followed by G2 with 114 appearances (13.7%), and LDC with 11 appearances (1.3%).

Table 2a. Distribution of bilateral complaints over complaints and respondent groups

Status complainant	Complainant	Status respondent			Grand total
		G2	IND	DEV	
G2	EC	49	32	54	135
	US	41	46	44	131
	G2 total	90	78	98	266
IND	Australia	23	9	12	44
	Bulgaria	2			2
	Canada	44	16	19	79
	Cyprus	2			2
	Czech Republic	2	1		3
	Hong Kong (China)	4	1	1	6
	Hungary	2	5	1	8
	Iceland	1			1
	Israel	1			1
	Japan	44	9	21	74
	Korea	17	3	7	27
	Malta	2			2
	Mexico	28	2	14	44
	New Zealand	17	4	7	28
	Norway	11	1		12
	Poland		2	1	3
	Romania	2			2
	Singapore			1	1
	Slovak Republic	2			2
	Slovenia	2			2
	Switzerland	6	4	11	21
	Turkey	2		3	5
	IND total	214	57	98	369
DEV	Antigua and Barbuda	1			1
	Argentina	14	1	7	22
	Barbados	2			2
	Belize	3			3
	Bolivia	1			1
	Brazil	28	6	3	37
	Chile	10	2	6	18
	China	8		1	9
	Chinese Taipei	4		4	8
	Colombia	11		5	16
	Costa Rica	5		5	10
	Côte d'Ivoire	3			3
	Cuba			2	2
	Dominican Republic	8			8
	Ecuador	10	1		11
	El Salvador	1		2	3
	Fiji	2			2

Table 2a. (continued)

Status complainant	Complainant	Status respondent G2	IND	DEV	Grand total
	Guatemala	9	2	6	17
	Guyana	2			2
	Honduras	10		3	13
	India	34	4	3	41
	Indonesia	2	1	1	4
	Jamaica	5			5
	Kenya	2			2
	Malaysia	1	1		2
	Mauritius	2			2
	Nicaragua	3	1	3	7
	Pakistan	6		2	8
	Panama	5		1	6
	Peru	6	1	2	9
	The Philippines	1	4	2	7
	Saint Lucia	3			3
	Sri Lanka	1		1	2
	St. Kitts and Nevis	2			2
	Swaziland	2			2
	Thailand	14	6	3	23
	Uruguay	1			1
	Venezuela	5			5
	Zimbabwe	3			3
	DEV total	230	30	62	322
LDC	Bangladesh	1		1	2
	Congo	2			2
	Madagascar	2			2
	Malawi	2			2
	LDC total	7		1	8
	Grand total	541	165	259	965

Table 2b. Distribution of bilateral complaints across complainant and respondent groups in percent

		Respondent G2	IND	DEV	Total
Complainant	G2	9.3	8.1	10.2	27.6
	IND	22.2	5.9	10.2	38.2
	DEV	23.8	3.1	6.4	33.4
	LDC	0.7	0.0	0.1	0.8
	Total	56.1	17.1	26.8	100.0

Table 3a. Propensity to join complaints rather than to complain

	Complainant												
	G2			IND			DEV			LDC			
Respondent	G2	IND	DEV	G2	IND	DEV	G2	IND	DEV	G2	IND	DEV	Total
Request for Consultations	62	49	46	59	22	20	68	18	34	0	0	1	379
Requests Join Consultations	28	29	52	155	35	78	162	12	28	7	0	0	586
Total	90	78	98	214	57	98	230	30	62	7	0	1	965
Joined as % of total	31.1%	37.2%	53.1%	72.4%	61.4%	79.6%	70.4%	40.0%	45.2%	100.0%	0.0%	0.0%	60.7%

Table 3b. Third party participation

G2		*DEV (cont.)*	
EC	58	Colombia	15
US	56	Costa Rica	6
G2 total	114	Côte d'Ivoire	4
		Cuba	16
IND		Dominica	3
Australia	38	Dominican Republic	2
Canada	58	Ecuador	7
Hong Kong – China	9	Egypt	2
Hungary	2	El Salvador	9
Iceland	6	Fiji	3
Israel	3	Ghana	1
Japan	65	Grenada	1
Korea	27	Guatemala	10
Mexico	38	Guyana	3
New Zealand	20	Honduras	9
Norway	21	India	43
Poland	1	Indonesia	3
Singapore	4	Jamaica	7
Switzerland	2	Kenya	3
Turkey	14	Malaysia	10
IND total	308	Mauritius	5
		Nicaragua	6
LDC		Nigeria	1
Bangladesh	1	Pakistan	4
Benin	1	Panama	1
Chad	1	Paraguay	13
Madagascar	3	Peru	7
Malawi	3	The Philippines	4
Senegal	2	Saint Kitts and Nevis	3
LDC total	11	Saint Lucia	3
		Saint Vincent and the Grenadines	1
DEV		Sri Lanka	3
Argentina	12	Suriname	1
Barbados	4	Swaziland	3
Belize	4	Tanzania	3
Bolivia	1	Thailand	24
Brazil	31	Trinidad and Tobago	3
Cameroon	1	Uruguay	4
Chile	15	Venezuela	16
China	39	Zimbabwe	1
Chinese Taipei	28	DEV total	398
		Grand total	831

Interestingly, more members have been third parties than complainants, despite the fact that only some of the disputes go to the panel stage, and despite our generous definition of complainants (which also include those that request to join in consultations; the numbers are 72 and 67, respectively). There is no complete overlap between the two categories: 12 Members appeared as third parties without having appeared as complainants. Importantly, all of them belong to the DEV/LDC groups (Dominica, Egypt, Ghana, Grenada, Nigeria, Paraguay, Saint Vincent & the Grenadines, Suriname, Tanzania, Benin, Chad, and Senegal).

3. Which agreements and provisions have been invoked?

We next turn to the subject matter of the disputes. We first consider the WTO Membership as a whole, and examine how the total number of disputes is distributed across agreements and provisions. We then turn to see if any broad pattern can be discerned with regard to the matters being raised.

(i) *A view across agreements*

Table 4 provides a broad overview of the total number of invocations of GATT with Annexes, GATS with Annexes, and the TRIPs.[6] In contrast to Section 2, where we relied on our notion of bilateral complaints, here we use Request for Consultation as our unit of account. An illustration may be warranted: if Arts. I and III GATT have been invoked in a Request for Consultation, we would count this as one invocation of GATT. Furthermore, we count it as one invocation, irrespective of the number of Members participating in the original request, and the number of Members joining in at a later stage. What we are looking for here is the response to the question: in how many disputes has, say, the GATT been invoked. If both GATT provision(s) and GATS provision(s) are invoked in a dispute, it will be counted in this table as one GATT invocation and one GATS invocation. Of course, this is by no means the only way in which this could be measured.

Table 4. Number of times the GATT, the GATS, and the TRIPs and their Annexes are invoked in Request for Consultations

Agreement	Number of disputes[a]	% of total
GATT and Annexes	657	94.1
GATS and Annexes	16	2.3
TRIPS	25	3.6
Total	698	100

[a]The GATT Annexes included here are AD, AG, ATC, CV, ILA, ROO, SCM, SG, SPS, TBT, TRIMS, and the Enabling Clause.

[6] For an explanation of the abbreviations of the agreements, see the Annex to this chapter.

As can be seen from Table 4, GATT (and the other Annex 1A agreements, that is the agreements regulating trade in goods) strands for the vast majority of invocations, or 94.1% of the total number. There are 50% more TRIPs invocations than GATS invocations, but they both dwindle in comparison to the invocations of the agreements governing trade in goods. This might *prima facie* look surprising. However, the fact that developing countries enjoyed a long transitional period to implement TRIPs, probably explains the few invocations of this agreement. GATS is still largely a *terra incognita* for most trading nations. This could tempt countries to complain, to clarify the law. But, the uncertainty concerning the outcome of a dispute may also deter countries from complaining. Also, empirical evidence suggests that it did not generate any meaningful trade liberalization beyond the status quo in 1995, which could be a part of the explanation for how rarely it has been invoked.

Table 5 specifies in more detail the WTO agreements that have been invoked. Not surprisingly, GATT 1947 completely dominates as the most frequently invoked agreement, accounting for roughly a third of all

Table 5. Agreements invoked in Requests for Consultations

Agreement	Invoked in number of requests[a]	% of total no. of invoked agreements
GATT	270	36.0
AD	71	9.5
SCM	70	9.3
AG	56	7.5
SG	34	4.5
ILA	33	4.4
TBT	33	4.4
WTO Agree	33	4.4
SPS	30	4.0
TRIPS	25	3.3
TRIMS	23	3.1
ATC	16	2.1
GATS	14	1.9
CV	12	1.6
DSU	11	1.5
ROO	5	0.7
GPA	4	0.5
Enabling Clause	4	0.5
ChinaAA	3	0.4
MDTruth	1	0.1
1979Understanding	1	0.1
ALL	749	99.8

[a]The number of times various WTO Agreements have been invoked in Request for Consultations. If reference is made to Arts. III.1 and III.2, this will count as one invocation. No account is taken of the number of complainants in the dispute.

instances. Then, there are three agreements that are invoked between themselves roughly as frequently, all of them being GATT Annexes: Agreement on Implementation of Art. VI of GATT 1994 (antidumping) (AD), Agreement on Agriculture (AG), and Agreement on Subsidies and Countervailing Measures (SCM). But with 9.5, 7.5, and 9.3%, they jointly do not stand for more than about a quarter of all invocations.

Tables 6–10 take further steps in disaggregating the data by considering the number of times specific provisions have been invoked. Starting with the use of GATT, Table 6 shows that the basic non-discrimination principles (Arts. I and III of the GATT) have been invoked in 29.2% of the disputes (193 out of 661 invocations). They are followed by concerns over alleged quantitative restrictions, which account for 12.1% of all GATT disputes (Art. XI, 80/661), and concerns over the lawful imposition of duties, which stand for 10.3% of all GATT disputes (Art. II, 68/661) (we disregard Art. XXIII invocations). Consequently, the total number of challenges concerning the legality of trade instruments is 22.4% of all GATT disputes ((80+68)/661). The transparency provision Art. X emerges

Table 6. General Agreement on Tariffs and Trade

Article	Number of times invoked in disputes[a]
I	91
II	68
III	102
V	5
VI	62
VII	6
VIII	9
X	60
XI	80
XIII	31
XV	2
XVI	6
XVII	6
XVIII	7
XIX	32
XX	5
XXI	2
XXIII	73
XXIV	8
XXVIII	6
ALL	661

[a]The number of times various provisions (Articles) have been invoked in the Request for Consultations by the original Complainants. An Article is counted only once even if referred to several times. Hence, if for instance, Arts. III.1 and III.2 have been invoked, the Table counts this as one invocation of Art. III.

Table 7. Agreement on implementation of Art. V1 of GATT 1994 (antidumping)

Article	Number of times invoked in disputes[a]
1	42
2	50
3	47
4	18
5	48
6	48
7	19
8	3
9	28
10	5
11	19
12	34
15	6
16	1
17	1
18	30
Annex I	5
Annex II	25
ALL	429

[a]The number of times various provisions (Articles) have been invoked in the Request for Consultations by the original complainants. An Article is counted only once even if referred to several times. Hence, if for instance, Arts. 3.1 and 3.2 have been invoked, the table counts this as one invocation of Art. 3.

as an important concern as well; in 9.1% of all GATT disputes, WTO Members have claimed that had been violated (60/661).

Next, let us take a look at how some of the other agreements have been used, starting in Table 7 with the AD. The most frequently invoked provision concern the definition of the dumping margin (Art. 2, 50 invocations, 11.7% of all invocations), the investigation process (Art. 5, 48, 11.2%), evidence (Art. 6, 48, 11.2%), injury (Art. 3, 47, 11.0%), principles (Art. 1, 42, 9.8%), and transparency obligations (Art. 12, 34, 9%).

Table 8 provides a breakdown for the SCM agreement, under which a WTO Member can challenge the legality of a subsidy and/or impose duties against injurious subsidies. The first possibility occupied 26.7% of all SCM claims (Arts. 3–7, 73 out of 273 claims), whereas the second 45.8% (Arts. 10–23, 125/273). The first category can be further broken down: 15.4% of all SCM claims concerned prohibited subsidies (Arts. 3 and 4, 42/273), 11.4% concerned actionable subsidies (Arts. 5–7, 31/273). Finally, 16.5% of all SCM claims concerned the constitutive elements of the subsidy definition in the SCM (Arts. 1 and 2, 45/273).

Table 9 breaks down invocations of the GATS, showing that its various provisions have been very sparsely invoked. This is of course not

Table 8. Agreement on Subsidies and Countervailing Measures

Article	Number of times invoked in disputes[a]
1	27
2	18
3	37
4	5
5	13
6	14
7	4
10	26
11	19
12	8
13	3
14	11
15	10
16	2
17	8
18	2
19	15
20	2
21	11
22	8
27	8
28	2
30	1
32	17
Annex I	2
ALL	273

[a]The number of times various provisions (Articles) have been invoked in the Request for Consultations by the original complainants. An Article is counted only once even if referred to several times. Hence, if for instance, Arts. 3.1 and 3.2 have been invoked, the table counts this as one invocation of Art. 3.

surprising given that the GATS as such has been rarely invoked. Consequently, it is probably premature to draw any conclusions from practice so far. But for what it is worth, we can point to two features: 39.2% of all claims concern specific commitments (Arts. XVI, XVII, and XVIII, 20/51); 41.1% of all claims concern alleged violations of the non-discrimination principle (Arts. II and XVII, 21/51), with the Most-Favored Nation and the National Treatment clauses being invoked almost as often.

Finally, the overall number of TRIPs invocations as well is, as noticed earlier, quite small. When invoked, the particular provisions mentioned in the Requests for Consultations tend to be remarkably evenly spread across the agreement, as demonstrated in Table 10. But three provisions stand out as the most frequently invoked: 12.0% of all TRIPs claims concern transitional arrangements (Art. 65, 14/117), 9.4% concern the existing

Table 9. General Agreement on Trade in Services

Article	Number of times invoked in disputes[a]
I	1
II	9
III	3
IV	1
VI	8
VIII	2
XI	1
XVI	7
XVII	12
XVIII	1
XXIII	3
TRP	1
AnnTelecoms	1
AnnMovPers	1
ALL	51

[a]The number of times various provisions (Articles) have been invoked in the Request for Consultations by the original complainants. An Article is counted only once even if referred to several times. Hence, if for instance, Arts. III.1 and III.2 have been invoked, the table counts this as one invocation of Art. III.

subject matter (Art. 70, 11/117), and a further 8.5% concern the patentable subject matter (Art. 27, 10/117).

(ii) *The pattern of complainants/respondents for selecting agreements and subject matters*

Tables 11 and 12 provide information on the invocation of five main agreements, broken down on the 16 possible constellations of complainant/respondent group. Tables 11 and 12 contain the same information, but exhibit a slightly different structure. Thus, in Table 11 the categorization is by country classification of the complainant, while in Table 12 it is of the respondent.

When constructing these tables, we face the question of how to treat disputes where complaining countries stem from different groups. For instance, countries A and B may file a Request for Consultation against country C, in which they invoke GATT. Assuming that A belongs to G2 and B to DEV, how should this be counted? One possibility would be to count this as both a G2 complaint under GATT and an IND complaint under GATT. But, this would raise the question of why not also take account of complainants that have joined in? It may seem natural to treat these countries in the same manner as the original complainants. Whereas, the problem with this is, however, that the initial complainants jointly referred to the GATT in their Request for Consultations, the countries joining in have not done this. If we treat them symmetrically with the original complainants, we must thus make the bold assumption that they

Table 10. Agreement on Trade-Related Intellectual Property Rights

Article	Number of times invoked in disputes[a]
1	1
2	4
3	6
4	4
9	4
10	2
11	2
12	2
13	2
14	4
15	1
16	3
17	1
18	1
19	1
20	3
21	1
22	2
24	2
27	10
28	4
31	1
33	3
34	1
39	2
41	5
42	3
49	1
50	4
51	1
61	3
62	2
63	6
65	14
70	11
ALL	117

[a]The number of times various provisions (Articles) have been invoked in the Request for Consultations by the original complainants. An Article is counted only once even if referred to several times. Hence, if for instance, Arts. 3.1 and 3.2 have been invoked, the table counts this as one invocation of Art. 3.

are implicitly invoking the same agreements. Its shortcomings notwithstanding, we will follow this approach.

Tables 11 and 12 show that, with regard to the GATT, IND dominates as complainant in absolute numbers with 332 (bilateral) invocations, followed by 290 for DEV, and 197 for G2 (we disregard LDC in this

Table 11. Invocation of agreements by complainant and respondent group

	Complainant																			
	G2					IND					DEV					LDC				
Respondent	G2	IND	DEV	LDC	Total	G2	IND	DEV	LDC	Total	G2	IND	DEV	LDC	Total	G2	IND	DEV	LDC	Grand total
GATT	62	52	83	0	197	194	46	92	0	332	212	21	57	0	290	6	0	1	0	826
AD	18	8	5	0	31	44	2	10	0	56	50	4	10	0	64	0	0	1	0	152
SCM	20	13	21	0	54	36	4	26	0	66	56	3	1	0	60	6	0	0	0	186
GATS	5	5	3	0	13	3	1	2	0	6	24	1	2	0	27	0	0	0	0	46
TRIPs	13	7	12	0	32	33	2	5	0	40	8	0	0	0	8	0	0	0	0	80

Note: The number of times five major WTO Agreements have been invoked in Request for Consultations by country group. Includes all bilateral disputes with both original and joining member countries.

Table 12. Invocations of agreements by complainant and respondent group

	Complainant																			
	G2					IND					DEV					LDC				
Respondent	G2	IND	DEV	LDC	Total	G2	IND	DEV	LDC	Total	G2	IND	DEV	LDC	Total	G2	IND	DEV	LDC	Grand total
GATT	62	194	212	6	474	52	46	21	0	119	83	92	57	1	233	0	0	0	0	826
AD	18	44	50	0	112	8	2	4	0	14	5	10	10	1	26	0	0	0	0	152
SCM	20	36	56	6	118	13	4	3	0	20	21	26	1	0	48	0	0	0	0	186
GATS	5	3	24	0	32	5	1	1	0	7	3	2	2	0	7	0	0	0	0	46
TRIPs	13	33	8	0	54	7	2	0	0	9	12	5	0	0	17	0	0	0	0	80

Note: The number of times five major WTO Agreements have been invoked in Request for Consultations by country group. Includes all bilateral disputes with both original and joining member countries.

discussion since the impact of this groups is marginal). G2 has been the main target of GATT complaints, having been so four times more often than IND (474 invocations compared to 119) and more than twice as often as DEV (233). The role of the GATT for IND as a complainant and G2 as a respondent can be seen from the fact that complaints by IND against G2 account for 23.5% (194/826) of all GATT complaints. But the complainant that has launched the most complaints against G2 is actually DEV, which account for 44.7% (212/474) of all GATT complaints against G2.

A similar pattern can be seen with respect to AD and TRIPs, where IND has been the most active invoker; in the case of AD they account for 36.8% (56/152), and in the case of TRIPs 50.0% (40/80), of all invocations. The prime target of such complaints has been G2, which in the case of AD was the target for 73.7% (112/152) of all complaints, and in the case of TRIPs for 67.5% (54/80) of all complaints. G2 is also the main target of SCM complaint: 63.4% (118/186) of all such complaints are directed against it; here, IND and DEV share the burden as complainants more equally, accounting for 35.5% (66/186) and 32.2% (60/186) of all complaints, respectively.

As we have already seen, there are very few GATS disputes. Examining the few invocations that have occurred, DEV complaints against G2 account for almost half of these instances, and G2 and IND have together been respondents in 84.8% (39/46) of the instances where its' GATS was invoked.

4. Winners and losers of legal claims

The data set contains information on the legal claims made by the parties and whether adjudicating bodies have accepted these claims or not.

A few preliminary observations are required. First, WTO disputes with multiple complainants have been disaggregated into a number of bilateral disputes equal to the number of complainants involved. The *unit of account* in the analysis is *legal claims*, as defined in the WTO case law on Art. 6.2 DSU (Dispute Settlement Understanding): a legal claim comprises a factual matter and the legal provision that it allegedly violates. A legal claim is, thus, an invocation of a provision, or even a paragraph of a provision, which has been violated allegedly by the action of a WTO Member. We have considered invocations already mentioned earlier, but the focus is now different. We are only concerned with the panel stage, since our ultimate concern in this section is whether claims are won or not, whereas in the earlier section, we looked at invocations in Requests for Consultation. Second, we follow the evolution of the EC membership in the sense that up to January 1, 2004 EC is EC-15, after that date EC-25 (since we do not reflect the recent expansion of the EU to 27 members).

There are in total 144 bilateral disputes with the definition just mentioned, involving a total of 2369 legal claims. Table 13 shows how

Table 13. **Distribution of number of legal claims by group pairing**

Complainant	Respondent			
	G2	IND	DEV	Total
G2	380	201	48	629
IND	971	37	81	1089
DEV	489	79	83	651
Tot.	1840	317	212	2369

Table 14. **Average number of claims within each group pairing**

Complainant	Respondent		
	G2	IND	DEV
G2	19	9.1	3.7
IND	27.7	7.4	11.6
DEV	14.8	19.8	16.6

these are distributed across pairs of complaining and responding Members, grouped by their country status. The IND group accounts for almost half (46%) of all the claims, DEV for 27.5% of all claims, whereas G2 for 26.5% of all claims.

Table 14 depicts the average number of claims for each pair (complainant group and respondent group). There is a significant variation, for each complainant group across respondents and vice versa. At the lower end, a G2 complaint against a DEV country on an average involves 3.7 claims, while an IND complaint against a G2 country on an average comprises almost 26 claims.

The distribution of the claims across agreements is shown in Table 15. The majority of claims are under the three contingent protection instruments AD, CVD, and SG (see Hoekman *et al.*, 2009 for an explanation of why this picture may exaggerate the quantitative importance of these disputes in the DS system).

The outcomes of the cases are classified in the data set on the basis of the findings by WTO adjudicating bodies as they appear in the Conclusions and Recommendations section of each panel report. We classify outcomes into three groups: (1) those claims where the complainant prevailed, (2) claims where the defendant prevailed, and (3) a residual group of claims where the outcome is unclear. While the last category is not self-explanatory given that in principle a panel should either find for or against a claim by a complainant, practice has made inclusion of this third category a necessity, for instance, because of the exercise of judicial economy.

Table 15. The distribution of claims across agreements/provisions

Provision/agreement	No. of claims
AD	615
ATC	13
AA	46
DSU:3.7	16
GATS	30
GATT:II	23
GATT:III	88
GATT:VI	69
GATT:X	46
GATT:XI	19
GATT:XIII	10
GATT:XIX	69
GATT:XX	25
SCM	269
SG	557
SPS	286
TBT	11
TRIPs	61
WTO:XVI.4	30

Table 16. Average percentage successful claims by group pairing, based on the sum of all claims for the pairing

Complainant	Respondent			
	G2	IND	DEV	Total
G2	62.4	63.2	89.6	64.7
IND	55.4	94.6	50.6	56.4
DEV	61.3	22.8	69.9	57.8
Total	58.4	56.8	67.0	59.0

For Table 16, the average number of successful claims is calculated by simply the total number of successful claims ("wins") for a given group by the total number of claims made by the group for a specific pairing. It can be noted that overall success rates are remarkably similar for the three active groups: when acting as complainants, G2, IND, and DEV win around 65% of the claims they advance, when calculated as a share of all the claims each group makes. Similarly, the total win percentage for the three complainant groups ranges between 56% and 65% of all the claims they advance. But the Table 16 also reveals a significant variability across different complainant–respondent constellations. Most successful are IND countries when complaining against other countries in the same group, winning almost 95% of the claims. It is also noticeable that G2 succeed with almost 90% of their claims against DEV. At the other end of the spectrum, we find the DEV group, which wins less than 23% of the claims they advance against IND.

5. Where do the panelists come from, who selected them, and how many panels have they served on?

Table 17 provides data on the nationality of individuals that have served as panelists (chair+non-chair) in the 154 panels in the data set; since each panel is composed of three panelists, the data set contains a total of 462 panelist-slots. A striking feature in this context is that individuals originating in IND and DEV have appeared as panelists (chair, non-chair) in 405/462 times, that is, in almost 88% of all times. Forty seven different nationalities have been represented, which means that more than two-thirds of all WTO Members have never had a panelist. But, only 57 times has a G2 citizen acted as panelist (chairman+non-chairman). This is less than 13% of all panelists used. The United States tops the list with 13 times (8 of which chair). However, US citizens account for 13/57 panelists, that is, less than 25% of the total G2 representation. Germany holds second position with 10 (2 chair) and Sweden third with 9 (8 chair) panelists.

53.4% of all panelists come from IND, the largest representation in this context. New Zealand tops the list with 45 (18 chair), and Switzerland comes second with 36 (17 chair). Australia is third with 28 (3 chair). Hong Kong (China) is fourth with 19 (14 chair). Canada comes fifth with 18 (5 chair). Singapore follows with 15 (3 chair), whereas Japanese citizens have been selected 12 times (1 chair). Eleven Koreans have been selected (4 as chair), and Icelanders have also been frequently represented (9 panelists, 8 chair). 34.2% of all panelists come from DEV. India tops the list with 27 (of which, 10 chair). Brazil is second with 19 (2 chair), followed by Chile 18 (2 chair) and South Africa with 18 (3 chair).

As revealed in Table 18, the composition of panels has been decided exclusively by agreement between the parties to the dispute on 64 occasions. Much more common has been that the DG has been involved in appointing the panel; this has occurred on 90 occasions. This does not mean, however, that on each of these occasions the DG has appointed all three panelists; it could well be the case that the DG appointed only two, or even one panelist and thus "completed" its composition (Art. 8.7 DSU).

Table 19 shows the propensity for panelists to serve more than once. As can be seen, a total of 195 individuals have served as panelists in 154 panel proceedings so far. Eighty eight individuals served only once as panelists, whereas 107 individuals served at least twice. Hence, more than 50% of the panelists have served more than once. Twenty out of 195, that is, 10.3%, have served five times or more. The record man among repeat players is Mohan Kumar from India, who served on 14 occasions, followed by

Table 17. Distribution of panelists by nationality and function

	Chair	Non-chair
G2 Member		
Austria	0	1
Belgium	1	4
Finland	1	4
France	0	2
Germany	2	8
Ireland	0	3
Italy	0	1
The Netherlands	0	1
Sweden	8	1
United Kingdom	0	7
United States	8	5
Total G2	20	37
DEV Member		
Argentina	1	7
Brazil	2	17
Chile	2	16
Colombia	3	7
Costa Rica	3	0
Ecuador	0	3
Egypt	7	4
India	10	17
Jamaica	0	1
Malaysia	0	1
Mauritius	0	2
Morocco	2	0
Pakistan	1	4
The Philippines	1	3
South Africa	5	13
Taiwan	0	1
Thailand	0	7
Uruguay	6	3
Venezuela	3	6
Total DEV	46	112
IND Member		
Australia	3	25
Bulgaria	0	1
Canada	5	13
Czech Republic	4	7
Hong Kong-China	14	5
Hungary	0	2
Iceland	8	1
Israel	0	6
Japan	1	11
Korea	4	7
Mexico	0	10
New Zealand	18	27
Norway	5	6

Table 17. (continued)

	Chair	Non-chair
Poland	6	5
Singapore	3	12
Slovenia	0	2
Switzerland	17	19
Total IND	88	159
	Percent of all panelists	
G2	12.3	
IND	53.5	
DEV	34.2	

Table 18. Composition of panels by the parties or the DG, and the respondent's country status

Chosen by:	Respondent			
	G2	IND	DEV	Total
DG[a]	53	20	17	90
Parties	36	17	11	64
Total	89	37	28	154

[a]Note that each dispute has its own DS number and therefore is counted separately. Accordingly, it is possible for a panelist to have served on more than one dispute involving more than one complainant although the respondent is the same for the particular dispute.

Table 19. Repeat panelists

Number of panels that panellist has served on	Number of panelists	Cumulative
1	88	88
2	43	86
3	36	108
4	8	32
5	6	30
6	4	24
8	3	24
9	4	36
10	2	20
14	1	14
Total	195	462

Mamoon Abdel-Fattah (Egypt, 10), Peter Palečka (Czech Republic, 10), Michael Cartland (Hong Kong, China, 9), Crawford Falconer (New Zealand, 9), Margaret Liang (Singapore, 9), Ole Lundby (Norway, 8), Hugh McPhail (New Zealand, 8), and Stefan Johannesson (Iceland, 8).

6. The duration of the process

Table 20 provides some simple data on the duration of the various stages of the DS process. Starting with the bilateral leg of the process – consultations – we observe that their average length is 210.2 days. Since the length of the consultations process depends solely on the will of the consulting parties, one cannot talk of delays, etc. However, with regard to the other DS stages, one can compare the statutory deadlines and the *de facto* duration and draw such conclusions. One should be careful, nevertheless, not to attribute responsibility for delays to the institution without further examination; the process can slow down because of the parties as well.

Charts 1–3 display the variation in terms of process length for the consultation stage, the panel stage, and the AB stage, respectively. In each chart the disputes are ordered horizontally according to increasing process length.

The statutory duration of the panel process is 6 months. This deadline for completion of the process can be extended to 9 months, if need be, but

Table 20. Average length of various DS processes

Proceeding	Average length of the process	Explanation
Consultations	210.2 days	From the date of Request for Consultations until the date the Panel was established
Panel	406.4 days	From the date the Panel was established until the date of the circulation of the Panel Report
Appellate Body	89.3 days	From the date of the Notice of Appeal until the date of the circulation of the Appellate Body report
RPT when awarded by arbitrator	12.0 months	The average RPT awarded by the arbitrator in the awards circulated
RPT when agreed bilaterally	9.5 months	Total length of agreed period between parties of RPT during which implementation must occur
Compliance panel	225.9 days	From the date of the request to establish a first compliance panel until the date of circulation of the Compliance Panel Report
Appellate Body (compliance)	87.7 days	From the date of the first Notice of Appeal until the date of circulation of the Appellate Body compliance report

Note: Average length of the period of time of the following dispute settlement proceedings under the *Dispute Settlement Understanding*.

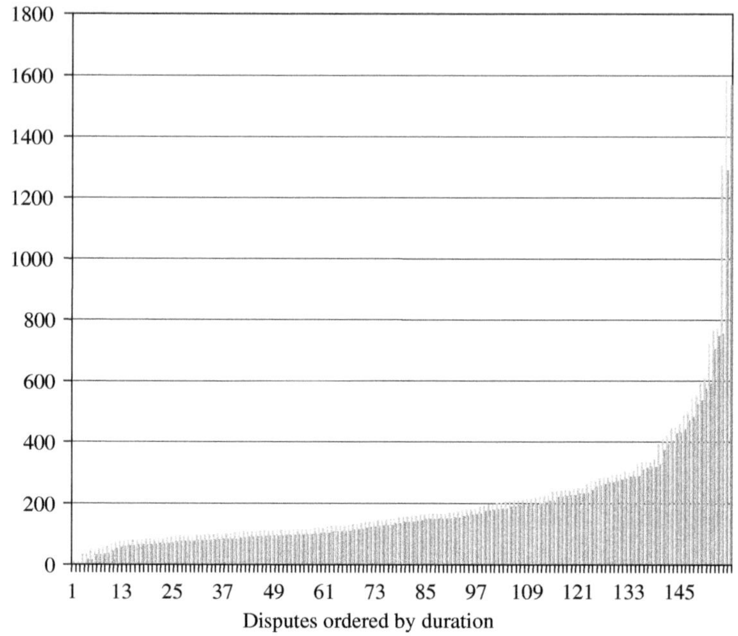

Chart 1. Duration of the consultation stage (days).

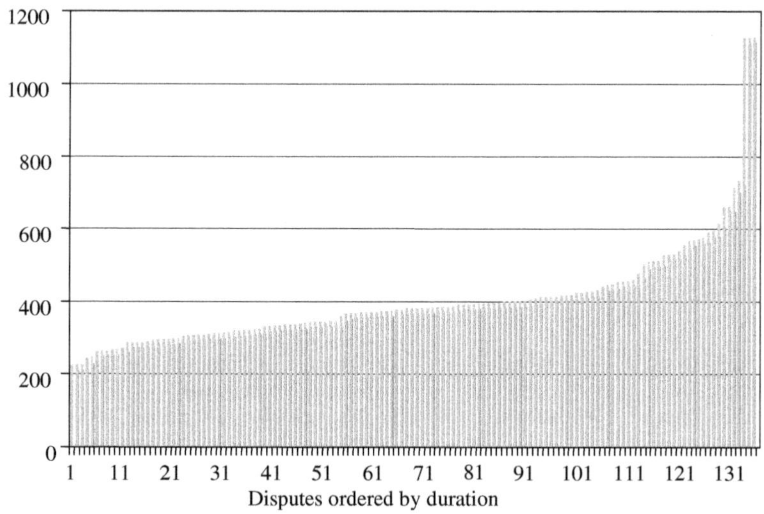

Chart 2. Duration of panel stage (days).

the DSU seems to suggest (Art. 12.9) that this period should not be extended any further. The average panel process of the disputes reflected in the data is 406.36 days, that is, over 13 months. Chart 2 (or rather the data underlying the chart) shows that the panel process had been completed

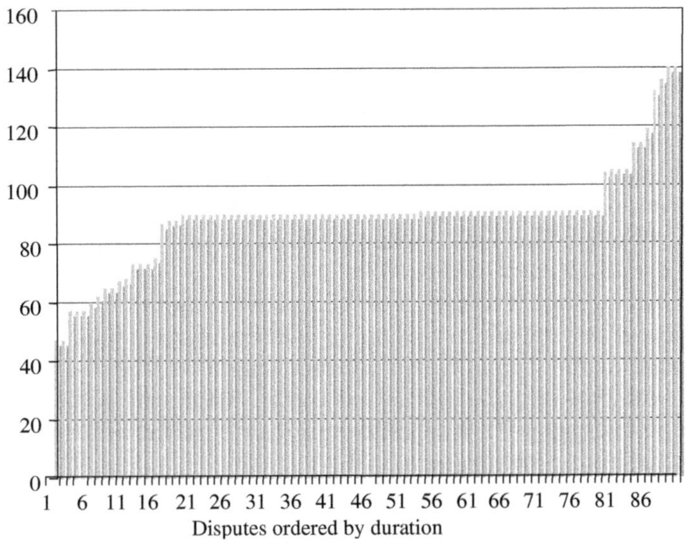

Chart 3. Duration of the AB stage (days).

within the statutory limits in only 10 instances. At the other end there are 23 disputes with duration of over 500 days.

Turning to the duration of the Appellate Body (AB) process, we first note that the statutory deadline for its completion is 60 days, but with the possibility to extend it to 90 days. *De facto*, the AB manages to complete its work within this deadline: the average duration is 89.31 days. On 78 out of 89 occasions, that is, 87.6% of the total number, the AB completed its work within the statutory deadline. There are only four disputes where the AB process exceeded 4 months.

Compliance panels (Art. 21.5 DSU) have to observe a statutory 90 days deadline. They can, however, take a longer time, if need be. Contrary to what is the case under Art. 12.9 DSU, Art. 21.5 DSU does not provide for a maximum delay of the process. Compliance panels enjoy some flexibility when deciding the time for completion of the process. In practice, they take on average 225.94 days to complete their work. The AB completes its work even faster when discussing an appeal against a compliance panel report (Art. 21.5 DSU) than when adjudicating an appeal against an ordinary panel report, on average it does so within 87.72 days.

Finally, Table 20 also yields information on the average reasonable period of time (RPT) for implementation of the WTO adjudicating bodies' recommendations/suggestions. The RPT has in practice been determined either through agreement between the parties, or through recourse to an Arbitrator. There are no statutory deadlines imposing a time frame during which parties to a dispute must reach an agreement as to the extent of the RPT, so the type of analysis undertaken earlier cannot be repeated for the bilateral determination of Rots. There is a statutory deadline that the Arbitrator must respect (Art. 21.3c). This is not, however, an interesting feature of the process and in what follows we focus on the length of the RPT that the Arbitrator has awarded, rather than ask the question whether he/she has respected the statutory deadlines when determining its extent. It should be noted that the DSU (Art. 21.3c) provides a guideline to the Arbitrator when it comes to fixing the RPT; it should not be longer than 15 months. The DSU acknowledges, however, that the RPT can extend beyond 15 months if need be.

What can be done, however, is to compare the awarded RPT depending on whether it is determined through a bilateral agreement or arbitration. As reported in the Table 20, the average length of bilateral RPT is 9.48 months, while the average RPT fixed by the Arbitrator being 12 months. Hence, the average RPT is significantly shorter when determined by the parties than by the Arbitrator.

7. Instead of conclusions

In the previous section we have merely displayed the data, and have not in any sense tried to statistically explain why the data looks the way it does, nor have we presented any benchmark against which to compare whether countries are over- or under-represented in the system, or whether it is working satisfactory in other respects. It is therefore impossible to draw any firm conclusions from the earlier discussion – the study is only meant to serve as food for further thought. There are in this regard a couple of features that we find somewhat striking.

A first observation, and there is no surprise here, is the almost complete absence of the large LDC group. One could add to this group a large number of countries in DEV that have never been active neither as participants in disputes nor in the adjudication process. It is therefore hard to escape the conclusion that a large fraction of the WTO Membership is passive as it comes to the WTO DS system.

A second observation is, to our mind, the surprisingly high participation rate by the DEV group. It should be recalled that we have classified as IND several countries that would in the WTO be treated as developing countries; this includes, for instance, Hong Kong (China), Korea, Mexico, and Turkey. These are all countries that are relatively active in the DS system. Despite having excluded them from the DEV group, the latter nevertheless appears as a significant player, as measured here.

Our third, and final, observation is that the G2 group is less dominant than we would have guessed. It tends to be much more often the subject of complaints than a complaining party, and G2 has a very low share of all panelists. This is not to take a stand on the "weight" of these countries in the organization, but just to point out how our numbers come out.

Annex: List of abbreviations of agreements

AD	Agreement on Implementation of Art. VI of GATT 1994 (antidumping)
AG	Agreement on Agriculture
ATC	Agreement on Textiles and Clothing
ChinaAA	China Accession Agreement
CV	Agreement on Implementation of Art. VII of GATT 1994 (customs valuation)
EnC	Enabling Clause
GATS	General Agreement on Trade in Services
GATT	General Agreement on Tariffs and Trade
GPA	Agreement on Government Procurement
IL	Illustrative List (annexed to the TRIMs)
ILA	Agreement on Import-Licensing Procedures
MDTruth	Ministerial Decision Regarding Cases where Customs Administrations have Reasons to Doubt the Truth or Accuracy of Declared Value
ROO	Agreement on Rules of Origin
SG	Agreement on Safeguards
SCM	Agreement on Subsidies and Countervailing Measures
SPS	Agreement on the Application of Sanitary and Phyto-Sanitary Measures
TBT	Agreement on Technical Barriers to Trade
TRIMs	Agreement on Trade-Related Investment Measures
TRIPs	Agreement on Trade-Related Intellectual Property Rights
TRP	Telecoms Reference Paper (GATS)
1979Und	1979 Understanding Regarding Notification, Consultation, Dispute Settlement and Surveillance

Acknowledgements

We would like to thank Henning Horn af Rantzien and Vilhelm Horn af Rantzien for excellent research assistance in the preparation of this version. We are also very grateful to the World Bank and the Marianne and Marcus Wallenberg Foundation for financial support.

Reference

Hoekman, B.M., Henrik, H., Petros, C.M. (2009), Winners and losers in the panel stage of the WTO dispute settlement system. In: Chantal, T., Joel, T. (Eds.), *Developing countries in the WTO legal system*. Oxford University Press, In Press.

CHAPTER 2

Issues of Fairness in Dispute Settlement

Andrew G. Brown[a] and Robert M. Stern[b]

[a]*P.O. Box 1763, Wellfleet, MA 02667, USA*
E-mail address: abrown@C4.net
[b]*Department of Economics and Gerald R. Ford School of Public Policy, University of Michigan, 735 S. State Street, Ann Arbor, MI 48109-3091, USA*
E-mail address: rmstern@umich.edu

Abstract
We first discuss what fairness may mean in the context of the dispute settlement process, noting the crucial relation between fairness in dispute settlement and the functioning of the trading system as a whole. We explore this relation further through an analysis of three main groups of dispute settlement cases. These are cases that turn around the question of defining fair competition; cases that arise from the use of contingency measures; and cases that draw the boundaries between domestic regulatory measures and the trade-related norms and rules of the WTO. There follows an analysis of experience with compliance and with the use of countermeasures in various cases. Finally, taking together the rulings of the Dispute Settlement Body and the procedures for compliance and the use of countermeasures, we conclude that while the present dispute settlement process serves to protect the fairness of the trading system as a whole, there are some aspects of dispute settlement that remain problematic from the standpoint of fairness.

Keywords: Trade, dispute settlement, fairness

JEL classifications: F02, F13, F53, F55

1. Introduction

We begin from the premise that ideas of fairness play some part in shaping the multilateral trading system. We derive this from the fact that the reciprocal exchange of rights and obligations has historically been at the core of the GATT/WTO system founded by the industrial countries.

Frontiers of Economics and Globalization
Volume 6 ISSN: 1574-8715
DOI: 10.1108/S1574-8715(2009)0000006005

Among these countries, or coalitions of these countries, all with significant economic power, reciprocity has assured a rough equivalence in perceived net benefits and therefore has seemed fair. As more developing countries have joined the system, however, the asymmetries in power have widened, and the cooperation of many countries has depended less on reciprocal exchanges among equal partners than on the desire of weaker countries to participate in the global trading system on acceptable terms. Still, so long as the leading powers, especially the United States, have sought to gain the voluntary cooperation of others rather than to impose its own will, some account has had to be taken of what others consider fair.

It is because the notion of fairness plays some part in sustaining the trading system that the dispute settlement process acquires importance. It represents the process that provides a channel through which disputes between individual countries may be resolved, or at least prevented from descending into trade wars. More generally, it is needed to sustain trust in the system of rights and obligations. It should reassure members that the mutually advantageous arrangements to which they have subscribed remain respected.[1] Thus, the process is expected to serve as the impartial expositor of what members collectively believe to be the norms and rules of the system; its envisaged duty is to interpret and apply the view of what is fair as embodied in the agreements that member countries have negotiated.

For the most part, we do not ask whether the rules of the GATT/WTO that the Dispute Settlement Body (DSB) is called upon to administer are themselves fair. These are reached by consensus, and there are many different opinions as to whether or not particular rules are fair. These affect assessments of DSB rulings, a fact that we cannot ignore. However, our main focus is on the narrower question of whether the arrangements for settling disputes under these rules raise issues of fairness.

This breaks down into two parts. The first is whether the process itself is equally accessible to all members and is seen as impartial. The second is whether the adjudicators interpret and apply the agreements of the WTO fairly in all, or nearly all, cases. In reviewing the performance of the DSB, which is carried out very largely by its subsidiary components, the panels and the Appellate Body, it is the second part that we concentrate on here. However, we would not want to underplay the importance of the first condition. If the way in which individuals assess the fairness of national courts is anything to go by, it is the accessibility and impartiality of the process that, more than anything, persuades

[1] Some economists interpret the function of the dispute settlement process quite differently, casting it in terms only of its economic rationale. They see it as a means of rebalancing trade relations so as to eliminate inefficiencies caused by protectionist measures and thereby to maximize national income (Bagwell and Staiger, 1999).

people to believe whether or not legal outcomes are fair.[2] The existing WTO procedures are not without their defects, and a number of valid criticisms have been voiced.[3] While most participants have appeared to believe that the established process meets high standards of impartiality, the question of accessibility raises serious doubts. Equal accessibility to the dispute settlement process clearly exists in name. As a practical matter, however, member countries differ widely in their capacity to use the process effectively. Such use requires that a member government has a body of trade lawyers, economists, and diplomats who have experience with the process and who can call upon a network of informed persons in government departments and private industry. The rational use of limited professional resources militates against the creation of such capacity in smaller and poorer countries. Moreover, in many developing countries – both large and small – the emergence of a formal legal system supported by a body of judges and lawyers who administer and practice commercial law is a development of only the last one or two generations. For such reasons, the richer, industrial countries are at an advantage in acquiring the expertise necessary to utilize the process advantageously.[4]

On the second condition of the fair interpretation and application of the WTO agreements, it is a common opinion that the DSB has performed its duties with creditable success most of the time. The Dispute Settlement Understanding (DSU) enjoins the DSB not "to add to or diminish the rights and obligations" provided in the agreements, and the latter, through its panels and Appellate Body, has clearly endeavored to stick to its last.[5] If some have found particular rulings of the DSB to be unfair, the problem may as readily lie in the WTO agreements themselves as in the DSB's deliberations. This said, however, the record of the DSB in resolving disputes has certainly not been above criticism even though the source of its deficiencies may not have necessarily been of its own making. It is an open question, for instance, whether some kinds of disputes that have broad economic or political ramifications can be resolved at all through the

[2] Social psychologists have found that how people assess the justice of the procedures heavily influences their readiness to accept the legal outcomes. Their judgment about whether the legal authorities have acted fairly are multifaceted and include such factors as their assessment of whether authorities were motivated to be fair, whether they were honest, whether they had ethical standards, whether they acted in a biased way, and whether adequate opportunities for representation were provided. See Tyler (1988) for a review.

[3] For an informative summary and commentary of reforms proposed officially during the Doha Development Round negotiations, see Mexico (2007). See also Hoekman and Mavroidis (2000).

[4] For a sociological analysis of why cases do, or do not, get submitted to the DSB – including a critique of the presumption of economic rationality – see Conti (2008).

[5] The sensitivity of governments on this point explains why precedent has not formally become part of WTO jurisprudence. For the DSB to build up a body of precedents would be seen as an infringement of the sovereign rights of members to negotiate their international rights and obligations.

distinctly rigid and legalistic dispute settlement process of the WTO. Moreover, the adjudicators in the dispute settlement process – the members of the panels and the Appellate Body – exercise considerable discretion in the interpretation and application of the agreements. Even where carefully crafted, the texts of the WTO agreements cannot be expected to describe all the highly specific circumstances found in individual cases. Moreover, most agreements contain inconsistencies and ambiguities in language. Indeed, the language of agreements has sometimes been deliberately left vague in order to facilitate the conclusion of negotiations. Furthermore, the interpretations placed on the rules and factual evidence depend on the beliefs and the expertise of the members of the panels and the Appellate Body.[6] Both their normative beliefs about the economic system and their technical understanding of the economic consequences of trade-related measures affect their interpretations. For these reasons, it is well to ask whether the DSB always make judgments in line with the collective view of fairness.

In this chapter, we attempt to evaluate the rulings and recommendations that the DSB has made up to mid-2007. Our underlying interest is not in the outcome of specific cases but in whether the dispute settlement process has been contributing effectively to the preservation of trust in the multilateral trading system as a whole. To do so, we have reviewed the hundred or so cases on which the DSB, through the panels and the Appellate Body, has made rulings and recommendations since the DSU came into force in January 1995 (Table 1). From these, we have selected a number of cases that we believe to illustrate the directions that the DSB has taken and the difficulties that the process has encountered. We make no attempt to provide a full account of all the legal, economic, and political facets of each case, and we do not quote chapter and verse of all the specific GATT/WTO articles quoted in individual cases. However, we do provide the WTO dispute settlement case numbers for those who might want to consult the DSB reports themselves (which are available on the WTO website). Complainants in many cases cite several GATT/WTO articles that the respondent has allegedly failed to comply with, but we restrict ourselves to what we regard as the key issues in each case.

2. *Fairness in trade relations*

Before we proceed any further, we should attempt to clarify what we mean by fairness. It is an elusive concept.[7] We know that it is a characteristic of

[6] While the members of the Appellate Body are distinguished jurists appointed for a (renewable) four-year term, panelists are selected on a case-by-case basis and vary widely in experience and background.

[7] The classic analysis of fairness is Rawls (1971). For a recent alternative view, see de Jasay (2006).

Table 1. Dispute settlement body: reports adopted, 1995–2007

	Total (1995–2007)
Panel reports adopted	108
Appeals notified (excluding Article 21.5)	75
Appellate Body reports adopted	68
Compliance Panel reports adopted (Article 21.5)	22
Appeals notified (Article 21.5)	14
Appellate Body reports adopted (Article 21.5)	14

Notes: Data for 2007 end in December 10, 2007. Article 21.5 of the Dispute Settlement Understanding provides that, if a complainant believes that the ruling and recommendations of the Dispute Settlement Body are not being complied with, it may request the Body, preferably through the original panel, to review compliance by the respondent.
Source: Adapted and updated from Wilson (2006).

relations among individuals and groups, but that these relations take many forms. We can offer no single definition of fairness that fits all occasions. However, most of us recognize intuitively what fairness means when we are confronted by particular sets of relations. In the context of the multilateral trading system, governments have codified their appropriate conduct in a number of agreements, and from these agreements, we can identify a few generalized sets of trade relations. Within each of these, we find that there is broad agreement, or fairly broad agreement, about what constitutes fairness.

The most elementary of these relations is how each government treats the products of another country at the point of entry in comparison with the products of third countries. Fairness is recognized to demand non-discrimination unless governments have collectively agreed that the criterion may be waived under certain specified circumstances. Another relation is that of a government to its own and to foreign producers within its domestic market; and in this situation, we generally recognize the national treatment of firms – another expression of non-discrimination – as our definition of fairness. A more complex relationship is how each government affects the market behavior of its own producers compared with how other governments affect theirs. The definition of fairness in this circumstance turns on our conception of fair competition, and there is less wholehearted agreement on this score.[8] Broadly, two views vie with each other. In the dominant view, governments should allow prices in a freely competitive market to determine outcomes for producers; there should ideally be an integrated world market in which producers from different

[8] For an interesting exchange of views on fairness in the U.S. context, see Ikenson and Lighthizer (2007).

countries compete with each other within the same institutional and regulatory framework. In the other view, governments may legitimately give domestic producers preferential treatment in order to promote national development. In this latter interpretation, equity qualifies the idea of fair competition. Fairness is not realized if account is not taken of the wide differences in income and wealth that exist among countries; equality of opportunity exists only formally if some lack the capacity to exploit the opportunity.[9]

Yet another set of circumstances that confront governments in their trade relations arises when any government feels obliged to defend its producers from import surges or from competition that it deems politically disruptive. Action against such competition is often rationalized as a defense against "unfair trade." Such interventions – the use of trade remedy measures – will appear arbitrary to other governments, and they only become acceptable if all are likewise free to act in similar circumstances. Fairness can only be approximated through agreement on these circumstances. However, if some governments exercise their freedom to act arbitrarily much more than others, that behavior is not likely to be considered fair by most people.

Finally, there are situations in which governments seek to override the obligations that they have accepted in their commercial relations with others because these clash with their social preferences. No one questions the freedom of governments to pursue their own policies in regard to domestic matters, but there are circumstances in which these may harm the trading interests of other countries. The protocol developed in the GATT/WTO to deal with these circumstances is that governments should first voluntarily agree on those national policies that may override the trading interests of other countries. When these exceptions are invoked, interventions in trade are accepted as fair. But when there is no prior voluntary agreement, the interventions are widely seen as unfair.

Needless to say, these general ideas about what constitutes fairness in trade relations do not provide any well-defined or objective set of yardsticks. Nor are they applicable to every specific circumstance. There are, moreover, valid differences of views about the appropriate definition of fairness to apply in particular circumstances. Despite these difficulties, the issue of fairness is present in most cases, and it is answered in one way or another. It merits inclusion in an analysis of disputes.

---

[9] There is, furthermore, a moral obligation to act justly toward the less fortunate. For a fuller exposition on the concept of fairness as applied to trade relations, see Brown and Stern (2007).

3. Interpretation and application of the WTO rules

We have grouped the dispute cases that we have studied into three main clusters:

1. Disputes that center around the ideas of non-discrimination and fair competition. These include cases that invoke the WTO rules relating to non-discrimination, national treatment, and subsidies. Also included is the rare case alleging restrictive business practices.
2. Disputes that concern the use of contingent trade remedy measures employed to deal with unforeseeable changes in economic or political circumstances. These include anti-dumping and countervailing duties and safeguard measures. (Both anti-dumping and countervailing duties could formally be included in the first cluster as measures concerned with fair competition. But it seems more realistic to treat them separately since governments can independently introduce them and since, especially in the instance of anti-dumping measures, political expediency rather than any firm idea of fair competition appears to dominate their use.)
3. Disputes that concern the boundary between WTO rules and social preferences in such matters as health and safety standards, public morals, and the environment.

While not all cases fit neatly into these three clusters, most are captured. The first two clusters have accounted for the majority of cases, with disputes about subsidies and anti-dumping duties being the leading issues. Compared to developing countries, industrialized countries have been decidedly the more active participants in the dispute settlement process, both as complainants and as respondents. The European Communities (EC) and the United States by themselves have accounted for more than a quarter of all complaints, and their practices have been challenged still more frequently (Horn and Mavroidis, 2006).

3.1. Non-discrimination, national treatment, and fair competition

The ideas of non-discrimination, national treatment, and fair competition have permeated much of the rule making in the GATT/WTO, and they underlie the criteria followed by the DSB in much of its adjudication. The implicit economic model is that of a freely competitive international economy where prices are not altered by governmental intervention. In so far as this applies, fairness equates with efficiency as defined in mainstream economics. However, the oldest expressions of fairness in trade relation are non-discrimination and national treatment, and these derive from a long history that predates the articulation of any specific economic model. The DSB has been quite rigorous in its application of these bedrock principles, and when countries have challenged practices accepted in the past as exceptions to the principles, it has tended to rule in their favor. This has sometimes raised questions about whether the ruling has resolved the dispute in a fair way.

3.1.1. Non-discrimination

In contributing to the preservation of trust in the GATT/WTO system of rules, the DSB is subject to at least one major limitation. It can pass judgment on an alleged misconduct only if an actual case has been presented to it. Regarding the principle of non-discrimination, by far the most frequent apparent infringement of the principle in recent years has been occasioned by the proliferation of free trade agreements (FTAs). One might therefore have expected that this would have generated numerous complaints to be considered by the DSB. But this has not been the case. In one sense, this may have been fortunate for the DSB since both the GATT and the WTO have been singularly unsuccessful in establishing criteria for assessing the consistency of FTAs with their rules.[10] More important, the anomalous situation reminds us that the DSB cannot resolve inconsistencies – and therefore possible causes of unfairness – that are inherent in GATT/WTO rules and practices.[11]

One of the few cases that addressed this issue was a complaint brought by India against Turkey (DS 34). It alleged that Turkey was implementing regulations that not only introduced new quantitative restrictions on imports of textiles and clothing but also discriminated against India's exports. Turkey's defense was that it was in the process of establishing a customs union (CU) with the EC and that, as part of this process, it was obliged to conform its regime for textile and clothing imports to that of the EC. The DSB ruled that the entry of Turkey into a CU did not exempt it from its obligation to conform to WTO rules. In introducing new quantitative restrictions and in applying them in a discriminatory way, Turkey was therefore in violation of these rules. (In this case, the DSB also gave precedence to the principle of non-discrimination over other international obligations of a member country.)

The GATT/WTO rules made an explicit exception to non-discrimination with the introduction of the Generalized System of Preferences (GSP);

---

[10] The ambiguity began early. The agreements establishing the European Economic Community were never submitted to the GATT for assessment of their consistency with the rules. Indeed, only one agreement has been declared consistent with GATT/WTO rules – the Czech-Slovak agreement.

[11] In view of the absence of formal challenges, we may ask, like Sherlock Holmes, why the dog did not bark in the night. The fact is that nearly all members of the WTO have had a direct interest in the definition of acceptable FTAs since they themselves are almost all parties to one or more such arrangements. There has apparently been a reluctance to challenges these arrangements in order to determine the circumstances in which non-discrimination should be upheld.

these preferences were expressly permitted in the GATT under its Enabling Clause. As the preferences granted under the GSP are determined by individual importing countries and are not part of any international commitment under the GATT/WTO, they are less subject to multilateral discipline. However, the DSB has placed some restrictions on the freedom of action of individual countries to broaden the use of these preferences. In a case brought against the EC, India complained that the tariff preferences granted by the EC under its Special Arrangements to Combat Drug Production and Trafficking were inconsistent with non-discrimination (DS 246). The EC treated these preferences, which were rewards for efforts to curtail drug production and trade, as part of its GSP scheme. The DSB ruled that these preferences could not be so justified and were therefore in violation of the principle of non-discrimination.

Some members have also appealed to the principle of non-discrimination in challenging waivers granted to member countries in the past for political or historical reasons. Undoubtedly, the best-known case on this score is the banana dispute between the EC on the one hand and the United States and some Latin American countries on the other (DS 27). This arose out of the long-standing preferential arrangements that EC member states have had with African, Caribbean, and Pacific (ACP) countries under the Lomé Conventions. These Conventions provided for non-reciprocal preferential arrangements in line with the Enabling Clause of the GATT. In fact, before the WTO was established, the EC had sought and been granted a waiver from GATT on the application of non-discrimination to its trade with the ACP countries.[12]

The event that triggered the banana dispute was the drive by the EC in the late 1980s and early 1990s to establish a Single Market within its borders. As part of that program, it drew up a common regime for bananas in 1993. Previously, each member country had pursued its own policy. In Germany and the Scandinavian countries, there was free trade or virtually free trade in bananas, and much of their imports came from Latin American countries. In some other EC countries, quotas and licensing arrangements favored imports from ACP countries. Under the new EC-wide regime, preferential treatment was accorded to imports from the ACP countries. In economic terms, the new regime brought about a redistribution of gains in the banana trade. The new regime favored the EC distributors and, to some extent, the ACP producers.[13] This change

[12] The EC believed that this legitimized its preferences to ACP countries. Officials in the Office of the U.S. Trade Representative, while "willing to concede that the waiver sanctioned the tariff on Latin American imports ... insisted that it left many additional trade violations unresolved" (Devereaux *et al.*, 2006, p. 113).

[13] A World Bank study concluded that most of the excess profits arising from the quota system flowed not to the Caribbean producers but to the EC distributors who bought and marketed the bananas (Borrell, 1994).

was at the expense of consumers in the EC, of Latin American producers, and of particular multinational corporations in the United States and Latin America that were distributors in the EC.

When the banana dispute came before the DSB, it ruled that most of the quota and licensing arrangements established by the EC under its new regime were not consistent with its obligations to respect non-discrimination and national treatment. In effect, the DSB did not question the waiver granted to the EC – it could accord a preferential tariff to the ACP countries – but it required that the system of quotas and licenses be as consistent as possible with the rule of non-discrimination. Even the allocation by the EC of specific quotas among individual countries within the ACP group was, for instance, a violation of non-discrimination. (As will be discussed later, EC compliance with the ruling presented substantial difficulties.)

In sum, the DSB itself has held closely to the principle of non-discrimination in its rulings. This obviously does not mean that, from a wider viewpoint, non-discrimination has been strictly observed in international trade relations. As noted, the trend has been toward the multiplication of preferential trading arrangements, justified mainly as FTAs. As a consequence, the non-discrimination rule, which was long a primary expression of fairness in international trade relations, has been losing its strength and clarity.

There is, moreover, still greater ambivalence about the fairness of the GATT/WTO system of rules when the concept is qualified by the notion of equity. Where new preferential arrangements by one major trading nation have adversely affected other large traders (by causing trade diversion), the latter have been able, for the most part, to offset the adverse effects by negotiating parallel FTAs themselves. Thus, it has tended to be poorer, third countries that have experienced the adverse consequences of these discriminatory arrangements. At the same time, the EC's preferential arrangements with ACP countries have been challenged in the WTO. Partly as a consequence, the EC has proposed to ACP countries that they forego their existing preferential arrangements with it – which, in a recognition of their need for development, were based on non-reciprocity – and that the arrangements be converted into reciprocal FTAs consistent with WTO rules. These inconsistent trends seem inequitable to many.

It is difficult to say therefore that, in the multilateral trading system operating under GATT/WTO rules, non-discrimination, as an expression of fairness, has been firmly upheld. The fault, however, has not lain with the DSB.

3.1.2. National treatment

Application of the national treatment rule appears to have been generally quite clear, and not many disputes have arisen on this score. Disputes have focused on domestic regulations that, intentionally or not, have differentiated between domestic and imported products. For instance, cases were brought against Chile, Japan, and South Korea on the grounds that their internal taxes on liquor discriminated in favor of domestic products through regulatory differentiation such as the alcoholic content of the liquor (DS 8, 10, 11, 75, 84, 87, 110). In these cases, the DSB found that the imported liquors were, in fact, "like products" that competed directly with domestic products and that the tax differentiation was therefore inconsistent with the national treatment rule. In the same vein, the DSB found that a soft drink tax and a distribution tax that were imposed by Mexico on imported sweeteners, soft drinks, and syrups were inconsistent with national treatment (DS 308). These appear to be fair applications of the rule.

Some developed country members have invoked the national treatment provision in quite another context. They have complained that certain emerging countries, in pursuing industrial policies that lay down conditions on foreign owned enterprises to utilize locally produced components or to meet certain export requirements, have violated the provision. In complaints brought against India by the EC and the United States, for instance, Indian performance requirements in the automobile industry were argued to be inconsistent with national treatment as well as with the import licensing rules and TRIMS (DS 146, 175). In line with the rules as they stand, the DSB found in favor of the complainants. From the viewpoint of fairness, however, many would argue that the rules fail to take account of equity. Poor countries seeking to rise out of poverty are intent on promoting the rapid indigenous development of new industry, and this legitimizes the use of the disputed measures as exceptions to the national treatment rule. This is an instance where the dominant norm of fairness hews too closely to the economists' static definition of efficiency as the optimal allocation of resources. A broader conception of fairness that was qualified by equity would recognize the relevance of a more growth-oriented model in which increasing returns played a central role. The same issue arises in a case relating to the Indonesian automobile industry, which is discussed in Section 3.1.3 (DS 54, 55, 59, 64).

3.1.3. Subsidies

Throughout the history of the GATT/WTO, subsidies have figured prominently among the allegations of unfair trade. International agreement on what constitutes unfair subsidies, however, has been slow to emerge. Some progress was made with the adoption of the Subsidy Code during the Tokyo Round. A much larger advance was made with the negotiation of the Subsidies and Countervailing Measures (SCM) Agreement during the Uruguay Round.

The SCM Agreement defined a subsidy in two ways: as a financial contribution by a government or a public body and as any form of income or price support affecting imports or exports that conferred a benefit. It drew a distinction between those subsidies that are of no concern to other countries and other subsidies that are prohibited or "actionable" because they directly affect trade relations; and they confine the latter to those that apply to individual industries or enterprises. Most of the disputes about subsidies over the last ten years or so have, in fact, related to export subsidies. The SCM Agreement was quite explicit on this score: it prohibited export subsides of non-agricultural products. In addition, the Agricultural Agreement placed limits on their use in exports of agricultural products. A number of the disputes about subsidies have turned on the appropriate definition of the terms in these agreements, and in clarifying these terms, the DSB has played an influential role in shaping the position of the WTO on subsidies.

The interpretation of the definition of subsidies by the SCM has been quite expansive – with implications that may have surprised the original drafters. This has been true particularly of national regulations affecting agricultural products. A fairly straightforward case was that brought by New Zealand and the United States against Canada on exported dairy products (DS 103, 113). Since Canada's official milk marketing arrangements provided for the sale of milk to export processors at below cost, the DSB deemed that, although no financial payment took place, a subsidy was being given. A somewhat more complex case was that brought against the EC on the export subsidization of sugar (DS 265, 266, 283). Under the EC regime regulating the production and sale of sugar, beet farmers were free to produce and sell sugar beyond their production quotas provided the sale was to export processors only (at unregulated prices). Although the EC made no payment to producers or processors and did not regulate the prices of raw or refined sugar, the DSB nonetheless ruled that the sugar exports were subsidized. It reasoned that the exports were cross-subsidized by the high prices received by producers for their sales in the domestic market. Producers were able to cover their fixed costs from their domestic sales and only had to cover their variable costs in order to benefit from their export sales. This implied that any products sold on the world market might be deemed to be subsidized if they benefited from domestic agricultural support programs, perhaps not something that the original drafters intended. Indeed, the EC observed to the Appellate Body that the finding in this case "blurs the distinction between domestic support and export subsidies."[14]

In the upland cotton subsidy case brought against the United States by Brazil, the DSB went in the same direction (DS 267). In effect, it questioned the consistency of some domestic agricultural support programs with WTO

[14] The Appellate Body asserted that its interpretation was based on the specific facts and circumstances of the sugar case and in particular that the sugar had to be exported (Powell and Schmitz, 2005, p. 37).

rules. Central to the dispute were two support programs. One consisted of direct payments to farmers, which were not related to prices or production but which the DSB nonetheless found to be actionable subsidies because the farmers receiving the payments were restricted in the alternative uses to which they could put their land (thus indirectly affecting prices and production). The other was the counter-cyclical payments that were introduced in the late 1990s when cotton prices fell. Although intended solely as support for farm incomes, the DSB noted that the base price in the program was well above world market prices, thus affecting world prices and making the payments actionable subsidies. Furthermore, the DSB found that, in suppressing world prices, the U.S. programs caused "serious prejudice" to the interests of the complainant, namely, Brazil. In this particular case, what gave rise to the dispute was not so much a failure on the part of the original drafters of the Uruguay Round agreements to appreciate their implications as a shift in the U.S. agricultural policies since the completion of the Round. With the collapse of cotton prices in the late 1990s, the balance of political forces had moved toward a partial reinstatement of the old policy of price supports, bringing support policy into conflict with WTO agreements accepted in the early 1990s.[15]

Analysis of the evidence rather than interpretation of the rules has been of primary importance in many cases. For instance, an important condition that the DSB has stipulated in its definition of export subsidies is that there should be a demonstrable link between the payment of a subsidy and actual export performance. The legal and institutional channels through which payments are made have therefore had to be studied. In a case brought by the EC against South Korea on the subsidization of commercial vessels, for instance, the complaint was that certain government agencies provided preferential financial terms to capital goods exporters (DS 273). The DSB noted, however, that there was no "mandate" requiring these agencies to provide export subsidies, and it ruled that only certain of their loans and guarantees could be identified as directly linked to export performance.

Appraisal of the evidence can demand careful and detailed economic analysis of local circumstances. It may not be easy, for instance, to determine whether payments made by a government were actually on terms below market rates and therefore constituted subsidies. Making fair comparisons of publicly and privately provided finance has been important in the cases brought by Canada against Brazil and Brazil against Canada on regional aircraft (DS 46, 70, 71, 222). Both countries are leading manufacturers of regional aircraft, have provided active governmental support to their manufacturers, and are close competitors.

[15] Canada has recently requested formation of a panel to settle a dispute about the U.S. corn subsidies. Other cases may be in the wings, awaiting the outcome of the Doha Development Round.

On both sides, the allegation was that financial arrangements made by governmental agencies in support of exports constituted prohibited export subsidies. In one phase of this long-running dispute, it was asserted that the Export Development Corporation (EDC) of Canada provided finance on terms more favorable than the private market. The DSB rejected this view, however, on the grounds that the EDC was able to provide highly favorable terms partly because it had acquired substantial expertise in this segment of the financial market and partly because its large portfolio allowed it to diversify its risks. Furthermore, it pointed to evidence of the competitiveness of the EDC; its net interest margin was better that that of some of the commercial banks.

On the Brazilian side, the initial complaint was that the government subsidized export financing through an interest-equalization account. (Brazil did not deny that this constituted a subsidy but argued that "payments are permitted in so far as they are not used to secure a material advantage in the field of export credit terms." The DSB rejected this reasoning, stating that the intention of the SCM Agreement was to impose a discipline on "subsidies which distort international trade.") In subsequent presentations, the focus shifted from broad complaints about the activities of governmental agencies to an analysis of the sources of financing in specific contracts negotiated with individual purchasers. Clearly, the DSB required considerable data and analysis – some of which has been withheld on grounds of commercial sensitivity – in order to make informed judgments. Yet there may be no clear yardstick of fairness in such cases since specific circumstances keep changing and plausible alternative assessments are always possible.

As well as the factual evidence, the more theoretical assumptions underlying the economic or financial analysis may also affect the rulings of the DSB. In assessing the evidence in specific cases, the DSB has been guided, unsurprisingly, by the more conventionally accepted assumptions. The case brought by the EC against the United States on the Foreign Sales Corporation (FSC) (and subsequent) legislation illustrates the role that such conventional beliefs may play in the interpretation and application of the rules (DS 108). The dispute raised the question whether certain national tax rebates or exemptions constituted export subsidies and therefore gave rise to unfair competition. Historically, some national tax measures have long been recognized as placing domestic producers or exporters at an unfair disadvantage in international trade. A manufacturer paying a sales tax on his product would, for instance, be at a competitive disadvantage if he were required to pay the same tax on his exports of the product; and it has been customary to exempt exports or to rebate the tax. Conversely, if imports did not attract the tax, domestic producers would be disadvantaged; and again, it has been customary to adjust border taxes to ensure national treatment of imported products. In brief, WTO rules have recognized indirect taxes as adjustable at the border. On the other hand, direct taxes such as corporate taxes have remained outside the scope of the rules.

When the EC countries began to introduce value-added taxes, these were treated as indirect taxes, an approach that was formally recognized in the Subsidy Code negotiated during the Tokyo Round in the 1970s. However, to U.S. producers and exporters, not working within a value-added tax system, it appeared that the European exporters received a tax rebate on their exports, whereas U.S. exports to the EC were subject to an additional tax. After the Tokyo Round, the United States introduced the FSC legislation, which gave American producers a measure of tax relief on their exports. Exporters were permitted to set up FSCs through which their export earnings were channeled, and they were allowed to defer taxes on a portion of these earnings. (Since deferment was for a number of years during which interest could be earned on the deferred taxes, the arrangement amounted to tax exemption.) After the adoption of the SCM Agreement, however, the EC challenged the legislation and the DSB ruled that, by the terms of the SCM Agreement, the U.S. tax relief fitted the definition of a prohibited export subsidy: revenue was foregone by the government, a benefit was conferred on the exporter, and the subsidy was contingent on export performance. The United States abandoned the practice after first attempting unsuccessfully to comply through modification of the legislation.

It has been trenchantly argued (Hufbauer, 2002) that the conventional view of taxes on which this ruling was based rests on weak economic analysis. In simple theory, the burden of an indirect tax falls wholly on the consumers who purchase the taxed product; unlike a direct tax, it does not affect production costs and the competitiveness of firms. In the case of a value-added tax, however, its incidence depends on several characteristics of the market and the tax itself. Producers may find it difficult to pass on the tax, and its incidence may fall mainly on their earnings – on the incomes of land, labor, and capital – and would therefore constitute a direct tax.[16] Thus, the distinction between rebates of direct taxes on export earnings and rebates of value-added taxes on exported products may be more blurred than conventionally assumed.[17]

---

[16] As Hufbauer observes, one of the characteristics that makes this more likely is whether or not adjustments are made at the border; a tax at the border would shift the incidence toward the income earners.

[17] As Hufbauer himself notes, the economic logic critical of the accepted convention can be taken even further. As others have argued, it does not matter in the end whether the tax policy subsidizes exports. In a regime of freely floating exchange rates, any advantage that a subsidizing country may obtain will be washed away by the effect of an improving trade balance in causing the currency to appreciate. However, as we know, this process takes time, and, moreover, other forces affecting the capital account may cause contrary movements in the exchange rate. The link is abstruse and uncertain. In the meantime, exporters are grumbling about the tax advantage of competitors and, in their world of more partial analysis, see the governmentally engineered tax advantage as unfair. It is with this more immediate world of national sentiment that the formal trading system must cope.

The particular economic analysis brought to bear on the evidence may clearly affect the rulings of the DSB. We may quote another, more extreme case on this score – one that concerned, not the subsidization of exports, but of domestic production in competition with imports. This was the case brought against Indonesia regarding certain measures affecting domestic car and car part production (DS 54, 55, 59, 64). Indonesia gave exemptions or rebates on import duties and sales taxes to companies that met certain local content requirements as well as to cars or car parts manufactured by Indonesian companies elsewhere and imported into Indonesia. The DSB found that the measures contravened several WTO rules, including non-discrimination, national treatment, and TRIMS. It also found that, under the terms of the SCM Agreement, the subsidies to domestic industry constituted actionable subsidies because they caused "serious prejudice" to the interests of the EC as an exporter. Thus, the ruling placed a restriction on Indonesian industrial policy, bearing out the criticism of many that the WTO rules and their interpretation were hostile to some of the developmental measures of poor countries. As in the case against India discussed in the section on national treatment, it appears that the economic model implicit in this judgment is one of comparative statics, not of economic growth. Had the judgment been backed by a more growth-oriented analysis, where development is seen as a succession of innovative investments that are actively supported by public policy interventions, it might well have been different. However, the DSB was probably reluctant to ask whether a subsidy was consistent with a member's development needs. The DSB panel in the case of Brazil's export subsidies of regional aircraft had noted that such was "an inquiry of a peculiarly economic and political nature, and notably ill-suited to a review by a panel whose function is fundamentally legal" (DS 46).

In various subsidy cases brought before the DSB, there has evidently been scope for differences of opinion about the fairness of its specific rulings. While the DSB has interpreted the definition of subsidies quite broadly, it has certainly remained within the terms of the SCM Agreement. However, in the analysis of the evidence in specific cases, there has been room for differences of opinion, deriving particularly from the assumptions underlying the economic reasoning. In assessing fairness, we have to recognize, therefore, that different but equally defensible constructions can be put upon the evidence.

3.1.4. Restrictive business practices

Restrictive business practices are also widely seen as another source of unfair competition. While there is no multilateral agreement under the WTO that covers these practices, they have been indirectly challenged through the dispute settlement process. The closest to a direct challenge came in the Kodak–Fuji complaint that the United States brought against

Japan (DS 44). The complaint was that governmental measures and business practices in Japan impeded foreign competition in the market for photographic film. Three sets of measures were criticized: distribution measures that allegedly created a market structure that prevented the access of foreign producers to traditional distribution channels; restrictions on the operation of large retail stores that allegedly prevented the growth of alternative distribution channels; and measures that restricted the use of sales-promotion techniques. Thus, the complaint was, in essence, directed at alleged deficiencies in Japanese competition policy.

In the absence of WTO rules relating to restrictive business practices, the complainant made the broad argument that its benefits under the WTO Agreements were being nullified or impaired by the measures (Article XXIII of GATT) and, in addition, that the Japanese distribution measures violated the national treatment provision. Some have said that, in this case, the United States was testing the boundaries of WTO jurisprudence. The nullification or impairment clause in the GATT provides a possible means of challenging measures of trading partners that are not specifically covered in the existing agreements; it accommodates "non-violation" complaints.

In the event, the DSB did not accept such a broad interpretation of the nullification or impairment clause. Nor did it directly address the absence of competition rules in the WTO. The DSB judged that the United States had failed to demonstrate that the Japanese measures had actually nullified or impaired its benefits under the WTO or that the measure conflicted with the national treatment provision. It thus assessed the complaint against the terms of the existing agreements and did not pass judgment on national laws or regulations that lay outside these agreements. To have done so would have been unfair since members of the WTO had not consented to any rules in the field of competition policy.

The story was quite different in the complaint brought by the United States against Mexico on telecommunications services (DS 204). The complaint was that Mexico maintained anti-competitive and discriminatory measures, tolerated certain market barriers employed in the private sector, and failed to take the needed regulatory measures. Since the matter concerned a service industry, the rules of the General Agreement on Trade in Services (GATS) applied, and it contains provisions that specifically relate to the measures being complained about. The DSB found that the measures were in violation of the GATS.

3.2. Contingent trade remedy measures and WTO rules

Our second cluster of disputes concerns contingent trade remedy measures. Three types of measures are provided for in the WTO Agreement: anti-dumping, countervailing, and safeguard measures. A WTO member is authorized, when certain contingencies are fulfilled, to impose such measures that might otherwise be inconsistent with the WTO Agreement. That is, under Article VI of the GATT 1994 and the Uruguay Round Anti-Dumping Agreement, anti-dumping duties can be imposed on a non-Most-Favored-Nation (MFN) basis on a producer or exporter and at levels in excess of WTO bindings in cases in which "dumped" imports cause or threaten "material" injury to a domestic industry. Under GATT Article VI and the Uruguay Round Agreement on SCM, countervailing duties can be used to offset a subsidy that benefits export producers and that is found to cause or threaten "material" injury to a domestic industry. Safeguard measures can be imposed in excess of bound rates or equivalent quantitative restrictions under GATT Article XIX and the WTO Agreement on Safeguards in the event of unforeseen developments in which imports cause or threaten "serious" injury to a domestic industry. Each type of contingent measure is subject to review at specified times. There is a "sunset" clause in the Anti-Dumping and SCM Agreements, which specifies that the measures should be terminated not later than five years after their imposition or the date of their most recent review, subject to determination that the expiration of the measures might likely lead to a continuation or recurrence of the injury involved. Safeguards are not to remain in effect for longer than four years although exceptions can be made for measures for up to eight years.

What distinguishes contingent trade remedies is that they are imposed initially by the importing country and without any form of advance authorization. As a consequence, as Krier (2005, p. 48) notes, the discipline of dispute settlement in these cases tends to focus on the *processes* by which the determination of the trade remedy is carried out by the national authorities. For anti-dumping and countervailing measures, this involves (p.49): "… the process by which investigations are initiated, transparency, due process and participatory rights of interested parties, public notice and explanation of determinations and judicial review." These same provisions, though less detailed, apply to safeguards. Dispute settlement panels thus are not initial finders of fact but rather are mainly concerned with how the investigations have been carried out.

3.2.1. Anti-dumping

In commenting on the rulings and recommendations of the DSB throughout this paper, our primary interest has been to ask whether the DSB has interpreted and applied the rules of the WTO fairly. The underlying assumption is that the rules themselves are accepted as reflecting a broad consensus about fair conduct in trade relations. As regards the Anti-Dumping Agreement, however, it is stretching belief to say that the anti-dumping practices allowed by the WTO rules are widely regarded as fair; they have been the subject of unrelenting criticism, particularly from economists. Anti-dumping provisions had been incorporated in the trade laws of a number of industrial countries long before World War II, and the anti-dumping rules of GATT and the WTO have largely been built around such legislation. The formal justification for the national laws has been the need for measures to counter "unfair trade" practices. However, the central criterion of "unfair trade" employed in the legislation is that the export price of a product is below the "normal" price in the home country; if this causes injury or threat of injury to producers in the importing country, it becomes the basis for justifying an anti-dumping duty.

There are many reasons why the export price may be below the "normal" price (which include the method of how these prices are measured), and a divergence may not be indicative of an "unfair trade" practice. The pricing strategies of firms within countries often use below-cost pricing for specific product lines, and the practice is regarded as quite consistent with national competition laws. It is only when an exporting firm operates from a "sanctuary" home market – one so protected that the firm can sell at a higher price at home – that the case for "unfair trade "can be argued. Such conditions are probably quite uncommon. Where they do not prevail, anti-dumping measures become no more than politically expedient measures to protect producers in the importing country.

Given the nature of the WTO rules, its dispute settlement process is severely limited in its ability to make rulings and recommendations that would be widely regarded as fair. It is confined to assessing whether national practices are consistent with the WTO rules, particularly in regard to the procedures and methodologies used by governments in arriving at decisions on the application of anti-dumping duties.

Since the inception of the WTO, 62 complaints about anti-dumping measures have been referred to the DSB. Respondents have been equally divided between industrial countries on the one hand and emerging market economies/developing countries on the other. The majority of cases against the latter have been settled through consultations or there was no settlement notified to the WTO. In contrast, many of the cases involving the EC and the United States have been much more drawn out through time in the panel and appellate process and in the implementation of the decisions handed down. The different experiences suggest that the anti-dumping issues involving the EC and the United States may be more complex, politically more sensitive, subject to different legal interpretations or given to delays in changing national laws and institutional practices to conform to WTO anti-dumping regulations. Yet the evidence suggests that the EC and the United States have finally responded when they are found in violation of WTO regulations.

Among the most troublesome cases that have resulted in protracted litigation are those involving the use of "zeroing" in calculating dumping margins, conflicts posed by U.S. laws, implementation of sunset reviews, and special circumstances in dispute settlement arising from the North American Free Trade Agreement (NAFTA).

"Zeroing" is a patently unfair practice used by some governments in determining anti-dumping duties. In the case brought by India against anti-dumping duties in the EC on bed linen, the practice was challenged (DS 141). It involves the establishment of a set of categories in the product under question. Within each category, a weighted average normal value is calculated by reference to home-country sales, third-country sales, or a constructed value. This normal value is then compared with a weighted average export price for that category. If the normal value is higher, the difference is treated as a positive dumping margin, that is, the goods are being exported at less than their normal value. If the normal value is lower than the export price, a negative dumping margin would exist. However, under EC practice, in calculating a total weighted average for all categories of the product under investigation, the negative dumping margins are changed to zero. As a result, the calculated dumping margin may be significantly overstated. The DSB ruled against the EC and in favor of India in this case. The United States has also been challenged successfully in a number of cases for its use of "zeroing" (DS 282, 294, 322, 325, 239).[18]

The consistency of national legislation with WTO rules has been another source of complaints. One such complaint was brought by the EC and Japan against the U.S. (DS 136, 162). This sought to invalidate the 1916 Act of the U.S., which was an anti-trust-based statute that addressed foreign-based predatory pricing (i.e., dumping), and made it a criminal offense that could result in the imposition of fines or imprisonment or recovery of treble damages. The United States argued that the 1916 Act was an internal matter and that it targeted predatory pricing more broadly, requiring that there be an intent to destroy, injure, or prevent the establishment of a U.S. industry or to restrain or monopolize trade. However, the DSB ruled that the Act violated the pertinent provisions of the GATT/WTO anti-dumping agreements. The U.S. subsequently repealed the 1916 Act in December 2004.

Several countries challenged another piece of U.S. legislation, best known as the Byrd Amendment (DS 217, 234). This complaint was lodged against the *Continued Dumping and Subsidy Offset Act of 2000*. This act changed the disposition of funds raised from duties on imports that the U.S. government determined to be dumped domestically. Before the Act, those funds were incorporated into the U.S. budget. The Act specified that the funds be distributed to the U.S. companies that filed pricing complaints. This meant that non-U.S. firms allegedly engaged in dumping could be fined and the funds given to the U.S. companies that made the

---

[18] See Ikenson (2005, esp. pp. 10–11) for an illustration of how anti-dumping margins can be inflated using zeroing and pp. 20–21 for a discussion of some of the WTO cases challenging the U.S. Import Administration's (IA) use of zeroing. He notes that the IA "… is adamantly opposed to changing its zeroing practice …," presumably "… to serve its mission of safeguarding American industries and jobs."

complaint initially. The duties could no longer be ostensibly argued as restoring fair price competition, and, indeed, they provided firms with a monetary incentive to initiate anti-dumping cases. The Byrd Amendment was ruled to be illegal in 2002. Following the imposition of sanctions on imports of selected U.S. goods by some of the complainants, the Byrd Amendment was repealed in January 2006, although the Act's provisions were to remain place until October 1, 2007, and the funds could continue to be redirected to the U.S. filing companies during this time.

As noted, according to the Anti-Dumping Agreement, measures should be terminated not later than five years after their imposition or the date of their most recent review, subject to determination that the expiration of the measures might likely lead to a continuation or recurrence of the injury involved. There have been several cases in which the implementation of the U.S. sunset procedures has been challenged (DS 281, 282, 244, 99, 268, 89, 225, 262).[19]

In at least two cases, differences in the dispute settlement mechanisms of the WTO and NAFTA have created some confusion and conflicts in coverage and interpretations. The U.S.-Canadian softwood lumber dispute is discussed completely in Section 4 but we may note here that, in addition to countervailing duties, the U.S. imposed anti-dumping duties on Canadian lumber. Canada challenged both the countervailing duties and the anti-dumping duties under Chapter 19 of NAFTA and in dispute settlement proceedings in the WTO. Canadian producers also filed claims against the U.S. government under the investor–state dispute settlement provisions of Chapter 11 of NAFTA. This extensive litigation resulted in a state of confusion. That is, on November 15, 2005, a WTO panel *accepted* a U.S. finding that Canadian imports of softwood lumber threatened to cause material injury to U.S firms. But, on August 10, 2005, a NAFTA Extraordinary Challenge Committee had confirmed an earlier NAFTA (Chapter 19) panel conclusion that did not support a finding of threat of material injury. The situation was further complicated by the claim filed under Chapter 11 of NAFTA. In the end, the lumber dispute, as we note later, was settled bilaterally.

A dispute between Mexico and the U.S. took much the same character. The issue was an anti-dumping duty imposed by Mexico on imports from the U.S. of high-fructose corn syrup (DS 101, 132). Each government had filed trade dispute cases before NAFTA and the WTO challenging the other's handling of the dispute. Again, in the end, the dispute was resolved bilaterally.

In the context of a discussion of fairness in dispute settlement, it is worth noting that two different dispute settlement bodies may arrive at opposite rulings on the same legal claims. How far this may be due to differences in

[19] Ikenson (2005, p. 21) suggests that the U.S. IA has been reluctant to bring U.S. sunset policy into conformity with the WTO Anti-Dumping Agreement and that the IA "... has turned what should be a temporary remedial measure into permanent protection."

the texts of the relevant agreements or in procedures or in the assessments of the evidence, we do not know. It does appear, however, that once a dispute settlement procedure has been initiated in either NAFTA or the WTO, one or the other forum is thereby excluded from further examining the issues at stake, and there may be no interaction between them.

More generally, the most we can say about the fairness of the WTO dispute settlement process in the area of anti-dumping measures is that in applying the Anti-dumping Agreement, the DSB has worked to remove some of the most egregiously unfair national practices.

3.2.2. Countervailing duties

The SCM Agreement requires that, before imposing a countervailing duty, member countries must undertake investigations that meet certain conditions: There must be sufficient evidence of the existence of a subsidy, of injury to the domestic industry, and of a causal link between the subsidized imports and the injury. Some of the key issues have been documented in the *European Journal of International Law* by Trachtman (2007) and others.

In one case of definition of a subsidy, Canada complained that the U.S. charged a countervailing duty on certain products on the grounds that Canada had imposed an export restraint on a product that was used in the production of the exported products (DS 194). The reasoning of the United States was that the restraint depressed the domestic price of the product and thus subsidized the exported products. The DSB panel, however, was of the opinion that the export restraint did not constitute a financial contribution and therefore did not qualify as a subsidy within the meaning of the SCM Agreement. (For other reasons, however, the DSB did not rule on this case.) In another such case of rule interpretation, the EC complained that, in a sunset review of a countervailing duty on certain steel products, the United States had failed to apply a *de minimis* standard as required by the SCM Agreement (DS 213). The interpretation of the DSB was that the Agreement did not require application of the standard.

Complaints about the imposition of countervailing duties have more often challenged the evidence presented in support of the duty. In at least two cases, the issue was whether, on privatization of a state-owned company, some part of the subsidies formerly granted to the state-owned company had been passed through to the new private firm. In the case of the countervailing duties imposed by the United States on certain steel products from the United Kingdom, the DSB ruled that the privatization extinguished the subsidy; the privatization had been carried out at arm's length and at fair market prices (DS 138). The conclusion was similar in a comparable case brought against the United States by the EC (DS 212).

Two complaints brought by South Korea against the United States and the EC concerned the imposition of countervailing duties on dynamic random access memory semi-conductors or chips (DS 296, 299). While approached differently by the DSB panels, the two cases turned similarly on whether the analysis of the factual evidence justified the duties. In both cases, the DSB found that a subsidy existed but that the analysis had failed to establish a link between the subsidized imports and injury to the domestic industry.

In the long-running dispute between Canada and the United States on softwood lumber that we have already mentioned, Canada initiated several complaints concerning the countervailing duties imposed by the United States (DS 236, 247, 257, 264, 277, 311). These cases dealt with different methodological and procedural aspects of the U.S. determination of the duties. In DS 257, for example, the DSB concluded that it was unable to determine whether the United States had correctly assessed the benefit accruing to Canadian industry from the recognized subsidy. The issue was how to treat a subsidy on primary goods that was passed on to further stages of processing. The DSB ruled in this case that a pass-through analysis was required in connection with sales of logs by tenured harvesters to unrelated sawmills. In DS 277, the DSB found that the United States had failed to demonstrate that the rise in imports was "substantial" or that there was a causal link between the imports and injury to the domestic industry. These cases were overtaken by events when, in October 2006, as discussed in Section 4, Canada and the United States signed a comprehensive bilateral agreement on softwood lumber that closed the dispute.

These cases in countervailing measures are a sub-category of the cases on subsidies, and from the viewpoint of fairness, much the same can be said about them. The issue of fairness has turned, for the most part, on the analysis of the evidence, and there has been room for differences of opinion about whether the evidence has been sufficiently or correctly assessed.

3.2.3. Safeguards

Safeguard measures differ from anti-dumping or countervailing measures in that they are not justified as a response to "unfair trade." These measures, which may take the form of increased tariffs or quotas, are designed to deal with unforeseen import surges resulting from earlier trade concessions that can be demonstrated to have "caused" serious injury in the importing country. They are intended to allow time for adjustment by an industry to a new trading situation. The justification of safeguard measures, which are permitted under Article XIX of the GATT and the Uruguay Round Agreement on Safeguards, is consequently expected to meet a higher standard (particularly of injury) than in the case of the other measures. Safeguard measures are also applied on an MFN basis on all imports of like products; and there may be compensation measures that are applied under special circumstances to exporting countries that are harmed by the imposition of safeguards.

Since 1995, there have been 31 safeguard actions filed in dispute settlement. Of these, 16 have been the subject of DSB reports (eight of these were complainant cases involved in settling the U.S. steel safeguard dispute). As with other measures, our particular interest is in whether the DSB – through its panels and Appellate Body – has interpreted and applied the rules fairly. In the case of safeguard measures, however, the language of the GATT Article and the Safeguards Agreement leaves notably large uncertainties about what the rules are. Sykes (2003) and Trachtman (2007, pp. 20–24) have noted a number of difficult interpretative issues that have arisen. Sykes has discussed these issues in the context of specific cases that have reached the Appellate Body of the DSB.

One source of difficulty is that, in accordance with GATT Article XIX, member countries may introduce safeguard measures to counter a larger than expected rise in imports if it takes place "as a result of unforeseen developments and of the effects of the obligations incurred" by a member, but it is unclear what constitute "unforeseen developments" and which obligations are relevant. Even though the Safeguards Agreement does not contain such language, the Appellate Body ruled in a case brought against South Korea relating to safeguard measures on imports of cotton and dairy products that the phrases remained a binding obligation (DS 98). Similar rulings were made in cases against Argentina on footwear (DS 121), and against the United States on lamb meat (DS 178). Sykes notes that the Appellate Body has not offered any meaningful guidance on how countries can satisfy the outmoded Article XIX requirements.

There is also a problem of measurement in defining what constitutes an import surge, which arose in the just mentioned case against Argentina. Sykes again notes that the Appellate Body has not provided guidance on the baseline to be used in measuring the "increased quantities."

There is a further problem in the definition of "serious injury." Sykes notes that the Appellate Body has not defined "serious injury" with any precision and has referred to the text of the Safeguards Agreement that states that "… the competent authorities shall evaluate all relevant factors of an objective and quantifiable nature having a bearing on the situation of that industry …" Thus, in the Argentina footwear case and in the case against the United States on wheat gluten (DS 166), the Appellate Body found that the safeguard measures implemented had not met the "all relevant factors" requirement. More broadly, the Appellate Body has ruled that serious injury should reflect "significant overall impairment," a condition that was found to be lacking in the Argentine footwear and the U.S. frozen lamb meat cases.

The causal relationship between increased quantities of imports and serious injury has figured in several cases. It can be very difficult to determine the causes of injury to an industry since there may be other factors such as changes in demand patterns rather than increased imports, which give rise to serious injury. In the aforementioned cases of Argentine footwear, U.S. frozen lamb meat and wheat gluten, as well as the case against the U.S. on carbon quality line pipes (DS 202), the Appellate Body did not address the conceptual issues involved in treating imports as a causal variable. Sykes thus concludes that: "… the Appellate Body offers no coherent guidance as to when safeguards are permissible and when they are not."[20]

The case against the United States on steel safeguards warrants separate attention. (DS 248, 249, 250–254, 258, 259) This case involved 10 safeguard measures that were applied and that were challenged by Brazil, China, EC, Japan, Korea, New Zealand, Norway, and Switzerland, with several additional countries requesting third-party representation. The Appellate Body ruled that all the measures were inconsistent with the U.S. obligations under Article XIX and the Safeguards Agreement, and all the claims were consolidated. This case has been discussed at length in Devereaux *et al.* (2006, Vol. 2), who note that the steel safeguard tariffs were imposed in response to the intense lobbying pressures of the domestic steel producers and union representatives to deal with the problems posed by the alleged surge of imported steel resulting from the foreign financial crises of the late 1990s.

The facts of this case were in dispute, and there was no clear evidence of substantial injury for the steel firms and workers involved. Yet the action was taken even though the Bush Administration knew that it would be challenged in the WTO, which turned out to be the case. The rationale for the Bush Administration appears to have been that, while WTO-inconsistent, the imposition of the safeguard tariffs would buy time for the aid to benefit the U.S. steel producers and workers. This is because of the various steps involved in implementing a dispute settlement action. It turned out that the Bush Administration removed the tariffs in the face of potential retaliation especially by the EC. This case thus illustrates how a country can "game" the WTO dispute settlement system at least for a while, but in the final analysis the WTO system becomes effective.

The WTO safeguard cases are significant in so far as practically every safeguard measure that has been challenged in the panel/Appellate Body process has been overturned. WTO member countries may thus be at a loss when it comes to designing safeguard actions that can meet panel/Appellate Body approval. What is needed therefore is recognition of this impasse and efforts to design guidelines and criteria that WTO members can attempt to follow without encountering the dead ends that they have experienced thus far.[21] If WTO member countries are reluctant to use safeguard measures for fear of their being overturned, it is quite likely that they may resort to other trade-remedy measures, in particular

---

[20] See Irwin (2003) for a review of WTO decisions involving causation and injury attribution in the U.S. escape clause cases and for a methodology for attributing injury to various factors that could be used to enable U.S. safeguards decisions to conform to the requirements specified in the WTO Safeguards Agreement.

[21] For suggested actions, see Sykes (2003, 2004) and for a critique of Sykes's views, see Jones (2004).

anti-dumping actions that do not have the same constraints as safeguard measures.[22] It is also possible that countries may decide to game the system to gain time in protecting domestic industries along the same lines as in the U.S. steel safeguard case noted above.

The vagueness in the rules relating to safeguard measures leaves open the question of whether the DSB has interpreted and applied the rules fairly.

3.3. National preferences and WTO rules

Another cluster of dispute cases arises from disagreements about how WTO rules should be reconciled with the many non-commercial regulations that nations apply domestically. While these regulations may impinge on external trade and affect the interests of trading partners, they also express social preferences that governments may view as overriding commercial concerns. This was recognized when the GATT was first drawn up in 1947. Members have always understood that they may claim exemption for their GATT/WTO obligations on certain non-commercial grounds – the most relevant in the present context being the protection of public morals, of the environment, and of the life and health of humans, animals, and plants. At the same time, they have been concerned that trading partners should not exploit such exemptions as a means of evading their trade obligations. The DSB has sometimes been called upon to define more precisely where the line lies between national preferences and WTO obligations.

The DSB has insisted that it does not question the right of members to determine their own domestic policies in these matters. However, it has usually maintained that, in application of these policies, members should respect the WTO rules about non-discrimination and national treatment. A recent example is in the case brought against the United States by Antigua and Baruda in regard to gambling and betting services (DS 258). The complaint arose out of restrictions that the United States had imposed on Internet gambling. The DSB found that, while the United States was certainly not barred from implementing measures that were deemed "necessary to protect public morals or to maintain public order," it was obliged to do so in a way that was consistent with its obligations under the WTO. The DSB noted that the commitments made in regard to these services by the United States under the GATS Agreement provided for full market access. Moreover, the U.S. regulations permitted certain exceptions such as interstate bets on horseracing and remote gambling conducted by Native American tribal entities, and these were not consistent with the obligation to apply measures in a non-discriminatory way.

Similar reasoning was applied in a complaint against the United States that its environmental regulations discriminated against imports of

---

[22] For an analysis along these lines, see Bown (2002).

gasoline from Brazil and Venezuela (DS 2, 4). Regulations adopted by the United States to implement a 1990 amendment to its Clean Air Act required domestic producers and importers of gasoline to meet certain standards that would reduce vehicle emissions of toxic air pollutants and ozone-forming compounds in the most air-polluted areas of the country. The regulations called for the establishment of certain baselines regarding the quality of the gasoline produced in 1990. The complaint was that the method used to determine baselines had the effect of discriminating against imported supplies. The DSB did not question the right of the United States to take measures to control air pollution. Clean air was an "exhaustible natural resource" whose protection justified an exception from WTO obligations. However, the DSB found that the measure violated WTO obligations because it was applied in a way that resulted in "unjustifiable discrimination" against imports from Brazil and Venezuela. Accordingly, it constituted "a disguised restriction of international trade" (the language in the chapeau to Article XX of GATT on general exceptions).

These cases were relatively straightforward applications of the idea of fairness expressed in non-discrimination and national treatment. In the more famous shrimp/sea turtle case brought by the United States against Thailand, the DSB entered more difficult terrain (DS 58). The case raised the question whether national regulations could override WTO obligations when the issue at stake was production methods used in foreign countries; this appeared to be unfair since it implied that the national preferences of one country could override those of another country.

The specific issue was a U.S. prohibition of shrimp imports from countries where the method of fishing endangered sea turtles since sea turtles were a protected species in the United States. As a general position, the DSB explicitly accepted that the international trading system should be wholly consistent with sustainable development. In this particular case, the United States could rightly seek an exception from its WTO obligations on the grounds that it was protecting an "exhaustible natural resource" (even though the resource being protected was beyond its territorial waters). However, the DSB questioned the U.S. regulation because it prescribed that domestic and foreign shrimpers had to use a particular production method – nets with a turtle extruder device – as a condition of being certified as suppliers to the U.S. market. This method of implementing the regulation was deemed to be both arbitrary and discriminatory and was therefore – as in the other environmental cases – in violation of WTO rules.

The DSB, however, went further, addressing the issue of the national preferences of one country overriding those of another. It stated that, as a condition of claiming an exception from WTO obligations, the United States should make good faith efforts to negotiate a bilateral or multilateral environmental agreement (MEA) that would protect sea turtles. In stipulating this condition, the DSB was apparently seeking a justification for encroachment on the sovereignty of the shrimp-exporting members.

It found grounds in the text of the Marrakech Decision that established the WTO Committee on Trade and the Environment. The DSB maintained that trade-related measures not based on international consensus were not the "... most appropriate means of enforcing environmental measures ..." and could lead to the "... imposition of unwanted constraints on the multilateral trading system."[23] In principle, the expression of national preferences in an MEA made the decision fair in the sense that all the trading partners had voluntarily consented to the action.

These interpretations of the rules as they relate to environmental measures have been careful to respect the ability of each member country to decide its own standards. However, when disputes have concerned exceptions to WTO obligations on the grounds of protecting human, animal or plant life, and health, the same has not been so. In these disputes, the DSB has been guided by a distinctly more stringent set of rules. Before national regulations for the protection of human, animal or plant life, and health may qualify as a legitimate exception to WTO obligations, they must clear the hurdle set in the Sanitary and Phytosanitary Agreement (SPS). It specifies that the need for regulation has to be justified by the scientific evidence, including an adequate assessment of risk. Members are expected to assess risk on the basis of the scientific evidence – as well as of other factors – while determining for themselves the level of risk that is acceptable. The Agreement, however, urges members to make use, so far as possible, of common international standards.[24]

A complaint brought by the United States against Japan illustrates the application of the main terms of the SPS Agreement (DS 245). The complaint concerned the quarantine restrictions that Japan imposed on imported apples to protect against the introduction of a disease known as fire blight. The DSB found that the restrictions were maintained in the absence of sufficient scientific evidence of their need. In addition, the DSB held that Japan had not undertaken an adequate risk assessment. Furthermore, Japan could not defend the restrictions on the grounds that they were provisionally necessary because the scientific evidence presently available was insufficient. (Japan complied with the ruling by introducing less rigorous standards.)

The complaint by Canada about Australia's prohibition of certain salmon imports was similar in key respects (DS 18). The DSB again found that the scientific evidence in support of the need for restrictions was insufficient and that an appropriate risk assessment had not been made.

---

[23] The DSB later found the United States to be in compliance after it had taken several steps. Besides providing technical assistance to foreign shrimpers, the United States modified its regulations to remove reference to a specific production method and to make its certification process non-discriminatory; and it initiated good faith efforts to negotiate bilateral or multilateral environmental agreements to protect sea turtles.

[24] Defining such standards is the work of the international Codex Alimentarius Commission, a scientific committee of FAO/WHO that assists it.

Furthermore, it found that arbitrary and unjustifiable distinctions were made in different salmon products to which the restrictions applied. Australia stated that it would comply with the rulings. However, although the case was first adjudicated in 1998, there has as yet been no satisfactory resolution. Australia has made successive adjustments to its regulations, but these have not been deemed sufficient by Canada or the DSB. There apparently remain differences of views between the Canadian and the Australian authorities on a valid interpretation of the scientific evidence.

In both the Japanese and the Australian cases, the application of the rules by the DSB appeared straightforward. It judged the scientific evidence insufficient and the assessment of risk inadequate. In the well-known hormone-fed beef case, however, the uncertainties surrounding scientific evidence came very much to the fore. The complaint brought by the United States and Canada was that the EC imposed a ban on imports of hormone-fed beef (DS 26, 48). The import prohibition was an extension of an internal ban that the EC had introduced in 1989 on the use of growth-promoting hormones in fattening cattle. If the DSB had taken the same approach as in the environmental cases, this fact would have been highly relevant since the key question would have been whether the regulations discriminated between domestic and imported products. However, the rules relevant to this case were those embodied in the SPS Agreement. While the Agreement stated that a higher standard than the international standard was permissible, there had to be some scientific evidence to justify it. In the event, the DSB focused on whether the assessment of the health risk associated with the use of the hormones was adequate; and it judged that this was not so. Therefore, the EC import prohibition was in violation of its WTO obligations. (We return to the subsequent history of this case in Section 4.)

At the heart of this dispute have been the different views on the assessment of risk that the complainants and respondent held (and still hold). The United States has taken the position that hormone-fed beef, which had been on the North American market for a number of years, should be deemed to be virtually risk free so long as there was no evidence to the contrary. The EC has taken the more cautious view that a new product should be assumed to be unsafe until all reasonable concerns about its safety had been proven false. Known as the precautionary principle, this latter view has wide application in the EC.[25] One possible contributory explanation for this divergence in risk assessment derives

[25] In defining the precautionary principle, the EC has stated that the introduction of new products or processes is subject to review in "cases where scientific evidence is insufficient, inconclusive, or uncertain and preliminary scientific evaluation indicates that there are reasonable grounds for concern that the potential dangerous effects on the environment, human, animal or plant life, may be inconsistent with the high level of protection chosen by the EU" (quoted in Rifkin, 2004, p. 327).

from the difference in political structures of the EC and the United States. The EC allows lobbies representing consumer safety and environmental interests greater political influence while producers' lobbies hold greater sway in the United States.[26]

The same clash over risk assessment arose in the dispute over biotechnical products. The complaint (DS 291–293) made by the United States and others was that the EC was unreasonably delaying the importation of genetically modified (GM) products and had, in effect, imposed a moratorium on them. Public concern in EC countries about the possible environmental impact of introducing genetically modified organisms (GMOs) as well as of the possible harmful effects of GM foods on human health had led the European Council in 1990 to introduce a complicated approval process before any GM crop or GM food could be sold on the market. In 1997, the regulations were further tightened, provoking the complaint. The DSB found that the *de facto* moratorium was in violation of the SPS Agreement; it was unreasonably delaying approvals. Interestingly enough, the DSB did not pass judgment on "whether biotech products in general are safe or not," instead stating only that the EC was engaging in procedural delay. (The EC stated that it would comply with the findings of the DSB and was given until November 2007 to do so.)

In both the beef hormone and the GM organism cases, the DSB has evidently been reluctant to pass any judgment itself on the scientific evaluations. The SPS Agreement, however, sought to reduce the abuse of health and safety regulations as a protectionist device by invoking scientific evidence as a more objective criterion for their justification. The problem is that risk assessment is an important element in the scientific evidence and that necessarily contains a subjective component. In a world where technological innovations are many and rapid, where there are consequences for human life, the ecology and the larger natural environment that are not readily foreseen, different degrees of risk assessment may be equally rational. From the viewpoint of fairness, it is difficult to say whether the rulings of the DSB were fair. On the SPS Agreement itself, it can be argued that, if its intent was to prevent protectionist abuse of health regulations while respecting national preferences, the rulings appear unfair. Accepting a more literal interpretation of the Agreement, however, the panels and the Appellate Body stayed within its terms and, in that sense, acted fairly. However, the crux of the matter in both cases was the assessment of the scientific evidence and the

[26] The clash in viewpoint about the assessment of risk has surfaced in other international bodies. The Codex Alimentarius Commission adopted the U.S. approach. On the other hand, the UN Protocol on Bio-Safety (the Cartagena Protocol) recognized the precautionary principle: a "lack of scientific certainty" could justify a refusal to allow the importation of genetically modified organisms (Article 10).

associated risk, and on these scores, there was room for differences in assessments that could all be defended as reasonable. It is not possible to express a consensus view of what is fair.

4. Compliance with DSB rulings and recommendations

In assessing the fairness of the dispute settlement process, we also have to consider the record of members in complying with the rulings of the DSB. If we believe that the DSB has ruled fairly in most disputes and if members have complied with the rulings in a timely way, then the dispute settlement process as a whole has been operating fairly. In fact, the record of compliance has so far been good. Between 1995 and March 2007, the DSB ruled on 109 dispute cases, and it found violations of WTO rules in nearly 90 per cent of these cases (Wilson, 2007). Almost all members declared their intention to comply with the rulings, and most did so within a reasonable time. In a number of cases, however, the complainant challenged the corrective action taken by the violating member as insufficient, and this set off a further lengthy round of adjudication. (Such delay could cause considerable financial loss to the complainant and be a source of unfairness.) When the violating members have sooner or later brought their laws and regulations into conformity with the DSB findings, the disputes have been settled.

Not all disputes that have come before the panels or the Appellate Body of the DSB have been successfully resolved by their rulings. In a few cases, the parties to the dispute have finally taken the matter out of the WTO process and resolved it through bilateral negotiation. In others, the complainant has felt compelled to resort to countermeasures in order to induce compliance. Up to March 2007, the DSB has authorized the complainants in some eight cases to take countermeasures in the form of withdrawal of concessions; and in five of these cases, the countermeasures were implemented. While, as discussed in Section 5, the countermeasures can be seen as a deterrent to "cheating," the need to resort to these measures may also be symptomatic of an honest reluctance on the part of the violator to comply. This would suggest that some disputes might not be expeditiously or fairly resolved within the rigid legalistic framework established by the DSU. Compliance with the terms of the DSB rulings, however fair they appear to be within the restricted remit of the DSB, may not always seem fair when seen in a broader context.

One dispute that the DSB was not able to resolve through conclusive rulings and that was eventually settled through bilateral negotiation was that between Canada and the United States on softwood lumber (DS 257, 277). The background to the case was that the effects of Canadian imports on the U.S. lumber industry had long been a source of political concern in the United States, and various measures had been taken over the years to restrict competition. After the WTO rules had come into force, the U.S. imposed countervailing duties (and later, anti-dumping duties). At the core of the U.S. case was the stumpage fees paid by Canadian sawmills for lumber. Since the timberland was mostly publicly owned, the fees were paid to the government, and, it was argued, since these were below market rates, they constituted a subsidy. Canada challenged the U.S. action both in the WTO and in NAFTA. In the WTO, Canada brought two main cases against the United States. One contested the U.S. claim that Canadian lumber exports were subsidized and caused injury to the U.S. industry (thereby qualifying as an actionable subsidy). The other challenged the methodological and factual grounds that the United States used in assessing the duties. While the DSB accepted the U.S. arguments that production was subsidized, it failed to determine whether there was also injury to the U.S. industry. It also found merit in the Canadian criticisms of U.S. methodology but, after the United States had modified its approach, ruled that on this score the United States was in compliance with WTO requirements. Over the four years of the formal dispute, however, the verbal exchanges between Canada and the United States had become increasingly acrimonious and were souring broader political and economic relations. After it had become a source of political embarrassment to both the governments, the dispute was finally settled through bilateral negotiations. Under the Softwood Lumber Agreement, Canada undertook to impose an export tax, optionally combined with export quotas, in the event that prices fell below a specified level, and the United States agreed to revoke the existing countervailing and anti-dumping duty orders and to refund duty deposits held by the U.S. customs authorities. Although the agreed solution was not necessarily consistent with WTO rules, it was at least regarded as sufficiently fair to restore good relations between the trading partners.

Resolution of the banana dispute between the EC and the United States was similar (DS 27). It will be recalled that, as discussed earlier, the DSB had been insistent on as close adherence as possible to non-discrimination in the preferential access that the EC accorded the banana producers of the ACP countries. The EC, however, faced substantial difficulties in devising a revised regime that was acceptable to all its member governments, the EC banana distributors, and the ACP banana producing countries, while also meeting the conditions laid down by the DSB. On the other side, the EC's long delay in moving toward compliance provoked the United States into seeking approval for, and introducing, countermeasures.

In the end, the dispute was settled in 2001 – at least for the time being – through bilateral negotiations. The violator and the complainant bargained with each other to arrive at a distribution of benefits from the revised regime that both found politically acceptable. The EC undertook to introduce a tariff-quota regime for non-ACP suppliers under which licenses would be granted according to historical shares in the EC market – and this favored the traditional U.S. multinational distributor. At the same time, the United States agreed that the EC could set aside a proportion of licenses for "newcomers" – and these included non-traditional EC distributors. Although the outcome in the banana dispute was consistent with DSB rulings, it could not have been determined by the DSB. What triggered the negotiated settlement was the mounting fear of an appreciable worsening in trade relations between the two major traders. The U.S. Congress was threatening to call upon the U.S. administration to rotate the products subject to retaliation on a six-monthly basis.[27] Such action might have provoked the EC to put into effect the countermeasures it had been authorized to apply in the FSC case but had so far refrained from acting upon.[28]

The continuing nature of some disputes – usually rooted in a lasting political need to defend highly valued constituent interests – suggests that they may not always lend them to resolution through the formal, semi-legal process of the DSU. When one or both parties are reluctant to abandon practices that may violate the rules, they may resort to the dispute settlement process, less to seek a resolution, than to defend their competing positions. The cases brought by Canada and Brazil against each other with regard to the export subsidization of regional aircraft took on some of this coloration (DS 46, 70, 71, 222). The DSB found that both provided prohibited export subsidies to their manufacturers. Both modified their regulations and financial practices, and both thereafter challenged whether the other was yet complying with the WTO rules. At one stage, both the governments were authorized to use countermeasures against the other.

The history of these cases is one in which the DSB has been called upon to make repeated judgments about whether the successive arrangements for financing exports constituted prohibited subsidies. Both parties have seen the actions of the other as commercially unfair. The legalistic interplay, however, has not appeared to resolve the dispute; it has been no substitute for a more pragmatic understanding between the two governments on what constitutes mutually acceptable financial relations that each government may have with its producers. A similar pattern of behavior could appear in the recently initiated Boeing–Airbus cases brought by the EC and the United States against each other on the same issue of subsidies to a key export industry (DS 316, 317).

A more intractable reason for the failure of the dispute settlement process to resolve a dispute is when both parties apply quite different

---

[27] In 2000, the U.S. Congress passed a trade bill that included the so-called carousel provision.
[28] We should note that the dispute was revived in 2005 when the EC proposed to introduce new MFN tariffs and new quotas for ACP countries. In 2007, in response to requests from Ecuador and the United States, the DSB agreed to consider again whether the new EC regime was in conformity with its rulings.

conceptions of fairness to the case. That is, the ruling of the DSB may conflict with strongly held social preferences on the part of the violator. This has been at work in the hormone-fed beef case (DS 26, 48). As discussed earlier, the DSB found in favor of the United States and Canada and against the EC in its banning of the importation of hormone-fed beef. Following the failure of the EC to comply, the United States and Canada in 1999 put into effect duly authorized countermeasures. In 2003, the EC returned to the DSB arguing that these measures should be lifted as it was now in compliance with the DSB rulings (DS 320, 321). It claimed that the ban on five of the six hormones used in fattening cattle was "provisional" pending further scientific research, a designation that was consistent with the SPS Agreement; and it stated that its ban on the sixth hormone – oestradiol 17 beta – had been made permanent, since a group of scientists had concluded that the hormone was potentially a carcinogen.[29] At the time of writing, the case is still under adjudication. At the root of the EC position is a conception of fairness holding that every person should be free to act provided the action does not harm anyone else. The conception applied by Canada and the United States is that everyone is bound by the "rules of the game" as embodied in the negotiated agreements of the GATT/WTO.

What do we infer from the several cases that we have just reviewed? Not all disputes can be resolved within the rather rigid, semi-legalistic framework of the DSU. In some, a more fruitful path is bilateral negotiations because these are not confined to the question of conformity with specific rules but can encompass broader concerns; and the resolution of the dispute may consequently be fairer. In others, disagreement about interpretation of the rules may be so profound that no resolution is possible, and the complainant is left with the only recourse of imposing countermeasures.

5. *The use of countermeasures*

In most cases, as we have already noted, countries have complied in a timely way with the rulings of the DSB. In our view, they have generally done so in order to preserve their reputation as reliable trading partners. As with participants in national markets, they recognize the value for long-lasting commercial relations of mutual trust exercised within a framework of common rules of conduct. Of course, there are always the possible participants who seek to advance their interest at the expense of others by

---

[29] The EC argued that one reason why the DSB had found it to be non-compliant was that it had failed to carry out a risk assessment within the meaning of Articles 5.1 and 5.2 of the SPS Agreement. It stated that an assessment had now been done by an independent scientific committee whose findings indicated that hormones posed a risk to consumers.

disobeying the rules, and so countries have invariably wanted to threaten retaliatory measures in order to deter such transgressors. Under the GATT regime, retaliatory measures could nominally be authorized, but, as the alleged violator of a rule could veto their use, they were never actually employed. Despite this fact, according to Hudec (2002), the record of compliance during the GATT years from 1947 to 1994 was rather good. In the DSU of the WTO, the scope for use of countermeasures was nevertheless strengthened. Violators could no longer block the authorization of countermeasures. Since 1994, as just noted, the DSB has authorized the use of such measures in several cases. It is an open question whether the greater use of such measures has enhanced the fairness of the dispute settlement process.

Under the terms of the DSU, authorized countermeasures may take the form of the withdrawal of concessions unless the complainant has agreed to accept compensation. Almost all complainants have opted for the withdrawal of concessions. On the face of it, these should work in favor of inducing compliance, at least so long as the complainant is not a small country and the violator is a large country. Provided the products affected are chosen with care so that the incidence of the measure falls heavily on politically articulate producers or consumers in the violating country, internal pressure may be brought on its government to comply. At least in the hormone-fed beef case, however, the countermeasures have evidently failed to weaken the reluctance of the violator to comply with the DSB ruling. In other cases that we have reviewed where the withdrawal of concessions has been authorized, it is difficult to say how influential the threat of withdrawal or actual withdrawal has been in advancing compliance. In the banana and FSC disputes, the actual or threatened withdrawal may well have reinforced more general concerns about national reputation in abiding by the WTO agreements. However, as noted earlier, the fear of both the EC and the United States that the use of countermeasures was deteriorating into a tit-for-tat game of retaliation and counterretaliation may have been more influential than the countermeasures themselves in bringing about compliance.

In one respect, a larger role for countermeasures to induce compliance with the rules clearly makes for greater unfairness in the dispute settlement process. Developing countries have long pointed out that when the complainant is a small country and the violator is large, familiar countermeasures such as raising tariffs on imports from the violating country may have little or no effect on the latter's behavior. Again, there is a bias in the process that works against small countries. This said, however, we should note that, in some circumstances, it may be possible for a small country to punch above its weight. In its case against the United States on on-line gambling, Antigua and Baruda proposed to rescind their commitments under the TRIPS Agreement to recognize U.S. trademarks and copyrights; and this could make Antigua and Baruda a safe haven for copiers of motion pictures and software.[30] The United States has objected to this proposed measure, and the issue is, at the time of writing, in the hands of an arbitrator.

It is unfortunate that countermeasures are so often cast in the role of a punishment intended to deter non-compliance. The DSU is itself not explicit on these measures; it only describes them as temporary measures applied in the expectation of full compliance. However, the DSB has been more forthcoming. In one case, it noted that "there is nothing (in the relevant provisions of the DSU) that could be read as justification for countermeasures of a punitive nature" (DS 27). Fairness would probably be better served if countermeasures were seen in a different light.

Some scholars have argued that the set of WTO agreements can appropriately be seen as a contract among members in which each accepts a balance of rights and obligations.[31] Like most contracts, however, it is incomplete in the sense that there are many uncertainties about future circumstances that cannot be spelled out when the contract is drawn up. In the theory of contracts, if one party to a contract comes to find a particular obligation too onerous and if the cost of compliance is greater than the benefit to the other party, it may propose an efficient breach of contract, offering full compensation for the lost benefit. In the WTO, such compensation – whether in the form of a financial payment or a revision of concessions – can be seen as restoring the balance between rights and obligations that members negotiated in the first place. This view of countermeasures introduces some flexibility into the obligation of compliance; these measures can be seen as compensation for efficient breaches of contract and as a deterrent only to inefficient breaches.

6. Conclusions

We have asked whether the dispute settlement process in the WTO has so far operated fairly. In so doing, we have – for the most part – not taken up the issue of whether the GATT/WTO rules applied in the dispute settlement process are themselves fair, though views on the rules must necessarily affect assessments of the outcomes from WTO dispute settlement.

Since there are no objective criteria for assessing fairness, there is no unequivocal answer to our question. However, there are some widely accepted principles applied in international trade relations that express ideas of fairness, and these have enabled us at least to make some partial assessments.

---

[30] The EC and Japan joined Antigua and Baruda in pressing the case against the United States, but they later withdrew their support after the United States offered them concessions in other service sectors (*Financial Times*, December 18, 2007).

[31] For a full exposition of this approach, see Schwartz and Sykes (2002).

We have noted that two questions can be asked. One is whether the procedures followed throughout the settlement of a dispute assure equal treatment to all parties, both powerful and weak. In some important respects, the procedures do meet this condition; for instance, no doubt has been raised about the impartiality of the persons appointed to adjudicate in dispute settlement cases. There are, however, two major weaknesses. First, effective participation of countries in the dispute settlement process demands a body of legal, diplomatic, and economic expertise in trade law that only large countries with long traditions in commercial law are well endowed with; and they are better able to press complaints or to defend themselves against alleged violations. Second, the use of countermeasures to induce compliance with WTO rules may be ineffective when employed by small and poor countries against their much larger trading partners.

The second question, to which we have devoted most of our attention, is whether the panels and the Appellate Body of the DSB have been able to interpret and apply the rules in ways that are widely regarded as fair. As just stated, we can give no conclusive answer. In some cases, the conformity of the rulings with widely accepted principles of fairness that are applied in international trade has been obvious. In many cases, however, while some ideas of fairness (and perhaps conflicting ideas such as equality of opportunity and equitable distribution of the benefits) may have lain behind the judicial reasoning, it is far from clear how any assessment could be made that might claim some objectivity. However, our review of individual cases suggests some observations that appear relevant to any assessment of fairness in the dispute settlement process. We list the most salient points below.

The panels and the Appellate Body of the DSB have done much to define and clarify what constitutes fair competition, especially with regard to subsidies. In their rulings on a number of cases, they have identified the kinds of governmental measures that give rise to subsidies and that may generate unfair competition. The more difficult task, however, has often been not the identification of a subsidy but the analysis of the evidence to establish the presence of a causal link between the subsidy and, say, export performance or injury caused to another member's industry through the depression of world prices. The rigor of the analysis, the assumptions, the methodology, and the normative and causal beliefs of the adjudicators may all be open to challenge and raise questions about the fairness of the ruling.

As noted, the DSB cannot compensate for any unfairness inherent in the GATT/WTO rules themselves. In dealing with anti-dumping cases, the panels and the Appellate Body have been successful in eliminating some of the more egregious national laws or practices that have appeared inconsistent with the WTO Agreement on anti-dumping measures. However, they have necessarily accepted the restrictions imposed by the Agreement on their capacity to assess the underlying rationale of anti-dumping measures or their consistency with the spirit of other GATT/ WTO agreements.

As others have observed, it is a weakness of the WTO dispute settlement process that there is no effective legislative mechanism through which agreements can be modified in light of accumulating juridical experience with individual cases. Since the DSB is enjoined not to add to, or subtract from, these agreements, its panels and Appellate Body are faced with a predicament when textual ambiguities need to be clarified, especially when these hide what many members may regard as policy issues. The analysis of Sykes (2003) in regard to the Agreement on Safeguards Measures illustrates just such a situation. One consequence is that the effectiveness of the Agreement is emasculated.

Experience with the dispute settlement process since 1995 has shown that, while the DSB has successfully brought most disputes to an end through the compliance of parties to the GATT/WTO rules, this has not always been so. In a few cases, a settlement regarded as fair by both parties has been beyond the ability of the DSB to achieve through its rulings and recommendations; its realization has required negotiations between the parties on a fair distribution of the benefits. Furthermore, in one or two cases where national preferences have conflicted with the rules, members have chosen to accept the imposition of countermeasures rather than to comply. It would be reasonable to view the countermeasures not as a penalty intended to induce compliance but as compensation for a breach of contract.

The borderline between member's obligations under the GATT/WTO Agreements and their own national preferences is an uncertain one. In principle, members recognize the rights of individual countries to override their obligations in certain areas such as public morals or health. However, if the assertion of national preferences is not to be exploited for protectionist purposes, a borderline has to be clearly demarcated. Particularly in view of rising global concerns about the environment, this may well become an increasingly sensitive issue. In this regard, the DSB was pointing in the right direction when it opined that the precondition for action by any one country that adversely affected the trade of others should be the existence of a multilateral or bilateral environmental agreement.

It is beyond the scope of our present effort to suggest or devise changes in the dispute settlement process that would deal with the various strains noted. So, we leave the unresolved issues to be addressed for a future occasion and for other specialists to consider.

Acknowledgement

We thank James Hartigan and Elizabeth Teague for their helpful comments on an earlier version of our paper.

References

Bagwell, K., Staiger, R.W. (1999), An economic theory of GATT. *American Economic Review* 89, 215–248.

Borrell, B. (1994), EU Bananarama III. Policy Research Working Paper 13/86. World Bank, Washington, DC.

Bown, C.P. (2002), Why are safeguards under the WTO so unpopular? *World Trade Review* 1 (3), 47–62.

Brown, A.G., Stern, R.M. (2007), Concepts of fairness in the global trading system. *Pacific Economic Review* 12 (3), 293–318.

Conti, J.A. (2008), The good case: decisions to litigate at the world trade organization. *Law and Society Review* 42 (1), 145–181.

de Jasay, A. (2006), When fair is not just and just is not fair. *Independent Review* 11 (2), 165.

Devereaux, C., Lawrence, R.Z., Watkins, D. (2006), *Case Studies in US Trade Negotiations, Vol 2: Resolving Disputes*. Institute for International Economics, Washington, DC.

European Journal of International Law. Current developments: decisions of the Appellate Body of the world trade organization. Available at http://www.ejil.org/archives.php

Hoekman, B.M., Mavroidis, P.C. (2000), WTO dispute settlement, transparency and surveillance. *World Economy* 23 (4), 527–542.

Horn, H., Mavroidis, P.C. (2006), *The WTO Dispute Settlement System 1995–2004: Some Descriptive Statistics*. World Bank, Washington, DC.

Hudec, R.E. (2002), The adequacy of WTO dispute settlement remedies: a developing country perspective. In: Hoekman, B., Mattoo, A., English, P. (Eds.), *Development, Trade and the WTO: A Handbook*. World Bank, Washington, DC.

Hufbauer, G.C. (2002), *The foreign sales corporation drama: reaching the last act?* International Economic Policy Briefs, Institute for International Economics, Washington, DC.

Ikenson, D.J. (2005), Abuse of discretion: time to fix the administration of the U.S. antidumping law. Cato Institute Trade Policy Analysis No. 31, October 3.

Ikenson, D.J., Lighthizer, R.E. (2007), Is the WTO dispute settlement system fair? Cato Institute Center for Trade Policy Studies, February 20–26. Available at http://www.freetrade.org

Irwin, D.A. (2003), Causing problems? The WTO review of causation and injury attribution in US Section 201 cases. *World Trade Review* 2 (3), 297–325.

Jones, K. (2004), The safeguards mess revisited: the fundamental problem. *World Trade Review* 3 (1), 83–91.

Krier, J. (2005), Contingent trade remedies and WTO dispute settlement: some particularities. In: Yerxa, R., Wilson, B. (Eds.), *Key Issues in WTO Dispute Settlement*. Cambridge University Press, New York.

Mexico. (2007), Diagnosis of the problems affecting the dispute settlement mechanism: some ideas by Mexico. *WTO Dispute Settlement Body: Special Session*, TN/DS/W/90. World Trade Organization, Geneva.

Powell, S.J., Schmitz, A. (2005), The cotton and sugar subsidies decisions: WTO's dispute settlement system rebalances the agreement on agriculture. *Drake Journal of Agricultural Law* 10 (2), 1–38.

Rawls, J. (1971), *The Theory of Justice*. Harvard University Press, Cambridge, MA.

Rifkin, J. (2004), *The European Dream*. Jeremy P. Tarcher/Penguin New York, NY.

Schwartz, W.F., Sykes, A.O. (2002), The economic structure of renegotiation and dispute resolution in the world trade organization. *Journal of Legal Studies* XXXI (January), 179–203.

Sykes, A.O. (2003), The safeguards mess: a critique of WTO jurisprudence. *World Trade Review* 2 (3), 261–295.

Sykes, A.O. (2004), The "safeguards mess" revisited – a reply to Professor Jones. *World Trade Review* 3 (1), 93–97.

Trachtman, J.P. (2007), Safeguards, antidumping and subsidies in the WTO (and in RTA/FTAs). In: Lukauskas, A. (Ed.), *Trade Policy for Development*. The World Bank, Washington, DC.

Tyler, T.R. (1988), What is procedural justice? Criteria used by citizens to assess the fairness of legal procedures. *Law and Society Review* 22 (1), 103.

Wilson, B. (2006), The WTO dispute settlement system and its operation: a brief overview of the first ten years. In: Yerxa, R., Wilson, B. (Eds.), *Key Issues in WTO Dispute Settlement*. Cambridge University Press, New York.

Wilson, B. (2007), Compliance by WTO members with adverse WTO dispute settlement rulings: the record to date. *Journal of International Economic Law* 10 (2), 397–403.

CHAPTER 3

Licence to Adjudicate: A Critical Evaluation of the Work of the WTO Appellate Body So Far

Petros C. Mavroidis

Parker Professor, School of Law, Columbia University, 435 W 116th Street, New York, NY 10027, USA
E-mail address: pmavro@law.columbia.edu

Abstract
In this chapter, I discuss the manner in which the Appellate Body (AB) has been completing the WTO contract through its case law. To do that, I first briefly examine the mandate given to the AB. Having established that, I move to discuss the manner in which the AB has handled its mandate. The AB is called to settle disputes among WTO members by following a certain methodology for interpreting the WTO contract. The main conclusions that I draw are that the AB has not, as a general remark, overstepped its authority and that it has, with few outliers, traditionally followed an (overly) textualist interpretative approach. This attitude is probably consistent with the incentive structure of a risk averse agent who can always turn back and request from its principals to write a more complete contract next time. It has led, nonetheless, to some unfortunate results. Assuming that the current WTO agreement and the interpretative tools are not negotiable (although a re-weighing of the various factors included in the latter is both feasible and warranted), it is the institutional design of the AB and its supporting Secretariat that should probably be re-thought.

Keywords: Appellate Body, case law

JEL classification: K33

1. Introductory remarks

The advent of the WTO, and the ensuing establishment of a two-level adjudication process (panels and the Appellate Body [AB]), marks the passage to a compulsory third party adjudication system, an oddity in international relations: as per Article 23 of the DSU, WTO adjudicating

Frontiers of Economics and Globalization
Volume 6 ISSN: 1574-8715
DOI: 10.1108/S1574-8715(2009)0000006006

bodies are the exclusive forum for adjudication of all disputes among WTO members with respect to issues coming under the purview of the covered agreements. This feature (exclusive adjudication) is certainly a contributing factor towards the substantial rise (compared to the GATT era) of dispute settlement reports that have been issued since 1 January 1995.[1] There is by now a critical mass of reports, which, to a large extent, provide the input for the evaluation of the record that follows.

No evaluation can take place, absent an understanding of the function of the adjudicating bodies being evaluated. Hence, in Section 2, I turn to the question what is expected from WTO adjudicating bodies. Section 3 contains a discussion of the record of the AB, whereas Section 4 includes suggestions for addressing some of the weaknesses that were discussed in Section 3. Concluding remarks are offered in Section 4.

2. *The function of WTO adjudicating bodies*[2]

2.1. Agents

Article 3.2 of the DSU clearly defines the role of WTO adjudicating bodies:

> The dispute settlement system of the WTO is a central element in providing security and predictability to the multilateral trading system. The Members recognize that it serves to preserve the rights and obligations of Members under the covered agreements, and to clarify the existing provisions of those agreements in accordance with customary rules of interpretation of public international law. Recommendations and rulings of the DSB cannot add to or diminish the rights and obligations provided in the covered agreements.

It follows that WTO adjudicating bodies cannot *extend or reduce* the policy space committed to the international plane by the framers, the WTO Members.[3]

---

[1] A look into Robert Hudec's (1993) monumental study reveals that fewer reports were issued between 1947 and 1993 than since 1995. There are of course many mitigating factors. As Henrik Horn *et al.* (2005) observe, with the advent of the WTO, there are more members and more agreements. Other things equal, it is quite reasonable to expect more disputes.

[2] This section draws heavily on Mavroidis (2007a).

[3] By this, I mean the precise amount of sovereignty that has been voluntarily transferred to the international plane from members acceding to the WTO.

2.2. Required to interpret …

Article 3.2 of the DSU also explains that adjudicating bodies are mandated to clarify (interpret) the covered agreements. Article 11 of the DSU further explains that, when interpreting a provision, adjudicating bodies are required to make an *objective assessment* of the matter before them. Now, it would have been quite odd to request that adjudicating bodies make a *subjective* assessment of the matter before them, would it not?[4] The last sentence of Article 11 of the DSU, however, is potentially in contradiction[5] with the obligation to perform an objective assessment: indeed, it could be that a bilateral solution agreeable between the players does not coincide with an objective assessment. This sentence is probably a leftover from the GATT 1947; the GATT 1947 has been described as a relational contract, a mix of diplomatic and legal approach. Over time, the area occupied by diplomacy was replaced by a more stringent, legal framework. Anyway, there is no instance, in the WTO era, where the (eventual) tension between the two tests has been put to practice: WTO adjudicating bodies have not felt constrained by this provision, and WTO Members have not attempted to sensitize their agents to this provision.[6] To conclude, WTO adjudicating bodies interpret and do not mediate.

2.3. An incomplete contract …

The term *incomplete contract* describes a contract that does not, in its original form, contain all information necessary for its operation. Such contracts are usually completed either through subsequent re-negotiation of the contract or by reference to other bodies of law (*default rules*) or through subsequent adjudication: a court of law, for example, might (assuming competence to this effect) borrow from default rules in order to clarify contractual terms and thus adjudicate a dispute.

The WTO contract is an incomplete contract. Take for example, the national treatment provision. As Horn and Mavroidis (2004) explain, for

[4] Any assessment by a judge is, of course, a subjective assessment. However, in light of the negative connotation that the term *subjective assessment* has, reference to it is, by convention, not made in a provision such as Article 11 of DSU.

[5] This point should be attributed to William J. Davey who made it in an oral conversation with the author.

[6] After all, parties to a dispute can always reach a mutually agreed solution, which is a restraining factor on the panel's exercise of jurisdiction. Affected third parties can of course challenge the consistency of such solutions with the multilateral rules. To this effect, they will have to introduce a new complaint before the WTO.

example,[7] negotiators, for good reasons, refrained from spending time trying to provide a complete list of all domestic instruments that should come under the purview of Article III of the GATT.[8] Another illustration of this point is offered by the fact that the DSU nowhere regulates the allocation of the burden of proof (burden of production *cum* persuasion). All the reports by WTO adjudicating bodies, however, have dealt explicitly or implicitly with this issue.

By interpreting the covered agreements, WTO adjudicating bodies "complete" the WTO contract,[9] by adding the missing information.[10] Such addition could be necessary in order to be in a position to apply a *generic* language (as is often the language of most provisions) to a *transaction-specific* context. When completing the contract, nonetheless, the WTO judge has to bear in mind the imperative in Article 3.2 of the DSU (*thou shall not undo the balance of rights and obligations as struck by the founding fathers*).

2.4. Which suffers from ambiguity as well …

As Posner (1995) pertinently, in my view, explains, there is tension between, on the one hand, the willingness of the legislator to draft laws using all-encompassing language in order to subsume the maximum number of transactions and, on the other, the limits inherent in our human nature to predict future events (state contingencies) on which we have, at the stage of drafting, imperfect information. This tension is present particularly in a contract such as the WTO, which is meant to regulate future trade relations, and it is not meant to be *transaction-specific*. As a result, negotiators will naturally privilege generic expressions, rather than precise definitions. The more we move away from a transaction-specific language, however, the more likely it becomes that we will be facing ambiguity. Take the term *like product*, for example, appearing in so many different places in the covered agreements: depending on the comparator

---

[7] On this score, see also Horn (2006).

[8] There is a positive correlation between the amount of information contained in a particular contract and what can be achieved through that contract. Adding information, however, represents negotiating costs. It is thus not excluded that negotiators might reach a point of diminishing returns: negotiations can take long time and, even if successful, might not yield satisfactory results. Negotiations *at the margin* will be decided following an assessment of the merits of including additional information (and the ensuing ambition); see on this score, the excellent analysis of Horn *et al.* (2008).

[9] To avoid any misunderstandings, the term *contract* is used in a neutral manner (i.e., equivalent to the term *agreement* or *treaty*).

[10] This is the role of the judge according to Battigalli and Maggi (2002), for example.

used,[11] one can reach different (internally coherent) interpretations. It is hence not paradoxical that different panels, and the AB itself, have struggled when interpreting this term.[12]

2.5. And compelled to use yet another incomplete contract in order to complete the original incomplete contract

Is the WTO judge free to choose any intellectual route when interpreting the contract (i.e., completing it by providing the additional information and setting aside the embedded ambiguity)? No, is the short answer. Article 3.2 of the DSU requires that the WTO judge have recourse to the customary rules of interpretation.[13] Since its very first report (judgment), the AB has equated customary rules with the general rule of interpretation embedded in the *Vienna Convention on the Law of Treaties* (*Vienna Convention*). The *Vienna Convention*, however, is far from being exact science; it reflects various elements of interpretation but falls short of establishing with precision the *weight* to be given to each one of them. The WTO judge, consequently, has to deal not with one but with two incomplete contracts. This is definitely not an envious position to be in.

Formal recourse to the *Vienna Convention* does not *ipso facto* yield consistent results.[14] It is not unheard of that, while applying the *Vienna Convention*, the AB has reached divergent decisions on more or less identical issues. Take the two decisions by the AB on non-recurring subsidies, *US – Lead and Bismouth II* and *US – Countervailing Measures on Certain EC Products*. The AB reached two diametrically opposite responses to the same question, that is, to what extent non-recurring subsidies pass through to the new owner who has paid a market price for the privatized entity? On both occasions, the AB had recourse, as it always does, to the *Vienna Convention*. On both occasions, it went through each and every element included in Article 31 of the *Vienna Convention*. Yet, the outcome is not the same: the first report stands for the proposition that an arm's length transaction always exhausts benefits received by the former owner,

---

[11] See on this score, Horn and Weiler (2003).

[12] See the comprehensive analysis in Horn and Mavroidis (2004).

[13] There is a presumption expressed in Article 3.2 of the DSU that recourse to the *Vienna Convention* is a guarantee, in principle at least, that the balance of rights and obligations, as struck by the founding fathers, cannot be undone by the judge.

[14] Not that I believe that consistency is in and of itself a value, for one can be consistently wrong. A court gains in institutional credibility, when it can show a linear evolution of its case law, nonetheless, assuming correct interpretations. In such cases, the presence and demonstration of distinguishing factors from one case to the other will sufficiently justify divergent outcomes.

whereas the second report takes the view that this is not necessarily the case.[15]

2.6. Being a WTO judge: not an enviable position to be in

As explained above, to fulfil their mission, WTO judges are requested to complete an incomplete, and often ambiguous, contract by using yet another incomplete contract.[16] This is not an enviable position to be in.[17]

3. Has the AB honoured its mandate?

The discussion so far aimed at establishing the role of the AB in the institutional equilibrium of the WTO: the AB, as per Article 3.2 of the DSU, is an agent charged with the interpretation of law and not a principal (a lawmaker). One natural way to start the discussion that will take us to a response to the question asked in the title of this section is by asking the question whether the AB has acted within the parameters of Article 3.2 of the DSU. Respecting its institutional role is only half the exercise; the AB must also complete the contract in a *reasonable* (*convincing*) manner. The former question (has the AB respected the institutional equilibrium as established by the framers?) is easier to answer: the response hinges on an evaluation of whether the AB kept its judgments within the policy space committed by the framers to the international (WTO) plane. The latter question (is the AB output reasonable/ convincing?) is the hard question where, unfortunately, recourse to increased subjectivity seems inevitable. The first question is discussed in Section 3.1, whereas Section 3.2 deals with the second.

3.1. An agent (most of the time)

An AB prone to false positives (type I errors) will be adding to the obligations of WTO members, whereas, through false negatives (type II errors), it will be diminishing their rights. Through such actions, however, it will not only be imposing costs to the addressees of its decisions, but it might also be creating institutional damage as well: it might reduce the

---

[15] In the view of Grossman and Mavroidis (2005), both reports are wrong.

[16] I am not arguing here that this is the reason why disputes occur in the first place. To my knowledge, we still lack a theory on why WTO disputes occur in the first place. The point here is simply that, assuming a dispute, this is what a WTO judge will be required to do.

[17] Of course, the judge can adopt a course of action that will minimize errors: minimalist judgments are highly recommendable for judges, and for WTO judges in particular, see the excellent analysis offered on this score by Sunstein (1999).

faith of WTO members in this form of dispute adjudication, in an era where compulsory third party adjudication is very much a rarity in international relations.

The AB has been predominantly faithful to its mandate.[18] There are, however, a few instances which, one could argue, show a tendency to behave more as a lawmaker rather than as a judge. For example, in all cases where the AB has completed the analysis, it has *ipso facto* deprived parties of their right to a two-stage adjudication. True, it has thus facilitated the speedy resolution of the dispute. However, to achieve this end, it cannot employ means that undo the balance of rights and obligations struck by WTO Members (and commit a *false positive*, a type I error).

There are few other examples. In *US – Softwood Lumber IV*, the panel faced an awkward situation: the United States (for good reasons probably) had used a benchmark other than those referred to in Article 14 of the SCM Agreement, and Canada challenged this arguing that the United States should have used one of the benchmarks reflected in Article 14. The language in this provision leaves no doubt as to the exhaustive character of the included list: it deals with the calculation of benefit and presupposes the existence of a market price in the exporting WTO Member; there was, nonetheless, no credible market price in the heavily subsidized Canadian lumber market, and this is why the US authority moved outside the four corners of Article 14 and used reasonable (in its view) benchmark. We are, arguably, dealing here with a case of legislative failure. The panel wisely signalled the issue concerning the incompleteness of Article 14 SCM, but refused to play legislator, and found against the United States for using a benchmark not sanctioned by the SCM Agreement. The AB reversed the panel, in principle, arguing that WTO Members could legitimately use other benchmarks. By doing that, however, it *added* a right that had not been contemplated in the original bargain. This is not its role, the solidity of arguments in favour of amending Article 14 of the SCM Agreement notwithstanding (type I error).[19]

In *US – Upland Cotton*, the AB majority opinion offers a reading of Articles 10.1 and 10.2 of the Agreement on Agriculture, which is difficult to reconcile with the wording, also with its negotiating history: if export credits came under the purview of Article 10.1, why would negotiators spend negotiating effort to introduce Article 10.2? Did they want to signal that they were prepared to exclude export credits from the disciplines of the Agreement through future action? This is a highly unlikely outcome,

[18] See the excellent analyses of Davey (2001) and Howse (2003), who largely share this view.

[19] By the way, the AB did not identify another appropriate benchmark and did not even establish the criteria that would help WTO Members in future practice use such alternative benchmarks. What is remarkable here is how an overly textualist court like the AB suddenly rejects textualism and pays lip service to the unambiguous wording of this specific provision.

since the whole negotiation was meant to discipline instruments and not the opposite. A contextual reading[20] of the two provisions amply supports the minority view, that is, that there was agreement as to the disciplining of many instruments, but no agreement on export credits, an issue left, as per Article 10.2, to future negotiations (type I error).

One could further discuss to what extent the interpretation in *US – Shrimp* of the terms "exhaustible natural resources" in Article XX(g) of the GATT is consistent with the legislative will. A review of the negotiating history supports the view that what the founding fathers had in mind were elements such as petrol and not animals, which come under the purview of Article XX(b) (type I error).[21]

Or, take even the discussion on the participation of NGO to the WTO. The AB was criticized rightly for inventing an interpretation of the term "to seek" featuring in Article 13 of the DSU, which manifestly did not correspond to the intention of the parties. It thus opened the way to NGO participation in WTO dispute settlement, an outcome at odds with the wish of the majority of the WTO Members, as discussions during a special session convened to this effect have shown.[22]

Such examples, however, are outliers among the over seventy reports and the hundreds of legal claims that the AB has entertained so far. In conclusion, the results of Davey (2001) and Howse (2003) are solid.

---

[20] This term needs some extra clarification in this particular context. I do not simply mean a look into the remaining provisions of the agreement but also a look into the circumstances surrounding the negotiation. The *Agreement on Agriculture* was meant to impose disciplines on instruments affecting farm trade. If Article 10.1 of the *Agreement on Agriculture* covers all instruments, then, for the AB to be correct, Article 10.2 can be understood as some sort of agreement to exclude, eventually, export credits from its coverage. But if there was uncertainty as to their inclusion why include them in the first place in Article 10.1? The negotiating history clearly shows that, if at all, the problem was to agree on disciplines and not to agree on indisciplined activities affecting farm trade. This is the first effort to bring farm trade under the auspices of the multilateral regime.

[21] There was some discussion, in a different group, which was discussing an international commodity agreement that would come under the aegis of the International Trade Organization (ITO), whereby the argument had been made that this term should cover living organisms as well. Charnovitz (1991) takes the view that, in light of this discussion, the negotiating record is nuanced on this score. This is a cautious and probably correct view. However, since these discussions were held in a different context (not in the context of the negotiation of Article XX(g) GATT), the better arguments lie with the approach advanced here, that is, that this term was meant to cover non-living organism. Recourse to preparatory work is an option only under the strict conditions of Article 32 VCLT (e.g., if the interpreter believes that, following exhaustion of the elements mentioned in Article 31 VCLT, the meaning of the term is still obscure, or simply in order to confirm an interpretation already reached). *De facto*, preparatory work has been used in the WTO context only for the latter purpose. In order to avoid any misunderstandings, I believe that the United States should have prevailed in this dispute anyway, irrespective of whether the case had been adjudicated under Article XX(b) or, more appropriately, under Article III:4 of the GATT 1994.

[22] See Mavroidis (2004) on this score.

3.2. Has the AB produced a convincing body of case law?

The AB is there not only to solve a particular dispute but also to make the adjudication of similar future transactions (more) predictable. It is not that the outcome (winner/loser) does not matter, it does. But it must be the natural (logical) consequence of the process, that is, the thought pattern that the AB will employ in order to respond to the questions submitted to it. The process, in other words, is as important as, if not more important than, the outcome.

It is the convincingness of the process that I purport to discuss in what follows. There is of course nothing like an exact measurement for convincingness, so relying on proxies is inevitable.

In what follows, I advance four (imperfect) proxies to discuss the convincingness:

(a) the consistency of the reasoning across cases;
(b) to what extent case law has led to less litigation over issues previously adjudicated;
(c) to what extent the principals have reacted negatively to the emerging case law;
(d) whether case law has influenced subsequent lawmaking.

The first proxy is almost a natural candidate in any discussion of this sort: courts are expected to apply similar reasoning across cases and not be guided by properties such as the identity of the players involved in a particular litigation. Consistency is, of course, not a value in and of itself, for one can be consistently wrong. Assuming, however, that this is not the case, it adds to a court's legitimacy to cite its prior (relevant) case law since this is one manner to signal predictability as to the outcome. Indeed, in the absence of distinguishing factors and/or new knowledge about an old issue, one would legitimately expect a court to repeat its prior case law.[23] In a similar vein, one should rationally expect that courts will not be consistently wrong: the principals will eventually react and try to minimize such risks by enacting laws that avoid such risk.[24]

It follows that absence of *collective* reaction by principals could be interpreted as a signal of tacit approval of the emerging case law. Unilateral reactions (by the loser) are not necessarily a concern of equal proportions: governments could, for domestic political economy reasons, for example, opt for strong reactions against a particular interpretation.

---

[23] The absence of *stare decisis* in the WTO legal order should, consequently, not be overstated.

[24] A caveat is warranted here: why did not he principals complete the contract *ex ante* and void the risk of consistently wrong interpretations? A number of factors, however, could explain why such has not been the case: it could be, for example, that case law exemplified why certain reasoning is wrong, something the negotiators did not anticipate at the negotiating stage.

A collective reaction, nonetheless, seems, *prima facie*, a good proxy for collective dissatisfaction. By this, I do not mean to equate convincingness of the reasoning in a particular WTO report with satisfaction of the principals. The point here is, rather, that one would be hard-pressed to find a common concern across 151 Members simultaneously dissatisfied with a particular outcome, were one to discard the intellectual coherence of a report as an explanatory variable.[25]

Assuming we understand that the role of the judge is to "complete" the contract, then one would expect that gradual completion will lead to less litigation, provided, of course, that the completion of the contract is authoritative in the eyes of WTO Members.

Finally, crystallization of case law into law is probably the best proof that case law has convinced (at the very least, the intended addressees, that is, the principals).

The first proxy is an investigation into the case law. The remaining three proxies require an investigation not only of the behaviour of the AB but also of the WTO Members. This is an argument in favour of weighing them differently than the first proxy. On the contrary, convincing case law might be discarded for "political", that is, non-intellectual reasons. As briefly alluded to, nonetheless, the risk that this is the case is quite small. Two factors constitute the institutional insurance policy against it:

(a) the heterogeneity of the current 151 WTO Members;
(b) decision-making in the WTO is based on consensus.[26]

3.3. Consistency across cases

Recall that we are discussing consistency with respect to the reasoning leading to an outcome. The WTO AB has sometimes expressed its reasoning in a very general, almost uninformative manner and sometimes in a functional manner. A good illustration of the former is the case law on national treatment, and more specifically, on the manner in which the AB will decide whether two products are directly competitive or substitutable (DCS), as per Article III:2 GATT. The AB has held that in order to decide

[25] The boundary between consistency, as discussed here, and predictability of the outcome is unclear. Nevertheless, I would rather be comparing the reasoning rather than the outcome itself, since the outcome could be influenced by factors other than the reasoning. There are papers in the literature that attempt to predict outcomes. Ruger *et al.* (2004), for example, discuss two models (one by political scientists and one by legal scholars) trying to predict the voting behaviour of the US Supreme Court Justices. There is of course risk of endogeneity here, in the sense that the desired outcome could influence the reasoning (in addition to the reasoning influencing the outcome).

[26] One could, and hopefully will, design other proxies or convincingly discard those mentioned in this chapter. But we do have to start this discussion somewhere, and, for the time being, the four proxies mentioned here seem appropriate to start the discussion.

whether two products are in a DCS relationship, it can rely on evidence including or not including econometric indicators. True, econometric indicators will not *always* yield satisfactory results. But to place the two approaches on equal footing without explaining under what the circumstances recourse to one or the other will be made simply does not make much sense either. Does the AB maintain that it is consumers that will decide whether two products are DCS *without* including price among the relevant criteria? Do consumers anywhere around the world purchase goods without thinking about their monetary resources?[27] We simply do not know the reasoning behind the AB decision to place the two approaches (use of econometric and non-econometric indicators to define a DCS relationship) on equal footing, except at a rather uninformative level, that is, that the two approaches are at equal footing. The AB will of course in subsequent case law apply its "reasoning" on a case-by-case basis. It thus confuses a case-by-case analysis with the necessity of methodology. A case-by-case analysis does not make the need for methodology redundant; to the contrary, it *presupposes* a methodology.

And then, there are cases where the AB has moved to details, where it has explained its reasoning in a functional manner. Take the privatization (pass-through) cases (*US – Lead and Bismouth II* and *US – Countervailing Measures on Certain EC Products*), for example. The question before it (on both occasions) was to what extent an arm's length privatization exhausts the benefits previously bestowed upon the companies that benefited from subsidies. In the first case, the AB held that the purchasing price matters: *any* time a market price has been paid, the benefits conferred to the original owner will be exhausted. Less than two years later, on the very same issue, the AB held that the price paid will not *always* exhaust the conferred benefits. In doing that, it cites to the first case. But the two cases are obviously mutually exclusive (*inclusio unius exclusio altrius*). The reasoning behind its finding in favour of absence of subsidization is inconsistent. Yet, the AB still managed to cite its first decision when deciding the subsequent case.[28]

And then, there are cases where it seems that the AB does not take its reasoning very seriously. Take the *US – Anti-Dumping Measures on Oil Country Tubular Goods* case: the US administration had circulated a *Bulletin* that investigating authorities should use when, *inter alia*, proceeding to review the necessity of continued imposition of anti-dumping duties. In the case at hand, the question before the AB was to what extent the standard of review adopted by the panel when examining the WTO consistency of the *Bulletin* was appropriate. In prior case law

[27] There are of course some goods for which demand is inelastic, but they constitute a very narrow exception in the world of goods.

[28] Grossman and Mavroidis (2005) take issue with both reports, arguing that the price paid is simply irrelevant.

(*US – Oil Country Tubular Goods Sunset Reviews*), the AB had accepted that the *Bulletin* as such was justiciable; it had also confirmed the panel's findings that a document such as the *Bulletin*, which the US administration uses in anti-dumping investigations, could be legitimately challenged before a WTO panel, since it was an act of normative character, applicable to an indefinite number of transactions.[29] However, in the subsequent report (*US – Anti-Dumping Measures on Oil Country Tubular Goods*), the AB faced a challenge by the United States against the panel's findings with respect to the justiciability of the *Bulletin* itself. The panel, reproducing faithfully in its view the AB's findings in the previous case (*US – Oil Country Tubular Goods Sunset Reviews*), held that the United States had violated its obligations under the *Anti-Dumping Agreement* by consistently finding (in application of the *Bulletin's* prescriptions) that continuation of anti-dumping duties was necessary. The panel had reviewed 206 cases, the overwhelming majority of which had been decided by reference to the waiver procedures, which were, in the AB's view, inconsistent with the requirements of the *Anti-Dumping Agreement*. So, the panel essentially had found that by applying consistently a WTO-inconsistent procedure (by virtue of the *Bulletin's* prescription), the United States was in violation of its obligations under the WTO. The AB rejected the panel's findings. In its view, the panel hastily rushed to conclusions; absent an inquiry into the rationale of the US domestic authority's decisions (all 206 of them), its conclusions were unfounded.[30] This is quite an odd statement. One can raise at least two legitimate concerns:

(a) Why does the rationale for the US investigating authority's decisions matter since the method used is anyway, as the AB itself ruled in a previous case, illegal?
(b) How can a panel inquire into the rationale of these cases without actually performing a *de novo* review, which it cannot do anyway, as the AB has ruled in prior case law?

The source of the confusion is the AB itself, which opens the door for justiciability of instruments such as the *Bulletin*, it then condemns the rationale for action embedded in the *Bulletin*, and to cap it all, it subsequently requests that panels review and discuss the (illegal) rationale when they find that the *Bulletin* is WTO-inconsistent, *since*, absent such discussion, their findings will be overturned.

And then, there are cases where the reasoning itself is missing altogether and, hence, it is impossible to evaluate consistency. Unfortunately, one of these cases concerns one of the pillars of the WTO edifice, the conditions under which special and differential treatment in favour of developing

---

[29] AB Report, *US – Oil Country Tubular Goods Sunset Reviews*, §§ 187 ff.
[30] AB report, *US – Anti-Dumping Measures on Oil Country Tubular Goods*, §§ 203 ff.

countries can be lawfully granted. In *EC – Tariff Preferences*, the AB introduces the idea that donors can use criteria other than those mentioned in the text of the *Enabling Clause* to legitimately distinguish across beneficiaries and thus accord asymmetric privileges. The AB further stated that such criteria, to the extent that they are *objective*, can be used in future practice. Even if the AB is right, *quod non* as Grossman and Sykes (2005) have persuasively demonstrated, does anyone know what kind of criteria the AB had in mind? The AB did not provide the defining characteristics of the *class* of criteria it had in mind, not even a mere *illustration* of specific criteria (e.g., an illustrative list) that would help it avoid at least type II errors in the future. But the AB is there to make outcomes predictable, or more predictable than they currently are. It is there to ease transaction costs. It is not there to add to the existing legislative ambiguity.

3.4. Less litigation in the future

Recall that the argument here is that the *completion* of the contract through case law has clarified the original contractual intent and, as a result, we observe less litigation post-clarification than before. As briefly alluded to above, this proxy should be taken with a substantial piece of salt: litigation does not depend *solely* on the clarity of the law. If this were the case (assuming clarity is symmetric for the players involved), we would only be observing bad faith cases and, at any rate, the gradual completion of the contract over the years would naturally entail fewer and fewer litigation. This is not the world we live in. With this caveat in place, I divide litigation in the WTO into two periods: 1995–2000 (A) and 2001–2006 (B). There are 219 cases in A and only 132 in B which, *prima facie*, seems to suggest that fewer cases see gradually the light of the day.[31]

At a more disaggregated level, litigation in anti-dumping and safeguards has picked up in B (33 to 38 and 11 to 22, respectively),[32] whereas litigation concerning domestic instruments and quotas has slowed down (66 to 36 and 57 to 25, respectively). This observation would, at a very superficial level, lend support to the argument that case law has in some areas made recourse to adjudication redundant.

[31] The unit of account is the DS number given to a dispute. It could be the case that some of the disputes involve more than one complainant. One can, of course, legitimately make the point that five years is too short a period and the twin point that it is too early to draw any conclusions. The data used here has been assembled by Horn and Mavroidis and is publicly available at http://www.worldbank.org/trade/wtodisputes

[32] A reminder that caution is warranted here: increase in adjudication could be the result of a downturn in the economy of the countries imposing AD duties. I am not using this information as demonstration of causality here: less litigation means the AB has done its job well, more litigation means the opposite.

Were one however, to look at a more detailed level, then one might have good reasons to doubt that this has indeed been the case. Take, for example, the case law on domestic instruments. The leading case in period B is *EC – Asbestos*, where the AB held that the test to define whether two products are like is in the marketplace. At the same time, nonetheless, the AB did not have recourse to consumer surveys or any other *market* information; it adopted a *reasonable* consumer test[33] and held that any consumer in knowledge of the different production processes would have privileged one product over the other; hence, the two products should be considered unlike.[34] But this test is of no much help to solve subsequent disputes: reasonableness in the abstract cannot be a marketplace test; if it were indeed the case, then Canadian consumers are obviously unreasonable (in the AB's eyes). The AB most likely construed its own view of the world as the reasonableness test it applied in this particular case.[35] It is, nevertheless, quite presumptuous to state that there is only one level of reasonableness, the one advocated by the AB: some risk averse societies, like France, might reasonably wish to impose an embargo on the type of products discussed here; Canada, reasonably as well, might wish to allow for sales of the same product, tax consumers who profit from lower prices (since the cost of this product will, arguably, be lower since a fixed element – public health protection – will be missing) and finance research aimed at combating cancer. It will be particularly hard to argue with the reasonableness of Canada's approach in case there is no uncertainty as to the risk distribution and the probability of it occurring is low (by reasonable standards). The point here is that two WTO Members might be asymmetrically risk averse without being necessarily unreasonable. The AB did not at all inquire into any of these scenarios. Moreover, it did not explain to us why France's standard (which it effectively adopted) is reasonable and Canada's is not: what is the methodology that when employed distinguishes between reasonable and unreasonable.[36]

---

[33] The term does not appear in the AB report, see Mavroidis (2007b) for additional explanation for its use.

[34] France has imposed an embargo on asbestos-containing construction material, based on scientific proof that exposure to buildings constructed with such material might be causing a form of cancer, mesothelioma. France allowed sales of asbestos-free construction material in its market. Canada complained because, in its view, the two products (asbestos-containing and asbestos-free material) were *like* and France, by treating them differently, was in violation of its obligations under the GATT.

[35] By this, I do not mean that a reasonableness test cannot ever take place in the marketplace. A consumer survey, nonetheless, would be the first *necessary* step in this process.

[36] As I have argued elsewhere (Mavroidis, 2007b), France should have prevailed anyway, but on different grounds: its measure was not "so as to afford protection" and, consequently, not in violation of Article III:4 GATT.

The test employed by the AB is not of much help for subsequent cases because we are in the dark as to what the AB might find reasonable in the future.

3.5. Reaction by principals

So far, there is not one single case where WTO Members collectively reacted to a decision by the AB. The closest we have come was the WTO Membership's reaction to the AB's initiative to invite *amici curiae* to participate in a pending litigation. Even there, nonetheless, there were a couple of notable dissents.

Collective reaction would be rather unusual in this context: one would, *normally*, expect that the WTO Member benefiting from a decision would have little incentive to voice its disagreement with it.

3.6. Influence on subsequent lawmaking

There is no evidence to this effect, but hardly any conclusions can be drawn from this observation. There has been no re-negotiation of the GATT since 1995 when the AB was established.

3.7. A partial conclusion

If at all, the above analysis suggests that some (tentative) conclusions can be drawn only from the first two proxies. Case law has been consistent only at an uninteresting (for providing a benchmark as to how adjudicate subsequent disputes) level of aggregation and, on occasion, inconsistent when the reasoning has been expressed at a sufficient (for providing a benchmark as to how to adjudicate subsequent disputes) level of disaggregation. I accept that the latter observation suffers from sample bias; the former, however, concerns the most basic of obligations assumed under the GATT – non-discrimination.

Less robust conclusions can be drawn from the second proxy (less litigation as a result of completion of the contract through case law): if at all, there are good arguments to support the conclusion that the AB cannot claim credit for those areas where the amount of litigation has been reduced; the absence of clear methodology that supports its outcomes suggests (at the very least) that fewer litigation is not the causal effect of *completion* of the contract through case law.

At the end of the day, the question, when evaluating the performance of the AB, will unavoidably be whether it has faithfully implemented the agreement? Absent an inquiry into the objectives of the agreement (Why was the agreement signed? What did drafters seek to address?), and subsequent construction of the words in this perspective *while* respecting the policy space committed to the WTO by its members, the AB will be bound to err when undertaking its tasks: for its task is not to proclaim winners and losers[37] but to reason why a particular claim should be accepted or rejected. This is why methodology is required. Sadly, this is what we have been missing so far.

4. Some suggestions (constructing the mold)

The WTO contract deals with some questions that are predominantly economics questions: what is a subsidy, for example, or, how should we calculate dumping margins, or how should injury be established when recourse to contingent protections is made, to name a few. Response to such questions requires an expertise that lawyers not trained in economics simply do not possess. Informed judgments on such issues crucially depend on input from the economics field. Yet, the AB (as is the case with most panels) does not include economists in its ranks, neither among judges nor among their clerks. Recourse to economics expertise has taken place informally so far in WTO adjudication and usually when authorization to apply countermeasures is requested.[38]

Recourse to economics, nevertheless, should not be confined to the calculation of countermeasures: economic analysis can help the AB avoid mistakes when analyzing legal rules. Consider the *US – Offset Act (Byrd Amendment)* report, to name one of the many examples on this score. Horn and Mavroidis (2007) show that subsidization of US companies might provide exporters with the exact opposite incentive than that contemplated by the AB – to dump even more aggressively. It would be highly advisable for the AB to hire economists (for its supporting services), and/or, assuming that the institutional arrangements in place allow it, establish formal links with the Economic Research Division of the WTO.[39]

Other steps will probably need to be taken as well, in order to increase the quality of the case law. But the lack of economic thinking in the treatment of economic issues is an obvious failing.

---

[37] Indeed, it is very difficult to conclude who the *real* winner or loser is in a given case. Mexico, for example, did not appeal the findings of the panel report on *Mexico – Telecoms* although, arguably, it would have a rather easy task before it, had it decided to do that, see Mavroidis and Neven (2006) on this. It became quite clear that Mexico used GATT as an excuse in this case in order to tame its national champion, Telmex. Mexico lost before the WTO, but probably won for all practical purposes.

[38] On this score, see Keck (2004).

[39] To avoid misunderstandings, I am not arguing here that recourse to econometrics, for example, will always provide us with a sound solution. It could be the case that it is not appropriate to use econometrics because the underlying data in the case is not good enough (e.g., not enough variation) to use it in order to identify statistically significant relationships. Where suitable, however, this should be the case.

Acknowledgements

I thank Kyle Bagwell, Chad Bown, Ivan Crowley, Henrik Horn, Jim Hartigan, Jorge Huerta-Goldman, and Alan Sykes for their very helpful discussions and comments.

References

Battigalli, P., Maggi, G. (2002), Rigidity, discretion and the costs of writing contracts. *American Economic Review* 92, 798–817.

Charnovitz, S. (1991), Exploring the environmental exceptions in GATT article XX. *Journal of World Trade* 25, 37–55.

Davey, W.J. (2001), Has the WTO dispute settlement system exceeded its authority? A consideration of deference shown by the system to member government decisions and its use of issue avoidance techniques. *Journal of International Economic Law* 4, 79–110.

Grossman, G., Mavroidis, P.C. (2005), Recurring misunderstandings of non-recurring subsidies. In: Horn, H., Mavroidis, P.C. (Eds.), *The WTO Case Law of 2002*. Cambridge University Press, Cambridge, UK, pp. 78–87.

Grossman, G., Sykes, A.O. (2005), A preference for development: the law and economics of GSP. *World Trade Review* 4, 41–68.

Horn, H. (2006), National treatment in trade agreements. *American Economic Review* 96, 394–404.

Horn, H., Mavroidis, P.C. (2004), Still hazy after all these ears: the interpretation of National treatment in the GATT/WTO case-law on tax discrimination. *European Journal of International Law* 15, 39–69.

Horn, H., Mavroidis, P.C. (2007), United States – continued dumping and subsidy offset act. In: Horn, H., Mavroidis, P.C. (Eds.), *The WTO Case Law of 2001, 2002, 2003*. Cambridge University Press, Cambridge, UK, pp. 622–656.

Horn, H., Maggi, G., Staiger, R.W. (2008), Trade agreements as endogenously incomplete contracts. *American Economic Review*, Forthcoming.

Horn, H., Mavroidis, P.C., Nordstrøm, H. (2005), Is the use of the WTO dispute settlement system biased? In: Mavroidis, P.C., Sykes, A.O. (Eds.), *The WTO and International Trade Law/Dispute Settlement*. Elgar Publishing, Aldershot, UK, pp. 454–486.

Horn, H., Weiler, J.H.H. (2003), EC – asbestos. In: Horn, H., Mavroidis, P.C. (Eds.), *The WTO Case Law of 2001*. Cambridge University Press, Cambridge, UK, pp. 14–40.

Howse, R.L. (2003), The most dangerous branch? The limits and role of the judicial power in the WTO. In: Cottier, T., Mavroidis, P.C. (Eds.), *The Role of the Judge in International Trade Regulation: Experience and*

Lessons for the WTO. University of Michigan Press, Ann Arbor, MI, pp. 11–41.

Hudec, R.E. (1993), *Enforcing International Trade law*. Butterworths, New Hampshire.

Keck, A. (2004), WTO dispute settlement: what role for economic analysis? *Journal of Industry, Competition and Trade* 4, 365–371.

Mavroidis, P.C. (2004), *Amicus curiae* briefs before the WTO: much ado about nothing. In: von Bogdandy, A., Mavroidis, P.C., Meny, Y. (Eds.), *In Honour of Claus-Dieter Ehlermann*. Kluwer, Amsterdam, pp. 317–330.

Mavroidis, P.C. (2007a), *Legal Eagles*? Mimeo, available at http://www2.gsb.columbia.edu/apec/APECStudyCenter,ColumbiaUniversity/Discussion%20Papers.html

Mavroidis, P.C. (2007b), *Trade in Goods*. Oxford University Press, Oxford, UK.

Mavroidis, P.C., Neven, D.J. (2006), El mess in Telmex: a comment on Mexico – measures affecting telecommunications services. *World Trade Review* 5, 271–296.

Posner, R. (1995), *Overcoming Law*. Harvard University Press, Cambridge, MA.

Ruger, T.W., Kim, P.T., Martin, A.D., Quinn, K.M. (2004), The Supreme Court forecasting project: legal and political science approaches to predicting Supreme Court decision making. *Columbia Law Review* 104, 1150–1209.

Sunstein, C. (1999), *One Case at a Time*. Harvard University Press, Cambridge, MA.

CHAPTER 4

The Evolution and Utilization of the GATT/WTO Dispute Settlement Mechanism

Pao-Li Chang

School of Economics, Singapore Management University, 90 Stamford Road, Singapore 178903
E-mail address: plchang@smu.edu.sg

Abstract
This chapter provides a theoretical framework of dispute settlement to explain the surge in blocking incidence of GATT panel reports during the 1980s and the variations in withdrawn incidence versus total disputes across different decades of the GATT regime. The study first suggests the role of the degree of legal controversy over a panel ruling in determining countries' incentives to block (appeal) a panel report under the GATT (WTO) regime. The study then analyzes the effects of political power on countries' incentives to use, and their interactions in using, the dispute settlement mechanism, given two-sided asymmetric information regarding panel judgement.

Keywords: Dispute settlement, legal controversy, block, appeal, two-sided asymmetric information, political cost

JEL classifications: F02, F13, K33, K41, K42

1. Introduction

Since its inception in 1947, the General Agreement on Tariffs and Trade (GATT) has evolved into a comprehensive framework of international trade laws as it exists today under the World Trade Organization (WTO). The operation of the GATT/WTO system has, to a large extent, hinged on the effectiveness of its dispute settlement mechanism. This procedure allows member countries to challenge other member countries' questionable trade measures with reference to the GATT/WTO agreements, and hence serves as a mutual surveillance and enforcement mechanism. Beginning with meager treaty clauses, the dispute procedure was elaborated increasingly during the GATT years, but it was the adoption

Frontiers of Economics and Globalization
Volume 6 ISSN: 1574-8715
DOI: 10.1108/S1574-8715(2009)0000006007

of the WTO dispute procedure in 1995 that fundamentally changed the nature of dispute settlement.

The customary practice under the GATT of requiring all decisions to be made by consensus posed a structural problem for the GATT dispute procedure. The defending party, by raising objection to consensus, could delay or block the procedure from moving forward, the most serious problem being the potential of the defending country to block an adverse ruling. The WTO dispute procedure established in 1995 altered several aspects of the GATT mechanism. The most significant was the removal of the consensus rule for adoption of rulings and hence the elimination of the blocking problem. A ruling made by a panel of experts will be deemed automatically adopted. To guard against possible legal errors made by the panel, an appellate procedure was added. A panel ruling can be appealed by either one of the disputing parties. If appealed, the dispute will proceed to an appellate panel whose judgment will be final and likewise adopted automatically unless there is a consensus against adoption.

Power politics, inherent in international relations, may have posed another threat to the efficient use of the GATT dispute settlement mechanism. Considerations of potential diplomatic cost (be it political, economic, or military) may influence countries' decisions of whether to initiate the formal procedure for resolving trade disputes. During the dispute settlement process, power politics may also affect countries' ability to extract bilateral settlements and carry on the litigation. The extent to which power politics may have intervened in the GATT legal system is likely to depend on the degree of international support for using the dispute procedure to resolve trade conflicts. The data on dispute cases under the GATT regime during the 1950s–1980s show a varied pattern in the number of filed complaints and their procedural outcomes across different decades. The pattern in the data corresponds to some interesting evolutions and movements in these decades, as will be documented later, which conceivably have affected countries' political considerations of using the GATT dispute procedure. Although not immune from the influence of power politics, the WTO procedure, given its more automatic and rule-based structure, leaves less room for power play. The procedure has since established itself as the norm for resolving trade conflicts in the international community. This is reflected in the dramatic increase of filed complaints under the WTO procedure.

Most studies on the GATT/WTO dispute settlement mechanism have been conducted by scholars of law or political science.[1] Bütler and Hauser (2000) was the first theoretical paper that systematically investigated this

[1] See, for example, Hudec (1993, 1999) and Jackson (1997, 2000) for analyses from legal perspectives, and Busch (2000) for investigations from political science perspectives.

mechanism from an economic perspective.[2] They, however, focused on the WTO dispute procedure; the incentives and interactions of countries in using the GATT dispute procedure were left largely unaccounted for. Furthermore, their theoretical model maintained a complete information framework and thus excluded the possibility of "withdrawn or abandoned" cases. We observe, however, a nonnegligible number of such cases during the GATT and WTO eras.

In a related literature on civil litigation, P'ng (1983), Nalebuff (1987), and Bebchuk (1988) present some potential frameworks toward understanding withdrawn civil disputes. In these papers, negative-expected-value suits can be filed with the presence of one-sided asymmetric information, and as a result, these suits are withdrawn or dropped if a settlement fails. Upon closer inspection, however, these papers are not so satisfactory in explaining withdrawn suits, because the withdrawal outcome in these papers either does not arise in the equilibrium or arise in the equilibrium only if it is costless for the plaintiff to file and then to withdraw a suit. In practice, countries typically have to incur (pecuniary or nonpecuniary) costs by bringing a dispute under the GATT/WTO procedure. Thus, the one-sided asymmetric information models discussed above cannot predict withdrawn cases and fully account for the interactions of disputing parties in international litigations.

In this chapter, I propose a theoretical framework of dispute settlement to explain the incidence of complaints filed and their disposition (withdrawn, settled, ruled – blocked or appealed) under the GATT/WTO procedures. I adopt a two-sided asymmetric information framework, which allows for potential litigation (political) cost, and explore the effects of political power on countries' incentives to use, and their interactions in using, the dispute settlement mechanism. The model's results indicate that as the political cost (relative to potential benefit) of using this mechanism to resolve trade conflicts increases for the complaining country, the dispute procedure is initiated less frequently, whereas the incidence of cases withdrawn or abandoned increases at first before decreases to zero.

This chapter then investigates the role of the degree of legal controversy over a panel ruling in determining countries' incentives to block or appeal a panel report. It is shown that under the GATT and WTO procedures, there exists an asymmetric disadvantage against the complainant. The potential benefit for the complainant to block or appeal an adverse panel ruling is uniformly less than the defendant, while the potential cost for both to do so is the same. This disadvantage against the complainant is diminished under the WTO procedure compared to the GATT's, but is not totally eliminated. It is also shown that as the level of legal controversy

[2] See Horn *et al.* (1999) for an empirical study of the WTO dispute settlement system. See also Bown (2002a, 2002b) for studies of the GATT/WTO dispute mechanism versus the safeguards provisions.

over panel rulings increases overall, the GATT panel reports are blocked at a higher frequency. The propensity to block a panel report under the GATT, however, is generally lower than the propensity to appeal a panel report under the WTO.

The rest of the chapter is organized as follows. Section 2 gives a more detailed account of the evolution of the GATT/WTO dispute settlement mechanism. Section 3 sets up the theoretical structure of the dispute mechanism. In Section 4, the theoretical model is developed and its results applied to explain the stylized facts observed in the data. Concluding remarks are collected in Section 5.

2. *Evolution of the GATT/WTO dispute settlement mechanism*

When the attempt to create an international trade organization in the late 1940s failed, the successfully negotiated trade agreement, the GATT, was left without a well-defined institutional structure.[3] Only a few clauses with regard to dispute settlement were contained in the original GATT, most of which centered around Article XXIII. The article states that a member country may request consultation with another member country, should it consider that its benefit expected under the GATT is being nullified or impaired by the other member country's trade measure. If no settlement is reached between the parties, the matter may be referred to the "Contracting Parties" (the member countries), which shall investigate and recommend action or give a ruling on the matter. In appropriately serious cases, the Contracting Parties may also authorize retaliatory actions. Despite the skeletal framework of Article XXIII, the dispute settlement in the early years of GATT worked rather smoothly, thanks to its small and homogeneous membership. Disputes were resolved in plenary meetings by rulings from the chair or consensus votes of member countries. As the procedure evolved, it began to delegate members' complaints to "working parties" formed by interested governments. One remarkable development occurred in 1952 when the GATT started using "the panel on complaints".[4] A panel composed of neutral government delegates would be established to hear and rule on a dispute. They would act in their own capacities and independently of any government interests. This development marked the beginning of third-party adjudication of legal claims brought under the GATT.

Because only the Contracting Parties had the power to decide on a matter, a panel report had to be adopted or approved by the Contracting Parties before its rulings became binding. Because it was a customary practice of GATT to require all decisions to be made by consensus, the procedure was inherently subject to delaying or blocking by the defending

[3] For more details, see Jackson (2000, p. 119).
[4] Hudec (1993, p. 30).

party, which by raising objection to consensus could keep the panel procedure from moving forward: the creation of the panel, the selection of the panelists, the adoption of the panel report, and the authorization of retaliation. However, this delaying or blocking problem did not begin to surface until the 1970s, the notorious example being the DISC case brought by the EC against the United States, and three US counterclaims.[5]

During the Tokyo Round negotiations conducted in 1973–1979, the GATT dispute settlement mechanism developed on dual tracks. On one hand, the negotiating efforts to strengthen the general dispute procedure of Article XXIII did not go very far. The resulting document "Understanding"[6] codified the established practices in implementing the procedure, but it was still ambiguous about whether the complainant had an absolute right to a panel process, and it did not take away the veto power of disputing parties in panel adoption. On the other hand, many of the new "Multilateral Trade Negotiations (MTN) Codes", resulting from negotiation efforts to restrain nontariff trade measures, also created their own dispute procedures. They varied in the degree of rigor and automaticity, but generally appeared to grant the complainant an automatic right to panel procedures. In this respect, the dispute procedures under these Codes were stronger than the GATT general procedure. The consensus rule, nevertheless, was still upheld for panel adoption in these various Code procedures.[7]

In 1995, the WTO was established following the completion of the Uruguay Round negotiations. The new Dispute Settlement Understanding (DSU) procedure under the WTO significantly renovated several aspects of the GATT mechanism. The separate procedures under the Tokyo Round Codes are no longer valid. The DSU governs all parts of the GATT/WTO system and serves as the single, unified mechanism for dispute settlement. Furthermore, the blocking problem that had plagued the GATT procedure is completely eliminated. A complaining country is granted an automatic right to have a panel created. Thus blocking is prevented at this early stage. Most importantly, a panel report is deemed automatically adopted by the new Dispute Settlement Body (DSB). Nevertheless, an appellate procedure is added as a safeguard against possible legal errors made by the panel. Either one of the disputing parties may consider appealing against the panel report to the Appellate Body (AB) whose judgment will be final and likewise adopted automatically unless there is a consensus against adoption. Thus, blocking a panel report has become virtually impossible under the WTO procedure.[8]

---

[5] See Hudec (1993), Complaint 69, 70, 71, and 72.

[6] "Understanding Regarding Notification, Consultation, Dispute Settlement and Surveillance."

[7] Hudec (1993, pp. 53–57).

[8] Jackson (2000, pp. 177–178).

3. Theoretical setup

The GATT and WTO dispute settlement procedures can be represented by the game trees in Figure 1. Suppose a trade dispute arises, the complaining country (C) detects that a trade-related practice implemented by the defending country (D) might be in violation of the GATT/WTO agreement or constitute "nullification or impairment" of benefits C expected under the agreement. C can consider whether or not to invoke the GATT/WTO dispute settlement procedure. If C decides not to file the case (*nf*), nothing happens and the status quo welfare remains, which is normalized to be zeros.

If C decides to file the case (*f*), it incurs (pecuniary or nonpecuniary) cost and benefit. The potential costs of bringing a complaint under the GATT/WTO include international political costs that result from an aggravated international relationship with the defending country. For example, the cost can be a loss of existing financial aid or preferential treatment provided by the defending country, or damage to the prospect of mutual cooperation between the countries in commerce or politics. Alternatively, the cost can be an increased likelihood of being challenged by the current defendant or other countries in the future via the GATT/WTO dispute settlement procedure.[9] However, a government usually brings a case under the GATT/WTO in response to a demand from a domestic industry or lobby group. By complying with their requests, the government earns political support from these industries or lobbies, which can mean more political contributions or electorate votes in the future. These potential international political costs and domestic political benefits are likely to vary with the disputing parties, the industries involved, and the degree of international support for the GATT/WTO dispute settlement procedure. Let K^f represent the political cost incurred by C in every period, net of domestic political benefit, by filing a complaint against D under the GATT/WTO. It is assumed that C incurs K^f in every period once it files the dispute, unless the dispute is settled or withdrawn, in which case K^f is incurred only for the period in which the dispute is present under the procedure.[10]

In practice, C invokes the GATT/WTO dispute procedure by requesting consultation with the defending country D. This is indicated by the beginning of Stage 0. The ensuing negotiations between the parties may

---

[9] Strategic – "retaliation" or "club" – motives were shown to be important in antidumping filings by Prusa and Skeath (2002). Blonigen and Bown (2003) showed that considerations of such strategic response by trading partners might in turn dampen the incentive to file antidumping cases in the first place. It is reasonable to suppose that such strategic considerations affect the filings of GATT/WTO trade disputes as well.

[10] In other words, it is assumed that the damage or benefit is permanent once the case is filed, but may be terminated before the dispute is escalated to the panel stage.

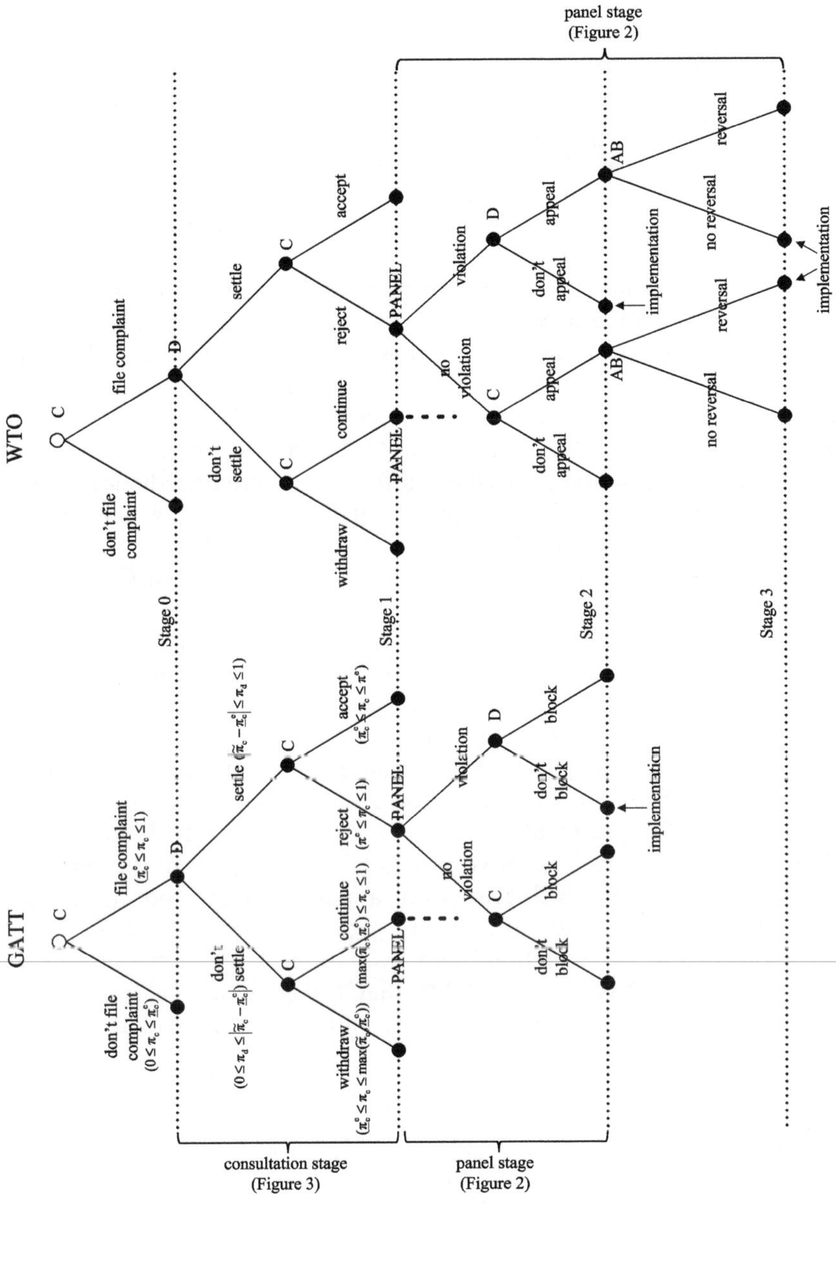

***Fig. 1.* Game tree of the GATT/WTO dispute settlement procedure.**

take various forms. Here the negotiation process is modeled as follows. Faced with a complaint, D decides whether to settle with C or not. If D chooses to settle, C then decides whether or not to accept D's proposed settlement terms. However, if D refuses to settle, C then decides whether to continue or withdraw from the litigation process. In reality, settlements in trade negotiations specify changes in policies or practices of D. It is assumed that the effects of such changes can be measured and summarized in monetary terms, the magnitude of which is denoted S. A positive settlement amount ($S > 0$) means D is willing to settle, and S represents the amount of welfare transfer from D to C as promised by the changes in D's policies.[11] Any zero or negative settlement offer by D is equivalent to D's refusal to settle.

If the dispute is neither settled nor withdrawn, it proceeds to the panel stage (Stage 1). When a case is brought before the panel, the disputing parties face two kinds of uncertainties: the uncertainty regarding the possible panel ruling (violation or no violation)[12] and the uncertainty regarding the quality of the ruling (the degree of legal controversy over the ruling). It is assumed that countries hold different interpretations about the GATT/WTO law and hence have different subjective predictions about possible panel rulings. This is represented by π_c and π_d, which are the respective probabilities that C and D predict that C's claim will receive a positive ruling. In other words, π_c and π_d are the "types" of C and D in terms of their own views of the likely panel judgement. It is assumed that each country owns some private information, which affects their predictions about the panel ruling and therefore one country's type is not known to the other. They each assume that the other's type is uniformly distributed on the closed unit interval [0, 1].

Before the panel, the parties are also uncertain about the quality of the ruling that will be made. Depending on the trade measure in dispute and the GATT/WTO agreements invoked, a panel ruling can be subject to different degrees of legal controversies. Let $L \in [0,1]$ represent the degree of legal controversy that will arise over a panel ruling, and $f(L|R)$ the probability density function of L given a certain ruling R, where $R = \{0,1\}$ corresponds to a "no violation" and "violation" ruling, respectively. In other words, $f(L|0)$ is the probability that L degree of legal controversy will arise over a "no violation" ruling, and $f(L|1)$ the probability that

[11] It is recognized that most trade measure changes exhibit nonzero sum natures. Zero sum is assumed here to simplify the analysis. This simplification also applies to the implementation phase of the dispute procedure discussed later.

[12] The classification of rulings as "violation" and "no violation" follows that of Hudec (1993, p. 275, 372). The "violation" category includes both rulings of legal violation and "nonviolation nullification and impairment." The "no violation" category includes cases in which no positive ruling is made on either legal violation or nullification and impairment, and cases in which the panel or the plenary body is unable to rule.

L degree of legal controversy will arise over a "violation" ruling. Intuitively, if the trade measure in dispute is more difficult or sensitive, higher degrees of legal controversies are likely to arise over the panel report. This will be represented by a rightward shift in the probability density function $f(L|R)$.

At the panel stage, a panel is established at C's request to hear and rule on the matter.[13] Under the GATT procedure, a panel ruling is not binding unless it is adopted by the Contracting Parties with consensus vote. Either party may consider blocking a panel report if faced with an adverse panel ruling. However, the diplomatic cost associated with blocking a report might prevent a country from doing so, unless the report is indeed subject to a large degree of legal controversy. This concept can be captured by a decreasing step function $K^b(L)$, which represents the diplomatic cost of blocking a report. This function has the simple interpretation that if the degree of legal controversy over a panel ruling is large enough ($L > \bar{L}$), blocking the report is diplomatically permissible and therefore it incurs no cost. Otherwise, the cost is prohibitively high. Regardless of whether or not C blocks a "no violation" report, no changes in D's trade practices will follow. However, when faced with a "violation" ruling, D can potentially avoid the implementation by blocking its adoption. Otherwise, the panel ruling will become binding and D will be obligated to begin the implementation at Stage 2.

Under the WTO procedure, the disputing parties lose their veto power over the panel report; however, they can challenge adverse rulings by resorting to the AB. The cost to appeal a report, K^a (such as lawyer fees), is assumed to be small relative to the value of the disputed trade measure. The dispute ends with no changes in D's trade practices if C does not appeal a "no violation" ruling. However, D is obligated to comply with the panel's recommendation if he does not appeal a "violation" ruling. The case proceeds to the appellate stage (Stage 2) if either party appeals. During the appellate stage, the AB reviews the legal aspects of the panel report and makes the final ruling on the case, which may reverse the original panel ruling in favor of the other party. I assume that the reversal probability of a panel ruling by the AB is equal to the degree of legal controversy L over the ruling. In other words, the higher the degree of legal controversy over a panel ruling, the more likely is the decision to be reversed by the AB. The appellate review is enforceable if a "violation" ruling against D is made. The implementation is assumed to take place beginning Stage 3.

The implementation of a "violation" ruling under the GATT or WTO procedure can take three potential forms: (i) the defendant removes the

---

[13] I abstract from the issue that the request for a panel might be blocked by D under the GATT. In practice, it was not as serious a problem as the blocking of a panel report, and usually a panel would eventually be established despite initial blocking.

disputed trade policy or practice, (ii) the defendant offers the complainant compensations, or (iii) the complainant withdraws substantially equivalent concessions.[14] The principle in all three recourses is to have the balance of reciprocity restored, although recourse (i) is the most preferred outcome of the system. Recourse (ii) can be carried out with the defendant offering trade concessions in other industries, but is typically not feasible due to domestic political constraints. If all else fails, recourse (iii) is the last resort.[15] In each of these outcomes, there will be a positive welfare transfer from D to C in every period. Let V denote this equivalent value of welfare transfer in these implementation outcomes.[16] We will also refer to V as the value of the disputed trade measure. C and D are assumed to have a common discount factor, δ, per period of time, where each stage of the process takes one period.[17]

4. *Theoretical model and implications*

The theoretical framework of dispute settlement introduced earlier exhibits the structure of a dynamic game with two-sided asymmetric information. The game can be solved backward starting from the panel stage. I first examine countries' incentives to block (appeal) panel reports under the GATT (WTO) regime at the panel stage, and then study their strategic interactions at the consultation stage. The perfect Bayesian equilibrium concept is used in deriving the results.

---

[14] In cases with a ruling of nonviolation nullification and impairment, the only legal rights established for the complainant are recourses (ii) and (iii).

[15] I have abstracted from the potential enforcement problem where the complainant does not or cannot retaliate, by withdrawing substantially equivalent concessions, after the defendant fails to remove the disputed trade policy or to compensate. This is beyond the scope of the chapter and the extension is left for future work. However, some speculations can be made. If we allow in the model the possibility that the implementation can fail, the defendant will similarly evaluate the benefit of noncompliance and the international diplomatic cost of doing so. Under the GATT, this comparison is in a way equivalent to that of whether or not to block an adverse panel ruling, absent any time-delay consideration. Thus, if a violation ruling is not blocked by a defendant, it is likely that the defendant will comply with the ruling. In Hudec (1993, p. 278), it is documented that 90% of cases with violation rulings under the GATT ended with a positive outcome, where at least some significant remedial action was taken by the defendant. If we take into account the fact that some violation rulings were blocked, the compliance rate with "adopted" panel reports is close to 100%, consistent with the above speculation.

[16] See Footnote 11.

[17] To keep the model analytically tractable, the game tree presented earlier is admittedly stylized. Some important realistic aspects of the dispute procedure that the chapter does not address include (i) strategic delays in the consultation or implementation stages, and (ii) settlements between the disputing parties at the panel stage before any ruling is adopted.

4.1. Panel stage

Under the GATT procedure, after the panel report is issued and its quality revealed, the disputing parties might consider blocking an adverse ruling given its degree of legal controversy. The benefit for D to block a "violation" ruling is to avoid the implementation, which has a continuation value of $V/(1-\delta)$. Taking into account the diplomatic cost of blocking a report $K^b(L)$, D will block the report if and only if the legal controversy over the report exceeds the threshold level ($L > \bar{L}$), Therefore, *ex ante* the probability that a "violation" ruling will be blocked by D is $1 - F(\bar{L}|1)$, where $F(L|1)$ is the cumulative distribution function associated with $f(L|1)$. This probability is indicated by the solid shaded area under $f(L|1)$ for the GATT procedure in Figure 2. However, C has no incentive

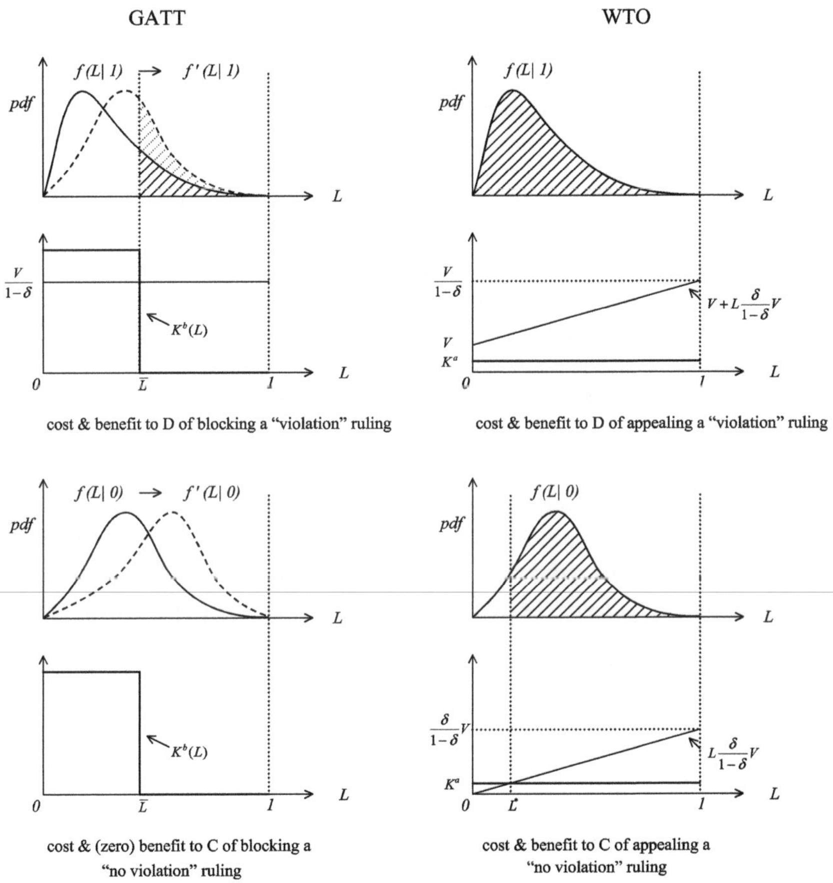

Fig. 2. Incentives and frequencies of disputing parties to block/appeal a panel report.

to exercise his blocking power given a "no violation" ruling, regardless of the quality of the report, because no economic benefits will accrue (no changes in D's trade practices will follow the blocking) but the blocking cost is nonnegative. Therefore, *ex ante* the probability that a "no violation" ruling will be blocked by C is 0.

Under the WTO with the new appellate procedure, the benefits and costs for disputing parties to challenge a panel ruling have changed as well. The expected benefit for D to appeal against a "violation" ruling is $V + L(\delta/(1-\delta))V$, where the first term is the gain in delaying the implementation for one period during which the appellate process takes place and the second term is the gain that the "violation" ruling may be reversed with probability L and D can avoid the implementation completely. The expected benefit of appeal increases if the panel report is subject to a higher degree of controversy. This relationship is indicated in Figure 2 under the WTO procedure. However, when C faces a "no violation" ruling, the expected benefit of appeal is $L(\delta/(1-\delta))V$, which is the gain that the "no violation" ruling may be reversed with probability L and implementation is required. Since the cost of appeal, K^a, is smaller than the value of the disputed trade measure, V, D will always appeal regardless of L. Therefore, *ex ante* the probability of a "violation" ruling being appealed by D is 1. However, C will appeal a "no violation" ruling if and only if the degree of legal controversy exceeds the critical level L^* such that $L^*(\delta/(1-\delta))V = K^a$. Thus, *ex ante* the probability that a "no violation" ruling will be appealed by C is $1 - F(L^*|0)$, where $F(L|0)$ is the cumulative distribution function associated with $f(L|0)$. The probabilities of appeal are indicated by the solid shaded area under $f(L|1)$ and $f(L|0)$ for the WTO procedure in Figure 2.

We summarize some observations regarding the disputing parties' incentives to block (appeal) panel reports in the following proposition.

Proposition 1. *(a) There exists asymmetric disadvantage against the complainant under the GATT and WTO dispute settlement mechanisms. (b) The disadvantage against the complainant is diminished under the WTO procedure compared to the GATT procedure, but is not totally eliminated. (c) The frequency of appeal under the WTO is higher than the frequency of panel reports being blocked under the GATT. (d) If the level of legal controversy increases overall, the frequency of panel reports being blocked under the GATT increases.*

Proof. (*a*) It is straightforward to see this by comparing the potential benefit and cost for C and D to block/appeal an adverse ruling under the GATT/WTO. The potential benefit for C to block or appeal an adverse ruling is uniformly less than D, while the same structure of cost applies to both parties. (*b*) The disadvantage against C is smaller under the WTO (V) than under the GATT($V/(1-\delta)$), but it still exists. (*c*) As illustrated in Figure 2, the frequency of appeal under the WTO is higher than the frequency of panel reports being blocked under the GATT. Both the defendant and the complainant appeal reports at a higher frequency under the WTO than the respective frequency at which they block reports under the GATT. (*d*) An increase in the overall level of legal controversy leads to a rightward shift in the probability density function, $f(L|R) \rightarrow f'(L|R)$, as illustrated in Figure 2. This leads to an increase in the frequency of panel reports being blocked under the GATT, as indicated by the dotted shaded area. Q.E.D.

The data on the GATT/WTO dispute settlement mechanism, as shown in Table 1, indicate that under the GATT regime, the defendant blocked the report at a higher frequency than the complainant given an adverse ruling. This may be explained to some extent by the asymmetric disadvantage against the complainant as claimed earlier. Table 1 also indicates that the frequency of appeal under the WTO (70%) is much higher than the frequency of panel reports being blocked under the GATT (12.5%). Finally, we see in Table 1 that under the GATT regime, there was a surge in the frequency of blocked panel reports in the 1980s compared to

Table 1. Incidence of panel reports blocked/appealed under the GATT/WTO

Regimes	Pre-Tokyo Round						Post-Tokyo Round		WTO
Decades	1950s		1960s		1970s		1980s		1995–2005
Total rulings	21		5		15		47		105
(No violation)		(6)		(0)		(7)		(7)	
(Violation)		(15)		(5)		(8)		(40)	
(Blocked by C)		(0)		(0)		(0)		(2)	
(Blocked by D)		(1)		(0)		(0)		(8)	
Blocked/appealed	1		0		0		10		74
Percentage of total rulings	5%		0%		0%		21%		70%

Note 1: For the GATT era, the data on "Total rulings" and outcomes of rulings, "No violation/Violation," were compiled from Hudec (1993, p. 289).
Note 2: For the GATT era, the blocked cases were identified from the Database of Hudec (1993) as follows. Cases with "Procedure" entry of "4" and "Plenary Action" entry of "1.2", "1.8", or "2.3" were first selected from Database Part II (pp. 588–608). Among them, whose panel reports were actually blocked were then identified using the information in Database Part I (pp. 417–585). The identified cases are Complaints 42, 103, 105, 107, 113, 132, 137, 149, 185, 191, and 196.
Note 3: The DISC case and its three counter-claims (Complaints 69–72, filed in 1973) were not included in the blocked cases. Their panel rulings were blocked at first but eventually the Council was able to reach decisions in 1982.
Note 4: The data for the WTO era were taken from Leitner and Lester (2006). The numbers (as of February 14, 2006) excluded circulated panel reports whose deadlines for appeal had not expired at the time mentioned earlier.

previous decades. This may be explained by the fact that the panel reports during the 1980s were subject to a higher degree of legal controversy, which according to Proposition 1 leads to a higher frequency of blocking. As discussed in Section 2, the Tokyo Round negotiations produced several new MTN Codes. These Codes broadened the GATT's scope significantly and submitted more contentious and sensitive nontariff trade measures to international discipline. Since it is more difficult to rule on the legitimacy of a nontariff measure than a technical tariff measure, we expect the panel reports to be subject to a higher degree of legal controversy overall in the 1980s following the Tokyo Round.

The proposition that the disputes invoking MTN Codes were more complex in nature and led to a higher degree of legal controversy over resulting panel reports and a higher frequency of blocking, is supported by the statistics shown in Table 2. In Table 2, we see that the disputes invoking MTN Codes were blocked at a much higher frequency (58%) than the overall complaints (21%) during the 1980s, confirming that the MTN Codes were the major contributing factor of the increase in blocked cases.

Table 2. Overall complaints versus complaints invoking MTN Codes during the 1980s

Procedural outcomes	Overall	MTN Codes	Blocking incidence	Overall	MTN Codes
Total complaints	115	35	Total rulings	47	12
Rulings	47 (41%)	12 (34%)	(No violation)	(7)	(2)
Settled	28 (24%)	8 (23%)	(Violation)	(40)	(10)
Withdrawn/abandoned	40 (35%)	15 (43%)	(Blocked by C)	(2)	(2)
			(Blocked by D)	(8)	(5)
			Blocked	10	7
			Percentage of total rulings	21%	58%

Note 1: The data on "Overall" complaints during the 1980s were compiled from Hudec (1993) as explained in the notes to Tables 1 and 3.
Note 2: The data on "MTN Codes" complaints were identified from the Database Part II (pp. 588–608) of Hudec (1993) as follows. The cases invoking MTN Codes were identified by the column "Legal Provisions". They are Complaints 97, 99, 103, 105, 106, 109, 111, 114, 115, 121, 123, 126, 128, 130, 134, 136, 137, 142, 147, 149, 151, 158, 159, 164, 165, 185, 188, 190, 191, 192, 196, 197, 203, 204, and 205. Their procedural outcomes were then identified using the following method. Cases with "Procedure" entry of "4" or "Plenary Action" entry of "3" were identified as cases with "Rulings"; cases with "Plenary Action" entry of "1" but not "Procedure" entry of "4" were identified as cases "Withdrawn/abandoned"; the remainder were cases "Settled". This classification was verified to reach the same aggregate number of procedural outcomes for overall complaints reported by Hudec (1993).
Note 3: Blocked cases that invoked MTN Codes could be easily identified by comparing the list of blocked cases (Note 2 to Table 1) and the list of MTN Codes cases (Note 2). They are Complaints 103, 105, 137, 149, 185, 191, and 196.

4.2. Consultation stage

We now proceed to the consultation stage. I first discuss the complainant's decision whether to continue or withdraw from the litigation if the defendant refuses to settle, and to accept or reject a settlement offer if the defendant proposes to settle. Given the complainant's strategy of paneling, I then analyze the defendant's settlement strategy. Finally, I derive the complainant's decision of whether or not to file the dispute, given the defendant's strategy of settlement. The equilibrium solution is derived for the GATT regime, although similar analysis can be carried out for the WTO regime.

As illustrated in Figure 1, if C files the complaint, the dispute will end up in one of three procedural outcomes: ruled by the panel, withdrawn, or settled. Under the GATT regime, before the panel, C predicts that the panel will give a "violation" ruling with probability π_c and that the ruling will be adopted successfully with probability $F(\bar{L}|1)$. In this case, C will receive the compensation-equivalent value of V in every period from the beginning of stage 2. C also predicts a probability $1-\pi_c$ of losing the case and receiving nothing. Once the case is filed, C also has to incur the political cost K^f in every period. Therefore, the expected welfare change in present value for C from a panel procedure is $E\Delta W_c^p = \pi_c F(\bar{L}|1)(\delta^2/1-\delta)V - (1/(1-\delta))K^f$. From D's perspective, D predicts a probability π_d that C will prevail in the trial and a chance $F(\bar{L}|1)$ that he will not block the ruling. Therefore, D's expected welfare change from the panel procedure is $E\Delta W_d^p = -\pi_d F(\bar{L}|1)\,(\delta^2/(1-\delta))V$. If the case is withdrawn, C incurs the political cost K^f for the period the case is present. Therefore, $\Delta W_c^w = -K^f$. However, if C withdraws the dispute, D maintains its status quo welfare: $\Delta W_d^w = 0$. If the case is settled at the terms S in present value, C receives the settlement amount but also incurs the political cost K^f for the period the case is present. Therefore, the payoff to C is $\Delta W_c^s = S - K^f$. The payoff to D by settling at the terms S, compared to the status quo welfare, is $\Delta W_d^s = -S$.

4.2.1. Complainant's decision to continue or withdraw from the litigation

If D does not offer to settle, C has to decide whether to continue or withdraw the complaint. A complainant is indifferent between the two if the expected payoff from the panel $E\Delta W_c^p$ equals that of withdrawal ΔW_c^w. That is

$$\pi_c F(\bar{L}|1)\frac{\delta^2}{1-\delta}V - \frac{1}{1-\delta}K^f = -K^f$$
$$\Rightarrow \pi_c = \frac{K^f}{\delta F(\bar{L}|1)V} \equiv \tilde{\pi}_c. \tag{1}$$

A complainant with $\pi_c \geq \tilde{\pi}_c$ expects a higher payoff from the panel proceedings, and therefore will choose to continue the litigation. However, a complainant with $\pi_c < \tilde{\pi}_c$ will withdraw the case. The threshold value $\tilde{\pi}_c$ as defined in Equation (1) equals the ratio of the political cost incurred by C relative to the value of the disputed trade measure, discounted by blocking probability and time lag in implementation. As $\tilde{\pi}_c$ increases, the dispute is politically more costly, relative to potential economic benefit, for the complainant to pursue. Therefore, there is less likelihood $(1 - \tilde{\pi}_c)$ that the complainant will proceed to the panel if the defendant refuses to settle. In this sense, the threshold value $\tilde{\pi}_c$ can be interpreted as an indicator of the degree of power politics at play.

4.2.2. Complainant's decision to accept or reject a settlement offer

If D offers to settle at the terms S, C is indifferent between accepting and rejecting the offer if the expected payoff from the panel proceedings is equal to the payoff from the settlement. The threshold level of π_c such that $E\Delta W_c^p = \Delta W_c^s$ is

$$\begin{aligned} &\pi_c F(\bar{L}|1)\frac{\delta^2}{1-\delta}V - \frac{1}{1-\delta}K^f = S - K^f \\ &\Rightarrow \pi_c = \frac{1-\delta}{\delta^2 F(\bar{L}|1)V}S + \tilde{\pi}_c \equiv \pi_c(S) \end{aligned} \tag{2}$$

A complainant with $\pi_c \geq \pi_c(S)$ is sufficiently optimistic about the panel ruling, and thus will continue the litigation. However, a complainant with $\pi_c < \pi_c(S)$ will opt to accept the offer S. The threshold type $\pi_c(S)$ is therefore the highest type of C that will agree to settle at the terms S if offered by the defendant.

4.2.3. Defendant's settlement strategy

Taking into account C's strategy of paneling as characterized by $\tilde{\pi}_c$ and $\pi_c(S)$, D decides on the settlement offer, given his type π_d. Suppose D's belief about the lowest type of C (C with the least optimistic prediction about panel rulings) that will file a complaint is $\underline{\pi}_c^b$. By proposing a settlement offer S, D expects $\pi_c \in [\underline{\pi}_c^b, \pi_c(S)]$ to accept the offer, while $\pi_c \in [\pi_c(S), 1]$ reject the offer and proceed to the panel stage. Therefore, D's expected payoff from proposing an offer S is

$$\begin{aligned} E\Delta W_d(S) &= -[\pi_c(S) - \underline{\pi}_c^b]S - [1 - \pi_c(S)]\bar{S}_d, \\ &\text{for } \max\{\underline{\pi}_c^b, \tilde{\pi}_c\} \leq \pi_c(S) \leq 1 \end{aligned} \tag{3}$$

where $\bar{S}_d = -E\Delta W_d^p$ is the expected welfare loss from the panel proceedings for D. The defendant has no incentive to offer more than enough to settle with all possible types of C such that $\pi_c(S) > 1$. For offers

S such that $\pi_c(S) < \max\{\underline{\pi}_c^b, \tilde{\pi}_c\}$, they are equivalent to D's refusal to settle. To see this, note that offers S proposed by D such that $\pi_c(S) < \tilde{\pi}_c$ correspond to negative offers, $S < 0$, and are equivalent to no settlement. For offers S proposed by D such that $\pi_c(S) < \underline{\pi}_c^b$, the offers are not large enough to settle with any type of C that files, so they are equivalent to no settlement as well. In the case without settlement, the complainant who files ($\pi_c \geq \underline{\pi}_c^b$) and who has enough confidence of winning ($\pi_c \geq \tilde{\pi}_c$) continues the litigation. Thus, the defendant's expected payoff is $E\Delta W_d(S) = -[1 - \max\{\underline{\pi}_c^b, \tilde{\pi}_c\}]\bar{S}_d$, for $\pi_c(S) < \max\{\underline{\pi}_c^b, \tilde{\pi}_c\}$.

We are ready to characterize the defendant's settlement strategy. Suppose S^e is the unconstrained optimal solution to $E\Delta W_d(S)$ in (3). Use the first-order condition: $\partial(E\Delta W_d)/\partial S = -[(\partial\pi_c(S)/\partial S)(S - \bar{S}_d) + \pi_c(S) - \underline{\pi}_c^b] = 0$ and the definition of $\pi_c(S)$ and $\bar{S}_d$. It is straightforward to show that

$$S^e = \frac{1}{2}\frac{\delta^2 F(\bar{L}|1)V}{1-\delta}(\pi_d - \tilde{\pi}_c + \underline{\pi}_c^b), \tag{4}$$

$$\pi^e \equiv \pi_c(S^e) = \frac{1}{2}(\pi_d + \tilde{\pi}_c + \underline{\pi}_c^b). \tag{5}$$

Note from (4) that the defendant's optimal offer rises as he is more pessimistic about panel judgement (higher π_d). The offer also increases if he believes that he is facing a potentially stronger opponent (higher $\underline{\pi}_c^b$). On the other hand, the defendant's optimal offer decreases if the dispute is more costly for the complainant to pursue (higher $\tilde{\pi}_c$) and there is less likelihood that the complainant will proceed to the panel if the defendant refuses to settle. As argued in the previous paragraph, the optimal offer S^e is truncated below at $\pi^e = \max\{\tilde{\pi}_c, \underline{\pi}_c^b\}$, where settlement fails, and above at $\pi^e = 1$, where the defendant has no incentives to further increase the settlement offer. It follows from (5) that a defendant relatively optimistic about panel judgement with $\pi_d \in [0, |\tilde{\pi}_c - \underline{\pi}_c^b|]$ will opt not to settle. However, a defendant relatively pessimistic with $\pi_d \in [|\tilde{\pi}_c - \underline{\pi}_c^b|, 1]$ will offer to settle following the optimal offer S^e. If $\tilde{\pi}_c + \underline{\pi}_c^b > 1$, the defendant's settlement scheme π^e is truncated above and all types of D with $\pi_d \in [2 - \tilde{\pi}_c - \underline{\pi}_c^b, 1]$ settle at the upper bound $\pi^e = 1$, which corresponds to an offer of $S^e = \delta^2 F(\bar{L}|1)V(1 - \tilde{\pi}_c)/(1 - \delta)$.

4.2.4. Complainant's filing decision and equilibrium outcomes

Given D's strategy of settlement as characterized earlier, C then decides whether or not to file the complaint. C's filing decision can be conveniently characterized by $\underline{\pi}_c^e$, which is the lowest type of C that will file a complaint at equilibrium. By perfect Bayesian equilibrium concept, D's belief should be consistent with C's strategy at equilibrium; therefore, the condition $\underline{\pi}_c^b = \underline{\pi}_c^e$ holds at equilibrium.

Given the presence of two-sided asymmetric information, it is likely for a complainant with $\pi_c < \tilde{\pi}_c$ to file a dispute. These types of C face a probability that D will not settle and as a result they will have to withdraw the case and incur loss. However, there is some probability that D might settle. If the prospect of a settlement and the magnitude of the settlement offer are large enough so that the overall expected payoff from filing is nonnegative, then this justifies their decision to file the complaint. This type of equilibrium corresponds to $\underline{\pi}_c^e < \tilde{\pi}_c$. On the other hand, another type of equilibrium $\underline{\pi}_c^e \geq \tilde{\pi}_c$ may arise, where all types of C that file will proceed to the panel unless a settlement is achieved. Figure 3 illustrates all the possible scenarios, where panels "FW1–3" represent three types of equilibria which include the possibility of withdrawal, and panels "FP1–3" represent three types of equilibria which do not.

In each panel, the type of defendant π_d and the type of complainant π_c are indicated on the horizontal and vertical axis, respectively. In scenarios "FW1–3", the lowest type of C that will file a complaint is smaller than the threshold type ($\underline{\pi}_c^e < \tilde{\pi}_c$). Following our analysis earlier, the defendant does not settle if $\pi_d \in [0, \tilde{\pi}_c - \underline{\pi}_c^e]$, and offers to settle according to the optimal scheme S^e if $\pi_d \in [\tilde{\pi}_c - \underline{\pi}_c^e, 1]$. The highest type of C that will accept D's offer S^e is illustrated by the linear schedule π^e. In "FW3", where $\tilde{\pi}_c + \underline{\pi}_c^e > 1$, the linear schedule π^e is truncated above and all types of D with $\pi_d \in [2 - \tilde{\pi}_c - \underline{\pi}_c^e, 1]$ offer to settle at the upper bound $\pi^e = 1$. In scenarios "FP1–3", the lowest type of C that will file a complaint is larger than the threshold type ($\underline{\pi}_c^e \geq \tilde{\pi}_c$). The defendant's settlement strategy can be similarly illustrated by the linear schedule π^e, with the lower truncation point of not settling for the defendant replaced by $\pi_d = \underline{\pi}_c^e - \tilde{\pi}_c$.

In each type of possible equilibrium, different outcomes emerge depending on the types of the disputing parties: π_c and π_d. These are indicated in Figure 3. The possible outcomes are "*nf*", where the complainant does not file the case; "*w*", where the complainant files and then withdraws the case; "*s*", where the complainant files the case and achieves a settlement with the defendant; and "*p*", where the complainant files the case and the case proceeds to a panel.

Take "FW2", for example. In this equilibrium, a complainant with $\pi_c \in [0, \underline{\pi}_c^e]$ will not file the case, while a complainant with $\pi_c \in [\underline{\pi}_c^e, 1]$ will file the case. If the complainant files the case, a defendant with $\pi_d \in [0, \tilde{\pi}_c - \underline{\pi}_c^e]$ will not settle; in response, a complainant with $\pi_c \in [\underline{\pi}_c^e, \tilde{\pi}_c]$ will withdraw, while a complainant with $\pi_c \in [\tilde{\pi}_c, 1]$ will proceed to a panel. However, in response to the complaint, a defendant with $\pi_d \in [\tilde{\pi}_c - \underline{\pi}_c^e, 1]$ will offer to settle according to the scheme S^e, which a complainant with $\pi_c \in [\underline{\pi}_c^e, \pi^e]$ will accept and a complainant with $\pi_c \in [\pi^e, 1]$ will reject and proceed to a panel. The size of the region for each outcome measures the likelihood of each outcome, since the types of the two disputing parties are assumed to be uniformly distributed on the closed unit intervals [0, 1].

We now characterize the equilibrium. Let $E\Delta W_c^f(\pi_c)$ denote the expected payoff from filing a dispute for a complainant of type π_c. Given

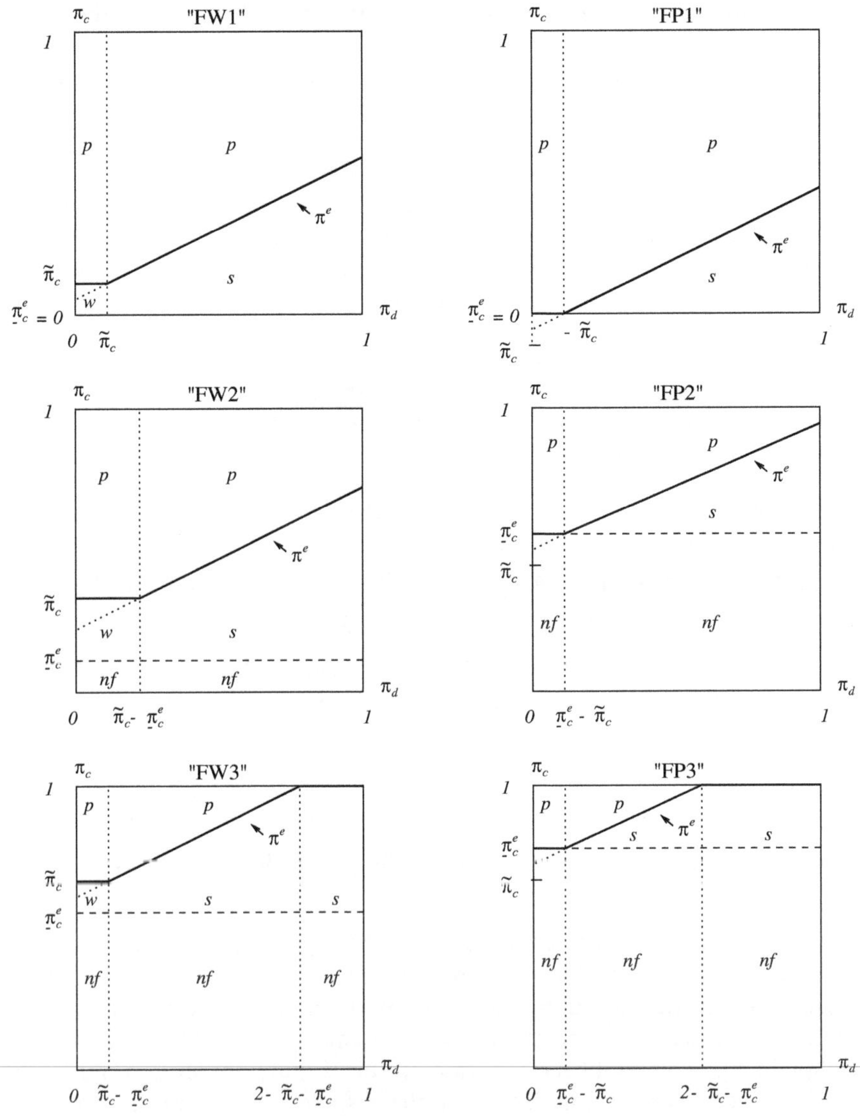

Fig. 3. ***Equilibrium scenarios as*** $\tilde{\pi}_c$ ***varies*** ($\tilde{\pi}_c < \delta$).

D's strategy of settlement, a complainant calculates its expected payoff from filing the dispute by evaluating the likelihood of each of the three possible procedural outcomes (withdrawal, settlement, and ruling) and their associated payoffs. Note that $E\Delta W_c^f(\pi_c)$ is a nondecreasing function of π_c. The equilibrium lower bound for the type of C that will file a dispute, $\underline{\pi}_c^e$, is determined by the zero cutoff condition, $E\Delta W_c^f(\underline{\pi}_c^e) = 0$, for $\underline{\pi}_c^e \in (0, 1)$. If $E\Delta W_c^f(\underline{\pi}_c^e) > 0$, lower types of C with

$\pi_c < \underline{\pi}_c^e$ will have incentives to file the dispute, which contradicts the definition of $\underline{\pi}_c^e$. On the other hand, if $E\Delta W_c^f(\underline{\pi}_c^e) < 0$, the complainant $\underline{\pi}_c^e$ is worse off by filing the case and will choose not to, which again contradicts the definition of $\underline{\pi}_c^e$. The corner solutions $\underline{\pi}_c^e = 0$ and $\underline{\pi}_c^e = 1$ arise respectively if $E\Delta W_c^f(0) \geq 0$ and $E\Delta W_c^f(1) \leq 0$.

The following proposition summarizes the dependence of the equilibrium scenario on the parameters of the dispute. The detailed derivations are provided in the appendix. In addition to the six equilibrium scenarios illustrated in Figure 3, define "NF" as the equilibrium scenario where the complainant does not file the dispute, regardless of his type.

PROPOSITION 2. *As the relative political cost $\tilde{\pi}_c$ increases for a complainant to pursue a litigation under the GATT, the equilibria "FP1", "FW1", "FW2", "FW3" ("FP2")", "FP3", and "NF" emerge sequentially, if the discount factor δ is relatively large (small).*

PROOF. As shown in the appendix, the condition on $\tilde{\pi}_c$ for the different scenarios of equilibrium to emerge is "FP1": $\tilde{\pi}_c \leq 0$, "FW1": $0 < \tilde{\pi}_c < (2-\delta)/\delta - 2\sqrt{1-\delta}/\delta$, "FW2": $(2-\delta)/\delta - 2\sqrt{1-\delta}/\delta \leq \tilde{\pi}_c < \min\{\delta/(4(1-\delta)), (1+\delta)/(2\delta) - \sqrt{1+2\delta-3\delta^2}/(2\delta)\}$, "FW3": $(1+\delta)/(2\delta) - \sqrt{1+2\delta-3\delta^2}/(2\delta) \leq \tilde{\pi}_c < (2\delta-1)/\delta$, "FP2": $\delta/(4(1-\delta)) \leq \tilde{\pi}_c < (1+\delta)/(2\delta) - \sqrt{1+2\delta-3\delta^2}/(2\delta)$, "FP3": $\max\{(1+\delta)/(2\delta) - \sqrt{1+2\delta-3\delta^2}/(2\delta), (2\delta-1)/\delta\} \leq \tilde{\pi}_c \leq \delta$, and "NF": $\tilde{\pi}c > \delta$. For $\delta > 2/3, (1+\delta)/(2\delta) - \sqrt{1+2\delta-3\delta^2}/(2\delta) < (2\delta-1)/\delta < \delta/(4(1-\delta))$; therefore, "FP2" does not arise. On the other hand, for $\delta < 2/3$, $(2\delta-1)/\delta < \delta/(4(1-\delta)) < (1+\delta)/(2\delta) - \sqrt{1+2\delta-3\delta^2}/(2\delta)$; therefore "FW3" is not sustainable. Q.E.D.

Figure 4 illustrates the dependence of the equilibrium scenarios on the parameters $\tilde{\pi}_c$ and δ. The equilibrium "FP1" arises if $\tilde{\pi}_c < 0$, which corresponds to the situation where the international political cost by filing the dispute is smaller than the domestic political benefit ($K^f < 0$) for the complainant. This is likely the case if the dispute involves a relatively powerful complaining country, or if the dispute attracts strong domestic political support from within the complaining country. The equilibrium "FW1" arises if the relative political cost $\tilde{\pi}_c$ turns positive, and the equilibrium "FW2" appears next if $\tilde{\pi}_c$ increases further. As the relative political cost continues rising, the equilibrium "FW3" ("FP2") emerges, if the discount factor δ is larger (smaller) than 2/3, followed by the equilibrium "FP3". Eventually with even higher $\tilde{\pi}_c$, the equilibrium "NF" emerges.

PROPOSITION 3. *As the relative political cost $\tilde{\pi}_c$ increases for a complainant to pursue a litigation under the GATT: (a) the incidence of complaints filed $(1 - \underline{\pi}_c^e)$ remains constant at first, before decreasing monotonically toward*

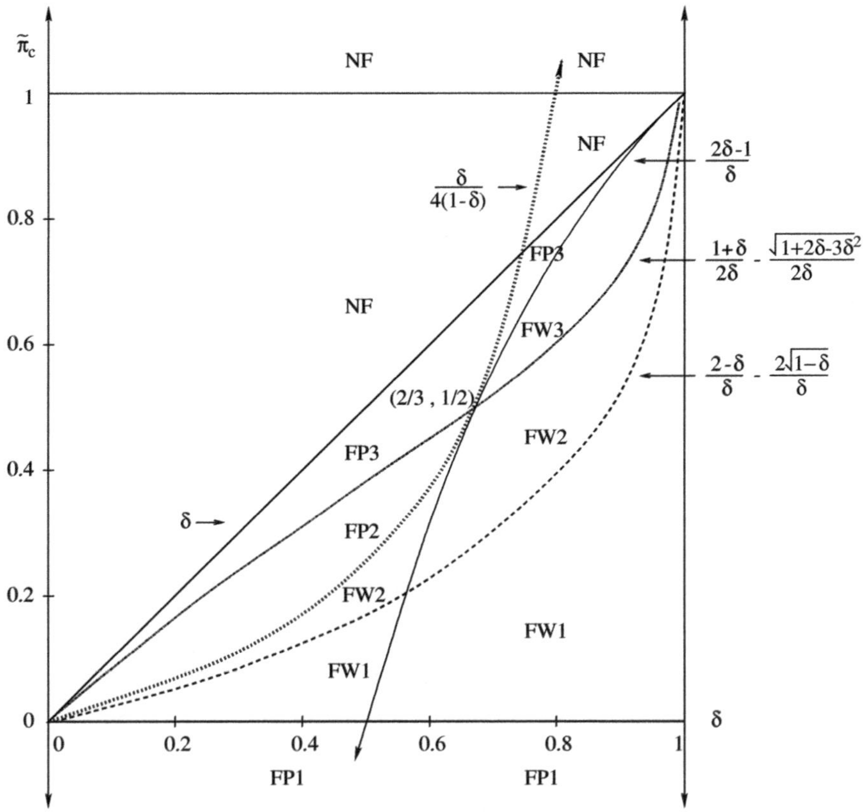

Fig. 4. Parameter space and equilibrium scenarios.

zero; (b) the incidence of complaints withdrawn increases at first, before decreasing toward zero.

PROOF. (*a*) As shown in the appendix, the lowest type of complainants that will file a case is "FP1": $\underline{\pi}_c^e = 0$, "FW1": $\underline{\pi}_c^e = 0$, "FW2": $\underline{\pi}_c^e = \tilde{\pi}_c + 2\sqrt{(1-\delta)/\delta}\sqrt{\tilde{\pi}_c} - 1$, "FW3": $\underline{\pi}_c^e = ((1-\delta)\tilde{\pi}_c)/(\delta(1-\tilde{\pi}_c))$, "FP2": $\underline{\pi}_c^e = \tilde{\pi}_c + 2\sqrt{(1-\delta)/\delta}\sqrt{\tilde{\pi}_c} - 1$, "FP3": $\underline{\pi}_c^e = ((1-\delta)\tilde{\pi}_c)/(\delta(1-\tilde{\pi}_c))$, and "NF": $\underline{\pi}_c^e = 1$. Thus, the incidence of complaints filed $(1-\underline{\pi}_c^e)$ remains constant from the equilibrium "FP1" to the equilibrium "FW1", as $\tilde{\pi}_c$ increases. It is straightforward to show that $\partial\underline{\pi}_c^e/\partial\tilde{\pi}_c > 0$ in the other equilibrium scenarios. Thus, the equilibrium-filing threshold $\underline{\pi}_c^e$ increases with the rise in the relative political cost $\tilde{\pi}_c$ through "FW2", "FW3" ("FP2"), and "FP3", until it reaches the upper bound $\underline{\pi}_c^e = 1$. The desired result therefore follows. (*b*) Recall the formula for the equilibrium-filing threshold $\underline{\pi}_c^e$ in each of the equilibrium scenarios from above. The incidence of complaints withdrawn can be represented by the region "*w*" in Figure 3. Since in "FW1", all types of complainants file ($\underline{\pi}_c^e = 0$), the region "w" increases with the relative political cost $\tilde{\pi}_c$. It can be shown that $\partial(\tilde{\pi}_c - \underline{\pi}_c^e)/\partial\tilde{\pi}_c < 0$ in the rest of equilibrium scenarios. Thus, the incidence of complaints withdrawn decreases as the relative political cost $\tilde{\pi}_c$ increases in "FW2" and "FW3", and eventually disappears when $\tilde{\pi}_c \leq \underline{\pi}_c^e$ as in "FP2" and "FP3". The desired result follows. Q.E.D.

When the international political cost of filing a dispute is dominated by its domestic political benefit for a complainant as in "FP1", the expected payoffs from all possible procedural outcomes are positive. Thus, the complainant will file the dispute regardless of his prediction of panel judgement ($\underline{\pi}_c^e = 0$). When the relative political cost $\tilde{\pi}_c$ turns positive but is relatively small as in the scenario "FW1", it is still sustainable for all types of complainants to file the dispute, and as a result, the higher the relative political cost $\tilde{\pi}_c$, the higher the incidence of complaints withdrawn. As the relative political cost $\tilde{\pi}_c$ continues rising, a complainant not sufficiently optimistic about panel judgement will quit filing ($\underline{\pi}_c^e > 0$) as in "FW2". Henceforth, the filing threshold $\underline{\pi}_c^e$ increases monotonically with the rise in the relative political cost $\tilde{\pi}_c$ and does so at a faster rate. Thus, the incidence of complaints withdrawn starts to decrease with the rise in the relative political cost $\tilde{\pi}_c$. This continues through "FW3" until the "withdrawal" outcome disappears, as in "FP2" and "FP3". With even higher relative political cost, the complainant will not file the dispute regardless of how optimistic he is about panel judgement ($\underline{\pi}_c^e = 1$); this is represented by the scenario "NF".

Proposition 3 implies that if the population of trade disputes are uniformly distributed across different pairs of subjective predictions (π_c, π_d), we should observe some systematic patterns of filing and withdrawal, corresponding to different levels of relative political cost $\tilde{\pi}_c$. When the relative political cost $\tilde{\pi}_c$ is very low, a lot of complaints will be filed but relatively few complaints withdrawn ("FW1"). When the relative political cost $\tilde{\pi}_c$ is medium, fewer complaints will be filed but a lot of them withdrawn ("FW2"). When the relative political cost $\tilde{\pi}_c$ is high, even fewer complaints will be filed and relatively few withdrawn ("FW3"). Finally, when the relative political cost becomes so high, very few complaints will be filed and none of them withdrawn ("FP3").

If we look at the statistics for the GATT regime in Table 3, we see that the pattern of total complaints and cases withdrawn varied across different decades. In the 1950s, 53 trade disputes were brought under the GATT legal system, 10 of which were withdrawn. In the 1960s, the system basically fell into a void. Merely seven times was the dispute settlement procedure invoked, and no complaints were withdrawn. In the 1970s, the legal activities seemed to thrive again with 32 new cases filed and five of them withdrawn. This momentum continued into the 1980s when we witnessed a surge in litigation (115 complaints) and withdrawals (40 cases).

Table 3. Procedural outcomes of complaints filed under the GATT and WTO

Regimes	Pre-Tokyo Round			Post-Tokyo Round	WTO
Decades	1950s	1960s	1970s	1980s	1995–2005
Total complaints	53	7	32	115	335
Cases in progress					159
Rulings	21 (40%)	5 (71%)	15 (47%)	47 (41%)	95 (54%)
Settled	22 (42%)	2 (29%)	12 (38%)	28 (24%)	52 (30%)
Withdrawn or abandoned	10 (19%)	0 (0%)	5 (16%)	40 (35%)	29 (16%)

Note 1: The data were compiled from Hudec (1993, p. 287) and WTO (2005, p. iii) for complaints filed under the GATT and the WTO regimes, respectively. WTO (2005) registers the number of *Panel Reports Adopted* (as of December 1, 2005) instead of *Panel Reports Circulated.* This accounts for the discrepancy in the numbers of Rulings between Tables 1 and 3.
Note 2: The percentages in brackets refer to the frequency of a certain procedural outcome with respect to the total number of completed complaints.

To understand the data, we can apply the results from Proposition 3 and assign to each decade a likely level of relative political cost $\tilde{\pi}_c$ that might be experienced on average by all countries utilizing the GATT dispute settlement system. Judging from the amount of complaints and withdrawn cases in each decade, the magnitude of relative political cost for each decade, ranging from small to large, is likely to be: 1980s, 1950s, 1970s, and 1960s. The corresponding representative equilibrium for these decades is likely to be: "FW2", "FW2/FW3", "FW3", and "FP3", respectively.

As documented by Hudec (1993), the GATT started with a small group of homogeneous countries. Most of them were small European states, which were accustomed to using international litigation procedure in resolving conflicts. Therefore, the dispute settlement procedure of the 1950s was dealt with as common practice, with no significant feeling of hostility about it. Therefore, the international political cost of using the GATT dispute settlement procedure in this decade is likely to be low.

In the 1960s, two major changes occurred to the system: the European Community was established, which replaced the original six smaller states with one larger trade negotiating entity; and the number of developing country members expanded rapidly. Both groups demanded major exemptions from the GATT obligations and the former advocated a diplomatic approach to all policy conflicts, contrary to the formal GATT legal procedure. This "antilegalist" position prevailed among developed countries, including the United States, such that it generated an atmosphere in which formal legal claims were regarded as unfriendly behavior. Therefore, it corresponds to a very high level of international political cost in the model for initiating a complaint during this decade.

In the 1970s, the GATT began to rebuild its legal system with the Tokyo Round negotiations. The United States reversed its antilegalist position, and among other countries there was a gradual awakening of interest in the dispute settlement system. Therefore, we can consider the political cost to have gradually come down in this decade, to the level of the 1950s, and to have continued to decrease throughout the 1980s after the Tokyo Round negotiations. The GATT dispute settlement procedure became a popular device for member countries to resolve trade disputes in this decade. Although we also witnessed earlier that a higher fraction of panel reports were blocked during this decade, and therefore the expected benefits from the litigation procedure for a complainant decreased, the decrease in political costs presumably exceeded the decrease in expected benefits so that overall, the relative political cost $\tilde{\pi}_c$ decreased for a complaint during the 1980s.

5. *Conclusion*

This chapter develops a theoretical model to explain the stylized facts observed for the GATT/WTO dispute settlement mechanisms. The chapter first studies the effect of legal controversy over a panel ruling on the incentives of countries to block (appeal) a panel report under the GATT (WTO) procedure. The chapter then examines the effect of political power on the incentives of countries to use, and their interactions in using, the dispute settlement mechanism, in a framework of two-sided asymmetric information. It is shown that the magnitude of the political cost, relative to potential benefit that a complainant stands to gain from using this mechanism, determines the pattern of filing activity and the frequency of various procedural outcomes. This result, when confronted with the statistics on disputes in different decades of the GATT regime, provides an indicator of how well the dispute procedure has worked during various decades, in terms of how much this procedure has been subject to potential power politics.

Appendix

This appendix derives the equilibrium conditional on the parameters of the dispute. The parameters of the dispute are summarized by $\tilde{\pi}_c$ and δ. In most of the equilibrium scenarios, the equilibrium-filing threshold $\underline{\pi}_c^e$ is derived as a function of the parameters of the dispute. The conditions on the parameters under which a particular equilibrium scenario arises are then derived.

Equilibrium "FP1": $\tilde{\pi}_c \leq 0$

If $\tilde{\pi}_c \leq 0$, it implies that $K^f \leq 0$ by (1). This represents a situation where the political benefit from domestic support by filing a dispute is larger than the international political cost. In this case, for all $\pi_c \in [0, 1]$, $E\Delta W_c^p \geq \Delta W_c^w = -K^f \geq 0$. Therefore, regardless whether D will offer to settle or not, C's payoff from all possible procedural outcomes by filing the complaint is nonnegative. In this case, C will file the complaint regardless of his type π_c. This is equivalent to $\underline{\pi}_c^e = 0$.

Equilibrium "FW1": $0 = \underline{\pi}_c^e < \tilde{\pi}_c, E\Delta W_c^f(0) > 0$

This is a scenario with corner solution, where $E\Delta W_c^f(0) > 0$ and C will file the complaint regardless of his type ($\underline{\pi}_c^e = 0$). However, the political cost of filing is positive. The expected payoff from filing for $\pi_c = 0$ is

$$E\Delta W_c^f(0) = \tilde{\pi}_c \Delta W_c^w + \int_{\tilde{\pi}_c}^1 \Delta W_c^s d\pi_d$$
$$= \tilde{\pi}_c(-K^f) + \int_{\tilde{\pi}_c}^1 (S^e - K^f) d\pi_d = -K^f + \int_{\tilde{\pi}_c}^1 S^e d\pi_d.$$

Use the formula S^e in (4) with $\underline{\pi}_c^b = 0$. It is straightforward to show that $E\Delta W_c^f(0) = (1/4)(\delta F(\bar{L}|1)V/(1-\delta))[-4(1-\delta)\tilde{\pi}_c + \delta(1-\tilde{\pi}_c)^2]$. This is positive if $\tilde{\pi}_c < (2-\delta)/\delta - 2\sqrt{1-\delta}/\delta$. Therefore, the condition on the parameters for this equilibrium to emerge is $0 < \tilde{\pi}_c < (2-\delta)/\delta - 2\sqrt{1-\delta}/\delta$.

Equilibrium "FW2": $0 \leq \underline{\pi}_c^e < \tilde{\pi}_c, E\Delta W_c^f(\underline{\pi}_c^e) = 0, \tilde{\pi}_c + \underline{\pi}_c^e < 1$

In this scenario, the relative political cost $\tilde{\pi}_c$ is larger, so that some types of complainants will not file the case. For $\pi_c = \underline{\pi}_c^e$, the expected payoff from filing is

$$E\Delta W_c^f(\underline{\pi}_c^e) = (\tilde{\pi}_c - \underline{\pi}_c^e)\Delta W_c^w + \int_{\tilde{\pi}_c - \underline{\pi}_c^e}^1 \Delta W_c^s d\pi_d$$
$$= (\tilde{\pi}_c - \underline{\pi}_c^e)(-K^f) + \int_{\tilde{\pi}_c - \underline{\pi}_c^e}^1 (S^e - K^f) d\pi_d = -K^f + \int_{\tilde{\pi}_c - \underline{\pi}_c^e}^1 S^e d\pi_d.$$

Use the formula S^e in (4) with $\underline{\pi}_c^b = \underline{\pi}_c^e$. We can show that $E\Delta W_c^f(\underline{\pi}_c^e) = (1/4)(\delta F(\bar{L}|1)V/(1-\delta))[-4(1-\delta)\tilde{\pi}_c + \delta(1-\tilde{\pi}_c + \underline{\pi}_c^e)^2]$. The zero expected payoff condition for $\underline{\pi}_c^e$ implies that $\underline{\pi}_c^e = \tilde{\pi}_c + 2\sqrt{(1-\delta)/\delta}\sqrt{\tilde{\pi}_c} - 1$. For this equilibrium to be borne out, the parameters have to satisfy the restrictions: $0 \leq \underline{\pi}_c^e < \tilde{\pi}_c$ and $\tilde{\pi}_c + \underline{\pi}_c^e < 1$. With some manipulations, it can be shown that this corresponds to the condition:

$$\frac{2-\delta}{\delta} - \frac{2\sqrt{1-\delta}}{\delta} \leq \tilde{\pi}_c < \min\left\{\frac{\delta}{4(1-\delta)}, \frac{1+\delta}{2\delta} - \frac{\sqrt{1+2\delta-3\delta^2}}{2\delta}\right\}.$$

Equilibrium "FW3": $0<\underline{\pi}_c^e<\tilde{\pi}_c, E\Delta W_c^f(\underline{\pi}_c^e)=0, \quad \tilde{\pi}_c+\underline{\pi}_c^e \geq 1$

In this scenario, the relative political cost $\tilde{\pi}_c$ is even larger ($\tilde{\pi}_c+\underline{\pi}_c^e \geq 1$), such that D's settlement offer π^e is truncated above at $\pi_d=2-\tilde{\pi}_c-\underline{\pi}_c^e$. In this case, the expected payoff from filing for $\pi_c=\underline{\pi}_c^e$ is

$$\begin{aligned}
E\Delta W_c^f(\underline{\pi}_c^e) &= (\tilde{\pi}_c-\underline{\pi}_c^e)\Delta W_c^w+\int_{\tilde{\pi}_c-\underline{\pi}_c^e}^{2-\tilde{\pi}_c-\underline{\pi}_c^e}\Delta W_c^s d\pi_d \\
&\quad +(\tilde{\pi}_c+\underline{\pi}_c^e-1)\Delta W_c^s|_{S^e=(1-\tilde{\pi}_c)\frac{\delta^2 F(\bar{L}|1)V}{1-\delta}} \\
&= (\tilde{\pi}_c-\underline{\pi}_c^e)(-K^f)+\int_{\tilde{\pi}_c-\underline{\pi}_c^e}^{2-\tilde{\pi}_c-\underline{\pi}_c^e}(S^e-K^f)d\pi_d \\
&\quad +(\tilde{\pi}_c+\underline{\pi}_c^e-1)\left[(1-\tilde{\pi}_c)\frac{\delta^2 F(\bar{L}|1)V}{1-\delta}-K^f\right] \\
&= -K^f+\int_{\tilde{\pi}_c-\underline{\pi}_c^e}^{2-\tilde{\pi}_c-\underline{\pi}_c^e}S^e d\pi_d+(\tilde{\pi}_c+\underline{\pi}_c^e-1)(1-\tilde{\pi}_c)\frac{\delta^2 F(\bar{L}|1)V}{1-\delta}.
\end{aligned}$$

Use the formula S^e in (4) with $\underline{\pi}_c^b=\underline{\pi}_c^e$. It can be shown that $E\Delta W_c^f(\underline{\pi}_c^e)= (\delta F(\bar{L}|1)V/(1-\delta))\left[-(1-\delta)\tilde{\pi}_c+\delta\underline{\pi}_c^e(1-\tilde{\pi}_c)\right]$. This equals zero if $\underline{\pi}_c^e= ((1-\delta)\tilde{\pi}_c)/(\delta(1-\tilde{\pi}_c))$. Using this equilibrium's conditions on $\underline{\pi}_c^e$, we can derive the corresponding condition on the parameters. It is

$$\frac{1+\delta}{2\delta}-\frac{\sqrt{1+2\delta-3\delta^2}}{2\delta}\leq\tilde{\pi}_c<\frac{2\delta-1}{\delta}.$$

Equilibrium "FP2": $\tilde{\pi}_c\leq\underline{\pi}_c^e, E\Delta W_c^f(\underline{\pi}_c^e)=0, \tilde{\pi}_c+\underline{\pi}_c^e<1$

This is the scenario where the relative political cost $\tilde{\pi}_c$ is so large that $\underline{\pi}_c^e<\tilde{\pi}_c$ is no longer sustainable. Instead, in the equilibrium, $\underline{\pi}_c^e\geq\tilde{\pi}_c$, so that if D refuses to settle, all types of C that file will proceed to the panel procedure. Note that in this case, the expected payoff from filing for $\pi_c = \underline{\pi}_c^e$ is

$$\begin{aligned}
E\Delta W_c^f(\underline{\pi}_c^e) &= (\underline{\pi}_c^e-\tilde{\pi}_c)E\Delta W_c^p+\int_{\underline{\pi}_c^e-\tilde{\pi}_c}^{1}\Delta W_c^s d\pi_d \\
&= (\underline{\pi}_c^e-\tilde{\pi}_c)\left(\frac{\delta^2 F(\bar{L}|1)V}{1-\delta}\underline{\pi}_c^e-\frac{1}{1-\delta}K^f\right)+\int_{\underline{\pi}_c^e-\tilde{\pi}_c}^{1}(S^e-K^f)d\pi_d.
\end{aligned}$$

Use the formula S^e in (4) with $\underline{\pi}_c^b=\underline{\pi}_c^e$. We can show that

$$E\Delta W_c^f(\underline{\pi}_c^e)=\frac{1}{4}\frac{\delta F(\bar{L}|1)V}{1-\delta}\left[\delta\underline{\pi}_c^{e^2}+2\delta(1-\tilde{\pi}_c)\underline{\pi}_c^e+\delta\tilde{\pi}_c^2+(2\delta-4)\tilde{\pi}_c+\delta\right].$$

The zero expected payoff condition for $\underline{\pi}_c^e$ implies that $\underline{\pi}_c^e=\tilde{\pi}_c+ 2\sqrt{(1-\delta)/\delta}\sqrt{\tilde{\pi}_c}-1$. To support this equilibrium such that $\tilde{\pi}_c\leq\underline{\pi}_c^e$ and

$\tilde{\pi}_c + \underline{\pi}_c^e < 1$, the parameters must satisfy the condition that

$$\frac{\delta}{4(1-\delta)} \leq \tilde{\pi}_c < \frac{1+\delta}{2\delta} - \frac{\sqrt{1+2\delta-3\delta^2}}{2\delta}.$$

Equilibrium "FP3": $\tilde{\pi}_c \leq \underline{\pi}_c^e,\ E\Delta W_c^f(\underline{\pi}_c^e) = 0,\ \tilde{\pi}_c + \underline{\pi}_c^e \geq 1$

In this scenario, the relative political cost is too large to support $\underline{\pi}_c^e < \tilde{\pi}_c$ and is so large that the defendant's settlement scheme π^e is truncated above at $\pi_d = 2 - \tilde{\pi}_c - \underline{\pi}_c^e$. In this case, the expected payoff from filing for $\pi_c = \underline{\pi}_c^e$ is

$$\begin{aligned} E\Delta W_c^f(\underline{\pi}_c^e) &= (\underline{\pi}_c^e - \tilde{\pi}_c) E\Delta W_c^p + \int_{\underline{\pi}_c^e - \tilde{\pi}_c}^{2-\tilde{\pi}_c-\underline{\pi}_c^e} \Delta W_c^s d\pi_d \\ &\quad + (\tilde{\pi}_c + \underline{\pi}_c^e - 1)\Delta W_c^s|_{S^e = (1-\tilde{\pi}_c)\frac{\delta^2 F(\bar{L}|1)V}{1-\delta}} \\ &= (\underline{\pi}_c^e - \tilde{\pi}_c)\left(\frac{\delta^2 F(\bar{L}|1)V}{1-\delta}\underline{\pi}_c^e - \frac{1}{1-\delta}K^f\right) + \int_{\underline{\pi}_c^e - \tilde{\pi}_c}^{2-\tilde{\pi}_c-\underline{\pi}_c^e} (S^e - K^f) d\pi_d \\ &\quad + (\tilde{\pi}_c + \underline{\pi}_c^e - 1)\left[(1-\tilde{\pi}_c)\frac{\delta^2 F(\bar{L}|1)V}{1-\delta} - K^f\right]. \end{aligned}$$

We can use the formula of S^e in (4) again with $\underline{\pi}_c^b = \underline{\pi}_c^e$ to show that

$$E\Delta W_c^f(\underline{\pi}_c^e) = \frac{\delta F(\bar{L}|1)V}{1-\delta}[\delta(1-\tilde{\pi}_c)\underline{\pi}_c^e - (1-\delta)\tilde{\pi}_c].$$

The condition that $E\Delta W_c^f(\underline{\pi}_c^e) = 0$ implies that $\underline{\pi}_c^e = ((1-\delta)\tilde{\pi}_c)/(\delta(1-\tilde{\pi}_c))$. Using this equilibrium's conditions on $\underline{\pi}_c^e$, we can derive the corresponding condition on the parameters. It is

$$\max\left\{\frac{1+\delta}{2\delta} - \frac{\sqrt{1+2\delta-3\delta^2}}{2\delta}, \frac{2\delta-1}{\delta}\right\} \leq \tilde{\pi}_c \leq \delta.$$

Equilibrium "NF": $\tilde{\pi}_c > \delta$

When $\tilde{\pi}_c$ is larger than δ, it can be shown that the various procedural outcomes will all render C negative payoffs regardless of his type π_c. First of all, note that $E\Delta W_c^p = 0$ when $\pi_c = \tilde{\pi}_c/\delta$. It follows that if $\tilde{\pi}_c > \delta$ all $\pi_c \in [0, 1]$ will have negative expected payoff from the panel procedure. Second, when $\tilde{\pi}_c > \delta$, the political cost of filing (K^f) is positive. Therefore, the payoff from filing and withdrawing a case is negative ($\Delta W_c^w = -K^f < 0$) for all types of C. Third, even if D is willing to settle at the upper bound $\pi^e = 1$, the payoff to C is

$$\Delta W_c^s = S^e - K^f = (1-\tilde{\pi}_c)\frac{\delta^2 F(\bar{L}|1)V}{1-\delta} - K^f = \frac{\delta^2 F(\bar{L}|1)V}{1-\delta}\left(1 - \frac{\tilde{\pi}_c}{\delta}\right),$$

which is negative if $\tilde{\pi}_c > \delta$. In sum, if C files, the expected payoffs are negative in all possible outcomes. Therefore, C will not file the complaint regardless of his type π_c. This scenario can be represented as $\underline{\pi}_c^e = 1$.

References

Bebchuk, L.A. (1988), Suing solely to extract a settlement offer. *Journal of Legal Studies* 17, 437–450.

Blonigen, B.A., Bown, C.P. (2003), Antidumping and retaliation threats. *Journal of International Economics* 60, 249–273.

Bown, C.P. (2002a), The economics of trade disputes, the GATT's Article XXIII, and the WTO's Dispute Settlement Understanding. *Economics and Politics* 14, 283–323.

Bown, C.P. (2002b), Why are safeguards under the WTO so unpopular? *World Trade Review* 1, 47–62.

Busch, M.L. (2000), Democracy, consultation, and the paneling of disputes under GATT. *Journal of Conflict Resolution* 44, 425–446.

Bütler, M., Hauser, H. (2000), The WTO dispute settlement system: a first assessment from an economic perspective. *Journal of Law, Economics, & Organization* 16, 503–533.

Horn, H., Mavroidis, P. C., Nordström, H. (1999), Is the use of the WTO dispute settlement system biased? CEPR Discussion Papers No. 2340.

Hudec, R.E. (1993), *Enforcing International Trade Law: The Evolution of the Modern GATT Legal System.* Butterworth Legal Publishers, New Hampshire.

Hudec, R.E. (1999), The new WTO dispute settlement procedure: an overview of the first three years. *Minnesota Journal of Global Trade* 8, 1–53.

Jackson, J.H. (1997), *The World Trading System.* The MIT press, Cambridge.

Jackson, J.H. (2000), *The Jurisprudence of GATT and the WTO.* Cambridge University Press, Cambridge.

Leitner, K., Lester, S. (2006), WTO dispute settlement from 1995 to 2005: a statistical analysis. *Journal of International Economic Law* 9, 219–231.

Nalebuff, B. (1987), Credible pretrial negotiation. *Rand Journal of Economics* 18, 199–210.

P'ng, I.P.L. (1983), Strategic behavior in suit, settlement, and trial. *Bell Journal of Economics* 14, 539–550.

Prusa, T.J., Skeath, S. (2002), The economic and strategic motives for antidumping filings. *Weltwirtschaftliches Archiv* 138, 389–413.

WTO. (2005), *Update of WTO Dispute Settlement Cases (WT/DS/OV/25).* The World Trade Organization, Geneva.

PART II

Politics and Trade Disputes

CHAPTER 5

Implementing the Agreement: Partisan Politics and WTO Dispute Settlement

David Epstein[a], Sharyn O'Halloran[b] and Amy L. Widsten[a]

[a]*Department of Political Science, Columbia University, New York, NY 10027, USA*
E-mail addresses: de11@columbia.edu; alw38@columbia.edu
[b]*George Blumenthal Professor and Professor of International and Public Affairs, Columbia University, New York, NY 10027, USA*
E-mail address: so33@columbia.edu

Abstract
This essay investigates the role of WTO Member States' political institutions in their decision to comply with adverse rulings. In the end, implementation of these rulings is a political act that Member States must undertake on their own. The decision to comply will thus be affected by domestic political pressures and institutions, including who wins and who loses if the decision is implemented, the locus of decision-making necessary to comply, and the overall structure of government. In this chapter, we explore the impact that domestic partisan preferences have on compliance rates among OECD countries. We construct a formal model of WTO implementation, predicting that when left-leaning parties, those who tend to favor protection for domestic labor and markets, control government, compliance rates should tend to fall. In contrast, right-leaning governments, those who weigh highly market access and returns to capital, should be more willing to comply with adverse WTO rulings. We test these hypotheses using data from WTO trade disputes involving twenty-five advanced industrialized countries and the European Union from 1970 to 2000, and find consistent support for our theory.

Keywords: WTO, trade dispute settlement, implementation, partisan politics, formal models of trade regulation

JEL classifications: F1, K2

> *"Consult before you legislate; negotiate before you litigate; compensate before you retaliate; And comply- at any rate."*
>
> Pascal Lamy, EU Trade Commissioner

Frontiers of Economics and Globalization
Volume 6 ISSN: 1574-8715
DOI: 10.1108/S1574-8715(2009)0000006008

On September 27, 2002, Brazil made a formal "request for consultations" with the United States on the issue of subsidies for Upland Cotton. Negotiations proved unsuccessful, and the case went to a World Trade Organization (WTO) dispute settlement panel. On September 8, 2004, the final panel report was delivered to the WTO Dispute Settlement Body as well as to the public, ruling in Brazil's favor. But the process did not end there; the United States immediately notified its intention to appeal 14 specific points of the final report to the WTO Appellate Body, and despite its loss again on appeal, the United States still refused to implement the mandated reduction of subsidies. To achieve $3 billion in retaliation, Brazil proposed to suspend tariff concessions as well as obligations under the WTO Agreement on Trade-Related Intellectual Property Rights and the General Agreement on Trade in Services. As of this writing the case has yet to be fully resolved, although the United States did relent on certain direct (stage 2) export subsidies to farmers.[1]

What explains patterns of compliance with dispute settlement decisions of the WTO and General Agreement on Tariffs and Trade (GATT)? This question has recently received considerable attention from scholars of international trade regimes. Charnovitz (2001) and Anderson (2002), for example, review the options available to complainants when respondent states refuse to implement WTO rulings, including sanctions. Busch and Reinhardt (2003) examine the compliance question from the standpoint of developed versus developing countries, showing that developed countries comply less when they lose decisions and elicit greater compliance, on average, when they win. And Smith (2003) investigates strategic aspects of the WTO's own decision-making procedures, arguing that they allow modifications of ad hoc committee determinations for the purpose of increasing eventual compliance.

This focus on compliance is entirely appropriate, for two reasons. First, it is clear that unimplemented WTO decisions not only fail to move policy; they also damage the organization's credibility. Second, Member States' compliance is the last domino in a series of strategic decisions, and as such is pivotal to the WTO's ability to support global movement toward trade openness. Indeed, the limits of compliance are the limits of globalization.

Garrett and Smith (2002) provide the micro-foundations for this logic, noting that anticipated compliance affects the WTO's rulings, which in turn affects states' willingness to settle complaints prior to a ruling, which in turn affects states' incentives to register complaints in the first place. Consequently, the Appellate Body of the WTO, which rules on disputes among Member States, is motivated to be forward-looking and strategic to

---

[1] This case will be examined in greater detail in Section 4 below.

increase its authority over international trade by securing Member States' compliance with its rulings.[2]

What is yet to be fully investigated, though, is the role of Member States' own domestic political institutions in their compliance decisions. In the end, implementation of adverse WTO rulings – whether by new legislation, executive order, administrative rulemaking, or some other device – is a political act that Member States undertake on their own. The decision to comply will naturally be influenced by international concerns, including the impact on the State's economic and diplomatic relations with the complainant countries and its effect on the global trading system. But these are not the only factors that come under consideration; domestic political pressures and institutions will also figure into the calculus: who wins and who loses if the decision is implemented, the locus of decision-making necessary to comply, and the overall structure of government, to name but a few. A complete theory of implementation must take these exigencies into account, and it is possible that compliance rates can be increased most efficiently by altering domestic, rather than international, trade institutions.

O'Halloran (2007) investigates the domestic politics of compliance with respect to the United States. Not only does the United States constitute, along with the European Union, one of the 500-pound gorillas of the international trading system; its institutions were specifically designed to make implementation difficult. Given its system of bicameralism and separate powers, the U.S. federal government is conservative in the classic sense of the word: change is difficult and requires large, sustained majorities. Nonetheless, O'Halloran argues that strengthening those institutions that (1) broaden the range of feasible outcomes, (2) limit the number of veto players, and (3) delegate authority to actors with the most liberal trade-oriented preferences would increase compliance rates.

In this chapter, we extend these insights to a comparative perspective, exploring the impact that domestic partisan preferences have on compliance rates among OECD countries. We find that when left-leaning parties, those who tend to favor protection for domestic labor and markets, are in control of government, trade compliance rates tend to fall. By contrast, we find that governments with a right-leaning orientation,

---

[2] Nonetheless, compliance is problematic for several reasons. First, the WTO has no direct enforcement authority over its sovereign members. Although, in contrast to its predecessor, the GATT, the WTO can authorize retaliatory sanctions by individual Member States, enforcement is decentralized, and so noncompliance is a persistent risk. Second, governments retain the discretion to boycott Appellate decision-making and pursue grievances outside the WTO system. For example, Garrett and Smith (2002) note that signatory states referred 53 complaints to panels between 1948 and 1959, but then effectively boycotted the panel system when developing countries pressed for changes in filing disputes, such that none were filed between October 1963 and December 1969.

those who weigh market access and returns to capital more highly, are more willing to comply with adverse WTO rulings.[3]

The next section reviews some basic data on compliance with GATT and WTO rulings. We then present a simple framework within which to understand the politics of the negotiation and implementation of GATT and WTO rulings. The fourth section provides a detailed case study of U.S. compliance with the WTO Upland Cotton ruling, and the fifth section concludes.

1. Patterns of compliance

One well-known statistic is that Member States comply with WTO rulings nearly 80% of the time, which is significantly higher than the 63% compliance rate under the GATT. But the real story is a bit more complicated.[4] In fact, if we disaggregate the data, we find that 66% of WTO rulings elicit full compliance, 13% some compliance, and 21% no compliance at all. Furthermore, the cases with no compliance tend to be the biggest in dollar terms, such as those involving Foreign Sales Corporation (FSC) tax benefits and softwood lumber.

So, who does not comply? Paradoxically, the richest countries (those with per capita GDP greater than $13,000) have the worst compliance records: if a poor country loses a ruling, they fully comply 81% of the time, compared with 68% for the rich. These differences are smaller than under the GATT, but they are still significant. Moreover, poor countries settle prior to a hearing 66% of the time, compared with 53% for wealthy countries. These differences in compliance patterns are illustrated graphically in Figure 1.

The graph also indicates a considerable amount of variation among wealthy states. For example, as shown in Figure 2, Finland complies 100% of the time, while the U.S. complies only 64% of the time. Chayes and Chayes (1993, 1995) note that, while compliance rates are in general good, noncompliance arises when treaties are ambiguous and indeterminate, when states face capacity limitations, and when changes in the social and economic environment are beyond a state's control.

Simmons (2000) highlights the role of reputation on compliance rates and finds that the peer pressure of other states in the region leads states to comply with IMF regulations: when a country violates an international agreement, it faces the costs of defaulting on its international obligation, including goodwill from other countries, embarrassment of being a

---

3 The focus of this paper will be on explaining variations in compliance rates. For a discussion of complaint initiation, see Widsten (2007).

4 The source of these data can be found in M. Busch and E. Reinhardt, "Developing countries and general agreement on tariffs and trade/world trade organization dispute settlement" (2003) 37(4) *Journal of World Trade* 719.

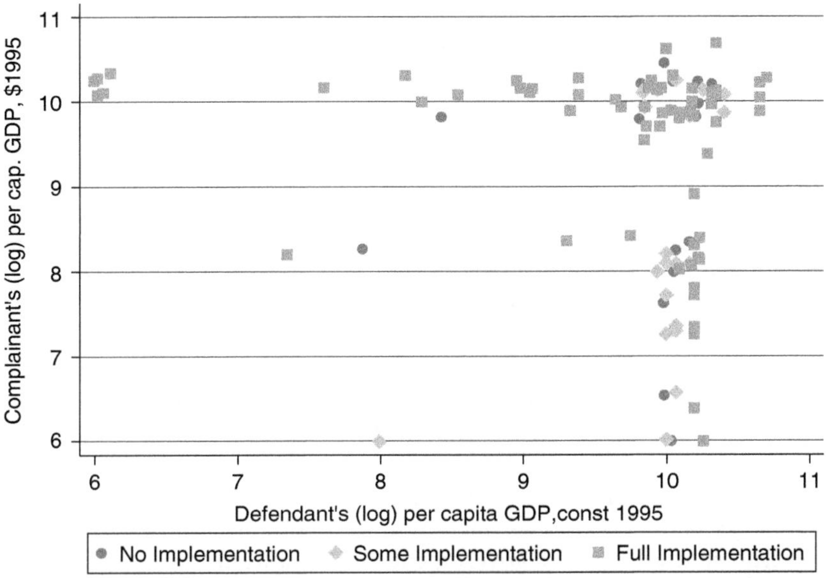

Fig. 1. Compliance patterns: by complainant and defendant GDP.

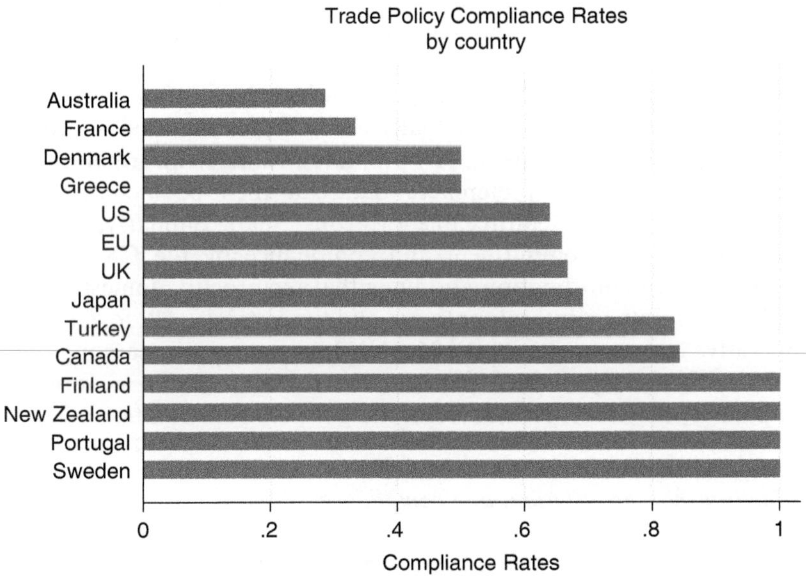

Fig. 2. Compliance rates.

cheater, and loss of credibility in negotiating future agreements (Simmons, 2000).[5] Therefore, international legal rules alter governments' incentives to comply by raising the reputational costs of reneging and allowing states to make a credible commitment to a policy stance.

In addition to these reputational issues, Slaughter (1995) argues that domestic regime type is essential to understanding compliance with international law. Governments possessing the rule of law and an independent judiciary are more likely to comply with international legal obligations. In the field of international environmental law, technical and administrative capacities, including financial resources, knowledge and training, authority, and access to relevant information are all requisites for compliance. (Weiss and Jacobson, 1998) Given that all these fundamentals are generally strong for the set of advanced industrial democracies it remains to be discovered what factors in domestic politics affect compliance.

Looking within domestic politics for answers to why states cooperate or fail to cooperate, variables including veto players, legislative control, electoral politics, divided government, and coalition politics may all be relevant. Tsebelis (1995), for example, argues that countries characterized by larger numbers of veto players in domestic politics are less likely to comply with international agreements, simply because the decision-making processes are more difficult (Tsbelis, 1995). According to this view, opening up the WTO to participation by interest groups, through *amicus curae* and other measures, and increased transparency invite more conflict into the WTO system.

Martin (2000) argues that legislatures, which have often been seen as bastions of isolationism, may actually aid in providing credible commitments under some circumstances by providing valuable information about legislative and societal preferences that can then be included in the agreement to make it enforceable (Martin, 2000). Similarly, Li (2001) studies patterns of commitment and compliance by the G8 to macroeconomic policy coordination and finds that reciprocity, domestic institutional constraints, electoral politics, and uncertainty all foster greater cooperative outcomes (Li, 2001). Nonetheless, cooperation among the G8 can be mitigated by divided partisan control or coalition governments. Compliance, therefore, reflects domestic political constraints.

2. *Partisanship, negotiation, and compliance*

The key issue, then, is how Member States can manage or balance the often-competing interests of good international citizenship and domestic resistance to compliance. The first task is to explain what drives states to

---

[5] See also Kovenock and Thursby, 1992.

come to mutually agreed solutions to their trade conflicts when those conflicts have escalated into the WTO apparatus. The second question is, given that states reached a mutually agreed solution, what are the factors that lead to compliance with international trade law?

We begin by noting that different governments will have different preferences for trading off domestic pressures and integration into the international system. In particular, left-wing governments will be less receptive to ratifying a market-liberalizing settlement, given that their constituency is likely to be more concerned about import penetration than export promotion, relative to right-wing governments. Left and right governments have distinct trade policy preferences, that is, with the right supporting export promotion and the left favoring intervention to protect vulnerable industries from import competition. The left tends to be associated with Keynesian welfare state economic policies, while the right tends to be associated with neo-classical economic policies.

To see how these observations affect dispute negotiation and rates of compliance, take a simple model of trade policy in which each dispute has a potential benefit $B>0$ to the plaintiff country, a probability of victory $p \in [0,1]$, and a cost of prosecution $C>0$. Before the case goes through the adjudication process, the defendant country can make a settlement offer $s>0$. If this is accepted the game ends. If not, then the plaintiff pays C, the case is decided, and the plaintiff wins with probability p.[6]

If the defendant country loses the case, it must decide whether or not to comply with the decision. The defendant country's cost E for evading an adverse judgment is unknown; with *ex ante* probability q the cost is $E>B$, so if the defendant loses it will choose to pay the judgment B. With probability $(1-q)$, $E<B$ and the defendant country will evade payment. As noted above, left governments are likely to place a lower value on the costs of not participating in the international trading system, so their value of q will be lower relative to right governments. The sequence of moves and payoffs to each player are illustrated in Figure 3.

The defendant country's type is unknown when it makes a settlement offer, so this is a signalling game and s may convey information about the defendant's cost of evasion. The game has no separating equilibrium; we thus analyze a semi-separating equilibrium where the defendant offers either $s = 0$ or $s = pB-C$. Defendants with low costs of evasion offer $s = 0$ for sure, while those with high costs randomize, offering $s = 0$ with probability π. The plaintiff country always accepts an offer of $pB-C$, and it accepts an offer of $s = 0$ with probability r.

The equilibrium in this game is characterized as follows:

$$r = \frac{C}{pB}$$

[6] One can add costs to the defendant for pursuing the case without affecting the equilibrium.

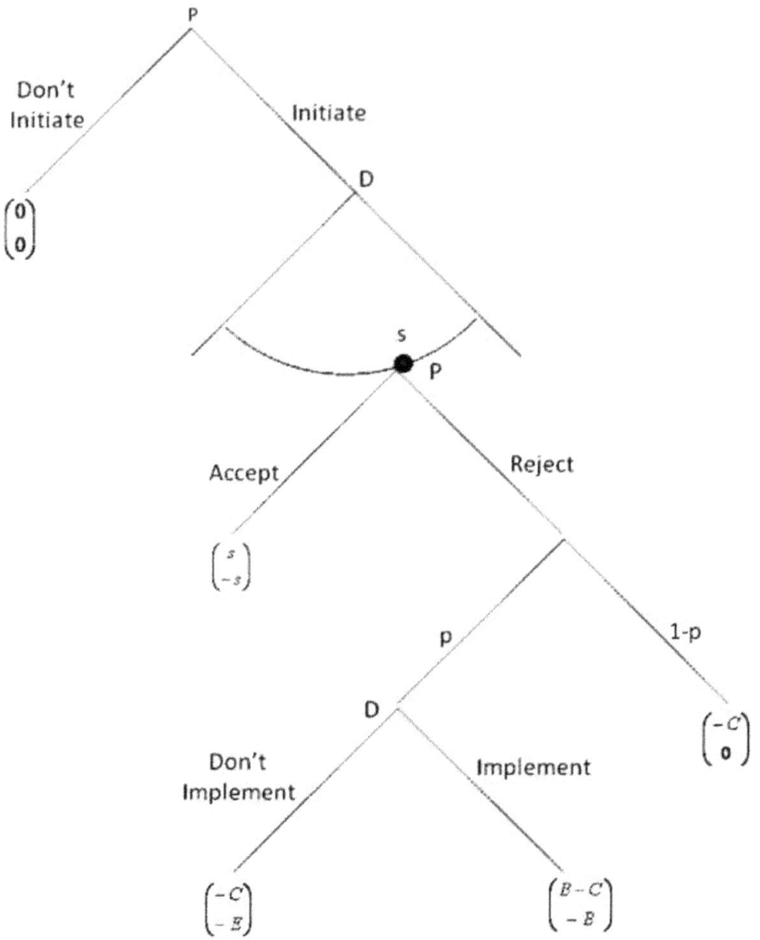

Fig. 3. Game tree.

$$\pi = \frac{1-q}{q}\frac{C}{pB-C}.$$

This equilibrium has a number of interesting implications. First, cases will only be brought if $pB-C \geq 0$. Holding the cost C of bringing the case constant, let us assume that left-wing governments value the benefits B of victory less than their right-wing counterparts. Then the cases brought by these governments would be expected to have higher values of p on average: left-wing governments, that is, will be more hesitant to bring cases in the first place, but when they do, the cases they bring will have higher probabilities of victory. The parameter p thus characterizes the plaintiff country, just as q characterizes the defendant, as noted above.

Furthermore, the equilibrium probability of settlement is r for low-cost governments and $r+(1-r)(1-\pi)>r$ for high-cost governments, so conservative defendants are more likely to settle before a case reaches its final decision. Once a case is adjudicated, the probability of evasion is $(1-q)(pB-C)/pB$. Taking derivatives with respect to p and q, evasion should be more likely with both left-wing plaintiffs and left-wing defendants.

We thus have three main hypotheses:

1) The probability of the plaintiff winning is higher in cases initiated by left-wing governments.
2) Settlement of suits prior to an official decision is more likely with right-wing defendants.
3) Adverse decisions are implemented less frequently with left-wing plaintiffs and defendants.

The type of enforcement mechanism used might also have an impact on the potential for compliance with international trade law. Multilateral institutions, like GATT and the WTO, and also regional mechanisms, offer public fora for dispute settlement where reputation plays an important role. Changes in the dispute settlement mechanism to a more stringent regime have resulted in fewer dispute settlement cases being launched by powerful countries, which now choose to pursue their goals through more politicized environments, including unilateral or regional mechanisms. If a country fails to comply or stands in breach of the agreement, it invites further censure and legitimates uncooperative behavior by countries both within and outside the mechanism. Furthermore, the existence of regional mechanisms may create more compliance within the group, but often divert trade outside it.[7]

On the other hand, international legal mechanisms may foster time inconsistency problems borne of the delays in the legal process. These legal rulings are not retroactive, so they create incentives to exacerbate the degree of noncompliance during the run-up to the ruling so as to maximize trade advantage until the ruling comes into effect. In the time during which countries deliberate over how and whether to retaliate against each other, the country in breach of the agreement continues to make inroads with continued violations.[8] During the U.S.–Japan trade negotiations in the 1980's, for example, the Japanese continued to make "inexorable" inroads in global high-technology markets as the negotiations took place (Tyson, 1992, p.6). And in the U.S.–EC steel negotiations in 1981 and 1982, the need for a transitional arrangement arose because of U.S. industry concern that the EC producers would take advantage of the time required to

[7] This claim has often been made about the EU.

[8] These violations can include trade barriers which prop up "infant" industries, aid to R&D, subsidies, etc.

implement the agreement to export all available steel, undermining the attempt to correct the problem (Levine, 1985).

Changes in economic conditions such as surges in imports or the exacerbation of the trade deficit may encourage governments to take a harder line to protect their home interests as well. Countries may also choose to forum shop, based on whether they are right or left. If a right-wing government wants to take a hard line, it may go outside the dispute settlement mechanism rather than surrender leverage to an international court.

3. Data and results

We test the hypotheses derived above with data from trade disputes involving 25 advanced industrialized countries and the EU from 1970 to 2000.[9] During this time period there were 442 cases of dispute settlement with a recognizable start date and end date, of which 192 went all the way through to a panel ruling.[10] Of these, the plaintiff won 150 cases and lost 42. In total, including cases settled before a formal panel ruling, there were 263 cases where a settlement was reached, and of these the defendant country complied fully 175 times (66.5%), 28 had partial compliance (10.6%), and 10 had no compliance (22.9%).

This latter measure – the degree of implementation – is the dependent variable for the last stage of the analysis. This variable, which we term *agreement*, measures whether or not the parties came to an agreement and whether there was a satisfactory resolution or mutually agreed solution recorded. We reviewed sources on trade disputes and determined when dispute settlement actions ended, generally after the adoption of a report and for which the paper trail completed its discussion of the monitoring and implementation process. The GATT era data were gleaned from Hudec (1993). The WTO data were gathered from the WTO website at www.wto.org. Cases from the EU Trade Barriers Regulation unilateral instrument and Canada's unilateral trade instrument are also included. For cases which were initiated but no agreement was reached, the *agreement* variable is coded as missing. We also recorded the duration of the case in months (*duration*) and whether or not the plaintiff won (*plaintwin*).

Our primary independent variables of interest are the plaintiff and defendant countries' partisan left–right orientations at the time the dispute was resolved. The data for these variables comes from the Comparative Manifestoes Project (CMP) dataset. (Budge, *et al.*, 2001) Party manifestoes

---

[9] My sample includes Australia, Austria, Belgium, Canada, Denmark, Finland, France, Germany, Greece, Iceland, Ireland, Israel, Italy, Japan, Luxembourg, the Netherlands, New Zealand, Norway, Portugal, Spain, Sweden, Switzerland, Turkey, the United Kingdom, and the United States.

[10] More recent cases and some longer ones were not included because they have not yet concluded.

are commitments by politicians of a particular party to adhere to a certain policy program. This dataset codes political party manifestoes using content analysis, recording the frequency of references to a particular philosophy or position (i.e. pro-protectionism, attitude toward government intervention in the economy, etc.) and is standardized across party systems and countries.[11] The variable is coded on a 10-point continuous scale, where 0 is the most right-wing and 10 is left.

To understand the inter-country dynamics of a particular dispute, we coded whether the case at hand was a countersuit, measured as the number of disputes launched by the defendant against the plaintiff in the prior year, and whether the plaintiff joined a suit already started by another country (*bandwagon*). For the political dynamics of the defendant country, we recorded its trade balance, whether an election occurred within three months of the cases's settlement, and the GDP ratio between the countries. Finally, to capture the international situation surrounding the dispute, we noted whether it took place during multilateral trade negotiations, and the dispute settlement mechanism used to adjudicate the case. Summary statistics for all variables are given in Table 1.

As a first look at the data, Tables 2 and 3 show the average duration of disputes and the probability that the plaintiff wins, given the ideology of the plaintiff and defendant governments. As indicated, disputes started by right-wing governments and with right-wing defendants tend to last longer, although the latter effect is less pronounced. This may indicate that right-leaning plaintiffs are more willing to initiate difficult, prolonged disputes than left-wing plaintiffs. And the overall success rate for suits started by left-wing governments is 86.8%, as opposed to 80.9% for more conservative governments, so left-wing plaintiffs are in general more successful, as the model predicts. Finally, Table 4 shows that implementation rates fall with both left-wing plaintiffs and defendants, so the politics of implementation also seem to be holding true to form.

We now subject these findings to more rigorous regression analysis, with the results given in Table 5. First, we encounter some surprising results when regressing the duration of a dispute on a number of independent variables; namely, left-wing plaintiffs are estimated to result in longer cases than right-wing governments, the opposite of the pattern indicated in Table 2. The reason seems to be the presence of the Dispute Settlement Mechanism variable, indicating that disputes settled under the WTO or GATT are resolved more efficiently than regional disputes.[12] Of course,

---

[11] The Comparative Manifestoes Project, in a massive undertaking, has developed standardized and comparable scores across the 25 advanced industrial societies used in this sample. We have added the European Union by creating standardized scores as an average of key EU countries over time.

[12] Running the same regression with separate indicators for the WTO and GATT venues confirms this suspicion.

Table 1. Descriptive statistics

Variable	Description	Observations	Mean	Standard deviation	Minimum	Maximum
Duration	Duration of case in months	441	19.18	22.26	1	124
Plaintiff wins	Defendant agrees to list of concessions	424	0.85	0.35	0	1
Agree	Defendant implements none (0), some (1/2), or all (1) concessions	304	0.67	0.45	0	1
Plaintiff party	Ideology of plaintiff (0 = right, 10 = left)	440	7.33	0.70	5.86	8.84
Defendant party	Ideology of defendant (0 = right, 10 = left)	440	7.47	0.66	5.86	8.84
Countersuit	Disputes launched against plaintiff	442	0.37	0.48	0	1
Bandwagon	Plaintiff bandwagoned onto the dispute	442	0.33	0.47	0	1
Defendant trade balance	Exports–imports	434	0.00	0.02	−0.06	0.10
Elected after	Election held 3 months after case resolved	441	0.25	0.43	0	1
GDP ratio	Ratio of plaintiff GDP to defendant GDP	441	0.50	0.31	0.0008	1.00
Multilateral trade negotiation	Multilateral trade round was in session	442	0.37	0.48	0	1
Dispute settlement mechanism	(1) Regional (2) GATT (3) WTO	442	2.27	0.75	1.00	3.00

Table 2. Average duration of dispute in months and party ideology

	Plaintiff		
Defendant	Right	Left	Average
Right	28.5	18.6	20.6
Left	27.3	16.1	19.0
Average	27.4	16.5	19.2

Table 3. Probability plaintiff wins dispute and party ideology

	Plaintiff		
Defendant	Right (%)	Left (%)	Average (%)
Right	76.9	83.7	82.2
Left	81.4	87.4	82.2
Average	80.9	86.8	85.3

Table 4. Probability losing side implements agreement and party ideology

	Plaintiff		
Defendant	Right (%)	Left (%)	Average (%)
Right	87.5	70.2	71.7
Left	89.5	61.4	65.6
Average	89.3	62.8	66.5

there are many reasons why a dispute might last a long time; perhaps it did not get settled and the loser implemented the agreement, or because there was no implementation and the dispute dragged on for many months or years. And the sign on the defendant party is in line with our expectations, though insignificant.

The next column confirms the prediction that cases started by left-wing plaintiffs do, in fact, result more often in victory than those started by right-wing governments. It is impossible to determine whether left-wing governments are more "picky" in the suits they start, meaning that they select those with a higher chance of victory in the first place, but the result of their calculations is in line with the theoretical predictions above.

Column 3 of the table shows a first pass at the results on implementation. Here, implementation is lowered when the plaintiff is left-wing, but the results on the defendant party are insignificant. However, as noted above, what we really want to do is separate out the impact of government ideology on the probability of settling before the

Table 5. Regression results

Dependent variable	Duration	Plaintiff wins	Agreement	Agreement	Agreement
Regression method	Robust regression	Probit	Ordered probit	Heckman selection equation	Heckman outcome equation
Plaintiff party	*2.89*	*0.28*	*−0.45*	*0.37*	*−0.12*
	(1.20)	(0.12)	(0.15)	(0.13)	(0.04)
Defendant party	1.15	*0.44*	−0.13	−0.38	*−0.12*
	(1.05)	(0.13)	(0.16)	(0.12)	(0.05)
Counter-suit	−1.87		−0.14	0.49	
	(1.34)		(0.18)	(0.16)	
Dispute settlement	*−5.51*		*−0.90*	1.00	
Mechanism	(1.23)		(0.28)	(0.14)	
Bandwagon	−2.26		0.30	−0.41	
	(1.51)		(0.21)	(0.17)	
Elected after			−0.10		
			(0.20)		
Defendant trade balance			*26.65*		*5.96*
			(6.46)		(1.34)
GDP ratio			−0.28		
			(0.30)		
Multilateral trade			−0.42		
Negotiation			(0.25)		
Constant	−1.37	*−4.24*		−1.58	*2.28*
	(11.70)	(1.38)		(1.29)	(0.51)
Observations	429.00	359.00	250	387	387
Censord				136	136
Uncensord				251	251
R-squared		0.05			
F	6.66				
Wald χ^2				8.41	
Arctan ρ				*0.87*	*0.87*
$\ln(\sigma)$				*−0.76*	*−0.76*
Cut lower			*−7.19*		
Cut upper			*−6.88*		

Note: Standard errors in parentheses. Italic coefficients significant at $p = 5\%$.

case comes to judgment, and then on implementation if and when a decision is reached.

This scenario is tailor-made for a Heckman selection model, which is reported in columns 4 and 5 of the table. The selection equation measures the probability that a case is settled prior to an official WTO ruling, while the outcome equation measures the degree of implementation if a ruling comes into effect. And indeed, the sign on a left-wing defendant is negative in the selection equation, meaning that they are less likely to settle, and negative in the outcome equation, indicating that they implement adverse decisions at a lower rate than right-wing governments. All effects are highly significant, as is the coefficient on implementation being lower against left-wing plaintiffs. Thus our theoretical predictions are borne out in the data analysis.

4. Case study

The Upland Cotton case is a good example of how domestic partisan concerns impact the implementation of WTO rulings. The United States is the second-largest producer of cotton in the world. From 2001 to 2003, U.S. cotton exports accounted for 40% of world trade, on average, while government subsidies averaged $3 billion per year (Schnepf, 2006). Cotton is a $2.1 billion export industry for the United States and averaged $4.6 billion per year in production during 1997–2002 (Schnepf, 2005). Cotton is grown across much of the southern United States, with Texas being the largest producer, accounting for an average of 26% of U.S. production since 1993. In 2002, 17 states reported cotton production valued at over $10 million (Schnepf, 2005).

In late 2002, Brazil, a major cotton export competitor, initiated a WTO case (DS267) against U.S. cotton subsidies and export credit guarantees. Brazil complained about four primary components of U.S. agricultural policy. First, that U.S. domestic support of cotton causes "serious prejudice" to Brazilian producers by depressing the world price of cotton and results in a larger U.S. share of the world cotton market. Second, that U.S. export credit guarantees are an export subsidy. Third, the Step 2 payments program is both an export subsidy and an import substitution policy and fourth, that tax credits and deferrals given for cotton to U.S. exporters amount to an export subsidy (Hudson *et al.*, 2005).

On September 8, 2004, a WTO dispute settlement panel ruled against the United States on several key issues involving prohibited and actionable subsidies. First, the panel found that U.S. domestic cotton subsidies exceeded permissible WTO levels, losing the protection afforded by the "Peace Clause," which shielded them from substantive challenges. Second, two major types of direct payments of U.S. farm programs – the Production Flexibility Contract of the 1996 Farm Act and the Direct Payments of the 2002 Farm Act – did not qualify for WTO exemptions from reduction commitments and should count against the "Peace Clause" limits. Third, Step 2 program payments are prohibited export subsidies. Fourth, U.S. export credit guarantees are effectively export subsidy commitments; and fifth, U.S. domestic support measures have resulted in excess cotton production and exports that have driven down international prices and resulted in serious prejudice to Brazil's cotton industry.

The panel failed to find compelling evidence that U.S. support programs would cause serious prejudice over the 2003–2007 period, though, and it found that other support programs, such as production flexibility contract payments, direct payments, and crop insurance did not cause serious prejudice to Brazil.

On October 18, 2004, the United States appealed to the WTO Appellate Body, which on March 3, 2005 confirmed the earlier DS panel findings against U.S. cotton programs. The panel found that the Step 2 program for cotton was a prohibited export subsidy and gave the United States until July 1 to end it or fix it. In addition, direct payments made under U.S. farm programs do not qualify for WTO exemptions from reduction commitments as "fully decoupled income support" and are not exempt from the Peace Clause (Lange, 2005).

On April 20, 2005, the U.S. representative to the WTO announced that the United States intended to implement the recommendations and rulings of the DSB in a manner that respected U.S. WTO obligations (U.S. Mission to the United Nations in Geneva, 2005). Subsequently, the Republican-controlled U.S. administration proposed legislation to Congress that would end Step 2. But the National Cotton Council, an industry group representing cotton producers, ginners, warehousers, merchants, cottonseed processors/dealers, cooperatives and textile manufacturers, openly questioned the wisdom of taking such a step. The NCC lobbied hard against any concessions and managed to stall the proposed measure in Congress.

By July 1, 2005, the U.S. had failed to meet its deadline on prohibited export subsidies and Brazil claimed the right to retaliate against $3 billion in U.S. exports to Brazil based on the prohibited subsidies, proposing $1 billion in retaliation-based subsidies. On July 4, 2005, Brazil requested authorization from the WTO to impose countermeasures against U.S. cotton subsidies. It threatened to revoke tariff concessions as well as obligations under the WTO Agreement on Trade-Related Intellectual Property Rights and the General Agreement on Trade in Services until the U.S. withdrew the $3 billion worth of export subsidies identified by the WTO (Schnepf, 2006).

The dispute dragged on until August 21, 2006, when Brazil submitted a request for a WTO compliance panel to review whether the United States had fully complied with the panel and appellate body rulings. This request gave the administration the leverage it needed to push through Congress a measure partially complying with the WTO ruling by eliminating the Step 2 program of export subsidies. Despite opposition from the farm lobby, the measure, which was included in the Deficit Reduction Act of 2005 (PL 109–171) passed both the House and Senate on partisan votes. In the House the count was 212–206, with all the Aye votes coming from Republicans. In the Senate the vote was tied 50–50, and the measure passed when Vice President Cheney cast the tie-breaking vote; again, only Republicans voted in favor of the measure.

Overall, then, this case illustrates the difficulty of implementing an unpopular WTO ruling, especially in a system of separate powers with rural overrepresentation in the Senate. The fact that the key points of dispute could only be implemented by positive congressional action made compliance difficult. Nonetheless, the Republican administration and most Republican lawmakers voted consistently on the side of upholding international obligations and acceding to the WTO ruling, difficult though it may have been politically.

5. Conclusion

Noncompliance undermines the credibility and viability of the WTO's rules-based multilateral trading system. Therefore, it is important to understand not only what inclines states to bring their disputes to this apparatus, but also why they tend to shirk from its pronouncements once handed down. The evidence suggests that left-wing governments tend to be less cooperative in dispute settlement implementation or compliance and process-tracing of the U.S. Upland Cotton case indicates, at least for the United States, that right-wing governments can be pragmatic in seeking the best deal, preferring the flexibility of international negotiations to the strictures of international trade law and implementing even unpopular adverse rulings.

Furthermore, the processes that leads states to initiate, escalate, and cooperate are not necessarily one and the same; different dynamics may be at work in each. The type of dispute settlement mechanism also plays are role in compliance with international law, with more stringent mechanisms less likely to lead to cooperation than less stringent ones. The evidence indicates that there are selection effects that come into play both in the political party of the plaintiff and defendant governments, as well as the dispute settlement mechanisms, that must be accounted for, as well.

References

Anderson, K. (2002), Peculiarities of retaliation in WTO dispute settlement. *World Trade Review* 1 (2), 123.

Budge, I., Klingeman, H., Volkens, A., Bara, J., Tannenbaum, E. (2001), *Mapping Policy Preferences. Estimates for Parties, Electors, and Governments 1945–1998*. Oxford University Press, Oxford.

Busch, M., Reinhardt, E. (2003), Developing countries and general agreement on tariffs and trade/world trade organization dispute settlement. *Journal of World Trade* 37 (4), 719.

Charnovitz, S. (2001), Rethinking WTO trade sanctions. *American Journal of International Law* 95 (4), 792.

Chayes, A., Chayes, A.H. (1993), On compliance. *International Organization* 47 (2), 175–205.

Chayes, A., Chayes, A.H. (1995), *The New Sovereignty: Compliance with International Regulatory Agreements*. Harvard University Press, Cambridge.

Garrett, G., Smith, J.M. (2002), The politics of WTO dispute settlement. Manuscript, UCLA, pp. 1–38.

Hudson, D., Rosson III, C. P., Robinson, J., Malaga, J. (2005), The WTO cotton case and U.S. domestic policy. http://www.choicesmagazine.org/scripts/printVersion.php?ID = 2005-2-10

Kovenock, D., Thursby, M. (1992), GATT, dispute settlement, and cooperation. *Economics and Politics* 4 (2), 151–170.

Lange, M. (2005) CEO National Cotton Council "Brazil cotton case and the WTO." http://www.cotton.org/issues/2005/langereptica.cfm?renderforprint = 1%

Levine, M.K. (1985), *Inside International Trade Policy Formulation: A History of the 1982 U.S.–EC Steel Arrangements.* Praeger, New York.

Li, Q. (2001), Commitment and compliance in G-7 summit macroeconomic policy coordination. *Political Research Quarterly* 54 (2), 355–478.

Martin, L. (2000), *Democratic Commitments: Legislatures and International Cooperation.* Princeton University Press, Princeton, NJ.

O'Halloran, S. (2007), U.S. implementation of WTO decisions. In: Janow, M. (Ed.), *The Tenth Anniversary of the WTO.* Columbia University Press, New York.

Schnepf, R. (2005), Background on the U.S.-Brazil WTO cotton subsidy dispute. CRS Report for Congress, July 11.

Schnepf, R. (2006), U.S. agricultural policy response to WTO cotton decision. CRS Report for Congress, September 8.

Simmons, B. (2000), International law and state behavior: commitment and compliance in international monetary affairs. *American Political Science Review* 94 (4), 819–835.

Smith, J.M. (2003), WTO dispute settlement: the politics of procedure in appellate body rulings. *World Trade Review* 2 (1), 65.

Tsbelis, G. (1995), Decision-making in political systems: veto players in presidentialism, parliamentarianism, multicameralism, and multipartyism. *British Journal of Political Science* 25 (3), 289–325.

Tyson, L. D'A. (1992), *Who's Bashing Whom: Trade Conflict in High Technology Industries.* Institute for International Economics, Washington, DC, p. 6.

U.S. Mission to the United Nations in Geneva. (2005), Press Release, "Statements by the U.S. Representative at the Meeting of the WTO Dispute Settlement Body," April 20.

Widsten, A. (2007), Partisan plaintiffs: partisan politics and international trade dispute initiation in twenty-five countries. Working Paper.

CHAPTER 6

Dispute Settlement, Compliance and Domestic Politics

Leslie Johns[a] and B. Peter Rosendorff[b]

[a]*Department of Political Science, UCLA, Los Angeles, CA 90095, USA*
E-mail address: ljohns@polisci.ucla.edu
[b]*Department of Politics, New York University, New York, NY 10012, USA*
E-mail address: peter.rosendorff@nyu.edu

Abstract

Many functionalist models of international cooperation rely on punishment by states to enforce cooperation. However, the empirical record suggests that such state-based accounts offer an incomplete explanation of international trade cooperation. We argue that when theoretical approaches are adjusted to incorporate aspects of domestic politics and institutions, two key insights emerge. First, political pressure from domestic industries can be key in creating demand for violations of trade agreements. Since such pressure is affected by stochastic shocks, the temptation of leaders to commit trade violations can vary over time. The presence of a dispute settlement procedure (DSP) provides flexibility that allows leaders to respond to such pressure by occasionally committing violations and then compensating their trading partners, if the DSP finds that the violation was not subject to exceptions in the trading agreement. This flexibility enhances the willingness of leaders to sign cooperative agreements in the first place. Second, domestic politics can function as an enforcement mechanism for ensuring compliance with international trade agreements and DSP rulings. Voters can condition their electoral decisions on whether their leader complies with socially beneficial trade agreements. The DSP plays an important role in this account as an information-provider. For voters to hold their leaders accountable, they need information about what choices their leader has made and whether his actions constitute compliance with an international agreement. The DSP provides transparency and reduces uncertainty about these factors.

Keywords: Dispute settlement, domestic politics, barriers to trade, compliance, punishment, retaliation, WTO

JEL classifications: F13, F53, F59, K33

Frontiers of Economics and Globalization
Volume 6 ISSN: 1574-8715
DOI: 10.1108/S1574-8715(2009)0000006009

1. Introduction

The world trading system has become significantly more "legalized" in recent times (Goldstein and Martin, 2000), with the adoption of the Dispute Settlement Understanding (DSU) as part of the agreements forming the World Trade Organization (WTO). However, the WTO has no enforcement powers, "no jailhouse, no bail bondsmen, no blue helmets, no truncheons, no tear gas" (Bello, 1996), to induce compliance. In the absence of any explicit and institutionally specific power of enforcement, what role does international adjudication play in facilitating cooperation and how might we think we about enforcement mechanisms that lie outside the institutional structure?

The standard view of the WTO is that institutions must be "capable of identifying and sanctioning (or at least authorizing sanctions against) cheating on the cooperative equilibrium" (Trebilcock and Howse, 1999, p. 54). Implicit in this notion is that cooperation can be sustained by repeated cooperative interactions if there is a threat of punitive retaliation for noncooperation. In this standard account, findings by the DSU panels or the Appellate board are complied with and offending measures are removed because of fear of punishment and retaliation, authorized or otherwise, from the plaintiff state. This intuition emerges from viewing the international trading system through the lens of the standard infinitely repeated prisoners' dilemma (PD). In this framework, the Pareto-superior condition of mutually low tariffs is sustained by the threat of punishment should one player unilaterally defect by raising trade barriers. Many of our functionalist models of international cooperation also rely more broadly, at some level, on punishment by states in order to enforce cooperation.

However, in the arena of international trade disputes, the empirical record provides many examples of states that fail to comply with their obligation to maintain low-trade barriers. Moreover, international punishment for such violations is almost nonexistent. Finally, empirical research on the relationship between the regime type of states and their willingness to join trade agreements and participate in the DSU contradict the theoretical implications of standard PD accounts on the relationship between patience and cooperation. These facts suggest that accounts of international trade that rely upon state-based punishments and retaliation (authorized by the DSU or not) in order to enforce cooperation offer an incomplete explanation. In this chapter, we argue that when our theoretical approaches are adjusted to incorporate aspects of domestic politics and institutions, two key insights emerge.

First, domestic politics can create demand for trade violations. If stochastic shocks such as changes in the state of the economy or the lobbying power of affected industries are possible, then the temptation of leaders to defect from cooperative trading and commit trading violations can vary over time. Adjudicatory mechanisms such as the dispute settlement procedure (DSP) can be key to sustaining trade agreements in such a world because the adjudicatory process injects flexibility into trading regimes: the existence of the DSP ensures that agreements can sometimes be violated and compensation granted. This allows cooperation to resume when the relative temptation to defect subsides. The flexibility provided by the DSP enhances the overall stability of trade agreements and institutions since it ensures that greater cooperation will take place in equilibrium and allows for cooperative arrangements to survive even after violations have occurred.

Second, domestic politics can be the mechanism by which leaders are punished for committing violations. If we abandon the heuristic of the unitary actor state and focus on the incentives of the leaders who are accountable to citizens, we can see that electoral incentives are one way by which leaders can be induced to engage in cooperation, rather than committing trading violations that only provide short-run benefits. The DSP is central to this account because it can both clarify uncertainty about whether a trading violation has occurred and provide transparency about the policy decisions of the leaders.

The DSP can facilitate punishment and enforcement mechanisms that are essentially *domestic* in nature, rather than state-based. Domestic, rather than international, punishments of policymakers more successfully explain observed evidence of compliance with international obligations and the findings of the DSU in particular.

We proceed as follows. First, we provide a brief overview of standard PD accounts of international cooperation and their empirical implications. Next, we show that the empirical record on international trade disputes directly contradicts many implications of these theoretical models. We then move on to a discussion of the relationship between domestic politics and trade disputes. We examine the role of domestic politics in generating demand for trade violations, and the role of the DSP in enhancing both the flexibility and stability of trading agreements. Then we discuss the use of domestic electoral incentives to enforce cooperative trading agreements and compliance with DSP rulings. Finally, we conclude.

2. *Punishment and patience in the standard PD framework*

Within the international-relations literature, Oye (1986) exemplifies the use of a 2×2 normal form structure where variation across issue areas is captured by varying the payoffs associated with each pair of actions. Games that address "collaboration" issues – such as international trade – are described as having a PD structure. While states would jointly benefit from cooperatively lowering their trade barriers and stimulating international trade, each state has the temptation to defect from such cooperation by unilaterally raising its own trade barriers. In the canonical form of the infinitely repeated PD in which two countries simultaneously set trade barriers over time, a number of models have examined how variation in the nature of punishment actions affects state behavior.

2.1. Standard PD theories of international cooperation

In the international trade literature, (Johnson, 1953–54) is an early work that characterizes the behavior of social welfare-maximizing governments when countries have monopoly power in trade. He shows that the Nash equilibrium in tariff setting yields Pareto-inefficient protectionism. With the popularization of the Folk theorem (Rubenstein, 1979), it became clear that payoffs on the Pareto frontier were supportable in equilibrium, and one manner by which such payoffs can be achieved is by the repetition of the one-shot game under the threat of grim trigger punishments for noncooperation and sufficiently large discount factors.[1]

In most approaches, the punishment applied along the equilibrium path is severe. Equilibria often rely on the grim trigger strategy, the most severe sequentially rational punishment that is possible, in which there is infinite reversion to the worst possible Nash equilibrium if players fail to act cooperatively. In other approaches, these punishments are limited in various ways. For example, the number of punishment periods can be limited (as in "tit-for-tat" or "tit-for-*n*-tats" where *n* is some finite number as in Downs and Rocke, 1995) or the magnitude of the punishment can be fixed (Ethier, 2001). In all of these accounts, for cooperation under the threat of a punishment strategy to be a Nash equilibrium to the repeated trade-barrier-setting game, the players need to be sufficiently patient. That is, in order for the fear of the punishment to be sufficiently dissuasive, the value that the players put on their returns in the future punishment periods must be sufficiently large in present-value terms.

These two theoretical elements of punishment and patience yield several key empirical implications. First, in this complete information environment, when there are violations of international trade agreements – "nullification or impairment of rights" in the language of the WTO – we should expect to see punishment or retaliation authorized and implemented without failure. Second, since punishment is key to sustaining cooperation, we should expect to observe severe punishments in order to increase the overall level of cooperation. Finally, if there is some mapping

[1] Fearon (1998) provides a recent example where, after a bargaining phase, enforcement of a PD game relies on the grim trigger strategy, in which if either player is observed to defect, then both defect forever afterwards.

from patience to polity type, we should see only the more patient polities joining trade agreements, abiding by their international obligations, and complying with rulings of the DSU. Democracies are often described as being less patient than autocracies: executives rarely look beyond the next election or at most the one after that, giving democracies shorter time-horizons relative to other polities (Olson, 2003; Schmidt, 2002). Hence the requirement of patience for sustaining cooperation in an infinitely repeated PD would suggest that democracies are less likely to join international trade agreements than other polity types.

2.2. Empirical contradictions of the standard PD theory

All these predictions are grossly contradicted by the empirical record. When violations of international trade agreements occur, they are rarely (if ever) followed by punishment and retaliation. Even when retaliations take place, they are rarely punitive in nature, which means that the severity of punishments is very limited. Finally, democracies are systematically more likely to join trade agreements and comply with DSU rulings than non-democracies. We consider each of these empirical regularities in turn.

2.2.1. Retaliation is rare following non-compliance

It is generally asserted that countries comply with the findings of the DSU. Hudec (2002), for example, describes compliance with dispute panel rulings as "good, although it has not always been rapid." Of course, compliance is a tricky thing to measure – the absence of the counterfactual makes for difficult measurement issues. That is, we do not know how states that have agreed to participate in an international regime, such as the DSU of the WTO, would have behaved in the absence of participation in the regime. The difficulty associated with attempting to measure how effective international organizations and agreements are in facilitating cooperation lies in dealing with this endogeneity problem. Have the signatories significantly changed their behavior in the presence of the obligation, relative to how they would have behaved in the absence of the international organization?[2] A number of empirical scholars have made serious attempts to address this question using the Heckman selection models (von Stein, 2005), examining duration effects rather than selection effects (Przeworski and Vreeland, 2000), or using propensity-score matching to control for selection bias (Simmons and Hopkins, 2005).

However, noncompliance does occur and is more easily measured. From the implementation of the revised DSU in 1995 to the end of 2007, the WTO

[2] Similarly, the relative frequency of compliance does not necessarily imply deep cooperation (Downs *et al.*, 1996; cf. Gilligan, 2004).

reports 369 DSU complaints. The appellate body has issued 78 reports over this period (Leitner and Lester, 2008). However, only a few countries (the United States, EU, Canada, Brazil, and Ecuador) have requested authorization to "suspend concessions" (the WTO term for retaliation) in a handful of cases. As for the actual implementation of retaliation, the United States (together with Ecuador in the Bananas case, and with Canada in the Hormones case) has retaliated against the EU, the EU has retaliated against the United States in the Foreign Services Corporation case, and Canada imposed retaliatory measures against the United States in the Byrd Amendment case. These three cases seem to be the only situations in which noncompliance has resulted in actual, implemented retaliation. While a credible international punishment mechanism is necessary to sustain cooperation in the standard PD account of trade policy, in practice states do not appear to be punished for violating their trade commitments.

2.2.2. Retaliation after non-compliance is not punitive

Moreover, when punishments are authorized by the DSU they are specifically limited in scope and duration. The WTO applies "the proportionality principle," which limits retaliation to a level that restores "balance" to the previously negotiated concessions. This is described as "compensation" – it is specifically not intended to be punitive and merely attempts to restore any harm done by the violation. Mavroidis (2000) states, "there is no room for punitive damages in the WTO context." This limit in the level of compensation following a violation is consistent with the WTO's "reciprocity" norm.[3]

Maggi (1999) shows that a system of unlimited punishments from multiple countries is superior to a bilateral punishment regime, especially when there are power-in-trade imbalances. Increasing the number of punishers is more likely to make retaliation more punitive, which in turn reduces the incentive of states to engage in non-compliance. Similarly, in the theory of international courts provided by Johns (2008), the central utility of the international court lies in transforming a bilateral dispute into a multilateral dispute since court rulings serve to coordinate endogenous costly enforcement by disinterested states. However, the WTO specifically limits standing and restricts any authority to retaliate only to those member states whose concessions have been nullified and impaired by the offending state's actions. An unharmed country is not entitled to compensation and cannot lawfully engage in retaliation (Trebilcock and Howse, 1999).

A key empirical implication of the theoretically repeated PD framework is that we should expect to observe severe punishments for noncompliance with DSU findings in order to increase the overall level of cooperation.

---

[3] Bagwell and Staiger (1999) argue that this norm serves a crucial function in limiting the use of tariffs to influence the terms-of-trade in the protecting country's favor.

However, the WTO texts explicitly limit compensation following a violation, which lowers the expected punishment from non-compliance.

2.2.3. Patient polities

Recall that in order for cooperation to be sustained in a repeated PD framework, states must be sufficiently patient by placing a high value on future cooperative payoffs relative to the short-term benefit from defecting from an international trade agreement. The electoral accountability mechanism in democracies ensures that democratic leaders are under more pressure than autocratic leaders to provide short-term public benefits for their constituents. Hence, as policy-makers are more accountable to their electorate, their time horizons are shorter since electoral accountability shortens tenure in office, *ceteris paribus*. Therefore, we would expect democratic polities to be less patient than autocracies, and an empirical implication of the repeated PD framework is that democracies will be less willing to comply with their international trade obligations or join these agreements than non-democracies. Similarly, democracies should be less willing than autocracies to comply with DSP ruling.

Much scholarship has shown that these expectations are false. For example, Russett and Oneal (2001) and Mansfield *et al.* (2000, 2002) have demonstrated the propensity of democracies to be more frequent joiners of regional and multilateral trading arrangements. Mansfield *et al.* additionally find that democratic countries are about twice as likely to form a preferential trading agreement as autocratic countries, and that pairs of democracies are roughly four times as likely to do so as autocratic pairs. This poses a substantial challenge to the canonical finding that patient players are more likely to cooperate than impatient players.

With respect to dispute settlement at the General Agreement on Tariffs and Trade (GATT), Busch (2000) establishes that cases are more likely to be paneled when the disputants are democracies. He additionally finds that these cases paneled by democratic dyads are more likely to end with concessions by the defendant state. Democracies are also more likely to be named in petitions filed by the United States in antidumping (AD) cases (Busch *et al.*, 2007). Since 1995, 44% of the total complaints have involved either the United States or the EU as the complainant, while 43% have the United States or the EU as the responding party, with 48 disputes between them (Leitner and Lester, 2008). Clearly democracies are willing to participate in the adjudicatory mechanism of the DSU and comply with its rulings.

In sum, the significant mismatch between the empirical record and theoretical implications of the standard repeated PD framework suggests that the use of this model as a basis for understanding compliance with international trade agreements and DSU rulings in particular is significantly flawed. More precisely, theoretical accounts of international trade that require punishment by other states and patience as the basis of international cooperation are insufficiently substantiated by the empirical facts. This leads us to consider the ways in which domestic politics can affect trading violations and the enforcement of DSP ruling.

3. Domestic politics: driver of compliance and enforcement?

What domestic factors might substitute for punishment at the international level after observed non-compliance with a state's obligations? A number of normative explanations have been offered. Perhaps countries comply with international law and rulings of the DSP because there is a pervasive belief that the law and courts should be obeyed. Such a norm is internalized within democracies, with independent judicial institutions and societal adherence to the concept of the rule of law, and can then be extended across borders (Chayes and Chayes, 1993). Even most interest-group accounts of the impact of civil society in enforcing international commitments, such as human rights agreements, rely upon the assumption that the normative value of adherence to an international commitment can change over time as societies grow to embrace the objectives of the law (Hafner-Burton and Tsutsui, 2005, 2007). In the realm of security studies, scholars commonly argue that democratic polities use law and institutions to settle conflicts rather than power (e.g. Doyle, 1986). As such, normative beliefs internalized at the domestic level can have an influence on international behavior.

Alternatively, a number of functionalist arguments that rely on domestic politics as enforcement devices have emerged and these approaches yield predictions that accord more closely with the observed empirical regularities in the area of international trade. It has been well understood since Putnam (1988) that decisions made at the international level – for example whether to join an international institution and whether to comply with the attendant obligations of these regimes – are substantially affected by domestic politics. A leader's willingness to comply with the rulings of an international court may be affected by the domestic political consequences of the treaty violations. Moreover, these domestic political concerns are heightened within democracies, providing an explanation for the empirical fact that democracies are more likely than autocracies to cooperate within international trade regimes, and participate more frequently in international dispute resolutions. We provide an overview of two different ways in which domestic politics can affect the willingness of a leader to commit trade violations and comply with DSB rulings. First, we examine the role of domestic politics in generating demand for trade violations and the role of the DSP in enhancing both the flexibility and stability of trading agreements. Then, we discuss the use of domestic electoral incentives to enforce cooperative trading agreements and compliance with DSP rulings.

3.1. Tolerated defection and the DSU: the flexibility theory

3.1.1. Overview

Recent work suggests that the international trade regime is designed not merely to facilitate cooperation on trade barriers internationally, but also to deal with domestic political problems faced by policymakers. Sometimes policymakers are faced with unanticipated but acute political pressure to protect particular industries. Rather than simply having their hands tied by an international obligation, the policymakers prefer to have the option to temporarily appease the domestic political constituency without excessively violating the terms of the international agreement or suffering international punishment. Policymakers who are accountable to domestic political interests need to know that the international system permits a degree of flexibility for the system to be functional. This has been labeled as the "Flexibility Theory" (Rosendorff, 2005; Kucik and Reinhardt, 2008).

A number of recent papers have picked up on this theme of international agreements that permit tolerated defection without excessive (or even any) punishment. The idea is traced to the legal concept of "efficient breach," where under unanticipated circumstances a violation of a contract's obligations may be more Pareto-efficient than fully abiding by the contract. If a court is able to ensure that *ex post* transfers compensate the injured party for the violator's failure to abide by the terms of the initial contract, political support for the international agreement can be enhanced by the tolerated breach of legally binding agreements.

Allowing for efficient breach in multilateral agreement accomplishes three ends that are well described by Kucik and Reinhardt (2008): (1) it defines legal standards that can constrain the abuse of such provisions; (2) it legitimizes the use of such provisions insofar as it meets those standards, which in turn can prevent excessive retaliation from other parties; and (3) it provides a mechanism to assess, and limit demands on, the compensation due to the adversely affected parties. Consider a period in which the political pressure to protect a particular industry is intense. The political leader experiencing this pressure may rescind the previous concessions made by his state or undertake some rebalancing of those concessions, leaving both countries no worse off than performing under the contract (Setear, 1997). Schwartz and Sykes (2002) have similarly claimed that the dispute settlement mechanism permits "rebalancing" by assessing the degree of infractions and authorizing capped levels of retaliation as a form of compensation.

Recent theorizing regarding the design of international organizations has posited that flexibility provisions – opportunities for signatories to temporarily deviate from their obligations under the treaty, perhaps at some cost – can act both to increase the willingness of states to join these agreements and permit them to commit to greater degrees of cooperation (at least in most periods). This allows the international regime to be more stable than would be the case in the absence of these provisions. Of course, too much flexibility leads to less cooperation. Therefore, the key design question is to choose the degree of flexibility that optimizes both stability and depth of cooperation.

3.1.2. Theoretical framework and results

Rosendorff (2005) models this as a game in which a country experiencing extreme but unforeseen domestic political pressure can choose to temporarily deviate from its low tariff obligations, pay some expected penalty as determined by the adjudication process at the DSU, and then return to the community of cooperating nations in the next period when political pressure subsides and returns to more "normal levels." In this model, two governments (a "home" government and a "foreign" government) must decide whether to abide by a trade agreement. Each government's one-period utility depends on the sum of consumer and producer surpluses, and tariff revenues.[4] Moreover, domestic political pressure that import-competing firms bring to bear is added to the objective function by weighting the firms' profit term. Let $a > 0$ denote the weight that the home government attaches to the profits of its import-competing firms. Similarly, let $\alpha > 0$ denote the weight that the foreign government attaches to the profits of its own import-competing firms. The stochastic political pressure parameters a and α are private information; each government knows the domestic political consequences that it will experience for its own compliance decision, but is uncertain about the level of political pressure that its trading partner is experiencing. Additionally, governments are uncertain about what levels of political pressure they will face in future time periods.

Each government simultaneously chooses a tariff level, where t denotes the tariff chosen by the home government and τ denotes the tariff chosen by the foreign government. If both governments agree to abide by a previously negotiated cooperative agreement, then tariff levels (t^C, τ^C) are implemented and each player receives a payoff that is a function of its domestic political pressure, $(C(a), C^*(\alpha))$. In contrast, if the home country decides to unilaterally deviate from the cooperative agreement, then his optimal deviation will be a function of his domestic political pressure, $t^D(a)$. So the foreign country's payoff from being the "sucker" and choosing the cooperative tariff rate, τ^C, while the home country deviates is a function of both domestic political pressure parameters a and α.[5] This yields payoffs of $(D(a), S^*(a,\alpha))$. Analogously, unilateral deviation by the foreign government yields payoffs of $(S(a,\alpha), D^*(\alpha))$. Finally, if neither player abides by the cooperative agreement, then the Nash equilibrium tariffs are chosen,

---

[4] Economic foundations for the model are explained in depth in Rosendorff (2005).

[5] The parameter α directly affects the foreign government's utility since it reflects the weight given to the profits of the import-competing firms within the foreign country, while the parameter a influences the foreign government's utility indirectly since it affects the choice of $t^D(a)$.

(t^N,τ^N), which yields payoffs of $(N(a,\alpha), N^*(a,\alpha))$. So the reduced-form stage game for a given period t when there is no DSP is as follows:

	C^*	D^*
C	$C(a),\ C^*(\alpha)$	$S(a,\alpha),\ D^*(\alpha)$
D	$D(a),\ S^*(a,\alpha)$	$N(a,\alpha),\ N^*(a,\alpha)$

where (in accordance with the PD nature of the game):

$$D(a) > C(a) > N(a,\alpha) > S(a,\alpha) \quad \text{for any pair } (a,\alpha).$$

This one-shot game is infinitely repeated and the players choose strategies to maximize the expected sum of their discounted one-period utility. In this adjusted form of the standard prisoner's dilemma, patience makes long-term cooperation more likely. However, there will always occur a domestic political shock in one or both states. This shock will sometimes be sufficiently large such that the leader may prefer to abrogate the agreement, maintain the political support of the affected industry, and exit the trading regime. The addition of some simple domestic politics brings the stability of the regime into question, even with the most patient of polities.

Suppose, instead, that if a violation of the cooperative agreement is committed in any given period, the violator's trading partner can file the dispute (i.e. request a panel) within the DSU. The panel hears the case and makes a decision. If the panel finds that an illegitimate violation has occurred, it then decides on a penalty.[6] Finally, the defendant decides whether to pay the penalty or not.

	$\mathcal{C}^*$	$\mathcal{DS}^*$	$\mathcal{D}^*$
$\mathcal{C}$	$C(a), C^*(\alpha)$	$S(a,\hat{\alpha}) + \theta L(\hat{\alpha}), D^*(\hat{\alpha}) - \theta L(\hat{\alpha})$	$S(a,\hat{\alpha}), D^*(\hat{\alpha})$
$\mathcal{DS}$	$D(\hat{a}) - \theta L^*(\hat{a}),$ $S^*(\hat{a},\alpha) + \theta L^*(\hat{a})$	$N(\hat{a},\hat{\alpha}) + \theta L(\hat{\alpha}) - \theta L^*(\hat{a}),$ $N^*(\hat{a},\hat{\alpha}) + \theta L^*(\hat{a}) - \theta L(\hat{\alpha})$	$N(\hat{a},\hat{\alpha}) - \theta L^*(\hat{a}),$ $N^*(\hat{a},\hat{\alpha}) + \theta L^*(\hat{a})$
$\mathcal{D}$	$D(\hat{a}), S^*(\hat{a},\alpha)$	$N(\hat{a},\hat{\alpha}) + \theta L(\hat{\alpha}), N^*(\hat{a},\hat{\alpha}) - \theta L(\hat{\alpha})$	$N(\hat{a},\hat{\alpha}), N^*(\hat{a},\hat{\alpha})$

The reduced normal form of the one-period game can be described in the matrix shown above. If dispute settlement is availed by either player, the *DS* action is taken. The court finds with probability θ that the defendant has violated the agreement, and authorizes retaliation in an amount commensurate with the loss incurred in expected value, L, by the

[6] Clearly, it will be common knowledge whether a violation has been committed. However, the panel only probabilistically finds the violator guilty (i.e. rules the violation illegitimate) because the panel may rule that the violation fell within the class of permissible exemptions (e.g. health, safety, or environmental measures).

plaintiff.[7] No external enforcement exits. If the defendant pays, it does so voluntarily.

Two key results emerge from this model. First, there exist equilibria in which a state under intense domestic political pressure sometimes commits violations, its trading partner files a case with the DSU, and the violator pays its penalty in order to return to cooperation. Moreover, equilibria can be supported with a wider range of discount parameters, significantly reducing the importance of patience in securing cooperative, compliant behavior. So, clearly the existence and use of the DSU is consistent with a theoretical account of domestic politics and international trade.

There is an additional implication regarding the willingness of states to enter cooperative trade agreements. If we compare a regime with and without the opportunity to bring a violation before the DSU panel, initial cooperative agreements can be reached for a larger set of parameters than if compliance was supported by a grim trigger strategy in which violators are forever excluded from cooperative trade agreements. If states know that they can commit violations when they are under intense political pressure, pay the penalty handed down by the court, and return to the cooperative regime, then they will be more willing to join the international regime in the first place. The flexibility provided by the ability to sometimes violate agreements ensures greater participation and stability of the institution than if a rigid punishment regime, such as the grim trigger, was in place.

This reverses a severe limitation of PD and patience-based models identified by Fearon (1998). He points out that "as the shadow of the future lengthens, both states choose tougher and tougher bargaining strategies on average, implying longer and longer delay till cooperation begins." That is, as the possibility of durable cooperation grows in the second-stage PD, the possibility of stalemate in the first-stage bargaining game rises. This leads Fearon to conclude that making agreements easier to enforce may make them harder to initially conclude, since the distribution of gains set initially will be so important and fixed throughout the future. The availability of the DSU may reduce this dynamic. That is, if in future periods, players can deviate, pay a penalty, and return to cooperation, this may mean that their initial distributional bargaining is not so important. The pattern of distributive gains agreed upon today may be altered in the future through the use of the panel procedure. Therefore, inclusion of dispute settlement may have another benefit: it may make agreements easier to conclude initially!

Fischer and Osorio (2006) expand this analytical approach to show that these results hold even in the absence of any actual compensation (but with

[7] While the shocks α and a are private information, the court (and the plaintiff) can infer something about the nature of the shock by virtue of the *DS* play – a deviation has been observed. Hence the court updates its beliefs about the domestic political shock and these updated beliefs are summarized by $\hat{a}$ and $\hat{\alpha}$.

verifiable political pressure). Countries will permit or tolerate the violation without punishment because they value the opportunity to renege temporarily in periods of intense political pressure that they might experience in the future. As such, there can exist a system of reciprocal nonenforcement of international obligations when domestic political pressure is intense. In return for the ability to occasionally violate an international agreement, a state will be willing to tolerate occasional violations by its trading partner. Bagwell and Staiger (2005) also explore this idea but let the compensation vary with the announcement made of the intensity of the political pressure faced by the incumbent government.

3.1.3. Empirical evidence

There is ample evidence to support the general dynamics of state behavior in the model above: domestic politics leads to deviation from a state's obligations, a panel ruling to cease the offending measure occurs, the defendant refuses to comply because the political costs of doing so are too high, and retaliation is authorized. For example, in 1996, the United States requested a DSU panel, arguing that the EU's prohibition on the imports of beef treated with hormones was inconsistent with its obligations under the WTO. The panel found that the EU ban was unjustified on a number of grounds, and the decision was upheld by the appellate body. Arbitration resulted in an agreement that the ban would be removed within 15 months. The EU did not comply with the finding and failed to remove the offending measure within that time-period. The panel authorized retaliation/compensation of \$116.8 million.[8] Hoekman and Kostecki (2001) remark that the EU was politically unable to comply with the initial ruling: "Political constraints reflecting a strong lobby in the EU that opposed the use of hormones in meat production made it (compliance) impossible" (p. 84). In addition, any increase in the productivity of European beef farmers would actually increase the costs of the common agricultural policy, something the EU could ill afford. Similarly, in 2002 the United States applied 30% steel tariffs under the "safeguard" provisions in order to protect steel workers in electorally pivotal states like West Virginia, Ohio, and Pennsylvania. The appellate body of the DSU ruled the tariffs illegal, and authorized compensation to the plaintiffs (the EU, China, South Korea, Brazil, Switzerland, Japan, New Zealand, and Norway) of \$2.2 billion.

A key element in the model above is that authorized retaliation is limited in magnitude to an estimate of the losses incurred. As discussed above, this is one of the key ways in which the practices of the DSU process diverge from the implications of standard PD accounts of international trading

---

[8] The panel also authorized retaliation/compensation of C\$11.3 million in a similar case filed by the Canadians.

regimes. Anecdotal evidence as to the EU's bargaining position during the Uruguay Round lends support to the argument that limits on retaliation are necessary for cooperation in the presence of political uncertainty. Section 301 of the US Trade Act of 1974 gave the US president the authority to unilaterally retaliate against the US's trading partners if their practices were deemed by the president to restrict US exports. This law was rendered more ominous by changes in 1988 (Super 301) that required the US Trade Representative to identify targets and set dates for retaliation. There was no limit to the number of countries or the value of the punishments. During the Uruguay Round negotiations, the EU Commission frequently expressed its concern about these provisions in US law for unilateral retaliation and saw the revised DSU as a measure to bind the United States to the same legal standard as other members. Under the DSU, all WTO members are precluded from making unilateral determinations as to violations; members must appeal to the DSU for such determinations. The EU was clearly more inclined to sign on to the new WTO as a result of the removal of the possibility of highly punitive, unilateral trade sanctioning measures (Bhagwati and Patrick, 1990).

The use of escape clauses in the WTO agreements also lends support to the flexibility theory. Temporary defection, either with or without compensation, is permitted under the WTO's business exceptions; for example, the safeguard provisions, its anti-dumping (AD) and countervailing duty codes (Rosendorff and Milner, 2001; Bagwell and Staiger, 2005). Additionally, Article XX exceptions are allowed to protect the health of people, animals and the environment, provided that they are applied in a nondiscriminatory manner. These exceptions are written into the agreements in order to add flexibility: governments do not fear retaliation because their trading partners tolerate their defection in these areas.

In addition to the evidence provided by the WTO DSU, there is also a large amount of evidence to support the flexibility theory in the areas of AD agreements and preferential trade agreements (PTAs). Kucik and Reinhardt (2008) empirically test the key idea that the decision to join an agreement and the level of cooperation are co-determined or endogenous. While they do not study the WTO DSU in particular, they investigate whether the availability of a similar flexibility-enhancing device in AD disputes increases the tendency of a country to join the international agreement, and whether its compliance is deeper than it would be otherwise. The WTO texts permit a state to apply an AD tariff – a temporary abrogation of its obligations – if a foreign firm is selling an item in the home market at "less than fair value" and causing "material injury." The WTO requires a state to adopt a specific institutional procedure before it may apply an AD tariff. This procedure is costly to establish and requires skills and capacity. As such, countries have varied across time in their adoption of an AD procedure. Viewing the adoption of an AD procedure as a signal of a state's intent to make use of the flexibility provisions of the WTO agreement, the authors use this variation to test the hypotheses of the flexibility theory of trading agreements. They show convincingly that countries joining the WTO are more likely to adopt an AD procedure than states that do not join the agreement. Additionally, countries with an AD code in place are more likely, *ceteris paribus*, to join the WTO, to agree to more tightly binding tariff commitments, and to actually implement lower tariffs.

While the theory above has focused on the institutions of the WTO, a similar logic applies to any PTA with a DSP with the characteristics described above. There is great variation in the design of these DSPs, with mechanisms varying from "soft" (e.g. ad hoc negotiations among the parties) to "hard" (e.g. standing independent tribunals whose determinations are legally binding). Smith (2000) constructs a measure of the degree of "legalization" of 63 post-1957 PTAs on a five-point scale. A higher measure indicates a DSP with stronger adjudicatory powers.[9] While this measure maps incompletely to the question at hand (i.e. is a DSP present and does it embody the proportionality principle?) the correlation is likely to be very close. Pevehouse *et al.* (2002) estimate a duration model of PTA survival and find that those that embody a DSP have a lower failure rate. Using a sample of 85 agreements, they show that the presence of a DSP is positively and significantly related to the duration of the PTA. They additionally use Smith's (2000) ranking of the degree of "legalization" of various PTA DSPs and find that more legalism results in longer-lasting agreements. Similarly, Rosendorff (2005) uses the Smith (2000) data to investigate whether the number of signatories rises with a DSP. The correlation between the number of members in an agreement and the Smith (2000) measure of legalism for the agreement is positive (0.27) and significantly different from zero at the 5% level ($p = 0.034$). Higher levels of legalism are associated with a larger numbers of signatories. Of course, this correlation is merely suggestive, but does lend some support to the hypothesis.

Overall, the flexibility theory establishes the insights of Sykes (1991), who argues that "without the safety valve [of some kind of formal flexibility provision], greater protection would arise ex post" (273).[10] A key element driving the optimality of the DSP in the arguments above is that

---

[9] A PTA gets a rating of 0 if a third-party review in the instance of disputes is unavailable. If a review is available, but the determination of the review panel is not binding, the PTA receives a coding of 1. If the ruling is binding but there is no standing tribunal of judges, the PTA is coded as 2. Finally, if a standing panel is present and only states have standing before it, the PTA is coded as a 3; but if treaty organs and individuals can also bring complaints, the PTA is then coded as 4.

[10] Similarly, Finger and Nogues (2005) argue that many Latin American countries used flexibility provisions in GATT/WTO as a quid pro quo to convince protectionist groups to accept broader trade liberalization.

any compensation or punishment that is actually applied cannot be too severe. Excessive demands for compensation, such as punitive awards, discourage the use of this temporary escape. While higher penalties may make for more per period cooperation, they risk making the entire system less stable. This is because the unexpected but intense political pressure to protect an affected industry, in the absence of any tolerated escape, may induce the executive to abrogate the agreement entirely. This, in turn, challenges the long-term stability of the multilateral system. Tolerated escape solves a domestic political problem and makes the international system more stable in the long run – at the cost of some per period failures to cooperate. This idea runs counter to the notion of "bindingness" – that tighter constraints lead to more cooperation and less defection (Goldstein and Martin, 2000) – and the more traditional notion that states sign these international agreements to credibly insulate themselves from domestic political pressure, especially when they are vulnerable to capture (Maggi and Rodriguez-Clare, 1998).

3.2. Domestic politics and punishment for trade violations

3.2.1. Overview

Another way in which domestic politics affects international trade disputes is by providing domestic enforcement for international commitments. All leaders must be concerned to some extent by the welfare of their constituents. Even highly repressive autocrats are subject to the threat of removal from office by their domestic supporters (Bueno de Mesquita *et al.*, 2003). While short-run violations of international trade agreements may provide a temporary benefit to leaders and their citizens, it can also compromise the ability of citizens to benefit from long-run cooperation in international trade. Although standard PD accounts of trading agreements treat states as unitary actors, it is important to recognize that foreign policy choices are in fact made by leaders, not states. The ability of citizens to remove office-seeking leaders from power allows for an alternative source of compliance of international agreements: domestic enforcement via electoral incentives.

3.2.2. Theoretical framework and results

This mechanism of domestic enforcement of international agreements has been most prominently and systematically promoted by the work on leader-specific punishments by McGillivray and Smith (2000, 2004, 2006). In their theoretical model, two leaders (rather than unitary-actor states) play the standard PD game. It is assumed that leaders derive inherent utility from remaining in power and the utility of domestic citizens is affected directly by the behavior of their leader. If leader x of state X defects in his interactions with leader y of state Y, then leader y punishes leader x by refusing to cooperate with him in any future periods. However, leader y credibly pledges that if the citizens of state X remove their leader, then leader y will cooperate with x's successor. As such, punishment at the international level is a grim trigger conditioned on the identity of leaders, not of states. Since citizens have the ability to remove leaders from power, this means that international punishments are endogenous to the actions of domestic citizens.

Of course, states vary with regard to the costliness of enacting a leadership change; it is less costly for leaders to be removed from office when there are electoral mechanisms in place than if citizens must launch a bloody revolution to enact a leadership change.[11] As such, when the costs of removing a leader from office are low, citizens are more likely to remove their leader from power in order to induce leader y to engage in cooperative behavior once again. Since leaders derive utility from remaining in office, leaders who are easily replaceable – such as leaders in democracies – have the greatest incentive to abide by their international commitments and engage in cooperative behavior. The promise to cooperate is most credible when it comes from a leader who is accountable to an electorate. While McGillivray and Smith (2004) focus on trade volumes rather than on accession to or compliance with international trade agreements, a similar logic suggests we would expect to see more democracies credibly comply with their obligations under international law.

A key assumption in the leader-specific punishment paradigm is that the citizens, who have incentives to remove leaders when they violate international obligations, are able to observe the behavior of the leader with some degree of accuracy. That is, voters must be able to observe, directly or indirectly, the policy choices and actions of their leaders in the international trading environment. Trade policies are sometimes obscure or their effects are difficult to estimate *ex ante*. Quotas will restrict imports, but voters may be unsure as to the degree to which the domestic economy will actually be affected. Nontariff barriers will redistribute income at some social cost; but there may be *ex ante* uncertainty as to who will bear the cost. Governments have an inclination to obscure rather than clarify any policy that redistributes income, especially when there are dead-weight losses attendant to the policy choice. In the context of the leader-specific punishment model, if citizens do not know whether their leader has committed a trade violation and refused to comply with a DSU ruling, their decision about whether to punish the leader by removing him from

[11] It is important to emphasize that in the leader specific punishment framework, the punishment imposed by the international trading partner – via the refusal to cooperate (i.e. return to the suboptimal Nash equilibrium) as long as the violating leader is in power – is key to supporting the willingness of citizens to engage in the costly action of punishing their leader by removing him from power. In the absence of such international punishment, citizens would be perfectly willing to accept the benefits of trade violations.

office will be made under uncertainty: sometimes leaders will be removed from office despite having made decisions that were expected to benefit the voter, and vice versa (Johns, 2006).

A crucial aspect of the WTO's DSP is that it publicizes information about whether a violation of an international agreement has occurred. This can ease the ability of domestic constituencies to punish leaders for violating agreements. While it is surely not the case that the average voter closely monitors DSU panel rulings, the transparency provided by the rulings can be beneficial to pro-trade constituencies and interest groups when they attempt to apply pressure to their domestic leader. As such, the transparency provided by a trade institution like the WTO DSU is key to supporting the leader-specific punishments discussed above.

The view of the WTO's trade court as an information-enhancing institution is at the center of the approach taken by Mansfield *et al.* (2002). Rather than having other states impose punishments until a leader is removed from power, the international system plays an informational role. In Mansfield *et al.* (2002), voters are unable to perfectly observe the policies chosen by their leaders. In a model where the political support minimizing tariff is larger than the social welfare maximizing tariff, the government attempts to increase political support from import-competing sectors without severely adversely affecting the social welfare on which the voters at large base their reelection decisions. Low tariffs and compliance with an international agreement signal to the electorate that the government is well behaved, less extractive, and responsible. Should a leader violate his obligations under a treaty, the international system does not punish; it merely signals to the domestic polity that the leader has violated its obligations and behaved in an extractive manner. Voters will condition their reelection rule on this information and punish agreement violators by removing them from elected office. Thus the international institution plays an important information-enhancing role.

This of course begs the question as to why a government would want to tie its hands in this way and be more bound to policies that benefit social welfare. Long-run social welfare is enhanced by the improved informational environment; but intuition would suggest that governments dislike having their hands tied once in office, However, the added information provided by the institution permits governments to survive re-election challenges in bad aggregate economic conditions. Consider an obscure informational environment: if the voters see poor performance at election time, then they cannot be sure whether the low incomes they experience are due to high tariffs or exogenous supply shocks. Voters may want to evict the incumbent even in periods in which the incumbent has been relatively well behaved. By acceding to the WTO and demonstrating its willingness to have its policies scrutinized by a credible third party (i.e. the court), the government ensures that the voters can condition their reelection rules on the information provided by the institution and not just merely on aggregate economic conditions. In periods where the government experiences a bad exogenous shock, it can rely on the absence of a finding of violation by the DSU panel to assure the voters that high prices are not due to extractive behavior by the state. This allows governments to survive in office during "tough times." Membership in the institution ensures that the leader is returned to office in bad periods (subject to good behavior) instead of being removed from power. The leader signs on to the WTO and trades away opportunities for rent extraction in return for not being "unfairly evicted" from office in bad times. The institution therefore solves a crucial signal extraction problem facing the voters while also rewarding leaders for compliance with international legal obligations.

The international institution as an information-enhancing device is also explored in the models of Rosendorff and Vreeland (2007a, 2007b). They construct a model of monetary policy in which voters must decide whether to keep or replace their leader based on the performance of the economy. In the baseline nontransparent environment, voters cannot observe the policies chosen by their leader. Since the strategic environment is noisy and policies translate into outcomes stochastically, voters sometimes replace leaders who chose a low-inflation rate and keep leaders who chose a high-inflation rate. However, leaders vary in the extent to which they are accountable to voters; for highly democratic societies, the decision of the median voter is decisive in determining whether the leader remains in office, while in less accountable governance systems, the leader is able to remain in power with some probability even if the median voter wishes to replace him. Rosendorff and Vreeland contrast the nontransparency case with a transparent environment in which there exists an international organization, such as the IMF or the World Bank, that provides reports on the policies chosen by leaders. The key theoretical finding provided by Rosendorff and Vreeland (2007a) is that a leader's preference for the transparent environment (as opposed to nontransparency) grows stronger as the leader is more accountable to the voter.

Additionally, Rosendorff and Vreeland (2007b) finds that in majoritarian systems of government, in which slight differences in vote-share translate into large differences in the allocation of legislative seats, leaders who are in power are less likely to prefer transparent environments because small changes in levels of electoral support have little impact on the allocation of legislative power. If majoritarianism is described as a political system in which votes are turned into seats in the legislature in a more "decisive" fashion, then majoritarian systems are characterized (on average) by a larger number of seats for the ruling party for any given share of the total votes. For instance, in a majoritarian system with single-member districts, 50% of the votes in 50% of the districts yields a majority in the legislature. So 25% of the total votes can lead to unconstrained policy-making. In contrast, in a purely proportional system, 25% of the total votes would lead to 25% of the seats, and hence a need to collaborate and compromise in the formation of economic policy. Therefore, we describe majoritarian systems as converting votes to seats in a more "decisive" fashion.

If policymakers are concerned both about seats and the opportunities for rent extraction (i.e. if these are substitutes in the policymaker's objective function), the marginal utility of the last seat is lower in the majoritarian system. In an economy in which there are stochastic shocks to the voters' pocketbooks, incumbents may be penalized if voters are unable to differentiate between bad aggregate economic conditions and extractive behavior by the policymaker. In a more transparent environment, voters are better able to assign responsibility for bad outcomes. If the loss associated with the last seat is low, policymakers might be willing to endure the risk of losing seats in bad aggregate conditions so that they might extract again in the future when conditions are better. Hence they will preserve a less transparent informational environment. The opacity of policy-making allows for greater extraction when conditions are good, and bearing the risk of eviction when conditions are bad is worthwhile because of the relative trade-offs between losing seats and rent extraction. On the other hand, if the loss associated with the marginal seat is high – as is the case in a less majoritarian system (e.g. a system with proportional representation) – then the incumbent might not be willing to bear the same risk of eviction when bad economic shocks materialize as in a more majoritarian system. Instead, such a policymaker can enhance the informational environment by providing opportunities for revelation of credible information about the incumbent's policies. Then the voters can better allocate blame for bad outcomes and are less likely to punish the policymaker. Of course, more information means that the policymaker has reduced ability to engage in extractive behavior. So when the loss associated with the marginal seat is high, the incumbent has an incentive to trade away future opportunities for rent extraction in exchange for reducing the likelihood of losing the marginal seat in the next election. Therefore. Rosendorff and Vreeland predict that majoritarian democratic polities (such as countries with single-member districts) will be less transparent than less majoritarian systems (such as countries with proportional representation).

Their empirical findings support claims from both models. First, democracies are more likely than autocracies to report (or report more accurately) their economic performance to international organizations like the IMF and World Bank. Second, democracies are more likely to report their economic performance in less majoritarian systems. This suggests that leaders will derive more benefit from the transparency provided by the institution – and hence be more likely to join trade agreements with such adjudicatory mechanisms – if they are more accountable to their domestic citizens and if the vote-seat share elasticity in their domestic legislature increases. As such, we believe that the implications of transparency on international cooperation – be it provided by international organizations like the DSU process at the WTO or domestic institutions – constitutes an important and exciting opportunity for further research.

In sum, electoral accountability is one manner in which compliance with international trading agreements can be induced. However, such a domestic enforcement system can only be effective if voters are able to observe the policy choices of their leader and know whether an illegitimate violation has occurred. As such, the DSU is key to supporting domestic enforcement of international trade agreements since it provides transparency by making policy choices observable to voters and provides information about whether a violation has in fact occurred.

4. Conclusions

Much of the theoretical literature on the study of international trade has been dominated by standard PD accounts of cooperation in lowering tariff barriers. These accounts generally assume that states are unitary actors and ignore the impact of domestic politics on international behavior. While these accounts of the impact of punishment and patience have given us valuable insight into strategic considerations that affect long-run cooperative behavior, they have also generated implications that are grossly contradicted by the empirical record on trade disputes. Incorporating elements of domestic politics into these accounts can help us to move away from the assumption of states as unitary actors and allow us to develop a more nuanced understanding of international trade cooperation and disputes.

Clearly, domestic politics plays an important role in the realm of international trade. First, political pressure from domestic industries can be key in creating demand for violations of existing trade agreements. Since such pressure is affected by stochastic shocks, the temptation of leaders to defect from cooperative trading and commit trade violations can vary over time. The presence of the DSP provides flexibility that allows leaders to respond to such pressure by occasionally committing violations and then compensating their trading partners if the DSP finds that the violation was not subject to exceptions in the trading agreement. This flexibility enhances that willingness of leaders to sign cooperative agreements in the first place.

Second, domestic politics can be a key enforcement mechanism for ensuring compliance with international trade agreements and DSP rulings. Since low tariff barriers enhance social welfare, voters can condition their electoral decisions on whether their leader complies with socially beneficial trade agreements. The DSP plays a key role in this account as an information-provider. In order for voters to hold their leaders accountable for their policy choices, they need information about what choices their leader has made and whether his actions constitute compliance with a pre-existing international agreement. The DSP provides transparency and reduces uncertainty about these factors.

While the analytical approaches considered here focus on the demand for trade violations and domestic enforcement of international agreements, there is also a considerable literature that focuses on the role of domestic politics at the negotiation stage. For instance, Martin (2000) argues that institutionalized participation by the domestic legislature at the negotiation stage ensures more cooperation once an agreement is reached. Similarly, Milner and Rosendorff (1996) show how domestic ratification in the presence of incomplete information and divided government can significantly affect both the likelihood that an agreement is reached and the nature of the agreement.

Overall, the resurrection of the PD paradigm depends on appealing to domestic political considerations for both flexibility and enforcement rather than severe international punishment for trade violations. This result is perhaps surprising. Yet the predictions derived from models with domestic political components are more consistent with the observed regularities than are those drawn from models that rely solely on international punishment for enforcement. These models also serve as a response to those who would toughen WTO penalties, make punishment more stringent, and increase the power of the DSP. Emerging results suggests that these may not be necessary and even perhaps be counter-productive in promoting international trade.

References

Bagwell, K., Staiger, R. (1999), An economic theory of GATT. *American Economic Review* 89 (1), 215–248.

Bagwell, K., Staiger, R. (2005), Enforcement, private political pressure and the GATT/WTO escape clause. *The Journal of Legal Studies* 34 (2), 471–513.

Bello, J.H. (1996), The WTO dispute settlement understanding: less is more. *American Journal of International Law* 90, 416–418.

Bhagwati, J., Palrick, H. T. (Eds.) (1990). *Aggressive Unilateralism: America's 301 Trade Policy and the World Trading System.* University of Michigan Press, Ann Arbor, MI.

Bueno de Mesquita, B., Smith, A., Siverson, R., Morrow, J. (2003), *The Logic of Political Survival.* MIT Press, Boston, M.A.

Busch, M.L. (2000), Democracy, consultation, and the paneling of disputes under the GATT. *Journal of Conflict Resolution* 44 (4), 425–446.

Busch, M.L., Raciborski, R., Reinhardt, E. (2007), Does the rule of law matter? The WTO and US antidumping investigations. Working Paper, Department of Government, Georgetown University.

Chayes, A., Chayes, A.H. (1993), On compliance. *International Organization* 47 (Spring), 175–205.

Downs, G.W., Rocke, D.M. (1995), *Optimal Imperfection? Domestic Uncertainty and Institutions in International Relations*. Princeton University Press, Princeton, NJ.

Downs, G.W., Rocke, D.M., Barsoom, P.B. (1996), Is the good news about compliance good news about cooperation? *International Organization* 50 (Summer), 379–406.

Doyle, M. (1986), Liberalism and World Politics. *American Political Science Review* 80 (December), 1151–1169.

Ethier, W.J. (2001), Punishments and dispute settlement in trade agreements. PIER Working Paper No. 01–021.

Fearon, J.D. (1998), Bargaining, enforcement and international cooperation. *International Organization* 52 (Spring), 269–305.

Finger, J. M., Nogues, J. J. (Eds.) (2005). *Safeguards and Antidumping in Latin American Trade Liberalization: Fighting Fire with Fire*. World Bank, Washington, DC.

Fischer, R., Osorio, M. (2006), Why do we need antidumping rules? Working Paper, Centro de Economía Aplicada, Universidad de Chile.

Gilligan, M. (2004), Is there a broader-deeper tradeoff? *International Organization* 58, 459–484.

Goldstein, J., Martin, L.L. (2000), Legalization, trade liberalization and domestic politics: a cautionary note. *International Organization* 54 (3), 603–632.

Hafner-Burton, E.M., Tsutsui, K. (2005), Human rights in a globalizing world: the paradox of empty promises. *American Journal of Sociology* 110 (5), 1373–1411.

Hafner-Burton, E.M., Tsutsui, K. (2007), Justice lost! The failure of international human rights law to matter where needed most. *Journal of Peace Research* 44 (4), 407–425.

Hoekman, B.M., Kostecki, M.M. (2001), *The Political Economy of the World Trading System: The WTO and Beyond*, second ed. Oxford University Press, New York.

Hudec, R.E. (2002), The adequacy of WTO dispute settlement remedies. In: Hoekman, B.M., Mattoo, A., English, P. (Eds.), *Development, Trade and the WTO: A Handbook*. The World Bank, Washington.

Johns, L. (2006), Knowing the unknown: executive evaluation and international crisis outcomes. *Journal of Conflict Resolution* 50 (2), 228–252.

Johns, L. (2008), Endogenous enforcement and jurisdiction in international adjudication. Working Paper, Department of Political Science, UCLA, Los Angeles, CA.

Johnson, H.G. (1953-54), Optimum tariffs and retaliation. *Review of Economic Studies* 21, 142–153.

Kucik, J., Reinhardt, E. (2008), Does flexibility promote cooperation? An application to the global trade regime. *International Organization* 62, 477–505.

Leitner, K., Lester, S. (2008), WTO dispute settlement from 1995 to 2007 – a statistical analysis. *Journal of International Economic Law* 11 (1), 179–192.

Maggi, G. (1999), The role of multilateral institutions in international trade cooperation. *American Economic Review* 89 (March), 190–214.

Maggi, G., Rodriguez-Clare, A. (1998), The value of trade agreements in the presence of political pressures. *Journal of Political Economy* 106, 574–601.

Mansfield, E.D., Milner, H.V., Rosendorff, B.P. (2000), Free to trade: democracies, autocracies and international trade. *American Political Science Review* 94, 305–322.

Mansfield, E.D., Milner, H.V., Rosendorff, B.P. (2002), Why democracies cooperate more: electoral control and international trade agreements. *International Organization* 56, 477–514.

Martin, L.L. (2000), *Democratic Commitments: Legislatures and International Cooperation.* Princeton University Press, Princeton, NJ.

Mavroidis, P.C. (2000), Remedies in the WTO legal system: between a rock and a hard place. *European Journal of International Law* 11 (4), 763–814.

McGillivray, F., Smith, A. (2000), Trust and cooperation through agent-specific punishments. *International Organization* 54 (4), 809–824.

McGillivray, F., Smith, A. (2004), The impact of leadership turnover on trading relations between states. *International Organization* 58, 567–600.

McGillivray, F., Smith, A. (2006), Credibility in compliance and punishment: leader specific punishments and credibility. *Journal of Politics* 68, 248–258.

Milner, H.V., Rosendorff, B.P. (1996), Trade negotiations, information and domestic politics. *Economics and Politics* 8 (July), 145–189.

Olson, M. (2003), Dictatorship, democracy and development. In: Knack, S. (Ed.), *Democracy, Governance and Growth.* University of Michigan Press, Ann Arbor, MI.

Oye, K. (1986), *Cooperation under Anarchy.* Princeton University Press, Princeton, NJ.

Pevehouse, J. C., Hafner-Burton, E., Zierler, M. (2002). Regional trade and institutional design: long after hegemony? Presented at the 2002 MPSA Meetings, Chicago, IL.

Przeworski, A., Vreeland, J. (2000), The effects of IMF programs on economic growth. *Journal of Development Economics* 62, 385–421.

Putnam, R.D. (1988), Diplomacy and domestic politics: the logic of two-level games. *International Organization* 42, 427–460.

Rosendorff, B.P. (2005), Stability and rigidity: politics and the design of the WTO's dispute resolution procedure. *American Political Science Review* 99 (3), 389–400.

Rosendorff, B.P., Milner, H.V. (2001), The optimal design of international trade institutions: uncertainty and escape. *International Organization* 55 (Fall), 829–857.

Rosendorff, B.P., Vreeland, J.R. (2007a), Electoral accountability and data dissemination: the effect of democracy on transparency. Working Paper, Department of Politics, New York University.

Rosendorff, B.P., Vreeland, J.R. (2007b), Majoritarianism and transparency. Working Paper, Presented at the 2007 Annual Conference of the International Political Economy Society.

Rubinstein, A. (1979), Equilibrium in supergames with the overtaking criterion. *Journal of Economic Theory* 21: 1–9.

Russett, B., Oneal, J. (2001), *Triangulating Peace: Democracy, Interdependence, and International Organizations*. Norton, New York.

Schmidt, M.G. (2002), Political performance and types of democracy: findings from comparative studies. *European Journal of Political Research* 41 (1), 147–163.

Schwartz, W.F., Sykes, A.O. (2002), The economic structure of renegotiation and dispute resolution in the World Trade Organization. *Journal of Legal Studies* 31, S179–S204.

Setear, J.K. (1997), Responses to breach of a treaty and rationalist international relations theory: the rules of release and remediation in the law of treaties and the law of state responsibility. *Virginia Law Review* 83, 1–127.

Simmons, B., Hopkins, D.J. (2005), The constraining power of international treaties: theory and methods. *American Political Science Review* 99 (4), 623–631.

Smith, J.M. (2000), The Politics of dispute settlement design: explaining legalism in regional trade pacts. *International Organization* 54, 137–180.

Sykes, A.O. (1991), Protectionism as a 'safeguard': a positive analysis of the GATT 'escape clause' with normative speculations. *University of Chicago Law Review* 58 (1), 255–305.

Trebilcock, M.J., Howse, R. (1999), *The Regulation of International Trade*, second ed. Routledge, New York.

Von Stein, J. (2005), Do treaties constrain or screen? Selection bias and treaty compliance. *American Political Science Review* 99 (4), 611–622.

PART III

Power and Inequities in Access to the DSU

CHAPTER 7

Developing Country Use of the WTO Dispute Settlement System: Why it Matters, the Barriers Posed

Gregory Shaffer

Melvin C. Steen Professor of Law, University of Minnesota Law School, Minneapolis, MN 55455, USA
E-mail address: shaffer@umn.edu

Abstract
This chapter examines the barriers posed for smaller and poorer World Trade Organization (WTO) members to challenge trade barriers under the WTO's dispute settlement understanding. It first addresses the implications of the judicialization of the WTO's dispute settlement system. It next examines reasons why participation in the WTO's dispute settlement system matters. It then summarizes the results of studies of the system's use and, in light of these findings, posits explanations for smaller developing countries' lack of engagement.

Keywords: WTO dispute settlement, developing countries, legal capacity, judicialization, implementation periods, aggregate stakes, participation, systemic effects, terms of trade, bargaining, legal shadow, litigation, enforcement, balance of power, legal consciousness, institutional bias, rule of law

JEL classifications: F13, F14, F53

1. Introduction

The legalized dispute settlement system of the World Trade Organization (WTO) has been hailed as a new development in international economic relations in which law, more than power, might reign. Nowhere has the international "rule of law" advanced more than in trade law. And yet, such declarations beg the question of who predominantly uses the legal system, who prevails, and how does it affect bargaining in the system's shadow? Can the legal system work for smaller countries and, in particular, for small developing countries? To what extent has legal capacity – the ability to

Frontiers of Economics and Globalization
Volume 6 ISSN: 1574-8715
DOI: 10.1108/S1574-8715(2009)0000006010

mobilize legal resources to prepare and litigate a WTO case – replaced the premium provided by market power? This chapter examines not trade barriers as we conventionally conceive of them but rather the barriers posed for smaller and poorer WTO members to challenge trade barriers.

Section 2 briefly addresses the judicialization of the WTO dispute settlement system and its implications for WTO member participation. Section 3 examines reasons why participation in the WTO dispute settlement system matters. Sections 4 and 5 respectively assess studies of the system's use and posit explanations for smaller developing countries' failure to use it. Section 6 concludes.

2. The judicialization of international trade dispute settlement

With the WTO's creation on January 1, 1995, international trade rules became more detailed, and their application more judicialized.[1] The rules comprise a package of eighteen multilateral agreements, numerous "understandings" and "protocols," and around 26,000 pages of text, including schedules of concessions. The negotiators of the package combined this substantive law with a more binding and independent judicial process. At least nominally, all WTO members are equal before the system, developed and developing countries alike, from the United States to Mozambique.

The WTO's Dispute Settlement Understanding created a notable appellate review system which has generated a more complex case law. The texts of WTO panel and Appellate Body decisions deploy sophisticated legal analysis, building on previous WTO jurisprudence as well as some public international law. The case law has burgeoned. WTO members filed [369] complaints over the first thirteen years (from January 1, 1995 to December 31, 2007).[2] Just to read through and understand the growing WTO case law is an immense task, including for specialized academics. While panel decisions under the GATT typically averaged around a dozen pages, under the WTO they range from 100 to 500 pages. While the GATT produced an average of 86 pages of panel findings per year from 1986 to 1995, the WTO produced 693 pages of panel findings in 1999 (Davey, 2003). If one counts the entire judicial reports and not just the sections on "findings," then, in 2000, there were 6,008 pages of WTO panel decisions, which mounts to 7,251 pages when one includes Appellate Body and arbitration decisions concerning implementation periods, compliance measures, and sanctions.[3] The case law now comprises "well over

[1] On the concept of *judicialization*, or third party dispute resolution, see Stone Sweet (1999, pp. 147–184).

[2] See Stone Sweet (1999).

[3] According to the WTO's web site, in 2000, there were eighteen panel decisions, eight Appellate Body decisions, fifteen implementation decisions (pursuant to DSU Article 21.3.c), seven compliance decisions (pursuant to DSU Article 21.5), and two decisions on sanctions

30,000 pages."[4] In short, WTO law involves greater legalization along the dimensions of binding obligation, precision of rules, delegation to a dispute settlement institution, and use.[5]

Greater legalization and judicialization of international trade dispute settlement, of course, do not come without costs. The demands on human resources have multiplied if a member wishes to invoke its international trading rights. Although the legalization of WTO dispute settlement constitutes a significant achievement in international law, the system remains far from a neutral technocratic process in its operation. Larger and wealthier countries are much better positioned to take advantage of the resource-demanding procedures of the legal system.

Analyses of law, from whatever academic discipline, risk reifying law as a relatively seamless, cost-free system, not subject to the effects of asymmetric information and resources, interpretation, and manipulation, implying that once the "rule of law" is created, rights will be neutrally enforced. Substantive law – however neutral, and whether it operates directly or diffusely – is of limited neutrality if weaker parties cannot mobilize legal resources in a cost-effective manner to pursue and defend their claims or negotiate them in the law's shadow.

Absolute trading stakes (the aggregate of a WTO member's exports and imports) appears to be the best predictor of a WTO member's use of the system.[6] That is not surprising. The more that a member trades, the greater its aggregate stakes in the system, and the greater its incentives to defend its trading rights, including as a result of pressure from affected constituencies. A number of studies suggest, however, that a residual explanation for discrepancies in participation lies in the greater difficulty that developing countries confront in mobilizing legal resources (what we refer to as legal capacity) so as to participate in an increasingly complex legal system (Busch and Reinhardt, 2002; Guzman and Simmons, 2005; Busch *et al.*, 2008a).

These two explanatory factors (aggregate stakes and legal capacity) are likely related. The larger a WTO member's economic stakes in the system,

---

(pursuant to DSU Article 22.6). These gave rise to 6,008 pages of panel decisions, 401 pages of Appellate Body decisions, 606 pages of decisions by compliance panels, 61 pages of arbitral decisions concerning the implementation period, and 75 pages of arbitral decisions concerning the amount of authorized sanctions.

[4] See Wilson (2008), available at http://www.wita.org/index.php?tg = posts&idx = List&forum = 3&thread = 99&views = 1. The Consultative Board to the WTO Director General reported in December 2004 that the first "81 cases for which reports are adopted, and reports whose adoption is pending, amount to more than 27,000 pages of jurisprudence." See WTO (2004).

[5] See Abbott *et al.* (2000) (characterizing international law in terms of variation in its precision, obligation, and delegation for third party dispute resolution).

[6] See Horn *et al.* (1999). They write, "Our tentative conclusion is that the seeming over-representation by G4 countries, or the mirror image under-representation of developing countries, to a large extent reflect differences in the diversity and value of trade." Id., p. 26. See also Francois and Horn (2008).

the more likely that member will invest in developing and mobilizing legal resources, including through coordinating with its private sector and outside legal counsel. This chapter nonetheless posits that the two explanatory factors do not fully overlap, so that legal capacity has some independent, explanatory value. The relationship of stakes and legal capacity to a country's use of the legal system do not appear to vary smoothly along a continuum. Rather, there appears to be a break at which point there is not so much differences in degree, but differences in kind between WTO members. As an advisor of least-developed countries skeptically observed, "the DSU does not have much relevance to the countries that I advise. It may be the last of their priorities."[7] In an article with Marc Busch and Eric Reinhardt, we surveyed the delegations of each of the member states in the WTO, including e-mails where those members did not have offices in Geneva, and composed an index measuring a member's WTO-related capacity.[8] We found that legal capacity matters at least as much as market power in explaining the use of the WTO legal system, as well as outcomes in antidumping investigations in domestic legal systems.[9]

The term "developing country" is an ambiguous one and does not clearly differentiate between those who are more likely to use the WTO legal system.[10] Certain developing countries, such as Brazil, India, and China, may have low per capita income, but they nonetheless can defend their interests in WTO litigation (at least more effectively than others) because of the scale and scope of their economies. In short, they have relatively high aggregate trading stakes. These aggregate economic stakes spur them to mobilize the requisite legal resources to deploy the legal system, typically through hiring and coordinating with outside legal counsel. They have used and have benefited from the WTO dispute settlement system.[11] Smaller developing countries, in contrast, have generally not used the system.

---

[7] Author interview with Esperanza Duran, Director, Agency for International Trade Information & Cooperation (AITIC), Geneva, June 6, 2002.

[8] Fifty-two delegations responded in full as of May 2007. The survey respondents included a broad range of member states, in terms of both income and geographical diversity. They comprised all major users of the WTO dispute settlement system and a broad representation of those who have never used it, including a large number of least developed countries. See Busch *et al.* (2008a).

[9] Busch *et al.* (2008a). Compare Guzman and Simmons (2005) and Bown (2005), available at http://papers.ssrn.com/sol3/papers.cfm?abstract_id = 546442.

[10] Countries falling within the category of "developing country" vary significantly in terms of their development and trading characteristics. The term, however, is used within the WTO legal texts and within the WTO system, so that it is also used in the media and scholarship.

[11] For a detailed study of Brazil, see Shaffer *et al.* (2008), available at http://papers.ssrn.com/sol3/papers.cfm?abstract_id = 1137905.

3. Why participation in WTO dispute settlement matters: tangible, systemic, and shadow effects

Participation in the WTO dispute settlement system can matter in four primary respects. First, it matters in specific adjudication to the extent that WTO legal decisions affect specific economic outcomes, as they have done. Busch and Reinhardt showed how around two-thirds of complaints "ending prior to a ruling (whether before or after the establishment of a panel), exhibited full or partial concessions by the defendant" (Busch and Reinhardt, 2000). Chad Bown found that these concessions have mattered economically. Three years after the date of adoption of a WTO judicial decision in favor of the complainant, imports of the complainant's affected goods increased substantially into the respondent member.[12] In other words, WTO dispute settlement has tangible effects by providing greater market access for individual industries.

Second, and conversely, the failure to participate in WTO dispute settlement can have terms-of-trade effects that adversely affect the overall social welfare of a country. If an importing country raises a trade barrier and that country exercises market power so that foreign exporters must lower their prices in order to sell in its market, then the exporting country's terms of trade are prejudiced. That is, the exporting country will need to sell a greater amount of its products (at the lower price) in order to obtain the same amount of imports. The removal or curtailment of the trade barrier following a successful WTO complaint can thus improve a country's terms of trade and overall social welfare because its exporters will no longer need to reduce their prices to overcome the foreign market access barrier.[13] As Bagwell and Staiger state, "the terms-of-trade consequences of trade-policy choices can be expressed equivalently in the language of market access, and so the terms-of-trade consequences and the market-access implications of trade-policy choices are different ways of expressing the same thing."[14] Whereas the first reason for participation focuses on the market access benefits to an individual industry, this second

---

[12] See Bown (2004b). Bown controls for other potential explanatory factors. See also Tomz *et al.* (2007) (finding that "GATT boosted trade among signatories, but it exerted at least as large an effect on colonies, newly independent states, and provisional applicants that had not acceded, but nonetheless possessed the rights and obligations of members"). The article responds to Rose (2004) (maintaining that there is "little evidence that countries joining or belonging to GATT/WTO have different trade patterns than outsiders," and thus it appears that GATT/WTO has not encouraged trade).

[13] According to Bagwell and Staiger (2002, p. 3), "The purpose of a trade agreement is to offer a means of escape from a terms-of-trade driven Prisoners' Dilemma."

[14] Bagwell and Staiger's (2002, p. 5) theory accounts for both economic and political motivations since member governments implicitly make commitments of greater market access to these industries in return for their political support during the negotiation and ratification of trade agreements. Id., p. 3. See also Schwartz and Sykes (2002, p. 179) and Milner (1997).

reason focuses on the welfare of a country as a whole on account of terms-of-trade effects.

Third, systemically, participation matters where WTO jurisprudence shapes the interpretation, application, and social perceptions of the "law" over time and thus affects future bargaining positions in light of these understandings. Just as in domestic law, the outcome of an individual WTO case has not only a tangible component but also a broader systemic one.[15] The tangible component is that a measure is found to either violate or comply with a legal obligation, and if it is in violation, it gives rise to a remedy, both benefiting the exporter and (potentially) a country's terms of trade. The systemic component affects the understanding of the law's application in subsequent cases. In short, participation affects the framing of cases, which affects judicial interpretation, which affects what the law means over time. As an interviewed developing country delegate states, "what they [panels] do is fill in the gaps of trade agreements; ... what they do is to finish the job negotiators did not perform," perhaps as part of an intentional compromise, when negotiations failed to define a provision with much precision, leaving its meaning to be resolved in the future.[16] Those who participate in WTO cases help to define that meaning through case law.

This systemic component leads to the most important fourth, and related, point. WTO law can affect domestic and bilateral political bargaining in the shadow of a potential case without any formal complaint being filed.[17] Domestically, the WTO legal system gives governments leverage over economic sectors that demand protection. Governments can now argue that such protection is costly because it can result in authorized trade retaliation (Staiger and Tabellini, 1999). Blonigen and Bown, for example, found statistical evidence that suggests that "retaliation threats substantially affect US AD [antidumping] activity from 1980 through 1998" by making it both "less likely [for private petitioners] to name a foreign import source in an AD petition" and "government agencies less likely to rule positive in their AD decision."[18] WTO law also provides strategic actors with arguments that they may deploy in domestic political debates regarding regulatory initiatives.[19]

---

[15] See, e.g., Galanter (1974).

[16] Author interview, July 13, 2005, Geneva.

[17] See, e.g., Shaffer (2003a). The book notes, among other matters, where Pakistan settled U.S. complaints against its automobile domestic content requirements, its system of differential alcohol tax rates, and its filing system for patents, in the shadow of successful U.S. litigation against other WTO members.

[18] See Blonigen and Bown (2003, p. 249) and Busch *et al.* (2008b), available at http://userwww.service.emory.edu/~erein/research/AD.pdf (finding statistical evidence "that suggests that the WTO legal regime deters protectionist practices against fellow members").

[19] As a Brussels lawyer confirms, "trade issues and trade arguments are very much used in the adoption of (EU) legislation. I have worked a lot in the EU proposed legislation on electronic take back and restrictions of hazardous substances in electronic products where we used a lot

Bilaterally, WTO law, jurisprudence, and legal procedures affect bargaining over trade disputes conducted in the legal system's shadow. As Marc Galanter reminds us regarding domestic litigation, "the career of most cases does not lead to full-blown trial and adjudication but consists of negotiation and maneuver in the strategic pursuit of settlement through mobilization of the court process."[20] Galanter calls this process "litigotiation." WTO members likewise settle the vast majority of their disputes over WTO obligations without litigation. Although the percentage of settled WTO claims is much lower than in domestic contexts,[21] over 65% of WTO requests for consultations have never produced a panel report.[22] GATT and WTO settlements have led to significant concessions, in fact, data show greater concessions from settlements on average than in fully litigated cases.[23] In short, WTO members, in the words of Canada's trade minister, pursue a "two-pronged approach – litigation and a negotiated settlement" – when faced with a trade dispute (Pruzin, 2004).

Two primary aspects of the law exercise shadow effects on bargaining: the law's substance and the law's procedures. First, the substance of WTO law, as set forth in the WTO agreements and as interpreted in WTO case law, inform and constrain settlement negotiations conducted in the law's shadow. As Mnookin and Kornhauser observe in their famous study in a domestic divorce law context, "the outcome that the law will impose if no agreement is reached gives each [party] certain bargaining chips – an endowment of sorts" (Mnookin and Kornhauser, 1979). Those WTO members who participate most actively in WTO litigation can "play for rules" and thus affect the nature of the bargaining chips. They are also

---

of trade arguments to defend US industry's interests. I think that focusing also in the legislative adoption phase changes somewhat the approach. The law firms are no longer specific trade law firms but regulatory law firms." E-mail from Candido Garcia-Molyneux (January 7, 2002).

[20] See Galanter (2001, pp. 577, 579) and see also Galanter (1984, p. 268).

[21] See Galanter (2004, pp. 459–570), noting that "the percentage of civil cases reaching trial has fallen from 11% in 1962 to 1.8% in 2002," replaced by "increases in settlements, in disposition by summary judgment, and in diversion into Alternative Dispute Resolution".

[22] As of July 24, 2008, 324 Requests for Consultations under the WTO that were filed by December 31, 2004, had resulted in circulation of 111 Panel Reports (constituting 34.3% of the total filings. In an earlier study, Busch and Reinhardt noted that "three-fifths of all [complaints] end prior to a panel ruling, and most of these without a request for a panel being made." See Busch and Reinhardt (2000, pp. 158–159). (This statement refers to GATT and WTO statistics combined.) The authors noted that no panel was ever established in roughly 55% of the cases. Id., p. 161 (chart noting increase in settled complaints from 58.2% in the period from 1989 to 1994 to 66.5% during the period from 1995 to 1999, the first five years of the WTO). See also Parlin (2000, pp. 565, 567–569).

[23] Busch and Reinhardt (2000). Since Busch and Reinhardt do not include disputes settled without the filing of a formal WTO complaint, the overall number of trade conflicts that resulted in concessions without the need for a WTO panel decisions is considerably higher.

more likely to be aware of the bargaining chips that they may deploy in order to use them strategically to their advantage.

Because of the WTO judicial system's weak enforcement powers, the judicial decision in a particular case should likewise be viewed in terms of its "shadow effect" on the resolution of a dispute. Cases are resolved through diplomatic negotiations (and private party bargaining behind-the-scenes)[24] that take place in the context of, and are informed by, judicial decisions. A judicial decision simply serves to help the parties resolve their dispute. Accordingly, following WTO legal rulings in the U.S.–Canadian lumber dispute over alleged Canadian subsidies, Canada's former ambassador to the WTO (working for a U.S. law firm on WTO matters) did not focus on compliance but focused on how the rulings can help "clear the way towards common ground on reaching an agreement."[25] In the words of one member representative to the WTO, "the end game ... ultimately involves negotiation informed by dispute settlement."[26] Amelia Porges concurs, noting, "every WTO dispute takes place between two negotiations: one negotiation that has failed to produce compliance and another negotiation on securing compliance after the dispute process is over."[27]

WTO members sometimes begin settlement negotiations only after the WTO ruling is issued. The U.S. Congress, for example, only seriously attended to modification of the U.S. "foreign sales corporation" tax subsidies after a WTO panel authorized the EC to sanction the United States by withdrawing trade concessions in an amount of US$ 4.043 billion dollars per year.[28] Years after the actual decision, the parties were still bargaining over how the United States would modify its tax regime and whether this modification was sufficient, in this case triggering further WTO litigation and bargaining in its shadow (Lam, 2005). As socio-legal scholars have shown, bargaining continues after legal decisions are rendered in

---

[24] To give an example from the GATT era, one of the judicial panelists in the GATT Section 337 case wrote to the author that, while "we were sitting in the second hearing, a telegram arrived that Akzo and Dupont [the private parties behind the suit] had reached an out-of-court agreement." Letter of January 9, 2004.

[25] See Pruzin (2004) (quoting former ambassador John Weeks who now works for the Geneva office of Sidley Austin Brown & Wood). The dispute concerned countervailing duties that the United States imposed against Canadian lumber on the alleged grounds that Canada had subsidized its lumber industry through charging low "stumpage fees" for the right to harvest trees on Canadian public lands.

[26] Author interview in Geneva, June 24, 2002.

[27] Porges (2003, pp. 141, 147). She continues, "It is the negotiation that will determine which of the range of possible outcomes emerges from a WTO dispute, and when."

[28] The WTO panel acted as arbitrator in determining the amount pursuant to Article 22.6 of the WTO Settlement Understanding, rendering its decision in August 2002. See Pruzin (2002, p. 1484) and Pruzin (2000, p. 1792) (the $4.043 billion amount "is based on the value of the subsidy granted by the US under the FSC scheme which the WTO found to be illegal earlier this year").

domestic legal systems as well.[29] Regarding U.S. contract law, Stewart Macaulay writes, "What appears to be a final judgment at the trial level may be only a step toward settlement. The judgment may affect the balance of power between the parties, but often it will not take effect as written." This phenomenon, however, is much more pronounced in the WTO legal system because the system wields no police powers for enforcement.

In addition, and perhaps more importantly, the law's "shadow" effects include the costs of deploying the law procedurally. As Herbert Kritzer points out regarding domestic litigation, "the ability to impose costs on the opponent and the capability of absorbing costs" affect how the law operates.[30] Where large developed countries can absorb high litigation costs by dragging out a WTO case, while imposing them on weaker complainants, they can seriously constrain a country's incentives to initiate a claim and correspondingly enhance a country's incentives to settle a dispute unfavorably. WTO law likely casts a weaker shadow for countries that lack lawyers conversant with WTO law, which tend to be smaller developing countries.[31] When a country is unable to mobilize legal resources cost-effectively, its threat to invoke WTO legal procedures against a country that wields greater legal resources has less credibility. It may not even consider the threat of litigation, knowing the challenges that it faces. It has less of an incentive to even study the details of WTO law, affecting what is called – in socio-legal studies – its "legal consciousness" (Cortese, 1966). It is this aspect of the WTO legal system, one which is rarely examined by legal and other academics other than in passing, which most adversely affects smaller and poorer members.

4. Some statistics on the system's use

Academics have increasingly mined statistics on the use of the WTO dispute settlement system to examine who are the primary participants and which of them are most successful. A number of scholars have examined how "developing countries" have fared compared to "developed countries."

The statistics show that the United States and EC remain by far the predominant users of the WTO legal system and thereby are most likely to advance their larger systemic interests through the judicial process and

---

[29] Macaulay (2003, pp. 44, 89) (for example, the case *Aluminum Corporation of America v Essex Group Inc.*).

[30] Kritzer (1991, pp. 73–75, 103–104, 132–133) (noting that the shadow of the law is also "the ability to impose costs on the opponent and the capability of absorbing costs"). See also Trubek *et al.* (1983, p. 72) (a study of litigation in the United States).

[31] Compare Jacob (1992, pp. 565, 586) (noting "the language in which a claim is initially framed combined with the manner in which attorneys are used and the success of consultation with personal networks are perhaps the key variables in determining the strength of the shadow of the law").

through bargaining in its shadow. Although their proportion of total WTO complaints has somewhat declined in the last few years, they continue to be the system's predominant users. Overall, during the WTO's first thirteen years (as of January 1, 2008), collectively the United States and EC were complainants in about 44% of the complaints filed and defendants in 43% of the total.[32]

These percentages dramatically increase when accounting for cases that have been fully litigated before WTO panels where the systemic impacts are greatest. The United States and EC are typically third parties when they are not a plaintiff or defendant. This raises their respective participation rates in cases fully litigated before WTO panels (from January 1, 1995 to December 31, 2007) to 99% (United States) and 85% (EC).[33] As of the end of 2007, the United States had participated as a complainant, defendant, or third party in every Appellate Body proceeding but one.[34] The U.S. and EC participation rates are much higher than their percentages of global trade, which in 2006 were about 12.6% and 18.1%, respectively, of world merchandise exports.[35] As parties and third parties, the United States and EC attempt to defend their systemic interests in shaping the interpretation of WTO rules over time.

Nonetheless, by many measures, the legal system has worked relatively well for the larger developing countries. Because of their participation, developing countries' overall relative and aggregate use of the legal system have increased significantly since the WTO's creation, as has their relative success.[36]

---

[32] Leitner and Lester (2008, p. 179). These figures are for all cases *filed*, not all Panel or Appellate Body decisions that were adopted. Compare Leitner and Lester (2005, pp. 231, 234) and Leitner and Lester (2003, pp. 251–253) (where collectively, the United States and EC were complainants in 48% and defendants in 41% of total complaints filed). From 1948 through the end of June 2000, the United States was either a complainant or defendant in 340 GATT/WTO disputes, constituting 52% of the total number of 654 disputes, while the European Community, which became more active over time, was a party in 238 disputes, or 36% of that total. See Busch and Reinhardt (2002, p. 462).

[33] See Shaffer (2003a, pp. 128–133, 157, Tables 6-1 and 7-1).

[34] Worldtradelaw.net, Participants and Third Participants in Appellate Body Proceedings, worldtradelaw.net/dsc/database/partiesab.asp (last visited June 19, 2008). Technically, the United States was not a third party in case DS290 (EC-Protection of Trademarks and Geographical Indications), but it was a complainant in the similar case that preceded it and which has the same title, DS174. These percentages have increased, in particular for the EC which has become a more systematic participant as a third party. See, e.g., Smith (2004, pp. 542, 561) ("Measured as a proportion of their opportunities to appear (i.e. the number of cases in which they are neither complainant nor defendant), the US has taken part as a third party participant in a remarkable 94% of appeals (15 of 16), while the EU has done so in 64% (18 of 28). The next most frequent participant is Japan at a much lower rate of 33 percent (10 of 30), followed by India (7 of 39) and Canada (6 of 34) at 18 percent.").

[35] UN COMTRADE Yearbook (2006). Compare Hoekman and Kostecki (2001, p. 59) (noting in 1999 that the corresponding figures were 16.8% and 20.1% of world merchandise exports).

[36] Compare Bown (2004a, pp. 59, 64) (noting an increase in developing country participation as complainants from "roughly 30%" of GATT disputes to "roughly one third" of WTO

A comparison of the numbers for the patterns for "complainants" under the GATT and WTO shows the following increase in developing country activity:

As a proportion of total bilateral complaints filed, developing countries have gone from around 31% (in the GATT) to almost 40% (in the WTO).[37]

Yet as Hunter Nottage points out, five developing countries account for 60% of developing country complaints, and thirteen developing countries account for 90% of them.[38] In total, 95 of the WTO's 120 non-OECD members had never filed a complaint before the WTO, and 62 had not even participated as a third party.[39] As regards countries from Africa and the Middle East, none has ever been a complainant before the WTO. No country in the region has been a respondent either, besides Egypt (four times) and South Africa (three times).

Moreover, the statistical data likely overstate the actual "in house" experience of developing country officials with the legal system, experiences that could be deployed for bargaining and litigation in future disputes. For example, in a number of cases, developing countries may participate through the direct financial and legal assistance of more powerful WTO members that promote their own interests, as when the EC provided funds for fourteen ACP countries to hire lawyers in Brussels to defend their interests as a third party (and indirectly, the EC's interests as a party) in the *EC-Sugar* case brought by Brazil and Thailand. Although some of these countries' Geneva representatives actively followed the legal arguments in the case, they were the exception.[40]

---

disputes) and Busch and Reinhardt (2002), pp. 466 467 (noting how, for data through 2000, "Developing countries constituted some 31 percent of GATT complainants, yet only 29 percent of WTO complainants, despite their ballooning proportion of the overall membership," although developing country membership in a 148-member WTO is much greater than that of the original 23-member GATT. These latter figures include the growing number of developing country cases against each other).

[37] This calculation, however, does not control or normalize for different factors, such as the increased number of developing country members, increased number of intra-developing country cases, levels of income, amount of trade, and so on.

[38] See Nottage (2008). Brazil and India in particular have been relatively active users of the WTO system, with Brazil having initiated twenty-three WTO complaints and India seventeen complaints during the first twelve-plus years. Calculated from WTO update as of May 2008. The World Trade Report 2007 lists WTO complaints filed through July 31, 2004, and finds that developed countries were complainants 199 times (or 58.7%) and developing countries 140 times (or 41.3%).

[39] These figures are as of December 31, 2007.

[40] Confirmed in a number of author interviews in Geneva, July 2005. The EC provided funding that it justified as technical assistance under the Cotonou Agreement. The EC's private sugar trade association, CEFS (Comite Europeen des Fabricants de Sucre), separately hired a law firm. EC lawyers worked closely with these teams of lawyers, as well as a Caribbean lawyer hired separately by the Caribbean sugar industry. Author interview with a private attorney working on the case, Chicago Illinois, May 28, 2004.

Likewise, the success of developing countries in WTO litigation (compared to under the GATT) appears to have increased in terms of gaining market access. Busch and Reinhardt found that "developing country complaints saw defendants fully liberalize disputed measures 36 percent of the time under the GATT, increasing to 50 percent under the WTO" (Busch and Reinhardt, 2003a). The economist Chad Bown's data, which is based on a calculation of actual liberalization measured in terms of increased imports to the defendant country three years after the legal decision, also suggest "that developing country plaintiffs are seeing greater success under the dispute settlement provisions of the WTO than was the case under the GATT."[41]

When broken down further, however, these statistics show signs of disparity in the legal system's use and in WTO member's success rates. Bown finds statistical support for the existence "of institutional bias" against smaller exporting countries' ability to use the legal system, in particular because of "the inability to make credible retaliatory trade threats against the respondent, the unwillingness to participate in disputes against respondents on whom exporters are reliant for bilateral aid, and the difficulty of affording legal representation because of the exporting countries' low levels of income."[42]

Developing countries have, in fact, been much more frequently targeted as defendants by all categories of countries. As Table 1 shows, a developing country is about 4.5 times more likely to be subject to a complaint under the WTO than under the GATT.[43] Of course, a major reason that developing countries have been much more likely to be defendants is that they assumed more legal obligations under the WTO than under the GATT, where they were subject to few binding tariff commitments and were often not subject to the side "codes," and there are now more developing country members.[44] Table 2 shows the nature of defendants.

Table 3 presents the number of complaints filed by developing countries, by period and target. It shows how developing countries are about twelve times more likely to target complaints against each other

---

[41] See Bown (2004a), pp. 66–67.

[42] See Bown (2005, p. 5) and Bown (2004b).

[43] See also Busch and Reinhardt (2002), pp. 466–467 (noting a developing country "is up to five times more likely to be subject to a complaint under the WTO"). See also Bown (2004a) (comparing 45% figure under WTO with an 11% figure under GATT). See also Hoekman and Kostecki (2001), pp. 394–395 (showing that, under the WTO, "the developing country share in terms of being a defendant rose to 37 percent" compared to "only 8 percent of all cases brought during the GATT years").

[44] Jackson *et al.* report that "the number of tariff lines 'bound' under Article II" of the GATT following the Uruguay Round negotiations and the creation of the WTO increased "from 78% to 99%" for developed countries and "from 22% to 72% for developing countries." See Jackson *et al.* (2002, p. 348). Similarly, the Agreement Establishing the WTO is famous for creating a "single package" where the old codes (as revised) and new substantive agreements were included as annexes to the agreement under a single institutional umbrella. Id., p. 219.

Table 1. Nature of complainant: developed or developing country[a]

Regime	Developed	Developing	Total
GATT	299	134	433
	69.05%	30.95%	100.00%
WTO	240	157	397
	60.45%	39.55%	100.00%

[a]This database covers all complaints filed through December 31, 2007. Country classifications as developed or developing are based on the WTO Dispute Settlement Database created for the World Bank by Henrik Horn and Petros C. Mavroidis ("Horn Database"), available at http://worldbank.org (search for "WTO Dispute Settlement Data Base") (last visited November 20, 2008); see also Chapter 1. For the purposes of this table, we have counted Korea as a developing country under the GATT and as a developed country under the WTO because its status has changed as it has developed over time. This categorization does not affect the central point highlighted by the table, since Korea was a complainant only once during the GATT. For GATT statistics, see Table 16 of the *World Trade Report* (2007), p. 269.

Table 2. Nature of defendant: developed or developing country[a]

Regime	Developed	Developing	Total
GATT	395	37	432
	91.44%	8.56%	100.00%
WTO	246	151	397
	61.96%	38.04%	100.00%

[a]This database covers all complaints filed through December 31, 2007. Country classifications as developed or developing are based on the Horn Database. We have counted Korea as a developing country under the GATT and as a developed country under the WTO due to its change in status over time. If Korea were considered a developed country under the GATT, the change would not affect the point highlighted by the table, since Korea was a respondent only four times during the GATT. For GATT statistics, see Table 18 of the *World Trade Report*, 2007, p. 271.

than they did under the GATT.[45] Correspondingly, they are relatively less likely to target complaints against developed countries.[46]

Smaller developing countries have also been less likely to defend their systemic interests within the WTO judicial system as third parties.

[45] Compare *World Trade Report* 175 (2003) ("Some 41 per cent of all complaints brought by developing countries since the entry into force of the WTO in 1995 have been directed against other developing countries, and this tendency has increased over the past years."). Although intra-developing country trade has increased, "more than two-thirds of intra-developing country trade originates and is destined to developing Asia." *World Trade Report* 25 (2003). These trade patterns are not replicated in dispute settlement patterns.

[46] Reinhardt documented earlier that developing countries are about "one-third less likely to file complaints against developed states under the WTO than they were under the post-1989 GATT regime." Unpublished manuscript cited in Busch and Reinhardt (2002), p. 467.

Table 3. Target of developing country complaints[a]

Regime	Developed	Developing	Total
GATT	123	5	128
	96.09%	3.91%	100.00%
WTO	84	73	158
	53.16%	46.84%	100.00%

[a]This database covers all complaints filed through December 31, 2007. Country classifications as developed or developing are based on the Horn Database. Korea has been counted as a developing country under the GATT and as a developed country under the WTO due to its change in status as it has developed over time. If Korea were considered a developed country under the GATT, the numbers would change only slightly and would not affect the analysis.

Once again, larger developing countries have increased their participation as third parties significantly in recent years. By December 31, 2007, thirteen developing countries had participated as a third party more than ten times, led by China (61), India (50), and Brazil (49).[47] Overall, however, most developing country members have never participated as either a party or third party in a WTO case.

The larger WTO members find that participation as a third party is important for them to keep abreast of WTO dispute settlement developments. A lawyer from a mid-sized developed country mission notes three primary reasons for participating as a third party.[48] First, an important procedural issue could arise affecting all future cases. Second, the interpretation of a point of substantive law could have implications for the country in future cases. Third, and perhaps most importantly, a country needs "to stay in touch with panel activity" in order to know how panels and the Appellate Body are working so that, when it has a complaint, it can tailor legal arguments and litigation strategies accordingly. WTO Appellate Body members and secretariat officials change over time. Just as in domestic litigation, a party needs to know the "institutional culture and personalities" of the judges and the tribunal.[49]

Finally, when developing countries have initiated complaints, their complaints have been less likely to result in favorable concessions than have those of developed countries. Importantly, Busch and Reinhardt have found that "the complainant's income (and, likewise, market size) has no effect on its prospects of winning a judgment, given that one is

---

[47] These figures are as of December 31, 2007. China has been proportionally quote active as a third party since it joined in December 2001.

[48] Author interview, Geneva, June 24, 2003.

[49] The quoted passages are excerpts from the interview.

going to be issued," suggesting that there is no statistically apparent political bias in the judicial system itself.[50] They likewise have found that "[a] rich complainant has no special advantage over a poor but equal-sized complainant in securing compliance from a defendant found in violation of WTO obligations," which can be explained, at least in part, by the non-compliance following a number of fully litigated U.S.–EC cases.[51]

However, Busch and Reinhardt found that developing countries have been less able to settle complaints advantageously during the consultation phase, which involves a significant percentage of WTO complaints, and ones that have triggered the greatest amount of market access concessions.[52] Their analysis showed that, overall, developed country complainants in WTO cases saw defendants fully liberalize disputed measures 74% of the time, compared to only 50% for developing country complainants (Busch and Reinhardt, 2003a). This discrepancy expanded significantly when one excludes the largest developing countries. Seventy-one percent of the cases in which developing countries benefited from full compliance involved complaints from the largest and wealthiest developing countries (Brazil, India, Korea, Singapore, Thailand, Mexico, Chile, and Argentina).[53] It is precisely in settlement negotiations after the filing of a complaint and before a WTO panel has issued a ruling that "rich complainants are much more likely to get defendants to concede...than poor complainants, holding GDP constant" (Busch and Reinhardt, 2003a).

These statistics suggest that developing countries are less able to convince a defendant of the eventual success of their case at any early stage and that a defendant may more likely drag out a legal case against a developing country plaintiff in order to impose legal costs that it is better positioned to absorb. Busch and Reinhardt maintain that "the WTO has exaggerated the gap between developed and developing complainants with respect to their ability to get defendants to liberalize disputed policies. In short, wealthy complainants have become significantly more likely to secure their desired outcomes under the WTO, but poorer complainants have not."[54] In other words, while developing countries have benefited

[50] See Busch and Reinhardt (2003a, pp. 719, 732). Compare Smith (2004, pp. 542, 568–569) (finding that the Appellate Body's "institutional interests, however, at times conflict with those of developing countries in the WTO, as these decisions on balance threaten to exacerbate existing inequalities, at least in the short term").

[51] Id., p. 732. Busch and Reinhardt note that greater concessions are obtained, on average, after a complaint is filed and before it is fully litigated, since full litigation indicates that a defendant may face severe domestic political constraints against modifying its trade restrictive national measures. Id., p. 474.

[52] They note that "the net effect of invoking adjudication, in the form of panel establishment, is to significantly increase the level of liberalization of disputed measures." Busch and Reinhardt (2002), p. 474. See also Busch and Reinhardt (2000, pp. 158, 162).

[53] Id., p. 726.

[54] Busch and Reinhardt (2003a), pp. 728–729.

from a legalized dispute settlement system, these studies suggest that they have been less able to obtain concessions than developed countries, whether the explanation is on account of legal capacity constraints or political considerations. This analysis further demonstrates the importance of bargaining effectively in the shadow of the WTO legal system.

5. Why smaller developing countries do not participate

Smaller developing countries are less likely to participate actively in WTO dispute settlement because of structural factors. On the benefit side, their exports are of a smaller aggregate value and variety, so that they have lower aggregate stakes in WTO complaints. In consequence, they will generally benefit less from a successful claim.[55] The WTO's weak remedies further reduce their incentives to initiate complaints. On the cost side, many developing countries have less effective governance systems, including less capacity to identify and pursue WTO complaints. I have previously identified the cost side factors in terms of the constraints of legal knowledge, financial endowment, and political power, or, more simply, of law, money, and politics.[56] These cost and benefit factors interact. Simply stated, for most developing countries, the prospective benefits from litigation are less likely to exceed the costs of litigation, including the economic and political costs.

Aggregate stakes matter most in the decision to file a complaint. A small developing country could have high *relative* stakes over a foreign trade restriction, so that WTO law could be of significant benefit to it. That is, a particular trade barrier could be of relative importance in relation to its total exports and economic production. In fact, a small developing country could have much higher relative stakes over a trade restriction in relation to its economy than the United States and EC. However, that country's case is likely to be of much smaller aggregate value. For example, in their study of U.S.–EC trade disputes, Busch and Reinhardt ranked a dispute that affects over US$ 150 million in annual trade as a "high stakes" dispute (Busch and Reinhardt, 2003b). However, a $150 million dollar claim only represented about .0015% of U.S. gross domestic product at that time (2001). A claim of comparable importance for Honduras would equal around US$ 255,000 dollars.[57] Honduras is not even a "least-developed country," and, not

---

[55] See the data in Nordstrom and Shaffer (2008).

[56] See Shaffer (2006, p. 177). The structural factors include internal governance challenges in many developing countries. See discussion in Shaffer *et al.* (2008).

[57] In 2001, the United States gross domestic product (GDP) equaled approximately US$ 10.1 trillion. In 2000, Senegal's GDP was about $16.2 billion, and Honduras' approximately 17 billion, in terms of purchasing power parity, such that a "high value" claim under Busch and Reinhardt's criteria, respectively, would equal from around $240,000 to $255,000 for these countries. See *CIA World Factbook*, available at https://www.cia.gov/library/publications/download/download-2001/index.html. U.S. GDP rose to 11.5 trillion dollars in 2003 and to

surprisingly, only one least-developed country (Bangladesh) had even filed a WTO complaint as of December 31, 2007. Even for relatively larger developing countries such as Peru, Malaysia, and Egypt, although a comparable "high stakes" claim would be valued at around US$ 2–4 million, respectively, the risk of procedural delays, loss, and non-compliance would significantly discount the case's value.[58] In short, Peru Malaysia, and Egypt will tend not to bring claims that are considered to be of "high stakes" for the United States and Europe, but only claims that affect a much larger percentage of their gross domestic products.

Legal costs have an invariant component that does not vary with the size of the complaint.[59] If the system is sufficiently complex to require a developing country to hire a foreign outside law firm in order to litigate effectively, the attorney's fees would likely cost at least US $400,000, and possibly much more.[60] In the case *Chile—Price Band System and Safeguard Measures relating to Certain Agricultural Products*, the Association of Argentine Edible Oil Industries (known by its Spanish acronym as CIARA) paid a law firm US $400,000 just to write the brief "for providing a first draft of the demand and being available for specific consultations," even though this limited legal work was found to be "less useful than expected."[61] Many claims, such as Brazil's against U.S. cotton subsidies, have resulted in significantly greater legal costs. In the cotton case, it is stated that Brazil's cotton trade association faced legal fees of around U.S. $2,000,000.[62] U.S. and EC-based multinational firms

---

11.75 trillion dollars in 2004, so that such a high stakes claim would constitute only .0013% of U.S. GDP in those years.

[58] Peru's GDP was around $123 billion, Malaysia's around $212 billion, and Egypt's around $258 million based on purchasing power parity. See *CIA World Factbook*, available at https://www.cia.gov/library/publications/download/download-2001/index.html.

[59] See further discussion in Nordstrom and Shaffer (2008).

[60] Litigation at the international level involves a distant forum in which legal expertise tends to be U.S. and Euro-centric, highly specialized, and expensive. In 2003, it was stated that complainants can face fees ranging from $300 to $600 or more an hour when they hire private law firms to advise and represent them in WTO cases. Confirmed in e-mail messages from two Washington DC trade lawyers, January 15 and Januray 18, 2003, and subsequent discussions, and these figures are rising. In 2001, Michalopoulos cited a figure of "$250–1000 an hour." Michalopoulos, (2001). See also Nordstrom and Shaffer (2008).

[61] See Tussie and Delich (2004). The case may be found at *Chile—Price Band System and Safeguard Measures relating to certain Agricultural Products*, Report of the Panel, WT/DS207. "To select the law firm, the [Foreign Affairs] Ministry suggested a list of three out of which CIARA picked one." CIARA also provided its own expertise, as did the Institute for International Agricultural Negotiations, or INIA, the think tank funded by the Argentine agribusiness sector. Id.

[62] Author interview, July 20, 2005 (noting a figure of $2 million). See Becker (2004, pp. C1, 7) ("the litigation has already cost $1 million"). As for the fees in the Brazilian cotton case, author interview with lawyers and trade association representatives in Sao Paulo, Brazil, April 2004 (referring to attorney fee estimates of between US$ 1–2 million dollars). Similarly, Indonesia's legal fees in the U.S. and European challenge to its national car program also

are willing to pay much more. In the U.S.–EC Boeing-Airbus dispute, it is estimated that fees were running at $1,000,000 per month and could reach $20,000,000 for each company if the case is not settled. Each company had hired a major U.S. law firm to represent it so as to provide the respective U.S. and EC trade authorities with maximum assistance to defend their commercial interests, including outside statistical analyses of the subsidies and their impact.[63]

The Advisory Centre on WTO Law enables developing countries to participate at subsidized rates and has represented an important development for the system (Shaffer, 2006). Yet, a country still needs legal capacity to provide the factual background and other back-up support necessary for the Advisory Centre or an outside law firm to litigate a case effectively. Those cases that are most factually-intensive brought by developing countries, and in particular the *US-cotton* and *EC-sugar* cases, involved Brazil's hiring of a U.S. law firm and U.S. and Brazilian economic consultants, respectively.[64]

The internal costs of identifying and supporting an individual case can be higher for a developing country because of economies of scale and scope. Since developing countries export a narrower array and smaller value of exports, they are less likely to have experience in WTO litigation. They are less likely, in socio-legal terms, to be "repeat players." Because they do not litigate multiple cases, as do larger countries, they do not benefit from economies of scale and scope when mobilizing resources for a single case. As a result, internal support costs in a single case should be higher for a developing country. In addition, a poor country must consider the greater opportunity costs confronting it on account of its scarce resources.

Legal expenses have been rising for all WTO members on account of the growing complexity of WTO jurisprudence. The WTO's more contextualized, case-specific jurisprudence has arguably increased the demand on lawyer time. To the extent that WTO panels and the WTO Appellate Body require higher standards of proof which involve greater use of statistical trade data as opposed to legal presumptions, legal costs will continue to rise. Interestingly, when members of the U.S. Congress expressed concern that Brazil's case could lead other countries to challenge U.S. agricultural subsidies, some analysts responded that there was little to fear. They concluded that the required legal fees would constitute "a sum that is prohibitive for the poor nations that suffer the most harm from cheap subsidized imports" (Becker, 2004).

---

allegedly rose to around $1,000,000 through the panel stage. Discussion with a lawyer in Geneva, February 7, 2003. However, Indonesia's fees in the auto case allegedly were not paid in full when the Suharto government fell in the wake of the Asian financial crisis. Discussion with former WTO secretariat member, February 12, 2003.

[63] Author interview with private attorney, July 20, 2005.

[64] See Shaffer *et al.* (2008).

In sum, the factors of trading stakes and the various costs of litigation are interrelated. As two socio-legal scholars write regarding domestic litigation, "[a]s costs rise, so does the threshold at which litigation becomes worthwhile" (Friedman and Percival, 1976). In the WTO context, simply put, the benefits for most developing countries to bring a case are less likely to exceed the threshold of litigation costs that make bringing a case worthwhile. Similarly, where the affected private sector in a developing country could finance the lawsuit, the potential benefits are less likely to justify the litigation costs, compared to the benefits for U.S. and European companies and trade associations. It is for this reason that 95 of the WTO's 120 non-OECD members have never filed a WTO complaint.[65]

6. Conclusions

To understand the operation of the WTO dispute settlement system, analysts need to engage in socio-legal and economic analysis. In particular, analysts need to assess how the legal system's design and jurisprudence affect participation and thus who defines what the law means over time. Analysts likewise need to assess how design and jurisprudential choices shape parties' relative abilities to bargain in the law's shadow, affecting economic outcomes for individual firms and for countries' terms of trade.

As any legal system, the WTO is far from perfect. It is subject to severe challenges for smaller and poorer members. Yet forsaking such law will not rid the world of systemic disadvantages either. A world without a legalized dispute settlement system for trade conflicts is beset by greater power imbalances. Critics of the WTO's legalized trade dispute settlement system only need to recall the use of more unilateral mechanisms in the years preceding its creation. WTO law can provide leverage to less powerful countries to ward off the threats of the more powerful.

The key issue is how countries should adapt to the legal system, on the one hand, and how the system's rules could be modified or jurisprudentially applied so as to reduce structural disadvantages, on the other. A central goal of the chapter is to provoke consideration of alternative choices in WTO dispute settlement. They include changes in WTO dispute settlement design that involve less legalization (such as the adoption of simplified procedures for smaller claims or claims between smaller countries),[66] or more legalization (such as the provision of stronger

---

[65] See Friedman and Percival (1976).

[66] One option is to create a distinct small claims procedure for smaller developing countries. In an article with Hakan Nordstrom, we show how the addition of a small claims procedure could benefit WTO members with small trade stakes. Depending on its design, such a procedure could enhance the system's equity and efficiency, without inflicting greater net political costs on government officials from a political economy perspective. See Nordstrom and Shaffer (2008).

remedies which will facilitate the use of outside law firms and their financing by private industry).[67] They also include key jurisprudential choices over rules of evidence, burden of proof, and the setting of clear rules or general (more fuzzy) standards that are more costly to litigate on a case-by-case basis. These design and jurisprudential choices all involve complex tradeoffs that entail imperfect institutional alternatives.[68]

Smaller and poorer countries also need to examine strategies for mobilizing legal resources that do not involve a change in dispute settlement rules. They need to do so since the WTO legal system will likely not be significantly changed and, in any case, lies outside of their control except through their use of it. This crucial issue of cost-effective strategies for mobilizing legal capacity to shape and benefit from WTO law is a separate subject.[69] Speaking generally, if developing countries are to participate meaningfully in the WTO dispute settlement system, they will need to continue to increase institutional capacity and coordination of trade policy at multiple levels, from the national to the regional to the global. They will need, in particular, to develop their own coordinative mechanisms to include private sector and civil society representatives. Capacity building endeavors generally will be most sustainable if they permeate broadly throughout institutions and societies.[70]

Since developing countries face different contexts, there is no single strategy that fits all of them. Exporting legal strategies across cultures regardless of context has never worked.[71] Each country will need to determine how best to adapt the strategies that this chapter explores in light of its particular circumstances. Many countries already have adopted many of them to a varying extent. The chapter's central purpose is to highlight options and provoke imaginative debate and experimentation with strategies that developing countries and their constituencies may adopt to better defend themselves in the international trading system.

Acknowledgements

My thanks to Jim Hartigan and Alec Stone Sweet for their comments on different versions of this article, as well as to participants at the WTO at 10 meetings in Sao Paulo, Brazil, and Cairo, Egypt, and workshops at the

[67] These choices include retrospective and monetary remedies, among others. See Shaffer (2003b, pp. 1–65).

[68] The phrase imperfect alternatives is used by Neil Komesar (1994) (a book calling for assessment of policy in terms of its likely handling by alternative institutions – be they courts, legislatures or markets – in which different parties will be better, or less well, represented).

[69] See Shaffer (2006) and Shaffer (2008) (regarding Brazil).

[70] If the focus of capacity building remains on individual capacity instead of larger societal and institutional capacity, then countries could simply be training individuals whose objectives and career paths are unpredictable. See Shaffer (2005).

[71] See, e.g., Trubek and Galanter (1974, p. 1062).

University of Wisconsin and Yale Law Schools and at an "International Dialogue on WTO Dispute Settlement Mechanism: Experience Sharing Among Developing Countries" in Beijing, China, where different versions of this chapter were presented. My thanks also to Kristin Bohl, Matt Fortin, Brian Larson, and Kyle Shamberg for their research assistance.

References

Abbott, K., Keohane, R., Moravcsik, A., Slaughter, A.-M., Snidal, D. (2000), The concept of legalization. *International Organization* 54 (3), 17–35.

Bagwell, K., Staiger, R. (2002), *The Economics of the World Trading System*. MIT Press, Cambridge, Mass.

Becker, E. (2004), Lawmakers Voice Doom and Gloom on W.T.O. Ruling, New York Times, April 28, pp. C1, 7.

Blonigen, B., Bown, C. (2003), Antidumping and retaliation threats. *Journal of International Economics* 60 (2), 249–273.

Bown, C. (2004a), Developing countries as plaintiffs and defendants in GATT/WTO trade disputes. *The World Economy* 27 (1), 59–80.

Bown, C. (2004b), On the economic success of GATT/WTO dispute settlement. *The Review of Economics and Statistics* 86 (3), 811–823.

Bown, C. (2005), Participation in WTO dispute settlement: complainants, interested parties and free riders. *World Bank Economic Review* 19 (2), 287–310.

Busch, M., Reinhardt, E. (2000), Bargaining in the shadow of the law: early settlement in GATT/WTO disputes. *Fordham International Law Journal* 24 (1, 2), 158–172.

Busch, M., Reinhardt, E. (2002), Testing international trade law: empirical studies of GATT/WTO dispute settlement. In: Kennedy, D., Southwick, J. (Eds.), *The Political Economy of International Trade Law: Essays in Honor Robert Hudec*. Cambridge University Press, Cambridge, pp. 457–481.

Busch, M., Reinhardt, E. (2003a), Developing countries and general agreement on tariffs and trade/world trade organization dispute settlement. *Journal of World Trade* 37 (4), 719–735.

Busch, M., Reinhardt, E. (2003b), Transatlantic trade conflicts and GATT/WTO dispute settlement. In: Petersmann, E.-U. (Ed.), *Transatlantic Economic Disputes: The EU, the US, and the WTO*. Oxford University Press, Oxford, pp. 465–486.

Busch, M., Reinhardt, E., Shaffer, G. (2008a), Does legal capacity matter? Explaining patterns of protectionism in the shadow of WTO litigation (February 1, 2008). Available at http://papers.ssrn.com/sol3/papers.cfm?abstract_id = 1091435.

Busch, M., Raciborski, R., Reinhardt, E. (2008b), Does the rule of law matter? The WTO and US antidumping investigations (May 14, 2008). Available at http://userwww.service.emory.edu/Berein/research/AD.pdf.

Cortese, C. (1966), A study in knowledge and attitudes toward the law: the legal knowledge inventory. *Rocky Mountain Social Science Journal* 3, 192–204.

Davey, W.J. (2003), The WTO dispute settlement mechanism, June 25. Illinois Public Law Research Paper No. 03-08.

Francois, J., Horn, H. (2008), Trading profiles and developing country participation in the WTO dispute settlement system (Research Institute of Industrial Economics Paper No. 730). Available at http://ideas.repec.org/p/hhs/iuiwop/0730.html.

Friedman, L., Percival, R. (1976), A tale of two courts: litigation in Alameda and San Benito counties. *Law and Society Review* 10 (2), 267–301.

Galanter, M. (1974), Why the haves come out ahead: speculations on the limits of legal change. *Law and Society Review* 9 (1), 95–160.

Galanter, M. (1984), Worlds of deals: using negotiation to teach about legal process. *Journal of Legal Education* 34 (2), 268–276.

Galanter, M. (2001), Contract in court; or almost everything you may or may not want to know about contract litigation. *Wisconsin Law Review* 2001 (3), 577–627.

Galanter, M. (2004), The vanishing trial: an examination of trials and related matters in federal and state courts. *Journal of Empirical Legal Studies* 1 (3), 459–570.

Guzman, A., Simmons, B. (2005), Power plays and capacity constraints: the selection of defendants in WTO disputes. *Journal of Legal Studies* 34 (2), 557–598.

Hoekman, B., Kostecki, M., (2001), *The Political Economy of the World Trading System,* second ed. Oxford University Press, Oxford.

Horn, H., Nordstrom, H., Mavroidis, P. (1999), Is the use of the WTO dispute settlement system biased? CEPR Discussion Paper 2340.

Jackson, J., Davey, W., Sykes, A. (2002), *Legal Problems of International Economic Relations: Cases, Materials and Text*, fourth ed., p. 348.

Jacob, H. (1992), The elusive shadow of the law. *Law and Society Review* 26 (3), 565–590.

Komesar, N. (1994), *Imperfect Alternatives: Choosing Institutions in Law, Economics and Public Policy*. University of Chicago Press, Chicago.

Kritzer, H. (1991), *Let's Make a Deal: Understanding the Negotiation Process in Ordinary Litigation 73–75, 103–104, 132–133*. University of Wisconsin Press, Madison.

Lam, E. (2005), Taxation U.S. appeals WTO ruling that jobs act's continued export breaks are noncompliant. *International Trade Reporter* 22 (46), 1883, November 24.

Leitner, K., Lester, S. (2003), WTO dispute settlement 1995–2002: a statistical analysis. *Journal of International Economic Law* 6 (1), 251–253.

Leitner, K., Lester, S. (2005), WTO dispute settlement 1995–2004: a statistical analysis. *Journal of International Economic Law* 8 (1), 231–244.

Leitner, K., Lester, S. (2008), WTO dispute settlement 1995–2007 – a statistical analysis. *Journal of International Economic Law* 11 (1), 179–192.

Macaulay, S. (2003), The real and the paper deal: empirical pictures of relationships, complexity and the urge for transparent simple rules. *The Modern Law Review* 66 (1), 44–79.

Michalopoulos, C. (2001), *Developing Countries in the WTO 94*. Palgrave, Houndmills, Basingstoke, Hampshire.

Milner, H. (1997), *Interests, Institutions and Information: Domestic Politics and International Relations*. Princeton University Press, Princeton.

Mnookin, R., Kornhauser, L. (1979), Bargaining in the shadow of the law: the case of divorce. *Yale Law Journal* 88 (5), 950–997.

Nordstrom, H., Shaffer, G. (2008), Access to justice in the WTO: the case for a small claims tribunal. *World Trade Review* 7 (4), 587–640.

Nottage, H. (2008), Trade and development. In: Bethlehem, D., McRae, D., Neufeld, R., Van Damme, I. (Eds.), *Oxford Handbook of International Trade Law*. Oxford University Press, Oxford.

Parlin, C. (2000), Operation of consultations, deterrence, and mediation. *Law and Policy in International Business* 31 (3), 565–572.

Porges, A. (2003), Settling WTO disputes: what do litigation models tell us? *Ohio State Journal on Dispute Resolution* 19 (1), 141–184.

Pruzin, D. (2000), European Commission News Release on Request to WTO Compliance Panel for Imposition of Sanctions in US, FSC Dispute, with Indicative Product List. *International Trade Reporter (BNA)*, vol. 17, November 23, p. 1792.

Pruzin, D. (2002), WTO Gives EU Green Light in Sanctions against United States over FSCs. *International Trade Reporter (BNA)*, vol. 19, September 5, p. 1484.

Pruzin, D. (2004), WTO Issues Two Rulings Favoring U.S. in Lumber CVD/AD Spats with Canada. *International Trade Reporter (BNA)* 21 (4), 116, January 22.

Rose, A. (2004), Do you really know that the WTO increases trade. *American Economic Review* 94 (1), 98–114.

Schwartz, W., Sykes, A. (2002), The economic structure of renegotiation and dispute settlement in the World Trade Organization. *Journal of Legal Studies* 31 (S1), S179–S204.

Shaffer, G. (2003a), *Defending Interests: Public–Private Partnerships in WTO Litigation*. Brookings Institution Press, Washington, DC.

Shaffer, G., (2003b), How to make the WTO dispute settlement system work for developing countries: some proactive developing country strategies. ICTSD Monograph, Geneva, pp. 1–65, March. Available at http://www.ictsd.org/pubs/ictsd_series/resource_papers/DSU_2003.pdf.

Shaffer, G. (2005), Can WTO technical assistance and capacity building serve developing countries? *Wisconsin International Law Journal* 23 (4), 643–686.

Shaffer, G. (2006), The challenges of WTO law: strategies for developing country adaptation. *World Trade Review* 5 (2), 177–198.

Shaffer, G., Sanchez, M.R., Rosenberg, B. (2008), Winning at the WTO: what lies behind Brazil's success. *Cornell International Law Journal* 41, 383–501.

Smith, J. (2004), Inequality in international trade? Developing countries and WTO dispute settlement. *Review of International Political Economy* 11 (3), 542–573.

Staiger, R., Tabellini, G. (1999), Do GATT rules help governments make domestic commitments? *Economics and Politics* 11 (2), 109–144.

Stone Sweet, A. (1999), Judicialization and the construction of governance. *Comparative Political Studies* 31, 147–184.

Tomz, M., Goldstein, J., Rivers, D. (2007), Institutions in international relations: understanding the effects of the GATT and the WTO on world trade. *International Organizations* 61, 37–67.

Trubek, D., Galanter, M. (1974), Scholars in self-estrangement: some reflections on the crisis in law and development studies in the United States. *Wisconsin Law Review* 1974 (4), 1062–1102.

Trubek, D., Sarat, S., Felstiner, W., Kritzer, H., Grossman, J. (1983), The costs of ordinary litigation. *UCLA Law Review* 31 (1), 72–127.

Tussie, D., Delich, V. (2004), The political economy of dispute settlement: a case from Argentina. Available at http://www.iadb.org/intal/aplicaciones/uploads/ponencias/Curso_BID-INTAL-OMC_2006_09_12_DIANATUSSIE1.pdf.

UN Comtrade Yearbook. (2006), Special Table A: total imports and exports by regions and countries or areas. Available at http://comtrade.un.org/pb/FileFetch.aspx?docID 1/4 1940 &type 1/4 special%20tables.

Wilson, B. (2008), WTO legal affairs division, WTO update: the dispute settlement understanding system. Address to the Washington International Trade Association (May 2). Available at http://www.wita.org/index.php?tg 1/4 posts&idx 1/4 List&forum 1/43&thread 1/4 99&views 1/4 1.

WTO. (2004), The future of the WTO: addressing institutional challenges in the new millennium. Report of the Consultative Board to the Director-General Supachai Panitchpakdi 51 (World Trade Organization).

CHAPTER 8

Why Are So Many WTO Disputes Abandoned?☆

Kara M. Reynolds

Department of Economics, American University, 4400 Massachusetts Avenue NW, Washington, DC 20016, USA
E-mail address: reynolds@american.edu

Abstract
Previous research on the success of the WTO dispute-settlement system may miscalculate the true benefits of the dispute process due to the nature of the datasets used. Approximately 33 percent of all disputes filed at the WTO are classified as pending or inactive and thus omitted from most studies. Further investigation reveals that many of these inactive cases were actually settled by the countries involved or considered in a similar WTO dispute, and, as a result, no further WTO action was taken. This suggests that the WTO dispute settlement process may be more effective in resolving disputes than otherwise thought. For those disputes not successfully resolved, I empirically estimate why countries may choose to initiate WTO dispute settlement action but fail to follow through, thus allowing the offending party to continue with the alleged WTO illegal activities. The results suggest that developing countries are less likely to resolve their complaints in the WTO dispute settlement system, a troubling implication for the equity of the system.

Keyword: WTO dispute settlement

JEL classifications: F13, K33

1. Introduction

When implemented in 1995, supporters heralded the World Trade Organization's (WTO) Dispute Settlement Understanding (DSU) as a

☆This project was supported by the National Research Initiative of the Cooperative State Research, Education and Extension Service, USDA, Grant #2005-35400-15849.

Frontiers of Economics and Globalization
Volume 6 ISSN: 1574-8715
DOI: 10.1108/S1574-8715(2009)0000006011

giant leap forward for the international trading system. Peter Sutherland, the director general of the General Agreements on Tariffs and Trade at the time said "the whole future of the WTO is inextricably bound up with the success of the dispute-settlement system," adding that the new system provided an assurance that countries would live up to their obligations under all current and future multilateral trade agreements (Zaracostas, 1994). Unfortunately, it is still unclear to what degree countries have lived up to their WTO obligations under the new dispute settlement procedures. Although Busch and Reinhardt (2003) note that countries failed to change their supposed non-WTO compliant laws in one-third of the 154 dispute settlement cases resolved between 1995 and 2000, countries only requested compensation for this non-compliance in 18 of these cases.

Moreover, most researchers compile the statistics used to analyze the success of the WTO dispute settlement process using only a small subset of the total number of disputes brought before the WTO. For example, although Busch and Reinhardt (2003) compile compliance statistics on the 154 disputes resolved between 1995 and 2000, in fact there were 219 disputes brought before the WTO during this time period.[1] Similarly, recent research has noted that many disputes are settled early, pointing to statistics that panels are established in only about half of all disputes initiated at the WTO. However, these researchers gloss over the fact that of those disputes that fail to result in a panel, the WTO is apprised of a settlement in only 25 percent of these cases. In fact, of the 324 disputes brought to the WTO between 1995 and 2004, 33 percent are still classified as pending, with no resolution in sight.

So what has happened to these disputes? Why are so many disputes apparently abandoned during the WTO dispute settlement process? Logic suggests a number of possible explanations. For example, it may be the case that the parties to the dispute have actually reached a settlement but failed to inform the WTO, although the DSU specifically states that "mutually agreed solutions to matters formally raised under the [dispute settlement process] shall be notified to the [Dispute Settlement Body]."[2] It may be equally likely that the complaining countries have failed to follow up on their initial complaints because they realize that the issues in question had little merit or because they lacked the resources or knowledge to move forward in the process.[3] The former may be more likely if the

---

[1] The dispute settlement process is initiated when a complainant country requests consultations with another WTO member over a particular trade policy complaint. If consultations fail, the complainant may request the formation of a dispute settlement panel after 60 days.

[2] There are no penalties specified for failure to notify the WTO regarding a settlement agreement.

[3] The DSU urges countries to "exercise its judgment as to whether action under the procedures would be fruitful" before bringing a case.

complainant files the dispute to retaliate for some earlier action by the defendant country or to harass the defendant country. The later possibility has particularly troubling implications for the equity of the dispute settlement process for developing countries.

Because WTO members are currently negotiating changes to improve dispute settlement procedures, it is important for policy makers to completely understand the current system's strengths and weaknesses. This research analyzes the disputes brought before the WTO in an effort to determine whether the large number of unresolved disputes are a sign of strength or weakness of the system. If, for example, most of the non-resolved cases have actually resulted in settlements between disputing countries, then the WTO system may be more successful in peaceful resolution than currently thought. Similarly, if the unresolved cases are primarily harassment complaints – or complaints without legal merit that are brought solely to extract concessions from trading partners – then the fact that these cases are unresolved is unsurprising. If disputes remain unresolved because developing countries lack the resources or knowledge to move forward in the dispute process, however, then the large number of unresolved cases may be indicative of a serious bias in the system against the developing world.

The paper proceeds as follows. Section 2 reviews the current WTO dispute settlement process, while Section 3 provides an overview of current research on dispute settlement, focusing on previous studies that analyze the outcomes of cases brought before the WTO. Section 4 summarizes the outcome of dispute settlement cases filed at the WTO between 1995 and 2004, paying particular attention to those cases that have apparently failed to be resolved. Sections 5 and 6 describe the data used in, and results from, an empirical estimation of what factors are significant determinants of whether a dispute is abandoned during the WTO dispute settlement process. Section 7 concludes.

2. *WTO dispute settlement procedures*

Although the General Agreement on Tariffs and Trade has included dispute settlement procedures since its inception in 1947, these procedures have changed dramatically over the years. The current system was first conceptualized in the 1979 Understanding on Dispute Settlement, but was strengthened by both the 1989 Dispute Settlement Procedure Improvements Agreement and, most recently, the 1994 DSU. The discussion below outlines current WTO procedures, while noting major changes made since the 1979 Understanding.

The Dispute Settlement Body (DSB), a body made up of ambassadors from all WTO member governments, administers the rules and procedures of the 1994 DSU. The dispute settlement process begins when a complainant country requests consultations with another WTO member over a particular trade policy issue. According to Parlin (2000), this request often follows unsuccessful efforts to resolve the dispute through bilateral diplomatic efforts. The consultation request must identify the measures of the other member that are being challenged and provide at least some indication of the WTO provisions that the member has allegedly violated. Although most requests are made by a single member, WTO regulations do allow for complaints by multiple members. Moreover, third parties with a substantial trade interest in the dispute can request to participate in the consultations and all subsequent actions. The respondent country, or defendant, must respond to the request within 10 days and must begin the consultations within 30 days.

If the consultations fail to produce a mutually satisfactory agreement, any of the complaining parties may file a request with the DSB for the establishment of a dispute settlement panel.[4] Although the 1979 agreement allowed the defendant to block the formation of a panel, both the 1989 Dispute Settlement Procedure Improvements Agreement and the 1994 DSU give complainants the right to a panel unless all DSB members decide by consensus not to establish a panel. Panels are made up of three to five "well-qualified" government and non-government officials from countries other than those parties to the dispute. The WTO maintains a list of eligible panelists.

Current regulations specify that the panel should attempt to issue a report within six months and must issue its report within nine months.[5] Although the 1989 agreement continued to allow a single country to block the adoption of a panel report, one of the major improvements of the 1994 DSU requires the DSB to adopt panel reports within 20–60 days after its circulation unless the DSB decides by consensus not to adopt the report or a party to the dispute formally notifies the body of its decision to appeal the decision.

If the decision is appealed, the WTO Appellate Body must review the decision and produce its report within no more than 90 days. The Appellate Body is a permanent, seven-member board established by the DSB. Members serve four-year terms and must be experts in the field of law and international trade and unaffiliated with any government. The Appellate Body report must be adopted by the DSB within 30 days of circulation unless the body as a whole decides against adoption.

A second major improvement of the 1994 DSU strengthened the enforcement capabilities of the WTO. If applicable, the defendant must

[4] A panel may be established in less than 60 days if both parties agree that consultations have failed. The complainant can alternatively use alternative dispute settlement procedures such as mediation, but few members have utilized these alternative measures.

[5] The DSU includes a shortened timeline for "urgent" cases, typically those that involve perishable products.

inform the DSB of its intentions to implement the panel or Appellate Body recommendations and rulings at a DSB meeting within 30 days of the adoption of the panel or Appellate Body report. Members are given a reasonable amount of time to implement the recommendations, typically a period proposed by the member and approved by the DSB, a period mutually agreed upon by the parties of the dispute, or a period determined through binding arbitration. The DSU specifies that this reasonable amount of time should not exceed 15 months, unless all parties involved in the dispute agree upon a longer time. Should the member fail to implement the recommendations within the agreed upon time, the complaining party has the right to compensation. If the parties to the dispute cannot agree upon compensation, then the complaining party can request permission from the DSB to suspend concessions equivalent to the level of nullification or impairment, as determined by an arbitrator.[6]

Members agreed to conduct a review of the DSU by December 31, 1999. The DSB began their review in 1997; during the review many members expressed dissatisfaction with the agreement and proposed changes to improve the process. For example, Hungary and Japan proposed strengthening the consultation process by requiring at least two consultation meetings, while the United States suggested shortening the consultation process. However, WTO members could not reach a consensus by the 1999 deadline. Instead, in November 2001, WTO members agreed to improve and clarify the DSU during the Doha Ministerial Conference. These negotiations, which are unrelated to the larger negotiations on the Doha Round, continue without a deadline. Negotiators are considering, among other things, third-party rights, panel composition, time-savings, and transparency. Before reaching an agreement, however, negotiators should consider outcomes under current dispute settlement procedures and, particularly, why so many cases are abandoned.

3. Literature review

Filings and outcomes of dispute settlement cases at both the GATT and the WTO have been of interest to a number of researchers. In particular, three primary questions have emerged in the previous literature. Obviously, the determinants of the actual policy outcomes of disputes and, in particular, the level of concessions made by the defendant are of primary interest to many researchers. However, this research is more closely tied to two questions regarding the filing and escalation of

---

[6] The WTO defines "nullification and impairment" as damage to a complainant country's benefits from its WTO membership due to another country's failure to carry out its WTO obligations.

disputes: what determines whether a country brings a complaint to the GATT/WTO dispute settlement system and why are countries able to settle some disputes while others escalate to a dispute settlement panel ruling.[7]

Previous research indicates that a number of country-specific factors significantly impact the likelihood of a country filing a dispute with the WTO. For example, Reinhardt (2001a) finds that democracies initiate, and are targeted in, more disputes than other countries, particularly developing countries. His estimates also indicate that countries that have a high degree of trade reliance on the defendant country are more likely to initiate disputes and that countries appear to retaliate against those countries that have initiated disputes against them in the past by initiating their own disputes. Bown (2004) specifically looks at country's decisions to bring antidumping cases to the WTO dispute settlement system and finds that the size of the economic market in the defendant country as well as the complainant's capacity to retaliate using DSU-authorized sanctions significantly impact the likelihood of bringing a dispute to the WTO. Using all dispute settlement cases, Bown (2005) finds that the size of exports at stake due to the WTO-inconsistent policy significantly impacts the decision to participate in dispute settlement; however, the country's retaliatory and legal capacity as well as its political–economic relationship with the defendant country also matters.

A number of papers have attempted to investigate why so many dispute settlements under both the GATT and the WTO are settled, particularly in light of the fact that GATT has little enforcement power.[8] Reinhardt (2001b), for example, develops a theoretical model in which the defendant wants to avoid retaliation by the complainant and thus often concedes before a panel ruling with a settlement offer that may be less costly than the potential result if the case proceeds to a panel.

Using disputes filed under the GATT 1947 agreement, Busch (2000) estimates the determinants of the probability of requesting a formal dispute settlement panel, as well as the probability of the defendant offering concessions at the consultation stage and at the panel stage. The author is particularly interested in whether the 1989 improvements to the GATT dispute settlement process, in which the defendant could no longer block the formation of a panel, resulted in more concessions and whether democratic regimes are more likely to request a panel or offer concessions. He finds, surprisingly, that the 1989 improvements had little

---

[7] Although this literature review includes only a subset of the studies most pertinent to this research, Busch and Reinhardt (2002) provides a more comprehensive overview of this research.

[8] Recall that although the 1994 DSU strengthened the enforcement capabilities of the system, countries still have the option to ignore WTO panel rulings although they may face retaliatory measures.

impact on the dispute settlement process. Democratic countries are more likely to offer concessions before the formation of a panel and more likely to request a formal panel should bargaining fail. Busch also finds that the likelihood of concessions falls with the number of complainants in a particular case and the level of openness of the defendant. Moreover, cases brought by developing countries are more likely to result in a formal panel, while the probability of concessions made at the panel stage falls with the ratio of the complainant's to the defendant's bilateral trade dependence. Busch and Reinhardt (2003) also find that developing countries are less likely to reach a settlement in their disputes, which is one reason why these countries are less likely to secure concessions from the defendant. They conclude that developing countries are less able to argue legal points during the consultation phase, thus failing to signal that the issue will be pushed to a successful conclusion at a dispute settlement panel.

Guzman and Simmons (2002) argue that settlement will be more difficult when the nature of the dispute is discontinuous. In other words, if the dispute centers around an issue in which the only possible settlement offer is complete compitulation on the part of the defendant, high transaction costs will prevent a settlement. The authors test this hypothesis using an empirical model similar to that used in Reinhardt (2001a) and Busch and Reinhardt (2003) and find democratic countries are less likely to settle disputes of this discontinuous nature, although the nature of the dispute does not seem to retard the ability of non-democratic countries from reaching a settlement. Most recently, Busch and Reinhardt (2006) find that the inclusion of third parties in the consultation phase makes early settlement less likely. The result supports the authors' theories that third parties increase the bargaining costs during consultations, thus disputes are more likely to end in a panel ruling. The inclusion of third parties does significantly influence the final outcome of panel decisions. The authors also find that settlement is likely in disputes between the United States and European Union, and the probability of reaching a settlement increases with the size of the defendant's economy. Finally, politically sensitive cases are less likely to be settled.

Although the research described earlier claims to investigate why some countries are able to settle their trade disputes, in fact the dependent variable used in the empirical analysis is whether a WTO dispute settlement panel released a ruling. In other words, the research implicitly assumes that countries reached mutually satisfactory settlements in all disputes that failed to reach the panel ruling stage.[9] An analysis of the

[9] Specifically, Guzman and Simmons (2002) define any case that had been pending for more than three years as "settled."

Table 1. Outcome of WTO dispute settlement cases, 1995–2004

	Number	Percentage of total
Total cases filed	324	100.0
Cases with no further action	107	33.0
Cases settled before establishment of panel	43	13.3
Cases withdrawn	8	2.5
Panel established	166	51.2
Settled before panel report circulated	37	11.4
Panel report adopted	129	39.8

outcomes of actual disputes filed at the WTO between 1995 and 2004 reveals that this might not be the case.

4. WTO disputes, 1995–2004

As noted earlier, between 1995 and 2004 WTO members formally requested consultations in 324 disputes. As can be seen in Table 1, a panel was established in slightly more than half of these cases. Many researchers have concluded from this fact that the WTO dispute settlement process is particularly successful in encouraging countries to settle their agreements.[10] In fact, countries reported reaching mutually acceptable settlement agreements before the release of a panel report in nearly 25 percent of all disputes initiated between 1995 and 2004. However, of more interest to this research is the fact that countries have failed to report a resolution of 33 percent of all disputes; yet they have also taken no further action by requesting a formal dispute settlement panel.

Countries may still be negotiating the outcomes of some of these disputes. Recall, however, that countries are allowed to request the formation of a panel after 60 days of consultations. Moreover, of those cases either settled before the establishment of the panel or in which a panel was established, the average number of days before one of these actions occurred was 447 days, slightly more than one year.[11] As Figure 1 illustrates, the cases that remain unresolved are distributed fairly evenly between 1995 and 2004. It seems unlikely that countries are continuing negotiations on a case brought over 10 years ago.

Further analysis of the pending cases reveals that many of these cases have actually been resolved, as illustrated in Table 2. Approximately

[10] See, for example, Reinhardt (2001b) and Busch and Reinhardt (2000).

[11] One case was settled within 44 days, while the maximum number of days before further action was four years.

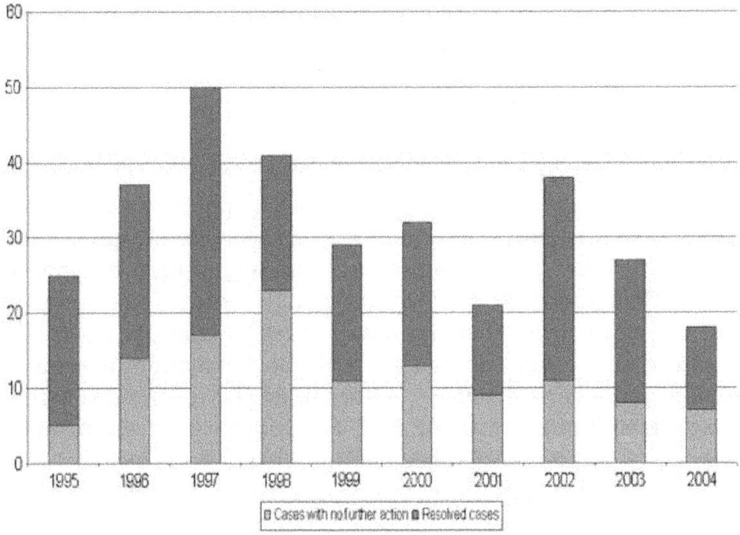

***Fig. 1.* Outcome of WTO dispute settlement cases, 1995–2004.**

***Table 2.* Outcome of pending WTO dispute settlement cases, 1995–2004**

	Number	Percentage of total
Total pending cases	107	100.0
Case brought to alternative venue	5	4.7
Issue taken up in alternative DSB case	29	27.1
Issue partially resolved or expired	46	43.0
No known outcome	27	25.0

5 percent of pending cases were resolved in alternative dispute settlement venues, including the U.S. Court of International Trade, the North American Free Trade Agreement (NAFTA) dispute settlement system, and the WTO's customs valuation committee. Similarly, the issues involved in 27 percent of the DSB cases listed as pending have been or are under consideration in other DSB cases. For example, in 2004 Thailand filed a case against the United States over a specific aspect of U.S. antidumping law commonly known as "zeroing." However, this same issue has already gone before a DSB due to a 2003 case initiated by the European Union, and the United States has announced that it intends to comply with the DSB Appellate Body Ruling.

I conducted an exhaustive search for possible resolution of all the remaining pending dispute settlement cases. Specifically, I searched newspapers, periodicals, and government publications for possible outcomes. In some cases, I also called government officials in departments involved in the case to confirm whether or not the issue had been resolved.[12] This research reveals that as much as 43 percent of "pending" dispute settlement cases have in fact been resolved in some way. However, in many cases, it is unclear to what extent these "resolutions" represent a victory for the countries that initiated the dispute rather than the natural expiration of defendant country's WTO-illegal regulations over what is sometimes a lengthy period of time. For example, often dispute settlement cases involving the imposition of antidumping duties become inconsequential when the defendant country later removes the antidumping duties in annual reviews. There is no way to tell whether the removal of the duties was a concession on the part of the defendant or would have happened regardless of the case.[13] Other domestic regulations targeted in DSB cases have limited shelf life such as temporary safeguard measures; thus, the cases automatically become nullified. Cases filed by Hungary against the Czech Republic and Slovakia became irrelevant when all parties joined the European Union.

Finally, my analysis suggests that approximately one-quarter of all "pending cases" at the WTO are truly pending; the countries have failed to resolve the issues involved in the case, but the complainants apparently lack the resources or the will to pursue the case by requesting the establishment of a panel.[14]

A review of those cases that are truly pending and those that have become irrelevant reveals some noteworthy patterns. As can be seen from the two-sample difference in means test statistics reported in Table 3, disputes filed by both developing and high-income countries are more likely to languish in the WTO dispute settlement process when they target developing countries when compared to those targeting high-income countries. There are a number of possible explanations for this pattern. For example, it is possible that cases filed against developing countries are more likely to be harassment suits designed to retaliate for some previous action by the defendant country or extract concessions from the defendant although the case has little legal merit. Alternatively, the benefits of pursuing a case against a developing country may be lower than pursuing

---

[12] Notes from this search are available from the author upon request.

[13] For example, India lifted antidumping duties in three of the seven antidumping cases targeted by the European Union in a dispute filed in 2004. In 2002, Argentina filed a dispute against Peru after Peru imposed preliminary antidumping duties on Argentinian vegetable oil. This case became obsolete when Peru imposed final antidumping duties on the same product, but this certainly does not represent a concession on the part of Peru. Cases such as these suggest that some disputes may be filed solely to pressure the defendant to rule a certain way in upcoming antidumping or countervailing duty cases, and not necessarily because the country has violated WTO provisions.

[14] For example, a U.S. official noted that U.S. complaints over the European Union's cheese subsidies, which were filed in 1997, "died off."

Table 3. Resolution of disputes, 1995–2004

	Developing complainants	All other cases	T-test[a]
Total cases	110	214	−0.882
Percentage unresolved	25.5	21.0	(0.379)
Cases against developing countries	55	66	−0.878
Percentage unresolved	36.4	28.8	(0.382)
Cases against high-income countries	55	148	0.527
Percentage unresolved	14.5	17.5	(0.599)
T-test	−2.688 (0.008)	−1.744 (0.080)	

[a] T-statistic associated with the hypothesis that the percentage of unresolved cases are equal across the two groups. P-values are reported in parentheses.

a case against a high-income country because of the size of the market. The summary statistics do not, however, provide evidence that developing countries lack the resources or knowledge to pursue a dispute settlement case at the WTO; developing countries successfully pursued 85.5 percent of the disputes they filed against high-income countries. The statistics suggest that further exploration of why some complaints languish in the WTO dispute settlement system is warranted.

5. *Empirical model and data*

I hypothesize that countries engage in the simple game illustrated in Figure 2, which occurs after a complainant country decides to file a request for consultations in the WTO dispute settlement system at a cost of C_F. During consultations, the defendant country makes a settlement offer ranging from full concessions to no concessions; this settlement would result in a net payoff to the complainant country in the amount of $B_S - C_{CS} - C_F$, where B_S represents the value of the settlement offer and C_{CS} represents the negotiating costs accruing to the complainant country. The complainant country has the option of accepting the settlement offer, requesting the establishment of a dispute settlement panel, or dropping the complaint. Note that in disputes involving multiple complainants, a single complainant may technically accept a settlement offer of partial concessions and decide not to pursue the matter further, while other parties to the dispute decide to request a dispute settlement panel. According to WTO records, none of the disputes filed by multiple complainants between 1995 and 2004 were settled by a subset of the complainants.

The payoff from requesting a dispute settlement panel is increasing in the expected value to the complainant of the decision by the panel, $E(B_P)$, but decreasing in the cost to the complainant of pursuing a panel, C_{CP}.

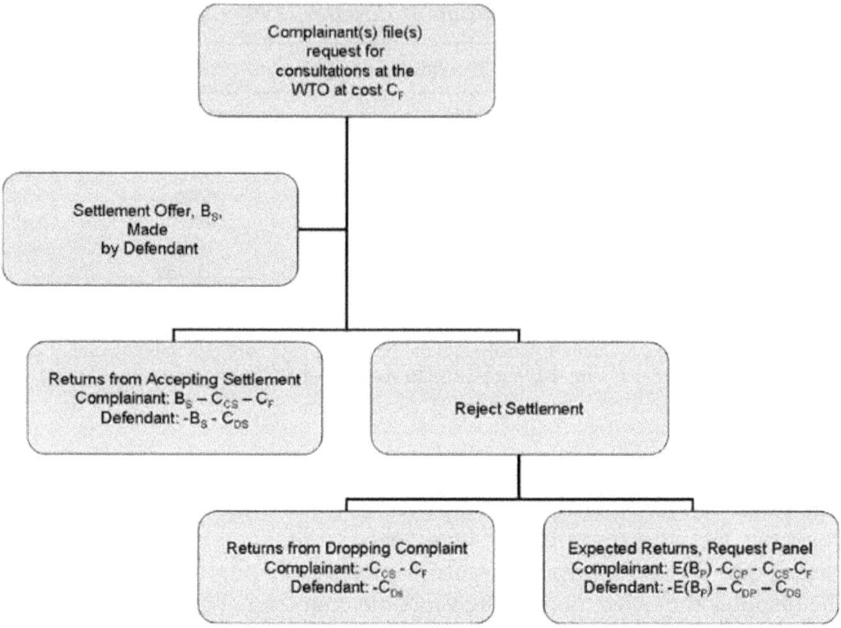

Fig. 2. Returns from filing a WTO dispute settlement request.

Clearly the complainant only requests a panel if the expected net payoffs from doing so exceed the net payoffs from the settlement offer, or if $E(B_P) - B_S - C_{CP} > 0$.[15]

In this model, the complaint will be dropped if the returns from both the settlement offer and the expected returns from requesting a dispute settlement panel are less than the returns from just dropping the dispute. Using the payoffs from above, this translates to the condition:

$$\mathrm{Max}[E(Bp) - C_{CP}, B_S] \leq 0.$$

In other words, the likelihood of a dispute languishing in the WTO dispute settlement process is an increasing function of the complainant's costs of pursuing a panel and a decreasing function of the expected value to the complainant of the decision by the panel; this expected value should solely be a function of the merits of the case, but may also depend on the

[15] In reality, many disputes are settled after the complainant requests the formation of a dispute settlement panel but before the panel reaches a final decision. As noted in Table 1, between 1995 and 2004 over 11 percent of cases sent to a panel were settled before the circulation of the panel report. To incorporate this possibility into the model, the expected benefits to the complainant of the decision by the panel, $E(B_P)$, should be reinterpreted as the expected benefits from requesting a panel, whether those benefits are due to a panel ruling or a pre-panel ruling settlement.

legal prowess of the complainant and defendant. The final term in the equation, B_S is the value of the settlement offer made by the defendant country. Even if the defendant country makes only a token settlement offer, the complainant country should prefer to accept the settlement offer rather than drop the dispute. If the dispute is dropped, therefore, it must be the case that the defendant failed to offer any concessions during the consultation phase/settlement negotiations. Similar to the bargaining model proposed in Reinhardt (2001b), I hypothesize that this settlement offer will be an increasing function of the expected value to the complainant of the decision of the panel, $E(B_P)$, and the cost accruing to the defendant from the panel, C_{DP}. The settlement offer will also be a function of the defendant's beliefs regarding whether the complainant will pursue a panel absent a settlement or simply let the dispute drop.

In a world of perfect information, the defendant will file the initial request for consultations only if they know that the returns from doing so will be positive. Thus, no cases will languish in the dispute settlement process.[16] Similarly, both the defendant and the complainant should want to avoid the additional legal costs associated with pursuing a panel. As a result, the defendant should make a settlement offer high enough that the dispute will be settled before the panel stage. The fact that disputes both languish in the WTO system and proceed to a panel is evidence that parties to these disputes must have both incomplete and asymmetric information about the outcome of the panel and/or the costs of pursuing the case.

To explain the likelihood of a dispute languishing in the WTO dispute settlement process empirically, I estimate a binary choice probit model of the complainant country's decision *not* to pursue a particular dispute using the model described earlier to inform my choice of explanatory variables. Although I do not observe the actual costs and benefits associated with each dispute, I include in the empirical estimation a number of explanatory variables that attempt to measure the potential costs and benefits of pursuing a case at the WTO. For example, I assume that the benefits of pursuing a case with merit are a function, in part, of the size of the defendant's economy and the importance of the trade relationship to the complainant country because the value of trade under dispute is likely to be higher.

Developing countries may have higher costs of participation due to less-developed legal systems or resource constraints that prevent them from pursuing a case at the WTO. Less-developed countries may also be less able to predict the expected returns from requesting consultations, increasing the probability that the case will languish at the WTO. If either of these conditions hold, disputes involving developing

---

[16] The exception to this rule is, of course, requests designed to retaliate against or otherwise harass a particular defendant.

complainants will be more likely to languish in the WTO. The theoretical model described earlier suggests that disputes involving developing defendants will be less likely to languish in the WTO if these countries have higher costs of participation because the defendants will make higher settlement offers in order to avoid the costs of a panel. On the contrary, the likelihood of a dispute languishing may be higher in cases involving developing defendants if these countries lack the resources or knowledge to make an adequate settlement offer. Moreover, the expected benefits from requesting a panel may be lower in cases involving developing defendants because the value to the complainant of unfettered market access may be lower. I include two variables, *GDP per Capita, Defendant and GDP per Capita, Complainant,* that measure the level of development of the defendant and complainant, respectively. One might expect the greater the ratio of the size of the complainant's to the defendant's economy, the lower the expected returns from pursuing the case and the more likely it will be dropped. I include the *Complainant to Defendant GDP Ratio* to account for this possibility. All three variables are from the World Bank's World Development Indicators.

Earlier studies have found that countries are more likely to file a dispute against a country that has previously targeted it in an earlier dispute settlement case. I expect that retaliatory disputes are more likely to be harassment disputes, have less merit than other disputes, and are more likely to languish in the WTO dispute settlement process. I construct a variable, *Tit for Tat*, to capture this possibility. This dummy variable equals 1 if the defendant country targeted the complainant country in a WTO dispute settlement action the year before the case.[17]

I include three case-specific dummy variables. The first, *Agriculture*, should capture whether cases involving politically sensitive agriculture industries are more likely to languish under the WTO dispute settlement process. The other two, *AD/CVD* and *Safeguards*, should capture the unique attributes involving antidumping, countervailing duty, and safeguard cases. I suspect that antidumping and countervailing duty disputes may be more likely to languish under the WTO dispute settlement process because WTO regulations require countries to review the imposition of antidumping and countervailing duty cases automatically every five years; moreover, most countries review the level of antidumping duties on an annual basis at the request of interested parties. Therefore, countries may be more likely to resolve these cases outside of the dispute settlement process.

As noted earlier, WTO dispute settlement rules allow countries to petition to be a "third party" in disputes. Third-party status affords countries the right to deliver written and oral testimony before panels and

---

[17] This is, admittedly, an imperfect measure as retaliatory cases may be filed multiple years after a particular case. Moreover, a dummy variable cannot capture the degree to which two cases may be tied together for retaliatory reasons.

receive the submissions of the complainants and defendants in the dispute. Third parties also have the informal right to participate in consultations before the establishment of a panel. Busch and Reinhardt (2006) find that third parties undermine or increase the cost of pre-trial negotiations, making it less likely that countries can reach a settlement in a particular dispute. In this analysis, I include the total *Number of Countries Involved,* including both third-party participants and complainants, as a possible explanatory variable for the likelihood that a case will languish at the WTO. The impact of this variable on the probability of languishing is ambiguous. The larger the number of participants, the higher the potential benefits of resolving the case and the more likely that at least one country will press forward with the case to ensure its resolution. On the contrary, coordination costs and the potential for free-riding may rise with the number of participating countries which may make it less likely that the countries will be able to reach a settlement or pursue the dispute further.

The impact of the complainant's trade dependence on the defendant, *Trade Importance to Complainant,* on the likelihood that a dispute is dropped is uncertain. I hypothesize that the greater the complainant's trade dependence on the defendant, the greater the expected benefits of pursuing a dispute by requesting a panel but the less bargaining power the complainant will have in the settlement negotiations and the lower the settlement offer. In contrast, the greater the defendant's trade dependence on the complainant, *Trade Importance to Defendant*, the less bargaining power the defendant will have and the higher the settlement offer, reducing the likelihood of the dispute being dropped. I measure the trade importance as the sum of total bilateral trade between the countries involved in the dispute in the year the dispute was filed divided by the nominal Gross Domestic Product of either the complainants or the defendant. Bilateral trade data are from the United Nation's Commodity Trade Statistics Database, while nominal Gross Domestic Product is from the World Bank's World Development Indicators.

Busch (2000) argues that democracies make greater use of the dispute settlement process and, more specifically, that democracies are more likely to request a panel in part because democracies are more used to legal norms of conflict resolution. I therefore include measures of the democratic tendencies of both the defendant and the complainants in the dispute settlement case, *Democracy, Defendant* and *Democracy, Complainant.* The Polity IV project's Political Regime Characteristics and Transitions, 1800–2002 Dataset creates a composite ranking each country's level of "Institutionalized Democracy" on a scale of 0–10.[18]

[18] "Institutionalized Democracy" is defined by three key characteristics: the presence of institutions and procedures through which citizens can express their preferences, institutionalized constraints on executives, and the guarantee of civil liberties. See Marshall and Jaggers (2002) for more detailed information on this variable.

Table 4. Summary statistics

	Mean	Std. error	Min	Max
Pending cases	0.35	0.48	0.00	1.00
Number of countries involved	1.07	0.64	1.00	9.00
Trade importance to complainant	0.04	0.11	0.00	0.54
Trade importance to defendant	0.03	0.09	0.00	0.53
Complainant to defendant GDP ratio	57.96	810.46	0.00	14,008.51
GDP per capita, defendant (thousands)	17.66	13.19	0.39	39.19
Max GDP per capita, complainants (thousands)	17.95	12.34	0.39	39.19
Democracy, defendant	8.78	1.89	0.00	10.00
Max democracy, complainant	8.98	1.45	0.00	10.00
AD/CVD	0.21	0.41	0.00	1.00
Agriculture	0.30	0.46	0.00	1.00
Safeguards	0.10	0.30	0.00	1.00
Tit for tat	0.29	0.45	0.00	1.00
US–EU dispute	0.13	0.34	0.00	1.00

The *Democracy, Complainant* variable is the maximum democratic ranking of all countries requesting consultations in the individual case.

The United States and European Community are by far the leading patrons of the WTO's dispute settlement system; disputes between these two trading partners accounted for 13 percent of all cases filed at the WTO between 1996 and 2004. To ensure that cases involving the United States and European Community are not biasing the results, I include in some specifications a dummy variable *US–EC Dispute*. Finally, I include an annual time-trend variable to capture whether cases filed early in the WTO's history are inherently different than those filed in later years. This time-trend variable should capture whether those cases filed late in the sample period are more likely to be unresolved simply because countries have not had enough time to request a panel or reach a settlement agreement.

The dataset includes the 299 disputes filed at the WTO between 1996 and 2004.[19] I employ two different forms of the dependent variable; in the first specification, I consider the dispute to be languishing, thus setting the dependent variable to equal 1, in all of the 105 disputes that the WTO currently considers "pending." In the remaining specifications, I define those disputes that have been considered in an alternative venue or an alternative DSU case as resolved. This reduces the number of disputes that are languishing, or truly pending, in the data sample to just 73. Summary statistics on each of the explanatory variables are presented in Table 4.

[19] I exclude those disputes filed in 1995 in order to construct the *Tit for Tat* variable.

6. Results

The marginal effects from the binary choice probit model are reported in Table 5. Specification (1) defines all those disputes that the WTO currently lists as pending as "unresolved," while the second and third specifications reduce the number of unresolved disputes by considering those disputes that have been examined in another venue or WTO dispute settlement case as successfully resolved. Results from the two definitions of the dependent variable are quite different, as discussed below.

Specification (1) shows that several of the variables that I hypothesized would be important determinants of the decision to abandon a dispute are

Table 5. Determinants of abandoning dispute marginal effects from probit estimation

	(1)	(2)	(3)
Number of countries involved	−0.046		
	(0.060)		
Trade importance to defendant	−0.799*	−0.282	−0.275
	(0.449)	(0.279)	(0.283)
Trade importance to complainant	0.222	−0.169	−0.162
	(0.310)	(0.231)	(0.237)
Complainant to defendant GDP ratio	−0.000	−0.001*	−0.001*
	(0.000)	(0.001)	(0.001)
GDP per capita, defendant	−0.010**	−0.004	−0.004
	(0.003)	(0.003)	(0.003)
Max GDP per capita, complainants	−0.004	−0.004*	−0.004*
	(0.003)	(0.002)	(0.002)
Democracy, defendant	0.028	0.009	0.010
	(0.020)	(0.012)	(0.013)
Max democracy, complainant	−0.003	0.045	0.046
	(0.025)	(0.029)	(0.029)
AD/CVD	0.139*	0.103	0.104
	(0.082)	(0.070)	(0.071)
Agriculture	0.163**	0.028	0.028
	(0.071)	(0.045)	(0.046)
Safeguards	−0.031	−0.058	−0.058
	(0.099)	(0.060)	(0.061)
Tit for tat	0.122*	0.073	0.071
	(0.072)	(0.058)	(0.060)
US–EC dispute			0.010
			(0.072)
Time trend	−0.010	−0.006	−0.007
	(0.012)	(0.008)	(0.008)
Pseudo-R-squared	0.086	0.086	0.087

Note: Standard errors reported in parentheses.
*Parameters significant at the 10 percent significance level.
**Parameters significant at the 5 percent significance level.

significant and of the expected sign. For example, I expected that the greater the importance of the trade relationship to the defendant country, the less bargaining power the defendant country would have, and the higher the value of the settlement offer to the complainant. Marginal effect estimates confirm that a one-standard-deviation increase in the importance of the bilateral trade relationship relative to the size of the defendant's economy reduces the likelihood that a dispute will languish at the WTO by slightly over 7 percent.

The estimates also suggest that the less developed the defendant country, the more likely the dispute will be abandoned; specifically, a $1,000 decrease in the per capita GDP of the defendant country results in a 1 percent increase in the likelihood that the dispute will never be resolved. This result could be driven by two possible explanations. First, the returns from pursuing a dispute with a developing country may be lower; thus, more of these complaints are abandoned. Second, and more troubling for the dispute settlement system, complainants may file more frivolous disputes against developing countries, hoping to force an early settlement with countries with fewer resources to fight claims.

As expected, the estimates imply that complaints that are filed to retaliate for earlier dispute settlement action, or *Tit for Tat* disputes, are 12 percent more likely to languish in the dispute settlement system, suggesting that these complaints may be more frivolous than other disputes.[20] Complaints involving antidumping and countervailing duty actions are approximately 14 percent less likely to be resolved in the dispute settlement system, confirming that these disputes are more likely to become irrelevant as countries reconsider antidumping actions in five-year sunset reviews, annual administrative reviews, or domestic court cases. Finally, complaints involving the agricultural sector are less likely to be resolved in the dispute settlement system.

Other variables that previous studies have shown to be important determinants in the outcome of disputes prove not to be significant in this analysis, including the level of democracy of the defendant and complainant and the number of countries involved in the dispute. Also insignificant in Specification (1) are the estimates associated with variables capturing the relative size of the complainant to defendant's economy and the level of development of the complainant.

The final two columns in Table 5 present the marginal effects from specifications using the alternative, more restrictive definition of an unresolved case. Note that although Specification (3) controls for potentially unique characteristics of the high number of disputes between

---

[20] Results from specifications in which the *Tit for Tat* variable is more broadly defined to equal 1 if the defendant country targeted the complainant country in a WTO dispute settlement action any time within the previous two years are not significantly different from those presented here. Specifically, *Tit for Tat* disputes are shown to be 11.3 percent more likely to languish in the dispute settlement system.

the United States and European Community using the *US–EC Dispute* dummy variable, the results are virtually identical to those presented in Specification (2).

As noted earlier, the results using the alternative definition of an unresolved case are significantly different from those from Specification (1). In fact, none of the variables that were shown to be significant in Specification (1) prove to be significant in the empirical analysis using the more restrictive definition. This may indicate that the variables that are significant in Specification (1) are not actually explaining the likelihood that a dispute will remain unresolved. Rather, these variables may be the important determinants explaining the likelihood that more than one WTO dispute will be filed regarding a particular issue or that countries will choose to pursue the issue in an alternative dispute settlement venue.

Three variables prove to be significant determinants of the likelihood that a dispute will truly remain unresolved. First, note that I exclude the variable *Number of Countries Involved* from the estimations using the alternative definition of the dependent variable. This is because the marginal effect associated with the number of countries involved cannot be identified because *all* the complaints that truly remain unresolved were filed by a single complainant. In other words, the raw data indicate that there is a zero percent probability and that complaints brought by more than one country will languish in the WTO dispute settlement system.

The other two variables that are significant suggest that complaints brought by smaller, less-developed countries are more likely to languish in the dispute settlement system. Specifically, a one-standard-deviation decrease in the size of the complainant's economy relative to the defendant's economy, *Complainant to Defendant GDP Ratio*, increases the likelihood that a dispute will remain unresolved by 81 percent. Similarly, a $1,000 decrease in the per capita GDP of the complainant country increases the likelihood that the dispute will remain unresolved by 0.4 percent. One possible explanation for these results is that smaller, developing countries are more likely to file frivolous complaints that they do not follow up upon.

However, the more troubling implication is that the results may instead be due to resource or knowledge constraints on the part of developing countries in the dispute settlement process. Smaller, developing countries may have less bargaining power and, therefore, lower returns from settlement offers. Developing complainants may be less able to predict the outcome of the dispute and incur the cost of filing a dispute that they later find out cannot be profitably resolved. Finally, developing countries may lack the legal knowledge and resources to pursue the complaint through the dispute settlement system; the costs of pursuing a panel may be higher for developing countries or budget constraints may force developing countries to abandon a dispute although it is sub-optimal to do so. Unfortunately, the results from this analysis cannot shed light on which of these potential explanations may be driving the results. Nevertheless,

I believe that WTO members should at least consider the possible implication that developing countries, and particularly developing complainants, are at a disadvantage in the dispute settlement system in their current review of the DSU.

7. *Conclusions*

As noted in the introduction, 33 percent of all disputes filed at the WTO are classified as pending or inactive and thus omitted from most studies analyzing the effectiveness of the dispute settlement system. This could significantly bias estimates of the effectiveness if the "inactive" cases have actually been resolved and, thus, misclassified.

My research suggests that approximately 5 percent of pending cases were resolved in alternative dispute settlement venues, including the U.S. Court of International Trade, the NAFTA dispute settlement system, and the WTO's customs valuation committee. Similarly, the issues involved in 27 percent of the DSB cases listed as pending have been or are under consideration in other DSB cases.

As many as 43 percent of the pending dispute settlement cases have been resolved in some way. However, in many cases, these resolutions do not represent a victory for the countries that initiated the dispute but rather the natural expiration of the defendant country's WTO illegal regulations over what is sometimes a lengthy period of time. Finally, my analysis suggests that approximately one-quarter of all pending cases at the WTO are truly pending, languishing in the dispute settlement system without resolution.

The empirical results analyzing the determinants of the likelihood that a dispute will fail to be resolved in either the WTO or some alternative DSB suggest that complaints brought by smaller, less-developed countries are less likely to be resolved. If this result is being driven by resource constraints or a lack of bargaining power on the part of developing complainants, it has troubling implications for the fairness of the WTO dispute settlement system. Countries should take these results into consideration during their review of the current WTO DSU.

References

Bown, C.P. (2004), Trade remedies and World Trade Organization dispute settlement: why are so few challenged? *Journal of Legal Studies* 34 (2), 515–555.

Bown, C.P. (2005), Participation in WTO dispute settlement: complainants, interested parties and free riders. *World Bank Economic Review* 19 (2), 287–310.

Busch, M.L. (2000), Democracy, consultation, and paneling of disputes under GATT. *Journal of Conflict Resolution* 44 (4), 425–446.

Busch, M.L., Reinhardt, E. (2000), Bargaining in the shadow of the law: early settlement in GATT/WTO disputes. *Fordham International Law Journal* 24, 158–172.

Busch, M.L., Reinhardt, E. (2002), Testing international trade law: empirical studies of GATT/WTO dispute settlement. In: Kennedy, D.M., Southwick, J.D. (Eds.), *The Political Economy of International Trade Law: Essays in Honor of Robert Hudec*. Cambridge University Press, New York and Cambridge.

Busch, M.L., Reinhardt, E. (2003), Developing countries and GATT/WTO dispute settlement. *Journal of World Trade* 37 (4), 719–735.

Busch, M.L., Reinhardt, E. (2006), Three's a crowd: third parties and WTO dispute settlement. *World Politics* 58 (3), 466–477.

Guzman, A., Simmons, B.A. (2002), To settle or empanel? An empirical analysis of litigation and settlement at the world trade organization. *The Journal of Legal Studies* 31, 205.

Marshall, M.G., Jaggers, K. (2002), Polity IV project: data users' manual. Working Paper. Center for Systematic Peace, George Mason University, Fairfax, Virginia.

Parlin, C.C. (2000), Operation of consultations, deterrence and mediation. *Law and Policy in International Business* 31 (3), 565–582.

Reinhardt, E. (2001a), Aggressive multilateralism: the determinants of GATT/WTO dispute initiation. Political Economy Working Paper 1999–4, Institute for Social Research, University of Michigan, Ann Arbor, MI.

Reinhardt, E. (2001b), Adjudication without enforcement in GATT disputes. *Journal of Conflict Resolution* 45 (2), 174–195.

Zaracostas, J. (1994), Dispute process crucial to WTO, Sutherland says. *Journal of Commerce* November 14, 1A.

CHAPTER 9

The Usage of the WTO Dispute Settlement System: Do Power Considerations Matter?

Sebastian Wilckens

Department of Economics, University of Kiel, Wilhelm-Seelig Platz 1, 24098 Kiel, Germany
E-mail address: sebastian.wilckens@gmx.de

Abstract
The usage of the WTO Dispute Settlement System (DSS) is dominated by high-income countries. Since the ultimate enforcement threat of the system is based on retaliation, countries may take their economic size as well as their specific bilateral retaliatory capacity into account when deciding whether or not to respond to a detrimental infringement of a trade agreement by filing a costly complaint. Hence, various scholars conjecture that lawsuits surfacing in the record of the WTO constitute only the biased tip of an iceberg of trade disputes. In order to investigate such a potential bias, this chapter sets up a sequential game of the DSS. Subsequently, a binary choice model is employed to empirically explain a country's decision whether or not to litigate against a trading partner. The results suggest that a country is more likely to file a complaint if (i) it is large, (ii) its trading partner is small, (iii) the trade value of the commodity at stake is large, and (iv) its retaliatory capacity is large.

Keywords: Developing countries, dispute settlement, WTO, retaliation, trade disputes

JEL classifications: F13, K33, O19

1. Introduction

With the establishment of the WTO in 1995, the Dispute Settlement Body (DSB) has gained much importance as an institution in the world trading system. While a panel's decision in the GATT era became a ruling only by consensus, the panel decisions under the WTO's Dispute Settlement System (DSS) become a ruling unless there is a consensus against it. This

Frontiers of Economics and Globalization
Volume 6 ISSN: 1574-8715
DOI: 10.1108/S1574-8715(2009)0000006012

modification is a candid commitment to encouraging complaints of members that have suffered from a contract breach of their trading partners. However, the WTO does not possess any supranational sovereignty to enforce compliance with the rules-based trading system by imposing sanctions or fines. As a consequence, the ultimate enforcement threat of a panel ruling is based on the retaliatory capacity of the victorious complainant. While it may be worthwhile for an economically large country to implement authorized retaliatory countermeasures against a trading partner, an economically small country may shoot itself in the foot by doing so.[1]

A prominent example of this discrepancy is found in the Bananas Dispute (DS16 and DS27), where the United States (US) and several Latin American countries complained against the bananas import regime of the European Communities (EC), which favored bananas from the African, Caribbean, and Pacific countries. Although the panel decided in favor of the complainants, the EC refused to bring their import regime into compliance with the ruling. Upon their request, Ecuador and the United States were authorized to suspend concessions to the EC as a retaliatory measure.[2] As an outcome of this dispute, the EC did not bring its import regime into conformity with the rules of the WTO and the United States implemented retaliatory measures, while Ecuador was reluctant to do so. Many scholars, such as Bronckers and van den Broek (2005) or Subramanian and Watal (2000), agree in arguing that Ecuador was virtually unable to implement retaliatory measures, unless it wanted to hurt its own economy even more.[3] At the end of the day of this dispute, the EC kept the benefits of maintaining an illegal import regime, the United States got at least a little compensated for the losses in the bananas business by the implementation of import barriers against the EC, while Ecuador was left with nothing but its injured bananas export sector.

Such a potential inability of economically smaller countries to enforce an offending trading partner's compliance may render the usage of the

---

[1] It is a well-known fact that a small country's optimal import tariff equals zero since it cannot influence world market prices. That is, it faces a completely elastic supply. Kennan and Riezman (1988) set up a two-country model to show by means of varying elasticities that once a country is large enough, it may gain from a tariff war as compared to free trade.

[2] Ecuador was authorized to suspend import concessions to the EC of an amount of 201.6 million US Dollars (USD), while the US were authorized to suspend concessions to the EC of an amount of 191.4 million USD.

[3] Note that even the arbitrators of this particular case acknowledged this problem in WT/DS27/ARB/ECU, para 177 by stating that "it could be that Ecuador may find itself in a situation where it is not realistic or possible for it to implement the suspension authorized by the DSB for the full amount of the level of nullification and impairment estimated by us in all of the sectors and/or under all agreements mentioned above combined." Moreover, the arbitrators notice that the Dispute Settlement Understanding (DSU) is not prepared for such a case in WT/DS27/ARB/ECU, para 177: "The present text of the DSU does not offer a solution for such an eventuality."

Table 1. Usage of the DSS by countries' income groups from 1995 to 2005

Complainant/defendant	High	Upper middle	Lower middle	Low	Sum
High	151	33	21	17	222
Upper middle	28	19	12	1	60
Lower middle	42	13	7	2	64
Low	14	5	2	1	22
Sum	235	70	42	21	368

DSS less attractive for smaller than for larger countries. This effect may show up in the data as a bias against smaller countries. Table 1 provides a breakdown of all complaining and defending countries from 1995 through 2005, grouped according to the World Bank's income classifications.[4] Clearly the figures of Table 1 show that economically larger countries filed the majority of all complaints. Moreover, these countries dominate the system as well among the defendants. However, this observation is not necessarily a proof for the claim that the DSS is biased against smaller countries. Horn *et al.* (1999) show that a model, in which countries encounter random violations proportional to the diversity and value of their trade, explains the observed pattern of disputes quite reasonably.[5] Hence, Horn *et al.* (1999) do not take the numbers of observable disputes as evidence of power considerations in dispute settlement. However, this approach has a caveat since it may be the case that the set of observable disputes constitutes only a biased subset of all disputes. There is reason to believe that the dark figure of disputes exhibits a pattern that differs from the pattern of the observable disputes. Smaller countries may not find it worthwhile to spend litigation costs on a complaint in anticipation of their inability to enforce an affirmative panel ruling. If this would prove true, the result of Horn *et al.* (1999) would have to be questioned since it would no longer mean that no power considerations are present at all, but rather that power considerations are absent among those countries that are already powerful enough to find complaining worthwhile. In other words, the Horn *et al.* (1999) approach may be based on a biased subset of disputes.

Bown (2005) proposes an approach that addresses this concern. He compiles a data set of those disputes, where all victim countries that have suffered from the defendant's offense are known with certainty.

[4] The figures on the notified disputes are taken from the author's own dataset, which is based on the record of disputes on the WTO's website. Income classifications of countries correspond to the World Bank's classification scheme.

[5] The underlying assumption of this class of models is that a dispute is generally undesirable for a country. In order to be still able to explain the occurrence of disputes, a demon, which possesses policymakers from time to time and leads them to irrational behavior, is introduced. This demon approach was first established by Kovenock and Thursby (1992).

Subsequently, Bown regresses the binary decision of whether or not a country has filed a complaint on several country- and dispute-specific variables. All in all, Bown's empirical results suggest that economically small countries indeed face a severe disincentive to complain as opposed to economically larger countries.

Yet another empirical approach is presented by Andrew Guzman and Beth Simmons. In their 2005 paper titled *Power Plays and Capacity Constraints: The Selection of Defendants in World Trade Organization Disputes*, Guzman and Simmons (2005) investigate the relationship between an offender's gross domestic product (GDP) and a complaining victim's GDP. On the one hand, they argue that a victim of a given size would rather complain against offenders that are not larger than the victim itself because of "power" considerations. On the other hand, a victim of a given size would utilize its legal capacity most efficiently if it complained in those cases where a high trade value is at stake. Since these latter cases are most likely to occur in a trading relation with a big country, a victim of given size could as well be expected to file complaints predominantly against bigger countries, according to Guzman and Simmons (2005). Based on these considerations, the authors postulate two opposing hypotheses. The *"Capacity Hypothesis"* states that "[a]s a country's income falls, a larger percentage of its complaints will be directed at High Income defendants," whereas the "*Power Hypothesis*" states that "[a]s a country's political power falls, a larger percentage of its complaints will be directed at states with little political power."[6]

In order to estimate the net effect of these two clashing hypotheses, the authors regress the logarithm of the offender's GDP on the logarithm of the complainant's GDP and several other exogenous control variables. Their central result is that the relationship between the logarithm of both parties' GDP is negative. They conclude from this result that, all else being equal, smaller countries are more likely to complain against bigger countries than against countries of about the same size. Furthermore, they draw the conclusion that the capacity effect dominates the power effect.[7]

Contributing to this literature, this chapter tries to shed light on the question of what determines whether a country does or does not file a complaint against an offending trading partner. It aims at providing a non-random theoretical explanation that allows for rationally acting

[6] The hypotheses are found at page 572 in Guzman and Simmons (2005).

[7] Note that a negative coefficient for $\log(GDP_V)$ in Guzman and Simmons' model means on the one hand that small countries complain against larger countries rather than against countries of about the same size. On the other hand, this result means that big countries also would rather file a complaint against a smaller country than against a country of about the same size. The authors state on page 583: "Although consistent with our results, we are unable to imagine a coherent theory under which poor states are prepared to file complaints against rich states but all else equal rich states are reluctant to do the same."

countries. Therefore, first a simple game theoretic model of the dispute settlement process is established and Nash equilibria are derived. Subsequently, suitable data to proxy for the game's payoff elements is identified. Based on data for 185 disputes where the importer has been adversely affected, ranging from 1995 to 2005, a probit model is estimated in order to explain a victim's binary decision whether or not to complain.[8] In particular, this binary complaining decision is regressed on the offender's and the victim's GDP, the trade value of the disputable commodity at stake, and a crude proxy for the retaliatory capacity of the victim. The results suggest that victims do take power considerations into account when deciding whether or not to file a complaint. Thereby, the findings of Bown (2005) are confirmed on a broader statistical basis, while the findings of Guzman and Simmons (2005) are questioned.

2. *Dispute settlement as a sequential game*

The handling of a dispute in the WTO occurs according to a clear-cut sequential scheme of escalation. The first stage foresees a consultation phase of 60 days, where the conflicting parties are supposed to settle their dispute in bilateral negotiations without any judge or panel. In case the opposing parties are unable to find an agreement within these 60 days, the establishment of a panel may be requested by either party. Once a panel has ruled on a dispute, the ruling can be appealed by either party, so that an appellate body will consider the issue again. If the final ruling on the dispute judges a defendant's policy to constitute an infringement of the WTO's rules, the offending party's government will be asked to bring its measures into conformity. Should the offending country refuse to do so within a "reasonable period of time," the victorious complainant may request the retaliatory "suspension of concessions." In practice, this suspension of concessions may constitute for example an import tariff or a quota that targets the complainant's imports from the defendant. Of course, the authorized extent of retaliation is dependant upon the magnitude of the initial offense. Formally, the DSU states that "[t]he level of the suspension of concessions or other obligations authorized by the DSB shall be equivalent to the level of the nullification or the impairment."[9] However, in legal practice there are various ways of how panels have interpreted this equivalence condition by calculating the authorized amount of retaliation. Jordan (2005) provides a discussion of the employed calculation methods. For those disputes that deal with trade in goods and violative import barriers, one particularly dominating approach is the counterfactual trade

[8] The 185 cases include both violation and nonviolation complaints.
[9] DSU Article 22, para 4.

value model.[10] This model first assesses the reduction in the trade value of the imported goods that have been subject to the defendant's disputable trade measure. This reduction in trade value is seen as the damage that was inflicted. Now in turn, the victorious complainant would be entitled to implement such a retaliatory import barrier on its own imports from the defendant that leads to a trade value reduction of smaller or equal size.[11] In other words, the retaliatory trade value distortion must not exceed the trade value distortion of the initial offense.

2.1. Setup of the game

Basically, this whole process can be seen as a sequence of decisions. At different points in time, the complainant and the defendant will choose actions, such as to complain, to comply, or to retaliate. By making these decisions, the players affect their own as well as their opponent's welfare, such that strategic behavior may result. Hence, one possibility to facilitate empirical analysis of the central question, which variables may trigger the complaining decision of an injured country, is to arrange the sequence of decisions in a game theoretical framework. In order to focus the model on the victim's decision whether or not to complain, rather than on the panel's ruling, it is convenient to employ one simplifying assumption right from the start.

Assumption 1-No Legal Failure. Whenever a violation of the WTO rules occurs, the panel correctly judges it to be a violation and consequently entitles the victim to retaliate against the offender if the latter does not comply with the ruling.

Given this assumption, the simplified sequence of decisions can be described as follows. Suppose an infringement of a bilateral trade agreement has already occurred. Let the offending country be denoted by "O" for offender, and let the country which is suffering from the offense be denoted by "V" for victim. Let the infringement cause a welfare loss of "D" ($\geqslant 0$) for the victim and a welfare gain (loot) of "Π"($\geqslant 0$) for the offender. Suppose further that O and V have been unable to reach a settlement of the dispute in previous (private) negotiations. Then, at the initial node "V_1" it is up to V to decide whether or not to file a complaint at cost "C" ($\geqslant 0$). If V decides not to complain, the game ends with V suffering from the offense, while O is enjoying the associated loot. If V decides to complain, the game arrives at node O, where the offender can decide whether to abolish the disputable trade measure (i.e. "comply") or

[10] This method was used for example in the following cases: DS26 EC-Hormones, DS27 EC-Bananas, DS160 US-Copyright.

[11] See Wilckens (2007) for a functional form of the counterfactual trade value model.

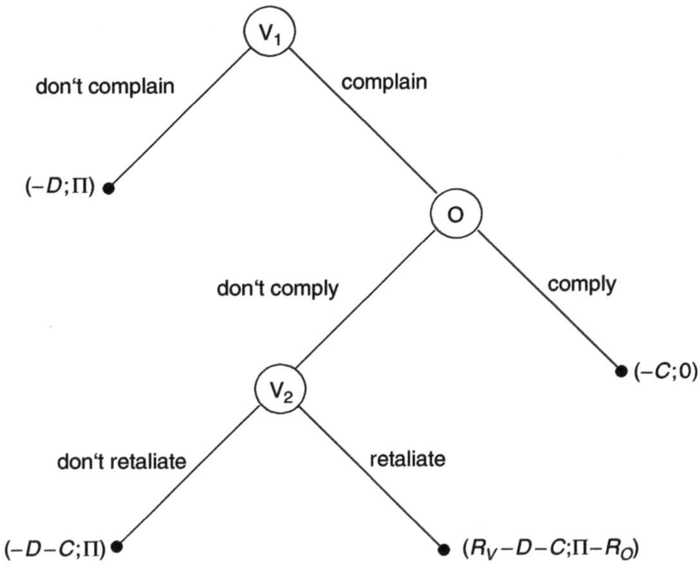

Fig. 1. A simplified game of dispute settlement.

to maintain it (i.e. "do not comply"). In case O complies, the game ends, and V is relieved of its welfare loss D, while O loses its loot Π. However, if O does not comply, the game arrives at node "V_2" where the victim can chose between "retaliate" and "do not retaliate". If no retaliation occurs, the game ends with V suffering from the damage and litigation costs, while O enjoys the loot. If retaliation á la WTO is implemented, the game ends as well, but retaliation affects both the victim's and the offender's welfare such that "R_V" ($\geqslant 0$) is added to the victim's payoff, while the offender's payoff decreases by "R_O" ($\geqslant 0$). Note that V's welfare gain from implementing retaliation does not necessarily have to offset its loss from the initial offense plus litigation costs. So independent of whether there is compliance or retaliation or none of either, the complainant may not be restored to the whole since WTO dispute settlement does not know any liability rule. Figure 1 depicts the structure of the described game in an extensive form of representation. The payoff vectors (π_V, π_o) are displayed at the end-nodes with π_V as the victim's payoff and π_o as the offender's payoff.

2.2. Strategies and Nash equilibria

Before the game may be solved, an assumption on the mode of information is needed.

Assumption 2-Perfect Information. The structure of the game and all payoffs are known to each player.

Moreover, strategies have to be defined. Obviously, the victim's set of strategies is given by

$S1_V :=$ (do not complain|do not retaliate)
$S2_V :=$ (do not complain|retaliate)
$S3_V :=$ (complain|do not retaliate)
$S4_V :=$ (complain|retaliate),
while the offender's set of strategies is
$S1o :=$ (do not comply)
$S2o :=$ (comply).

Recall that the central purpose of the game theoretic foundation is to identify those equilibria that are characterized by a complaining victim. For the game at hand, two Nash equilibria involving "complain" can be identified.

Proposition 1-Nash Equilibria. *The game exhibits two Nash equilibria in "complain":*

(i) *{(complain|retaliate), (do not comply)} is a Nash equilibrium iff* $\Pi > R_O \wedge R_V > C$.
(ii) *{(complain|retaliate), (comply)} is a Nash equilibrium iff* $\Pi \leq R_O \wedge D > C$.

Proof. See Appendix A.1.

Note that the two Nash equilibria in "complain" exclude each other since $\Pi > R_O$ excludes $\Pi \leq R_O$ and vice versa. Hence,

$$R_V > C \wedge D > C \tag{1}$$

is a sufficient condition for observing "complain" in equilibrium. In line with basic intuition, the following results can be verbalized.

2.2.1. Intermediate results

A country that is suffering from the infringement of a bilateral trade agreement would be expected to file a complaint in equilibrium if

(i) litigation costs are low;
(ii) the victim's gain from retaliation is large;
(iii) the victim's damage from the initial offense is large.

3. *Payoff proxies for the binary decision model*

Up to now, the payoff elements of the game that have been found to influence a victim's binary decision whether or not to complain are entirely unobservable variables in a theoretical framework. Therefore, this section discusses the selection of appropriate "real world" proxies for these payoff elements after a brief introduction into the general structure of binary decision models.

3.1. General setup of the probit model

Let y_i represent the choice of the *i*th victim, which takes the value 1 if the victim files a complaint and 0 otherwise. Consider that a rational individual would prefer to complain, whenever doing so yields more utility than not complaining, but that these utility levels are unobservable. Let the *i*th victim's utility from complaining be denoted by U_{i1} while utility from not complaining is denoted by U_{i0}. Moreover, define $y_i^* := U_{i1} - U_{i0}$. Then it holds that

$$y_i = \begin{cases} 1 & \text{if } y_i^* > 0 \\ 0 & \text{if } y_i^* \leq 0. \end{cases} \qquad (2)$$

Note that in Equation (2), y_i apparently is observable as opposed to y_i^*. The insights from the dispute settlement game suggest that a particular victim's utility from complaining and not complaining would be determined by a vector of exogenous and observable variables. Consequently y_i^* is as well determined by a vector of these exogenous variables. In particular, let

$$y_i^* := x_i'\beta + \varepsilon_i, \qquad (3)$$

where x_i' denotes the vector of exogenous variables, β denotes the vector of unknown parameters, and ε_i are random errors. Furthermore, let P_i denote the probability for $y_i = 1$. Then $1-P_i$ is the probability for $y_i = 0$. Consequently, it follows from Equations (2) and (3) that

$$P_i = \; Prob(y_i = 1) = Prob(y_i^* > 0) = Prob(\varepsilon_i > -x_i'\beta). \qquad (4)$$

Assuming a symmetric probability distribution, like the normal, it holds as well that

$$P_i = \; Prob(y_i = 1) = Prob(y_i^* > 0) = Prob(\varepsilon_i < x_i'\beta). \qquad (5)$$

Hence, the probability for a complaint can be compactly written as

$$P_i = F(x_i'\beta) \qquad (6)$$

where $F(\cdot)$ denotes the cumulative distribution function of the standard normal in case of the probit model.[12]

[12] For a discussion of the nonlinear probit approach that is used here, see Greene (2003), chapter 21 or Judge *et al.* (1988), chapter 19.

3.2. Selection of payoff proxies

The components of the payoffs in the game theoretic model are generally unobservable in reality. In order to be able to empirically test the theory's predictions (i.e. Proposition 1 and its associated verbalization), it is necessary to find observable data for the vector of exogenous variables x' that can be employed as a proxy for each of the model's payoff elements.

3.2.1. Litigation costs

The victim's costs of litigation may contain various elements. One prerequisite in the course of the preparation of a complaint is to collect data on the scope of the infringement. Another one is to calculate the precise monetary value of the injury, using plausible price elasticities, which need to be estimated in advance. In order to conduct these kinds of economic assessments, the trade mission of the victim country would either have to hire consultancies that are specialized in this field, or it would have to use the working capacity of the trade mission's permanent employees. In addition to these economic calculations the complaint needs to be prepared by lawyers that have a sound knowledge of the particular legal aspects of the GATT/WTO agreement. Finally, in a lengthy dispute there will be traveling costs for several flights, hotel stays, etc. Nordström (2005) emphasizes the role that litigation costs play in deterring especially smaller countries from using the dispute settlement system. Nordström reports that "[t]he fees charged by top-notch law firms in Brussels and Washington D.C. are in the range of $500 to $1.000 per hour plus expenses [...]" (Nordström, 2005, p. 1). Moreover, lawyers are reported to have charged their clients fees in excess of 10 million dollars (Shaffer *et al.*, 2003). Bown and Hoekman (2005) report similar figures. In line with Nordström's findings, it may be assumed that the level of litigation costs rises with the complexity of a case, but that it is independent of the value of the traded goods at stake in a particular dispute.

One argument that could be made to tie the level of litigation costs to a country specific variable is as follows. It may be plausible to assume that richer countries' governments have already sunk a significant part of their litigation costs by running a large permanent trade mission in Geneva and having several trade economists and lawyers permanently on their payroll. As opposed to this, poorer countries that do not have a "standing army" of economists and lawyers may regard substantial parts of the litigation costs as variable costs. However, Bown (2005), who uses data on the number of a country's delegates at the WTO Secretariat finds no evidence of such a potential influence on a country's decision whether or not to file a complaint. Guzman and Simmons (2005) model the role of litigation costs as a problem of limited legal capacity. In particular, they assume that the larger a country is in terms of its GDP (in an alternative model they use the

GDP per capita), the larger is the number of disputes this country can handle.

All in all, litigation costs may be either regarded as decreasing in the victim's GDP (GDP_V) or they may be regarded as completely independent. Furthermore, there is no theory which predicts that a victim's litigation costs increase in its GDP. Hence it may be expected that $\partial C/\partial GDP_V \leq 0$.

Yet a different factor that may influence the litigation costs for a particular victim are other complainants whose complaints target the same disputable trade measure of the same defendant. These situations may be distinguished into (i) disputes where there are multiple complainants who file a complaint jointly, and (ii) disputes where the defendant and the subject coincide with other complaints.[13]

Let the dummy variable indicating the occurrence of the first situation be called $MC1$, while the dummy variable for the second situation should be called $MC2$. The common purpose of these dummy variables is to capture potential cost synergy effects in the course of the joint preparation of a complaint, as well as a potential increase in political pressure on the defendant, which may shorten the trial procedure when there are multiple complainants.[14] While the narrowly defined concept of $MC1$ may serve to capture only those effects that emerge from a jointly filed complaint, the broader scope of $MC2$ covers potential effects that emerge from other disputes on the same disputable trade measure of the same defendant. Both dummy variables would be expected to have a dampening effect on the victim's litigation costs.[15]

3.2.2. The victim's gains and losses from import restrictions

Proposition 1 includes R_V as a variable reflecting a gain from an import restriction for the active (tariff setting) country and D as a variable that reflects a loss from an import restriction for the passive country.

There are two economic reasons why the active country may benefit from implementing an import restriction. First, countries may put more weight on the producer surplus of their domestic import substituting industries than on consumer surplus in the market for a particular commodity. This stronger weight on producer surplus could be explained by industry lobbying efforts, hence by political economy models, whose

[13] An example for the first situation would be DS16, where Guatemala, Honduras, and the United States jointly filed a complaint against the European Union. For the second situation consider as an example DS2 and DS4, where Venezuela and Brazil both targeted the United States' "Standards for Reformulated and Conventional Gasoline", each complainant litigating by means of a separately filed complaint.

[14] The idea of introducing dummies for these situations is taken from Guzman and Simmons (2005). Note however, that Guzman and Simmons (2005) define the "bandwagon" dummy, which corresponds to the $MC2$ dummy, in a slightly different way.

[15] Formally, $\partial C/\partial MC1 < 0$ and $\partial C/\partial MC2 < 0$ would be expected to hold.

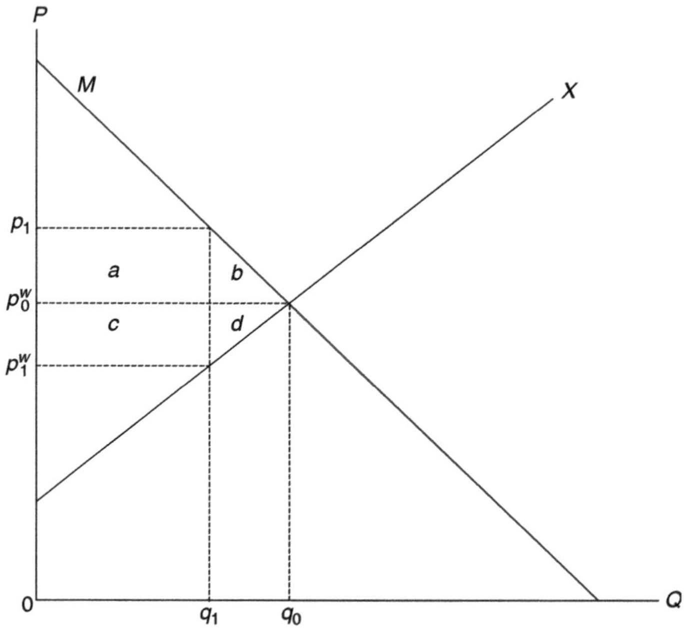

Fig. 2. Welfare effects of an import tariff.

empirical verification would require information on lobbying intensities in the affected countries. The second economic reason is one that applies to those countries that are large enough to influence world market prices. These countries can influence the terms of trade in their favor such that they realize a net welfare gain from the imposition of an import barrier. Figure 2 schematically depicts the effects of an import tariff, levied by a large country. The downward sloping line *M* represents the country's import demand while the upward sloping line X represents global export supply. Initially, when there is no tariff, the world market price p_0^w equals the domestic price p_0, while q_0 indicates the initially traded quantity. Suppose that the importing country now levies a tariff of τ. Then the domestic price rises to p_1 and reduces import demand to a quantity of q_1. Since the global export supply is not completely elastic, the reduction in import demand leads to a reduction of the world market price to p_1^w. The effects on the welfare of the importing country are ambiguous. That is, on the one hand, consumer surplus is reduced by the trapezoid area $a + b$, but on the other hand, a tariff revenue of the rectangular area $a + c$ is gained. So the net welfare gain for the importer is $c - b$.[16] Clearly this difference

[16] Any increase of a potentially existing domestic import substituting producer's surplus is out of the scope of this analysis.

decreases as the global export supply gets more and more elastic. Finally, if the importer faced a completely elastic export supply, the area c would vanish, such that the complete tax plus the deadweight loss had to be borne by domestic consumers. Consequently, a net welfare loss would be the result if the export supply was sufficiently elastic. Thus, if the offender is a large supplier on the world market for the retaliation goods, its more elastic export supply function is likely to reduce the retaliatory gain for the victim. On the basis of exports to the European Union, Nordström (2005) finds empirical evidence for the claim that larger or richer countries are larger suppliers on the world market, both overall and in individual commodities. Moreover, Nordström finds that "[a] subdivision of GDP into population and per capita income does not change the result very much. In other words, it does not matter if the supplying nation is small because of a small population or poor population" (Nordström, 2005, p. 8). Hence, it may be conjectured that the offender's GDP (i.e. GDP_O) reduces the victim's gain from retaliation:

$$\frac{\partial R_V}{\partial GDP_O} < 0.$$

Furthermore, the elasticity of the importing country's demand plays a role as well. Consider the consequences of a less elastic (i.e. steeper) import demand curve on the net welfare gain $c - b$. Obviously b would increase when holding c fixed or, vice versa c would shrink when holding b fixed, so that the net welfare gain would decrease.

The bottom line message from this little exercise is that bigger victim countries are more likely to be able to extract a large gain (i.e. large R_V) from imposing a retaliatory import restriction because (i) bigger countries usually have a more elastic import demand since they are more likely to produce domestic substitutes and (ii) bigger countries are more likely to be able to influence world market prices and consequently face a less elastic export supply, especially if the targeted exporter is small. In a theoretical analysis, Anderson (2002) emphasizes these difficulties that are predominantly faced by smaller countries that consider the implementation of retaliatory measures. In a two-country model of trade, Wilckens (2007) shows that a country's welfare gain from setting a (retaliatory) tariff increases from its own size. Broda *et al.* (2006) found empirical evidence that mirrors this result in the data. In their empirical study they show that countries indeed seem to take the relevant elasticities into account when setting their tariffs. Thus it may be concluded that $\partial R_V/\partial GDP_V > 0$.

Furthermore, two additional variables play a crucial role for the gains from retaliation. First, the value of the victim's imports from the offender constitutes an upper bound for the implementation of retaliation since retaliation can apparently only target these imports. Hence, for the trade value of the exports from the offender to the victim (X_{OV}) it may be assumed to hold that $\partial R_V/\partial X_{OV}>0$. Second, since the WTO's equivalence condition authorizes retaliation up to the magnitude of the initial damage, the trade value of the disputed commodities (DTV) limits the extent of retaliation as well. Hence, it may be conjectured that $\partial R_V/\partial DTV>0$.

What is left to proxy for, are the detrimental effects of the initial import restriction on the victim. Tariff equivalents of the offense would be a desirable but rarely available proxy since the files of most disputes' cases lack precise information on the concrete scale of the offense. Moreover, many dispute settlement proceedings came to an end before a panel ruled on the issue, such that there are virtually no numbers available. However, all else being equal, the magnitude of the initial damage D should be positively correlated with the trade value of the disputed commodity. Hence it seems likely that $\partial D/\partial DTV>0$.

3.3. Summary of hypotheses

Bringing together the selected proxies with the insights of the dispute settlement game, a link between empirically observable data and the expected behavior of a victim country can be established. In particular, the probability for observing that an injured country files a complaint is given by $P_i = F(x_i'\beta)$, where x' now incorporates the observable variables. Consequently, previous arguments lead to the following hypotheses:

$$\text{(H1)} \quad \frac{\partial P_i}{\partial GDP_V} = \overbrace{\frac{\partial P_i}{\partial R_V}}^{(+)} \overbrace{\frac{\partial R_V}{\partial GDP_V}}^{(+)} + \overbrace{\frac{\partial P_i}{\partial C}}^{(-)} \overbrace{\frac{\partial C}{\partial GDP_V}}^{(-)} > 0$$

$$\text{(H2)} \quad \frac{\partial P_i}{\partial GDP_O} = \overbrace{\frac{\partial P_i}{\partial R_V}}^{(+)} \overbrace{\frac{\partial R_V}{\partial GDP_O}}^{(-)} < 0$$

$$\text{(H3)} \quad \frac{\partial P_i}{\partial MC1} = \overbrace{\frac{\partial P_i}{\partial C}}^{(-)} \overbrace{\frac{\partial C}{\partial MC1}}^{(-)} > 0$$

$$\text{(H4)} \quad \frac{\partial P_i}{\partial MC2} = \overbrace{\frac{\partial P_i}{\partial C}}^{(-)} \overbrace{\frac{\partial C}{\partial MC2}}^{(-)} > 0$$

$$\text{(H5)} \quad \frac{\partial P_i}{\partial DTV} = \overbrace{\frac{\partial P_i}{\partial D}}^{(+)} \overbrace{\frac{\partial D}{\partial DTV}}^{(+)} + \overbrace{\frac{\partial P_i}{\partial R_V}}^{(+)} \overbrace{\frac{\partial R_V}{\partial DTV}}^{(+)} > 0$$

$$\text{(H6)} \quad \frac{\partial P_i}{\partial X_{OV}} = \overbrace{\frac{\partial P_i}{\partial R_V}}^{(+)} \overbrace{\frac{\partial R_V}{\partial X_{OV}}}^{(+)} > 0.$$

4. *Data and estimation*

4.1. Sample selection

Both the variables of the game theoretic model and the suggestions on how to proxy for these are based on the assumption that the initial offense has been any measure that adversely affects imports. As a consequence, the model may not be applied to disputes dealing with, for example, export subsidies or violations of intellectual property rights. Moreover, it is required that the bundle of affected commodities can be determined. Practically, this means that only those disputes dealing with import restrictions will be included for which there is information available on the harmonized system (HS) codes of the disputable commodities. This information is generally found in the WTO's case records, which are publicly available on the webpages of the WTO.[17]

Furthermore, since the value of the bilateral trade flow of the disputable commodity is of major interest, the data for the particular HS codes has to be available for the selected disputes. The UN COMTRADE database provides data on the vast majority of all bilateral trade flows up to 2005. Since trade flows from 2006 are not yet covered sufficiently, this analysis includes disputes from 1995 to 2005. Out of the total number of 335 disputes that have arisen throughout this period, 185 deal with measures that adversely affect imports.[18]

Among these 185 disputes the most frequently involved articles and agreements are National Treatment (60 disputes), Most-Favoured-Nation Treatment (50 disputes), Antidumping and Countervailing Duties (41 disputes), the Agreement on Subsidies and Countervailing Measures (30), the Agreement on Technical Barriers to Trade (21), and the Agreement on Safeguards (21). Note that in the majority of the disputes the complainant addressed more than one agreement or article. Moreover, in several of these 185 disputes there are multiple complainants such that the number of countries complaining is 198.

Clearly, it is plausible to assume the 198 complainants have been injured by the 185 offenses. But who else suffered from these offenses and did not

---

[17] For some cases this information has been taken from Horn and Mavroidis (2006), who provide a comprehensive database on disputes from 1995 through early 2004.

[18] See Appendix A.2 for a list of these disputes.

complain? There is no certain answer to this question because for most cases there is virtually no information on the "dark figure" of victims available. The approach used here defines a victim according to the following assumption.

ASSUMPTION 3-DEFINITION OF A VICTIM. A country is assumed to have suffered from an offender's disputable import restriction if it

(i) has been a WTO member in the year of the initiation of the dispute or the year before;
(ii) exported the disputable commodity to the offending country either in the year of the dispute or in the year before.[19]

In other words, Assumption 3 postulates that each of the 198 complaints before the WTO constitutes only the tip of a much larger iceberg of countries that have been injured by the particular disputable trade measure. Practically, the underwater parts of these icebergs, which consist of the injured but non-complaining countries, are identified according to the following three-step procedure. First, the HS classification of the disputable commodity is determined from the above-mentioned sources. Second, all suppliers of the disputable commodity that exported to the offender's market either in the year of the dispute or the preceding year are determined from the UN COMTRADE database. Third, all WTO members in this set are considered as victims. Applying this procedure to each of the 185 disputes and dropping observations with missing data yields a total number of 3,735 victims – 195 complainants and 3,540 silent victims.[20]

4.2. Data description

In order to test hypotheses H1 through H6, the following variables are compiled for each of the 3,735 victims.

- log(DTV) denotes the logarithm of the trade value of the disputable commodity's exports from the victim to the offender in the year before the complaint in US dollars. Exports are determined according to the HS

[19] The disputable commodity is specified with a precision of four digits according to the HS classification system. Note that most import restrictions specify the targeted commodities with a precision of four digits. Consequently the WTO's case records as well as the database of Horn and Mavroidis (2006) is dominated by four digit HS precision. Moreover, especially for many lower-middle and low-income countries, four digits is the highest degree of precision for most reported bilateral trade flows.

[20] Note that the earlier number of 198 complaining countries has been reduced by three. This is due to the unavailability of trade data for the Dominican Republic, who is a defendant in disputes 300, 302, and 333. In particular, log(X_{OV}) is not available for these three disputes.

classification with a precision of four digits.[21] Information on the HS codes is taken from the WTO's "Documents Online"[22] web page and from Horn and Mavroidis (2006). Bilateral trade values are taken from UN COMTRADE.[23]

- $\log(GDP_O)$ denotes the logarithm of the gross domestic product of the offender in the year of the complaint in US dollars. Data on this variable is taken from the World Bank.
- $\log(GDP_V)$ denotes the logarithm of the gross domestic product of the victim in the year of the complaint in US dollars. Data on this variable is taken from the World Bank.
- $\log(X_{OV})$ denotes the logarithm of the trade value of all exports that are shipped from the offender to the victim in the year before the complaint.[24] Data on this variable is taken from UN COMTRADE.
- $MC1$ and $MC2$ are dummy variables indicating by a value of one (zero otherwise) that there has been at least another complainant, either in the same case ($MC1$) or in the same issue with the same defendant ($MC2$).

Table 2 reports mean and standard deviation for these variables, separately for complaining and non-complaining countries. A noteworthy observation in the pattern of Table 2 is that the 195 complaining countries exhibit higher means in (i) their own GDP, (ii) the disputable trade value, and (iii) their exports to the offender as compared to the 3,540 non-complaining countries. Moreover, the offender's GDP exhibits a lower mean for the subset of complaining countries as opposed to the subset of non-complaining countries, while the subset of complaining countries shows slightly higher means in $MC1$ and $MC2$. Thus, the considerations that emanate from the game theoretical model appear to be mirrored in the raw data.

Table 3 provides a correlation matrix of the exogenous variables. The victim's aggregated exports to the offender exhibit a moderate positive correlation with the victim's own GDP, the disputable trade value, and the offender's GDP, while the victim's GDP is positively correlated with the disputable trade value. These observations are not too surprising since we know from gravity equation models that GDP and trade value tend to be positively correlated. More interesting may be the finding that the

[21] Since this variable should capture the amount of goods targeted, it is plausible to use the trade value at $t-1$ in order to deal with the problem that the disputable trade measure may have already reduced the trade value at time t.

[22] See http://docsonline.wto.org/

[23] See http://comtrade.un.org/db/

[24] It may be the case that for some disputes, for example disputes where the offender fails to comply with its tariff commitments, there is immediate recognition of non-compliance. Therefore bilateral trade flows may already have been affected by the trade dispute in the year of the filing of the complaint. To avoid this potential endogeneity problem, the trade flow at time $t-1$ is used.

Table 2. Descriptive statistics of exogenous variables

Subsample	Complaining		Non-complaining		All	
Variable	Mean	Std. dev.	Mean	Std. dev.	Mean	Std. dev.
$\log(DTV)$	17.5549	3.1641	14.5534	3.4808	14.7101	3.5283
$\log(GDP_O)$	27.9138	2.1423	28.8350	1.6909	28.7870	1.7292
$\log(GDP_V)$	27.4505	2.1526	24.9767	2.2388	25.1059	2.3009
$\log(X_{OV})$	22.4739	2.6478	20.8308	2.4552	20.9166	2.4922
$MC1$	0.0872	0.2828	0.0249	0.1557	0.0281	0.1653
$MC2$	0.3795	0.4865	0.3633	0.4810	0.3641	0.4812
Observations	195		3,540		3,735	

Table 3. Correlation matrix of exogenous variables

Variable	$\log(DTV)$	$\log(GDP_O)$	$\log(GDP_V)$	$\log(X_{OV})$	$MC1$	$MC2$
$\log(DTV)$	1	0.1596	0.3457	0.4675	0.0053	0.0899
$\log(GDP_O)$		1	−0.2858	0.3963	0.0922	0.0872
$\log(GDP_V)$			1	0.5580	−0.0254	−0.0701
$\log(X_{OV})$				1	0.0510	−0.0184
$MC1$					1	−0.1206
$MC2$						1

victim's and the offender's GDP are negatively correlated, such that opposing countries are rather of unequal size than of equal size:

4.3. Estimation and results

Treating all observations as being individual (e.g. the US complaining in 1995 is a different victim from the US complaining in 1996), there are no repeated observations available. So the reaction of one and the same individual in more than one environment of explanatory variables does not occur. The estimation method will therefore require the maximization of the log likelihood function, which is $\ln \ell = \sum_{i=1}^{T} y_i \ln F(x_i'\beta) + \sum_{i=1}^{T} (1 - y_i) \ln[1 - F(x_i'\beta)]$, where $F(\cdot)$ is again the cumulative distribution function of the normal distribution. The maximization of this function via β is conducted using the numerical iterative Newton–Raphson method.[25]

[25] See Greene (2003, p. 670 ff). for a more detailed description of the properties of the Newton–Raphson estimation method. The alternative maximization algorithm method of Quadratic Hill Climbing as well as the Gauss–Newton algorithm confirm the results of the Newton–Raphson algorithm by producing similar results. The software used for the estimation of the following models is EViews 5.0.

Table 4. Probit regression results

Variable	Model 1		Model 2		Model 3	
	Coefficient	SE	Coefficient	SE	Coefficient	SE
Constant	−2.7680***	1.0738	−2.4259**	1.0834	−2.765***	1.0733
log(DTV)	0.1105***	0.0173	0.1250***	0.0164	0.1099***	0.0174
log(GDP_O)	−0.1768***	0.0314	−0.2086***	0.0321	−0.1772***	0.0314
log(GDP_V)	0.1274 ***	0.0273	0.1382***	0.0280	0.1274***	0.0273
log(X_{OV})	0.0496*	0.0259	0.0475*	0.0272	0.0501*	0.0260
$MC1$			1.2838***	0.1863		
$MC2$					0.0243	0.0804
Log likelihood	−610.8268		−585.4150		−610.7831	
McFadden R^2	0.2021		0.2352		0.2022	
Akaike	0.3298		0.3167		0.3303	
Schwarz	0.3381		0.3267		0.3403	
Hannan-Quinn	0.3327		0.3203		0.3338	

Table 4 presents the results of three different probit regressions, where y is regressed on a vector of the previously introduced exogenous variables and a constant. Standard errors (SE) are computed according to Huber/White (quasi-maximum likelihood), while *, **, and *** indicate a variable's significance on a 10, 5, and 1% level, respectively.[26] A first glance at the results shows that all coefficients confirm the signs that are predicted by hypotheses 1 through 6. That is, the disputable trade value and the victim's GDP have a positive effect, while the offender's GDP shows a negative effect. Moreover, these coefficients are significant on the 1% level in all three models of Table 4. However, the aggregated exports from the victim to the offender show the predicted positive effect, but the coefficient is considerably less significant, at the 5.59, 8.04, and 5.43% level, respectively. Recalling the correlation matrix, the poorer explanatory power of X_{OV} may be attributed to this variable's higher degree of correlation. Among the two dummies, which control for the occurrence of multiple complainants, the narrowly defined case-dummy $MC1$ exhibits the predicted positive sign on a 1% significance level, while the broadly defined issue-dummy $MC2$ lacks significance even on the 10% level. Based on the likelihood ratio statistic, the joint null hypothesis that all slope coefficients are zero can be rejected on a 1% level for each of the three models. According to the values of the log likelihood function, McFadden R^2, Akaike-, Schwarz-, and Hannan–Quinn-criteria, the second model is consistently preferred to the other models.

[26] Employing other computational concepts of standard errors, such as generalized least squares, leads only to minor changes in the significance levels. The changes in significance are small enough to ensure that all *, **, and *** notations remain valid for every variable in each model.

4.4. Robustness

The regression design, the selection of variables, and the definition of injured countries constitute a very specific setup. Hence, it should be checked whether the results can be sustained qualitatively when this setup is modified. There are two fundamental starting points that could be subject to changes. First, the definition of an injured country may be changed, resulting in a different set of observations. Secondly, the regression design and the set of explanatory variables may be altered.

Regarding the first point, Assumption 3 could be seen as just a necessary condition for defining an injured country. That is, it may be the case that some but not all exporters of the targeted goods suffered from the offender's infringement. One possibility of determining whether one of those countries that already satisfy the necessary condition has been affected by an offense, is to look for "suspicious" variations in the trade flow of the disputable commodity. Common sense would suggest that, all else being equal, the implementation of an import barrier should lead to a reduction in trade flows in the year of the dispute (or the year before the dispute) compared to the average trade flows of the previous years. Using a small data set from Bown (2005), where those countries that imported the targeted goods but did not suffer from the violation can be distinguished from those countries that did suffer, a statistical criterion can be derived for each country i to separate the affected from the unaffected countries.[27] Let Φ_k^i denote the criterion, where k refers to the first pre-dispute period that is included. Φ_3^i for example, is the value of the criterion for the ith country that reaches back to three years before the notification of the dispute. Employing the sample of Bown (2005), a cutoff level $\Phi_k^{\text{cut}}(\alpha)$, where α denotes the probability of an alpha error,[28] may be constructed. Since the criterion is constructed such that low levels of Φ indicate a decrease in trade value, while high levels of Φ go along with an increase in trade value, a country may be assumed to have suffered from an offender's disputable trade measure if and only if

$$\Phi_k^i \leq \Phi_k^{\text{cut}}(\alpha) \tag{7}$$

as an additional sufficient condition. Computing this additional condition for different values of k and α and selecting countries accordingly leads to different subsets of those 3,540 non-complaining victims that already satisfy the necessary condition of Assumption 3. For example $\Phi_4^{\text{cut}}(0.05)$ yields 2,214 silent victims, whereas the greater alpha error in $\Phi_4^{\text{cut}}(0.1)$ produces 2,143 silent victims. Table 5 provides an excerpt of regression results for different sample selection criteria using level data. Obviously, all

---

[27] For a detailed explanation of the criterion see Appendix A.3.

[28] That is erroneously judging an injured country to be non-injured.

regression results can be sustained qualitatively. Note that the results are as well robust to logarithmic data specification, with or without constant, and to sample selection criteria with an alpha error of 1%.

The second possibility of alteration is to include additional explanatory variables. In order to control for potential differences in litigation costs, one may want to include the offender's and the victim's GDP per capita (i.e. $GDPPC_O$ and $GDPPC_V$). Furthermore an index of economic freedom for the victim (i.e. EF_V) may serve to address concerns that governments of less economically free countries may refer less of their exporters' complaints to the WTO than governments of more economically free countries. For some models that include these variables, Table 6 shows that the central results remain qualitatively unchanged. Additional non-reported regressions include combinations of variables in logs and levels, different selection criteria, case and issue dummies, as well as GDP ratios,

Table 5. Probit results for level data under various sample selection criteria

Variable/criterion	$\Phi_4^{cut}(0.05)$	$\Phi_4^{cut}(0.1)$	$\Phi_3^{cut}(0.05)$	$\Phi_3^{cut}(0.1)$
Constant	−1.2927***	−1.2772***	−1.3544***	−1.332***
GDP_O	−6.40E-14***	−6.41E-14***	−6.14E-14***	−6.19E-14***
GDP_V	7.11E-14***	7.00E-14***	7.50E-14***	7.47E-14***
DTV	5.11E-11**	5.06E-11**	5.22E-11**	5.13E-11**
X_{OV}	5.99E-12***	6.00E-12***	6.01E-12***	6.00E-12***
McFadden R^2	0.1451	0.1436	0.1466	0.1465
Akaike	0.4848	0.4959	0.4586	0.4707
Schwarz	0.4968	0.5082	0.4699	0.4823
Hannan-Quinn	0.4891	0.5003	0.4627	0.4749
Observations	2,409	2,338	2,599	2,506

Table 6. Probit results for logarithmic data and additional variables under $\Phi_4^{cut}(0.05)$

Variable	Model 1	Model 2	Model 3	Model 4	Model 5
Constant	−3.159760***	−2.0897*	1.1998	−3.3650	−3.3622
$\log(GDP_O)$	−0.1590***	−0.2005***	−0.2220***	−0.2188***	−0.2193***
$\log(GDP_V)$	0.1687***	0.1302***	0.1296***	0.1841***	0.1841***
$\log(DTV)$	0.1127***	0.1056***	0.1063***	0.1053***	0.1053***
$\log(X_{OV})$		0.0568*	0.0792**	0.0840***	0.0839***
$\log(EF_V)$			−0.7554***	0.3798	0.3798
$\log(GDPPC_V)$				−0.2054***	−0.2054***
$\log(GDPPC_O)$					0.0010
McFadden R^2	0.1813	0.1836	0.1887	0.1965	0.1965
Akaike	0.4635	0.4631	0.4610	0.4575	0.4583
Schwarz	0.4731	0.4751	0.4755	0.4743	0.4775
Hannan-Quinn	0.4670	0.4675	0.4663	0.4636	0.4653

and ratios of GDPs with trade values. The gist of these calculations is that the signs of the coefficients for GDP_O, GDP_V, DTV, X_{OV}, and $MC1$ are robust to all conducted changes.

5. Excursus: a note on Guzman and Simmons (2005)

Recall the central finding of Guzman and Simmons (2005) that the relationship between both parties' GDP is negative, that is, all else being equal, smaller countries are more likely to complain against bigger countries. Consequently, their result contrasts this chapter's results as small victims have been found to be deterred from complaining against bigger offenders.

A possible explanation for this discrepancy may lie in the way how Guzman and Simmons take their Capacity Hypothesis to the data. Consider that a low endowment of legal resources may be understood as a high level of litigation costs. Hence, along the lines of Guzman and Simmons, small countries face a high level of litigation costs. Recall that this chapter's model produced the trivial insight that either the initial damage or the gain from retaliation must exceed litigation costs in order to render a complaint worthwhile.[29] So, if we are concerned that poor countries lack legal resources, we should be tempted to say that these countries will predominantly engage infringements that cause a high damage which lets them break even with their high level of litigation costs.[30] Still in line with this, Guzman and Simmons speak of a *"large market"* (see Guzman and Simmons, 2005, p. 572), but what they indeed use to control for the size of the affected market in their regression, is the offender's GDP. Granted, the market size or the disputable trade value at stake could be positively correlated with the offender's GDP, but note that this correlation may be very weak.[31] This is due to the fact that log(DTV) varies extremely across the individual disputes. Hence, the information that is incorporated in the trade value at stake is close to orthogonal to the offender's GDP.

It would be an interesting question to ask, whether the relationship between both parties' GDPs would remain negative if one augmented a regression of the Guzman and Simmons fashion by log(DTV). Thus, it would be possible to distinguish between a victim's incentive to complain

[29] See Equation (1).

[30] Guzman and Simmons (2005, p. 572) argue analogously: "All else equal, the capacity hypothesis suggests that a capacity-constrained state will be able to pursue only a limited number of cases. The state must prioritize the list of potential defendants and will tend to pursue larger markets rather than smaller markets. Thus, a low-capacity complainant may pursue only one case, and that case will be against a defendant with a large market."

[31] Note Table 3 showing a rather low correlation coefficient of 0.1596 between log(DTV) and log(GDP_O).

Table 7. Feasible general least squares results for Equation (8)

Variable	Coefficient
Constant	23.3059***
$\log(GDP_V)$	0.0804***
$\log(DTV)$	0.0422***
$ECorUS_O$	3.4968***
$MC1$	0.2398**
R^2	0.9969
Adjusted R^2	0.9968
Akaike	2.1779
Schwarz	2.2609
Observations	198

against infringements of large markets on the one hand and its disincentive to mess with bigger countries on the other hand. From previous insights, we would hypothesize that, all else being equal, the GDP of an offender should be increasing in the disputable trade value and in the victim's GDP. This is because a complaint against a big country is more likely to be profitable if the complainant himself and/or the trade value at stake is large. Equation (8) describes the regression approach, where the logarithm of the offender's GDP is regressed on a constant, the logarithm of the complaining victim's GDP, the logarithm of the disputable trade value, a dummy that equals one if either the EC or the US are the offender ($ECorUS_O$), a dummy that equals one if there are multiple complainants in a dispute, and a random disturbance term ε.[32]

$$\log(GDP_O) = \alpha + \beta_1 \log(GDP_V) + \beta_2 \log(DTV) + \delta_1 ECorUS_O + \delta_2 MC1 + \varepsilon. \tag{8}$$

Equation (8) is estimated on the basis of the 198 complaints for which the vector of disputable trade values has already been compiled in the preparation of this chapter's central (binary) model. Using feasible general least squares and consistent standard errors, the results of Table 7 are obtained.[33] The results show that the estimated coefficients for the victim's GDP as well as for the disputable trade value are positive and significant on a 1% level. This change in the sign of the coefficient for the victim's GDP means that, all else being equal, small countries would rather complain against small countries than against large countries. Hence, it may be the case that Guzman and Simmons' result is driven by the

[32] Both dummies are part of the original Guzman and Simmons model.
[33] Again, the estimation is conducted using EViews 5.0.

omission of the trade value at stake, which has been found to have a highly significant influence.

6. Concluding remarks

Initially a simple game theoretical model has been used to produce the predictions that a violated country's incentive to file a complaint increasesaccording to its own economic size, the value of the commodities at stake, and its retaliatory capacity. The level of litigation costs as well as the economic size of the offender have been found to be detrimental to a violated country's incentive to file a complaint.

These theoretical predictions are generally conformed by the coefficients' signs that result from the binary regression model, using data on 195 complaints from 1995 through 2005. The results have been shown to hold under (i) several other methods of selecting injured countries and (ii) different regression designs including additional variables. Moreover, the empirical results reproduce the findings of a similar approach by Bown (2005), who focuses on 54 disputes from 1995 through 2000, for which there is certain information on the affectedness of victims available.

The findings may have implications for the interpretation of the results in Guzman and Simmons (2005) who find that a small victim is more likely to file a complaint against a bigger offender than against an offender of about the same size. Without the inclusion of the disputable commodity's trade value, the data set at hand reproduces the Guzman and Simmons result. However, once controlling for the disputable commodity's trade value, the Guzman and Simmons result, that countries rather tend to file against countries of different than of equal size, is reversed.

Furthermore, the empirical findings of this paper raise implications for a potential bias of the DSS' usage. The estimated coefficients of the model predict that the observed set of complainants is biased towards those cases where the victim is large, the offender is small, the disputable trade value is high, and the victim's retaliatory capacity is large. Moreover, the disentanglement of the separate effects of these variables unambiguously suggests that, all else being equal, bigger countries do have a greater incentive than smaller countries for using the DSS.

While this study answers the question whether the use of the system is biased towards large countries in the affirmative, it may be complementary to the results of Horn *et al.* (1999), who find that the number of product market pairings serves to explain how often a country has been involved in a dispute. However, their analysis is based on the set of those disputes that have been notified to the WTO, and, from what has been argued in this study, this observable subset should not be representative, but rather biased. Merging the results of both studies suggests that while the binary decision of whether or not to complain depends upon the identified variables that are specific to countries and commodities, a country's frequency with which it faces an infringement may very well be proportional to the number of bilateral product market pairings.[34]

Acknowledgement

I would like to thank Horst Raff and Rolf J. Langhammer as well as participants of the Brown-Bag-Seminar at the University of Kiel, the European Trade Study Group Conference at the University of Athens, and the Midwest International Trade Conference at the University of Illinois for helpful comments and suggestions.

Appendix

A.1. Proof of Proposition 1

Potential Nash equilibria (PNE) including "complain" are:

PNE1 = {(complain|do not retaliate), (do not comply)}
PNE2 = {(complain|do not retaliate), (comply)}
PNE3 = {(complain|retaliate), (do not comply)}
PNE4 = {(complain|retaliate), (comply)}

PNE1 does not not constitute an equilibrium since complaining and not retaliating is strictly worse than not complaining, when the offender plays "do not comply".
PNE2 does not constitute an equilibrium since "comply" is not a best response to "do not retaliate".
PNE3 constitutes a Nash equilibrium iff $\Pi > R_O \wedge R_V > C$.
PNE4 constitutes a Nash equilibrium iff $\Pi \leqslant R_O \wedge D > C$.

[34] The author cannot imagine a reason why the number of a country's product market pairings should affect the binary decision of whether or not to complain, given a particular offense. However, the number of infringements that a country commits or suffers from may very well be proportional to its product market pairings if one assumes that offenses occur randomly and separately in each product market pairing. Consequently, a sequential two-step model would be needed to predict the number of a country's observed participation as a complainant. In the first step, countries would be offended randomly and proportional to their number of product market pairings in the spirit of the Horn *et al.* (1999) approach. In the second step, the binary decision whether to complain against each of these infringements would be made according to the binary decision model presented in this study.

A.2. Included disputes

The following list of numbers refers to the numbers of the disputes as filed in the records of the WTO.

1, 2, 3, 4, 6, 7, 8, 10, 11, 12, 13, 14, 16, 17, 18, 19, 21, 23, 24, 25, 26, 27, 29, 31, 34, 41, 44, 48, 49, 52, 54, 55, 56, 58, 60, 62, 63, 64, 65, 66, 67, 68, 72, 74, 75, 76, 77, 78, 81, 84, 85, 87, 89, 97, 98, 99, 101, 102, 105, 109, 110, 112, 119, 121, 122, 123, 132, 134, 137, 138, 140, 141, 142, 143, 144, 145, 146, 147, 148, 151, 154, 155, 156, 157, 158, 159, 161, 164, 165, 166, 167, 169, 175, 177, 178, 179, 180, 181, 182, 184, 185, 187, 189, 191, 195, 202, 203, 205, 206, 207, 208, 209, 210, 211, 212, 213, 214, 215, 216, 218, 219, 223, 225, 226, 227, 229, 230, 231, 233, 235, 236, 238, 240, 241, 243, 244, 245, 247, 250, 255, 256, 257, 260, 262, 263, 264, 269, 270, 271, 272, 276, 277, 278, 280, 281, 286, 287, 288, 295, 296, 297, 299, 300, 302, 303, 305, 306, 308, 309, 310, 311, 312, 313, 314, 319, 323, 326, 327, 328, 329, 330, 332, 333, 334, 335

A.3. Construction of a statistical sample selection criterion

In order to derive an appropriate sufficient condition that is based on a variation in trade flows, data from Bown (2005) is being exploited in the following way. There are 19 cases dealing with import restrictions in Bown (2005), where not all trading partners of the disputable commodity have been affected by the offense of the respondent. For these 19 cases, Bown succeeds in identifying those trading partners that have suffered from the offense.[35] In the next step, this list of injured but non-complaining trading partners of the 19 offenders is augmented by all non-complaining trading partners that exported the particular commodity to the 19 offenders. When comparing the non-injured non-complaining trading partners to the injured non-complaining trading partners, it becomes apparent that indeed the exports of the injured countries exhibit a dip, as opposed to the exports of the non-injured countries. Hence, a criterion, based on this observation, may be used in order to distinguish between injured and non-injured countries. In order to avoid distortions arising from variations in output levels, let the criterion be based on the relative share of exports of the disputable commodity that are shipped from the ith potential victim to the offender at time t, where t denotes the year of the dispute. Let TV_t^{io} denote the ith

[35] I am grateful to Chad Bown, who was so kind to send me data on the countries which have suffered from the 19 offenses, that Bown (2005, p. 9) describes as follows. "[...] 19 WTO-inconsistent policies in the sample were applied on at least a' 'quasi'-MFN basis, in that even though an MFN-violation is a key element of the dispute, we were still able to identify from other, non-WTO sources the other exporting countries in addition to the complainant facing the discrimination of the WTO-inconsistent policy."

potential victim's exports to the offender at time t, and let TV_t^{iw} denote the ith potential victim's exports to the world at time t. Then the share of exports that is shipped from the ith victim to the offender at time t is simply

$$S_t^i := \frac{TV_t^{io}}{TV_t^{iw}} \tag{A.1}$$

Consequently, the average share of exports that have been shipped from the ith victim to the offender from time $t-k$ until time $t-l$, with $k>1$, is

$$\mu_{kl}^i := \frac{1}{k-l+1}\sum_{j=l}^{k} S_{t-j}^i. \tag{A.2}$$

Building on this, let the criterion be defined as the share of exports at time t over the average share of exports from $t-k$ to $t-2$. The trade flows in the year before the official filing of the complaint (i.e. $t-1$) may already be affected by the offense. To avoid complications that could arise due to the potential endogenous character of the trade flow in $t-1$, this period is being omitted. Thus, the criterion Φ_k^i is

$$\Phi_k^i := \frac{S_t^i}{\mu_{k2}^i}. \tag{A.3}$$

The sample's distributional properties of the two alternative criteria Φ_3^i and Φ_4^i are displayed in Table 8. For Φ_3^i the number of injured (non-injured) countries is 56 (247). For Φ_4^i the number of injured (non-injured) countries is 44 (196).[36] Table 8 shows that injured countries exhibit lower values of both alternative criteria than non-injured countries. A test for different means of Φ_3^i and Φ_4^i in the two subsamples rejects the Null hypothesis of a common mean.[37] Thus, the criteria may serve to select injured countries from the population of those countries that already satisfy the necessary condition for being injured. In particular, the approach taken here defines a cutoff level for Φ_4^i, so that all countries which exhibit a Φ_4^i below this cutoff level will be judged as injured.[38] To formalize the cutoff level, let μ_1 and σ_1 denote the mean and the standard

[36] This difference in the number of observations is due to the fact that the Φ_k^i criteria require the availability of bilateral trade data with a precision of four digits for several consecutive years. While Φ_3^i requires data for only three years (i.e. t, $t-2$, and $t-3$), Φ_4^i requires data for four years (i.e. t, $t-2$, $t-3$, and $t-4$).

[37] The hypotheses are H_0: $\mu_1-\mu_2=0$ vs. H_1: $\mu_1-\mu_2\neq 0$, where μ_1 represents a criterion's mean in the subsample of injured countries, and μ_2 represents a criterion's mean in the subsample of non-injured countries. Furthermore, let D be the difference of the subsample means. It follows that $D(\Phi_3^i)=1.728862975$ and $D(\Phi_4^i)=0.673370718$. Using a pooled standard deviation s, the test statistic $\Theta = D/s$ is asymptotically normal distributed. In particular, $\Theta_{\Phi_3^i} = 2.670699463$ and $\Theta_{\Phi_4^i} = 3.150306819$. Hence, the Null hypothesis can be rejected for both criteria on all reasonable significance levels (i.e. 10, 5, and 1% in a two-sided test).

[38] The test for different means suggests that Φ_4^i is slightly more powerful than Φ_3^i for distinguishing between injured and non-injured countries. A disadvantage of Φ_4^i as opposed to Φ_3^i clearly is the more excessive data requirement and its implications for a sample selection bias.

Table 8. Distribution of selection criteria in the sample

Subsample	Injured countries		Non-injured countries	
Criterion	Φ_3^i	Φ_4^i	Φ_3^i	Φ_4^i
Mean	1.004962804	1.001819577	2.733825779	1.675199294
Std. dev.	0.446674356	0.632216268	10.10916218	2.66398746
Observations	44		196	

deviation of Φ_4^i in the subsample of injured countries, respectively. Moreover, let α denote the probability of an alpha error, i.e. erroneously judging an injured country to be non-injured. Then the cutoff level is denoted by

$$\Phi_4^{\text{cut}}(\alpha) := z_{1-\alpha}(\mu_1, \sigma_1) \tag{A.4}$$

where $z(\cdot)$ denotes the α quantile of a normal distribution with mean μ_1 and standard deviation σ_1. Finally, a country is assumed to have suffered from an offender's disputable trade measure if and only if

$$\Phi_4^i \leq \Phi_4^{\text{cut}}(\alpha). \tag{A.5}$$

References

Anderson, K. (2002), Peculiarities of retaliation in WTO dispute settlement. *Centre for Economic Policy Research Discussion Paper Series*, 3578.

Bown, C.P. (2005), Participation in WTO dispute settlement: complaints, interested parties and free riders. *World Bank Economic Review* 19 (2), 287–310.

Brown, C.P., Hoekman, B.M. (2005), WTO dispute settlement and the missing developing country cases: engaging the private sector. *Journal of International Economic Law* 8 (4), 861–890.

Broda, C., Limao, N., Weinstein, D.E. (2006), Optimal tariffs: the evidence. *National Bureau of Economic Research Working Paper Series*, 12033.

Bronckers, M., van den Broek, N. (2005), Financial compensation in the WTO. *Journal of International Economic Law* 8 (1), 101–126.

Greene, W.H. (2003), *Econometric Analysis*, fifth ed. Prentice Hall, Upper Saddle River, NJ.

Guzman, A.T., Simmons, B. (2005), Power plays and capacity constraints: the selection of defendants in WTO disputes. *Journal of Legal Studies* 34, 557–598.

Horn, H., Mavroidis, P.C., Nordström, H. (1999), Is the Use of the WTO Dispute Settlement System biased? *Centre for Economic Policy Research Discussion Paper Series 2340*.

Horn, H., Mavroidis, P.C. (2006), The WTO dispute settlement data set. *The World Bank.*

Jordan, M. (2005), Sanktionsmöglichkeiten im WTO-Streitbeilegungsverfahren. *Hamburger Studien zum Europöaischen und Internationalen Recht 41.*

Judge, G.G., Hill, R.C., Griffiths, W.E., Lütkepohl, H., Lee, T.-C. (1988), *Introduction to the Theory and Practice of Econometrics*, second ed. Wiley, Malden, MA.

Kennan, J., Riezman, R. (1988), Do big countries win tariff wars? *International Economic Review* 29 (1), 81–85.

Kovenock, D., Thursby, M. (1992), GATT, dispute settlement and cooperation. National Bureau of Economic Research Working Paper Series 4071.

Nordström, H. (2005), The cost of WTO litigation, legal aid and small claim procedures. Discussion Paper at the 2005 Conference of the Center for World Affairs and the Global Economy (WAGE) at the University of Wisconsin, Madison.

Shaffer, G., Mosoti, V., Qureshi, A. (2003), Towards a development-supportive dispute settlement system in the WTO. *International Center for Trade and Sustainable Development Resource Paper 5.*

Subramanian, A., Watal, J. (2000), Can TRIPS serve as an enforcement device for developing countries in the WTO. *Journal of International Economic Law* 3 (3), 403–416.

Wilckens, S. (2007), Should WTO dispute settlement be subsidized? CeGe Discussion Paper Series 62.

PART IV

Specific Issues in Dispute Settlement

CHAPTER 10

Agricultural Trade Disputes in the WTO

Tim Josling

Freeman Spogli Institute, Encina Hall, Stanford University, Stanford, CA 94305, USA
E-mail address: josling@stanford.edu

Abstract
Agricultural trade has generated more than its share of disputes in the past fifty years. Lack of a clear structure of rules to constrain government activity in these markets, coupled with the particularly sensitive nature of trade in basic foodstuffs, has been the main cause of this disproportion. New rules agreed in the Uruguay Round provided an improved framework for government policy in this area, and a temporary exemption was given to certain subsidies from challenge in the WTO (the Peace Clause). However, the expiry of the Peace Clause in 2003 and a growing willingness on the part of exporters to challenge domestic farm programs in other countries through action under the Dispute Settlement Understanding has once again stirred the agricultural pot. Now trade disputes are frequently leading to litigation, encouraged by the slow progress in the Doha Round of trade negotiations. In particular, the scope for domestic subsidies, under the Agreement on Agriculture and the Agreement on Subsidies and Countervailing Measures, has increasingly become the subject of litigation. Countries may have to further modify their domestic policies so as to reduce their vulnerability to challenge in the WTO.

Keywords: WTO trade disputes, agricultural trade conflicts, trade litigation

JEL classifications: F13, F53

1. Introduction

Agricultural trade accounts for a small and declining share of global merchandise trade.[1] But its share of trade disputes is large and shows few signs of declining.[2] For the first fifty years of the General Agreement on

[1] Agricultural exports now make up 8 percent of global exports.
[2] Of the 367 requests for consultations made to the Dispute Settlement Board, 100 have primarily been about agricultural trade, a share of 27 percent.

Frontiers of Economics and Globalization
Volume 6 ISSN: 1574-8715
DOI: 10.1108/S1574-8715(2009)0000006013

Tariffs and Trade (GATT)/WTO multilateral trade system, one could have put this down to imprecise rules and inadequate enforcement mechanisms in that sector (Josling *et al.*, 1996). With the introduction of the Uruguay Round Agreement on Agriculture (URAA) much of the ambiguity was removed, but this did not stem the flow of disputes. Indeed, the strengthened legal provisions of the Dispute Settlement Understanding (DSU) gave encouragement to complainants to attempt to settle long-standing disputes that had eluded the weaker GATT dispute settlement process.

New disputes also emerged, reflecting changing trade concerns. Many of these new disputes related to health and safety issues, took advantage of the more structured rules included in the sanitary and phytosanitary (SPS) Agreement. Others dealt with market access issues, in part over the interpretation of the new obligations. Recently, agricultural disputes have challenged the scope for domestic and export subsidies, under the Agreement on Agriculture and the Agreement on Subsidies and Countervailing Measures (SCM). In the absence of an agreement in the Doha Round one might expect these conflicts to intensify, as countries attempt to use litigation to achieve what might otherwise be gained through negotiation. And if the Agreement on Agriculture does become revised in a successful Doha conclusion, there will be no doubt that several more issues will need to be resolved through the DSU. The prospect of litigative peace in agriculture remains remote.

This chapter reviews the agricultural disputes since the end of the Uruguay Round. After a section that provides an overview of the 100 or so cases that focus on agricultural products, the chapter identifies several disputes that have been taken through all the stages of the dispute settlement process, and have therefore shed significant light on the obligations that countries adopted in the Uruguay Round. Following a discussion of these cases, a concluding section reviews their significance for trade and policy developments in agriculture.

2. *An overview of agricultural trade disputes under the WTO*

There have been about 100 disputes over agricultural trade notified to the Dispute Settlement Body (DSB) over the lifetime of the WTO.[3] Figure 1

[3] The definition of an "agricultural" case is somewhat arbitrary. In this chapter I include all cases that deal largely with agricultural trade even if the dispute is over an aspect of the SPS Agreement. However, in these cases I do not dwell on the implications for the SPS Agreement, but focus on the importance for agricultural trade and policy. I have excluded cases dealing with fish and fish products. Where the disputes have a broad scope (such as the challenges to India's use of quantitative restrictions) I have chosen to exclude them, although many agricultural products may have been affected.

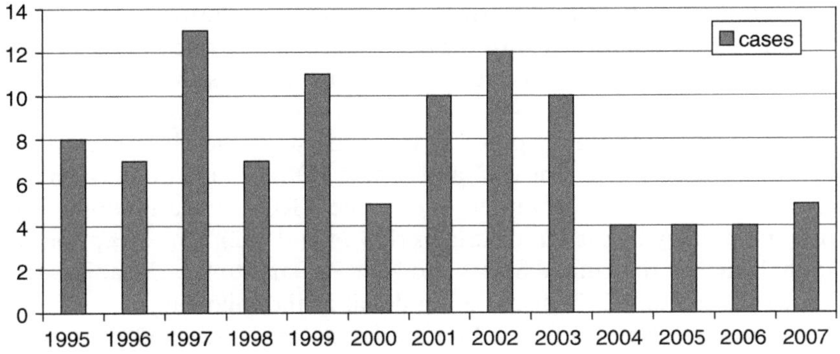

Fig. 1. WTO disputes: agricultural cases. Source: Annex Table.

shows the distribution of these agricultural cases over time.[4] On an average there have been about eight disputes every year that can be classified as agricultural.[5] In the first couple of years of the WTO 15 agricultural disputes were notified to the DSB. Four of these agricultural disputes focused on issues of implementation by the European Community (EC) of the Uruguay Round commitments (DS 9, 13, 17, and 25; see Annex Table).[6] Over this period, the United States initiated three disputes with Korea about the treatment of imported agricultural products, reflecting a long-running concern by US exporters (DS 3, 5, and 41). And two of the most prominent of the agricultural disputes were litigated in 1996, both with their origin in the GATT and each involving the United States and the EC (as was typical of many of the trade disputes at that time). These "legacy" disputes were over the EC's (1992) import regime for bananas (DS 16, 27, and 105) and the (1988) EC regulations over the use of hormones in beef (DS 26 and 48).[7] At least in the United States, the justification for the strengthening of the GATT dispute settlement process through the DSU was in part based on the prospect of finally resolving these conflicts.

As these disputes were being adjudicated, a burst of new litigation occurred in 1997, with 13 disputes that year, perhaps reflecting the lag

---

[4] For the purposes of this chapter a dispute is initiated by the request for consultations that is notified to the Dispute Settlement Board. It is then given a "DS" number. The WTO website keeps track of these individual disputes, and records any action taken.

[5] The average number of requests for consultation notified to the CSB has been 28 per year since 1995.

[6] The convention followed by the WTO of referring to the European Union as the EC (European Community) is adopted here. Although technically correct, this convention may seem a little anachronistic to the reader.

[7] Another dispute that had been prominent in the GATT era was over the EC subsidies to oilseeds. The final agreement that ended this dispute was negotiated at the same time that the modalities for agriculture in the Uruguay Round were agreed between the United States and the EC, at Blair House in November 1992.

from commercial concern to formal request for consultations. Most of the 1997 cases were concerned with the operation of tariff rate quotas (TRQs) and other import regulations, representing the tensions that accompanied the process of "tariffication" and the removal of non-tariff import barriers. Typical of the disputes at this time were the challenges to the operation of TRQs by the EC and Brazil (DS 69) on poultry and by New Zealand (DS 72) on butter, and to the TRQs of the Philippines on pork and poultry by the United States (DS 74 and 102). One exception was the challenge by the United States and New Zealand to the Canadian dairy policy (DS 103 and 113, discussed in detail in the following).

Disputes in 1998 also focused on market access issues, and the number of cases fell into more "normal" levels. Among these complaints was a challenge by Canada to transport restrictions on cattle, hogs, and grain by the United States (DS 144) that also reflected an attempt to settle an older dispute using the newfound legal structure of the WTO.[8] A renewed burst of activity in 1999 was followed by a less contentious year in 2000, with the focus again on import regulations in both the years.[9] The year 2001 saw a number of safeguard complaints, in part due to the weakening of world prices at the turn of the century.

A significant shift in the type of agricultural disputes is noticeable in 2002, with the challenge by Australia, Brazil, and (later) Thailand to the EC sugar regime. The conflict was over the extent to which that regime in effect provided export subsidies about the scheduled limits. This was followed by a challenge from Brazil to the US policy toward upland cotton, on this occasion questioning the subsidies given to US producers. Thus the emphasis had shifted from disputes over import regulations and contingent protection to the farm policies that were becoming exposed to legal scrutiny. Litigation began to be discussed as a complement to the slow-moving Doha Round in the effort to curb subsidies notably in the United States and EC. The cat was out of the bag.

The year 2003 saw another 10 disputes on agricultural issues reported to the DSB. Two cases reflected the changed nature of food trade: the resurrection of an earlier challenge by the United States to the EC's system of protecting Geographical indications (GIs), and a challenge by three countries to the slow process of authorizing the release of biotech products on the EC market (DS 291, 292, and 293).[10] At the end of 2003 the Peace Clause expired, widening the net of subsidies that could be appealed

[8] For a more detailed history of US–Canadian agricultural trade disputes see Barichello *et al.*, 2005.

[9] An interesting issue was raised by Brazil (DS 154) on the preferential treatment for coffee imported by the EC from competitor countries under regional trade agreements.

[10] The original US GI case (DS 174) had been held in abeyance, and was revived following a new policy initiative by the EC. Australia took out a case in 2003 (DS 290) that then was joined with the earlier case.

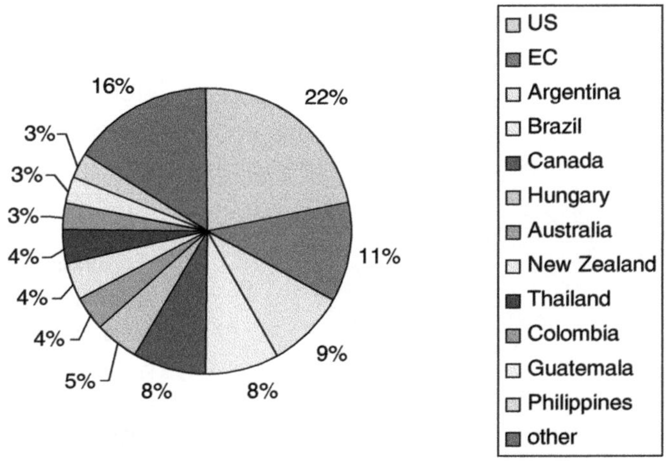

Fig. 2. Shares of requests for consultation on agricultural trade, by complainant. Source: Author's calculations based on WTO website.

under the SCM.[11] There was no immediate rush to litigation, though a number of countries actively explored the possibility for successful challenges. The panel report on the US-cotton dispute (DS 267) emerged in September 2004 and that on EC-sugar (DS 265, 266, and 283) was circulated in October 2004. The reports and their broad confirmation by the Appellate Body gave renewed hope to those who saw the DSU as an effective way of forcing policy change in the EC and the United States. But, in fact the number of new cases initiated since 2004 has been markedly less than before, perhaps reflecting the influence of continued negotiations in the Doha Round. Nevertheless, the most significant cases in the past three years have been those that have challenged US domestic support notification (DS 357 and 365), again reflecting the emphasis since 2002 on using current agreements to rein in farm support policies.

In contrast to the GATT dispute settlement process, which was used primarily by developed countries, the DSU mechanism has been used by a number of developing countries to resolve agricultural disputes.[12] The number (and percentage) of cases brought by individual WTO members is shown in Figure 2. About half of the complaints have been lodged by four countries, namely, the United States, the EC, Argentina,

---

[11] For more detail on the effect of the Peace Clause on agricultural disputes see Steinberg and Josling, 2003.

[12] For a comprehensive treatment of the difficulties faced by developing countries in using the GATT dispute settlement process see Barton *et al.*, 2006.

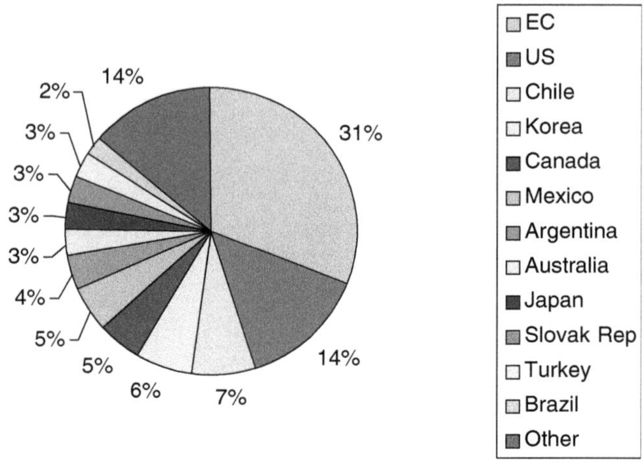

Fig. 3. Shares of requests for consultation on agricultural trade, by respondent. Source: Author's calculations based on WTO website.

and Brazil. It is of course normal for exporters to bring challenges to the policies of importing countries, and for the larger countries to be able to afford the expense of litigation. Small countries may hesitate to use the dispute settlement mechanism knowing that even if successful they have little chance of achieving the desired policy change. But the fact that 23 countries initiated requests for consultation (and many more joined disputes as third parties) shows that there appeared to be a need for such an outlet for commercial tensions in agricultural trade.

If agricultural cases are initiated by frustrated exporters it is natural that their complaints would be focused on the major (and most protected) import markets. Imports of agricultural products tend to be less concentrated than agricultural exports, reflecting the balance between population and land. But the same concentration of disputes among a few countries is evident from the list of respondents. Figure 3 shows the distribution of post-WTO agricultural disputes by respondent.

The distribution of respondents does not appear to reflect the trade pattern. Once again, 23 countries have been named as respondents in requests for consultations, and many of these are exporters. In fact, the EC, the United States, and Chile have had to respond to over one-half of all complaints. And exporters such as Argentina, Australia, Brazil, Canada, Hungary, and Mexico have all been the respondents in agricultural disputes. This emphasizes the often overlooked feature of agricultural trade policy that exporters are sometimes as protectionist as importers when it comes to parts of the agricultural sector that are less than competitive. Therefore, the disputes are often among exporters for

Table 1. Classification of agricultural cases in the WTO, 1995–2007

	Number of cases	Panels established	
		Number	Percent
Market access	40	13	33
Domestic support	3	3	100
Export subsidies	7	5	71
SPS	11	6	55
A/D, CVD	15	4	27
Safeguards	11	7	64
UR Implementation	4	2	50
Other	9	4	44
Total	100	44	44

Source: Author's calculations based on WTO website.

whom domestic politics often complicates commercial diplomacy and leads to ambivalence in trade policy.[13]

It was indicated earlier that many of the cases involving agricultural trade were focused on import regulations and other aspects of market access. This is confirmed in Table 1, where the 100 disputes are grouped on the basis of the grounds for challenge. Forty percent of the requests for consultations were on market access issues: if one includes challenges over health and safety standards imposed by importers and the contingent protection through antidumping duties, countervailing levels and safeguards, the share increases to 77 percent. By contrast, only 10 percent of the disputes were over issues related to domestic support and export competition.[14]

As with other disputes, agricultural challenges are often settled without the aid of a panel and formal litigation. Table 1 also shows the proportion of cases in each category that resulted in the establishment of a panel. The relationship between the grounds for complaint and the likelihood of a panel being established is significant. Forty-four percent of agricultural disputes reached the panel stage. But in the case of market access challenges, only one-third of the cases resulted in a panel: only one-quarter of the disputes over antidumping and countervailing duties reached that stage.

[13] One would expect these intra-exporter conflicts to be less when trade negotiations are in progress, as the tendency will be for exporters to focus on importing countries. But the Doha Round has progressed so haltingly that disputes among exporters have not been noticeably muted.

[14] The Agreement on Agriculture distinguishes between market access, domestic support, and export competition. This distinction is not always useful when considering disputes. Nor is the distinction between complaints under the URAA and other parts of the WTO (GATS, SCM, etc.). Complainants regularly include multiple grounds for challenge. The categories in the table are therefore based on a subjective view of the main issues involved and not a listing of the legal grounds for challenge.

Table 2. Current status of agricultural disputes in the WTO

	Number of cases
Adopted by DSB	32
Report awaited	8
No report issued	2
Withdrawn	2
Replaced	1
Resolved	12
Resolution not notified to DSB	43
	100

Source: Author's calculations based on WTO website.

So these cases are apparently easier to resolve, in part because the trade remedies and often the challenged import regulations are themselves temporary.[15] Disputes over export subsidies and domestic support tend to be more intractable, and involve potentially significant domestic policy changes.

The current (January 2008) status of the agricultural cases considered here is shown in Table 2. Of the 44 panels established to consider agricultural cases, 32 have reported and a further 8 have yet to report.[16] In the other four cases the challenge was withdrawn, or the panel has been in abeyance for several years; a further case was replaced by another one covering the same complaint.[17] Twelve cases were notified to the DSB as having been resolved bilaterally, without the need for as panel, and a further 43 cases were presumably resolved, though the DSB was never notified of the outcome.[18]

The number of disputes that are notified to the DSB overstates the number of policies or procedures that are actually in dispute. It has been common for two or more countries to complain about the same alleged violation of WTO rules. Correcting for this duplication, and for the fact that some countries revise or extend their complaints, the number of separate perceived violations falls to 83. The number of these that actually went to panels also overstates the number of panel decisions. In a number of cases, similar complaints have been grouped and dealt with by the same panel.

[15] Note, however, that the SPS cases more often resulted in the establishment of panels, as many of these trade barriers are less likely to be transitory (Josling *et al.*, 2004).

[16] In the two cases, the DSB has agreed to establish a panel but the panelists are yet to be appointed.

[17] A challenge by Colombia against Chilean safeguards (DS 228) was replaced by a similar challenge with slightly revised complaints (DS 230).

[18] The reluctance of the parties to a dispute to report the successful resolution of that dispute to the DSB is understandable in strategic terms. However, one assumes that all interested parties are aware of the details of the solution, so it would make the assessment of the significance of the DSU simpler if notification were mandated.

Indeed, many of the most contentious cases have been brought by countries acting in concert: the grouping of countries in the banana disputes, the EC-hormones case, the EC-GI case, and the EC-biotech case are examples of coordination among complainants. The number of separate cases that went to panels is therefore 35, generating 31 separate legal opinions.

To see the impact of these opinions, it is necessary to consider the details of several of the most important cases. Six such cases are discussed here: three of them relate to issues of market access and import regulations, the other three to subsidies given to domestic producers under farm support programs. The market access cases include the banana case, with a rich history of market discrimination by the EC in favor of its own former dependencies and colonies; the beef hormone case, considered a landmark in the litigation over health and safety standards; and the EC-GI case that touched upon the provisions of the TRIPS that mandate the protection of regionally named foods. The subsidy cases include the landmark Canada-dairy case that addressed the question of whether export subsidies could result from domestic price setting; the US-cotton case that explored the application of the SCM Agreement to agricultural subsidies; and the EC-sugar case that extended the Canadian dairy ruling.

3. Market access complaints in agriculture

3.1. Bananas

Trade in bananas has elicited a series of disputes over the years, pitting the postcolonial regimes of the EC countries against the US-based multinational companies that had a foothold in those parts of Europe that did not have tropical colonies. The banana controversy in the GATT was stimulated initially by the changes in the European import rules implied in the EC's policy of "Completing the Single Market," which were introduced at the start of 1993.[19] Moving from the varied import systems run by individual countries to an EC-wide policy that could be operated without internal trade barriers proved to be a challenge. "Dollar" bananas appeared to lose some of their market access to those coming from the former colonies of France and the United Kingdom. Some countries in Latin America settled on a market sharing deal with the EC but others complained to no avail.

The Uruguay Round, with its strengthening of the Dispute Settlement process, came along at an opportune time for the disaffected group. Two panel reports under the GATT, in 1993 and 1994, had failed to improve

[19] For more detail on the Banana case see Josling (2003), Chapter 9.

the market position for dollar bananas.[20] The third panel, reporting on May 22, 1997, proved to be more effective. "Bananas III," as the report became known as, found the EC in multiple violation of trade rules (WTO, 1997a). The various steps taken to resolve this conflict continue to this day.

As a "pure" market access case, the banana issue would have been interesting. But the case tackled much more than the conflicts over postcolonial discrimination. It was the first panel to consider an argument that a country had contravened the General Agreement on Trade in Services (GATS). By allocating import licenses to domestic firms based on past shipments, the banana import regime gave valuable trading permits to the competitors of the US-based multinationals. The EC had agreed to end discrimination in "wholesale trade services" in the Uruguay Round. This aspect of the case increased its importance and provided a potentially useful clarification of the relationship between rules for goods trade and those for trade in services.

Four different stages in the unfolding dispute can be distinguished. The first stage was that leading up to the request for consultations in September 1995. During this stage, the dispute was essentially one of market access by Central American companies in the EC market as a result of the consolidation of import quotas when the Single Market regime was adopted. The process of accommodation of these bananas was not easy, but the Banana Framework Agreement (BFA) at least in part met these concerns. The second phase began when the impact of the BFA became apparent and the firms that felt that they were losing market opportunities began to pressure their governments for action. This phase continued through the adoption of the panel report as amended by the appeal process and the EC's announcement that it would change its policies to comply. The third stage of the process started with the realization by the complaining parties that the change in regulations had not in fact solved the problem and that further action was needed. This stage continued for another year, and could only be resolved by a change in policy that was safe from WTO challenge. Such a change was finally agreed between the EC and the United States on April 11, 2001, about eight years after the deliberations of the first banana panel. The changes revolved around the substitution of the import license regime for a "tariff only" approach, while keeping the preferential tariff for African, Caribbean and Pacific (ACP) suppliers. The fourth phase of the dispute (still under consideration) centers on the height of the most favored nation (MFN) tariffs faced by the Central American exporters.

Though GATT and WTO complaints often cite more than one Article which the offending country is supposed to have violated, the banana case is unusual for the lengthy list of purported violations. To illustrate this, the list of legal bases for complaints in the banana case is given in

[20] The panel reports had no impact. The EC effectively prevented their adoption by the General Council, following a long GATT tradition of blocking unfavorable reports.

Table 3. Basis for complaints about the EC banana import regime

GATT Article I:1	Non-discrimination
Article II	Schedule of concessions
Article III	National treatment
Article X	Transparency
Article XI	Elimination of quantitative restrictions
Article XIII	Non-discriminatory administration of quantitative restrictions
Import Licensing Agreement Article 1	General provisions
Article 3	Nonautomatic licenses
Agricultural Agreement Article 4.2	No discretionary import licensing
GATS Article II	Most favored nation treatment
Article XVI	Market Access
Article XVII	National treatment
TRIMS Article 2	National treatment and quantitative restrictions

Source: Josling (2003).

Table 3. The essence of the case was the discriminatory allocation of quotas and the license procedures used to affect the quotas. But non-discrimination as a principle recurs throughout the GATT and the GATS, and thus the same policy measures can be in multiple violation. The EC may have thought that the Lomé waiver was satisfactory cover, but this did not survive the scrutiny of the panel.

The failure of the BFA to satisfy the varied interest of the Latin American producers led directly to the request on February 5, 1996 by Ecuador, Guatemala, Honduras, Mexico, and the United States for consultations with the EC. After the necessary consultations had reached no conclusion the complainants requested the formation of a panel.[21] The panel was established by the DSB on May 8, 1996.

The list of complainants is also of interest. Columbia, Costa Rica, Nicaragua, and Venezuela had been the "beneficiaries" of the BFA, and apparently were not willing to risk the wrath of the EC by trying to better their access. But the EC had not managed to satisfy Guatemala, and that country joined with Honduras in an exactly parallel complaint. Ecuador had joined the WTO only on January 26, 1996, and so was anxious to test its newly acquired rights.[22] The United States had originally intended to stay on the sidelines: it would not have been consistent with the attempt to

[21] The EC was to argue before the panel that this period of consultation had been inadequate: given the long gestation period of this conflict it seems unlikely that any further interchange of information or explanations would have improved the situation.

[22] The EC indicated in its submission to the panel that Ecuador had been persuaded with undue haste (only two weeks after its membership) to join the others as a co-complainant. But one imagines that the Ecuadorian government had anticipated such action before its membership was approved.

build up relations with the Caribbean to be seen to challenge the EC's preferences in that region. But 1996 was an election year. Having sold the WTO to the US Congress partly on the basis of the strengthened DSU, it was vulnerable to the argument that holding the EC to the trade rules was an important aspect of US trade policy. Direct pressure from the US-based multinational corporations, in particular the Chiquita corporation, swung the Clinton administration behind the complaint. At a stroke, this raised the stakes and turned a thorny issue of preference systems into a matter of high principle and policy.[23] Along with the beef hormone dispute the banana case focused attention on the willingness of the EC to subjugate its policy preferences to the judgment of a WTO panel. If it proved unwilling, this would not be lost on those whose support for the extension of multilateral trade rules was tenuous at best.

The substantive issues covered by the GATT that were considered by the panel were of three types: tariff questions, quota allocation questions, and the legality of the import-licensing regime. Several of these issues had also to be considered in the light of agreements that came out of the Uruguay Round, including the Licensing Agreement as well as the Agreement on Agriculture and the Trade-Related Investment Measures (TRIMS) Agreement. In addition, the panel considered the compatibility of the licensing regime with the EC's obligations under the GATS.

The tariff issue was perhaps the easiest of the three. The complainants charged that the differential tariff rates that applied between third country bananas and non-traditional ACP imports was a violation of MFN.[24] No objection was lodged against the duty-free imports from the ACP where these were necessary to conform to the requirements of the Lomé Convention. The WTO had granted the EC a waiver from its Article I obligations in December 1994 (extended in October 1996): the EC argued that this was adequate to cover the whole import regime, and not just the traditional ACP imports. The only tariff question of particular interest to the panel, then, was whether this waiver covered non-traditional imports from ACP countries. They decided that as the waiver was not specifically limited to the traditional trade quantities, it must be assumed that "the preferential tariff for the non-traditional ACP bananas is clearly a tariff preference of the sort that the Lomé waiver was designed to cover." (WTO, 1997a, p. 333) As a consequence, the EC "won" the tariff

---

[23] Mexico followed the lead of the United States in part because of the Mexican ownership at that time of one of the firms (del Monte) and in part as an expression of North American solidarity on a matter of WTO principle.

[24] Guatemala and Honduras, in their joint complaint, added a further tariff issue, arguing that the tariff on third country bananas was above the bound rate of 20 percent. This was in violation of Article II, which refers to the schedules of bindings.

argument and defined in part the relationship between the Lomé Convention and the WTO.

The EC was less fortunate in the case of quota allocation. The argument over the allocation of quotas went to the heart of the complaints over the EC banana regime. At its simplest, the argument revolved around whether the quotas under which banana imports are allowed were allocated in a way consistent with Article XIII of the GATT, which stipulates that they should be allocated in a non-discriminatory way and one that disturbs trade as little as possible. The chapeau of Article XIII:2 states that

> In applying import restrictions to any product, Members shall aim at a distribution of trade in such product approaching as closely as possible the shares which the various Members might be expected to obtain in the absence of such restrictions…
>
> (WTO, 1995)

The complaining parties charged that the EC had allocated the banana import quotas in a way that was inconsistent with this Article. Some countries (the ACP and those that had signed the BFA) had country-specific quotas, while other countries had no such quotas but had to compete for the "other" category of imports. Moreover, they argued that the quotas given to those countries were too large and did not reflect market developments. The allocation method also gave the BFA countries exclusive right to fill any shortfall in supplies under the BFA quotas.

The EC argued that the WTO waiver covered any discrimination under Article XIII as well as Article I. It further argued that it was in effect running two import regimes in parallel, and thus any discrimination between countries covered by different quota schemes was not in violation of the GATT. The traditional ACP bananas were given preference, but this was undoubtedly covered by the waiver and thus could be put on one side: the rest of the banana imports were covered by a tariff quota as entered in the EC schedule, although ACP countries received a (waiver consistent) preference on the tariff to be paid. The panel pointed out that this was the first time a whole quota regime had been called into question, as opposed to the operation of an isolated quota provision. It could also have been said that the spread of tariff quotas that emerged from the Agreement on Agriculture made this an issue of much greater significance. The allocation of quotas (as well as the distribution of licenses, as discussed in the following) is of increasing interest in agricultural trade policy.

The panel found that the EC only had one quota regime for purposes of analyzing its compatibility with Article XIII, regardless of how the EC has chosen to administer the different quotas (WTO, 1997a, para. 7.82). The EC had reached an agreement with the BFA countries, allocated shares in respect of non-traditional ACP bananas, and granted country-specific quotas to ACP countries. This was the regime as laid down in Regulation

404/93. Moreover, it did discriminate against the countries outside the BFA and the ACP. Columbia and Costa Rica had a substantial interest in the EC market and thus could reasonably have been included in the BFA: Nicaragua and Venezuela did not have such a substantial interest and had less of a claim than some of the complaining countries (Guatemala, Honduras, and Mexico).[25] The EC's quota allocation scheme thus violated Article XIII and would have to be modified. However, the panel found that the quota allocation for the ACP bananas, even if in violation of Article XIII, was covered by the WTO waiver for the Lomé Convention.[26]

If the quota allocation system ran afoul of Article XIII, the licensing system that gave expression to the quotas came in for the most severe condemnation by the panel. This system was judged with respect to its transparency and its tendency to discriminate. The system itself was complex, which in itself made for a lack of transparency. But the complaining parties charged that the intention of the license system was to favor firms that had historically imported bananas from the Windward Isles and French overseas territories. This discrimination was contrary to Articles I (non-discrimination) and III (national treatment) of the GATT. It was also claimed that the CMOB violated Article X of the GATT that requires that countries administer trade measures, including licenses, "in a uniform, impartial and reasonable manner." Moreover, it was argued that the EC's licensing system contravened the Agreement on Import Licensing Procedures (Licensing Agreement) that had been incorporated into the basic rules of the WTO at the conclusion of the Uruguay Round.[27] In addition, it was charged that the arrangement violated the TRIMS agreement, which contains a list of trade-related investment measures such as purchasing requirements that are deemed to be inconsistent with national treatment in the GATT. The requirement that firms have to purchase bananas from the ACP to apply for "B" Licenses was therefore a violation of this provision.

Perhaps, the most significant challenge to the import-licensing regime was the suggestion that it was inconsistent with the GATS. The GATS was one of the major innovations of the Uruguay Round, putting service trade on a similar footing to that in goods. Non-discrimination and national

---

[25] Ecuador and Panama were not GATT/WTO members at the time of the BFA. Ecuador was deemed by the panel to have the right to challenge the quota allocation of the BFA upon joining ("all Members have rights") though as the EC pointed out it might have been better to have dealt with this issue in the Protocol of Accession.

[26] The Appellate Body later reversed this finding (WTO, 1997b).

[27] The Licensing Agreement provided more detail on the way in which licensing measures were to be administered, and is included as an Annex 1A agreement in the Marrakesh Agreement which established the WTO.

treatment are fundamental principles of the GATS, as they are in the GATT. But the GATS contains some restrictions on the applicability of these principles. The banana case was the first major test of the scope of these rules and their relation to those in goods trade.

The first task of the panel was to clarify the relationship between the GATT, with its emphasis on the conditions under which goods are traded, with the GATS, which deals with services. Clearly, the trading of goods requires a number of services. If goods markets are distorted by discriminatory trade policies, does it follow that the provision of services that accompany those goods and effectuate the trade is also distorted? Or would that constitute "double jeopardy" for the country implementing such contested regulations? The EC argued before the panel that it should not be made to justify its policy under both the GATT and the GATS, as it was not imposing any measure that discriminated directly on the provision of services. The fact that the "necessary" quota system impacted service providers was not enough to establish a violation of the GATS. The United States argued that, to the contrary, the way the license system worked was to make it much more difficult and expensive for the US corporations to compete with those based in Europe.[28] Thus the licensing system was indeed contrary to GATS.

The panel had little difficulty in deciding that the same measure can violate both GATT and the GATS. Indeed, the specificity with which the import regime for bananas distributed licenses, by operator category and activity, made it difficult to argue that measures had no effect on the competitiveness of particular firms.[29] The panel found that the EC regime did indeed violate the non-discrimination and national treatment provisions of the GATS. The Lomé waiver was of no help here, of course, as it related to the obligations under the GATT, specifically Article I. Once again, though, the issue was not the import of traditional ACP bananas but the BFA quotas and the third-country quotas. The panel ruled that the EC be required to change its import regulations to avoid conflict with the GATS.

---

[28] The US had a particular reason to push the GATS complaint, as it had championed the inclusion of services in the WTO. As with the DSU, the GATS was a major selling point within the US to convince skeptics that the WTO was worthwhile. To have at hand a convenient case to explore the implications of the GATS was fortunate. The EC, in general content to include services in the Uruguay Round, chose to nominate "wholesale trade services" as one of the sectors in its liberalization offer. This meant that it was subject to the general "national treatment" provision of the GATS, along with "non-discrimination".

[29] An important aspect of the GATS is that it takes the WTO a significant step toward considerations of the impact of policies on firms as opposed to goods. Thus, the arguments that the panel had to consider dealt with the competitive position of companies and involved commercially sensitive information.

3.2. Beef hormones

Similar to the banana case that started well before the establishment of the WTO, the beef hormone dispute was also a legacy from the GATT. The events leading up to the EC ban on the domestic use of hormones in cattle raising and hence on imports of hormone-treated beef are important in explaining the political longevity of this US/EC dispute.[30] European livestock producers were searching for ways to stimulate growth in cattle, and took eagerly to the use of hormones, but sometimes with inadequate knowledge of the consequences of misuse of such chemicals.[31] Regulatory control sometimes slipped between the cracks, as coordination and harmonization of national regulations progressed haltingly in the EC.

European authorities first proposed a hormone ban in response to public anxieties that emerged following highly publicized reports of "hormone scandals" in the late 1970s. The first incident was reported in 1977, when some schoolchildren in northern Italy exhibited signs of premature hormonal development that investigators initially suspected was linked to illegal growth hormones in veal or poultry served in school lunches. Although exhaustive examination of possible causes of the abnormalities produced no concrete conclusions, a public furor arose over the use of hormones in livestock production. The second incident occurred three years later, again in Italy, when numerous samples of veal-based baby food were found to contain residues of the illegal hormonal drug diethylstilbestrol (DES), further alarming European consumers.[32] Consumer organizations called for a boycott of veal that had a significant adverse effect on the market and incidentally on the administration of the agricultural market policy which at that time supported veal as well as beef prices.

The United States took the issue of the EC hormone ban to the GATT in March 1987, alleging that there was no legitimate basis for the ban under the Tokyo Round Standards Code. When bilateral consultations between the EC and the United States failed to resolve the matter, the United States requested that a technical expert group be convened

---

[30] The discussion in this section draws heavily from Josling *et al.*, 2006.

[31] Naturally occurring hormones in cattle and humans can be added to feed or applied to increase the rate of animal growth (growth promotion purposes), to synchronize the estrus cycles of dairy cattle to lower production costs (zootechnical purposes), or to correct certain endocrine dysfunctions (therapeutic purposes). "Synthetic" hormones, which mimic the action of natural hormones, are only used for growth promotion.

[32] DES is a synthetic estrogen that had been widely used since the late 1930s for both human and animal health purposes until epidemiological evidence linked the use of DES by pregnant women to the development of cervical cancer in their daughters. Medical and livestock uses of DES were eventually banned in the United States (in 1979) and in Europe (in 1981).

pursuant to Article 14.5 of the Code to examine the issue of scientific support for the EC's measure. Under the GATT rules, the EC blocked formation of the group, arguing that its ban was related to a processing standard (known as PPM, for production and processing method) rather than a product standard (PS) that was not covered. The EC had argued that its sole obligation under the Standards Code was to abstain from the *intentional* circumvention of the disciplines by formulating its measures as PPMs rather than PSs.

As this dispute escalated, both sides publicly considered trade restrictions against the other.[33] When the ban went into effect, the United States retaliated with 100 percent *ad valorem* duties on a range of products imported from Europe. The EC requested a panel to examine the legitimacy of the retaliation, but this request was blocked by the United States. Later in 1989, a joint US–EC Task Force agreed to a limited compromise to allow imports of some US beef products that were certified to be "hormone free" (the ban previously applied to all US beef, as hormones are widely used in the US cattle sector) as well as other beef products destined for pet food. The United States, in response, withdrew some products from its retaliation list.

Further compromise, however, was precluded by the increasing polarization of domestic political forces on both sides of the Atlantic. The US beef industry was convinced that the ban was a protectionist device aimed at restricting trade. The US government worried that in addition to the technical criteria of effectiveness, safety and reliability, a "fourth criterion" of the economic and social impact of the adoption of a particular technology was being endorsed by the EC in its standard for veterinary and other substances, and would become established as an excuse for protecting other agricultural markets. The European producer was determined that US beef should not escape the hormone ban, and the Parliament appeared desirous of hanging onto a popular cause even at the expense of some embarrassment for the Commission. The legal stalemate and ensuing exchange of tit-for-tat measures was widely viewed as one of the more visible failures of the GATT dispute settlement mechanisms. It was the hormones dispute, more than any other case, which motivated negotiation of stronger disciplines on technical regulations in the GATT Uruguay Round. Yet, even knowing that the hormones issue was going to re-emerge under these stronger rules, the EC did not thwart the adoption of the SPS Agreement.

---

[33] For example, in 1988, the US Food Safety and Inspection Service (FSIS) began to request certification from EC authorities that meat produced in EC countries met US safety requirements for hormone residues and conformity assessment procedures were equivalent to US standards. The EC responded with the announcement of a counter-retaliation valued at $360 million (that it never implemented) that targeted products such as California walnuts (Kramer, 1989).

With new Uruguay Round rules for SPS measures and dispute settlement procedures in place, the United States renewed its complaint against the beef import ban. In January 1996, the United States requested formal consultations with the EC, which were joined by Australia, Canada, and New Zealand. The United States charged that the EC ban violated not only the basic GATT provisions, but the technical barriers to trade (TBT) and SPS agreements as well. The central claim was that the ban was not based on science. The EC responded that the ban was the only feasible option for meeting its very high public health goals. The parties met in March, but a mutually satisfactory solution could not be found. The following month, the United States requested that the WTO establish a panel to hear the dispute. The EC countered by requesting a panel to review the legitimacy of the US retaliatory tariffs, whereupon the United States unilaterally rescinded them in July 1996. The first meeting of the panel to hear the complaint by the United States (later joined by Canada) against the EC hormone ban was set for October 1996. As long anticipated, the *Hormones* dispute became the bellwether test of the new disciplines in the SPS Agreement.

The outcome of the Hormones case was favorable to the United States and Canada. In its report issued on August 18, 1997, the WTO dispute settlement panel concurred with the complainants that the EC ban on beef treated with hormones for growth-promotion purposes was inconsistent with its obligations under the SPS Agreement. In support of these findings, the panel noted that the scientific evidence that the EC had reported as informing its regulatory decision fell into two categories. Those studies which had specifically evaluated the potential toxic effects of hormones used to promote growth in cattle concurred that, at present, there was no indication that these substances posed public health risks when properly used. Other research, which the EC argued raised serious questions about the methodology or conclusions of these studies, examined the carcinogenic or genotoxic potential of entire categories of hormones or the hormones at issue in general. As such, the panel stated, these latter studies did not qualify as a risk assessment – in this case, an evaluation of the consequences of consuming beef from cattle treated with growth hormones – as defined in the SPS Agreement.[34]

It was anticipated that, whatever the outcome, the Appellate Body would be asked to review the panel's decision, and indeed, all three parties to the dispute requested a review of both procedural and substantive findings in the panel's report. The Appellate Body released its report in January 1998, ruling on 14 issues. The Appellate Body overruled

[34] Moreover, the panel noted, the scientific experts that it had consulted during its proceedings (under the terms of Article 13 of the DSU) had concurred that this evidence did not invalidate or contradict the scientific conclusions that had been reached by the first group of studies.

the panel on several points, but concurred with the panel that the EC measure was not in conformity with all of the SPS Agreement disciplines.[35] Following the appeal, the EC said that it required four more years to conduct additional risk assessments before policy changes could be considered. The United States and Canada countered that this did not constitute implementation, so the matter went to arbitration in Geneva. The arbitrator concluded that 15 months was a reasonable time to comply.[36] The arbitrator also noted that requests for additional time to conduct new studies or consult experts to demonstrate consistency of a measure was not consistent with the requirement for prompt compliance.

The EC then announced that it would proceed with scientific studies regardless of the arbitrator's decision. In the interim, United States and Canada discussed potential compensation schemes or trade concessions that the EC could offer to compensate the beef producers for loss of the market access due to the hormone ban. Among the options discussed was labeling. The United States agreed that it could label hormone-treated beef as "a product of the USA." It could not agree to a label that would indicate the level of hormones in the beef was higher than a comparable product from the EC, arguing that it is unclear that the level would be higher and such a label would be potentially misleading to consumers.

With no compensation scheme in place, the WTO offered retaliation to the United States and Canada in the form of increased tariffs on EC exports totaling about $128 million. In the meantime, the EC has proceeded with its scientific evaluation of the six hormones through the Scientific Committee on veterinary measures for public health. The Committee opined that it could establish no acceptable daily intake for the hormones. On the basis of this opinion, the EC proposed a permanent ban on estradiol, and a provisional ban on the other five hormones until another committee could review the evidence again to determine if these five hormones might be safely used for therapeutic and technical purposes. The matter was then put before the European Council, but it has not been acted on to date.

---

[35] The Appellate Body held that the statement in the SPS Agreement that a measure shall be based on an international standard where one exists (except as otherwise provided for in the agreement) does not imply that measures need to conform to international standards. If this were so, contended the judges, the SPS Agreement would vest international standards (that are recommendations under the terms of the Codex) with obligatory force and effect. To sustain such an assumption, the Appellate Body argued, language far more specific and compelling than that found in Article 3 of the SPS Agreement would be necessary.

[36] The arbitrator that established a May 1999 deadline for compliance had noted that "It would not be in keeping with the requirement of prompt compliance to include in the reasonable period of time, time to conduct studies or to consult experts to demonstrate the consistency of a measure already judged to be inconsistent." (WTO, 1998).

The effect that the legal resolution of this landmark dispute would have on the issue of the regulation of hormone use and other food safety cases remains uncertain. But, it has defined the scope of the SPS Agreement and made more public the dilemma that regulations face in balancing consumer safety based on science with consumer sentiment based on perception.[37] The beef hormone case has dramatically demonstrated the limits of the DSU in imposing politically unacceptable solutions on powerful countries. It has also shown that not all legally sanctioned results of SPS dispute settlement cases give desirable trade outcomes. This landmark case has thus (for the moment at least) resulted in less rather than more international trade. Trade sanctions are by far the least preferable of the possible outcomes of the WTO dispute settlement process. But the granting of authorized retaliation under the rule of law may still be superior to undisciplined unilateral tit-for-tat measures, such as those that occurred between the United States and EC in the 1980s, which can be described as the equivalent of "vigilante justice" in trade. Sanctions are tolerated by the EC, as they are small in cost and diffuse in impact. Short of a change of heart by the US beef industry, which might eventually accept compensating market access for additional hormone-free beef into the EC, it is not easy to see a resolution to this conflict.

3.3. EC-GIs

Trade disputes in agriculture in the area of intellectual property have been almost absent. But, as with other sectors of the economy, the establishment of intellectual property rights has become an important aspect of trade and global commerce. The TRIPS agreement addresses agricultural and food products directly, in the provisions (in Articles 22 and 23), which define members' obligation to protect GIs within their

[37] The WTO dispute over EC measures regulating biotech products raised some of the same legal issues as the hormones case. Argentina, Canada, and the United States argued that the EC Commission's failure to complete the process set out in its own directives and regulations for the premarketing review of 27 biotech products between October 1998 and August 2003 constituted a *de facto* ban on these products, which was not based on a risk assessment. The complainants also argued that nine specific prohibitions by EC member states on biotech products that had been formally approved by the EC were likewise not based on a risk assessment. The EC argued that there have been no undue delays in its scientific approval processes, that were "premised on the application of a prudent and precautionary approach." The WTO panel issued its report in this highly visible dispute in September 2006, concurring with the complainants that the EC had maintained a *de facto* ban on biotech products that violated its obligations under the SPS Agreement. Specifically, the panel noted that "it is clear that application of a prudent and precautionary approach is, and must be, subject to reasonable limits, lest the precautionary approach swallow the discipline" imposed by the SPS Agreement. The panel likewise agreed with the complainants that the prohibitions maintained by EC member states were not based on a risk assessment.

markets. The TRIPS provisions on GIs have been the subject of a trade dispute that led to the setting up of a WTO Dispute Settlement Panel. This has given the opportunity to clarify some key issues. The challenge was initiated by the United States in June 1999, when it requested consultations with the EC on the alleged lack of protection for US trademarks and GIs in the EC. Specifically, the United States contended that the EC did not accord as much protection to US GIs or similar trademarks as it did to EC producers. Such a situation would be a violation of the WTO principle of "national treatment," which holds that foreign and domestic products should be subject to the same rules. It would also violate several provisions of the TRIPS Agreement, which reasserts the right of national treatment in the case of intellectual property protection.

Initially, the United States objected to the Regulation 2081/92 governing GIs (except in the wine sector), as amended. This led to inconclusive talks but neither a resolution nor the selection of a panel. But the revision of the legislation in the EC in April 2003 raised more concerns in the United States, and this time the United States was joined by Australia in the complaint. A panel was requested by the United States and Australia in August 2003, and agreed in October of that year. The panel ruled in April 2005 that the EC has indeed failed to give the US trademark holders adequate protection, as required. The main points of the Panel decision, as confirmed by the Appellate Body, are summarized in Table 4.

The outcome of the WTO case managed to give comfort to both sides to the dispute. The EC was able to claim that its GI protection program was not WTO-incompatible as such and the United States could point to the fact that the EC was found to have violated WTO articles in the way in which it implemented that policy. The EC would have to change its policy regarding the registration of foreign products in the EC market considerably.[38] Its own GI regime will in essence have to be opened to all countries selling GI goods into the EC market. This could undermine the strategy of encouraging quality improvements through regional product protection over time. Having other countries protect EC GIs in their markets, as they are requesting in the current WTO negotiations, would restore some measure of balance in this respect.

The regulations at issue in the WTO case did not apply to wines and spirits. But some aspects of the ruling do relate to this area of trade. The panel report clarified one aspect of the complications of having GI and trademark systems intersect, by considering the issue of the rights to the names Bud and Budweiser. This contentious issue, involving one of the world's largest food-and-drink firms, had been simmering for a century, ever since Adolphus Busch emigrated from Germany to the United States and chose a German-sounding name (actually the German translation of a

[38] Subsequently, the EC has simplified its registration requirements for foreign GIs.

Table 4. Summary of WTO panel ruling on GIs

Issue	Ruling
Violation of Article III: discrimination against non-EC firms and producer groups	EC GI regulation discriminates against non-EC persons and products. EC cannot deny protection on the grounds that the foreign government does not grant "equivalent protection" nor can the EC make protection conditional on "reciprocal" protection in another country.
Violation of Article III: interpretation of process of challenge of GIs by foreign firms	Non-EC firms should be able to register and challenge GIs directly without requiring intervention by their governments. Private rights holders should receive protection under domestic law without needing the intervention of their own government.
Violation of Article 16.1 of TRIPS dealing with potential conflicts between trademarks and GIs	EC regulations should allow holders of preexisting trademarks to prevent confusing use of GI. The EC argument that TRIPS allows for coexistence of GIs and pre-existing trademarks but limits trademark holders' rights was rejected by the panel. The EC should take steps to avoid registering GIs where there is a "relatively high" likelihood of confusion with a trademarked product. This protection against confusion was specifically extended to the registration of GIs that used a translation of a trademarked term.

Note: Complain dealt with GIs for products other than wines and spirits, which are covered by different EC regulations.
Source: Author, based on WTO panel report following Josling (2006).

Czech town name Budjovice) to the dismay of the brewers in that town who had several centuries of experience. When the Czech Republic emerged from the blanket of central planning and tried out the competitive marketplace they persuaded four countries to grant GI status to Budweiser as well as its Czech language equivalent. The EC took over this protection when the Czech Republic joined the EC, and hence had to defend its actions when the United States challenged the EC Regulation.[39]

Although the complaint against the EC has been settled, Anheuser-Busch still has outstanding complaints against Budejovicky Budvar, the current Czech brewer of the beer in question. The UK courts have allowed both brewers to use Bud and Budweiser as trademarks in that markets,

[39] Under the TRIPS Agreement, trademarks that overlap with GIs are granted protection. The EC was thus, in the view of the United States, delinquent in not protecting the Bud and Budweiser names. They could register the Czech name as a GI but not its German translation.

and a similar ruling in Japan allows both to use the term Budweiser (O'Connor, 2004, p. 226). Resolution to this issue is still pending in other large markets such as Russia. Coexistence could be a reasonable outcome to this dispute if no consumer confusion is demonstrated.

4. *Agricultural subsidy cases*

Although the cases that actually involve subsidies (domestic and export) are a minority of the total agricultural conflicts, they have the most significance for rule changes through negotiations. Four such subsidy cases are discussed in this section: the Canada-dairy case, US-cotton and EC-sugar, and the Canadian and Brazilian cases against the United States notification of its trade-distorting support – the Total Aggregate Measure of Support (AMS) (US-TAMS). It is these four disputes that are redefining the concept of a subsidy and the usefulness of the "boxes" of the URAA. A brief account of each of these cases is given in the following sections.

4.1. The Canadian dairy case

In the aftermath of the Uruguay Round, the Government of Canada instituted a new policy designed to assist exporters of dairy products (mainly cheese) made with expensive domestic milk. A separate "export" class of milk was defined which could be sold at a price lower than that for domestic use.[40] The architects of the policy no doubt assumed that, as no government funds were involved, such a scheme would not be seen by trading partners as an export subsidy.

New Zealand, supported by the United States, took issue with the policy and, after the requisite consultations, it became the subject of a WTO dispute.[41] The panel ruled that the program did indeed constitute a subsidy to exports as it resulted from government action even though no funds were involved. The Canadian policy was changed to reduce the role of

[40] Before 1995, the Canadian Dairy Commission, the Federal body charged with the management of the dairy market and the coordination of the Provincial Milk Marketing Boards through the National Milk Marketing Plan, assisted exports through levies paid by dairy farmers. The new regulation at issue established five Special Milk Classes (Classes 5(a) through 5(e)) for milk and dairy products not exclusively for the domestic market. This Class 5 milk is sold at negotiated prices or set by formula based on US industrial milk. The Special Milk Classes 5(d) and (e) were the focus of the dispute, and covered exports of cheese and dried milk mainly to the United States and the United Kingdom, as well as surplus milk from the domestic market.

[41] The dispute also included a complaint about the administration of Canadian dairy import regulations, but that raised different issues and will not be discussed here (WTO, 1999).

the government, leaving it up to the private sector to negotiate sales of the milk for processing and sale to export destinations.[42] New Zealand and the United States were not convinced that this had solved the problem. The panel was asked to rule on the new policy, and again found it to be in violation of Canada's export subsidy commitments on the grounds that the price of domestic milk was controlled by the government and that this in itself could be enough to subsidize exports.[43] Importantly, the Appellate Body in ruling on the second case directed the panel to use the test of whether the cost of the milk to the export processors was less than the cost of production incurred by the farmers. The panel reconvened and decided that as most farmers produced for both the domestic and the foreign market that they in effect sold the milk surplus to their domestic allotment at a "subsidized" price (WTO, 2001).

The case was settled when the Canadian provinces abolished their CEM programs. Changes in the Federal programs are ongoing. New Zealand and the United States have withdrawn their request for sanctions, and argued that the outcome vindicated the working of the dispute settlement machinery. But the significance of the outcome of the challenge by New Zealand and the United States to the Canadian dairy policy was soon obvious to export interests in other countries. If selling farm products for exporting (or processing for export) at a price less than the cost of production was indeed regarded as an export subsidy then any situation where high, administered domestic prices coexisted with exports might be shown to be contrary to the WTO – or at least would need to be counted against the export subsidy commitments. Sugar policies in the EC were an obvious target, but other cases could subsequently emerge.

In the present context this outcome has another implication. The WTO rules and commitments are based on the notional separation of domestic support from market access and export competition. These aspects are clearly linked economically and politically, but it was assumed that they were at least possible to separate in administrative terms. But if an administered price can grant a subsidy on exports, then the link between domestic support and export competition is exposed. In other words, the legal avenue has made obvious what the pillars of the URAA had attempted to conceal: that the root cause of trade problems is high domestic prices set by farm policy and that these have not been effectively reduced by the constraints imposed on the "at the border" instruments or on domestic subsidies.

---

[42] Canada abolished the Special Milk Class 9(e) and restricted sales under Class 5(d) to conform to its export subsidy commitments. A new milk category of Commercial Export Milk (CEM) was established.

[43] The challenge to Canadian dairy policy was not covered by the Peace Clause as it charged that the export subsidy commitments had been violated.

4.2. The US cotton case

The case against US cotton subsidies appears also to question the distinction between amber and green boxes.[44] The rulings of the panel are best summarized by considering the nine elements of the US programs that were the subject of the challenge by Brazil. Five of these elements (direct payments, production flexibility contract payments, market loss assistance payments, counter-cyclical payments and marketing loan payments) relate to the major instruments of farm policy adopted for the "program crops" in the Farm Bills that cover the period 1999–2003.[45] Two more are specific to cotton (Step 2 subsidies and cottonseed payments), and the other two are of more general application (crop insurance and export credit guarantees). The panel ruled basically on two issues: whether these subsidies were allowed or prohibited and whether they caused "serious prejudice" (even if allowed) to Brazil.

The two subsidies that were not price-related (and which had therefore been notified by the United States as being in the green box) were found not to be the cause of "price suppression" in world markets. They were, however, found to contain provisions that made them ineligible for the green box: specifically the restrictions on the alternative crops that farmers could grow on cotton land. These, the panel decided, could keep more acres in that crop than would totally "decoupled" payments have done. The three subsidies that were price-related were found to have caused price suppression through their impact on keeping cotton production high in the United States at a time of low world prices.[46]

The panel ruled that the Step 2 subsidies paid to domestic users were prohibited under the SCM and the Step 2 subsidies available to export users were prohibited because they were not included in the US schedule of subsidies. Moreover, the Step 2 subsidies also caused significant price suppression in world markets. Cottonseed subsidies and crop insurance

---

[44] Brazil requested consultations with the United States on September 27, 2002. After three abortive discussions, a panel was established on May 19, 2003 and issued a report on June 18, 2004 (WTO, 2004b). This ruling was appealed by the United States, and the Appellate Body issued its report on March 3, 2005. The report as amended was adopted on March 21, 2005 (WTO, 2005).

[45] The two Farm Bills in question are the 1996 FAIR Act and 2002 FSRI Act. Production flexibility contract payments were authorized under the FAIR Act, and marketing loss assistance payments were added as emergency measures in 1998–2001. The FSRI Act replaced these with direct payments and counter-cyclical payments. Marketing loans for cotton have been in place since 1986 and Step 2 subsidies since 1990. The cottonseed payments are emergency payments authorized by the ARP Act in 2000. Crop insurance is authorized by separate legislation, the Federal Crop Insurance Act.

[46] The panel rejected the US argument that the low world prices were from other causes and that the high US exports were an exception rather than the rule.

payments were deemed not to have caused price suppression, and were not prohibited subsidies.

The final aspect of the US programs on which the panel ruled was the set of export credit guarantees that are available to US firms when they sell into overseas markets where credit risks are a factor. The finding in this case was that the export credit guarantees given to cotton producers constituted an export subsidy, and since no such subsidy had been included in the US schedule it was in effect prohibited.[47]

The panel ruling required the United States to end the prohibited subsidies within six months of the adoption of the report or by July 1, 2005 at the latest. This ruling applied to the Step 2 payments, to both domestic and export users, and to the export credit guarantees for cotton. The United States decided that it could make these changes in legislation without having to await the next Farm Bill at that time expected in 2007.[48] The Administration urged Congress to scrap the Step 2 payments, and these will cease at the end of the crop year, in August 2006. The USDA has also proposed changes to the export credit arrangements by eliminating the 1 percent cap on the fees that are charged for borrowing through the GSM-102 program, and by terminating the GSM-103 program that provides for longer repayment periods.

More problematic for the United States is how to adjust the programs that the panel found to cause significant price suppression. Withdrawing the marketing loan and counter-cyclical payments would require major changes in the US legislation and could not easily be done outside the context of the next Farm Bill. Taking other steps to remove the adverse impacts on Brazil might seem easier to achieve, but any attempt to restrict US cotton exports could prove difficult. Compensation to Brazil for lost exports would also seem politically implausible, and a deal to boost Brazilian exports of other commodities would be similarly unpopular. So the prospect is for no change in these aspects of US policy at least until the 2007 Farm Bill, at which time the policies may in any case need to be modified as a result of the Doha Round.

An interesting side issue raised by the panel report is the conclusion that the direct payments and production flexibility contract payments are not eligible for the green box. This would seem to indicate that countries might ask the United States to resubmit notifications of domestic support for the years in question. This would almost certainly put the United States in excess of its amber box limits, and raise serious problems with trading partners. If this were to be resolved by litigation (an easier task since no serious prejudice issues would be relevant) then the United States

[47] The ruling also declared the export credit guarantees for rice exceeded its allowed export subsidy limit, but did not find fault with other aspects of the program

[48] The Farm Bill was eventually passed in early 2008.

would have to make major changes to its farm policy. But again, the chances are that these issues will be resolved in the context of the Doha Round.

The signal importance of the cotton case for WTO jurisprudence is that it clarifies several aspects of the application of WTO rules to agricultural subsidies. The Peace Clause effectively dissuaded members from challenging agricultural subsidies under the SCM before 2004. Though the panel ruled that the Peace Clause did not provide shelter for the US subsidies in question, the case is best considered as the first "post-Peace Clause" challenge to farm subsidies. The consistency of agricultural subsidies with the provisions of the SCM is a fertile ground for speculation. But the panel indicates that, at least in this case, these restrictions are both onerous and comprehensive. Though the ruling on serious prejudice was based on the impact of US subsidies on world cotton prices, the same provision of the SCM also includes the effect of subsidies in impeding exporters in domestic and third country markets as well as the impact on market shares. Moreover, though it was not found germane to this case, the SCM has provisions for cases where the "threat" of serious prejudice exists.

The case may or may not usher in a flurry of similar litigation; much depends on the success of the Doha Round in reducing subsidies. But the panel report certainly gives encouragement to countries that have refrained from making challenges because they felt that panels would have difficulties in finding evidence of serious prejudice. In markets where there are many factors contributing to the export performance of particular countries, establishing causal relationships is problematic. But the panel seemed to be un-phased by the conflicting opinions of expert witnesses on the magnitude and direction of the impact of US subsidies on world cotton prices. They made their ruling on the basis of a preponderance of evidence from economic studies that production of cotton in the United States has a significant impact on the world market price. Although they avoided linking their decision to any particular study, they certainly paid more attention to such evidence than many previous panels. So the cotton panel continues the trend toward rulings based on economic reasoning and quantification as a way of bringing precision to terms such as "substantial" and "significant" that pepper the rules on the trade impacts of subsidies (Table 5). The cotton case is likely to be cited in many panel reports in future years.

4.3. The EC sugar case

The impact of the Canadian dairy case on the approach taken by exporters toward farm policies in other countries can be seen in the challenge brought by Brazil, Australia, and Thailand against the EC sugar

Table 5. US cotton programs and main elements in the cotton panel ruling

Program	Panel ruling
Direct payments (DP)	Not eligible for green box because of restrictions on use of land Do not cause significant price suppression on world markets
Production flexibility contract payments (PFC)	Not eligible for green box because of restrictions on use of land Do not cause significant price suppression on world markets
Market loss assistance payments (MLA)	Caused significant price suppression on world market
Counter-cyclical payments (CCP)	Caused significant price suppression on world market
Marketing loan payments (ML)	Caused significant price suppression on world market
Step 2 payments	Caused significant price suppression on world market For domestic users, payments were import substitution subsidy For export users, payments were export subsidies not included in US schedule
Cottonseed payments	Do not cause significant price suppression on world markets
Crop insurance	Do not cause significant price suppression on world markets
Export credit guarantees	Credit guarantees for cotton (and several other products) were export subsidies and were not included in US schedule. (Rice export subsidy exceeded its scheduled level)

Source: Author, based on WTO Panel Report following Josling (2005).

subsidies.[49] Complaints about EC sugar policy are not new. Australia had challenged the EC sugar regime in 1979 in the GATT and Brazil followed in 1980, but these were complicated by the fact that there was an International Sugar Agreement (ISA; to which the EC was not a signatory) that restricted exports. Under such circumstances, the panels were unable to determine the extent of injury that the plaintiffs had suffered and the policies continued unchecked (Josling and Tangermann, 2003). The United States also challenged the CAP sugar policy in the GATT in 1982, but no panel was established. The EC indicated its willingness to join the ISA, and proceeded in turn to challenge the US sugar regime.

---

[49] The Australian and Brazilian challenges were initiated in September 2002 and Thailand joined the complaint in March 2003. The dispute numbers are DS265, DS266, and DS283, respectively. The panel report was presented on October 15, 2004 and was appealed. The Appellate Body gave their opinion on April 28, 2005 and the DSB accepted the report as modified (WTO, 2004a).

One of the contentions of these sugar exporters in the recent WTO case was that the EC grants *de facto* export subsidies by means of the high price paid for sugar used on the domestic market. The domestic market price is maintained for sugar produced under two quotas (the "A" and "B" quotas): production over those quotas (usually called "C" sugar) cannot be sold on the domestic market and receives no direct subsidy. At issue is whether the C sugar benefits indirectly as farmers can cover their fixed costs from returns from the high-price quotas. The analogy with the exported milk products from Canada is close if not exact. The complainants maintain that if such subsides were included, the EC would be in breach of its export subsidy commitments under the URAA.

A second contention was that the EC exports the equivalent of the 1.4 million tons of sugar that is imported under preferential agreements enshrined in the Cotonou Agreement with former colonies. This sugar is sold to the EC at the internal price but re-exported at the world price. This was not notified as a part of the EC's schedule of exports that benefit from subsidies: it was explicitly excluded in a footnote.

The panel found, and the Appellate Body agreed, that the EC was in breech in both respects. The exports of C sugar did benefit from the high price of A and B quotas awarded to the same farms. As the C sugar was solely destined for exports, the effect was to cross-subsidize.[50] By implication, if C sugar were sold on the internal market to any extent, the argument would have required a further stage of showing that the exports were harming other exporters. But as the implicit financial benefits to producers of C sugar were not notified as export subsidies, they were *de facto* prohibited regardless of their market impact. Similarly, the panel found that the re-export of the ACP (and Indian) sugar was prohibited as it did not appear in the EC schedule. Thus, the EC sugar case differs from that of US cotton in that it centers primarily on the notification of export subsidies. The fact that these notifications were not challenged at the time raises questions about how the activities of the Agriculture Committee might be linked more usefully to the issue of the nature of these policies.

The sugar case is complicated by an additional element. If the EC cannot either re-export the ACP imports or sell C sugar on the world market, then the domestic price has to be reduced and/or the quotas have to be reduced. The EC Commission realized this link with reform of the EC sugar regime, and used the argument effectively to persuade member states of the need for policy change. The political decision was made by the

[50] Investigations of subsidies in nonagricultural markets often explore the possibility of cross-subsidization within firms. The economics of cross-subsidization is not as well accepted as the accounting conventions.

EC's Council of Ministers on November 22, 2005, to undertake a reform that cut the sugar price support level by 36 percent and compensated farmers with decoupled payments. Although the support price will stay significantly above the world price level, the incentive to produce for export (over and above the quota volume) will be significantly reduced. If the output falls as expected, the EC will come into compliance with the Panel ruling: cross subsidized production will not find its way into export markets, and the ACP sugar will be absorbed largely in the domestic market.

Suppliers of raw sugar to the EC have also been promised compensation. Under the Cotonou Agreement, these suppliers benefit from guaranteed access at internal prices, and so will lose from the reduction in price levels. Although this preferential access is already under threat from the opening up of tariff and quota-free access to the least developed countries under the "Everything but Arms" agreement of the EC, it remains of economic and political importance to a number of countries. Furthermore, they will also benefit from reductions in the sales of "C" sugar on world markets. Thus the link with the trade negotiations is more complex than just the connection with the reform of the EC sugar regime.

5. Conclusion

The proliferation of agricultural cases in the WTO reflects both the ambivalent nature of the multilateral trade rules in the sector and the sensitive nature of the trade itself. In addition, the perceived vulnerability of the major farm programs of industrial countries to challenge under the URAA and the SCM has led to some recent high-profile disputes. The nature of technological changes in food production, particularly the uneven adoption of biotech seeds, has led to other disputes. Countries are still grappling with the trade policy consequences of the search for attributes in production that are desirable to consumers. The dividing line between providing consumers with adequate decisions on which to base decisions and cooperating with domestic producers to restrict imports is often difficult to determine. More of these issues will be tested in the WTO in future years. Indeed, it would be risky to predict any sharp decrease in the numbers of agricultural disputes brought before the DSB in the next decade.[51]

---

[51] In some areas of trade, complaints can trigger retaliatory filings as an element of trade strategy. This does not seem to be a problem in agriculture at present but it may emerge as more sensitive cases are litigated.

The URAA constituted a negotiated solution to several market access issues in agriculture. The URAA mandated the removal of non-tariff border measures and the binding of most tariffs. It introduced the Special Safeguard for Agriculture (SSG) as new safeguard mechanism and TRQs to maintain access in cases where non-tariff measures were converted to tariffs. In addition, the URAA helped to clarify the issue of subsidies that had proved to be so difficult to discipline under the GATT. The URAA circumscribed the use of export subsidies, obliging countries to notify all such aids and include schedules for their reduction. New export subsidies were banned. For domestic subsidies the URAA introduced a classification of domestic support instruments that attempted to limit the use of the more trade-distorting subsidies. The URAA also implemented notification procedures to track compliance with the provisions and the schedules of commitments.[52] But each of these issues left room for interpretation and were grist for the litigation mill.

Market access issues were the most important in the early days of the WTO, as countries explored through the DSB the practical implementation of the new rules and the agreed schedules. The process of tariffication was fairly smooth, and the introduction of the SSG also was without major problems. However, the establishment of TRQs did lead to several conflicts, as one might imagine in cases where government decisions had immediate commercial impact. The success in limiting trade-distorting subsidies has been somewhat more elusive. Export subsidies that were included in the schedules in general caused few disputes, in part because the limits were well above actual levels. But panels examining country policies unearthed several policies that acted as export aids within the terms of the WTO but had not been notified as such. Thus the major challenges to domestic farm programs in the EU and the United States came from other exporters complaining that the export subsidy restrictions were being circumvented.

Cases brought against particular types of domestic support have been infrequent. With inconclusive debates in the Committee for Agriculture and without the guidance of panel reports, countries were able to decide largely for themselves whether particular policies were consistent with the definitions of the green and blue boxes, and hence not subject to reductions. As long as countries were way below their limits on domestic

[52] Commitments on subsidy levels are treaty provisions, and the commitments in a Member's Schedule are "an integral part" of the URAA and other WTO agreements (WT/DS265/R, paragraph 7.128). Conformity with scheduled commitments is a necessary but not a sufficient condition for escaping challenge. Panels have made clear that compliance with a Domestic Support commitment in a Member's Schedule does not in itself preempt or exclude the operation of other WTO obligations (WT/DS267/R, paras. 7.1066 and 7.1067).

support, it was not a priority to challenge the notifications themselves. But the jump in funding for the 2002 US Farm Bill caused a re-think of this situation, with the possibility that the limits may have been breached if notifications had been erroneous. The statement of the US cotton panel that some of the expenditures that the United States had claimed as "green" may have been mislabeled, turned this possibility into a contestable proposition.

The current case brought by Canada and Brazil, challenging the level of US farm subsidies as notified under the categories used by the URAA, illustrates that ambiguity still exists.[53] On the one hand, it is a remarkable case, which if it ever went to a panel would clarify the somewhat fuzzy nature of the "boxes." On the other hand, it refers to past notifications that were alleged to wrongly classify certain subsidies. So the remedy in the event of a successful challenge is presumably to oblige a re-notification by the United States of its domestic support for several historical years. But the United States could well argue that in the current period of high prices, support levels are already well below the limits set in the schedules even with renotification. So it would not be clear what the United States could do to make amends: changing current policies would not be an appropriate remedy, and compensation for past violations is not contemplated in the DSU.

This does not drain the interest away from the case. The reclassification of direct payments in the United States away from the green box in a revised notification would indeed be a small prize for competing exporters. But added the possibility of a new set of limits in the Doha Round, and the case becomes critical. If the Doha Round succeeds in reducing allowable trade-distorting subsidies (as calculated by the AMS), the allocation of subsidies to these boxes becomes sensitive. The prospect exists that the major driver of change in US farm policy could indeed be the WTO dispute settlement process, and the decisions on the classification of subsidies. That could also set up some controversy over the role of WTO rules when they clash with powerful political interests. Agricultural trade will continue to provide vexing issues for the multilateral trade system and its judicial processes.

---

[53] The two cases brought by Canada and Brazil (DS 357 and 365 respectively) have been merged. The complaint is that United States exceeded its Total AMS limits in several recent years.

Annex

***Table A1.* WTO Disputes initiated since January 1995 related to agricultural products**

Date	DS#	Complainant	Respondent	Commodity	Issue
1995	3	United States	Korea	Agricultural products	Import testing
1995	5	United States	Korea	Agricultural products	Shelf life
1995	9	Canada	EC	Cereals	UR implementation
1995	13	United States	EC	Grain	UR implementation
1995	16	Guatemala, etc.	EC	Bananas	Import regulations
1995	17	Thailand	EC	Rice	UR implementation
1995	22	Philippines	Brazil	Coconut	CVD
1995	25	Uruguay	EC	Rice	UR implementation
1996	26	United States	EC	Meat	SPS
1996	27	Ecuador, etc.	EC	Bananas	Import regulations
1996	30	Sri Lanka	Brazil	Coconut milk	CVD
1996	35	Argentina, etc.	Hungary	Agricultural products	Export subsidies
1996	41	United States	Korea	Agricultural products	Import testing
1996	48	Canada	EC	Meat	SPS
1996	49	Mexico	United States	Tomatoes	A/D
1997	66	EC	Japan	Pork	Import measures
1997	69	Brazil	EC	Poultry	TRQ
1997	72	New Zealand	EC	Butter	TRQ
1997	74	United States	Philippines	Pork, poultry	TRQ
1997	76	United States	Japan	Agricultural products	Quarantine
1997	98	EC	Korea	Dairy	Safeguards
1997	100	EC	United States	Poultry	SPS

Table A1. (continued)

Date	DS#	Complainant	Respondent	Commodity	Issue
1997	102	United States	Philippines	Pork, poultry	TRQ
1997	103	United States	Canada	Dairy	Export subsidies
1997	104	United States	EC	Processed cheese	Export subsidies
1997	105	Panama	EC	Bananas	Import regulations
1997	111	Argentina	EC	Groundnuts	TRQ
1997	113	New Zealand	Canada	Dairy	Export subsidies
1998	133	Switzerland	Slovakia	Dairy	Import restriction
1998	134	India	EC	Rice	Import restriction
1998	143	Hungary	Slovak Rep	Wheat	Import duties
1998	144	Canada	United States	Cattle, swine, and grain	Transport restrictions
1998	145	EC	Argentina	Wheat gluten	CVD
1998	148	Hungary	Czech Rep	Wheat	Import regulations
1998	149	EC	India	Nonspecific	Import quotas
1999	154	Brazil	EC	Coffee	Differential treatment
1999	158	Guatemala, etc.	EC	Bananas	Import regulations
1999	161	United States	Korea	Beef	Import regulations
1999	166	EC	United States	Wheat gluten	Safeguards
1999	167	Canada	United States	Cattle	CVD
1999	169	Australia	Korea	Beef	Import regulations
1999	174	United States	EC	Agricultural Products	GIs
1999	177	New Zealand	United States	Lamb	Safeguards
1999	178	Australia	United States	Lamb	Safeguards
1999	180	Canada	United States	Sugar	Classification
1999	185	Costa Rica	Trinidad	Pasta	A/D

2000	187	Costa Rica	Trinidad	Pasta	A/D
2000	203	United States	Mexico	Live swine	A/D
2000	205	Thailand	Egypt	Tuna in oil	Import regulations
2000	207	Argentina	Chile	Agricultural products	Price band
2000	210	United States	Belgium	Rice	Import duties
2001	220	Guatemala	Chile	Agricultural products	Price band
2001	223	United States	EC	Corn gluten	TRQ
2001	226	Argentina	Chile	Edible oils	Safeguards
2001	228	Colombia	Chile	Sugar	Safeguards
2001	230	Colombia	Chile	Sugar	Safeguards
2001	235	Poland	Slovakia	Sugar	Safeguards
2001	237	Ecuador	Turkey	Bananas	Import regulations
2001	238	Chile	Argentina	Peaches, preserved	Safeguards
2001	240	Hungary	Romania	Wheat/flour	Import prohibition
2001	241	Brazil	Argentina	Poultry	A/D
2002	245	United States	Japan	Apples	SPS
2002	250	Brazil	United States	Citrus products	Florida excise tax
2002	256	Hungary	Turkey	Pet food	SPS
2002	263	Argentina	EC	Wine	Import regulations
2002	265	Australia	EC	Sugar	Export subsidies
2002	266	Brazil	EC	Sugar	Export subsidies
2002	267	Brazil	United States	Cotton	Domestic support
2002	269	Brazil	EC	Poultry	Classification
2002	270	Philippines	Australia	Fruit and vegetables	Quarantine
2002	271	Philippines	Australia	Pineapple	Quarantine
2002	275	United States	Venezuela	Agricultural Products	Import licensing
2002	276	United States	Canada	Wheat	Import restrictions, STE
2003	283	Thailand	EC	Sugar	Export subsidies

2003	284	Nicaragua	Mexico	Black beans	SPS
2003	286	Thailand	EC	Poultry	Classification
2003	289	Poland	Czech Republic	Pigmeat	Import duties
2003	290	Australia	EC	Agricultural Products	GIs
2003	291	United States	EC	Biotech products	Import regulations
2003	292	Canada	EC	Biotech products	Import regulations
2003	293	Argentina	EC	Biotech products	Import regulations
2003	295	United States	Mexico	Beef, rice	A/D
2003	297	Hungary	Croatia	Meat	SPS
2004	310	Canada	United States	Hard wheat	A/D
2004	314	EC	Mexico	Olive oil	CVD
2004	320	EC	United States	Beef	Continued suspension
2004	321	EC	Canada	Beef	Continued suspension
2005	329	Mexico	Panama	Milk products	Classification
2005	330	EC	Argentina	Olive oil, etc.	CVD
2005	334	United States	Turkey	Rice	TRQ
2005	338	United States	Canada	Corn	CVD, A/D
2006	341	EC	Mexico	Olive oil	CVD
2006	349	Argentina	EC	Garlic	TRQ
2006	351	Argentina	Chile	Milk products	Prov. Safeguards
2006	356	Argentina	Chile	Milk products	Def. Safeguards
2007	357	Canada	United States	Agricultural products	Domestic support
2007	361	Colombia	EC	Bananas	Import duties
2007	364	Panama	EC	Bananas	Differential treatment
2007	365	Brazil	United States	Agricultural products	Domestic support
2007	367	New Zealand	Australia	Apples	Quarantine

Source: WTO website.

References

Barichello, R., Josling, T., Sumner, D. (2005), *Agricultural Trade Disputes Between Canada and the United States: Costly but Diminishing*, Commentary, No. 224, December, CD Howe Institute, Toronto.

Barton, J.H., Goldstein, J., Josling, T., Steinberg, R.H. (2006), *The Evolution of the Trade Regime: Politics, Law and Economics of the GATT and WTO*. Princeton University Press, Princeton, NJ.

Josling, T. (2003), Bananas and the WTO: testing the new dispute settlement process. In: Josling, T.E., Taylor, T.G. (Eds.), *Banana Wars: The Anatomy of a Trade Dispute*. CABI Publishing, Wallingford, pp. 169–194.

Josling, T. (2005), Unraveling the cotton case. *Bridges*. Year 9, No. 4, April–May, pp. 3–5.

Josling, T. (2006), The War on *Terroir:* geographical indications as a transatlantic trade conflict. *Journal of Agricultural Economics* 57 (3), 337–366.

Josling, T., Tangermann, S. (2003), Production and export subsidies in agriculture: lessons from GATT and WTO disputes involving the US and the EC. In: Petersmann, E-U., Pollack, M. (Eds.), *Transatlantic Economic Disputes*. Oxford University Press, Oxford.

Josling, T., Roberts, D., Orden, D. (2004), *Food Regulation and Trade: Toward a Safe and Open Global System*. Institute for International Economics, Washington, DC.

Josling, T., Tangermann, S., Warley, T.K. (1996), *Agriculture in the GATT*. Houndmills, London and New York.

Josling, T., Zhao, L., Carcelen, J., Arha, K. (2006), Implications of WTO litigation for the WTO agricultural negotiations. *IPC Policy Brief*.

Kramer, C.S. (1989), Food safety and International Trade: the US-EC Meat and Hormone Controversies. In: Kramer, C.S. (Ed.), *The Political Economy of US Agriculture*. National Center for Food and Agricultural Policy, Resources for the Future, Washington, DC, pp. 210–211.

O'Connor, B. (2004), *The Law of Geographical Indications*. Cameron May, London.

Steinberg, R.H., Josling, T.E. (2003), When the peace ends: The vulnerability of EC and U.S. agricultural subsidies to WTO legal challenge. *Journal of International Economic Law* 6 (2), 369–417.

World Trade Organization. (1995), The results of the Uruguay Round of multilateral trade negotiations, The Legal Texts, WTO, Geneva.

World Trade Organization. (1997a), European Communities-regime for the importation, sale and distribution of bananas, complaint by the United Sates, Report of the Panel, WT/DS27/R/USA, May 22, 1997.

World Trade Organization. (1997b), European Communities-regime for the importation, sale and distribution of bananas, Report of the Appellate Body, WT/DS27/AB/R, September 9.

World Trade Organization. (1998), EC – measures concerning meat and meat products (hormones), WTO/DS26 & 48/AB/R, February 13.

World Trade Organization. (1999), Canada – measures affecting the importation of milk and the exportation of dairy products, WT/DS103/R and WT/DS113/R.

World Trade Organization. (2001), Canada – measures affecting the importation of milk and the exportation of dairy products, Report of the Appellate Body, WT/DS103&113/AB/RW.

World Trade Organization. (2004a), European Communities – export subsidies on sugar, Reports of the Panels, WT/DS265/R, WT/DS266/R, & WT/DS283/R.

World Trade Organization. (2004b), United States – subsidies on Upland cotton, Report of the Panel, WT/DS267/R.

World Trade Organization. (2005), United States – subsidies on Upland cotton, Reports of the Appellate Body, WT/DS265/AB/R, WT/DS266/AB/R, & WT/DS267/AB/R.

CHAPTER 11

WTO Dispute Cases Relating to Food Safety Issues

Mitsuo Matsushita[☆]

Nagashima, Ohno, Tsunematsu, Kioicho Building 3-12, Kioicho, Chiyoda-Ku, Tokyo 102-0094, Japan
E-mail address: mitsuo_matsushita@noandt.com

Abstract
There are several agreements within the framework of the World Trade Organization that have an impact on the issue of food safety. These include the prohibition against quantitative restrictions of GATT 94, the general exceptions of Article XX, the Agreement on Sanitary and Phytosanitary Measures, the Agreement on Technical Barriers to Trade, and the Agreement on Trade-Related Aspects of International Property Rights. This chapter analyzes the primary disputes pertaining directly or tangentially to matters of food safety and representation under each of these agreements that were impaneled under the dispute settlement understanding. Particular attention is given to the EC/Hormones and the EC/genetically modified organisms (GMO) cases.

Keywords: Food safety, Article XX, Sanitary and PhytoSanitary Agreement, Agreement on Technical Barriers to Trade, Chapeau, GATT 1994, EC/Hormones, EC/GMO, Cartagena Protocol, form and nature of a measure, national treatment, burden of proof, Enabling Clause, Appellate Body

JEL classifications: F13, K33, K41, Q18

1. WTO agreements relevant to food safety issues

1.1. Major WTO agreements relevant to food safety issues

The GATT 1994 generally prohibits quantitative restrictions of trade by way of import quota or any other form, as well as the imposition of tariffs above

[☆] Mitsuo Matsushita is a Professor Emeritus of Tokyo University and a former member of the WTO Appellate Body.

Frontiers of Economics and Globalization
Volume 6 ISSN: 1574-8715
DOI: 10.1108/S1574-8715(2009)0000006014

the concession rate. It also prohibits Members from imposing a measure favoring its own products in discrimination against products of another Member if those products are "like products." A Member is prohibited from imposing a measure that favors a product of another Member in discrimination against products of third Members if those products are like products. However, Article XX of the GATT 1994 provides certain exceptions from the above prohibitions even if a measure falls under one of such prohibitions provided that the requirements of Article XX are satisfied.

There are several other agreements within the framework of the WTO which have bearings on food safety issues. One is the SPS Agreement (The Agreement on Sanitary and Phytosanitary Measures, hereafter referred to as "the SPS"). The SPS permits Members to take a measure to protect life and health of humans, animals, and plants. But Members may do so only to the extent necessary for this purpose. The measure must be scientifically justifiable and based on sufficient scientific evidence.

The other is the TBT Agreement (The Agreement on Technical Barriers to Trade, hereafter referred to as "the TBT"). This agreement deals with labeling and representation of products and enforcement of mandatory and optional product standards. This agreement mandates that the principles of national treatment and most favored nation treatment apply to products imported from other Members with regard to the TBT measures. The SPS is a special law in relation to the TBT and when both a provision of the SPS and a provision of the TBT are applicable to the same subject matter, the provision in the SPS prevails over the provision in the TBT. The Agreement on Trade-Related Aspects of Intellectual Property Rights (TRIPS) is aimed at protecting intellectual property rights. Although the TRIPS provides that all products should be patentable, Article 27.2 of the TRIPS allows Members to exclude inventions from patentability if it is necessary to protect life and health of humans, animals, and plants, as well as the prevention of serious damage to environments.

1.2. The GATT 1994

As mentioned earlier, the GATT 1994 prohibits the imposition of import and export restrictions and discriminatory measures regarding products. However, Article XX of the GATT provides for exceptions and, as long as a measure of a Member that falls under the prohibition of the GATT satisfies the requirement of exceptions, it enjoys the immunity from the prohibitions of the GATT.

Article XX consists of the introductory part (this is often referred to as "Chapeau") and 10 exceptions, that is, exceptions (a–j). If a measure of a Member falls under one or more of items (a–j), the measure is exempted from the prohibition of the GATT on restrictions of trade. However, Chapeau provides for the conditions necessary for a measure to meet in order to enjoy exemption. Among the items included in Article XX of the GATT, Article XX(b) is most relevant. Article XX(b) exempts a measure that is necessary to protect life and health of humans, animals, and plants.

In the past, several GATT dispute settlement cases dealing with food safety and health issues interpreted Article XX(b) of the GATT 1947. In the Thai Tobacco Case,[1] the Thai Government took a measure to restrict sale of tobacco domestically and also its imports from the United States for the reason that tobacco created risk to health. The United States petitioned to the GATT on the ground that the Thai measure violated Article XI (the prohibition against quantitative restrictions) of the GATT. The panel considered the matter and judged that the Thai measure fell under Article XX(b), since smoking of tobacco was harmful to health, and a policy to reduce smoking was covered by Article XX(b). However, the panel stated that the measure in question must be "necessary" to accomplish this purpose, and to satisfy "the necessity test," there should be a circumstance in which there was no other alternative way, which was less trade restrictive. In the view of the panel, the Thai measure did not meet this standard and was struck down as a violation of Article XI of the GATT.

In the Tuna/Dolphin Case,[2] the U.S. Government imposed import prohibition of tuna and tuna products from countries that did not take steps to protect dolphins when their fishing vessels harvested tuna. In this case, the panel held that the imposition of import ban on tuna was not necessary to accomplish the purpose of protecting dolphins and that the U.S. measure was contrary to Article XI of the GATT. In the U.S. Gasoline Case,[3] the U.S. Government imposed restrictions on domestic production and sale of gasoline and also on imports in order to accomplish the purpose of preventing air pollution caused by the emission of harmful substances from automobiles. The panel and the Appellate Body held that, although the U.S. policy to prevent air pollution was covered by Article XX(b), the import restriction did not meet the necessity test since there would have been less trade restrictive alternatives.

In the Asbestos Case,[4] the French Government prohibited the use and import of asbestos because of hazardous nature of this product. Canada claimed that this amounted to a prohibited discrimination of Canadian asbestos since there were three other domestic products with similar features but were allowed to be used. The Appellate Body upheld the

---

[1] Thailand-Restrictions on Importation of and Internal Taxes on Cigarettes, adopted on 7 November 1990, BIASD 375/200.

[2] United States-Restrictions on Imports of Tuna, circulated on 3 September 1991, not adopted, BISD 395/155.

[3] United States-Standards for Reformulated and Conventional Gasoline, Appellate Body and Panel Report, adopted on 20 May 1996, WT/DS2/9.

[4] EC-Measures Affecting Asbestos and Asbestos-Containing Products, Report of the Panel, 18 September 2000, WT/DS135/R; Report of the Appellate Body (AB-2000-1), 12 March 2001, WT/DS135/AB/R.

French decree primarily on two grounds. (a) Asbestos and similar products that could be used as materials for architectures were not "like products" for the reason that users of such substances (builders of architectures) were conscious of hazard of asbestos compared with other similar substances, and in judging whether asbestos and other substances were like products, this should be taken into consideration. (b) The prohibition of asbestos could be covered by Article XX(b) of the GATT 1994.

1.3. The SPS agreement

The SPS specifically addresses issues of food safety and international trade. The SPS tries to balance the need to protect life and health of humans, animals, and plants with that of preventing excessive control of international trade under the name of protecting life and health. The SPS allows Members to take "SPS measures" to protect life and health of humans, animals, and plants by imposing the prohibition of imports of certain items and the requirement for labeling with regard to some products. However, the SPS requires, in Article 5.7, that Members take such SPS measures only to the extent necessary to protect life and health. SPS measures cannot be maintained unless they are supported by sufficient scientific data established by appropriate risk assessment.

Also SPS measures taken by Members need to be based on international standards, guidelines and recommendations, if there are any. If an SPS measure is based on an international standard, guideline or recommendation, such a measure is presumed to be necessary to protect life and health of humans, animals or plants and compatible with the SPS and the GATT. However, under special circumstances, Members can deviate from this obligation of basing their standards on international standards. This is Article 5.7 of the SPS that recognizes the precautionary principle in a limited way. According to this provision, Members can take a provisional SPS measure when there is not enough scientific evidence to support the measure. However, the Member must endeavor to obtain additional information regarding the measure and, in due course, must review it.

1.4. The TBT agreement

The TBT provides that domestic mandatory standards need to be based on international standards with regard to product safety, product testing and product representation. Provisions of the TBT generally apply to food safety matters unless such matters are covered by the SPS.[5] Therefore,

[5] Article 1.5 of the TBT Agreement states: "The provisions of this Agreement do not apply to sanitary and phytosanitary measures as defined in Annex A of the Agreement on the application of Sanitary and Phytosanitary Measures."

depending on the nature of issues, the TBT can be applied to domestic standards that deal with food safety. According to the established WTO jurisprudence, mandatory domestic standards need to be based on international standards regardless of whether the domestic standard came into effect before the taking effect of the TBT or *vice versa*.[6]

The Sardine Case[7] is a WTO dispute settlement case, which deals with food representation issues. Although this case did not deal with food safety issue directly, holdings of the Appellate Body in this case may have some bearing on food safety issues. Involved in this case was a regulation of the European Communities (EC), which provided that the word "Sardines" could be used only on canned foods made from fish caught in the Black Sea, the North Sea and the Mediterranean Sea. The Codex Alimentarius which was an international standard regulating food representation provided that, although the word "Sardines" could be used only in connection with canned foods made of fish caught in those areas, the word could be used for canned foods made of fish of similar type caught in other areas as long as prefix "X" was attached such as "Peruvian Sardines" or "Pacific Sardines." In this sense, therefore, there was a difference between the EC regulation and the Codex Alimentarius.

Peru brought a claim against EC in the WTO, which argued that the EC regulation was inconsistent with Article 2.4 of the TBT which requires that a mandatory domestic standard needs to be based on an international standard if such exists or its enactment is imminent. Both Panel and the Appellate Body held that the EC regulation was contrary to Article 2.4 of the TBT. EC argued that this regulation was necessary so that consumers in Europe would not be misled to believe that all of canned foods with the label of "Sardines" are made of fish caught in the Black Sea, the North Sea and the Mediterranean Sea. However, the Appellate Body rejected this claim by stating that the EC claim was not based on substantial evidence.

2. WTO dispute cases relating to food safety issues

Although there were some GATT panel reports on health matters before the coming into being of the WTO such as the Thai Tobacco Case mentioned earlier, there are only five cases so far which were handled by the Dispute Settlement Body of the WTO in which SPS issues

---

[6] See note (7), *infra*.

[7] EC-Trade Description of Sardines, Report of the Appellate Body (AB 2002-3), 26 September 2002, WT/DS231/AB/R. For a critical review of this case, see Robert Howse, "The Sardines Panel and AB Rulings – Some Preliminary Reactions", Legal Issues of Economic Integration 29(3), 2002, pp. 247–257.

were raised. These cases are the EC Hormones Case,[8] the Australian Salmon Case,[9] the Japan Apple Case (I),[10] the Japan Apple Case (II)[11] and the EC/GMO Case, which will be discussed below. The Australian Salmon Case dealt with the issue of health of salmon, and the Japan Apple Cases were concerned with quarantine of agricultural products. Therefore, the only cases in the WTO in which food safety and SPS issues were dealt with are the EC Hormones Case and the EC/GMO Case.

2.1. The EC Hormones case

In the EC Hormones case, the EC imposed a ban on domestic sale and import of beef taken from animals treated with six kinds of hormones. An international standard formulated by the Codex Commission stated that, with respect to two hormones, beef product involved no recognizable risk as long as the residue of hormones remained within the limit stated in the standard. The United States and Canada filed a complaint with the WTO alleging that this EC measure was contrary to the SPS. The Panel stated that the measure in question was contrary to the SPS. The Appellate Body upheld the Panel's finding and held also that the EC measure was contrary to the SPS.

First, the EC argued that its measure was based on the precautionary principle[12] and should be justified. The Panel and the Appellate Body, however, stated that the precautionary principle was not recognized as a principle in international law. Also, Article 5.7 of the SPS incorporated a provisional precautionary principle into the SPS and any application of precautionary principle that would permit a wider scope of precaution than this would not be permitted.

---

[8] EC-Measures Concerning Meat and Meat Products, Complaint by Canada, Report of the Panel, 18 August 1997, WT/DS48/R; EC-Measures Concerning Meat and Meat Products, Complaint buy the United States, Report of the Panel, 18 August 1997, WT/DS26/R/U.S.A.; EC-Measures Concerning Meat and Meat Products, Report of the Appellate Body, 13 February 1998, WT/DS26/AB/; WT/DS/48/R.

[9] Australia-Measures Affecting Importation of Salmon, Report of the Panel, 12 June 1998, WT/DS18/R; Australia-Measures Affecting Importation of Salmon, Report of the Appellate Body, WT/DS18/AB/R.

[10] Japan-Measures Affecting Agricultural Products (Apples), Report of the Panel, 27 October 1998, WT/DS76/R; Report of the Appellate Body (AB-1998-8), 22 February 1999, WT/DS76/AB/R.

[11] Japan-Measures Affecting the Importation of Apples, Report of the Panel, 15 July 2003, WT/DS24/R; Report of the Appellate Body, 26 November 2003, WT/DS245/AB/R.

[12] Under the precautionary principle, measures to prevent risks can be taken even if scientific evidence showing that there are risks does not exist or is not sufficient. The precautionary principle is sometimes used in domestic legislation dealing with food safety, for example, in some pieces of legislation, the approval of using food or additives is not allowed unless they are proven to be safe. The Cartagena Protocol, which is a protocol to the U.S. Biodiversity Convention, provides for the precautionary principle. According to the Cartagena Protocol, the signatories can take a measure to prevent genetically modified organism even without scientific evidence that it causes a risk to human, animal or plant life and health and that it has a detrimental effect on the environment.

Second, with regard to burden of proof, the Panel held that it was incumbent on the party that had imposed a SPS measure to adduce evidence that there was a sufficient risk assessment. The Panel also held that it was the responsibility of the party that had invoked a measure not based on an international standard to justify this measure. The Appellate Body reversed both of those holdings of the Panel. The Appellate Body stated that the party challenging an SPS measure of another Member was responsible to prove that the measure was contrary to the SPS and also that the measure could not be justifiable by a provision for derogation.[13] In this way, the Appellate Body imposed a stringent responsibility on a complaining party to prove a violation of the SPS on the part of the defending party and to prove that there was no justification for deviating from general principles.

Third, the matter involved in this case was highly scientific in nature. The Panel sought views of scientists, and they filed their views concerning the risk involved in hormone-treated beef. The majority of the scientists stated that, as long as the residue of hormones remained within the range stipulated in the Codex standard, there was no recognizable risk. One scientist stated that there was still a risk that one out of one million persons who took beef in which the residue of hormones remained within the range of Codex standard may get cancer. The Panel accepted the majority view and held that the EC measure was not based on a proper risk assessment. The EC appealed this holding to the Appellate Body and argued that the Panel violated Article 11 of the Dispute Settlement Understanding by ignoring the view of the minority scientist. The Appellate Body upheld the holding of the Panel in this regard but stated that, under some circumstances, a minority scientific view with regard to food safety issue could be accepted.

This last holding of the Appellate Body decision raises an important evidentiary issue. Although it may seem commonsensical that a majority view with respect to food safety should be accepted, it may be justified, under some circumstances, to accept a minority view with regard to food safety issue. Especially if a human life issue is involved, the abundance of precaution should be taken and even a minority view holding that a substance might involve risk to human life and health may be worthy of respect. Article 5.3 of the SPS states that, in assessing the risk to animal or plant life or health, Members shall take into account relevant economic factors, including the costs of control in the importing country and the relative cost-effectiveness of alternative approaches to limiting risks. It is to be noted that the word "humans" is absent from Article 5.3. *A contrario* interpretation is that the SPS does not allow economic factors such as costs to play a role in deciding whether a measure to protect life and health

---

[13] Generally, a derogation clause provides that one can choose not to adhere to the rule established in another provision of a law or treaty under the conditions stipulated in the clause.

of humans is justified, whereas, with regard to animals and plants, such economic factors can be an important test. Therefore, in the SPS, human life and health cannot be dealt with on the same basis of cost-effectiveness as that of animals and plants. An implication is that the SPS makes a distinction between human life and health on the one hand and those of animals and plants on the other and that the standard of proof for a risk in a substance related to food with regard to humans is different from that for animals and plants.

There may be a mixed situation where a measure has a primary effect on animal and plant but has a secondary effect on humans. If its effect on humans is adverse, it should be regarded as a measure affecting humans rather than animals and plants. For example, a use of antibiotics on animals for their health may have secondary effect of human health, which is detrimental. In this instance, there should be no cost consideration in assessing the appropriateness of this measure.

Fourth, although the legal aspects of the EC Hormones Case were resolved by the adoption of the Panel's report and the report of the Appellate Body by the Dispute Settlement Body of the WTO, this case raises an important political issue. In the EC, the ban on hormones was the result of long-standing discussions and considerations within the communities. This matter was discussed at the level of national governments, the decision-making bodies of the EC such as the Council of Ministers and the European Commission. Therefore, the ban on hormones, in a sense, reflected the democratic decision-making process of the EC. There is a sentiment in Europe that an important political decision which reflects the political process of Europe should not be so easily overturned by an international organization. Of course, there is a counter-argument that the EC acceded to and signed WTO agreements and it should be bound by it. Legally this is a correct answer. However, this shows that an intervention of WTO disciplines into domestic policies of Members may create political tension, and, if it goes too far, this may cause non-compliance of WTO disciplines.

2.2. The EC/GMO case

In 2003, the United States, Canada and Argentina took the EC to the WTO on the ground, *inter alia*, that the EC violated provisions of the SPS by imposing moratorium with respect to approval of import of agricultural products produced with biotechnology (GMO products). After 3 years, the Panel published a report in 2006 in which it approved some EC measures but invalidated some others.[14] This is an extremely complex case, and the panel report is over 1000 pages in which many issues are discussed.

[14] EC-Measures Affecting the Approval and Marketing of Biotech Products, WT/DS291, 292, 293/R.

One issue involved is a series of regulations adopted by the EC for approval of GMO products.[15] The EC imposed moratorium on approval of GMO products for marketing in 1998 and, since then, maintained the moratorium. The claimants argued that the EC violated provisions of the SPS because of undue delay in approval, the lack of transparency in the procedure and the lack of sufficient scientific evidence to justify the delay in approval. Another issue was temporary safeguards applied by six EC Member States (Austria, France, Germany, Greece, Italy and Luxemburg) by which they prohibited marketing of GMO products in their territories. On this issue, the EC argued that the temporary safeguards are justified by Article 5.7 of the SPS, which permits temporary measures based on the precautionary principle.

The Panel report incorporates many complex issues. The procedural and systemic issues include, *inter alia*, (a) whether separate reports are necessary for the claims by the United States, Canada and Argentina, (b) whether scientific experts and the relevant international organizations should be consulted with for their expert opinions, (c) whether information should be provided to the parties in accordance with Article 13 of the DSU, (d) whether measures in question should be specified under Article 6.2 of the DSU, (e) what is the relationship between WTO agreements and other principles of international law in interpreting WTO agreements, (f) the relationship between the TBT and the SPS, (g) the issue of leakage of the interim report, (g) whether new pieces of evidence should be accepted at the state of interim review, (h) the issue of new evidence concerning the measures in question, (i) the issue of translating evidence to other WTO official languages than English language.

The Panel report also deals with substantive issues which include, *inter alia*, the following: (a) whether provisions of the SPS are applicable to the EC approval system, (b) whether there was a moratorium of approval of GMO products in the EC between 1999 and 2003, (c) whether the EC measures that deal with the approval of GMO products are an application of procedure and come under Annex A(1) of the SPS which provides for requirements or procedure, (d) whether the moratorium of approval of GMO products by the EC was a measure under Article 5.1 and Annex A(1) of the SPS, (d) whether the delay of approval by the EC amounted to a violation of Annex C(1)(a) and Article 8 of the SPA, (e) whether there was a discrimination as alleged by Argentina between imported GMO and domestic non-GMO products regarding the approval system and (f) whether safeguards (temporary prohibition of marketing of GMO products by EC Member States) were SPS measures and therefore prohibited by the SPS.

---

[15] EC-Measures Affecting the Approval and Marketing of Biotech Products, WT/DS291, 192 and 193.

In essence, the Panel found that the delay of approval of GMO products by the EC violated provisions and Annex of the SPS. The Panel also found that safeguard measures taken by the EC Members did not satisfy the requirement of temporary safeguards as provided for in Article 5.7 of the SPS. The items discussed in the Panel report are too many to be dealt with in this paper. Therefore, the writer has taken liberty to choose a few topics of interest.

2.3. The relationship between the SPS and other principles of international law in the WTO dispute settlement procedure

In this dispute, the EC argued that WTO agreements should be interpreted in accordance with principles established in international law norms in the UN Biodiversity Convention and the Cartagena Protocol. The EC argued that the binding international norms are the Biodiversity Convention and the Cartagena Protocol.[16] The Cartagena Protocol allows a Member to take a measure to prohibit or control imports of GMO products even if there is no scientific evidence to support such a prohibition. In this sense, the Cartagena Protocol permits the precautionary principle much more widely than the SPS.

Preamble of the Cartagena Protocol states that the Protocol and the other international agreements including WTO agreements are mutually supportive and the Protocol does not restrict rights and obligations of the participants under other international agreements. This suggests that if a state is a Member of the WTO and, at the same time, a Member of the Cartagena Protocol, rights and obligations of both agreements apply to that Member. However, what happens if there is conflict between rights and obligations of one agreement and those of the other? There may be a situation where a Member of the Protocol takes a precautionary measure to prohibit imports of a GMO product without a clear evidence of risk to human life and health and another Member challenges this measure in the WTO. One of the parties to the dispute may be a Member of the WTO and the Cartagena Protocol or both of them may be Members of WTO and the Cartagena Protocol.

In the EC/GMO Case, the Panel cited Article 31(3)(c) of the Vienna Convention which states that, in interpreting a treaty, all the rules of international law as applied to the parties to a dispute should be taken into account. The Panel stated that only those rules of international treaties to which both disputing parties at a WTO dispute are signatories need to be taken into account.[17] Argentina, Canada and the EC have ratified the UN Biodiversity Convention, and the United States has signed but not yet

[16] Para 51–54 of the Panel report.
[17] Para 68 of the Panel report.

ratified it. With regard to the Cartagena Protocol, the EC joined it, Argentina and Canada signed but have not yet ratified it, and the United States did not sign it. The Panel held that one of the parties to the dispute before the Panel, the United States, was not a party to the Cartagena Protocol, and, therefore, there was no need to take into account of the principles of the Cartagena Protocol in this dispute.

The Panel reasoned that it did not have to take into account the principles of the UN Biodiversity Convention and the Cartagena Protocol in this dispute for the reason that one of the parties to the dispute was not a party to those international treaties. Article 31(3)(c) seems to clearly provide that the norms of other treaties should be considered in a dispute regarding a treaty if the disputing parties are parties to those other treaties. Therefore, the interpretation of the Panel seems to be reasonable when it stated that the principles of UN Biodiversity Convention and the Cartagena Protocol were irrelevant since the United States, one of the parties to the dispute, was not a party to them.

However, the issue of the relationship between WTO agreements and the Cartagena Protocol is so important in interpreting the SPS in future that it deserves some comments on a hypothetical basis.[18]

Article 3.2 of the SPS states that if an SPS measure of a Member is based on an international standard, guideline or recommendation, such a measure is presumed to be in compliance with WTO agreements even if this measure is not supported by scientific evidence. Annex A2(a–c) of the SPS identifies that standards promulgated by the Codex Alimentarius Commission, the International Office of Epizootics, and the International Plant Protection Convention are such international standards. In order for any standards formulated and promulgated by the Cartagena Protocol and the UN Biodiversity Convention to be qualified as an international standard in the above sense, it must be identified by the SPS Committee by consensus.

A decision of the SPS Committee to identify standards established by the Cartagena Protocol as an international standard, guideline or recommendation must be made by consensus. The United States, which is not a party to the Cartagena Protocol, is not likely to vote for the identification of the Cartagena Protocol as a qualified international standard in the sense of the SPS. Also Article 3.2 of the SPS creates only a presumption that an SPS measure based on an international standard is in

[18] For detailed analysis of conflicts and relationships between treaties, see Joost Pauwelyln, Conflict of Norms in Public International Law: How WTO Law Relates to other Rules of International Law (Cambridge University Press, 2003); Gabrielle Marceau, "A Call for Coherence in International Law-Praises for the Prohibition against"Clinical Isolation" in WTO Dispute Settlement, 33 Journal of World Trade 5 (October 1999), pp. 87–152; Steve Charnovitz, "Linking Topics in Treaties", 19 University of Pennsylvania Journal of International Economic Law 2 (Summer 1998), pp. 329–345.

conformity with WTO agreements if such a measure is based on an identified international standard. The word "presumption" is used instead of "deemed to be." Therefore, such a presumption may be overturned by adducing sufficient evidence to the contrary. The precautionary principle as provided in the Cartagena Protocol, if adopted by the SPS Committee, will drastically change principles in the SPS. It may even amount to a *de facto* amendment of Article 5.7 of the SPS. Such a major change in the SPS will substantially change rights and obligations of WTO Members in respect to the SPS. It is doubtful whether this change would be allowed without a decision of the Ministerial Conferences.

2.4. The EC approval procedure of GMO products and Annex A(1) of the SPS

The Panel examined whether the EC approval procedure of GMO products was an SPS measure in the sense of Annex A(1) of the SPS. Annex A(1) of the SPS provides, as SPS measures, "laws, decrees, regulations, requirements and procedures."[19] The Panel distinguished two categories of these, the "form" and "nature" of a measure. The Panel states that the EC measures in question in this case are regulations promulgated by the European Council of Ministers and the European Parliament and that they amounted to "laws" in the sense of Annex A(1). According to the classification of the Panel, "nature" of SPS measures is "requirements and procedures" and that, within the category of procedures, "testing, inspecting, certification and approval procedures" are included. The Panel held that the EC regulations amounted to procedures in the sense of Annex A(1) and that this signified "nature" of the measures.

There seems to be no textual justification for this dichotomy between "form" on the one hand and "nature" on the other in the wordings of Annex A(1) of the SPS. A more natural reading of Annex A(1) seems to be that it enumerates "laws, decrees, regulations, requirements and procedures" and treats them as equal in nature, although form may be different. In the interpretation adopted by the Panel, a measure must satisfy the "form" requirement as well as the "nature" requirement. This interpretation may unnecessarily narrow the scope of SPS measures in Annex A(1) of the SPS.

---

[19] It also adds "end product criteria, processes and production methods, testing, inspection, certification and approval procedures, quarantine treatments including relevant requirements associated with the treatment of animals or plants, or with the materials necessary for their survival during treatment, provisions on relevant statistical methods, sampling procedures and methods of risk assessment and packaging and labeling requirements directly related to food safety."

The Panel further stated that the general moratorium exercised by the EC did not disapprove every application for approval and did not satisfy the "form and nature" requirement.[20] This reading of Annex A(1) seems to be too narrow. If the Panel had read the five words in Annex A(1) as of equivalent nature with some differences in form, the only question would have been whether the general moratorium of the EC on GMO products amounted to one of those five categories and was covered by Annex A(1) of the SPS. In substance, there seems to be little difference between a general moratorium of approval and a partial ban of a product.

2.5. National treatment in Annex C.1(a) of the SPS[21]

Argentina argued that specific measures of the EC concerning different products were a violation of Annex C.1(a), second sentence, and Article III: 4 of the GATT. Annex C.1(a) of the SPS prohibits Members from discriminating imported products compared with like domestic products in the testing and approval of products and unduly delaying the procedures. Argentina argued that, in this case, GMO products were being treated unfavorably relative to non-GMO products. The Panel stated that Members are authorized to treat differently (less favorably) imported products compared with domestic products in their approval procedures because that difference may have come from the difference in safety features unless that differential treatment was made due to the difference in origin of products. Therefore, a mere differential treatment *per se* constitutes a violation of neither Annex C.1(a) of the SPS nor Article III:4 of the GATT. The Panel pointed out that Argentina did not adduce evidence to show that the differential treatment was based on the difference in the origin of products.[22]

The Panel did not examine whether imported GMO products and domestic non-GMO products were like products due to judicial economy considerations.

Issues of national treatment have been dealt with under various provisions in WTO agreements including Article III:2 of the GATT. It is the first time that national treatment was an issue in connection with approval procedures of products, and, in this sense, this Panel report is a valuable precedent. Generally, panels and the Appellate Body investigate whether an imported product and domestic product are like products and,

---

[20] Para 7.137 of the Panel report.

[21] Generally, the principle of national treatment means that a WTO Member shall accord to a product of other Member treatment no less favorable to that accorded to a like domestic product. For example, if a WTO Member imposes higher liquor tax on imported alcoholic beverage than it does on a similar domestic alcoholic beverage, it is contrary to the principle of national treatment.

[22] Para 7.2415 of the Panel report.

when they find that those are like products, examine whether there is discrimination in favor of the domestic products. In this case, the Panel skipped the process of examining whether imported GMO products and domestic non-GMO products were like products for the reason that the difference of treatment between them did not necessarily come from the difference in the origin of them and the difference of treatment did not constitute a violation in itself.

There are many precedents regarding the concept of like products in which the tests were physical similarities, the end uses, tariff classifications and consumers' perceptions.[23] One question, which may arise is whether the consumers make a sharp distinction between GMO products and non-GMO products, and, for this reason, these two should be regarded as non-like products. In the EC/Asbestos Case,[24] the Appellate Body held that asbestos and other three products with similar physical characteristics were non-like products since the risk of asbestos was widely recognized among users, consumers, international organizations and the public in general. In GMO products, it seems that views of consumers are more widely diversified. In Europe and Japan, there is suspicion that GMO products may be a cause of unpredictable consequences in the future, whereas, in the United States and Canada, there is less sense of this nature.

In any event, this finding of the Panel seems to have established the priority of order in reviewing the appropriateness of approval procedures of products under the SPS, for example, that there would be a review of whether the approval procedure that treats imported product less favorably than domestic product does so due to the difference in the origin of the products and, if this is proven, whether these two products are like products.

2.6. Burden of proof issues in the SPS[25]

As mentioned earlier, six Members of the EC invoked temporary safeguards against import of GMO products, and the complainants challenged this. The EC invoked Article 5.7 and argued that the measures in question are justified by this provision. The Panel examined the relationship between Articles 2.2 and 5.1 of the SPS on the one hand and Article 5.7 of the SPS on the other. Article 2.2 of the SPS requires that Members base their SPS measures on sufficient scientific evidence, and

---

[23] For a detailed analysis of the concept "like products," see _Wong-Mog Choi: "Like Products" in International Trade Law-Toward Consistent GATT/WTO Jurisprudence (Oxford University Press, 2003) and cases cited in this article.

[24] See note 4, *supra*.

[25] A detailed study of the issue of the burden of proof in WTO law is found in Michelle T. Grando, "Allocating the Burden of Proof in WTO Dispute – A Critical Analysis", Journal of International Economic Law, Vol. 9, No. 3, September 2006, pp. 615–656.

Article 5.1 requires that Members run risk assessment with regard to SPS measures[26] that they intend to adopt and allows them to enforce such measures only when such measures are supported by sufficient scientific evidence. On the contrary, Article 5.7 of the SPS allows Members to adopt temporary SPS measures on the basis of available evidence in accordance with the requirements stipulated in that Article when sufficient scientific evidence is not available. The question here is which party bears the burden of proof with respect to the relationship between Article 2.2 and Article 5.7 of the SPS and Article 5.1 and Article 5.7 thereof.

The Panel made a general statement by citing the EC/Tariff Preferences Case[27] that when a provision of a treaty permits a measure under certain conditions which would be inconsistent with another provision of the treaty but for the existence of these conditions and one of the provisions refers to the other, the claimant who alleges a violation of the provisions bears the burden of proving that the measure in question is inconsistent with the latter provision and that it does not satisfy the conditions for permission. The Panel then examined the relationship between Article 2.2 of the SPS and Article 5.7 thereof.

Article 5.7 of the SPS permits Members to take temporary SPS measures when there is not sufficient evidence to take SPS measures in accordance with Article 2.2 of the SPS. Article 2.2 refers to Article 5.7 by the phrase "except as provided for in paragraph 7 of Article 5." For this reason, the Panel said that Article 5.7 is not an exception to Article 2.2, but creates an independent right for a party invoking it. The Panel held, citing the EC/Sardines Case[28] and the EC/Tariff Preferences Case, that the claimant alleging a violation of Article 2.2. by the respondent's SPS measure must prove that the respondent measure is not permitted by Article 5.7 of the SPS. Likewise, the Panel held that the claimant is responsible to prove that the respondent's SPS measure is inconsistent with Article 5.1 as well as that it is not allowed by Article 5.7. In conclusion, the Panel held that the EC measures were in violation of Article 5.1 and were not permitted by Article 5.7.

The Panel's finding as explained earlier can be formulated as follows. If Provision A prohibits Measure X, Provision B permits it and either

[26] Risk assessment in a narrow sense means a scientific examination of whether a substance generates hazards to life and health. In a broad sense, however, it includes an assessment of "risk management," that is, an assessment of the manageability or controllability of risk. For example, a risk may be small in scientific experiment, but there may be circumstances in which it is difficult administratively to prevent such risk from spreading widely. Properly risk assessment should take into account both scientific aspect and administrative or managerial aspects.

[27] EC-Conditions for the Granting of Tariff Preferences to Developing Countries, Report of the Panel, 1 December 2003, WT/DS246/R; Report of the Appellate Body, 7 April 2004, WT/DS246/AB/R.

[28] See note 7, *supra*.

Provision A or Provision B refers to the other by such phrase as "except as provided for in Provision B," then the permission as provided for in Provision B is not an exception from Provision A, but is an independent right of Members and a claimant who alleges that the respondent violates Provision A is responsible to prove not only that the respondent's measure is in violation of Provision A but also that it is not permitted by Provision B.

In the past, there have been several Appellate Body rulings in which the issue was the burden of proof. Such cases include the U.S./Shirts and Blouses Case,[29] the EC/Hormones Case,[30] the EC/Tariff Preferences Case and the Brazil/Aircraft Case.[31] In the U.S./Shirts and Blouses Case, the Appellate Body stated that a party asserting the affirmative of a matter is responsible to prove it, and, when it is successfully made, the burden of proof shifts to the other party. In the EC/Hormones Case, the Appellate Body referred to the relationship between Articles 3.1 and 3.3 of the SPS and noted that Article 3.1 referred to Article 3.3. The Appellate Body held that whoever claimed that a measure was in violation of Article 3.1 was also responsible to prove that the measure was not permitted by Article 3.3. In the EC/Sardines Case, the Appellate Body held that whoever asserts that a measure violates Article 2.4 of the TBT Agreement is responsible to prove that the measure not only violates the prohibition in Article 2.4 but also is not qualified to be permitted by the derogation clause in Article 2.4 of the TBT Agreement. Also in the Brazil/Aircraft Case, the Appellate Body held that the sentence in Article 27.2 of the SCM Agreement, which states "The prohibition of paragraph (a) of Article 3 shall not apply to: (a) developing country Members referred to in Annex VII, (b) (omitted)," does not grant an exception from Article 3.1(a) which prohibits subsidies but conferred an independent right to Members invoking it.

On the contrary, the Enabling Clause states "Notwithstanding the provisions of Article I of the General Agreement," Members can confer preferential tariffs to developing country Members. In the EC/Tariff Preferences Case, the Appellate Body took note of this phrase and stated that the Enabling Clause is an exception to Article I of the GATT. It is generally recognized that Article XX of the GATT is an exception to prohibitions contained in other parts of the GATT. When a Member invokes Article XX of the GATT, that Member is responsible to prove that the measure in question satisfies the requirement for exception as provided for in Article XX of the GATT. However, Article XX of the

---

[29] United States-Measures Affecting Imports of Woven Wool Shirts and Blouses from India, Report of the Appellate Body, 25 April 1997, WT/DS33/AB/R.

[30] See note 8, *supra*.

[31] Brazil-Export Financing Programme for Aircraft, Report of the Appellate Body, 2 August 1997, WT/DS46/AB/R.

GATT states "nothing [no provision] in this Agreement shall be construed to prevent the adoption or enforcement by any contracting party of measures:...," and, therefore, Article XX of the GATT also refers to other provisions of the GATT. In light of the above analysis, there seems to be little difference in the textual structures between the SPS and the TBT on the one hand and the Enabling Clause and Article XX of the GATT on the other.

A brief review of the Appellate Body holdings together with the Panel report in the EC/GMO Case reveals that holdings in reports of the Appellate Body are rather confused and not quite consistent with each other. The Appellate Body, in some cases, interpreted words such as "Notwithstanding" and "Except for" to confer an independent right while interpreting similar words as granting exceptions in other cases. In other words, the Appellate Body made a distinction between "exception" and "conditional right" and, with regard to conditional right, allocated the burden of proof to the party challenging the measure in question to prove that the defending party violated a provision of a WTO agreement *and* that the defending party was not qualified to invoke the provision for such conditional right.

In all such cases, however, the following formulae seem to apply, that is, Provision A prohibits Measure X, Provision B allows it and either Provision A or Provision B refers to the other. However, the Appellate Body has not explained the rationale why a certain rule on the burden of proof should be adopted in relation to Article XX and Enabling Clause on the one hand and another rule of the burden of proof in relation to the SPS and the TBT on the other.[32]

It may be that the Appellate Body took into account the purposes and objectives of the SPS and the TBT in dealing with burden of proof issues, for example, some "political" or "policy" considerations may have crept into the process of decision making of the Appellate Body. The SPS and the TBT cut into the realm of "sovereignty" of Members more deeply than mere border measures such as tariffs and import restrictions in the sense that the former require that Members adopt SPS and TBT measures, which would apply to the domain of domestic regulations. For example, the SPS requires that Members adopt SPS measures based on international standards as identified by the SPS Committee regardless of whether products subjected to the standards are imports or domestically produced. There is a potential tension between the international disciplines

[32] For critical reviews of this holding of the panel, see Oren Perez, "Anomalies at the precautionary Kingdom: Reflections on the GMO Panel's Decision", The International Law Forum of the Hebrew University of Jerusalem Law Faculty (Research Paper No. 13-06, October 2006) (http://www.ssrn.com/abstractid=940907); Tomer Broude, "Genetically Modified Rules: The Awkward Rule-Exception-Right Distinction in EC-Biotech", *supra*. (Research paper No. 14–06, December 2006) (http://www.ssrn.com/abstractid=949623).

incorporated in the SPS and the TBT on the one hand and the realm of domestic authorities of Member states on the other. The Appellate Body may have paid respect to domestic authorities by imposing a heavy burden of proof on claimants challenging SPS and TBT measures of another Member and thereby somewhat easing the responsibility of Members challenged by the SPS and the TBT.[33] If so, however, the details of this reasoning should be made clear. Moreover, the Preamble of the SPS states that the purpose of the SPS is "to elaborate rules for the application of the provisions of GATT 1994 which relate to the use of sanitary or phytosanitary measures, in particular the provisions of Article XX(b)." This Preamble suggests that the SPS is an elaboration of Article XX(b) of the GATT and should be read together with it. The consequence is that the same burden of proof should be applied to Article XX(b) as the SPS.

The Panel in the EC/GMO Case faithfully followed precedents as established by the Appellate Body in previous cases. Therefore, if there is confusion and unclearness in the holding of the Panel, it is not the Panel which should be criticized. It is rather the holdings of the Appellate Body which should be critically reviewed again.

Under the present rule on the burden of proof, a claimant has to prove not only that the respondent's measure is in violation of a provision of a WTO agreement but also that such a measure is not permitted by the derogation clause. This puts a heavy burden on the claimant. One consideration is that the burden of proof should be imposed on the party, which is in a good position to prove the matter of which a proof is required. In the present rule, a claimant has to prove that there are no conditions in the territory of the respondent to justify the derogation. Yet it is the respondent, which is in a better position to adduce evidence that such conditions exist in its territory. Of course, the ease of adducing evidence should not be the only consideration when deciding the issue of who has the burden of proof. However, this deserves some attention.

3. Concluding remarks

By looking through the two WTO cases regarding food safety issues, one can see that there are some problems still left to be addressed. One is that of the burden of proof. Under the Appellate Body jurisprudence established through the EC/Hormones Case and the EC/GMO Case, a heavy burden of proof is imposed on a claimant challenging a SPS measure of another WTO Member. This may cause difficulty to developing country Members when challenging SPS measures of a developed country Member for the lack of legal and economic resources.

---

[33] World Trade Law net, European Communities – Measures Affecting the Approval and Marketing of Biotech Products (WT/DS291.292.293/R), Updated 30 October 2006.

It is submitted that the burden of proof under the SPS should be carefully reconsidered and, if necessary, modified.

Another potential issue is the relationship between the SPS and other rules of international law, especially the UN Biodiversity Convention and the Cartagena Protocol. Negotiators were aware of this issue when they gathered together in Doha, Qatar, to launch the Doha Development Round (DDR).

Paragraphs 31–33 of Doha Declaration are concerned with environmental issues. Paragraph 31 states that Members negotiate on "(i) the relationship between existing WTO rules and specific trade obligations set out in multilateral environmental agreements (MEAs)." It continues to provide "The negotiations shall be limited in scope to the applicability of such existing WTO rules as among parties to the MEA in question. The negotiations shall not prejudice the WTO rights of any Members that are not a party to the MEA in question..." Paragraph 32 provides, in part, that "the negotiations carried out under Paragraph 31 (i) and (ii) shall not add to or diminish the rights and obligations of members under existing WTO agreements, in particular the Agreement on the Application of Sanitary and Phytosanitary Measures, nor alter the balance of these rights and obligations, and will take into account the needs of developing and least-developed countries."

This ambiguity of the meaning of the Doha Declaration raises several issues.

1. The negotiation will take place only with regard to the applicability of existing WTO rules as among parties to the MEA.
2. The rights of WTO members that are not members of the MEA will be unaffected by the result of the negotiations.
3. Generally, the results of the negotiation will not affect the rights and obligations of members under existing WTO agreements in particular the SPS Agreement.
4. The needs of developing and least-developed countries will be taken into account.

The terms of reference of the negotiations are primarily focused on clarifying the relationship between WTO agreements and MEAs for members of the WTO as well as the MEAs. It does not cover the relationship between WTO agreements and the MEAs for WTO members that are members of MEAs and for those that are non-members of the MEAs. Therefore, the effect of the result of negotiations will be rather limited. If a dispute arises between Country A that is a member of the WTO and a member of a MEA and Country B that is a member of the WTO but not a member of the MEA, it will not be covered by the result of the negotiation.

Although the Doha Development Agenda includes terms of reference for negotiations on the relationship between WTO agreements (especially the SPS), there are many difficulties for negotiation, including agricultural issues. It is highly unlikely that any meaningful negotiations will be held on this issue in near future.

However, the ultimate solution of the issues discussed earlier is an amendment of Article XX, that is, an addition to Article XX of a provision which would provide that measures which implement the UN Biodiversity Convention and the Cartagena Protocol would be exempted from the application of GATT provisions. This would be Article XX(k) of the GATT 1994 providing that measures, which implement environmental protection or MEAs, would be exempted from the application of GATT provisions. This option requires an adoption of resolution to amend Article XX and requires consensus of the whole of WTO members. Such a consensus may be difficult to achieve. There may be claims by some WTO members that such a drastic proposal is outside the scope of Doha Declaration. In practice, chances of this option being adopted are rather slim. However, the process of reform must begin sometime, and it is time to think more seriously about the issues surrounding SPS reforms.

CHAPTER 12

Trade Dispute Diversion: The Economics of Conflicting Dispute Settlement Procedures between Regional Trade Agreements and the WTO

James H. Cassing

Department of Economics, University of Pittsburgh, Pittsburgh, PA 15260, USA
E-mail address: jcassing@pitt.edu

Abstract
A somewhat underappreciated aspect of the burgeoning rush to regional trade agreements (RTAs) is a discrepancy between the dispute settlement procedure (DSP) embodied in the original World Trade Organization (WTO) Dispute Settlement Understanding (DSU) and that found in the language of many RTAs. This chapter explores the issue in the context of a dynamic repeated game of trade agreements. As is well known, the institutional alternatives available in negotiating multilateral freer trade agreements – regional agreements, side agreements, trade dispute settlement punishments, and so on – can proscribe the limits and shape the nature of self-enforcing trade agreements. Here, we suggest the extent to which deviations from the WTO DSP embodied in RTAs – for example, "private interest access," "third party procedures," and "choice of forum" – can not only work against the interests of "weaker parties" but furthermore undermine multilateral agreements closer to free trade.

Keywords: Regional trade agreement, dispute settlement procedure, dispute settlement understanding, World Trade Organization, dynamic repeated game, self-enforcing agreement, choice of forum

JEL classifications: F13, F15, F53

1. Introduction

Disagreements between sovereign parties to trade agreements ("trade disputes") are inevitable as economic interests change and commitments

 ISSN: 1574-8715
DOI: 10.1108/S1574-8715(2009)0000006015

require clarification or interpretation. Of course, the attendant clarifications of commitments also require credible mechanisms of enforcement, or "punishment." The World Trade Organization (WTO) foresaw this need and embodied a dispute resolution mechanism or Dispute Settlement Procedure (DSP) in the Dispute Settlement Understanding (DSU) of the original agreement. Similarly, the recent explosion of regional trade agreements (RTAs) creates new avenues for trade disputes and so has itself been accompanied by the incorporation and extension of particular dispute resolution mechanisms. However, a somewhat underappreciated aspect of the burgeoning rush to RTAs is a discrepancy between the DSP embodied in the original DSU and that found in the language of the RTAs. This is true of both US free trade agreements such as NAFTA or the various bilateral agreements and European Union Partnership agreements. As it happens, this can matter substantively for trade and welfare as parties attempt to tailor DSP rules in line with particular interests and to divert disputes to their preferred forum.[1]

This chapter explores the issue in the context of a dynamic repeated game of trade agreements. As is well known, the institutional alternatives available in negotiating multilateral freer trade agreements – regional agreements, side agreements, trade dispute settlement punishments, and so on – can proscribe the limits and shape the nature of self-enforcing trade agreements. Here, we suggest the extent to which deviations from the WTO DSP embodied in RTAs – for example, "private interest access," "third party procedures," and "choice of forum" – can not only work against the interests of "weaker parties" but furthermore undermine multilateral agreements closer to free trade.[2]

The chapter proceeds as follows. In Section 2, we review briefly the essence of a DSP and its role in shaping and supporting trade agreements. We also highlight some of the key elements in the DSP of the WTO and some RTAs, emphasizing the discrepancies. Section 3 reviews some of the economics and political science literature on why discrepancies in DSP arise and on how these discrepancies might matter. In Section 4, we present a more formal model of the DSP and derive some conditions under

---

[1] Woolcock (2006, p. 5) has observed that "there is thus nothing new in rules being devised or evolving from a multilevel process. What is new is the emergence of the regional level as one of the most important…This multilevel nature of trade and investment policy has been recognized in policy circles. For example, the OECD Ministerial Declaration of 2001 called for efforts to ensure that regional and multilateral regimes are complements and not substitutes for one another…"

[2] A number of papers have investigated the impact of RTAs on multilateral cooperation, but the mechanisms driving the impact, for example, "tariff complementarity," are very different from the mechanism explored here. See especially Saggi (2006), Saggi and Yildiz (2007), and Maggi (1999) and the references therein for a nice review of this literature along with some interesting new results. For a more "political" model dealing with trade agreements and time inconsistency, see Maggi and Rodriguez-Clare (2007) and references to some of their earlier papers.

which the options available in a regional DSP can have the perverse effect of weakening support for a stronger WTO DSP. Since it is the harshness of the potential punishment that underwrites a more liberal trade regime, we will argue that any such weakening of support will in turn weaken support for a more cooperative freer multilateral trade regime. Indeed, a number of authors have portrayed RTAs as "stumbling blocks rather than building blocks" and lamented the distraction away from the multilateral process. Section 5 discusses nuances and offers some conclusions.

2. *The role of the DSP in shaping trade agreements*

2.1. The procedural mechanisms

On the surface, a DSP is needed as part of any trade agreement simply to codify, however loosely, what are the procedures of redress should one of the parties to the agreement be accused of deviation. Also, it is recognized that a forum for clarification of obligations will invariably be required on occasion in the future. After all, even a trade agreement as simple as one to lower tariffs still involves numerous definitions, formulae, and modalities. In fact, the reach of the WTO agreements goes far beyond that – covering non-tariff barriers and so on – and many RTAs go even further, entering the uncharted waters of labor and environmental concerns, for example, while going well beyond the WTO in dealing with intellectual property rights (IPR).

As a practical matter, when structuring a DSP, there is an inevitable tension between a more or less legalistic approach, the latter deferring instead to more reliance on negotiation of disputes. Typically, the contrast is made as in Jackson (2000) between the "rule-oriented approach" and the "power-oriented or diplomacy approach." Roughly, the WTO leans toward the former and various RTAs toward the latter, presumably because the WTO is a multilateral forum where power is somewhat diffused whereas the most important RTAs tend to be between a large developed country – especially the United States or EU – and a smaller less developed country pursuing deeper integration than is offered by the WTO but compelled by the larger country to accept less legalism in the DSP, or at least legalism more favorable to the larger country such as embodied in "TRIPS-plus" or more generally "WTO-plus" (Drahos, 2007).[3] Cognizant

[3] Interestingly, it was the United States that pressed for the more rule-oriented approach in the WTO while it is at the same time notorious for exerting its superior bargaining position and rule-bending in RTAs. Presumably, the US negotiators were well aware of the more limited bargaining power advantage in adjudicating disputes in the more multilateral WTO forum. See Drahos (2007) for a characterization of the US approach to trade negotiations. Also of interest for a historical perspective is Petersmann (1997). Girvan (2008) offers a perspective on asymmetry in the European Partnership Agreement (EPA) negotiated with the

of the power asymmetry accompanying many RTAs, the less powerful partner has often insisted on a "choice of forum" provision, which permits the complainant in a dispute to select either the DSP of the RTA or the DSP of the WTO. At the same time, while the less powerful country typically has in mind shifting a trade dispute away from the RTA forum to the WTO, the more powerful country often welcomes "choice of forum" to move the dispute in the other direction. This in effect links a country's attitude toward the DSP negotiated in the WTO with that negotiated in an RTA.

The WTO DSP follows guidelines laid out in the Understanding on the Rules and Procedures Governing the Settlement of Disputes ("Dispute Settlement Understanding") which addresses jurisdiction, procedures, and substantive content. (See, e.g., Mavroidis and Sykes, 2005, and the references to a vast literature therein.) In sum, the procedure mandates *consultation* among parties in a dispute – *investigation*, *ruling*, and *recommendation* by a panel – and potentially authorization for the aggrieved parties to *suspend obligations* ("retaliate") against the violator. In practice, retaliation has not been so common, suggesting that the "threat of punishment" has itself been sufficient to deter deviations from the trade agreement – that is, the agreement is "self-enforcing" and the level of freer trade cooperation is "supported" by the punishment threat inherent in the DSP.

The DSP accompanying various RTAs – for example, as outlined in Chapter 20 of the North American Free Trade Agreement (NAFTA) – is also nominally legalistic and follows the DSU in spirit (WTO, 1995; Gantz, 1999).[4] However, there are some important differences. First, the initiation of a trade complaint is government to government in the WTO. The private sector and non-governmental organizations (NGO) do not have standing to force actions by the WTO.[5] However, according to the rules of the EU,

---

Carribean Community and writes, "The absence of clearly specified and time-bound commitments in support of economic adjustment and transformation [by the EU] contributes to a major asymmetry in the architecture of the EPA. In contrast Cariforum's import liberalization commitments in goods and services are defined by international classification categories and are time-bound; with specified implementation procedures, provisions for dispute settlement, and authority to apply trade sanctions in the event of non-compliance. Clearly the EC and the 27-member EU have vastly superior resources to those of Cariforum states to devote to the monitoring of implementation obligations. This asymmetry is going to be a major factor in the on-going relationship between the two sides."

[4] See Smith (2000) for an integrated summary of the key features of most of the post-1957 RTAs. Table 3 (p. 156–7) indicates levels of legalism in dispute settlement design using the characteristics of third party review, third party ruling, judges, standing, remedy, and implied level of legalism.

[5] In spirit, private entities in a complainant country may have access to courts in a respondent country to file a lawsuit if the respondent country has not complied with a WTO ruling. In fact, that right is somewhat empty. In the United States, for example, Congress was explicit that there are no rights enforceable by US law embodied in the wording of the WTO

NAFTA, and various bilaterals, it happens that unions, business groups, and activists have the ability to press complaints. For example, in the NAFTA, labor unions and environmental groups have initiated complaints, and there are special DSPs afforded private parties with investment disputes against governments (NAFTA, supra note 1, Chapter 9). Such access to the trade dispute apparatus cannot help but politicize the DSP and give an advantage to the larger, more powerful country's narrower interests. (See Levy and Srinivasan, 1996; Robertson, 2006).

Second, the consultation and adjudication stage forums for a trade dispute have different structures. In the WTO, non-disputant third party countries have access to the process. This enhances the ability of disputant parties to build coalitions in pressing their cases. Also, only third parties – representatives of three non-disputant countries – comprise the panel if that stage is reached in the dispute. And, while there is a right of appeal, the rulings and recommendations of the panel cannot be vetoed by either disputant as in the pre-1995 GATT. If an offending trade action persists, retaliation (suspended obligations) is proscribed within the context of the DSU and Article XXVIII ("Compensation"). In contrast, for most RTAs, non-members are not privy to the consultations even if they have important interests. Furthermore, as in NAFTA Chapter 19 ("Antidumping and Countervailing Duty Matters"), national rather than regional or international law is sometimes given precedence.[6] Furthermore, the variety of mechanisms for resolving disputes can itself be confusing and open to interpretation, which admits a far larger role for the "power-oriented approach" over the "rules-oriented approach" in resolving trade disputes (Gantz, 1999). As for arbitration, the analogue of the WTO panel in an RTA typically comprises representatives of the RTA member countries, which, as with NAFTA's "Free Trade Commission" consisting of the trade ministers of the three NAFTA countries, issues and recommends implementation of an arbitral report. Thus, the adjudication of disputes potentially gives more weight to self-interest and power politics. Once again, the DSP is likely biased in favor of the larger, more powerful partner to the regional agreement.

Finally, there is the option in most RTAs – including NAFTA, the US bilaterals, and the EU Partnerships – of "choice of forum." While a complainant in an RTA has access to the regional DSP, there is also the

("the doctrine of self-execution"). There is a similar interpretation in the EU ("the doctrine of direct effect").

[6] While commercial treaties imply a certain standard of behavior, domestic law can supersede treaty commitments. In the United States, for example, the courts have been extremely reluctant to rule that treaties, especially WTO and other trade treaties, have any force of law in the US courts. The issues flow from Article 6 of the Constitution regarding "supreme law." The US approach is "dualist" and courts have made it hard to enforce treaty obligations as law.

option of taking the complaint to the WTO where appropriate. (Some RTAs limit choice of forum on some issues; e.g., NAFTA requires that certain environmental disputes listed in Article 104 be settled under the NAFTA's Chapter 20 rather than under the GATT/WTO mechanism. For more detail on the legal requirements controlling choice of forum, see Gantz, 1999.) In light of the differences in the procedural structure discussed above, this is an important option since third party access, coalition building, panel composition, and so on are all affected by the choice. Roughly, in a trade dispute, a weaker bargaining power country would prefer the WTO forum while the country with more bargaining power would prefer the regional forum where that power cannot be diluted (Drahos, 2007). For example, in a case involving agricultural products tariffication (US versus Canada), the United States chose the NAFTA forum essentially because it would have been difficult to argue that Canada had violated the WTO Agreement on Agriculture even though it was Canada's implementation of its obligations under the WTO that led to the charges of NAFTA violations in the first place (Gantz, 1999).

Suggestively at least, these discrepancies between the multilateral and the regional DSP are substantive in that they influence complainant access to the resolution mechanism, potential for more or less coalition formation, and discretion as to which forum to exploit. Consequently, nations have an interest in DSP design. And, although multilateral and regional trade negotiations occur in distinct and separate policy venues, the character of the multilateral (WTO) DSP sometimes has force in both venues due to "choice of forum." As we next discuss, this linkage is important because it is the DSP that shapes how much trade cooperation can be achieved. Therefore, more powerful nations potentially pursuing future RTAs and hoping to bolster the use of the more favorable (for them) regional DSP are given an incentive to weaken the multilateral DSP which in turn weakens the extent of possible cooperation within the WTO. That is, what a country agrees to regarding the WTO DSP could potentially erode its bargaining power in an RTA and so have an effect on what can be achieved in regional trade negotiations.[7]

We now turn to review informally the logic of recent economic (game theoretic) explanations of the DSP as an institution which in fact shapes and limits cooperative trade agreements. Roughly, the notion is that a DSP creates institutional friction, which dissipates the incentives for countries simply first to break trade agreements and then, when detected, just quickly renegotiate back to where they were before the violation. But then, there would be no "punishment" to deter deviation from the agreement in the

---

[7] Woolcock (2006, p. 3) notes that incompatible rules at the regional and multilateral levels can be problematic and observes that "difficulties may arise…when regional or bilateral enforcement results in interpretations of general norms that diverge from those of the WTO or other global bodies." See also Woolcock (1996) for a discussion of rules competition.

first place – and so no agreement. In subsequent sections, we will formalize this notion and introduce conflicting regional and multilateral DSPs.

2.2. The self-enforcement underpinnings

While on the surface the DSP is a quasi-legalistic mechanism to clarify, adjudicate, and reconcile trade disputes, economists have recently focused on the linchpin role played by a DSP in supporting credible cooperative trade agreements (Ludema, 2001; Bagwell and Staiger, 2002; Klimenko *et al.*, 2008).[8] From this perspective, the world is portrayed as a collection of sovereign nations, which can gain from cross-border transactions – trade and investment. Thus, there is an incentive for countries to cooperate in order to create an economic environment absent trade barriers or other commercial impediments and so conducive to the globally first-best state of free trade. But, for any particular country, there is an incentive to unilaterally impede commerce as through an optimum tariff/non-tariff barrier, which moves the terms of trade in a favorable direction or, more subtly for example, lax enforcement of patents or copyrights which allows the local citizenry to obtain valuable property by distributing "pirated" material at very low prices. However, as all countries start unilaterally to deviate from more cooperative free trade, the end result is trade restriction and reduced welfare for all. Typically, this is portrayed as reversion to the non-cooperative "Nash equilibrium" wherein all nations erect "optimal response" trade barriers, which maximize national welfare given the ("optimal response") trade barriers of the other nations. Although all nations would benefit by cooperatively restoring free trade, there is now no incentive for any one country to lower its barriers given the trade barriers of the others.

So the question emphasized in the economics literature is how sovereign nations can obtain maximum cooperation – free trade – while discouraging narrowly self-motivated defections. At first face, the answer is of course a free trade agreement. But in order to discourage deviation from the agreement, there must be some sort of credible punishment to discourage the deviation. This credible punishment which imposes discipline on agreement member nations is said to "support" the agreement. While this will be discussed more formally below, in sum the DSP can be viewed as the "punishment" for violating a trade agreement in that the violation results in a retreat toward the Nash equilibrium and reduced welfare for some period of time which could be prolonged as the trade dispute is resolved within the institutional context of the DSP. It is precisely this restriction on instantaneously restoring the initial agreement conditions that constitutes the extent of the punishment. In a sense, the DSP is an institution that makes history (behavior) matter. And so, any nation

[8] See especially Keck and Schropp (2007) for a thoughtful critical review of this literature.

cognizant that unilateral deviation results in retribution that cannot be quickly negotiated away will not deviate in the first place so long as the short run gain does not outweigh the discounted present value of the long term loss. Or, to use the terminology of game theory, at every point in time, the agreement must be "subgame perfect" or "self-enforcing."

Importantly, just how much cooperation can be supported – how close to free trade the world can get – depends on the nature of the DSP since this is what governs how quickly a violator will be caught and how severely punished. A very vigilant, streamlined DSP (rapid detection of violations) entailing very harsh punishment (lengthy loss of potential cooperative gains) supports the most cooperation, and in the limit free trade. In what follows, we will treat the character of the DSP as the sole determinant of the trade agreement. Of course, it is the trade agreement itself that is negotiated and then the DSP put into place. But "rule-making" is totally contingent on enforcing the rules, and this is what the DSP does. As Woolcock (2006, p. 13) observes:

> Rules mean little unless they are enforced, and all trade and investment agreements contain some degree of ambiguity that requires interpretation. Dispute settlement provisions, review procedures and the scope for non-state actors to bring cases of non-compliance are therefore important elements in rule-making... Regional interpretations of rules may, however, set precedents for wider multilateral rules and thus challenge WTO rules.

3. The causes and consequences of differing DSPs

In this section, we review some of the sources of variation in DSPs across trade agreements and then reflect on some of the consequences for how these differences temper trade agreements. At the heart of the differences, of course, are the ambitions and the relative bargaining power of the would-be member countries. Then, in the next section, we explore how the differences in DSPs in conjunction with "choice of forum" may limit the extent of multilateral cooperation.

3.1. Different rules for settling disputes

A number of studies have noted substantive differences in the rules and adjudication procedures applied in various trade agreements (Hudec, 1990; Smith, 2000; Woolcock, 2006). Since the goals of various trade agreements as well as the bargaining power of potential member countries differ, it is not surprising that no one DSP is institutionalized for, nor suits, all trade agreements (Schott, 2004; Aggarwal and Fogarty, 2004). For example, the regional goals of the Southern African Development Community (SADC) with a focus on transport logistics and freer trade corridors between relatively poor countries contain potential trade disputes far different from, say, the US–Jordan Free Trade Agreement with a focus on a deeper integration for credibility reasons from one side and for securing substantial intellectual property guarantees regarding pharmaceuticals from the other. Or, in the context of the original Canada–US Free Trade Agreement, there was clearly concern by Canada about application of anti-dumping (AD) and countervailing duty (CVD) laws that led the Canadians to press for what is now Chapter 19 of NAFTA providing (then) for a binational panel review of disputes of AD/CVD policies. In particular, national law must be applied in AD/CVD cases within NAFTA, and parties are prevented from interfering with the panel process. (This is in contrast to the more "power-oriented" approach of Chapter 20.) Similarly, the EU integration of its internal market was bolstered only after the move to qualified majority voting that restricted individual countries' prerogative to veto unfavored decisions (Sandholtz and Zysman, 1989; Moravcsik, 1991; Garret, 1992; Yarbrough and Yarbrough, 1997). And, in EU-centered RTAs, investment is typically excluded since it does not fall under European Community competence (Reiter, 2006).

In their seminal study of dispute settlement mechanisms, Yarbrough and Yarbrough (1997) offer a good framework for thinking about alternative DSPs and when each might emerge. First, they characterize alternatives as running from least forceful ("self-help") to most forceful ("pure third party enforcement").[9] Specifically, they identify four sorts of DSPs:

1. third party information gathering and dissemination, but no external enforcement other than unilateral retaliation;
2. non-binding third party adjudication and recommended remedy, but no external enforcement other than retaliation;
3. binding third party adjudication, no retaliation allowed when no violation found, and enforcement through permissible retaliation by aggrieved party;
4. binding third party adjudication and enforcement, as happens for example in a national legal system.

The distinction between the first two and last two DSPs is essentially the possibility of legal non-compliance in the first two. DSP 2 characterizes NAFTA and many RTAs, as well as the GATT DSP before the Uruguay Round, as the only recourse to any disagreement with a report is retaliation since any panel finding can be overridden by a disputant and compliance is not mandatory. In fact, in the pre-1995 GATT, the

[9] Smith (2000) offers a similar taxonomy recounting the key features of institutional design that make a dispute settlement procedure more or less legalistic. See also Smith (1995).

defendant in a trade dispute could refuse to permit panel formation, could veto adoption of a panel finding which required consensus, and could block authorization of retaliation. Thus, the DSP which characterizes many RTAs is typically somewhat skewed toward the "power approach" discussed above where unequal bargaining power can be exploited more easily.

In contrast, DSP 3 is closer to the current WTO panel system wherein the panel formed in a trade dispute retains some independence and compliance with the recommendations is mandatory. This approach is generally more "rules oriented" and would somewhat blunt the advantages and disadvantages of asymmetric bargaining power. Also, this mechanism must result in an end to a dispute, although of course the resolution might entail a required remedy and punishment.

So there is a spectrum of potential DSPs, and which will be chosen depends on the nature of the set of countries negotiating a trade agreement. Beth Yarbrough and Robert M. Yarbrough cast the outcome as the result of a "coordination game" wherein agreement negotiators' preferences differ with respect to the nature of the dispute settlement mechanism and the accompanying enforcement. In such games, the DSP that emerges depends on the participants' perceived costs of coordination failure and costs of compromise.[10] Thus, what emerges in an RTA between a large nation, for whom the cost of failure is low and the cost of compromise is high, and a smaller nation, for whom the opposite holds, is a DSP like DSP 2 more amenable to the larger country exploiting its power or ameliorating its particular domestic special interests. And, in the context of a broader, more balanced set of negotiating countries as with the WTO, what emerges is a DSP like DSP 3 which is more even-handed and favorable to less powerful interests.

Smith (2000) explores the issue econometrically matching 63 post-1957 RTA treaty texts with characteristics of the RTA partners to predict DSP design outcomes. He concludes (p. 173), "Thanks to their market size and lesser dependence on trade, relatively large countries tend to prefer less legalism than their smaller counterparts…In almost every pact with high asymmetry, legalism is absent."[11] Drahos (2007) seems to concur with this view and further motivates the next section when he notes that "what the United States does in trade dispute resolution matters to the evolution of the trade regime" (p. 192).

---

[10] Schelling (1960) discusses communication, announcements, and solutions in the so-called pure coordination games.

[11] See Rosendorf (2005) for a discussion of this and other empirical studies of DSP design, but with the somewhat different focus of agreement stability.

3.2. The main differences and how they matter

While the discrepancies in the wording and coverage between the WTO and the various RTA DSPs can be subtle and complex, generically there are three classes of differences that matter:

- private party access ("complaint initiation");
- non-disputant representation ("third-party procedures");
- choice of forum.

In this section, we discuss the first two differences and in the next section show how, in light of the first two differences, the third difference might create an undesirable link to the WTO. In essence, the argument will be that the first two differences encourage more powerful countries (in terms of bargaining power) to divert trade disputes to the regional forum and away from the multilateral forum if they can. The opposite holds for the less powerful countries. At the same time, the third difference weakens the ability of the more powerful country, when it is the alleged transgressor, to shift a dispute to its preferred regional forum and so creates an incentive to undermine the less preferred multilateral forum.

3.2.1. Private party access

A number of legal scholars have noted that whereas the DSP of the WTO gives only official government entities direct access to the dispute settlement mechanism, many RTAs – for example, NAFTA with respect to the side agreements on labor and environmental issues – and the rules of the EU go further in giving private interest groups some ability to press complaints (Levy and Srinivasan, 1996; Trebilcock and Howse, 1999). For example, recently, a leading US labor coalition and an industry group have filed a complaint with the U.S. Trade Representative asking that it formally sanction the government of Jordan for "gross workers' rights violations" under the free trade agreement with the US and Israel. Specifically, the case by the AFL-CIO, the largest trade union confederation in the US, and the National Textile Association (NTA) marks the first time a business association has formally joined in seeking a workers' rights complaint under a trade agreement (IPS, August 11, 2008).

Whether such access is desirable is not clear, but seems doubtful. On the one hand, Kahler (1995) suggests that domestic political interests' linkage to political institutions is a strength of the EU as connections to policy become more substantial. Others, however, fear that narrow business interests and aggressive NGOs are driving the new regionalism in a direction not necessarily in the interests of poorer countries or even sometimes of the larger, more powerful countries' other diplomatic objectives. (See Robertson (2006) and some of the references therein.) The argument here is that the poorer countries have little power to resist the demands of powerful interest groups such as pharmaceutical, labor, or environmental interests, and direct private access to the DSP removes the firewall which a larger country government might well want to preserve in pursuing its broader agenda in contrast to the narrowly defined self-interest of the businesses, unions, and NGOs.

Politically, such access by private interests creates a constituency with a bias in favor of RTAs, where they can have direct influence on behavior in the other country, and against the WTO, where they have only more muted, arms-length ability to participate in disputes. Consequently, some governments may feel politically compelled to entertain trade disputes in the regional forum rather than in the WTO (Levy and Srinivasan, 1996). Drahos (2007, p. 209) summarizes:

> (T)he current proliferation of FTAs represents something of a crossroads for the DSU. By constituting many possible trade courts, the United States and the EU are creating a system in which their respective influential domestic trade interests will lobby them to go to the trade court in which those interests are most likely to obtain satisfaction. How much such a system will help to improve trade liberalization that leads to real economic gains is an open question.

3.2.2. Non-disputant representation

Another difference between the DSP of the WTO and that of most RTAs concerns the treatment of interested parties to a trade dispute that have no standing in the RTA, the so-called third-party procedures. As outlined in the DSU of the WTO, certain procedural aspects of dispute resolution allow for third party participation in a dispute between two WTO members (DSU, supra note 2, Articles 9.1, 10.1, 10.2). At the initial consultation stage, so long as the third party has substantial trade interest, that party may be enjoined in the consultations based on Article XXII of the GATT. More substantively, once the panel stage is reached, third parties have a right to be heard, to make written submissions, to receive written submissions, and even to bring their own actions (Article 10 of the DSU). Importantly, this means that weaker parties in a dispute are afforded the opportunity to enlist support through cooperation and collective action in both defending and bringing trade actions (Gantz, 1999; Drahos, 2007). In an RTA, such coalition building is simply not available when the forum is the RTA DSP because participation is limited to RTA members. Of course, for the United States or EU with increasingly many bilateral agreements, this means no coalition building opportunity at all for the partner country in many trade disputes.

Drahos (2007) has argued forcefully that the procedures of the DSU that facilitate coalition building are especially important to weaker states. In particular, a coalition "signals to a panel that there are aggregated interests of the WTO membership at work in the dispute rather than just the individual interests of one strong State and one weak State" (p. 201). This in turn can suggest to the WTO panel interpretations more considerate of the entire WTO membership (Smith, 2003). In contrast, as Drahos writes, in an RTA trade dispute, particularly within a bilateral agreement, "the capacities and power of the two parties are what they are." Several case studies and other empirical evidence seem to support this view (Shaffer, 2003; Bown, 2005; Busch and Reinhardt, 2005).

In sum, the DSP of the RTA once again works against the interests of the weaker party in a dispute. Of course, as discussed above, the weaker party apparently agrees to the somewhat disadvantageous procedures of the RTA DSP because the agreement itself has redeeming value. But, if possible, the weaker state would prefer to fight all of its trade dispute battles in the more favorable multilateral WTO forum. In fact, a feature of most RTAs, "choice of forum," makes this possible for many trade disputes. However, if the regional agreement DSP favors the more powerful country's interests – either due to catering to private party self-interest or because the process favors the stronger party procedurally – then that country has an incentive to weaken any alternative adjudication forum that may be available to a trade dispute adversary. We now turn to this issue and its implications for the WTO.

4. "Choice of forum" and the link to the WTO

One counterbalance to the asymmetric large country advantage of an RTA DSP would seem to be the option of taking a regional trade dispute to the WTO. A recurring feature of all US RTAs and most other RTAs, including the EU and implicit at least in the Partnership Agreements, is the so-called choice of forum.[12] This feature gives the complaining party in a trade dispute wherein both regional and multilateral agreement obligations have been breached the choice as to which DSP is to be applied, that of the RTA or the WTO. For reasons discussed above, there would appear to be an advantage to the stronger party channeling complaints to the regional forum and the weaker party to the WTO forum. When the government or special interests in the more powerful country are the complainants, and when the country has in place a number of RTAs, the dispute can in fact often be moved to the more favorable forum. In fact, it has been suggested that this is precisely why a more powerful country might seek a web of

[12] Busch (2007) writes, "Indeed, in reviewing the texts of all trade agreements containing a formal dispute settlement chapter, as listed in the Dartmouth Tuck Trade Agreement Database, I found only a few exceptions that, like the CARICOM–Colombia agreement, make no mention of the opportunity for forum shopping. See Tuck School of Business at Dartmouth, Tuck Trade Agreements Database+ Available at (http://cibresearch.tuck.dartmouth.edu/trade_agreements_db/). Accessed 21 March 2007+".

RTAs (Bhagwati, 1994; Drahos, 2007).[13] As a practical matter, it is really only the United States and the EU that have extensive networks of bilateral RTAs and whose complainant interests stand to benefit most from diverting trade disputes away from the WTO DSP. Indeed, it has been argued that the choice provision is largely the creation of the "highly organized intellectual property lobby groups in the United States" (Drahos, 2007, p. 192).

Of course, on the surface at least, smaller, weaker partners to RTAs can themselves use the provision when they are the complainants in order to shift the trade dispute to their favored forum, presumably the WTO. This, however, links the RTA to the DSP of the WTO and creates an incentive for the stronger member of an RTA to weaken this option, that is, to weaken the WTO DSP. We next discuss the consequences of this incentive in a more formal model of trade disputes and the DSP.

4.1. The model

Recently, economists have focused on the theoretical underpinnings of DSPs and the connection with the overlying trade regime. The basic idea is that credible commitments to mutually beneficial trade agreements must be self-enforcing and so require that any contemplated deviations confront potential punishment sufficiently harsh to discourage violations aimed to secure short-term gains.

Formally, suppose initially that there are two ("large") countries, Home (H) and Foreign (F), engaged in free international trade as in a standard competitive trade model. While the simple formal model presented here couches trade agreements in terms of tariffs, and so countries are taken to be "large" so that they can have an incentive to deviate from the agreement by imposing an optimum tariff, clearly the spirit extends easily to investment guarantees, IPR protection, and so on. In this sense, virtually every country is "large" in that each can affect world prices of some things that it imports. Indeed, many trade disputes recently, mostly informal rather than formally notified, have been between economically quite disparate countries and, in the case of the United States, have revolved around IPR ("pirating and patenting") and investment access issues.

Using capital letters for home country variables, denote by M and X (m and x) the quantities of imports and exports, respectively, of H (F).

[13] Or, as Reiter (2006) has bluntly observed, "Of course, given the very asymmetric character of many agreements and the US interest as a capital exporter in securing access and protection for investment in its RTA partners' markets (and not the reverse), the United States has everything to gain from applying the open-ended disciplines of the NAFTA model in combination with investor-state dispute settlement. In asymmetric agreements such stringent rules pose no real threat to US interests in terms of the risk of legal challenges from foreign investors. NAFTA-type investment rules are therefore typically part and parcel of the US FTAs (and BITS)."

In equilibrium, $M = x$ and $X = m$. Both countries have the option of imposing import tariffs, T and τ. Social welfare for each country is assumed to be a continuously differentiable, quasi-concave function defined over consumption of the goods. Welfare can be written in implicit form as a continuous function of the tariff levels, $W = W(T, \tau)$ and $w = w(T, \tau)$, with welfare in autarky normalized to zero (see, e.g., Mayer 1984).

Each country now has a best response tariff conditional on the tariff level of the other country. In a one period game, given the assumptions made, there exists an interior Nash equilibrium and we denote the solution T_n and τ_n. Note that prohibitive tariffs that take trade to autarky are also trivially a Nash equilibrium.

Now suppose that the game is an infinitely repeated one which unfolds over a sequence of discrete intervals t, $t = 0, 1, 2, 3, \ldots$. A (cooperative) trade agreement beginning in period $t = 0$ is represented by a pre-set level of negotiated tariffs T_t and τ_t at each period (stage) yielding welfare levels of $W(T_t, \tau_t)$ and $w(T_t, \tau_t)$ for H and F, respectively. Suppose that an agreement sets tariff levels at a constant T^* and τ^* for all time. In a cooperative agreement with $T^* < T_n$ and $\tau^* < \tau_n$, welfare W and w are higher than in the non-cooperative Nash equilibrium.

Denote by ω_t the one period gain to H deviating from the agreement in period t – for example, by imposing an optimum tariff in t – and by W_{pt} the value of the "punishment payoff" which would ensue beginning in the next period – for example, the Nash response by F to the H tariff. Note that "no punishment" in a recurrent trade agreement with the possibility of renegotiation would mean that the agreement is simply reinstated after the violation is detected. But then, W_p would just coincide with the initial agreement payoff after period $t = 0$ no matter what, and so it would always pay to "cheat" until caught. As it turns out, W_p will entail reversion to a Nash equilibrium for some finite period of time.

Then, using δ to denote the discount factor at each stage and normalized by $(1 - \delta)$, a necessary and sufficient condition for the agreement to be a subgame perfect equilibrium (SPE) in period $t = t'$ is given for H by:

$$\sum W(T, \tau)_{t'} > (1 - \delta)\omega_{t'} + \delta W_{pt'} \tag{1}$$

where $\sum W(T, \tau)_{t'} = (1 - \delta) \sum_{t=t'}^{t=\infty} \delta^t W(T, \tau)$.

That is, the LHS which represents the discounted present value at period t' of adhering to the agreement must exceed the RHS, which comprises the immediate value of deviating from the agreement (as with an optimum tariff) and the discounted value of the punishment payoff that would ensue upon detection the next period.[14]

---

[14] The normalization $(1 - \delta)$ is introduced to facilitate comparisons across time and $W_{pt'}$ is discounted by δ because punishment takes place in the next period (Ludema, 2001).

The trade agreement as represented here is then the jointly determined solution to the H problem max W subject to Equation (1) and the analog for F. In much of the literature, it is assumed that H and F are symmetric in order to simplify the mathematics involved, but this is not necessary. Nonetheless, it is convenient to maintain the assumption when we refer to the WTO trade agreement. Thus, T will be the same for all members and we can suppress τ in the notation. Also, we can then allow that there are more than two countries in the WTO agreement.

4.2. The solution with and without renegotiation

Since W_p decreases the more severe is the punishment, the most severe punishment which is an SPE would seem to be a permanently prohibitive tariff resulting in autarky forever. That is, $W_p = 0$ as the violator loses the gains from trade for the rest of history. This, in turn, would support the trade agreement closest to free trade since the temptation to deviate for a short-run gain comes at a very high cost. Or, in terms of condition (1), LHS > RHS would hold for the relatively lowest tariff levels given any δ. The level of tariff would itself be the lowest consistent with the inequality holding (weakly). However, in a recurrent trade agreement, such a punishment path is not itself credible in that it is not "renegotiation proof." That is, if one country violated the trade agreement, the other country could then impose autarky forever: But why would they? Once in the no trade state, it would behoove both nations to renegotiate at least *some* mutually beneficial trade and both would be better off by simply moving to the interior Nash equilibrium, T_n and τ_n.

So the question addressed in the literature (Ludema, 2001; Klimenko *et al.*, 2008; and others) is to find the feasible (renegotiation proof) punishment path which in turn then determines the character of the trade agreement that is supportable. Following Ludema, such a punishment path that would support the tariff agreement with tariffs at the level T^* entails, upon detection of a violation, reverting to the Nash equilibrium for some length of time and then reestablishing the initial agreement. The punishment in the symmetric game for H and F is given by a path through time:

$$\{(T_{\mathrm{n}}, T_{\mathrm{n}}) \text{ for } t^* - 1 \text{ periods, } Q_{t^*} \text{ for 1 period,}$$
$$\text{and } (T^*, T^*) \text{ for } t^* + 1 \text{ and beyond}\}$$

where Q_{t^*} is a randomized tariff pair and serves a technical convexifying role.[15]

[15] Ludema's seminal portrayal of the DSP in this context (Ludema, 2001) proves the existence of this punishment path to support a tariff agreement and discusses the convexification assumption. Klimenko *et al.* (2008) derive a similar punishment path characterization of the DSP and argue that it will only exist if it can be externally imposed. Note also that the

Importantly, it is precisely the friction created by the DSP – detection, hearings, and adjudication – which takes t^* periods to run its course that creates the punishment (loss of freer trade benefits) that in turn supports a trade agreement. That is, if renegotiation after a trade agreement violation were costless, then countries would continually violate the agreement and the only equilibrium to emerge would be the Nash equilibrium forever (Klimenko *et al.*, 2008). The more severe is the punishment – the longer is t^* – the closer to free trade will be the trade agreement.

So we can think of the trade agreement that might emerge as a search for t^* which in turn determines the lowest tariff level T which is supportable or consistent with the SPE condition (1). For what follows, it is convenient to adopt the approach of Ludema wherein the optimal trade agreement values – tariffs and length of reversion to the Nash equilibrium – is reduced to maximizing welfare of the punishment path. And this, in turn, can be simplified to the problem:

$$\max_{T,\Lambda}[(1-\delta^{\Lambda})W(T_{\mathrm{n}})+\delta^{\Lambda}W(T)] \tag{2}$$

subject to the SPE condition (1), and where Λ is the "effective punishment length" and approximately t^*, the number of periods before the dispute is resolved and the initial agreement tariff levels reestablished. There is only one argument in the welfare function reflecting the symmetry assumption in the WTO forum. The problem can be further simplified by noting that the tariff level T can be written $T(\Lambda)$ since it is the lowest T consistent with the SPE condition (1). Also, $\mathrm{d}T/\mathrm{d}\Lambda<0$ since more "punishment" supports lower tariffs. The solution to problem (2) obtains at Λ^* and $T^* = T(\Lambda^*)$.

Geometrically, the solution is illustrated as in Ludema (2001), but with different notation, in Figure 1.

For convenience, call the country represented the home country H. In Figure 1, $W(T_n)$ represents welfare in H associated with Nash reversion. $W(T(\Lambda))$ reflects the welfare associated with the trade agreement which depends on the tariff level, T, which in turn depends on the severity of punishment for deviation from the agreement, that is, the length of reversion to the Nash equilibrium, Λ. The higher is Λ, the higher will be welfare since lower tariffs can be supported in the cooperative equilibrium. The welfare of the punishment path $W_p(\Lambda)$ is itself the maximand of Equation (2) which is a convex combination of Nash reversion for all time, $W(T_n)$, and welfare of no deviation from the agreement, $W(T)$.

Now consider the shape of the "punishment path" welfare $W_p(\Lambda)$ as it relates to the "length of punishment" Λ. Note that at $\Lambda = 0$, there is no

punishment path of the model supposes that punishment is meted out without delay while the legal process unfolds, whereas in reality, short-term or insignificant violations could go unpunished except for a loss of future credibility. Both papers also provide an excellent discussion of the institutional underpinnings for characterizing a DSP as a reversion to a Nash equilibrium for some finite period of time.

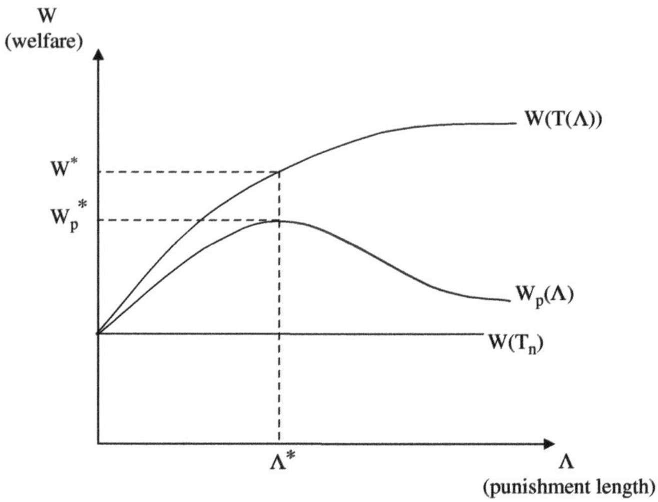

Fig. 1. Equilibrium trade agreement.

punishment for deviation and so the Nash equilibrium obtains. As Λ approaches infinity, δ^{Λ} tends to zero and so again W_p coincides with the Nash equilibrium value $W(T_n)$. Somewhere in between these extremes, W_p achieves a maximum - Λ^* – and this supports the tariff agreement $T^* = T(\Lambda^*)$ with welfare $W^*(T^*(\Lambda^*)$.

4.3. The impact of choice of forum

Suppose now that there is a multi-country WTO Agreement fashioned as above by more powerful states like H and F along with weaker states who are also members of the WTO. Furthermore, suppose that H is negotiating or has negotiated an RTA with a fellow WTO member country that is a relatively weaker state, f. For example, we might think of H as the United States and f as Colombia. While H is taken to be more powerful than f in a bargaining sense, we assume that the bargaining power of H is relatively weaker in the multilateral setting and stronger in the bilateral regional setting. This follows from the above discussion of the possibilities for coalition building available to weaker countries in the more global forum of the WTO and the presence of counterbalances represented by other powerful countries to any one powerful nation. Suppose also, for clarity and following Maggi (1999), that we can treat the spillover *economic* (trade) consequences of the trade negotiation outcomes in the RTA as independent of the WTO negotiations. That is, essentially we rule out significant trade diversion owing to trade policies adopted in the regional setting on the wider group and vice versa. Then we will suppose that welfare from the WTO Agreement and the RTA is additively separable so that we can use the above analysis as a starting point. (For example, similar to the three-country model of Maggi with separable bilateral relationships, assume that each pair of countries trade two distinct goods that are neither supplied nor demanded by the third country.)

Now in the absence of choice of forum, the trade agreements would not be linked directly in that each country, say H and f, would negotiate for the most favorable agreement in the forum in question. Again, we assume that H is a large country endowed with stronger bargaining power relative to f, but that H has less relative leverage in the multilateral forum, where the bargain is among many nations, and more in the regional forum, where the bargain is just with f. Since it is the DSP that supports the agreement in this model, the DSP negotiated in the WTO will look different from the DSP of the RTA, and so too will the agreements, or supportable levels of obligations in the WTO versus the RTA. In particular, in the regional agreement, H will be able to fashion a DSP which is more favorable to its export trade-opening or IPR interests and more tolerant of its self-motivated or protectionist trade agreement violations than would be the case in the multilateral forum. For example, in both the US-Morocco FTA and the Jordan-US FTA, the United States was able to obtain with "TRIPS-plus" concessions regarding patent protection and pharmaceutical generics, which go far beyond any WTO TRIPS obligations.[16]

Next, suppose that there is a choice of forum provision in the RTA. In modeling the impact of choice of forum, we will maintain the assumption of symmetry of countries in the WTO agreement negotiations but not in the RTA negotiations where we assume H to have a bargaining advantage over f. Besides being mathematically convenient to retain symmetry in representing the WTO Agreement, this seems plausible in that in the WTO forum, narrow country self-interest is more difficult to advance given the possibilities of coalition building. For example, in the Doha Round, many developing countries were able to hold negotiating positions credibly that simply would not have been possible in a bilateral agreement with the EU or the United States. Roughly, for example, Colombia is less malleable when negotiating in the WTO than it is in negotiating the US-Colombia Free Trade Agreement. And, this is also consistent with the incorporation into the US bilaterals of many features championed by US business interests and NGOs which go well beyond what is achievable in

[16] While we do not model the RTA explicitly, technically it would emerge in a model similar to the WTO portrayal above except the "threat point" in the bargaining when an agreement breaks down would be an asymmetric Nash bargaining game solution. Klimenko *et al.* discuss this in terms of "frontier punishment" wherein the punishment reversion is to the frontier of supported repeated game payoffs (worse than cooperation) and just where along the frontier is determined by the relative bargaining power of countries.

the WTO – specifically, some clauses on market access, investment guarantees, IPR, labor, and environmental conduct. (Alternatively, and equivalent for the model below, we could think of the WTO Agreement as being shaped by a few strong states – like H and F above or the United States and EU – who are also engaged in RTAs with a number of weaker states without any influence in the WTO beyond membership – like f or Colombia.)

Now, with a choice of forum provision, although H would by assumption be able to negotiate a more favorable DSP with the weaker f in the RTA, any DSP negotiated in the WTO can in some sense be extended at least partially to the RTA, thus weakening H's bargaining position – that is, imposing more balanced discipline on H – in the RTA. Specifically, the forum is chosen by the complainant and is relevant in the case of a "double breach" of overlapping obligations in the RTA and the WTO. Consequently, H has an incentive to incorporate this downside into its WTO negotiations and attitude toward that forum's DSP.

Mathematically, the trade agreement welfare maximization problem now must be amended to incorporate a term Z(Λ), which will enter negatively, meant to capture the reduction in H welfare when the WTO DSP is strengthened because this undermines H's ability when it is the trade dispute "respondent" (defendant) to divert disputes into the more favorable (for H) DSP of the RTA due to choice of forum. Although we will not model the RTA negotiations explicitly, the term Z(Λ) should be considered as a reduced form representation of the extent to which access to the WTO DSP benefits f (at the expense of H) in any RTA trade dispute where f is the complainant. By construction, we write $Z(\Lambda)>0$ with the derivative $dZ/d\Lambda>0$ to reflect that a harsher WTO DSP – that is, larger Λ – gives the weaker RTA member f the ability to hold H more accountable in a trade dispute over an agreement violation. Presumably $Z(0)=0$.

Thus, the WTO trade agreement will emerge as before from the maximization of the modified problem:

$$\max W - Z$$

subject to the SPE condition.

As before, in the WTO negotiations, the effective punishment length and tariff levels are determined by solving the now modified problem:

$$\max_{T,\Lambda}[(1-\delta^{\Lambda})W(T_n)+\delta^{\Lambda}\{W(T)-Z(\Lambda)\}] \tag{3}$$

subject to the SPE condition (1).

The problem is the same as Equation (2) except for the presence of $Z(\Lambda)$ meant to capture that a harsher (harder to manipulate for stronger parties) DSP in the WTO, that is, a higher value for Λ, reduces H welfare by weakening its power-oriented negotiation ability in the other (RTA) forum. The Z term arises in the modified problem (3) because the punishment path welfare is a weighted sum of the welfare of the trade agreement and the reversion to the Nash equilibrium.

Now denote the maximand of the initial problem (2) above as $B = [(1-\delta^{\Lambda})\,W(T_n) + \delta^{\Lambda}\,W(T)]$ and write the maximand in (3) as

$$B - \delta^{\Lambda} Z(\Lambda). \tag{4}$$

At the maximum, and noting that $T = T(\Lambda)$, we have

$$dB/d\Lambda - [\Lambda\delta^{\Lambda-1}Z(\Lambda) + \delta^{\Lambda}dZ/d\Lambda] = 0. \tag{5}$$

Evaluating the expression at the original equilibrium value for Λ that solves problem (2), Λ^*, reveals

$$dB/d\Lambda - [\Lambda\delta^{\Lambda-1}Z(\Lambda) + \delta^{\Lambda}dZ/d\Lambda] < 0 \tag{6}$$

since $dB/d\Lambda = 0$ at Λ^* and $[\Lambda\,\delta^{\Lambda-1}Z(\Lambda) + \delta^{\Lambda}\,dZ/d\Lambda] = d(\delta^{\Lambda}\,Z)/d\Lambda > 0$.

Intuitively, of course, this is because the original agreement ignores the deleterious indirect effect on H welfare of a stronger WTO DSP. Now, as before, B is increasing in Λ up to the maximum and then decreasing, as in Figure 1. However, since $dB/d\Lambda = 0$ at the maximum in the original problem, as in Figure 1, and since $d(\delta^{\Lambda}\,Z)/d\Lambda > 0$, it follows that, at the new maximum welfare solution, Λ must be smaller, noting that in the vicinity of the original solution value $dB/d\Lambda = 0 < d(\delta^{\Lambda}\,Z)/d\Lambda$.[17]

The new equilibrium, Λ^{**} and T^{**}, along with the initial equilibrium, are illustrated in Figure 2.

Total welfare of the trade agreement is now given by $W(T(\Lambda)) - Z(\Lambda)$. The punishment path is again a convex combination of agreement compliance total welfare and the Nash equilibrium (reversion) welfare, which together can be written as $W_p(\Lambda) - \delta^{\Lambda}Z(\Lambda)$. As before, at $\Lambda = 0$ the Nash equilibrium is obtained, recalling that $Z(0) = 0$. And, as Λ approaches infinity, all of the weight in the convex combination is put on the Nash equilibrium.[18] Hence, $W_p(\Lambda) - \delta^{\Lambda}Z(\Lambda)$ achieves a maximum somewhere in between at Λ^{**} which supports the tariff agreement T^{**}. As discussed above, $\Lambda^{**} < \Lambda^*$ because of the presence of the Z term reflecting the spillover effects into an RTA.

Two points are of interest. First, at Λ^{**} – representing the new WTO DSP – the supportable WTO tariff is higher than in the absence of an RTA. This is due to the "choice of forum" provision which H negotiators

---

[17] In general, if a function $f(x)$ achieves an interior maximum at x^*, and if $g(x)$ is increasing in X, then $f(x) - g(x)$ achieves a maximum at $x' < x^*$.

[18] A natural assumption is that $W(\Lambda) - Z(\Lambda) > 0$ everywhere, but this is not necessary. All that is required in order to avoid a corner solution at $T^{**} = T_n$ is that $W(\Lambda) - Z(\Lambda) > 0$ from the right in the vicinity of $\Lambda = 0$. The corner solution would represent the extreme case where the RTA is so important and advantageous for H that any enforcement at all in the WTO, given "choice of forum", is too destructive in the RTA.

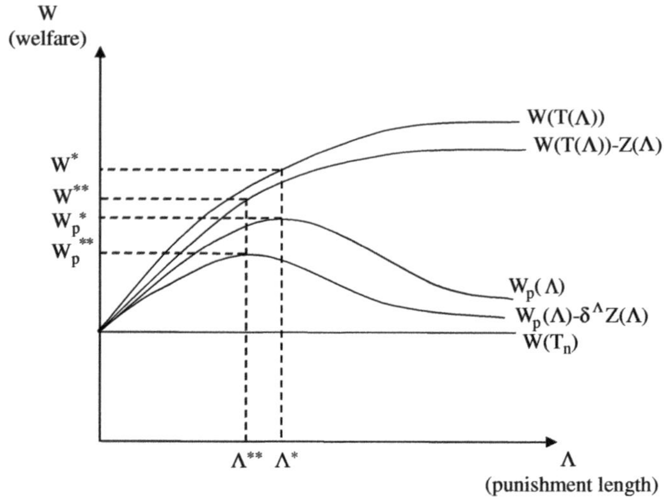

Fig. 2. The impact of choice of forum.

realize allows f to impose stricter enforcement in an RTA than H could otherwise negotiate by using its superior bargaining power in an RTA. That is, the dilution of H's bargaining power in the WTO forum seeps into the RTA forum. So, H dilutes the WTO DSP in response.

Second, since it is the DSP that underwrites the self-enforcing tariff level in the WTO, the resulting WTO tariff is now higher – $T^* < T^{**}$. Note that H welfare arising from the WTO agreement is now lower, W^{**}, for two reasons: (1) The WTO DSP is now weakened and so Λ is lower and cooperative tariffs higher and (2) at the lower Λ, H welfare is further reduced by $Z(\Lambda)$ because any WTO DSP at all can be used against H in the RTA due to "choice of forum." (This would not happen if the WTO DSP and the RTA DSP were exactly the same institution, but then H would not be securing more favorable treatment in the RTA despite enhanced bargaining power.)

Naturally H welfare will be reduced on account of higher WTO tariffs, but this ignores that there are offsetting gains in the RTA where H can now obtain a more favorable regional agreement. Of course, overall welfare for H, including welfare obtained from the RTA, will be higher. As in Figure 2, the gain in the RTA must exceed the loss on account of H taking the RTA into account, which is given by $W^* - W^{**}$. Therefore, the extent to which RTA negotiations erode the multilateral process depends on the magnitude of the spillover costs $Z(\Lambda)$. Apparently, these costs depend on the extent of H's asymmetric power in an RTA and on how much gain can be achieved by exploiting this power in the regional forum.

4.4. Some preliminary evidence and indications

Empirically, the extent to which the choice of forum option erodes multilateral cooperation is difficult to assess. Case studies in Drahos (2007) suggest it might be extensive, although this was not the focus of that study. He does conclude though that "it is worth noting that these choice-of-forum provisions to be found in US FTAs do not sit very comfortably with the goal of strengthening the multilateral trading system." Also, consistent with at least the developing world's perception of an erosion in and increasingly nonchalant attitude toward the WTO DSP by the United States and the EU is the large coalition of developing countries' persistence in the Doha Round in advocating a strengthening of the WTO dispute settlement apparatus (ICTSD, 2008).

Gantz (1999), Busch (2007), and many others certainly document well that choice of forum both matters and diverts trade disputes to the forum viewed as more favorable by the complainant. But these studies do not address directly the forum diversions' potential role in weakening the WTO. Nonetheless, Drahos (2007, p. 209) implies as much in concluding his case studies when he writes

> One priority that developing countries should be thinking about is to argue for provisions in these dispute settlement chapters that require the parties in the case of double breach to take the matter to the WTO. That would also be consistent with the aim of the DSU to strengthen the multilateral trading system. The effect of creating a web of bilateral dispute resolution fora will be to give the United States and the EU more opportunities to play for rules.

Bown (2005) investigates developing country participation in the WTO and finds that the existence of RTAs negatively affects the participation of these countries in the WTO. In light of this, Drahos (2007) observes that as the United States and the EU enter into more FTAs with developing countries, the coalitional possibilities of the WTO DSP will be weakened for developing countries as a group. Also, developing countries in the WTO but with an RTA with the United States or the EU may become reluctant to join a coalition in a trade dispute against either for fear that this would create other costs in the RTA. Again, the WTO DSP would be weakened. Whether these adverse consequences for the WTO are an explicit aim of US or EU policy motivated by choice of forum, of course, is not proven by these observations.

Finally, since the welfare gain in the RTA must offset the loss in the WTO on account of weakening the latter DSP, it is at least possible to entertain reasonable conjectures. Roughly, the United States would probably not be willing to give up cooperative gains in the WTO in order to enhance its bargaining position with a small country where there is little to gain – say, Singapore – but might be more sensitive when there is a potentially large market RTA like Korea, or where the RTA is with an important trade partner eager to make some substantial concessions for domestic political reasons – say, Mexico. The model and logic presented above suggest that these latter agreements could indeed ultimately impair the WTO DSP and so the extent of multilateral cooperation.

5. Summary and conclusions

International trade agreements give rise to trade disputes. DSPs proscribe the mechanisms by which disputes are to be resolved. The WTO DSP is broadly outlined in the DSU of the Uruguay Round. Recently, however, the increasing presence of RTAs in international commerce – now counted at over 250 by the WTO – has given rise to a host of parallel DSPs which are subtly different from each other and that of the WTO.

At one level, this chapter has described some of these differences in DSPs and suggested that some countries are generally treated more favorably by the regional DSP and other countries by the WTO DSP. The reasons largely have to do with the disparate extent of bargaining power or political/economic leverage available in a regional versus a more multilateral forum. There is some evidence that the regional forum favors the stronger state because it reduces the possibility of coalition building for the weaker state. And certainly the regional forum favors certain private interests – business, labor, NGOs – in the stronger state because they are given standing and the ability to initiate complaints according to many regional DSP.

Now, in a number of trade disputes, nations which hold concurrent membership in the WTO and an RTA can choose which DSP to use in resolving a complaint. Since the DSPs differ, this choice of forum creates an incentive to divert a complaint to the more favorable DSP, so-called forum shopping. There is considerable evidence that this in fact occurs. But this also gives an incentive for nations to weaken the DSP to which potential adversaries in a complaint might try to divert a trade dispute. Since stronger states, like the United States and EU, and private interests, like the pharmaceutical industry in the United States, tend to prefer the regional forum, these interests gain an incentive to weaken the WTO DSP.

The issues involved now become deeper and potentially more important in light of the current economic view of the role of a DSP portrayed in the international trade and political science literature. There the DSP is cast as the linchpin in free trade agreements, determining the extent to which freer trade can be achieved. This view builds on contract theory.

Central to any mutually beneficial cooperative contract is the belief by the contractors that the agreement will be fully and faithfully executed. Within nations, courts and cops enforce such behavior and so serve to underwrite the mutual gains which accrue to the contracting parties.

Deviations from the terms of an agreement can be punishable offenses. Between sovereign nations, there are no such external forces to ensure compliance with the terms of international agreements. Generally, it is only the parties to the agreement themselves that have the wherewithal to punish cheaters. (By analogy, it is the victim that must punish the criminal.)

In the realm of commerce, unimpeded international trade and investment is mutually beneficial for all nations, but any one nation can do even better by discriminating against foreigners in favor of its own citizens. Of course, when all nations then revert to such discrimination – optimum tariffs/NTBs, pirating, international fraud, and so on – the gains from trade are reduced and could be enhanced through an international agreement not to discriminate so much. But, in the absence of credible courts and cops, international cooperative agreements need to be self-enforcing; That is, the perception of punishment that could credibly be meted out by partners to the agreement must outweigh any gains derived from cheating. And, the harsher is the perceived punishment, the more is the cooperation that can be supported – that is, the closer the world comes to free trade.

In international cooperative trade agreements, the DSPs can play an important punishment role. When an agreement violation occurs, not only do counterparties withdraw trade benefits (retaliate), but the DSP requires that the trade dispute be adjudicated in a proscribed manner that takes time. Thus, the violator is institutionally prevented from apologizing and returning immediately to the initial cooperative agreement on the previous more favorable terms. If it were not for the DSP, it would otherwise be in everyone's interest to let the violator do so, thus inadvertently undermining any cooperative agreement in the first place.

But now return to the "choice of forum" feature of many RTAs. States are given an incentive to weaken the least favorable forum. For stronger states, this forum is often that of the WTO. So, there is an incentive to weaken the WTO DSP. But since it is the DSP that underpins the extent of trade liberalization in the first place, the result is less cooperation in pursuing freer trade and investment. Thus, the explosion of RTAs may undermine the multilateral process in yet one more way.

References

Aggarwal, V., Fogarty, E. (Eds.) (2004). *EU Trade Strategies: Between Reionalism and Globalism*. Palgrave, Basingstoke.

Bagwell, K., Staiger, R. (2002), *The Economics of the World Trading System*. The MIT Press, Cambridge.

Bhagwati, J. (1994), Threats to the world trading system: income distribution and the selfish hegemon. *Journal of International Affairs* 48 (Spring), 279–285.

Bown, C.P. (2005), Participation in WTO dispute settlement: complainants, interested parties and free riders. *World Bank Economic Review* 2, 287–310.

Busch, M.L. (2007), Overlapping institutions, forum shopping, and dispute settlement in international trade. *International Organization* 61 (Fall), 735–761.

Busch, M.L., Reinhardt, E. (2005), Three's a crowd: third parties and the WTO dispute settlement. Processed for Conference on WTO Dispute Settlement and Developing Countries: Use, Implications, Strategies, Reforms. University of Wisconsin, Madison, 20–21 May.

Drahos, P. (2007), Weaving webs of influence: the United States free trade agreements and dispute resolution. *Journal of World Trade* 41 (1), 191–210.

Gantz, D.A. (1999), Dispute settlement under the NAFTA and the WTO: choice of forum opportunities and risks for the NAFTA parties. *American University International Law Review* 14, 1025–1106.

Garret, G. (1992), International cooperation and institutional choice: the European community's internal market. *International Organization* 46, 533–560.

Girvan, N. (2008). Implication of the Cariforum-EC EPA. Trinidad and Tobago Review, 7 January, http://www.normangirvan.info/wp-content/uploads/2008/01/girvanimplicationsepa10jan.pdf

Hudec, R. (1990), Dispute settlement. In: Schott, J.J. (Ed.), *Completing the Uruguay round.* Institute for International Economics, Washington, D.C.

ICTSD (International Centre for Trade and Sustainable Development). (2008), MFN in the cariforum EPA is no threat to South-South trade. *Trade Negotiations Insights: News, Analysis and Views on Economic Partnership Agreements and the WTO from a Sustainable Development Perspective* 7 (4).

IPS. (2008), Labour: U.S. Union, Business Group Slam Jordan Sweatshops. Inter Press Service News Agency, 11 August, http://ipsnews.net/news.asp?idnews = 34904

Jackson, J. (2000), *The Jurisprudence of GATT and the WTO*. Cambridge University Press, Cambridge.

Kahler, M.A. (1995), A world of blocs: facts and factoids. *World Policy Journal* 12, 19–27.

Keck, A., Schropp, S. (2007), Indisputably essential: the economics of dispute settlement institutions in trade agreements. Staff Working Paper ERSD-2007-02,World Trade Organization, Geneva.

Klimenko, M., Ramey, G., Watson, J. (2008), Recurrent trade agreements and the value of external enforcement. *Journal of International Economics* 74, 475–499.

Levy, P.I., Srinivasan, T.N. (1996), Regionalism and the (dis)advantage of dispute-settlement access. *AEA Papers and Proceedings* (May), 93–98.

Ludema, R.D. (2001), Optimal international trade agreements and dispute settlement procedures. *European Journal of Political Economy* 17, 355–376.

Maggi, G. (1999), The role of multilateral institutions in international trade cooperation. *American Economic Review* 89, 190–214.

Maggi, G., Rodriguez-Clare, A. (2007), A political economy theory of trade agreements. *American Economic Review* 97 (4), 1374–1406.

Mavroidis, P.C., Sykes, A.O. (2005), *The WTO and International Trade Law/Dispute Settlement*. Edward Elgar, Cheltenham.

Mayer, W. (1984), Endogenous tariff formation. *American Economic Review* 74 (5), 970–985.

Moravcsik, A. (1991), Negotiating the Single European Act: national interests and conventional statecraft in the European community. *International Organization* 45, 19–56.

Petersmann, E.-U. (1997), *The GATT/WTO Dispute Settlement System: International Law, International Organizations and Dispute Settlement*. Kluwer Law International, London.

Reiter, J. (2006), International investment rules. In: Woolcock, S. (Ed.), *Trade and Investment Rule-making: The Role of Regional and Bilateral Agreements*. United Nations University Press, Tokyo.

Robertson, D. (2006), *International Economics and Confusing Politics*. Edward Elgar, Cheltenham.

Rosendorf, B.P. (2005), Stability and rigidity: politics and design of the WTO's dispute settlement procedure. *American Political Science Review* 99 (3), 389–400.

Saggi, K. (2006), Preferential trade agreements and multilateral tariff cooperation. *International Economic Review* 41 (1), 29–57.

Saggi, K., Yildiz, H.M. (2007), Bilateral trade agreements and the feasibility of multilateral free trade. Paper presented to the Royal Economic Society Annual Conference 2007 (http://faculty.smu.edu/ksaggi/FTAs.pdf).

Sandholtz, W., Zysman, J. (1989), 1992: recasting the European bargain. *World Politics* 42, 95–128.

Schelling, T. (1960), *The Strategy of Conflict*. Harvard University Press, Cambridge.

Schott, J.J. (2004), *Free Trade Agreements: US Strategies and Priorities*. Peterson Institute, Washington, D.C.

Shaffer, G. (2003), How to make the WTO dispute setttlement work for developing countries: some proactive developing country strategies. *Towards A Development-Supportive Dispute Settlement System in the WTO*. ICTSD Resource Paper No. 5, ICTSD, Geneva.

Smith, J.M. (1995), The limits of legalization: dispute settlement in NAFTA. Stanford Center on Conflict and Negotiation Working Paper 49, Stanford Law School, Stanford.

Smith, J.M. (2000), The politics of dispute settlement design: explaining legalism in regional trade pacts. *International Organization* 54 (1), 137–180.

Smith, J.M. (2003), WTO dispute settlement: the politics of procedure in appellate body rulings. *World Trade Review* 2 (1), 65–100.

Trebilcock, M.J., Howse, R. (1999), *The Regulation of International Trade*. Routledge, London.

Woolcock, S. (1996), Competition among rules in the single European market. In: McCahery, J., Bratton, W.W., Picciotto, S., Scott, C. (Eds.), *International Regulatory Competition and Coordination: Perspectives on Economic Regulation in Europe and the United States*. Clarendon Press, Oxford.

Woolcock, S. (Ed). (2006), *Trade and Investment Rule-Making: The Role of Regional and Bilateral Agreements*. United Nations University Press, Tokyo.

WTO. (1995), *Regionalism and the World Trading System*. World Trade Organization, Geneva.

Yarbrough, B., Yarbrough, R.M. (1997), Dispute settlement in international trade: regionalism and procedural coordination. In: Mansfield, E.D., Milner, H.V. (Eds.), *The Political Economy of Regionalism*. Columbia University Press, New York.

CHAPTER 13

The ADA and the DSU of the WTO

James C. Hartigan

Department of Economics, University of Oklahoma, Norman, OK 73019-2103, USA
E-mail address: hartigan@ou.edu

Abstract

Beginning with the assumption that antidumping laws are used to address adverse shocks in import-competing industries, this chapter provides an explanation for the infrequent utilization of the Dispute Settlement Understanding under the Antidumping Agreement. It does so with a very simple model that represents the shock by a one-dimensional random variable. This is found on an interpretation of the ADA as a *de facto* escape clause. ADA signatories are homogeneous, which enables the representation of the expected frequency of shocks over each member's import-competing sectors by the binomial distribution with identical parameters. The explanation for the infrequency of utilization of the DSU invokes a repeated Prisoners' Dilemma with two levels of cooperation in an infinite horizon game. The high level is free trade in all sectors. The low level is the application of ADA duties in sectors incurring the shock in a manner that is consistent with the ADA. The high level of cooperation in all sectors in every period is not sustainable for any degree of patience. A convex combination of the high and low levels of cooperation is sustainable for some degrees of patience under the folk theorem. However, this combination of cooperation is attainable only with the support of the DSU. The extent of importance of the DSU depends on the completeness of information with which signatories are endowed. With complete information, dispute resolution does not occur in equilibrium. However, its presence supports cooperation through its mandate to sanction retaliation. If filing were prohibitively costly, disputes would never arise, and cooperation would be expected to evaporate. In the instance of incomplete information with costless filing, disputes would occur in equilibrium whenever an AD action was taken. In the most realistic circumstance, that of incomplete information and nonprohibitive filing costs, disputes would arise only when the number of AD actions exceeded their (common) expectation. This provides a conceptual explanation for the observations of Tarullo (2002) and Bown (2005) that ADA disputes are infrequent.

Frontiers of Economics and Globalization
Volume 6 ISSN: 1574-8715
DOI: 10.1108/S1574-8715(2009)0000006016

Keywords: Antidumping, dispute settlement, adverse shock, WTO, DSU, ADA, retaliation, prisoners' dilemma

JEL classifications: F13, K33, K42

1. Introduction

Although it has not been extensively invoked in the context of the Antidumping Agreement (ADA), the Dispute Settlement Understanding (DSU) of the World Trade Organization (WTO) provides a mechanism for redress of grievances under Article VI. The DSU has corrected or ameliorated several structural flaws of dispute settlement under the General Agreements on Tariffs and Trade (GATT). First, it is unified, encompassing nearly all parts of the GATT/WTO system. Second, each complainant has the right of consultation with the member that is the subject of a complaint. Third, each complainant has the right to have the process initiated. Fourth, there is an appellate procedure. A fundamental difference from the GATT is that the DSU has been interpreted as requiring the consensus to block, rather than a consensus to adopt, a panel report.[1] Given these enhancements to the rights of plaintiffs, a pertinent issue is an explanation for the paucity of formal complaints under the ADA. Bown (2005) discloses that a retaliatory antidumping (AD) filing may serve as a substitute for the filing of a formal dispute in US actions.[2] Bown (2005) and Tarullo (2002) consider the possibility that Article 17.6(i) of the DSU, which requires deference to national investigative authorities in AD verdicts, may explain the infrequency of filings of complaints. Neither Bown, using inferential statistics, nor Tarullo, utilizing legal reasoning, find support for this hypothesis. In fact, Tarullo notes that at the time of his writing, all disputes under the ADA had been decided in favor of the complainant.[3]

There are other reasons that, to my knowledge, have not been considered in the literature. One pertains to burden of proof.[4] Incurring the burden of proof as a defendant is contrary to most civil and

[1] See Jackson (1997) and www.wto.org. With a consensus to adopt, a single objection (including by the loser) could preclude implementation of the panel report. Under a consensus to block, the losing member has to persuade all members of the panel (including its adversary) to oppose implementation.

[2] Capacity to engage in a reciprocal or retaliatory filing is measured by the value of production that is exported to the affected foreign country. Other authors who have documented retaliation in filings include Prusa and Skeath (2005), Feinberg and Reynolds (2006), and Vandenbussche and Zanardi (2008).

[3] Tarullo also notes that the standard for a successful complaint is rather weak, as it requires the plaintiff to prevail on only a single point.

[4] By burden of proof, I intend to convey the burden of persuasion. This contrasts, of course, with the standard of proof, which is an evidentiary requirement.

administrative proceedings.[5] The U.S. AD investigative proceedings, which form a model for AD laws in other signatories, conducts a bifurcated proceeding. The U.S. International Trade Commission (USITC) conducts the material injury investigation. The burden of proof in this investigation falls on the domestic industry. The ITA of the Department of Commerce conducts the investigation of the allegedly unfair act. Here the burden of proof is the responsibility of the foreign exporters.[6] After the exporters incurred the burden of proof in the initial AD investigation, the signatory for whom the exporting firms are a constituent would incur it again in filing a dispute.[7] The extent to which exporting interests absorb this burden may be a deterrent to contesting administrative protection decisions at the WTO. A higher burden of proof in the initial investigation, as well as in the pursuit of a dispute, is likely to be associated with less effort in contesting administrative protection judgements through the DSU.

Although the allocation of the burden of proof is suggested as a hypothesis for the paucity of formal disputes noted in the literature, the focus of this chapter is on another explanation, namely, the trigger strategy in an infinite horizon Prisoners' Dilemma. The standard Prisoners' Dilemma is characterized by a discrete strategy space consisting of a pair of possible actions for each player. These may be termed cooperate and defect. In our context, these typically may be viewed as free trade or protection. Since this chapter is concerned with the ADA, it would be natural to consider defection as invoking an AD law and imposing duties. However, this chapter takes a different view. It enlarges the set of actions that are deemed cooperative to include the assessment of AD duties. The justification for this characterization is that as long as the imposition of AD duties is in accordance with the ADA, it is a cooperative action. It certainly is not as cooperative as free trade, however.[8] Thus the set of possible cooperative actions is not degenerate. It contains a pair of discrete actions as elements.[9] Defection is construed as imposing an AD duty in a

---

[5] Fundamental administrative principles establish that an agency or institution bears the burden of proof in an enforcement action. See Peabody Coal vs. Ralston (Ind. Ct. App. 1991). Thus it would be expected that this burden in U.S. AD investigations is the domain of the International Trade Administration (ITA), as it should be construed as enforcing "fair" pricing. This burden generally falls on the complainant in civil litigation.

[6] The high percentage of affirmative decisions by the ITA (see Boltuck and Litan, 1991), the increasing utilization of constructed value by the ITA (see Blonigen, 2006), and reading of investigative reports (see www.usitc.gov and ia.ita.gov) suggest this inference.

[7] This is mitigated by the consultation phase of a dispute.

[8] Frischmann and Hartigan (2008) take this approach in analyzing the escape clause (EC) in international treaties, as do Hartigan and Vandenbussche (2008) in discussing the diffusion of AD laws and their usage.

[9] It is conceivable that the set of cooperative actions could be continuous. Cooperation could vary continuously with the level of AD duties or the number of import-competing sectors protected by such duties.

manner that is not considered consistent with the ADA. Salient examples of this include the Continued Dumping and Subsidy Offset Act of 2000, commonly known as the Byrd Amendment, and zeroing. This act was determined to be a violation of the ADA by the Dispute Settlement Body (DSB) in 2004. It permitted the distribution of revenues, collected from the levying of AD and countervailing duties (CVD) on imports from firms that were identified in the AD or CVD investigations as unfair traders, to U.S. firms that supported the initial petition. This was to defray the costs of qualified expenditures.[10] In the terminology of Tarullo, this should be construed as a legal misinterpretation of the ADA. Such a material misinterpretation can be considered as defection from the ADA in our context.

The use of zeroing may be regarded as a procedural dispute. The ITA calculates AD margins through a weighted average method. However, when a foreign firm's export price to the United States is at least as great as its national market price, the AD margin for such a transaction comparison is set to zero. In this manner, AD margins, and the protection they provide, are inflated. This procedure continues to be a subject of dispute by the DSB.

Because cooperation in any period of the discrete time infinite horizon game can occur at two levels, free trade should not be expected to be an equilibrium in every period. Neither should be the imposition of AD duties in every period and in every import-competing sector, as such a protectionist outcome readily is obtainable without the ADA or the formation of the WTO. Thus the equilibrium to this game will include periods of high and low levels of cooperation. The imposition of AD duties is construed as a response to an adverse shock that could not have been anticipated with certainty at the time of negotiation of the ADA. This shock must cause material injury to domestic producers.[11,12] Formal disputes may or may not be expected to arise in equilibrium. Whether or not they do depend on the structure of information in the game. Under complete information, disputes will not arise in equilibrium. They may

---

[10] Qualified expenditures include the purchasing of inputs, the training of personnel, the acquisition of technology, investment in plant and equipment, and engaging in research and development.

[11] Note that I am ignoring the nonattribution requirement that stipulates the injury that reasonably might have another cause must not be attributed to imports. This is in keeping with practice, which does not appear to enforce nonattribution. For more information, see Durling and McCullough (2005). It also is in keeping with a criticism of AD implementation under which the higher standards for an affirmative EC verdict relative to those for a positive AD decision induce the inappropriate use of AD as a *de facto* EC. See Cass and Knoll (1998) for an elaboration.

[12] Ethier (2002) explains unilateral deviation (administered protection) in the context of a sequence of multilateral trade liberalization negotiations through the realization of a positive (technology) shock to the exporters to the deviator.

under incomplete information. This is broadly consistent with actual experience under the ADA. It is also consistent with the aforementioned studies concerned with proliferation of AD laws and their usage. An appropriate question, then, is to ask what is the purpose of the DSU as applying to the ADA? My interpretation is that it imposes a discipline that keeps play on the equilibrium path under either complete or incomplete information. That is, it precludes abuses in procedures, factual determination, and legal interpretation.[13] The paper now continues with a development of the model underlying this interpretation of the ADA and the DSU.

2. *A model*

The approach assumes an infinite horizon in discrete time. There are $n : n \geq 2$ signatories of the ADA, where n is finite. For simplicity, each signatory is assumed to be identical at the time of agreeing to the ADA. Each signatory contains $m : m \geqslant 1$ import-competing– and exporting industries, where m is also finite.[14] The game entails three stages. In the first stage, which only occurs in the initial period, negotiation and ratification of the ADA occurs. The second stage occurs in every period. In it, each signatory may incur a shock $S : S \in \mathbb{R}$ in import-competing industry i.[15] Thus S is a random variable, for which positive realizations increase the cost of production. It is distribution function is $g(S)$; which has finite support on $\mathbb{R}$. Its expectation $E(S) = 0$. That is, it is not expected that a shock will occur in any industry in any period. Let $\Omega = \mathbb{R}^+$ and its absolute complement Ω^C be a partition of $\mathbb{R}$ where Ω denotes an adverse shock occurring in import-competing sector i.[16] Furthermore, let $\Omega_A \subset \Omega$ be a proper subset of Ω indicating those shocks satisfying the material injury criteria of the ADA. The conditional density function $g\ (S|\Omega_A)$ has finite

[13] See Tarullo (2002) for an elaboration of these abuses.

[14] This entails cross hauling, in the sense of Brander and Krugman (1983) and Murray and Kurdaliev (1999).

[15] Although Safeguards may be a more appropriate venue under which to address adverse shocks than the ADA, the injury standard under the ADA is weaker (material versus serious). It is relatively easy to get AD duties extended (repeatedly) under the 5-year sunset provision (see Liebman, 2004). Safeguards are introduced initially for 4 years and can be renewed once for 4 additional years. The ADA does not require a national interest clause, although one can be introduced. Safeguards typically do take national interest into account. Although Safeguards are not required to abide by Most Favored Nation (MFN) principles, they do so with reasonable frequency. AD duties do not abide by MFN. AD duties, however, tend to be much higher than Safeguard protection. Hence the ADA may be serving as a *de facto* Safeguard.

[16] Negative values of S; which (including $S = 0$) constitutes Ω^C, are favorable shocks. When exporters in industry i incur a favorable shock and home producers draw $S = 0$, this could be construed as an adverse relative shock, which may be actionable under an interpretation of the ADA. For simplicity, I do not consider this interpretation.

expectation $E(S|\Omega_A) = S_{\Omega_A}$. Define by 1_{Ω_A} the indicator function taking the value 1 on the set Ω_A and taking the value zero elsewhere on $\mathbb{R}$. The absolute complement of Ω_A is Ω_A^C: Thus it can be stated that the probability $p_i : p_i = (0, 1)$ that a shock satisfying the material injury standard in sector i occurs is

$$p_i = 1_{\Omega_A}\Omega_A + 1_{\Omega_A}\Omega_A^C \tag{1}$$

The shock satisfying the material injury standard is a binary variable: either it occurs or it doesn't. The ADA agreement determines the threshhold level of S that constitutes a material shock. This is $\inf(\Omega_A)$, and is denoted by $\tilde{S}$. The probability that a shock is realized is inversely related to the value of $\tilde{S}$. Thus $dp_i/d\tilde{S}<0$. The shocks are independently and identically distributed (iid) across sectors, countries, and time.[17] Hence we denote the probability of a shock by p. An adverse shock can be in the form of a decrease in the price of competing imports, an increase in the cost of production, or a decline in demand, for a nonexhaustive set of examples. For convenience, I assume that such shocks are transitory. That is, there is no persistence or autoregression.[18] Hence the duties remain in place for a single period. Given the iid probability of an adverse shock in each of the m import-competing sectors in each signatory, we can invoke the binomial distribution ($S \sim B(m, p)$) to state that the probability of invoking the ADA to address s shocks in any period for each member is

$$f(s; m, p) = \binom{m}{s} p^s (1-p)^{m-s} \tag{2}$$

If none of the n countries realizes a shock in any of its import-competing m industries in the second stage, then the play in that period concludes. If a shock or shocks do occur, then an investigation or investigations transpire resulting in the assessment of an AD duty or duties protecting the pertinent sector or sectors. The play then proceeds to the third stage. A decision is made at this stage by governments with adversely affected exporting firms as constituents regarding whether or not to file a dispute with the DSB. If a complaint does not take place, the play proceeds to the succeeding period. If a filing occurs, a decision then is rendered by the DSB. If the complaint is denied, the AD duty remains in place for that period. If the filing is affirmed, the DSB requests that the duty be revoked. In practice, the government losing the dispute can appeal. If the panel's decision is affirmed, then the losing government is given a reasonable period of time to

[17] This may seem objectionable. In particular, a negative demand or cost shock may affect an array of domestic sectors in any given period. Hence this assumption is made for modelling convenience.

[18] As I will note below, the presence of persistence or autoregression in shocks would limit the degrees of freedom of the AD authority in each signatory. That is, the opportunity to protect additional industries that incur adverse shocks would be constrained.

bring an offending policy into compliance.[19] If it does not, then permission from the DSB for retaliation can be requested.[20] It may appear that several moves may transpire in stage three. As we shall see, however, these moves are collapsed into a single stage because a dispute will not take place in the equilibrium of this model under complete information as to whether an adverse shock has transpired in any sector. A dispute may arise in equilibrium when information as to whether or not adverse shocks have occurred is incomplete. However, I do not address the process of dispute settlement. I mention that process to disclose that the model is not inconsistent with the provisions of the DSU. The equilibrium concept is subgame perfection, and hence I begin with stage three.

2.1. Stage three: dispute resolution

As was mentioned in the preceding section, there is no basis for a dispute under the ADA in the absence of the application of AD duties in any sector in any signatory. Hence, no dispute is an equilibrium for the third stage in this instance.

Before considering the stage three response to the application of AD duties in the second stage, I will briefly review defection from cooperation in trigger strategy games. When a player defects, the game shifts to a punishment phase. The length of this phase can be infinite, as in the case of grim trigger strategies. With a grim trigger, cooperation is never restored. However, cooperation can be restored after expiration of an exogenously given punishment phase. It can also be restored endogenously through a penance strategy in which those players that were harmed by defection do not cooperate until the period following a return to cooperation by the defector. The generic trigger strategy game does not include a player (an institution) whose objective is to facilitate cooperation amongst the other players. Given that the n noninstitutional players voluntarily formed the institution (WTO), the grim trigger outcome is not a reasonable candidate equilibrium. This outcome was available without the formation of the WTO and negotiation of the ADA. Thus, some return to cooperation is envisaged after defection. In contrast to the generic trigger strategy game, it is not wholly up to those players incurring harm from defection whether or not to retaliate. It is their choice whether or not to file a complaint, but they must request permission from the WTO to retaliate if their complaint

[19] In this context, the offending policy would be an AD duty imposed by the government incurring an adverse shock in an import-competing sector. The government of the country that has constituent exporting sectors that are affected adversely by these duties does not have an offending policy.

[20] For the discussion of penalties and retaliation for noncompliance in treaties, see Nzelibe (2005).

is validated. This imposes at least two responsibilities upon the DSB for it to have credibility. One is that the process must be impartial and thorough. In the absence of the fulfillment of these responsibilities, the incentive to defect increases. A signatory will believe that it has a greater probability of successfully pursuing a policy that it expects is either a violation or nonviolation complaint under a biased or manipulated DSU.[21,22] That is, if it expects to be a beneficiary of bias. The second responsibility is that there must be material penalties or retaliatory acts that can be authorized by the DSB in the event of defection. In the absence of such deterrents, the incentive to cooperate may be insufficient. If the DSU fulfills these requirements, then the incentives for cooperation will be sufficient and disputes will be infrequent in equilibrium. The presence of the DSU is to ensure that cooperation is the equilibrium path of the game.

It was indicated in the introduction that although disputes under the ADA are not frequent, particularly relative to the number of AD actions in place, they still do occur. As Howse and Esserman (2006) have contended that the WTO has maintained a healthy balance between its political and judicial (dispute settlement) institutions, and has successfully resisted political pressure on the DSB, it is not unreasonable to look to the second responsibility as source of the failure to deter disputes. Kovenock and Thursby (1992) and Mitchell (1997) have discussed the prospective punishment scheme that is generally utilized by the DSB to address violations and N&I of expected benefits under the treaty establishing the WTO. With prospective punishments, a signatory does not incur a penalty or retaliatory act if it complies within a reasonable period of time. The criticism of prospective punishments is that because a signatory can avoid liability for any losses imposed on other members by its offending policy through reasonably prompt compliance with a panel decision of the DSB, they are an insufficient deterrent to the adoption of policies that are probable inducements to disputes.[23] With incomplete satisfaction of the second requirement, disputes may occur on the equilibrium path of the game.[24] However, the (sufficiently strong) prospective punishments will eventually have bite, so that ultimately

[21] Nonviolation complaints refer to the nullification and impairment (N&I) of expected benefits under the treaty.

[22] Given that our signatories are homogeneous, it is much less likely that a signatory can exert undue influence on the dispute process than is the case in the WTO. The WTO has members of different size and economic stature, which may affect the equity of resolution. See Horn *et al.* (1999) and Reynolds (Chapter 8, this volume) for more on this matter.

[23] Chakraborty and Hartigan (Chapter 18, this volume) establish that prospective punishments are rational when disputes arise from misinterpretation of obligations and commitments.

[24] This, of course assumes that use of prospective punishments are themselves consistent with an equilibrium model of the formation of the WTO. This is considered by Chakraborty and Hartigan (Chapter 18, this volume).

compliance will occur.[25] While acknowledging this possibility, I will give more credence to incomplete information as to whether or not an adverse shock transpired together with nonprohibitively costly dispute settlement to explain the occurrence of AD disputes, recalling they will not take place on the equilibrium path of this (simple) game under complete information.

2.2. Stage two: compliance with the ADA

As was stated in the introduction, the compliance decision selects from a nondegenerate discrete set of actions in each sector. Let this set be $\alpha_j = \{\alpha_F, \alpha_A, \alpha_D\}$ where α_F denotes free trade or the relatively stronger form of cooperation in industry $j \in \{1, m\}$. Given the assumption of cross hauling in each of the m sectors, each member will choose an export and an import policy. Since my focus is the ADA, the export policy will always be α_F. The weaker form of cooperation entails the filing of an AD action in one of the m import-competing sectors of the economy in any period. This is denoted by α_A. Defection is denoted by α_D.[26] The choice of α_j is determined by the realization of S, with $d\pi^i/dS < 0$. Thus payoffs are inversely and monotonically related to shocks. As was noted earlier, the probability of imposing AD duties in every sector in a given period cannot equal unity. As was also noted, because the probability of adverse shocks is nonzero, free trade would not be expected in every period. Because the horizon is multiperiod (infinite), a discount factor $\delta : \delta = (0, 1)$ is assumed. The per period (stage game) payoff to each signatory $i \in \{1, n\}$ in sector j is given by $\pi^i_j\,(\alpha^i, \alpha^{-i})$, where α^i is the strategic choice of member i and α^{-i} are the strategies of signatories $\{1, i-1, i+1, n\}$ pertaining to protection from imports in that sector. The trigger is a legal misinterpretation of the ADA, and/or procedural and factual determinations that result in excessive play of the lower form of cooperation. This is a defection from or violation of the ADA. Recall that the probability of an adverse shock in any of the m sectors in the n members is given by p. The threshhold level of p will be established endogenously in stage one. It satisfies our purpose at this juncture to state that $\forall\ \tilde{p} > p = (0, 1)$, where $\tilde{p}$ is the probability of sectors receiving AD protection in any period, play proceeds to a dispute in stage three. The expected value of the binomial distribution, the density function

[25] Additional explanations for compliance include the McGillivray and Smith (2006) contention that the credibility of punishment for noncompliance with an agreement is enhanced by the threat of punishment of specific leaders through refusal of additional cooperation. This is because voters can depose opportunistic leaders that jeopardize future national welfare. Mansfield *et al.* (2002) portray the DSB as enhancing information for voters as to the degree of responsibility of their government.

[26] Because abrogation of a treaty is rare, defection is characterized as a violation. In practice, this could be deliberate or unintentional.

of which is given by (2), is

$$E(S) = mp \tag{3}$$

Given the number m of import-competing sectors and the probability of an adverse shock p, (3) gives the number of sectors that are expected to be protected by AD duties in any period in each signatory. Hence each member does not protect $m(1-p)$ sectors. The number of markets that are expected to be protected by AD duties to which firms located in country i export is denoted by $(n-1)\,mp$. Hence the number of markets that are not protected is given by $m(n-1)(1-p)$. Thus the condition for cooperation in any period t for values of δ exceeding some threshhold is given by[27]

$$\begin{aligned}(1/(1-\delta))[m(n-1)(p\pi^i(\alpha^i_F,\ \alpha^{-i}_A)+(1-p)\pi^i(\alpha^i_F,\ \alpha^{-i}_F))\\ +m(p\pi^i(\alpha^i_A,\ \alpha^{-i}_F)+(1-p)\pi^i(\alpha^i_F,\ \alpha^{-i}_F))]\\ \geq m\pi^i(\alpha^i_D,\alpha^i_F)\end{aligned} \tag{4}$$

As was mentioned in the introduction, the set of actions that are deemed cooperative is nondegenerate, containing α_F and α_A as elements. Given that each of the $n-1$ other signatories are expected to protect mp import-competing sectors on the equilibrium path, defection (violation of the ADA) must yield the highest stage game payoff for it to be attractive in any sector j.[28] If it does not, the solution becomes trivial. Not only would defection never occur, it would be trivial to establish conditions to demonstrate that it is off the equilibrium path. Since a country will not defect in a sector in which foreign firms have not incurred an adverse shock if it will not do so when foreign countries trade freely, I can state the condition as

$$\pi^i_j(\alpha^i_D,\ \alpha^{-i}_F) \leq \max\left(\pi^i_j(\alpha^i_F,\ \alpha^{-i}_F),\ \pi^i_j(\alpha^i_A,\ \alpha^{-i}_F)\right)\quad \forall\ j\in\{1,m\} \tag{5}$$

In comparing $\pi^i_j(\alpha^i_F,\ \alpha^{-i}_F)$ and $\pi^i_j(\alpha^i_A,\ \alpha^{-i}_F)$, it is consistent with this approach to assume that a signatory will impose an AD duty on imports in a sector that has incurred an adverse shock if the realized number of sectors incurring shocks in any period $s \leq mp$. In this instance, the lower level of cooperation yields a larger payoff than the higher cooperative level. That is, $\pi^i_j(\alpha^i_A,\ \alpha^{-i}_F) > \pi^i_j(\alpha^i_F,\ \alpha^{-i}_F)$ whenever any shock occurs meeting the definition under the ADA. Since the protection of mp sectors by any signatory is anticipated by the other signatories along the equilibrium path, it will not undermine cooperation for sufficiently patient members. In characterizing the equilibrium, two questions remain. Will a signatory

[27] The functions π^i are evaluated at the pertinent expectations for S. Thus, (4) is an *ex ante* (before realization of S in all industries) condition for cooperation. This is justified by the assumption that an act as profound as defection from a treaty is not episodic.

[28] I normalize payoffs in the periods subsequent to defection to be zero. This presumes that cooperation under the ADA collapses, and signatories receive a payoff equivalent to what they would receive in the absence of the ADA.

protect *mp* sectors when $s < mp$ and will a signatory protect more than *mp* sectors when $s > mp$? The answer to the first question depends on the relative values of $\pi_j^i(\alpha_F^i, \alpha_F^{-i})$ and $\pi_j^i(\alpha_A^i, \alpha_F^{-i})$ in the absence of a shock. That is, is free trade preferrable except in the instance of a shock? If so, it is preferrable to eschew protection of any import-competing sector in which no shock has occurred. Alternatively, is acting opportunistically the better alternative? In that case, a signatory will desire to protect at least *mp* sectors in every period. However, if *mp* sectors are protected if the number of shocks $s \leq mp$; protection of $s > mp$ cannot be along the equilibrium path, as the expected number of protected sectors then would exceed *mp*. That is, beliefs (expectations) would be inconsistent with the strategies being played. Hence the number of sectors protected in any period must equal the number of adverse shocks that are elements of Ω_A.

In any period in which the ADA is in effect, it is possible that $s > mp$ in stage two. That is, a country could legitimately protect more that its expectation of protection. That is, it would be in compliance with the ADA in doing so. Other signatories can respond by either filing or not filing a dispute. If signatories were completely informed about the existence of shocks, a dispute would not be filed.[29] However, in the presence of incomplete information, in which members were endowed only with knowledge of the probability distribution over shocks, filing a dispute serves a purpose. The dispute settlement procedure could inform the complainant as to whether or not a shock transpired. If filing a complaint was costless and information were incomplete, a dispute would arise in equilibrium in *every* instance of application of an AD duty.[30] However, if the dispute process were sufficiently (but not prohibitively) costly and information was incomplete, complaints would occur in equilibrium only when $s > mp$. In the case of incomplete information, the DSU serves as a more comprehensive role than that of sustaining cooperation on the equilibrium path without ever being invoked, which is its purpose when information is complete. When information is incomplete, another purpose of the DSU is to deter opportunistic breach.

The AD disputes are infrequent, suggesting that the assumptions of incomplete information combined with costless dispute resolution is not the most reasonable. There is no reason for sufficiently patient signatories to engage in a dispute when information is complete, irrespective of whether or not disputes are costly. If information was incomplete and

---

[29] Unless, of course, the purpose of the DSU is for the renegotiation of commitments. In this context, that would not occur because there are no power disparites amongst the signatories of the ADA. Furthermore, the probability of a shock is known at the time of negotiation of the ADA, and is invariant with respect to time.

[30] This is to deter opportunistic breach of the ADA by claiming an adverse shock when none is manifest. See Frischmann and Hartigan (2008) for a discussion of spurious breach in the context of the escape clause.

disputes were costless, they would be frequent. Because disputes do occur, albeit infrequently, it suggests that information is incomplete and there is a nonprohibitive cost to invoking the DSU.

Given that a dispute does not occur with every instance of the invocation of AD duties, what prevents opportunistic breach? That is, what precludes a member from claiming a shock and imposing AD duties when no adverse shock has occurred? It is that each signatory expects to protect, on average, *mp* import-competing sectors in every period. The opportunity for spurious breach occurs only when $s < mp$: Protecting $\tilde{s}$: $\tilde{s} = (s, \ mp]$ sectors in any period will result in the inability to protect some sectors in any period in which $s > mp$. If a country does try to protect $s > mp$ after engaging in opportunistic breach, it will invite a dispute alleging that its AD procedures violate the ADA. Thus the presence of the DSU sustains cooperation as the equilibrium path of the game. However, it could not serve this function if its invocation were prohibitively costly.

2.3. Stage one: negotiation of the ADA

Given that incomplete information regarding adverse shocks in import-competing sectors with nonprohibitive costs of dispute resolution is a plausible characterization of international trade under the ADA, consideration of the negotiation of the ADA will take place with that as the assumption. Since intuitive arguments have established that neither free trade nor protection of all import-competing sectors by AD duties are plausible equilibria, the negotiation of the ADA will establish the threshhold level of S that constitutes a material adverse shock. That is, a realization of a shock under which protection of an import-competing sector is in compliance with the ADA. It was assumed in the preceding section (succeeding stage) that a signatory will protect as many sectors as sustain an adverse shock, however the theshhold level of shock is defined. An overly protectionist global economy is detrimental to exporting sectors and economic efficiency. Hence, $\tilde{S}$ will be bounded away from zero. The threshhold level of shock determines the probability of a sector being protected by an AD duty in any period, or from (2), the percentage of sectors receiving protection. To determine the level of $\tilde{S}$ that is negotiated by the ADA, find the subset of Ω for which (4) holds. To do so, let Π^i be the difference between the left and right sides of (4). Since the countries are assumed to be homogeneous, this subset will be defined as

$$\widehat{\Omega} : \Pi(S) \geq 0 \tag{6}$$

By subgame perfection, $\widehat{\Omega} = \Omega_A$. Given the aforementioned criticisms of the effectiveness of WTO-sanctioned retaliation and the eschewing of penalties for noncompliance, it is not unreasonable to conclude that $\tilde{S}$ may be arbitrarily close to zero. However, as the studies of retaliation in AD actions indicate, reciprocal usage of AD laws may provide a more effective lower bound for Ω_A. Thus, it may not be surprising that signatories do not utilize the DSU to address being targeted by another member's AD law. Retaliation, however, has its limitations. Whether it targets the industry that filed against an industry in a signatory, or a different industry in that member, it is a sector-specific instrument. Filing a dispute can be a broader approach to addressing dissatisfaction with a country's implementation of the ADA. It can target a general policy of implementation, such as, the Byrd Amendment. It would be less effective to use retaliatory filings to address a broad policy matter like Byrd or zeroing. That is, however, unless other signatories invoked policies like Byrd, which would represent a downward ratcheting of cooperation under the ADA.

3. Conclusion

Beginning with the assumption that AD laws are used to address adverse shocks in import-competing industries, this chapter provides an explanation for the infrequent utilization of the DSU under the ADA. It does so with a very simple model that represents the shock by a one-dimensional random variable. This is found on an interpretation of the ADA as a *de facto* EC. ADA signatories are homogeneous, which enables the representation of the expected frequency of shocks over each member's import-competing sectors by the binomial distribution with identical parameters. The explanation for the infrequency of utilization of the DSU invokes a Prisoners' Dilemma with two levels of cooperation in an infinite horizon game. The high level is free trade in all sectors. The low level is the application of ADA duties in sectors incurring the shock in a manner that is consistent with the ADA. The high level of cooperation in all sectors in every period is not sustainable for any degree of patience. A convex combination of the high and low levels of cooperation is sustainable for some degrees of patience under a folk theorem analog. However, this combination of cooperation is attainable only with the support of the DSU. The extent of importance of the DSU depends on the completeness of information with which signatories are endowed. With complete information, dispute resolution does not occur in equilibrium. That is, unless it serves as a forum for the renegotiation of commitments. However, its presence supports cooperation through its mandate to sanction retaliation. This will not arise in my framework. If filing were prohibitively costly, disputes would never arise, and cooperation would be expected to evaporate. In the instance of incomplete information with costless filing, disputes would occur in equilibrium whenever an AD action was taken. In the most realistic circumstance, that of incomplete information and nonprohibitive filing costs, disputes would arise only when the number of AD actions exceeded their (common) expectation. This provides a conceptual explanation for the observations of Tarullo (2002) and Bown (2005) that ADA disputes are infrequent.

References

Blonigen, B.A. (2006), Evolving discretionary practices in U.S. antidumping activity. *Canadian Journal of Economics* 39, 874–900.

Boltuck, R., Litan, R.E. (1991), *Down in the dumps*. Brookings Institution, Washington, DC.

Bown, C.P. (2005), Trade remedies and world trade organization dispute settlement: why are so few challenged? *Journal of Legal Studies* 34, 515–555.

Brander, J.A., Krugman, P.R. (1983), A "reciprocal dumping" model of international trade. *Journal of International Economics* 15, 313–321.

Cass, R.C., Knoll, M.S. (1998), The economics of "Injury" in antidumping and countervailing duty cases: a reply to professor sykes. In: Bhandari, J.S., Sykes, A.O. (Eds.), *Economic Dimensions in International Law: Comparative and Empirical Perspectives.* Cambridge University Press, Cambridge.

Durling, J.P., McCullough, M.P. (2005), Teaching old laws new tricks: the legal obligation of non attribution and the need for economic rigor in injury analyses under US trade law. In: Choi, E.K., Hartigan, J.C. (Eds.), *Handbook of International Trade Vol. II: Economic and Legal Analyses of Trade Policy and Institutions.* Blackwell, Oxford.

Ethier, W.J. (2002), Unilateralism in a multilateral world. *Economic Journal* 112, 266–292.

Feinberg, R.M., Reynolds, K.M. (2006), The spread of antidumping regimes and the role of retaliation in filings. *Southern Economic Journal* 72, 877–890.

Frischmann, B.M., Hartigan, J.C. (2008), Compliance institutions in treaties (working paper).

Hartigan, J.C., Vandenbussche, H. (2008), Why are antidumping laws WTO legal? (working paper).

Horn, H., Mavroidis, P.C., Nordstrom, H. (1999), Is the use of the WTO dispute settlement system biased? www.cepr.org/pubs

Howse, R.L., Esserman, S. (2006), The appellate body, the WTO dispute settlement system, and the politics of multilateralism. In: Sacerdoti, G., Yanovich, A., Bohanes, J. (Eds.), *The WTO at Ten: The Contribution of the Dispute Settlement System.* Cambridge University Press, Cambridge.

Jackson, J.H. (1997), *The world trading system: law and policy of international economic relations.* MIT Press, Cambridge, MA.

Kovenock, D., Thursby, M. (1992), GATT, dispute settlement, and cooperation. *Economics and Politics* 4, 151–170.

Liebman, B. (2004), ITC voting behavior on sunset review. *Weltwirtschaftliches Archiv* 140, 446–475.

Mansfield, E.D., Milner, H.V., Rosendorff, B.P. (2002), Why democracies cooperate more: electoral control and international trade agreements. *International Organization* 56, 477–514.

McGillivray, F., Smith, A. (2006), Credibility in compliance and punishment: leader specific punishments and credibility. *Journal of Politics* 68, 248–258.

Mitchell, S.K. (1997), GATT, dispute settlement, and cooperation: a note. *Economics and Politics* 9, 87–93.

Murray, T., Kurdaliev, N. (1999), Universal dumping of homogeneous products. *Review of International Economics* 7, 580–589.

Nzelibe, J. (2005), The credibility imperative: the political dynamics of retaliation in the world trade organization's dispute resolution mechanism. *Theoretical Inquiries in Law* 6, 215.

Peabody Coal vs. Ralston (1991), Indiana Court of Appeals, 578, N.E. 2nd, 751.

Prusa, T.J., Skeath, S. (2005), Modern commercial policy: managed trade or retaliation? In: Choi, E.K., Hartigan, J.C. (Eds.), *Handbook of International Trade Vol. II: Economic and Legal Analyses of Trade Policy and Institutions*. Blackwell, Oxford.

Tarullo, D.K. (2002), The hidden costs of international dispute settlement: WTO review of domestic anti-dumping decisions. *Law and Policy in International Business* 34, 109–168.

US Department of Commerce, International trade administration, www.ita.doc.gov

US International Trade Commission, www.usitc.gov

Vandenbussche, H., Zanardi, M. (2008), What explains the proliferation of antidumping laws? *Economic Policy* 23, 94–138.

World Trade Organization, www.wto.org

PART V

Compliance, Enforcement, and Remedies

CHAPTER 14

Trade Agreements and Dispute Settlement in the WTO System

Wilfred J. Ethier

Department of Economics, University of Pennsylvania, Philadelphia, PA 19104-6297, USA
E-mail address: ethier@econ.sas.upenn.edu

Abstract
This paper develops a theory, consistent with empirical evidence, of trade agreements as the exchange of market access. The WTO dispute settlement process is discussed in this context. The role of that process is neither to deter nor to punish violations of trade agreements, but to maintain reciprocity.

Keywords: Exchange of market access, reciprocal conflict, substantially equivalent withdrawal of concessions, commensurate punishment

JEL classifications: F02, F13

Multilateral trade liberalization under the auspices of the General Agreement on Tariffs and Trade (GATT) culminating in the creation of the World Trade Organization (WTO) may well constitute the most successful deliberate exercise of economic policy in human history.

The early GATT contained a dispute settlement procedure (DSP). The Uruguay Round, which established the WTO, significantly changed this procedure in the hopes of increasing its use. These hopes have been realized.

To address the DSP, I require a theory of the WTO itself. Although there is a large theoretical literature addressing trade agreements, it is not very relevant to the WTO. Thus, I first provide such a theory.

1. Introduction

Building on Harry Johnson's classic paper (1953–1954), scores of contributions developed and elaborated what can be called the "Received Theory" of trade policy and trade agreements. The deservedly influential

Frontiers of Economics and Globalization
Volume 6 ISSN: 1574-8715
DOI: 10.1108/S1574-8715(2009)0000006017

work of Bagwell and Staiger (1999, 2002) has triumphantly completed the research agenda implied by Johnson nearly half a century earlier.

An emphasis[1] on political economy emerged in the 1980s. Grossman and Helpman (1994, 1995, 2002) provide its most widely used component. The current state of the Received Theory is therefore conveniently described in two recent books by Bagwell and Staiger (2002) and Grossman and Helpman (2002).

However, the Received Theory is dramatically inconsistent with reality.[2] The central premise of the Received Theory is that trade agreements arise *solely* because countries with market power are concerned, to at least *some* degree, with the fact that trade barriers, imposed for *whatever* reason, can move the terms of trade in their favor, shifting real income there from the rest of the world.

As pointed out in Ethier (2004), this is inconsistent with actual multilateral trade agreements, which do *not* prevent countries from trying to influence their terms of trade,[3] the Terms-of-Trade Puzzle:

(i) Actual trade agreements do not prevent countries from manipulating their terms of trade with export taxes; (ii) Countries nevertheless do not, by and large, implement such taxes.

If the interests of owners of factors specific to export sectors are sufficiently important, governments will not wish to tax exports, so the Export-Tax Puzzle disappears. But this introduces a new problem, the Export-Subsidy-Transfer Puzzle:

In equilibrium, exporting nations will (i) offer large export subsidies, which will (ii) be incompletely countervailed by importing nations, who (iii) would decline to implement actual countervailing duty laws (which require complete countervailing).

Thus, the Received Theory necessarily implies equilibria that are dramatically counterfactual. Furthermore, the source of these counterfactual predictions is exactly the distinguishing feature of the Received Theory: the central role played by the terms of trade and/or by trade tax revenue (Ethier, 2007).

However, the Grossman–Helpman model (2002) has received considerable empirical attention (Goldberg and Maggi, 1999; Gawande and Bandyopadhyay, 2000; Mitra *et al.*, 2002; McCallum, 2004). These papers have been uniformly supportive of the theory, but in a highly selective

---

[1] See Hillman (1982, 1990), Hillman *et al.* (1995), and Hillman and Moser (1996). Surveys of the literature on the political economy of trade policy may be found in Nelson (1988), Hillman (1989), Magee (1994), and Rodrik (1995).

[2] See Ethier (2006a, 2007).

[3] Although the Received Theory assigns the central role to terms-of-trade considerations, they are ignored virtually without exception by trade lawyers and policymakers. See Regan (2004) for an argument that the public rhetoric of trade, the specific provisions of trade agreements, and the full range of policy behavior of countries are not well explained by terms-of-trade considerations.

way. They have not investigated the predictions that reflect the central presumptions of the Received Theory (import subsidies for all politically unorganized import-competing sectors and export taxes for all politically unorganized export sectors.) But they have given powerful evidence that, in politically organized import-competing sectors, protection is negatively related to the import–penetration ratio, presumably reflecting the tug between sectoral special interests and consumer surplus central to most political economy approaches to trade policy. Also in such sectors, protection appears to be negatively related to the domestic elasticity of import demand. Furthermore, this literature argues persuasively that distinguishing between politically organized and unorganized sectors is crucial to understand this dependence.

This paper takes seriously both the theoretical argument that the Received Theory generates dramatically counterfactual predictions, because of its central presumption, and the empirical evidence that the conflict between sectoral interests and consumer surplus matters for policy and that political organization determines how it matters. I construct a model on this basis, and I then investigate the role of trade agreements in such a context. I do not attempt a microeconomic explanation of this basis.

The paper proceeds as follows. The next section describes an economic model, simplified for transparency, and the following section adds a model of lobbying. I then describe a non-cooperative equilibrium in trade policy setting and investigate the potential role of a trade agreement. The resulting framework is then used to analyze the role of the WTO dispute settlement mechanism.

2. *The model: economics*

Assume two countries (*H*ome and *F*oreign), two factors (*K*apital and *L*abor), and $N + 1$ traded goods $(0, 1, \dots, N)$. Good 0 is a numeráire good, produced by labor alone. Goods 1 to N are produced by capital and labor, with capital specific to each of these sectors. H imports goods *1* to n and exports goods $n + 1$ to N.

Ownership of each specific factor is distributed uniformly over a fraction α_i of the population (labor force), with each individual owning some of just one of the specific factors. Normalize so that $L = 1 = \alpha_1 + \dots + \alpha_N$. Choose units so that a unit of good 0 is produced by a unit of labor. Thus, if good 0 is produced, the wage $w = 1$.

Each individual in each country has preferences summarized by the utility function $U = c_0 + u_1(c_1) + \dots + u_N(c_N)$, where c_i denotes consumption of good i. This implies individual demand functions $d_i = d_i(Q_i)$, $i = 1, \dots, N$, where Q_i denotes the relative price of good i in terms of good 0. Residual income is all spent on the numeráire good 0. I assume that endowments in both countries are such that each produces and consumes good 0.

Each country may tax or subsidize either imports or exports. For H, let Q_i and P_i denote, respectively, the domestic and international relative price (in terms of the numeráire) of good i, and τ_i one plus the *ad-valorem* trade tax t_i. Thus, $Q_i = \tau_i P_i$ for $i = 1, \ldots, n$, and $Q_j = P_j/\tau_i$ for $j = n + 1, \ldots, N$. Analogous F variables are distinguished by asterisks.

2.1. International trade

Equilibrium in the world market for good i, $i = 1, \ldots, n$, is represented by $M_i(\tau_i P_i) = X_i^*(P_i/\tau_i^*)$, where M_i and X_i^* respectively denote H import demand and F export supply. H's import tax and F's export tax thus determine P_i, independently of other sectors. This in turn implies the following.

$$\frac{\tau_i}{P_i}\frac{dP_i}{dt_i} = -\frac{e_i}{e_i + f_i^*}$$

and

$$\frac{\tau_i}{Q_i}\frac{dQ_i}{dt_i} = \frac{\tau_i}{P_i}\frac{dP_i}{dt_i} + 1 = \frac{f_i^*}{e_i + f_i^*}$$

where $e_i \equiv (-\tau_i P_i M_i'/M_i) > 0$ and $f_i^* \equiv (P_i X_i^{*\prime}/\tau_i^* X_i^*) > 0$.

Similarly, equilibrium in the world market for goods $n + 1$ to N can be represented by $M_j^*(\tau_j^* P_j) = X_j(P_j/\tau_j)$. Thus,

$$\frac{\tau_j}{P_j}\frac{dP_j}{dt_j} = \frac{f_j}{f_j + e_j^*}$$

and

$$\frac{\tau_j}{Q_j}\frac{dQ_j}{dt_j} = \frac{\tau_j}{P_j}\frac{dP_j}{dt_j} - 1 = -\frac{e_j^*}{f_j + e_j^*}$$

H imports of goods $1 \ldots n$ need not equal in value H exports of goods $n+1 \ldots N$: trade balance is reached with a net exchange of good 0.

3. *The model: policy formation*

I next describe the political economy side of the model. This is a reduced-form model of policy formation consistent with the evidence discussed earlier.

3.1. Lobbies

The owners α_i of each specific factor i potentially organize a lobby to bargain with the government over t_i. Nobody lobbies for policy regarding the numeráire good. The sectors differ in the abilities of the associated factor owners to organize as well as in the abilities of those that do organize to bring pressure to bear on the government (Olson, 1965).

If a sector does not organize, and so does not lobby, the government leaves trade policy unchanged at its existing level, which, for convenience, I assume to be free trade. Organized sectors elicit a government response. In this response, the government wishes to increase the specific factor income $\pi_i(Q_i)$ of the associated lobby, but is also reluctant to reduce consumer surplus $S_i(Q_i) \equiv u_i(c_i(Q_i)) - Q_i d_i(Q_i)$.

W_i denotes the objective function of the government if in that sector the α_i group is organized and, thus, does lobby.

$$W_i(t_i) = (\delta_i - 1)\pi_i(Q_i) + s_i(Q_i). \tag{1}$$

Here, $\delta_i \geq 1$ denotes the importance the government attaches to the welfare of the α_i lobby. The government wishes W_i as high as possible, but it is constrained by a reluctance to drive consumer surplus too low:

$$S_i(Q) \geq \frac{1}{\varepsilon_i}. \tag{2}$$

The parameters δ_i and ε_i both reflect the political influence of the ith lobby: Higher values imply more influence. For simplicity assume that they are consistent in the sense that

$$\delta_i > \delta_j \text{ if and only if } \varepsilon_i > \varepsilon_j. \tag{A1}$$

Number each country's imports in decreasing order of political influence and likewise for each country's exports.

3.2. Policy choice

Differentiating (1) yields, for each import-competing sector (the sector subscript i is omitted):

$$\frac{t}{Q}\frac{dW}{dt} = \left[\delta \frac{x}{M} - 1\right] M \frac{f^*}{e + f^*} \tag{3}$$

where x denotes domestic production. A tariff is called for when the term in brackets is positive. This will be more likely the greater the degree δ of political influence possessed by that sector's lobby. For a given degree of influence, this will be more likely the smaller the import penetration ratio M/x. If the term in brackets is negative, the sector's organized interest group lacks the power to influence policy: thus, it will not lobby and the government will not depart from free trade.

If dW/dt is positive, the government will impose a tariff. Doing so will both increase x and reduce M; dW/dt will remain positive. Thus, the government will raise t until (2) binds. Thus, other things equal, the greater the degree ε of political influence, the greater the tariff t and the lower the import penetration ratio M/x.

Next, from (2),

$$\frac{\varepsilon}{t}\frac{dt}{d\varepsilon}=\frac{d}{S}\frac{f^*}{e+f^*}$$

More political influence ε implies a higher tariff t, but how much higher is negatively related to the import elasticity e.

PROPOSITION 1. *An import-competing interest group is more likely to lobby the lower the import penetration ratio. For those that do lobby, the tariff will be positively related to the degree of political influence and negatively related to the import–penetration ratio and to the elasticity of import demand.*

REMARK 1. This simple model predicts just those properties that empirical investigations of the Grossman–Helpman model have supported.

Turning to export sectors,

$$\frac{t}{Q}\frac{dW}{dt}=\left[-\delta\frac{x}{X}-1\right]X\frac{e^*}{e^*+f}<0. \tag{4}$$

Thus, the government will wish to subsidize the exports of all politically organized sectors. If it does so, the resulting increase in the domestic relative price will reduce domestic demand, so that X/x will rise with the subsidy. From (2),

$$\frac{\varepsilon}{t}\frac{dt}{d\varepsilon}=-\frac{d}{S}\frac{e^*}{e^*+f}.$$

Thus, an increase in sectoral influence will increase the subsidy the government is willing to offer, and it will increase it more the smaller is the domestic export elasticity f.

PROPOSITION 2. *The government will be willing to subsidize the exports of all organized export sectors. The government's desired subsidy will be positively related to the degree of political influence and negatively related to the export–production ratio and to the elasticity of export demand.*

4. The non-cooperative equilibrium

Next, consider the non-cooperative, trade-policy equilibrium between H and F. Because of the partial equilibrium structure of the model, the various sectors can be analyzed independently. So look at good 1, which H imports and F exports, and whose respective specific factor owners are organized and sufficiently potent to influence policy in each country. Then by Propositions 1 and 2, the H government wishes to tax imports of good 1, and the F government wishes to subsidize its export.

4.1. Best responses

Let Q_1^A solve $S_I(Q_1^A) = 1/\varepsilon_1$. Let τ_1^A denote the value of τ_1 that will cause $Q_1 = Q_1^A$ when $\tau_1^* = 1$, that is, H's best response to $\tau_1^* = 1$. In like manner, $\tau_1^{*B} = 1$ denotes F's best response to $\tau_1 = 1$.

The set of all combinations of τ_1 and τ_1^* implying $Q_1 = Q_1^A$ is the locus of solutions to

$$M_1(Q_1^A) = X_1^*\left(\frac{Q_1^A}{\tau_1\tau_1^*}\right),$$

the rectangular hyperbola defined by $\tau_1\ \tau_1^* = \tau_1^A$. Since Q_1^* is uniquely related to Q_1 through the market-clearing condition for good 1, it is also constant in this locus.

Now, suppose F were to depart from A by imposing an export subsidy $dt_1^* < 0$. Then an increase in the H tariff of $dt_1 = -\tau_1\ dt_1^*$ will hold Q_1 and Q_1^* unchanged. This will maintain the initial situation except that F pays an export subsidy, which H taxes away with an equivalent increase in its tariff. This countervailing increase in its tariff constitutes a beneficial H response to F's adoption of an export subsidy.

4.2. Equilibrium

In like manner, the locus $\tau_1\tau_1^* = \tau_1^{*B}$ is F's best-response curve. Since the two loci (both rectangular hyperbolae) correspond to different values of the domestic prices, they cannot intersect. There is no Nash equilibrium in t_1 and t_1^* alone! Moving along either loci leaves all demands and supplies unchanged: The only effect is to shift trade-tax revenue between F and H.

An equilibrium can be obtained if we slightly enlarge each country's set of policy instruments. Suppose that, in addition to setting its trade taxes or subsidies, each country can decide whether to implement, or not to implement, a countervailing duty law. Such a law would mandate that imports of goods receiving a foreign export subsidy would be subject to a matching tariff, in addition to whatever trade tax or subsidy the importing country might otherwise wish to implement.

If H, for example, were to implement such a law and also to set τ equal to the value that would cause $Q_1 = Q_1^A$ when $\tau_1^* = 1$, those actions would credibly commit H to be on its best-response curve. Then F's best response, assuming it does not want simply to give government revenue to H, would be τ_1^A.

PROPOSITION 3. *There is a non-cooperative equilibrium in trade policy. Each country adopts a countervailing duty law and employs neither export taxes nor export subsidies. Import-competing sectors with sufficient political influence receive protection and those without do not. Such tariffs will be higher the higher the degree of political influence, and the lower the import penetration ratio and the elasticity of import demand.*

REMARK 2. Countervailing duty laws emerge here as the result of non-cooperative choices by the two governments, *not* as a result of a trade agreement.

In reality it is true that the GATT, in Article XVI, attempts to curtail the use of export subsidies and also provides a code of conduct regarding countervailing duty laws for WTO members. But such laws were in existence *long* before the GATT. Another implication of the endogenous introduction of countervailing duty laws is the following.

REMARK 3. Each government is powerless to offer its export lobby anything in Nash equilibrium.

This will turn out to be the essential reason for trade agreements of the sort actually observed. This environment is *not* assumed; it is a direct consequence of the requirements for a non-cooperative equilibrium given the political climate of policy described here.

REMARK 4. Proposition 3 displays those predictions of the Grossman–Helpman approach that have found empirical support and does not display those predictions that appear counterfactual.

5. Trade agreements

Now suppose that the H and F governments can undertake negotiations for a trade agreement that would stipulate the trade taxes or subsidies. In the event of such negotiations, each interest group would lobby its government about the taxes in the agreement that pertain directly to it. I inquire whether there is a basis for such negotiations.

5.1. The exchange of market access

A large literature insists that trade agreements seek to *exchange market access*: I will grant your exporters increased access to my market in exchange for increased access to your market for my exporters.[4] Bagwell and Staiger (2002, pp. 28–29) however, state, "we may interpret 'cost shifting,' 'terms-of-trade gain,' and 'market-access restriction' as three phrases that describe ... [a] single economic experience." The earlier literature, it seems clear, had "something else" in mind, but when it expressed its ideas in formal terms, used models that, as Bagwell and

[4] See Hauser (1986), Finger (1988, 1991), Moser (1990), Hillman *et al.* (1995), Hillman and Moser (1996), and Ethier (2008).

Staiger (2002, p. 20) correctly observe, were very often special cases of their own.

The present analysis provides a formal basis to define trade agreements based on the exchange of market access and to distinguish them from those that are not. The basic idea behind the exchange of market access seems to be that each country, for whatever reason, agrees to allow increased imports of a particular good in exchange for increased exports of another particular good. That is, such trade agreements are necessarily *inter-sectoral*.

This model possesses extensive separability: Equilibrium policies in each sector are determined independently of those in the other sector. This has so far been a matter of expositional convenience, but now it serves another purpose as well. With policies in each sector determined independently, there could be an incentive for independent sector-by-sector international negotiations not involving inter-sectoral trade-offs, such as the 1965 US–Canada automobile agreement. In such an *intra-sectoral* negotiation, the governments would bargain over t_1 and t_1^*, with any implied change in $M_1 = X_1^*$ settled by a change in the trade volume of the numeráire good.

I can now pose the following question. With policy determination in each sector independent of that in the other sector, is it *necessary* for trade negotiations to address inter-sectoral trade-offs to serve a useful purpose? If so, I regard the negotiations as motivated by a desire to exchange market access.

Definition. *Trade agreements are said to be based on the exchange of market access if and only if there is no reason for sector-by-sector negotiations.*

5.2. Trade agreements to exchange market access

The equilibrium described in Proposition 3 offers no opportunity for an intra-sectoral trade agreement. In sector 1, for example, F is implementing no policy and so can offer H nothing in return for a lower tariff. Thus, any trade agreement must be based on the exchange of market access.

Consider a simple trade agreement involving only goods 1 and $n + 1$. The motive for a trade agreement based on the exchange of market access would be to enable each government to offer its export sector something while taking something less from its import-competing sector. It is true that, with the non-cooperative equilibrium, each government is powerless to offer its export sector something in any other way. But it is not clear that it will be tempted to use this way. The reason is that, since retreating from the t_1 in the non-cooperative equilibrium would impose a first-order cost on H, doing so would be tempting to H only if the implied negotiated benefit for good $n + 1$ is large enough. It is not clear that a trade agreement can be found that would do this for both countries simultaneously.

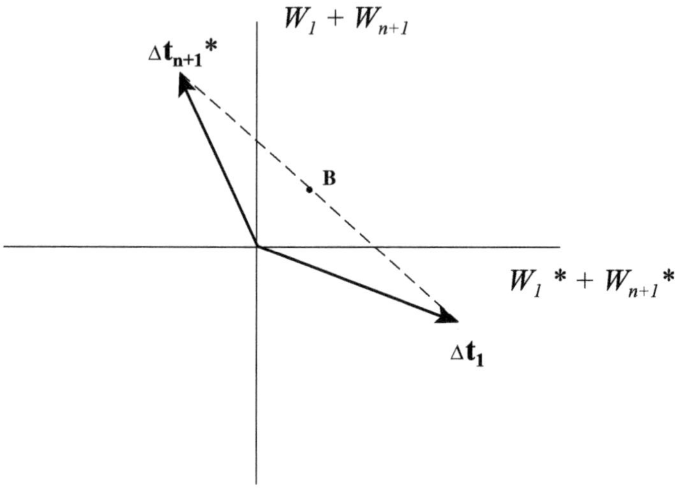

Fig. 1. Mutually beneficial exchange of market access.

Now consider a hypothetical trade agreement stipulating $dt_1 < 0$ and $dt^*_{n+1} = \alpha\, dt_1$ for some α. Such an agreement will raise the joint surplus in each country, and so be perceived as beneficial by each government, if and only if the following holds.

$$\frac{\partial W_1}{\partial t_1} + \alpha \frac{\partial W_{n+1}}{\partial^*_{n+1}} > 0$$

$$\frac{\partial W_1^*}{\partial t_1} + \alpha \frac{\partial W^*_{n+1}}{\partial^*_{n+1}} > 0$$

This will in turn be possible for some $\alpha > 0$ if and only if the following condition is met.

$$\left(\frac{\partial W_1^*}{\partial t_1}\right)\left(\frac{\partial W_{n+1}}{\partial t^*_{n+1}}\right) > \left(\frac{\partial W^*_{n+1}}{\partial t^*_{n+1}}\right)\left(\frac{\partial W_1}{\partial t_1}\right) \tag{5}$$

Figure 1 illustrates how satisfaction of (5) is equivalent to the existence of a mutually beneficial trade agreement. The vectors labeled $\mathbf{\Delta t_1}$ and $\mathbf{\Delta t^*_{n+1}}$ depict the effects of reductions in the respective tariffs on the two joint surpluses. When these vectors have the relative slopes illustrated, reflecting (5), an appropriate linear combination, such as at point **B**, will be mutually beneficial.[5]

[5] The attentive reader will recognize this logic as that behind the familiar Hawkins-Simon (1949) condition for the feasibility of an input–output system.

Condition (5) in effect requires that, at the margin, tariffs have relatively greater impact on export lobbies than on import lobbies. This is intuitively understandable, and since in Nash equilibrium the tariffs were set with exclusive reliance on the effects on the latter lobbies, unlikely to be demanding. So we have the following result.

PROPOSITION 4. *With (5) a mutually-beneficial trade agreement is feasible. This agreement is based on the exchange of market access, and it need not constrain export taxes.*

The existence of a bargain based on the exchange of market access requires only that the analog of (5) hold for *some* pair of goods from both countries. Denote by $\mathbf{B}_{ij} = (t_i^0, t_j^{0*})$ a bargain in which the home country exchanges access to its good-i market for access to the foreign good-j market, Home changing its tariff to t_i^0, and Foreign changing its tariff to t_j^{0*}. The actual pair is determined by bargaining between the two countries, a delicate process into which I, dear reader, shall not intrude. I do assume, however, that such a bargain is efficient: At the new tariffs established by the bargain, any tariff change that increases $W_1 + W_2$ necessarily lowers $W_1^* + W_2^*$ and *vice versa*. Also, at the bargained rates, condition (2) does not bind for either good.

A trade agreement $\mathbf{TA} = \{\mathbf{B}_{ij}\}$ consists of a set of such bargains. There is no reason to expect such an agreement to be unique or to include all goods. Proposition 4 establishes its existence.

6. Dispute settlement

With a theory of trade agreements consistent with available evidence, I now turn to dispute settlement. This section offers a description and interpretation of the WTO dispute settlement process, and Section 7 relates it to the present model.[6]

The GATT/WTO trade liberalization has had to deal with numerous trade disputes between individual countries, and the need to address these has produced a multilateral response. This can be summarized by the following stylized facts.

1. Trade disputes are inherently *bilateral*, not multilateral.

The direct participants to trade disputes (whether two or several), and only they, initiate the disputes, force their timing, undertake negotiations to settle, and inflict punishments.[7] Indeed, a major purpose is to keep

[6] See Bütler and Hauser (2000) and Ethier (2006b).

[7] Third countries with a vital interest in a matter under dispute between major countries sometimes sign on as participants (the banana war between the United States and the EU being a notable example). This can be the easiest way for small countries to participate in the system.

disputes bilateral by inducing aggrieved nations to go before a panel of experts rather than to seek allies among third countries.

2. The DSP of the WTO has almost always decided, to at least some significant degree, in favor of the complainant (*C*) and, therefore, against the defendant (*D*).

Countries file complaints only when confident (usually rightly) that their complaints are justified.

3. Defendants have (much more often than not, at least since the institution of the WTO procedure) abided by the decisions of the DSP. But a number of important, highly visible cases, involving major countries, have resulted in prolonged violations of DSP decisions.

The decisions to abide have been widely viewed as evidence of the "success" of the WTO DSP, whereas the violations have been viewed as "failures" that threaten the viability of a "rules-based" system.

4. Punishments for alleged violations of past agreements have been *delayed.*

Use of the DSP implies that punishment will be postponed until that procedure has run its course and the defendant has failed to abide by its decision.

5. Punishments for alleged violations of past agreements are *commensurate with the violations* (*i.e.*, tit-for-tat) and cease when the violations cease.

This can be regarded as just one facet of the principle of *substantially equivalent withdrawal of concessions*, pervasive throughout the GATT (see Articles XIX, XXIII, and XIV of the GATT).

Points 4 and 5 together imply that a country is in effect free to violate its WTO commitments without punishment for the duration of the adjudication process (typically about 20 months), provided it does abide by the final ruling. This strongly suggests that the deterrence and the punishment of violations of trade agreements is not the purpose of the DSP. For example, in March 2002, the United States implemented safeguard measures on steel imports. The financial press widely advanced the views that the purpose of the measures was to influence the Congressional elections upcoming in November 2002 and that the measures were in violation of WTO rules. Several steel-exporting countries brought the case before the DSB, whose panel ruled against the United States in July 2003. The United States appealed, but the Appellate Body upheld the panel's ruling in November 2003. The US suspended its measure in December 2003. By then, the elections that had been the apparent motivation had come and gone, and the United States escaped all punishment for its actions.

Trade agreements are necessarily incomplete contracts because the subsequent state of the world is not known when negotiations take place. Any agreement must reflect this. The most straightforward way to deal with it is to negotiate *state-contingent* agreements. But these have severe limitations: The negotiation of even state-invariant changes in recognized policy instruments has become enormously complicated and time consuming. So, negotiated trade agreements necessarily remain, by their very nature, incomplete contracts. This is implicitly acknowledged in the GATT itself, where Articles XXII and XXIII allow response to a "nullification or impairment" of concessions not necessarily the result of an explicit repudiation of a trade agreement.

Trade agreements address a limited number of policy instruments that pertain directly to trade, but governments care about economic outcomes, not about the instruments that can be negotiated. And trade is one aspect of the general equilibrium that depends on *all* economic instruments. So, *ex post*, governments will be doing things that influence trade and that have not been explicitly addressed by trade agreements: a recipe for disagreement about the constraints implied by those agreements.

Each country is aware, *ex ante*, that it may find itself, *ex post*, harmed by a policy that some trading partner wishes to make. So the former will want a recognized punishment procedure as a deterrent. But that country will also be aware, *ex ante*, that it might find, *ex post*, itself in a position where it would be costly not to take some policy action that would harm a partner. This is the *reciprocal–conflict problem*: Each country knows that it might turn out to be either the accuser or the accused. Thus, it is in no country's interest, *ex ante*, to agree that, *ex post*, either the accuser should be unconstrained in its ability to punish or the accused should be unconstrained in its ability to proceed without punishment. This generates a role for a dispute settlement mechanism.

Resolving basic uncertainty about whether specific policies are in fact consistent with trade agreements does not seem to be a central purpose. As noted above, WTO DSP decisions normally go against the defendant, and, in the more visible cases, the financial press routinely and correctly predicts in advance which way decisions will go. So, I assume away any uncertainty about whether a policy under dispute does in fact violate trade agreements. The purpose of a DSP instead will be (i) to supply a formal international statement that such a policy is in fact a violation, (ii) to specify explicitly how it is in violation, and (iii) to provide, if necessary, a neutral assessment of the "damage" caused by that policy.

This implies that punishments *must* be delayed, because the implementation of a controversial policy by some country cannot be required to wait until the dispute settlement mechanism renders its verdict. The reason the mechanism exists in the first place is that no one knows in advance what will come into dispute: Trade agreements are incomplete contracts. So the only way to delay such implementation is to require that this be automatically required for any policy action that is disputed, and this would in effect give each country a temporary veto over every economic policy action of every other country.

7. *Dispute settlement in the theory of trade agreements*

I now present a model of a DSP motivated by the earlier considerations. First, I must modify the sequence of events within each period to include the operation of a DSP.

7.1. Trade-related actions

Suppose that, *ex post,* some country may determine an action, a, which directly influences that government's level of political support and also affects that country's willingness to import. I am especially concerned with two types of uncertainty to which such an action would be subject *ex ante*: (1) uncertainty (or complete ignorance) about what actual policy situation (environmental issues, health or safety concerns, etc.) might give rise to such a potential action and (2) uncertainty about the identity of the country in which the situation might emerge. To focus sharply on these concerns, I assume away all other sources of uncertainty.

The first aspect is incorporated in the requirement that the trade agreement be an incomplete contract. Next, I suppose that exactly one issue will arise and that it will induce a trade-related action by one country or the other, with an equal probability (1/2) of either outcome.

In general, a trade-related action by some country may or may not be welcomed by its partners. But this paper concerns trade *disputes.* Consequently, I assume that such actions are always unwelcome: They cause the country undertaking the action to display more protection rather than less.

Specifically, I assume that implementing an action a (>0) affects the country's demand for imports in the same way as would an increase in its tariff in the proportion a. Thus, the trade-related action in effect reduces the country's tariff from the negotiated rate t to the rate $t-a$, independently of its effect on the country's trade.

7.2. The sequence of events

Each period now consists of the following sequence of events.

1. Countries negotiate a bargain $\mathbf{B}_{ij}$ as discussed in Section 5, but now they also determine a DSP.
2. One country (the potential *defendant*) is then induced to make a trade-related action a not explicitly covered by the trade agreement.
3. The trading partner (the potential *complainant*) then utilizes the DSP.
4. The DSP renders a decision for the complainant, and the defendant must then decide whether to abide by the decision or to defy it. If it decides to abide, it abandons a, and the sequence comes to an end.

5. If the defendant decides to violate the DSP decision, the complainant retaliates with trade restrictions proportional to the trade effects of the action a:ρa. The degree of proportionality ρ is fixed by the trade agreement.

A negotiated bargain can now be written as $\mathbf{B}_{ij}(\boldsymbol{t}_1, \boldsymbol{t}_2^*, \rho)$. Let $t_1 = \boldsymbol{t}_1^0$ and $t_2^* = \boldsymbol{t}_2^{0*}$ denote what the negotiated tariffs would be if there were no possibility of a trade-related action. I refer to such a tariff pair as the *optimal degree of liberalization.* The parameter ρ can be interpreted as stipulating in advance the principle (e.g., the equivalent withdrawal of concessions if $\rho = 1$) to be applied to such settlements, and a purpose of this section is to endogenize the choice of ρ more generally than just in a DSP. But as the balance of this paper will specifically deal with a DSP, I shall continue to employ the language of the latter.

The Home country may find itself *ex post* in the role of either D or C. If D refuses to abide by a DSP ruling, or if a settlement is made, the Home objective functions in the two cases become:

$$W_D = W_i(t_i - a) + W_j(t_j^* - \rho a)$$

$$W_C = W_i(t_i - \rho a) + W_j(t_j^* - a)$$

Analogous expressions apply to the Foreign country.

Consider the bargain $t_i = \boldsymbol{t}_i^0 + a,\ \ t_j^* = \boldsymbol{t}_j^{0*} + a$, and $\rho = 1$. Regardless of which country is induced to make the trade-related action, this bargain will *ex post* deliver the optimal degree of liberalization. This is independent of the magnitude of a, so $\rho = 1$ is appropriate for all bargains; that is, it will be stipulated in the trade agreement **TA** itself. Thus, the **TA** will feature such liberalization for each commodity pair for which it is known that *one* country will be induced to make a trade-related action, it will feature $t_i = \boldsymbol{t}_i^0,\ \ t_j^* = \boldsymbol{t}_j^{0*}$ for each commodity pair for which it is known that no country will be induced to make such an action, and it will feature $\rho = 1$.

This result is a direct reflection of the reciprocal-conflict property that I have argued and is essential to understand the role of the DSP in the WTO system. To make this clear I am content to simplify by assuming both that the magnitude of a is known and that it is known that just one country will be induced to make the action with equal probability of which country that will turn out to be. But I have also so far considered only commodity pairs for which it is known with certainty either that one country will be induced to make such an action or that neither will.

Such certainty is not essential to the nature of the DSP. So suppose that, for some commodity pairs, there is a probability, strictly between 0 and 1, that a trade-related action will be induced. *Ex post* having $\rho = 1$ will still be desirable. But the *ex ante* bargain will now feature $\boldsymbol{t}_i^0 < t_i < \boldsymbol{t}_i^0 + a$, and $\boldsymbol{t}_j^{0*} < t_j^* < \boldsymbol{t}_j^{0*} + a$. Once again, I do not intrude on the delicacies of the bargaining process. Thus, *ex post*, actual realized protection will be deficient if the trade-related action does emerge and excessive if it does not.

PROPOSITION 5. *The negotiated trade agreement will feature commensurate punishment. It will deliver,* ex post, *the optimal degree of liberalization if it is known with certainty that a violation will occur. Otherwise, the* ex post *liberalization will be deficient if a violation does occur and excessive if it does not.*

The above argument assumes that if a country denies access to some market, its trading partner suspends access to its own market that had been bargained for the former. But in reality, if a defendant refuses to abide by a DSB ruling, the complainant may *choose* which substantially equivalent concessions to withdraw. This gives the complainant the potential to maximize the political discomfort felt by the defendant. (In the steel case noted earlier, the EU had indicated that it would behave in such a way.) This is arguably the sole potentially punitive component of the DSP.

Consider from the perspective of Proposition 5 the hormone-fed beef case, widely regarded as a "failure" of the WTO system and as a threat to a "rules-based" international order for trade policy. An alternative interpretation might go as follows. "If governments thought that trade agreements would prevent them from responding to unforeseen deep political pressures, they would never sign on to those agreements in the first place. If they thought that such pressures would allow their trade partners to depart from reciprocity, they also would never sign on to such agreements. Under these circumstances, the experience of the hormone-fed beef case is probably the best feasible outcome, from the viewpoint of long term trade liberalization." Perdikis *et al.* (2001, p. 381) observe, "It has always been recognized that for the WTO to be politically acceptable there have to be provisions which allow governments to ignore their WTO commitments when domestic pressure for protection becomes politically unmanageable." In other words, violation of DSP decisions can be thought of as an *extra-legal* counterpart, applying to a residual of unforeseen circumstances, to various GATT provisions (e.g., Articles XXII and XXIII) allowing the *legal* withdrawal of concessions.

8. Concluding remarks

The Received Theory of international trade agreements, the result of half a century of research by international trade theorists, suffers from fundamental puzzles that call into question its very relevance to reality.

- This paper has utilized a simple formulation of the political economy of protection based directly on a trade-off between the income of special interests and consumer surplus. The model delivers the predictions that appear to be supported by the empirical evidence, but is free of the puzzles exhibited by the Received Theory.

- Neither government can unilaterally deliver anything to its export lobby, nor can sector-by-sector negotiations achieve anything. The two governments have an incentive to negotiate a trade agreement to exchange market access, and such an agreement would resolve the puzzles.
- Trade agreements are of necessity incomplete contracts because trade can be affected by all sorts of potential policies that countries can neither foresee nor be willing to negotiate about.
- The negotiated trade agreement will induce the defendant to violate the DSP and will deliver, *ex post*, the optimal degree of liberalization.
- This suggests a central role, in the process of multilateral trade liberalization, for an *implicit* agreement to allow countries to violate agreed commitments if the violation implies no retreat from reciprocity. It also provides an argument for the principle of *the equivalent withdrawal of concessions*, which has permeated the GATT from its very beginning.

The principle of the equivalent withdrawal of concessions – or of commensurate punishment – has a vital implication for negotiated trade liberalization. A trade agreement can, in the end, deliver liberalization no greater than that desired, *ex post*, by the more reluctant liberalizer.

References

Bagwell, K., Staiger, R.W. (1999), An economic theory of GATT. *American Economic Review* 89 (1), 215–248.

Bagwell, K., Staiger, R.W. (2002), *The Economics of the World Trading System*. The MIT Press, Cambridge, MA.

Bütler, M., Hauser, H. (2000), The WTO dispute settlement system: a first assessment from an economic perspective. *The Journal of Law, Economics, and Organization* 16 (2), 503–533.

Ethier, W.J. (2004), Political externalities, nondiscrimination, and a multilateral world. *Review of International Economics* 12 (3), 303–320.

Ethier, W.J. (2006a), Selling "protection for sale". *Asia-Pacific Journal of Accounting & Economics* 13 (2), 153–162.

Ethier, W.J. (2006b), Punishments and dispute settlement in trade agreements: the equivalent withdrawal of concessions. *Keio Economic Studies* 42 (1–2), 1–23.

Ethier, W.J. (2007), The theory of trade policy and trade agreements: a critique. *European Journal of Political Economy* 23 (3), 605–623.

Ethier, W.J. (2008), International trade agreements. In: Margit, S., and Yu, E.S.H. (Eds.), *Contemporary and Emerging Issues in Trade Theory and Policy*. Emerald, Bingley, UK, pp. 381–395.

Finger, J.M. (1988), Protectionist rules and internationalist discretion in the making of national trade policy. In: Vosgerau, H.-J. (Ed.), *New Institutional Arrangements for the World Economy*. Springer-Verlag, Heidelberg, pp. 310–323.

Finger, J.M. (1991), The GATT as an international discipline over trade restrictions. In: Vaubel, R., Willett, T.D. (Eds.), *The Political Economy of International Organizations*. Westview Press, Boulder, pp. 125–141.

Gawande, K., Bandyopadhyay, U. (2000), Is protection for sale? Evidence on the Grossman–Helpman theory of endogenous protection. *Review of Economics and Statistics* 82 (1), 139–152.

Goldberg, P.K., Maggi, G. (1999), Protection for sale: an empirical investigation. *American Economic Review* 84 (4), 1135–1155.

Grossman, G., Helpman, E. (1994), Protection for sale. *American Economic Review* 89 (5), 833–850.

Grossman, G., Helpman, E. (1995), Trade wars and trade talks. *Journal of Political Economy* 85 (4), 667–690.

Grossman, G., Helpman, E. (2002), *Interest Groups and Trade Policy*. Princeton University Press, Princeton.

Hauser, H. (1986), Domestic policy foundation and domestic policy function of international trade rules. *Aussenwirtschaft* 41, 171–184.

Hawkins, D., Simon, H. (1949), Some conditions of macroeconomic stability. *Econometrica* 17, 245–248.

Hillman, A.L. (1982), Declining industries and political-support protectionist motives. *American Economic Review* 72, 1180–1190.

Hillman, A.L. (1989), *The Political Economy of Protection*. Harwood Academic Publishers, Chur, Reprinted 2001, Routledge, London.

Hillman, A.L. (1990), Protectionist policies as the regulation of international industry. *Public Choice* 67, 101–110.

Hillman, A.L., Moser, P. (1996), Trade liberalization as politically optimal exchange of market access. In: Canzoneri, M., Ethier, W.J., Grilli, V. (Eds.), *The New Transatlantic Economy*. University Press, Cambridge, pp. 295–312.

Hillman, A.L., Long, N.V., Moser, P. (1995), Modeling reciprocal trade liberalization: the political-economy and national-welfare perspectives. *Swiss Journal of Economics and Statistics* 131, 503–515.

Johnson, H.G. (1953-54), Optimum tariffs and retaliation. *Review of Economic Studies* 21, 142–153.

Magee, S.P. (1994), Endogenous protection: a survey. In: Mueller, D.C. (Ed.), *Handbook of Public Choice*. Basil Blackwell, Cambridge, MA.

McCallum, P. (2004), Protection for sale and trade liberalization: an empirical investigation. *Review of International Economics* 12 (1), 81–94.

Mitra, D., Thomakos, D.D., Ulubaşoğlu, M.A. (2002), Protection for sale' in a developing country: democracy vs. dictatorship. *Review of Economics and Statistics,* 84 (3), 497–508.

Moser, P. (1990), *The Political Economy of the GATT*. Verlag Ruegger, Grüsch.

Nelson, D. (1988), Endogenous tariff theory: a critical survey. *American Journal of Political Science* 32, 796–837.

Olson, M. (1965), *The Logic of Collective Action*. Harvard University Press, Cambridge, MA.

Perdikis, N., Kerr, W.A., Hobbs, J.E. (2001), Reforming the WTO to defuse potential trade conflicts in genetically modified goods. *The World Economy* 24 (3), 379–398.

Regan, D.H. (2004), Why do we have trade agreements? And why does it matter? – A lawyer's view of some economic theory. University of Michigan (unpublished manuscript).

Rodrik, D. (1995), Political economy of trade policy. In: Grossman, G., Rogoff, K. (Eds.), *Handbook of International Economics*. North-Holland, Amsterdam, pp. 1457–1495.

CHAPTER 15

WTO DSU-Enforcement Issues

Joseph Pelzman[a] and Amir Shoham[b]

[a]*Department of Economics, The Elliott School of International Affairs, George Washington University, 2115 G Street NW, Washington, DC 20052, USA*
E-mail address: jpelz@gwu.edu
[b]*School of Business Administration, College of Management, Rishon LeZion 75190, Israel*
E-mail address: amirsho@bgu.ac.il

Abstract
The WTO dispute settlement process is an improvement to the original GATT dispute settlement mechanism. However, it fails to assure a timely implementation and enforcement of the dispute settlement body (DSB) recommendations. To this date, the issue of mandatory enforcement is still open to interpretation. The number of 'matters' that have been subject to WTO dispute settlement stands at 266 over the 1995–2006 period. The number of implementation disputes has increased since 1998 and stand at 34 as of January 1, 2007. This chapter reviews the process of dispute settlements and enforcements since 1995 and to argue for the interpretation of 'WTO agreements' as 'binding contracts' whose breach must be evaluated as either 'efficient' or 'non-efficient' when discussing enforcement. In this context the non-compliance issue may be viewed as an 'efficient breach' where the only efficient remedy is a 'fine' rather than the usual practice of 'suspension of concessions or other obligations' to the Respondent. What sets our approach apart from earlier discussion is that it does not view 'suspension of concessions' as a sufficiently burdensome and efficient sanction. A 'fine' on the other hand may serve as a 'buy out' of a Respondents WTO obligations, and can be transferred to the negatively affected domestic producers in the Complainant's market as compensation for losses.

Keywords: WTO, Dispute Settlement System or Understanding (DSU), GATT, enforcement issues, efficient contract, efficient breach, suspension of concessions or obligations, efficient 'fine' system

JEL classifications: F1, F13, K12, K33, K42

Frontiers of Economics and Globalization
Volume 6 ISSN: 1574-8715
DOI: 10.1108/S1574-8715(2009)0000006018

1. Introduction

The WTO Dispute Settlement System or Understanding (DSU) substantially improved the General Agreement on Tariffs and Trade (GATT) rules for settling disputes between members. However, compliance remains substantially an elective choice. Normally, if a measure is found to be in violation then the Respondent has a number of choices. The first best option from the perspective of the institution would have the Respondent abide by the decision of the WTO and come into compliance with the ruling by withdrawing the offending measure(s). The first best option from the perspective of the Respondent may be to continue to maintain the offending measure(s) and provide compensatory benefits to the Complainant. A third option that is more complicated and would involve sanctioned retaliation would have the Respondent continue the offending measure(s) and decline to provide compensation. This would induce WTO-sanctioned retaliation against its exports and have a negative reputation effect on the integrity of the WTO DSU process.

In theory, the WTO dispute settlement system is expected to ensure the implementation of the dispute settlement body (DSB) recommendations to maintain the balance of negotiated concessions and preserve the sanctity of the WTO agreements.[1] In reality, when trade issues rise above some critical threshold to a Respondent, the theory behind the DSU enforcement breaks down and the well-meaning legal system only leads to prolonging the dispute rather than resolving it. Consequently, there is a continuing discussion for greater empowerment and reform of the DSU. But as one would expect in an international body such as the WTO, there are a large number of suggested modifications and disagreements regarding how and to what extent the DSU should be rebuilt.[2]

Despite the fact that the prevailing paradigm is that the key improvement of the trading system from the GATT to the WTO is the nondiscretionary panel proceedings under the DSU, the issue of mandatory enforcement is still open to interpretation.[3] As of January 1, 2007, there have been 356 WTO complaints filed under the DSU. The number of 'matters' that have been subject to WTO dispute settlement stands

---

[1] The 'Member concerned' is the party to the dispute to which the DSB recommendations are directed. Understanding on Rules and Procedures Governing the Settlement of Disputes (DSU), Article 19.1. GATT Secretariat, the results of the Uruguay Round of multilateral trade negotiations, the legal texts (Geneva 1994), 404. See in particular DSU, Article 22.

[2] See WTO, 2004.

[3] See Alvarez, 2002, Antoniadis, 2007, Bello, 1996, Bourgeois, 2001, Brewster, 2006, Bronckers, 2001, Cameron and Gray, 2001, Carmody, 2006, Charnovitz, 2001, Charnovitz, 2004, Chayes and Chayes, 1995, Davey, 2005, Mavroidis, 2000, Mavroidis and Sykes, 2005, Pauwelyn, 1998, 2003a, 2003b, Peters, 2003, Petersmann, 1999, Schoenbaum *et al.*, 1998, Schoenbaum, 1998, Schowalter, 2004, Taniguchi *et al.*, 2007, Van Den Broek, 2003, Weiss, 2000, World Trade Organization, 2002, and Yerxa and Wilson, 2005.

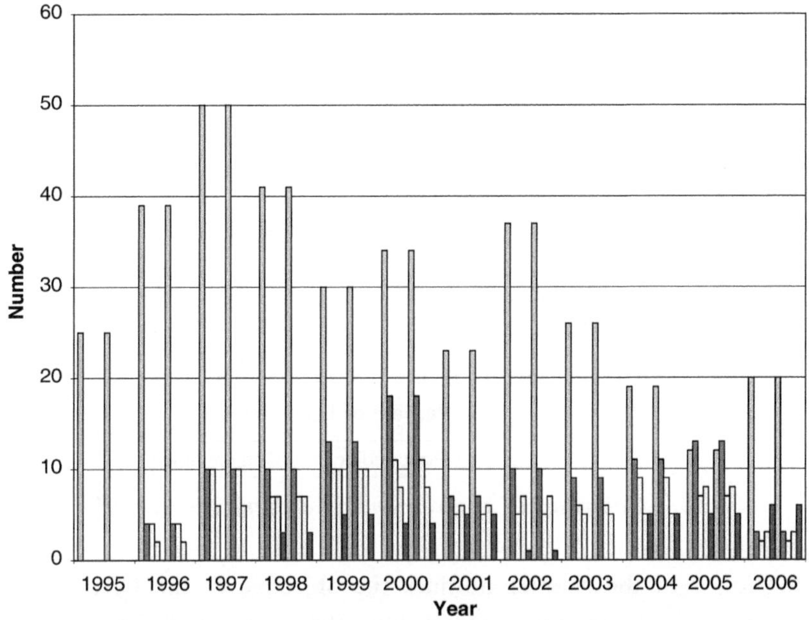

Fig. 1. WTO DSU process in numbers.

at 266 over the 1995–2006 period. The number of implementation disputes under DSU Article 21.5 has increased since 1998 and stands at 34 as of January 1, 2007. Despite the fact that the WTO DSU process is being implemented, the process breaks down when it has to assure implementation of WTO decisions, post appeal (Figures 1 and 2).[4]

The intent of this chapter is to review the process of dispute settlements and enforcements as dictated by the WTO DSU since 1995 and argue for the interpretation of 'WTO agreements' as 'binding contracts' whose breach must be evaluated as either 'efficient' or 'non-efficient' when discussing enforcement. In this context, the non-compliance issue may be viewed as an 'efficient breach' where the only efficient remedy is a 'fine' rather than the usual practice of 'suspension of concessions or other obligations' to the Respondent.[5]

---

[4] See Figures 1 and 2 which summarize the results through 2006. An annual statistical reporting of the WTO dispute settlement system is provided by Leitner and Lester, 2003, 2004, 2005, 2006 and 2007.

[5] See Schwartz and Sykes, 2002.

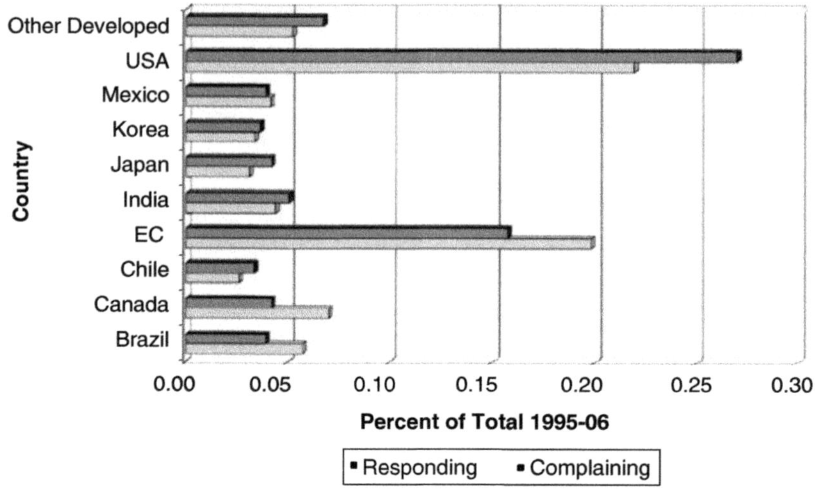

Fig. 2. ***Complaining and responding country concentration.***

Section 2 of the chapter outlines the objective of the DSU process. Section 3 discusses the mechanisms that are designed to ensure implementation along with a discussion of their strengths and weaknesses. Section 4 presents a review of a number of recent WTO cases where enforcement was the critical issue and a form of 'efficient breach' was established. We show that this breach always concludes with sanctioned retaliation by the Complainant without any modification of the DSU process ensuring enforcement. Consequently, the 'process' is maintained but the enforcement problem is shifted in time to the Complainant, raising the transaction costs of disputes. Section 5 presents a proposed solution to the enforcement problem. We propose an efficient 'fine' system that will result in compensation equivalent to the damage, despite the existence of breach. Under our suggested enforcement rules, it may be possible for a Respondent to continue to breach her obligations to the WTO contract while simultaneously compensating for damages created by the offending measure. The end result will be more efficient than the current system of diplomatic maneuvering designed to pressure the Respondent to remove or modify the offending measure.

2. *Objectives of the DSU*

The DSU contains rules and procedures whereby an aggrieved party can request consultations and commence a dispute proceeding if another Member's measures (the Respondent) are inconsistent with the WTO agreements. Article 3.2 of the DSU explicitly states the objective function underlying the WTO dispute settlement system. It states that 'the dispute settlement system of the WTO is a central element in providing security and predictability to the multilateral trading system.' Furthermore, Article 3.3 of the DSU, states that WTO Members recognized the importance of 'the prompt settlement of situations in which a Member considers that any benefits accruing to it directly or indirectly under the covered agreements are being impaired by measures taken by another Member is essential to the effective functioning of the WTO.' Article 3.7 provides that 'the aim of the dispute settlement mechanism is to secure a positive solution to a dispute.' It further adds, 'a solution mutually acceptable to the parties to a dispute and consistent with the covered agreements is clearly to be preferred.'

Figure 3 provides a schematic of the DSU process and time line. There are a number of unique elements contained in the DSU process. First, there is a strict time limit for every stage of the dispute settlement process; second, a supervisory subgroup of the WTO, DSB, was created to oversee the operation of the DSU; third, explicit procedures for consultations were established; fourth, panels can be established automatically if the parties fail to settle the dispute within 60 days of consultations; fifth, panel and Appellate Body reports are automatically adopted unless there is a consensus to the contrary by the DSB; sixth, the Appellate Body, while not an Appeals Court, was created to review legal issues and interpretations of panel reports; seventh, there is a presumption that the losing respondent is

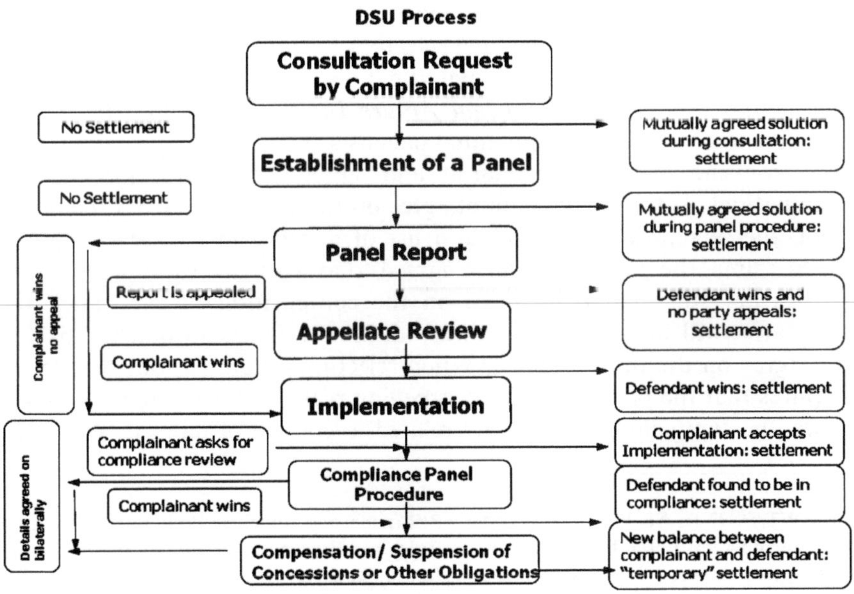

Fig. 3. ***DSU process. Source: Zimmermann, WTO dispute settlement at ten.***

required, in a reasonable period of time (RPT), to implement the DSB recommendations. Baring that, the Complainant is entitled to request permission to retaliate. Members are expected to abide by the rules and procedures of the DSU on issues pertaining to the WTO agreements and are not permitted to take unilateral retaliatory actions. Typically, a case that goes through the Appeals process may take 18 months to complete. Enforcement, however, may take years. Consequently, the present value of economic losses associated with a dispute that proceeds to the end is enormous.

The first stage of the dispute settlement process starts with consultations pursuant to Article 4 of the DSU. Article 4.2 states that each Member is to 'afford adequate opportunity for consultation.' Under Article 4.3, a Member is to reply within 10 days and 'enter into consultations in good faith' within 30 days after the receipt of the request for consultations. The panel in *Korean Liquor Taxes* stated that the 'conduct of consultations is not the concern of a panel but that the panel need only concern itself with the question whether consultations took place ... The only requirement under the DSU is that consultations were in fact held ... and that a period of 60 days has elapsed.'[6]

If consultations fail to settle the dispute within 60 days following the receipt of request for consultations, the complaining party can make a request for the establishment of a panel. The Respondent can block the creation of a panel once. However, when the DSB meets for a second time, the appointment can no longer be blocked.

Once a panel is established, panelists must be selected within 20 days. If one were to compare this panel selection to 'jury selection' or selection of a panel of judges as in a US civil litigation, one would be disappointed. The actual process has the *Legal Affairs Division* providing the parties with five to seven names of potential panelists. The disputing parties would then convene with the secretariat and either accept or reject various nominations. If the parties cannot agree on three panelists from the initial pool, the secretariat will provide a list of another five to seven names. By this time, the parties will have agreed to at least two candidates. If the parties are still unable to agree on the composition of the panel, the secretariat will provide two to three additional names so that the parties can agree on the third panelist. When rejecting a nomination, Article 8.6 requires that the party provide 'compelling reasons' for doing so. In most cases 'the compelling reasons' are related to conflict of interest. When the

---

[6] See WT/DS27/R, AB-1997-3, WT/DS69/AB/R (panel and Appellate Body Reports adopted on September 25, 1997); Understanding on Rules and Procedures Governing the Settlement of Disputes, Article 4.2; and *Korean Liquor Taxes*, Panel Report. It would be correct to view the consultation stage as the 'discovery' stage in US civil litigation. But that flies in contradiction to Article 4.6 of the DSU, which states 'consultations shall be without prejudice to the rights of any Member in any further proceeding.'

parties cannot agree on the composition of a panel within 20 days, the Director General is to determine the composition of the panel.[7]

Once the panelists have been appointed, the issue shifts to the timing of the first written submission. The Respondent is given only three to four weeks to prepare and submit its written submission. In contrast, the Complainant(s) usually have had a much longer time to prepare their written submission. Under the WTO jurisprudence, the Complainant must present evidence to prove that fact.[8] Once the Complainant establishes a fact, the Respondent must rebut that presumption with its own evidence and argument. The DSU does not impose a strict time limit on when evidence must be submitted to a panel and the Working Procedures of Appendix 3 of the DSU does not provide compulsory deadlines with which a panel must comply.

Apart from the specific complaints concerning Respondent behavior, any and all violations of a WTO commitment may according to Article XXIII:1 of the GATT 1994, be construed as a 'nullification or impairment' of a Member's rights. In fact, despite the language of Article 3.7 of the DSU requesting the exercise of judgment, Members file the charge of 'nullification or impairment' as if it was a catchall complaint.[9]

With respect to a Complainant's 'standing,' in EC – Bananas III,[10] the European Communities (EC) claimed that the Complainant, the United States, did not have a legal interest in its claims since the United States had only a token production of bananas and did not (and could not within the foreseeable future) export bananas to the EC. Therefore, the EC requested the panel not to rule on the claims made by the United States. The panel and the Appellate Body rejected the EC's request. In particular, the Appellate Body stated that a Member is not required to show legal interest to bring a matter before a panel. However, the Appellate Body held that 'a general rule that in all international litigation, a (Complainant) must have a 'legal interest' in order to bring a case' was not applicable to the WTO dispute settlement system. Furthermore, it stated that in the WTO dispute settlement system, a complaint might be admissible before a panel without proving a Complainant's legal interest as long as the Complainant 'considers' in good faith that its benefits under the WTO Agreements are being 'nullified or impaired' and that a recourse to the procedures under the DSU 'would be fruitful.'[11] In fact, Article 3.8 of the DSU merely

[7] There are cases where the parties cannot agree and the Secretariat had to appoint a Panel. This was the case in the *Korean Liquor Taxes* case and *United States – Anti-dumping Duty on Dynamic Random Access Memory Semiconductors (DRAMS) of one Megabit or above from Korea.*

[8] United States – Measures Affecting Imports of Woven Wool Shirts and Blouses from India, AB-1997-1, WT/DS33/AB/R (Panel and Appellate Body Report adopted on May 23, 1997), at 13–14.

[9] GATT 1994, Article XXIII:1. See also DSU, Article 3.3.

[10] See WTO (1997).

[11] GATT 1994, Article XXIII:1; DSU, Articles 3.3 and 3.7. Appellate Body Report, EC – Bananas III. See also Martha (2001).

confirms that every infringement of WTO obligations presumably entails the nullification or impairment of the benefits of another Member or Members. In fact, one cannot separate the obligation of the WTO Agreements and the benefits of the Members. An infringement of these obligations almost inevitably 'nullifies or impairs' the benefits.

Perhaps the most important aspect of the WTO dispute settlement process is the right to appeal to the Appellate Body. Parties to the dispute, not third parties, may appeal to the Appellate Body on issues pertaining to law and legal interpretations.[12] If there is no appeal within 60 days after the circulation of a panel report, the panel report is to be adopted by the DSB.[13] If a case is appealed the Appellate Body may uphold, modify or reverse the panel's findings, but it cannot remand the matter for further consideration to the original panel. In that sense it differs from normal US civil appeal processes.[14]

What are the implications for enforcement or 'bindingness' nature of the DSB recommendations? It is widely acknowledged that the Member concerned whose measures have been found to be in violation of the WTO Agreements is 'bound' or bears a 'legal obligation' to implement the DSB recommendations.[15] Nevertheless, persistent skepticism exists with regard to the 'bindingness' of the DSB recommendations.

3. Mechanisms to ensure implementation of the DSU recommendations

The question of 'bindingness' of the DSB recommendations can be addressed by focusing on the second sentence of Article 19.1 of the DSU that provides that a 'panel or (the) Appellate Body may suggest ways in which the Member concerned could implement' the DSB recommendations. Should this be interpreted as 'binding?' As of the end of 2005,[16] the panels have made suggestions in only 10 cases and, occasionally, they have

[12] DSU, Article 17.4.

[13] DSU, Article 16.4.

[14] An appeal begins by filing a Notice of Appeal with the Appellate Body Secretariat and providing a written notification to the DSB. Ten days after filing the Notice of Appeal, the appellant must submit its written submission to the Appellate Body and also must provide a copy to the other parties to the dispute and third parties. [Appellate Body Rule XXI.] The Appellee wishing to respond to the allegations raised in the appellant's written submission must provide its response no later than 25 days after the filing of the notice of appeal. [Appellate Body Rule XXII(1)]. A typical Appellee will therefore have access to appellant's documents for 15 days.

[15] Despite the fact that the text of the DSU is unclear about the 'bindingness' of the DSB recommendations, it has been argued that Articles 3.7, 21.1, 22.1, and 26.1 shows a clear preference for compliance with the recommendations. See Jackson (1997), Jackson (2004), Lowenfeld (2002), Hudec (2000), Sykes (2000).

[16] See WorldTradeLaw.net, 'WTO Case Law Index,' available at http://www.worldtradelaw.net/dsc/wtoindex.htm

rejected an explicit request made by the complaining party to make a suggestion under Article 19.1. To date, the Appellate Body has not made a suggestion under Article 19.1 in any case. This outcome is troubling given that the Complainant occasionally specifies a certain way to implement the DSB recommendations and requests that a panel suggest the specified way as one of the implementation options.[17] If the DSU process were supposed to mirror a judicial process then it would be unreasonable to expect the DSB to take a Complainant's recommendations and assess the appropriate implementation options.

This confusion over the 'bindingness' of the DSB recommendations highlights a more disturbing confusion about the objective of the DSU. Within the dispute system of the WTO there are apparently two conflicting objectives. One is the objective of 'compliance' while the second is the 'settlement of a dispute.' One could argue that the latter is concerned with the integrity of the trading system while the former is concerned with a narrower 'balancing' standard. The DSU states that a 'solution mutually acceptable to the parties ... is clearly to be preferred,' and goes on to say 'in the absence of a mutually agreed solution, the first objective of the dispute settlement mechanism is *usually* to secure the withdrawal of the measures concerned if these are found to be inconsistent with the provisions of any of the covered agreements.'[18]

If one or the other of these objectives is not met, the Complainant can start the process to provide for 'compensation' by the Respondent or to 'suspend WTO concessions or other WTO obligations on a discriminatory basis.' Both responses have both country-specific ramifications as well as generally negative 'system specific' outcomes. Consequently, the DSU describes the first action as a 'temporary' measure while the second action as the 'last resort.'[19]

The obvious questions are how one gets to this 'last resort' and how many complaints reach that 'wall of non-compliance.'[20] The first step in the diplomatic process is for the Complainant to secure a judgment[21] from the WTO (panel or Appellate Body) that the Respondent is maintaining measures inconsistent with its WTO obligations. The resulting report is customarily adopted by the WTO DSB. In line with Article 21.3, the Respondent gets a RPT for implementation. Is this action merely one of

[17] See WTO (2005).

[18] DSU, Article 3.7.

[19] DSU, Article 3.7 noting that the first step is a 'temporary measure pending the withdrawal of the ... measure.' See Charnovitz, 2002, who has effectively popularized this 'last resort' terminology.

[20] See Pauwelyn (2000, p. 338).

[21] In US civil litigation, the 'judgment' is requested as part of the initial litigation, not as a separate procedure with the requisite time delays.

precluding the inevitable? What of the economic losses incurred by the Complainant's private sector, once the discussion shifts to a RPT?

The DSB is quite clear in its expectation that 'members concerned shall implement the DSB recommendations *immediately* after the adoption of a panel or Appellate Body report.'[22] However, if this is *impractical*,[23] the Respondent is entitled to a RPT that is determined through either a proposal made by the Respondent and approved by the DSB or a mutual agreement between the parties. Otherwise, the parties may request an arbitrator to determine the RPT pursuant to Article 21.3(c) of the DSU. The RPT should not exceed 15 months from the date of adoption of the panel or Appellate Body report; however, the RPT may be shorter or longer, depending on the particular circumstances of a case. Under Article 21.3(c), this arbitration is expected to ensure that the time period for implementation is not prolonged unnecessarily.

To date, 21 awards have been made under Article 21.3(c).[24] These award ranges from 6 months to 15 months, and the average RPT is approximately 11.82 months, which is only about two-and-a-half months longer than that determined by an agreement between the parties pursuant to Article 21.3(b) of the DSU.[25] In most cases, the arbitration under Article 21.3(c) functioned effectively and provided prompt implementation of the DSB recommendations. Article 21.3 represents the diplomatic approach to the DSU. It does not take into account the economic costs to the Complainant's private sector caused by delayed removal of the offending measures. If one views the DSU process as a diplomatic process to resolve disputes than the 'value of time' is irrelevant.[26]

How does one determine if the Respondent is in fact implementing the required corrective steps? Does the Complainant have to provide compelling evidence? Or does the Respondent provide periodic implementation reports? Article 21.6 of the DSU provides that '[t]he DSB shall keep under surveillance the implementation of adopted recommendations.' Under this provision, any Member may raise the issue of implementation at a DSB meeting at any time following the adoption of the recommendations. The issue of implementation shall be placed on the agenda of the DSB meetings until it is resolved. The Respondent shall provide the DSB with a status report of its progress. In effect, Article 21.6 attempts, in theory, to improve the transparency of the implementation measures.

---

[22] DSU, Article 21.3(a) and (b).

[23] This term is not well defined.

[24] WorldTradeLaw.net, 'List of all Article 21.3(c) "Reasonable Period of Time" Arbitration Awards,' available at http://www.worldtradelaw.net/dsc/database/rptawards.asp

[25] See WTO (2000, 1998); and WorldTradeLaw.net, 'Average Implementation Time Periods (in months),' available at http://www.worldtradelaw.net/dsc/database/implementaverage.asp.

[26] WorldTradeLaw.net, 'Implementation Period: Provisions Used,' available at http://www.worldtradelaw.net/dsc/database/implementationprovision.asp

In reality, it succeeds to a relatively limited degree. The interesting question is who should bare the responsibility for compliance monitoring the institution itself (DSB) or the Complainant?

In the event that the Respondent has not taken any reasonable steps toward compliance, the DSU process adds a further time-consuming loop. The Complainant in this case is entitled to initiate an 'Article 21.5' expedited panel and Appellate Body review process.[27] The system defaults and leaves the process of surveillance in the hands of the Complainant who is assumed to have a strong economic interest in strict performance. Thus, the Complainant's private sector whose benefits are 'nullified or impaired' by the violating measures plays the primary role in monitoring whether the Respondent has brought its measures into conformity with the WTO Agreements through the appropriate implementation of the DSB recommendations. To date, 29 cases have had recourses to Article 21.5.[28]

Under the current accepted practice in the WTO, the measures of a Member are presumed to be in conformity with the WTO Agreements until they are found otherwise in the DSU. The same applies to the implementation measures, i.e., the implementation measures taken by the Member concerned in good faith are presumed to be in conformity with the DSB recommendations and the WTO Agreements. Under this set of acceptable presumptions, any allegations of non-compliance and non-implementation of the DSB recommendations, requires that the complaining party shall first have recourse to the Article 21.5 review. In effect, this puts a stop to a Complainant's attempt to seek authorization for suspension until the procedures under Article 21.5 are complete.[29]

In the event that these recommendations and rulings are not implemented within a reasonable period of time, the diplomatic process has a few more time-consuming steps. Although the language of DSU Article 22.1 is quite clear in providing that '[c]ompensation and the suspension of concessions or other obligations are available (temporarily).' The Respondent at this point shall first, if so requested, 'enter into negotiations with any party having

---

[27] Article 21.5 provides that the panel shall circulate its report within 90 days after the date of referral; however this time limit is not rigorously followed. The time period given to an Article 21.5 panel is approximately a half of what is given to the original panel under Article 12.8. The text of Article 21.5 of the DSU is not clear on whether the Appellate Body may review the 'disagreement' regarding the implementation; however, in practice, the Appellate Body accepts an appeal to the findings made by a panel under Article 21.5. See also Kearns and Charnovitz (2002) and Charnovitz (2002).

[28] See WorldTradeLaw.net, 'List of all WTO complaints brought pursuant to DSU Article 21.5,' available at http://www.worldtradelaw.net/dsc/database/searchcomplaintscompliance.asp. Nineteen matters have been referred to Article 21.5.

[29] In United States – Import Measures on Certain Products from the European Communities, Report of the Appellate Body, WT/DS165/AB/R, ¶¶ 126–127 the WTO Appellate Body held that an Article 21.5 panel determination is a prerequisite to undertaking a suspension of concessions. (December 11, 2000).

invoked the dispute settlement procedures, with a view to developing mutually acceptable compensation.' Only, if the negotiations on compensation fail, the Complainant 'may request authorization from the DSB to suspend the application to the Member concerned of concessions or other obligations under the covered agreements.' According to Article 22.4 of the DSU, '[t]he level of the suspension ... shall be equivalent to the level of the nullification or impairment.' If the Respondent objects to the level of the suspension requested or to procedural errors in the request, the matter shall be referred to arbitration under Article 22.6 of the DSU. Only after this arbitration, shall the Complainant receive authorization from the DSB to 'suspend concessions or other obligations' within this 'balancing' paradigm. The concept of rebalancing of benefits, an approach incorporated as early as the GATT 1947, is central to the issue of 'compensation and suspension of concessions or other obligations.'

Given the high profile that Article 22.6 panel attract in the literature it is surprising that a very small number of disputes get to this 'last resort.' Despite the limited number of 'last resort' cases, these cases have received brand-name recognition in the popular press and the political arena. They include the two Banana cases (US and Ecuador complaints against the EC), the two Hormones cases (Canada and US complaints against the EC), the Export Financing for Aircraft case (Canada's complaint against Brazil), and the Foreign Sales Corporations case (the EC's complaint against the United States. In two less well-known cases, the parties agreed on tariff reductions as compensation,[30] while in the other case, monetary compensation was agreed upon.[31] The incredibly small number of compensation actions can be interpreted as the Complainant's willingness to accept suspension as the preferred instrument rather than a monetary fine.[32] The question of preferred response has sparked a boom in the reform literature beyond the Sutherland Report.[33] To choose among these responses one needs to determine which of the recommended measures lead to the minimum trade distortions.

Under the current DSU the Respondent must choose a set of tariff items where the tariff reductions would result in a 'balanced' compensation. By relying on the Respondent to choose products where she is to obtain an agreement on compensation, one removes the Complainant from any meaningful choice as to the items chosen and means to enforce

---

[30] Japan – Alcoholic Beverages II, Dispute Settlement Body, Minutes of Meeting, WT/DSB/M/41, February 26, 1998, at 2; Turkey – Textiles, Dispute Settlement Body, Minutes of Meeting, WT/DSB/M/116, January 31, 2002, at 20.

[31] United States – Section 110(5) of US Copyright Act (US – Section 110(5)), Notification of a Mutually Satisfactory Temporary Agreement, WT/DS160/23, June 26, 2003.

[32] Anderson (2002), believes that this choice of remedy reflects a deterrence value.

[33] See, The LDC Group (2002), Pauwelyn (2000), Rosas (2001), Bronckers and Van Den Broek (2005).

the compensation. In effect, we are at the same point as before in the implementation stage of relying on voluntary payment by the Respondent. Furthermore, this compensation could serve as an excuse for the absence of proper implementation of the DSB recommendation. This may be the real outcome despite the language of Article 22.1 of the DSU, which clearly states that 'compensation is a temporary measure,' and the parties need to continue interactions to seek the implementation of the DSB recommendations while agreeing on compensation that compensates for the loss incurred until the implementation is achieved.

As an alternative, one can imagine a system where compensation can take the form of monetary compensation. Thus, the Respondent may find it relatively easier to agree on monetary compensation rather than on changes in border measures. The Complainant may be able to simply distribute the monetary compensation to economic actors that are actually injured by the violating measures or to invest the money in a governmental project to rebuild the injured industry.[34] Monetary compensation would not lead to any trade distortions as compared to tariff concessions.

To date the number of 'suspension of concessions or other obligations' stood at 27 cases and of those 15 were authorized. The arbitrators under the authority of Article 22.6 have provided 16 awards.[35] Does the existence of this 'last resort' of 'suspension of concessions or other obligations,' induce the implementation of the DSB recommendations by the Respondent? The evidence, to date, suggests that this is not the case. The world's largest economies with the largest stake in the trading system as such and the WTO rules in particular, are the United States and the EC, and they have the worst record with regard to the implementation of the DSB recommendations.[36]

In part, this may be explained by the perception that the final 'compensation' can never rise to the threshold initial economic harm and the further economic losses incurred during the institutional time path mandated by the DSU process.[37] In theory, the level of countermeasures shall be equivalent to the level of 'nullification or impairment of benefits caused by violating measures.' The arbitrators under Article 22.6 have consistently maintained that the term 'equivalent' connotes a 'correspondence, identity or balance' between the two levels.[38] Based on this understanding, the arbitrators calculate the level of 'nullification or impairment' by comparing the trade value in an actual WTO-inconsistent situation with the trade value that would be expected under a WTO-consistent

---

[34] See O'Connor and Djordjevic (2005).

[35] See WorldTradeLaw.net, available at http://www.worldtradelaw.net/dsc/database/retaliationrequests.asp. and www.worldtradelaw.net/dsc/database/suspensionawards.asp

[36] See Bronckers and Van den Broek (2005).

[37] This is similar to the complaints one finds in US civil litigation where a judgment is viewed as meaningless paper if it is not enforceable with limited delay.

[38] See Article 22.6 Arbitrators' Award (US), EC – Bananas III, ¶¶ 4.1, 6.5.

'counterfactual' situation, and then require the level of countermeasures to be identical to the calculated level of nullification or impairment.

4. Recent WTO decisions dealing with enforcement – the process of burden shifting

As we have demonstrated in the discussion earlier, implementing the final DSU Appellate report is the most challenging and important aspect of the entire WTO dispute settlement system. The report itself, along with all appeals and maneuvering have no value unless offending practice is removed. The very objective of attaining 'security and predictability' of the entire WTO legal system depends on the compliance and enforcement of these reports. In theory, the DSU provides a rule-based, time-bound procedure, which is enumerated in Articles 21 and 22 of the DSU. In theory, the most important achievement of the compliance and enforcement procedure is that it should provide an automatic remedy of 'suspension of concession' in case of non-compliance, and the determination of whether there is non-compliance and the amount of retaliation is to be made by WTO panel, rather than the Complainant unilaterally.

In reality, the diplomatic maneuvering makes compliance an uncertain event. The evidence to date clearly demonstrates that the issue of enforcement begins with the question of the value of time and lost economic resources suffered by the private sector of the Complainant. The WTO DSU process ignores this question of the 'value of time' and 'opportunity costs' of non-compliance preferring instead to focus on the *length* of the RPT based on the determination of the criteria of 'peculiar circumstances' for granting longer RPT, and only then on what is required of a Respondent while the reasonable period is underway. Should there be a fine imposed, a cessation of concessions or other sanctioned retaliation instruments? Despite the potpourri of suggested reforms by a wide group of Members, none appear to have been taken seriously.[39]

Article 21.6 of the DSU provides for the reporting on the status of implementation of the recommendations and rulings of the DSB at each DSB meeting. This paragraph has been divided into three subparagraphs.[40] The new subparagraph (b) of Article 21.6 states that the Respondent 'shall start to report from the *midpoint of the length of the reasonable period of time* or 6 months after the date of adoption of the recommendations and rulings of the DSB, whichever is earlier.'

---

[39] See Bolivia, Canada, Chile, Colombia, Costa Rica, Ecuador, Japan, Korea, New Zealand, Norway, Peru, Switzerland, Uruguay, and Venezuela (WT/MIN(01)/W/6).

[40] No change has been made in the first two sentences of the article 21.6, which forms the subparagraph (a) which reads 'The DSB shall keep under surveillance the implementation of adopted recommendations or rulings. The issue of implementation of the recommendations or rulings may be raised at the DSB by any Member at any time following their adoption.'

This change was made to accommodate the situation where the reasonable period of time is less than six month. The new subparagraph (c) provides for written notifications that need to be submitted to the DSB, as regards the implementation measures taken by a Respondent.

Under the WTO DSU, the members are left with two possible procedural recourses if the Respondent fails to comply fully. This procedural recourse is provided in Articles 21.5 and 22 of the DSU. But the DSU fails to specify the relationship between the two procedures. The procedure set forth in Article 21.5 provides that if there is disagreement with respect to the measures taken to comply with the recommendations and rulings, such disputes shall be decided 'through recourse to these dispute settlement procedures' as provided under the DSU.[41] However, the second procedure set forth in Article 22 provides that if the Respondent has neither implemented the WTO ruling within the compliance period nor negotiated mutually accepted compensation within 20 days after the reasonable period expires, the DSB, upon request, shall grant authorization to suspend concessions or other obligations.[42] This so-called 'sequencing problem' was brought out in the EC – Banana case.[43] In this case, the EC (the offending Respondent) argued that Article 21.5 compliance review should be resorted to *before* requesting the DSB for suspension of concessions as per Article 22. However, the United States (the winning Complainant) countered that it can request authorization to suspend concessions within 20 days after the end of the compliance period, without resorting to Article 21.5 compliance review.

Disputes over the implementation of panel and Appellate Body decisions continues to be a primary part of the DSB agenda, with parties challenging the time period or method of implementation (or lack thereof) in a number of key disputes.

In late 2004, the Complainants in the US Continued Dumping and Subsidy Offset Act of 2000 (the Byrd Amendment) dispute – Brazil, Canada, Chile, the EC, India, Japan, Korea, and Mexico – were authorized to suspend concessions against the United States for its failure to implement the decision of the Appellate Body.[44] While several bills were

---

[41] See Article 21.5, DSU.

[42] See Article 22.2, DSU.

[43] See WT/DS27.

[44] Decision by the Arbitrator, United States–Continued Dumping and Subsidy Offset Act of 2000, WT/DS234/ARB/CAN (Aug. 31, 2004). In accordance with the Byrd Amendment, the United States redistributes antidumping and countervailing duties to US producers who meet certain criteria. The distributions under the Byrd Amendment amount to hundreds of millions of dollars each year, and the current countervailing duties being held in the US treasury for ultimate distribution in the lumber case alone total more than $5 billion. WTO Panels and the Appellate Body ruled that these disbursements are in violation of the WTO Agreements. See Panel Report, WT/DS294/R, supra note 82; Appellate Body Report, United States–Final Dumping Determination on Softwood Lumber from Canada, WT/DS264/AB/R (Aug. 11, 2004).

presented to Congress that would repeal the Byrd Amendment, Congress failed to repeal the legislation by the end of 2005. Consequently, in early 2005, Canada, the EU, Mexico, and Japan began retaliating against the United States by imposing taxes on imports of a variety of US goods, including live swine, cigarettes, paper, agricultural products, textiles, machinery, oysters, and fish products.[45] On February 1, 2006, Congress passed legislation to repeal the Byrd Amendment.[46] However, the repeal did not take effect until October 1, 2007. As a result, the EU trade commissioner responded with 'regret' that the United States has chosen to include a transition period rather than ending the payments immediately.[47] The retaliation continued until the legislation was repealed.

In October 2004, the United States enacted the American Jobs Creation Act of 2004 that repealed both the Extraterritorial Income Exclusion and its predecessor, the Foreign Sales Corporation provision; two laws that had been deemed *de facto* export subsidies to US exporters.[48] As a result, on January 1, 2005, the EC lifted tariffs but then sought consultations on whether the new law complied with the prior decisions and threatened to re-impose the tariffs if a panel agreed that the new law was insufficient. On September 30, 2005, the panel in the second proceeding, US Tax Treatment for 'Foreign Sales Corporations,' determined that new US law continued to violate the Agreement on Subsidies and Countervailing Measures (SCM) and Agriculture Agreements, given that the new law maintained the same inconsistent subsidy programs through a grandfathering clause.[49] The panel reauthorized the EC to impose retaliatory tariffs.

In 2003 a WTO panel and the Appellate Body determined that restrictions imposed by Japan to prevent disease (fire blight) in domestic apples were inconsistent with the Agreement on the Application of Sanitary and Phytosanitary Measures (SPS Agreement).[50] In response,

---

[45] See International Trade Canada, Canada's Retaliation Notification to the WTO, (April 29, 2005), available at http://www.dfait-maeci.gc.ca/tna-nac/disp/byrd-lettre-en.asp; European Commission, US Byrd Amendment: Commission Proposes Sanctions on US Products (March 31, 2005), available at http://europa.eu.int/comm/trade/issues/respectrules/dispute/pr310305_en.htm

[46] Press Release, Office of the US Trade Representative, Congress Takes Important Action: Byrd Repeal Brings US Into Compliance with WTO Ruling (Febraury 1, 2006), available at http://www.ustr.gov/Document_Library/Press_Releases/2006/February/Congress_Takes_Important_Action.html

[47] Press Release, European Commission, EU Welcomes Repeal of Byrd Amendment; Regrets Transition Period (Febraury 2, 2006), available at http://europa.eu.int/rapid/pressReleasesAction.

[48] See Appellate Body Report, United States–Tax Treatment for 'Foreign Sales Corporations,' WT/DS108/AB/R (February 24, 2000).

[49] See Panel Report, United States–Tax Treatment for 'Foreign Sales Corporations,' WT/DS108/RW2 (September 30, 2005).

[50] Appellate Body Report, Japan–Measures Affecting the Importation of Apples, WT/DS245/AB/R (November 26, 2003); Panel Report, Japan–Measures Affecting the Importation of Apples, WT/DS245/R (July 15, 2003).

Japan made certain modifications to its restrictions, including the lifting of certain import prohibitions if the imports met specified criteria. The United States then sought recourse to the DSB, complaining that the new measures continued to violate the SPS Agreement and requesting authorization to impose retaliatory measures in the amount of US$143.4 million annually.[51] On June 23, 2005, the panel issued its report in Japan – measures affecting the importation of apples, agreeing with the United States that Japan's measures continued to violate the Agreement because they were 'not supported by sufficient scientific evidence,'[52] and they were 'more trade-restrictive than required to achieve Japan's appropriate level of phytosanitary protection.'[53] On August 30, 2005, Japan and the United States notified the WTO of a mutually agreed solution in which Japan had amended its legislation, as of August 25, 2005, to bring it into compliance with the SPS Agreement.[54]

On January 31, 2005, the EC notified the WTO of a proposed new bound tariff for most-favored nation (MFN) countries that would take effect January 1, 2006, while maintaining an existing preference for African, Caribbean, and Pacific (ACP) countries.[55] Several countries in Latin America contested the new tariff rate, complaining that the new bound rates would disadvantage MFN countries by giving increased market access to the ACP countries (and consequently decreased market access for MFN countries).[56] The arbitrator agreed, noting that the new bound tariff system 'would not result in at least maintaining total market

---

[51] See Request for the Establishment of a Panel, Japan–Measures Affecting the Importation of Apples, WT/DS245/11 (July 20, 2004); Recourse to Article 22.2 of the DSU by the United States, Japan – Measures Affecting the Importation of Apples, WT/DS245/12 (July 20, 2004).

[52] Panel Report, Japan–Measures Affecting the Importation of Apples, ¶8.120 WT/DS245/RW (June 23, 2005); see also Recourse to Article 22.2 of the DSU by the United States, WT/DS245/12., Ibid.

[53] Panel Report, WT/DS245/RW, Ibid., ¶ 9.1(c).

[54] Notification of Mutually Agreed Solution, Japan–Measures Affecting the Importation of Apples, WT/DS245/21 (September 2, 2005).

[55] As part of the Doha Ministerial conference in November 2001, WTO members negotiated a waiver (commonly referred to as the Doha Waiver) that allows the EU to give preferential market access to banana exports from ACP countries, with the caveat that third parties, such as countries in Latin and Central America, would have the right to request consultations or arbitration should the EU modify its tariff quota system. See International Centre for Trade and Sustainable Development, WTO Arbitrator Rules Against New EU Tariff Rates for Bananas, Bridges Weekly Trade News Digest (August 3, 2005), available at http://www.ictsd.org/weekly/05-08-03/BridgesWeekly9-28.pdf. The requests for arbitration in this case were made under this Doha Waiver. See Award of the Arbitrator, European Communities–The ACP-EC Partnership Agreement–Recourse to the Arbitration Pursuant to the Decision of 14 November 2001, WT/L/616 (August 1, 2005); Award of the Arbitrator, European Communities–The ACP-EC Partnership Agreement – Second Recourse to the Arbitration Pursuant to the Decision of 14 November 2001, WT/L/625 (October 27, 2005).

[56] See Award of the Arbitrator, WT/L/616ibid.; Award of the Arbitrator, WT/L/625 ibid.

access for MFN banana suppliers' as is required under the ACP–EC Partnership Agreement.[57]

In response to the arbitrator's award, the EC further modified its tariff proposal by lowering the new bound rate for MFN countries.[58] At the same time, however, the EC raised the available quota for ACP countries. This outcome was unacceptable to the complaining Members and on September 26, 2005, the EC requested further arbitration over the matter.[59] In its second decision, the arbitrator determined that the EC failed to rectify the matter because MFN banana suppliers would continue to receive diminished market access under the new proposal.[60]

The US softwood lumber cases led to a number of WTO disputes over implementation in 2005. In the United States, Final Countervailing Duty Determination with Respect to Softwood Lumber from Canada, Recourse by Canada to Article 21.5 of the DSU, Canada challenged US implementation of the Panel and Appellate Body rulings, asserting that the United States failed to conduct a proper pass-through analysis because, although it performed a limited analysis with regard to some transactions, it failed to determine if a pass-through of benefit actually occurred with regard to a majority of transactions between unrelated parties.[61] The Panel agreed with Canada, and on December 5, 2005, the Appellate Body upheld the Panel's decision.[62]

Canada not only challenged the US failure to comply with regard to its §129 re-determination in the original investigation but also charged that the US pass-through methodology as applied in the first administrative review resulted in a failure to comply with the DSB ruling. The panel agreed, determining that both the §129 determination and the administrative review results amounted to a failure to properly implement the rulings of the DSB. In response to the failed implementation, Canada requested authorization from the DSB to retaliate in the amount of C$200 million annually. In a separate article 21.5 dispute involving the US lumber injury determination, the US-Investigation of the International Trade Commission in Softwood Lumber from Canada, an arbitration panel affirmed the US §129 implementation determination, finding that the United States' renewed finding of threat of injury was not inconsistent with the antidumping (AD) Agreement.[63] As a result, the WTO

---

[57] Award of the Arbitrator, WT/L/616, Ibid., ¶ 94.

[58] See Notification by the European Communities, Eurpoean Communities–The ACP-EC Partnership Agreement (September 13, 2005); Award of the Arbitrator, WT/L/625, op. cit.

[59] Award of the Arbitrator, WT/L/625, op. cit.

[60] Ibid. ¶ 127.

[61] See Appellate Body Report, United States–Final Countervailing Duty Determination with Respect to Certain Softwood Lumber from Canada, WT/DS257/AB/RW (December 5, 2005).

[62] Ibid.

[63] See Panel Report, United States–Investigation of the International Trade Commission in Softwood Lumber from Canada, WT/DS277/RW (November 15, 2005).

determination pertaining to the US finding of injury did not result in revocation of the AD and countervailing duty orders. Canada has not yet indicated whether it intends to appeal the US-Softwood Lumber Injury Panel decision to the Appellate Body.

The trail of mixed enforcement that we have highlighted in the recent WTO cases suggests that the DSU reinforces our conclusion that a revision in the compliance mechanism is overdue. Despite the small number of cases that reach the 'last resort' the negative reputation effect of these large and passionate disputes on the entire trading system is not insignificant.

5. Proposed solution to the implementation problem

Schwartz and Sykes (2002) and Sykes (2000) among others have suggested that a solution to the enforcement problem can be found in contract theory. If the WTO Agreements are viewed as incomplete contracts, then a remedy for breach of obligations is the withdrawal of equivalent concessions by the Complainant. By introducing a liability rule into the legal mix, the WTO permits a Respondent to violate a WTO obligation when the cost to the Respondent of being compliant exceeds its benefits. This so-called 'efficient breach' theory[64] suggests that, in certain cases, it may be preferable to choose not to perform the obligations of a contract and pay damages instead. If we apply this to the WTO, one may argue that the WTO Agreements are 'incomplete contracts,' and that a Member should be given the 'option' to not comply with the WTO Agreements or the DSB recommendations and instead to pay 'damages' in the form of compensation or suspension of concessions or other obligations. If this argument prevails it would make the DSB recommendations similar to a court order requiring specific performance.

The 'efficient breach' theory in US contract law is concerned with the choice of remedies in the case of violation of contracts. This theory recommends whether a court should award damages or order-specific performance, on the premise that these two remedies are available in the US courts. It guides a court in choosing an appropriate remedy option. However, it is definitely not an indication of the 'nonbindingness' of either a contract or a court order of specific performance. As we have seen from case history, while the DSB recommendations may appear similar to an order of specific performance, they do not specify concrete ways to bring the violating measures into conformity. Compensation and suspension of concessions or other obligations are available only 'in the event that the recommendations ... are not implemented within a reasonable period

[64] See Sykes (2000), Schwartz and Sykes (2002), Dunoff and Trachtman (1999). An alternative view is presented by Lawrence (2003).

of time,'[65] and they are not an alternative remedy option of equal value. Consequently, the existing remedy under the DSU should not be considered as the 'efficient' remedy suggested by the 'efficient breach' theory.

From contract theory, we know that the key to compliance is the price of breach: where the price of a breach is sufficiently high, compliance will result. For this proposition to be tractable in WTO law, one first needs to measure the price of breach in terms of Complainant's damages and create an institution within the WTO to mandatorily enforce the payment of damages.[66] This would streamline the WTO procedure, shorten the time for enforcement and prevent unilateral action by the Complainant. To date, the WTO, as we can see from earlier discussion lacks the institutions that can provide for payment of damages. Consequently an 'efficient breach' rule appears, at first blush, to be impracticable.[67] In fact, there are some in the enforcement debate that argue that enforcement is not in the purview of the WTO. The resulting behavior that we see in the latest WTO cases does however approach the 'efficient breach' concept in that the WTO-inconsistent measure may remain in place after a DSB recommendation and retaliation is the only efficient solution. This unfortunately raises the transaction costs associated with international trade disputes which was to be reduced with the WTO DSU process.

As an example of these higher transaction costs one need only review the effect of the recent Trade and Development Act of 2000, signed into law in May 2000, which strengthen §301 of the Trade Act of 1974, by adding a degree of uncertainty and complexity to the list of tariff items subject to retaliation. The Act amended §301 trade program requiring the office of the "United States Trade Representative" (USTR) to 'carousel,' or rotate, a retaliation list when a country does not implement a WTO dispute settlement. It requires the USTR to rotate items 120 days after the first list of items and every 180 days thereafter. The USTR would not be required to rotate the list if compliance was imminent, or if both the USTR

[65] DSU, Article 22.1.

[66] US contract law, in general, provides for four major ways of awarding damages. *Expectation damages* represent the amount of money that would put the non-breaching party in the position in which it would have been if the contract had been performed, that is, if the non-breaching party's expectations had been fulfilled. *Reliance damages* represent the amount of damages sufficient to place the non-breaching party in its pre-contract position. Courts order *specific performance* of a contract obligation if the subject matter of the contract lends itself to performance, such as where the seller of a home breaches his agreement to sell. Finally, courts order *restitution* of money that has been transferred to the breaching party. In this case, the non-breaching party may choose the measure of damages. When the DSB finds that a WTO-inconsistent measure must be removed, it is similar to specific performance. The time gap till removal may result in financial money damages similar to reliance or expectation damages.

[67] The compensation principle has been justified by the theory that some breaches of contracts are efficient; that is, the aggregate benefits of breach outweigh the aggregate costs.

and the petitioners agreed that rotation was not necessary in that particular case. The legislation is designed to place pressure on foreign governments, through their domestic exporters, to change their position on the disputed practice.[68]

From the discussion thus far, it is obvious that the DSU has solved the problem of the initial Panel creation but has failed to address the issue of implementation. This was not the intent but the outcome of a dispute process that focused more on the 'process' and less on the outcome. Moreover, if one views the entire DSU process as a diplomatic attempt to negotiate compliance then there is no failure in the system. However, if one views the WTO commitment as a contract than the lack of enforcement of the DSB recommendations, is a breach of that contract. To induce Member states to comply with the DSB, one needs to avoid tolerating these breaches. An effective way of doing that involves the creation of a monetary fine system and not the removal of concessions.

The use of fines is more efficient than alternative remedies in that it will not introduce negative externalities. The fine structure we recommend will not only reimburse the Complainant's loss in profits thus serving as compensation for lack of specific performance, but will also, if implemented at every time period till performance serve as a 'punitive' damage with the self-correcting signaling to other Member countries contemplating breach of their WTO commitments.

Consider the following two situations:

$$E(\pi)_t^C < E(\pi)_t^R \tag{1}$$

When expected profits of the Complainant are less than that of the Respondent then there are three specific alternatives fines.

	Fines	Expected profit of Respondent	Expected profit of Complainant	DSB status
Option 1	$E(\pi)_t^C < E(\pi)_t^R < F_1$	0	π_t^C	Compliance
Option 2	$F_2 < E(\pi)_t^C < E(\pi)_t^R$	$\pi_t^R - F_2$	F_2	Efficient breach/ less than full compensation
Option 3	$E(\pi)_t^C \leq F_3 < E(\pi)_t^R$	$\pi_t^R - F_3$	F_3	Breach/full compensation

[68] In his statement introducing S. 1619, Senator DeWine said that 'some [WTO] member nations are simply undermining this entire [dispute] process by refusing to comply with the final dispute settlement decision, even after losing their cases on appeal.' See Congressional Record, September 22, 1999, p. S11260.

where

F_i = the specific fine implemented;
$E(\pi)_t^R$ = expected profit of Respondent at time t;
$E(\pi)_t^C$ = expected profit of the Complainant at time t.

Under the first option where the fine is greater than the expected profit of the Respondent, the Respondent will comply with the DSB recommendations since the penalty is greater than her profits. In the second case, where the fine is less than the expected profit of both the Complainant and the Respondent, the Respondent continues to breach and if the fine is enforced will make a net profit $[\pi_t^R - F_2]$. The plaintiff will receive the fine which will not fully compensate her for expected losses. In the third case, where the fine is less than the expected profits of Respondent, the Respondent continues to breach and if the fine is enforced will make a net profit $[\pi_t^R - F_3]$. However, in this case, the Complainant will receive a fine equal to his losses in expected profits. One can envisage a case here where the fine exceeds the expected losses of the Complainant. This alternative is not suggested because it will serve to induce rent-seeking behavior on the part of the Complainant. To assure that the damaged Complainant will receive her full compensation, the fine must be set at the expected losses of the Complainant. Without punitive damages, the Respondent will continue to breach until her expected profits equal the fine. (See Figure 4).

Consider the second situations:

$$E(\pi)_t^R < E(\pi)_t^C \tag{2}$$

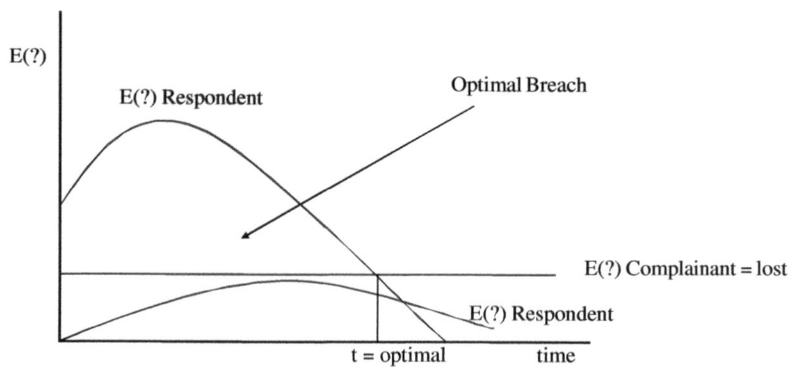

Fig. 4. Compliance scenarios.

When the expected profits of the Respondent are less than that of the Complainant then there are three specific alternatives fines.

	Fines	Expected profit of Respondent	Expected profit of Complainant	DSB status
Option 1	$E(\pi)_t^R < E(\pi)_t^C < F_1$	0	π_t^C	Compliance
Option 2	$F_2 < E(\pi)_t^R < E(\pi)_t^C$	$\pi_t^R - F_2$	F_2	Efficient breach/less than full compensation
Option 3	$E(\pi)_t^R \leq F_3 < E(\pi)_t^C$	0	π_t^C	Breach/full compensation

Under the first option where the fine is greater than the expected profit of the Respondent and the Complainant, the Respondent will comply with the DSB recommendations since the penalty is greater than her profits. In the second case, where the fine is less than the expected profit of the Complainant and Respondent, the Respondent continues to breach and the fine enforced will make a net profit $[\pi_t^R - F_2]$. The Complainant will receive the fine but the amount will not fully compensate her for the expected losses. In the third case, where the fine is less than the expected profits of Complainant but greater than that of the Respondent, the Respondent ceases the breach and the fine is enforced at the level of losses to the Complainant (π_t^C). As in the earlier case, to assure that the damaged Complainant will receive her full compensation, the fine must be set at the expected losses of the Complainant. (See Figure 4).

What sets this approach apart from that of Schwartz and Sykes is that it does not view 'suspension of concessions' as a sufficiently burdensome and efficient sanction. If the WTO, after a 'reasonable time' permit such a 'suspension of concessions' the Complainant government will have to devise a domestic mechanism to fully compensate the losses incurred by its negatively affected sector(s). Remember that 'suspension of concessions' amounts to a war of trade volumes not lump sum transfers, with lots of negative second round effects. A 'fine' on the other hand may serve as a 'buy out' of a Respondent's WTO obligations, and can be transferred to the negatively affected domestic producers in the Complainant's market as compensation for losses.[69] Applying such a fine

[69] A recent article by Schowalter (2004) also supports the use of fines based on efficiency grounds.

system would restore the Complainant's aggrieved sector to its *ex ante* position before breach, without introducing any second round trade distortions.

References

Alvarez, J.E. (2002), The WTO as linkage machine. *The American Journal of International Law* 96 (1), 146–158.

Anderson, K. (2002), Peculiarities of retaliation in WTO dispute settlement. *World Trade Review* 1, 123–134.

Antoniadis, A. (2007), Unilateral measures and WTO dispute settlement: an EC perspective. *Journal of World Trade* 41 (June 3), 605–627.

Bello, J.H. (1996), The WTO dispute settlement understanding: less is more. *The American Journal of International Law* 90 (July 3), 416–418.

Bourgeois, J.H.J. (2001), Some reflections on the WTO dispute settlement system from a practitioner's perspective. *Journal of International Economic Law* 4 (March 1), 145–154.

Brewster, R. (2006), Rule-based dispute resolution in international trade law. *Virginia Law Review* 92 (2), 251–288.

Bronckers, C.M. (2001), More power to the WTO? *Journal of International Economic Law* 4 (March 1), 41–65.

Bronckers, C.M., Van Den Broek, N. (2005), Financial compensation in the WTO: improving the remedies of WTO dispute settlement. *Journal of International Economic Law* 8, 101–108.

Cameron, J., Gray, K.R. (2001), Principles of international law in the WTO dispute settlement body. *The International and Comparative Law Quarterly* 50 (April 2), 248–298.

Carmody, C. (2006), WTO obligations as collective. *The European Journal of International Law* 17 (2), 419–443.

Charnovitz, S. (2001), Rethinking WTO trade sanctions. *The American Journal of International Law* 95 (October 4), 792–832.

Charnovitz, S. (2002), The WTO's problematic 'last resort' against noncompliance. *Aussenwirtschaft* 57 (Heft IV), S409–S439.

Charnovitz, S. (2004), Recent developments and scholarship on WTO enforcement remedies. In: Lacarte, J., Granados, J. (Eds.), *Inter-Governmental Trade Dispute Settlement: Multilateral and Regional Approaches. Chapter 6*. International Law and Policy, Cameron May Ltd., London, pp. 151–165.

Chayes, A., Chayes, A.H. (1995), *The New Sovereignty: Compliance with International Regulatory Agreements*. Harvard University Press, Cambridge.

Davey, W.J. (2005), The WTO dispute settlement system: the first ten years. *Journal of International Economic Law* 8 (March), 17–49.

Dunoff, J.L., Trachtman, J.P. (1999), Economic analysis of international law. *Yale Journal of International Law* 24 (Winter), 1–42.

Hudec, R.E. (2000), Broadening the scope of remedies in the WTO dispute settlement. In: Weiss, F. (Ed.), *Improving WTO Dispute Settlement Procedures: Issues & Lessons from the Practice of Other International Courts and Tribunals*. Cameron, London.

Jackson, J.H. (1997), The WTO dispute settlement understanding: misunderstandings on the nature of legal obligation. *American Journal of International Law* 91 (January), 60–64.

Jackson, J.H. (2004), International law status of WTO dispute settlement reports: obligations to comply or option to "buy out"? *American Journal of International Law* 98 (January), 109–125.

Kearns, J.E., Charnovitz, S. (2002), Adjudicating compliance in the WTO: a review of DSU Article 21.5. *Journal of International Economic Law* 5 (2), 331–352.

Lawrence, R.Z. (2003), *Crimes and Punishments? Retaliation under the WTO*. Institute for International Economics, Washington, DC.

Leitner, K., Lester, S. (2003), WTO dispute settlement 1995–2002: a statistical analysis. *Journal of International Economic Law* 6 (1), 251–261.

Leitner, K., Lester, S. (2004), WTO dispute settlement 1995–2003: a statistical analysis. *Journal of International Economic Law* 7 (1), 169–181.

Leitner, K., Lester, S. (2005), WTO dispute settlement 1995–2004: a statistical analysis. *Journal of International Economic Law* 8 (1), 231–244.

Leitner, K., Lester, S. (2006), WTO dispute settlement 1995–2005: a statistical analysis. *Journal of International Economic Law* 9 (1), 219–231.

Leitner, K., Lester, S. (2007), WTO dispute settlement 1995–2006: a statistical analysis. *Journal of International Economic Law* 10 (1), 165–179.

Lowenfeld, A.F. (2002), *International Economic Law*. Oxford University Press, New York.

Martha, R.S.J. (2001), The duty to exercise judgment on the fruitfulness of actions in world trade law. *Journal of World Trade* 35, 1036–1040.

Mavroidis, P.C. (2000), Remedies in the WTO legal system: between a rock and a hard place. *European Journal of International Law* 11 (4), 763–813.

Mavroidis, P. C., Sykes, A. O. (Eds.) (2005). *The WTO and International Trade Law/Dispute Settlement*. Edward Elgar Publishing Inc., MA.

O'Connor, B., Djordjevic, M. (2005), Practical aspects of monetary compensation: the US – copyright case. *Journal of International Economic Law* 8 (1), 127–142.

Pauwelyn, J. (1998), Evidence, proof *and* persuasion in WTO dispute settlement: who bears the burden? *Journal of International Economic Law* 1, 227–258.

Pauwelyn, J. (2000), Enforcement and countermeasures in the WTO: rules are rules – toward a more collective approach. *American Journal of International Law* 94 (2), 335–347.

Pauwelyn, J. (2003a), How to win a World Trade Organization dispute based on non-World Trade Organization law?: Questions of jurisdiction and merits. *Journal of World Trade* 37 (6), 997–1030.

Pauwelyn, J. (2003b), A typology of multilateral treaty obligations: are WTO obligations bilateral or collective in nature? *European Journal of International Law* 14 (November 5), 907–951.

Peters, A. (2003), International dispute settlement: a network of cooperational duties. *European Journal of International Law* 14 (1), 1–34.

Petersmann, E.-U. (1999), Dispute settlement in international economic law-lessons for strengthening international dispute settlement in non-economic areas. *Journal of International Economic Law* 2, 189–248.

Rosas, A. (2001), Implementation and enforcement of WTO dispute settlement findings: an EU perspective. *Journal of International Economic Law* 4 (1), 131–144.

Schoenbaum, T.J. (1998), WTO dispute settlement: praise and suggestions for reform. *The International and Comparative Law Quarterly* 47 (3), 647–658.

Schoenbaum, T.J., Nakagawa, J., Reif, L.C. (1998), *Trilateral Perspectives on International Legal Issues: From Theory in to Practice*. Transnational Publishers, NY.

Schowalter, J.M. (2004), A cruel trilemma: the flawed political economy of remedies to WTO subsidies disputes. *Vanderbilt Journal of Transnational Law* 37, 587–630.

Schwartz, W.F., Sykes, A.O. (2002), The economic structure of renegotiation and dispute resolution in the World Trade Organization. *The Journal of Legal Studies* 31 (1), Part 2: Rational Choice and International Law, (January), pp. S179–S204.

Sykes, A.O. (2000), The remedy for breach of obligations under the WTO dispute settlement understanding: damages or specific performance? In: Bronckers, M., Quick, R. (Eds.), *New Directions in International Economic Law: Essays in Honor of John H. Jackson*. Kluwer Law International, Boston, pp. 347–351.

Taniguchi, Y., Yanovich, A., Bohanes, J. (2007), *The WTO in the twenty-first century: dispute settlement, negotiations, and regionalism in Asia*. Cambridge University Press, United Kingdom.

Van Den Broek, N. (2003), Power paradoxes in enforcement and implementation of World Trade Organization dispute settlement reports: interdisciplinary approaches and new proposals. *Journal of World Trade* 37 (1), 127–162.

Weiss, E.B. (2000), Strengthening national compliance with trade law: insights from environment. In: Bronckers, M., Quick, R. (Eds.), *New Directions in International Economic Law: Essays in Honor of John H. Jackson*. Kluwer Law International, Boston, pp. 463–467.

World Trade Organization. (1997), Appellate Body Report, European Communities – regime for the importation, sale and distribution of bananas (EC – Bananas III). WT/DS27/AB/R. (adopted September 25).

World Trade Organization. (1998), Article 21.3(c) Arbitrator's Award, EC – Bananas III. WT/DS27/15. (circulated on January 7).

World Trade Organization. (2000), Article 21.3(c) Arbitrator's Award, Canada – patent protection of pharmaceutical products (Canada – pharmaceutical patents). WT/DS114/13. (circulated on August 18).

World Trade Organization. (2002), Negotiations on the dispute settlement understanding: proposals by the LDC Group. (October 9) TN/DS/W/17.

World Trade Organization. (2004), The future of the WTO: addressing institutional challenges in the new millennium. Geneva.

World Trade Organization. (2005), Article 21.5 Panel Report, United States – final countervailing duty determination with respect to certain softwood lumber from Canada (US – softwood lumber IV). WT/DS257/RW. (adopted December 20).

Yerxa, R., Wilson, B. (Eds.) (2005). *Key Issues in WTO Dispute Settlement: The First Ten Years*. Cambridge University Press, New York.

CHAPTER 16

Retaliatory Trade Measures in the WTO Dispute Settlement Understanding: Are There Really Alternatives?

Bryan Mercurio

Faculty of Law, Professor, The Chinese University of Hong Kong, Sha Tin, NT, Hong Kong SAR
E-mail address: b.mercurio@cuhk.edu.hk

Abstract
The appropriateness of retaliatory trade measures in the World Trade Organization dispute settlement process have increasingly come under scrutiny in recent years. Several Members and commentators alike have recommended large-scale amendments to the Dispute Settlement Understanding (DSU) to provide alternatives to retaliatory measures, with the most notable including compensation, collective retaliation, and increased special and differential treatment for developing countries and/or widespread loss of privileges for non-conforming respondents.

Unfortunately, many of the proposals failed to first identify the aims and objectives of the retaliatory phase, or even of dispute settlement more generally. This chapter takes a more holistic approach in its analysis of whether any of the current proposals will improve (or harm) the system. In doing so, this chapter will first assess the effectiveness and appropriateness of retaliatory trade measures by evaluating the goals and objectives in which it is designed to achieve. It will then evaluate some of the more prominent proposals for amending the DSU under the same framework. Taking such an approach will allow for a more comprehensive review and will reveal not only the problems with retaliatory trade measures, but also its positive aspects, and not only the positive aspects of the suggested alternatives but also where they may be detrimental to the system.

Keywords: International trade law, dispute settlement, trade retaliation, compensation

JEL classifications: K19, K42

Frontiers of Economics and Globalization
Volume 6 ISSN: 1574-8715
DOI: 10.1108/S1574-8715(2009)0000006019

1. Introduction

The DSU has served an integral role in increasing the legitimacy of the multilateral trading system by providing a rules-based, binding and impartial forum for WTO Members to resolve their disputes.[1] Members have, by and large, respected the process and the decisions of panels, and the Appellate Body have, by and large, been carefully considered and reasoned.[2] But no system is perfect, and both Members and commentators have now had over ten years, more than 350 complaints and over 200 panel and Appellate Body reports, to consider the operation of the system. While no Member or serious commentator is calling for the dismantling of the DSU or even for a substantial re-writing of the agreement,[3] several procedural and systemic issues have been raised throughout the course of the DSU Review, which warrant further consideration.

This chapter focuses on one area of the DSU that has increasingly gained the attention of Members and commentators alike – the implementation phase of the dispute settlement process and more specifically the appropriateness of trade retaliation. In this area, several Members and commentators have recommended large-scale amendments to the DSU to provide for increased and more targeted compensation, suspension of rights/ concessions and increased retaliatory rights.[4] This chapter will assess the effectiveness and appropriateness of retaliatory measures by first discussing the working of the system as well as its aims and objectives. It then will evaluate some of the more prominent proposals for amending the DSU under the same framework. Finally, the chapter will conclude that although the current system has its failings, radical change is not needed and slight

---

[1] While dispute settlement in the GATT increasingly became legalistic and formalized, an element of diplomacy remained. For instance, the adoption of panel reports could be blocked by either party to a dispute. See generally, John Croome, Reshaping the World Trading System: A History of the Uruguay Round (Geneva: World Trade Organization, 1995). For detailed information on the DSU, see Yang Guohua, Bryan Mercurio and Li Yongjie, WTO Dispute Settlement Understanding: A Detailed Interpretation (Kluwer Law International, 2005).

[2] Former Director-General Supachai Panitchpakdi noted: "[The dispute settlement system] has largely been successful because WTO member governments have been prepared to implement Panel and Appellate Body rulings and to bring their laws and regulations into conformity with WTO rules should a Panel decision go against them". Available at http://www.wto.org/english/news_e/spsp_e/spsp35_e.htm

[3] See, for example, Virachai Plasai, "Compliance and Remedies Against Non-Compliance Under the WTO System" ICTSD Issue Paper 3, p. 4 (stating "Members should aim for an improvement, and not a major overhaul of the system"). There have, however, been some proposals that would, if implemented, radically change parts of the system. For instance, the EC called for both permanent panelists and the ability of the Appellate Body to remand disputes back to panels. See TN/DS/W/38 (23 January 2003) paras 14 and 21.

[4] Member proposals can be found at http://www.law.georgetown.edu/iiel/research/projects/dsureview/synopsis.html. See also, Joel P. Trachtman, 'The WTO Cathedral' (2007) 43 Stanford Journal of International Law 127, footnote 3 (citing at 20 such commentator proposals).

tweaks are more appropriate given the negative or undetermined implications resulting from some of the more far-reaching proposals.

2. *The dispute settlement process*

The DSU provides for the resolution of disputes between WTO Members through a number of various interconnected articles. At the outset, the DSU contains a clear preference for a mutually agreeable solution to be reached between the parties to the dispute. Article 3.7 of the DSU states in relevant part:

> The aim of the dispute settlement mechanism is to secure a positive solution to a dispute. A solution mutually acceptable to the parties to a dispute and consistent with the covered agreements is clearly to be preferred ...

In the absence of a mutually agreed solution, Article 3.7 states, "the first objective of the dispute settlement mechanism is usually to secure the withdrawal of the measures concerned if these are found to be inconsistent with the provisions of any of the covered agreements". In absence of a mutually agreed solution or the withdrawal of the inconsistent measures, the DSU offers the complaining party two avenues with which to resolve the dispute. First, the responding Member may provide compensation to the complainant Member. The offer of compensation is voluntary, and compensation is understood to be on a temporary basis until the inconsistent measure is withdrawn (Article 22.1). If an agreement on compensation cannot be reached and the Member concerned fails to remove a measure found to be inconsistent with its obligations (i.e. to "bring its measure at issue into conformity with its obligations" (Article 19.1)) under the covered agreements within a "reasonable period of time" (Article 21.3),[5] the aggrieved Member may seek to obtain authorization from the Dispute Settlement Body (DSB) to suspend concessions or other obligations that are extended to the non-compliant Member under the covered agreements. If the parties cannot agree on the extent of retaliation, an arbitrator will determine the amount (Article 22.6). Following this step, the complaining party can exercise its option to suspend concessions or other obligations against the non-compliant Member.

The suspension of concessions or other obligations is commonly referred to as "retaliation", as concessions or other obligations are suspended only when the Member complained against fails to implement the rulings

[5] For commentary on this issue, see Bryan Mercurio, 'The Future of Dispute Settlement in the WTO: The Implementation Phase Under Scrutiny' in Ross Buckley (Ed.), The WTO and the Doha Round: The Changing Face of World Trade (Kluwer Law International, London: 2003) pp. 115–143. If the non-compliant Member has modified its measures and claims to have brought them in line with the rulings and recommendations of the panel/Appellate Body, then the complaining Member must challenge the claim and receive a ruling from the panel/Appellate Body that the measures remain inconsistent with WTO obligations. See Article 21.5 of the DSU.

of the DSB. The suspension can take numerous forms, but, in terms of trade in goods, includes temporary increases in tariff rates by the complaining Member on certain selected products from the non-compliant Member. Tariff increases have been in the order of 100% ad valorem.

The DSU makes clear that seeking and applying retaliatory measures is the option of "last resort", only to be applied when all other avenues such as "mutually acceptable solution" and "voluntary compensation" have been exhausted. As a general rule, Article 22.3(a) of the DSU provides that complaining parties should first seek to suspend concessions or other obligations with respect to the same sector(s) as that in which the panel or Appellate Body has found a violation or other nullification or impairment. Thus, if the violation relates to the GATT, the retaliatory measures should target goods. However, while all goods are grouped as one sector, this is not the case for every covered agreement. For instance, trade in services (GATS) is classified into 12 sectors (such as business services, communication services, construction and related engineering services, distribution services, educational services), and retaliatory measures should first be sought within the specific sector of the infringing measures. If the complaining party does not consider it practicable or effective to suspend concessions or other obligations with respect to the same sector(s), it may seek to suspend concessions or other obligations in other sectors under the same agreement. For instance, if the non-compliant measures relate to the patent sector under the TRIPS Agreement, but the complaining party does not consider it practicable or effective to suspend concessions or other obligations with respect to the patent sector, its retaliation may target another sector within TRIPS, such as the trade mark sector. Finally, if the complaining party does not consider it practicable or effective to suspend concessions or other obligations with respect to other sectors under the same agreement, and the circumstances are serious enough, Article 22.3(c) of the DSU allows the complaining party to suspend concessions or other obligations under another covered agreement (this is commonly referred to as "cross-retaliation").

3. Dispute settlement: in practice

3.1. Goals of dispute settlement

Retaliation plays a prominent role in the success of the DSU, even though there is some disagreement as to the goal of retaliation. This is primarily due to the fact that the DSU does not explicitly provide the aim or objective of the suspension of concessions.[6] The DSU does, however,

---

[6] The arbitrators in *US–Offset Act* called attention the problems caused by a lack of stated purposes: "it is not completely clear what role is to be played by the suspension of obligations in the DSU and a large part of the conceptual debate that took place in these proceedings could have been avoided if a clear 'object and purpose' were identified". WT/DS217/ARB/BRA, 31 August 2004, para. 6.5.

provide some guidance as to the aims and objective of the dispute settlement mechanism. For instance, Articles 3.7 and 3.3 of the DSU, read together, state that the DSU should be used to "secure a positive solution to a dispute" between Members as promptly as practicable. Article 3.7 also provides that, when disputing Members cannot reach a mutually acceptable solution, the first objective of the DSU is the removal of any measures that are found to be inconsistent measures with the covered agreements. The DSU also makes clear that compensation and the suspensions of concessions are "temporary measures" and that neither is preferred "to full implementation of a recommendation to bring a measure into conformity with the covered agreements".[7] The DSU additionally states that "prompt compliance with the recommendations and rulings of the DSB is essential"[8] and furthermore directs the DSB to "continue to keep under surveillance the implementation of adopted recommendations or rulings, including those cases where compensation has been provided or concessions or other obligations have been suspended but the recommendations to bring a measure into conformity with the covered agreements have not been implemented".[9] Most commentators therefore believe that Members are under an obligation to comply with the rulings and recommendations of adopted panel and Appellate Body reports.[10]

---

[7] DSU Article 22.1.

[8] DSU Article 21.1.

[9] DSU Article 22.8.

[10] However, as Judith Hippler Bello stated in a provocative think piece: "[T]he WTO has no jailhouse, no bail bondsmen, no blue helmets, no truncheons or tear gas". Judith Hippler Bello, 'The WTO Dispute Understanding Mechanism: Less is More' (1996) 90 American Journal of International Law 416, 417. This piece sparked a series of retorts and rebuttals regarding the obligation to implement an adopted report, see John H. Jackson, 'The WTO Dispute Settlement Understanding—Misunderstandings on the Nature of Legal Obligation' (1997) 91 American Journal of International Law 60; Warren Schwartz and Alan Sykes, 'The Economic Structure of Renegotiation and Dispute Resolution in the World Trade Organization' (2002) 31 Journal of Legal Studies 179; John H. Jackson, 'International Law Status of WTO Dispute Settlement Reports: Obligation to Comply or Option to "Buy Out"?' (2004) 98 American Journal of International Law 109. See also, Robert E. Hudec, Broadening the Scope of Remedies in WTO Dispute Settlement, in *Improving WTO Dispute Settlement Procedures* (Friedl Weiss & Jochem Wiers, Eds.) (London, Cameron May Publishers, 2000) at pp. 345–376; Trachtman, supra note 4, at 146, who states: "Even assuming [WTO law is mandatory], a legal realist, and a legal economist, would ask not what the formal law specifies, but what it does in response to breach. Ubi ius ibi remedium. Here, the law in action clearly does not operate as a property rule. States that violate WTO law are not subject to enforceable specific performance-type remedies, nor do they experience any penalty for their violation beyond the potential authorization of withdrawal of equivalent concessions (outside of the export subsidies context). So, as a matter of fact and practice, if not as a matter of legal doctrine, the WTO legal system is best characterized as employing a liability rule, rather than a property rule. As suggested above, it is a rather modest liability rule".

With that in mind, some commentators argue that the objective of the ability to suspend concessions is to rebalance the tariff concessions and other obligations that Members have agreed to. Thus, if one Member is violating the rules and thereby nullifying or impairing benefits, the other Member can violate the rules as well in order to restore the original balance.[11] The rebalancing viewpoint thus allows the complaining Member to take action to remedy an injustice by removing concessions granted through negotiations to the non-compliant Member, thereby restoring the trade relationship balance.[12]

On the contrary, some commentators believe the purpose of the ability to suspend concessions is to induce the Member complained against to comply with its obligations under the covered agreements.[13] As evidence, advocates point to the fact that retaliatory measures often target powerful interest groups from the territory of the Member complained

---

[11] For the rebalancing view, see D. Palmeter, 'The WTO Dispute Settlement Mechanism, Compliance with WTO Rulings and other Procedural Problems' (2001) 4(2) The Journal of World Intellectual Property 291; D. Palmeter and S. Alexandrov "'inducing compliance' in WTO dispute settlement" Political economy of international trade law: essays in honor of Robert E. Hudec. by (eds) D.L.M. Kennedy and J.D. Southwick (Cambridge: Cambridge University Press, 2002) 647–654.

[12] Several commentators, however, believe the current system does not provide a consistent model for calculating "equivalence". See, for example, H Spamann, 'The Myth of "Rebalancing" Retaliation in WTO Dispute Settlement Practice' (2006) 9 Journal of International Economic Law 31; Kym Anderson, 'Peculiarities of Retaliation in WTO Dispute Settlement' CIES Discussion Paper No. 0207 (March 2002). Moreover, Anderson points out that "ensuring equivalence between the damage and the retaliation in terms of the gross value of trade between the respondent and the complainant does not mean that retaliation has the same economic welfare effect on the respondent as the initial damage is having on the complainant. The bilateral trade value necessarily exaggerates the negative effect on both parties' economic welfare, but it does not do so equally (except by coincidence)". Id at 7. For a discussion on "equivalence" in the calculation of damages as well as to the inconsistency and flaws of "rebalancing", see Trachtman, supra note 4, 156–162. It is also worth noting that the arbitrators in *EC–Bananas* found it difficult to establish the equivalent suspension of TRIPS concessions. See *EC–Bananas*, para. 159.

[13] See, for example, Steve Charnovitz, 'The WTO's Problematic "Last Resort" Against Noncompliance' downloaded from ssrn.com, p 21; Marco Bronckers and Naboth van den Broek, 'Financial Compensation in the WTO. Improving the Remedies of WTO Dispute Settlement' (2005) 8 Journal of International Economic Law 101, 112. Of course, if this is the case, the question must be asked why the system does not provide for punitive levels of retaliatory measures. That being said, some believe the system has evolved, post-Uruguay Round negotiations, in such a manner so that compliance is now the focus of retaliatory measures. For discussion on whether "equivalent" retaliatory measures can induce compliance, see Joost Pauwelyn, 'WTO Victory on Steel Hides Deficiencies', Jurist Legal Intelligence, 23 January 2004, available at http://jurist.law.pitt.edu/forum/Pauwelyn1.php (stating equivalent retaliation is "a simple tit-for-tat or zero-sum game where, in principle, no more pressure is put on the violating country (by the trade sanction) than on the victim (by the original violation)). See contra, Robert Z. Lawrence, Crimes and Punishments? Retaliation Under the WTO (2003, Institute for International Economics).

against in order to encourage them to lobby for compliance. For instance, in *EC—Bananas*, one of the complaining parties, the United States, suspended the concessions on certain meat products, pecorino cheese, sweet biscuits, candles, bed linen, electrothermic coffee and tea makers and handbags, even though the original matter concerned restrictions on the importation and distribution of bananas.[14] Under this view, the suspension of concessions or other obligations is designed to be a temporary measure pending full implementation of the DSB report. Thus, the ultimate goal is to have the offending measure brought into compliance, and suspension is designed to achieve this outcome. Under this view, equivalence between damage and retaliation is likely not to be seen as particularly relevant. Instead, the retaliatory measure should simply be sufficiently costly to the Member concerned so that it chooses to absorb the (lesser) cost of compliance instead of the (higher) cost of the retaliation.

The "induce compliance" viewpoint has until recently been supported by the reports of several Article 22.6 arbitrations. For instance, the arbitrators in *EC–Bananas I* stated:

> [T]the authorization to suspend concessions or other obligations is a temporary measure pending full implementation by the Member concerned. ... this *temporary* nature indicates that it is the purpose of countermeasures to *induce compliance*. But this purpose does not mean that the DSB should grant authorization to suspend concessions beyond what is *equivalent* to the level of nullification or impairment. In our view, there is nothing in Article 22.1 of the DSU, let alone in paragraphs 4 and 7 of Article 22, that could be read as a justification for counter-measures of a *punitive* nature.[15]

The arbitrators in *EC–Hormones* agreed with and quoted the above paragraph,[16] while the arbitrators in *EC–Bananas II* likewise found that in order to have "effective" retaliatory measures, "the party seeking suspension to ensure that the impact of that suspension is strong and has the desired result, namely to induce compliance by the Member which fails to bring WTO-inconsistent measures into compliance with DSB rulings within a reasonable period of time".[17] However, the

---

[14] See *EC–Bananas*, Recourse by the United States to Article 22.2 of the DSU, WTO Doc. No. WT/DS27/43 (14 Jan 1999), at 3.
[15] WT/DS27/ARB, para. 6.3
[16] WT/DS26/ARB, para. 40
[17] WT/DS27/ARB/ECU, para. 72. See also, *Brazil–Aircraft*, WT/DS46/ARB, para. 3.44; *US – FSC*, WT/DS108/ARB, para. 5.52; *Canada–Aircraft*, WT/DS222/ARB, para. 3.48.

arbitrators in *US–Offset Act* recently cast doubt upon the theory when it stated:

> The concept of "inducing compliance" ... is not expressly referred to in any part of the DSU and we are not persuaded that the object and purpose of the DSU – or of the WTO Agreement – would support an approach where the purpose of suspension of concessions or other obligations pursuant to Article 22 would be exclusively to induce compliance. Having regard to Articles 3.7 and 22.1 and 22.2 of the DSU as part of the context of Articles 22.4 and 22.7, we cannot exclude that inducing compliance is part of the objectives behind suspension of concessions or other obligations, but at most it can be only one of a number of purposes in authorizing the suspension of concessions or other obligations. By relying on "inducing compliance" as the benchmark for the selection of the most appropriate approach we also run the risk of losing sight of the requirement of Article 22.4 that the level of suspension be *equivalent* to the level of nullification or impairment.[18]

Other commentators, however, have slightly differing views such as that the principles of contract law and the efficient allocation of resources are the driving force behind retaliation implementation.[19]

The importance of this debate cannot be understated, as the present system cannot truly be judged, nor can any modifications be recommended, until clear aims and objectives of the DSU are set. It seems that this point is central to any discussion of reform, yet it has been virtually ignored by government officials, practitioners and academics alike. Commentators have simply skipped over the issue and continued, without clear direction from the DSU, into why their favoured amendment would resolve one "problem" or another. Such diverse views have created a situation where the DSU is being judged by various competing, and sometimes contradictory, standards. Throughout this chapter, and indeed in any discussion regarding the success (or failure) of the DSU and any potential amendments, the important yet often ignored point regarding the lack of clarity of the aims and objectives of the DSU must be taken into consideration. We shall come back to this point in section 3.2 and throughout this chapter.

3.2. Success of dispute settlement

The DSU has successfully managed and resolved the vast majority of Member disputes. As of January 2008, 369 formal complaints have been

---

[18] Para 3.74

[19] See, for example, Schwartz and Sykes, supra note 10.

filed comprising 273 matters resulting in 246 panel requests. These claims have resulted in 219 panel and Appellate Body adopted reports and 39 arbitral awards. Of these, only eight disputes have reached the Article 22.6 arbitration stage (resulting in 17 arbitral decisions).[20] With only eight disputes reaching the Article 22.6 stage,[21] there is an unusually large amount of commentary on an area that has been so infrequently invoked. This leads one to ask whether there are so few requests for retaliation because compliance with panel and Appellate Body reports is exceedingly high, whether the mere threat of retaliatory measures encourages compliance or whether Members do not see the value in requesting and implementing retaliatory measures. There is support for each position, and therefore, a combination of factors probably is at work. For instance, Members successfully implement panel/Appellate Body rulings and recommendations in 83% of disputes (signifying high compliance Davey, 2005); the threat of retaliatory measures by Canada is likely to have influenced Australia to ultimately comply with the decision in *Australia–Salmon* (signifying that threats encourage compliance)[22] and a number of complainants in *EC–Bananas* did not seek to impose retaliatory measures (signifying that retaliatory measures are not effective).[23] Of course, the situation is even more complicated, as retaliatory measures have failed to elicit compliance in a number of high profile disputes (namely *EC–Hormones* and *EC–Bananas*, although in the latter instance, retaliatory measures likely played a major role in the ultimate resolution of the matter). Likewise, compliance has not been achieved where Members have received but opted not to impose any retaliatory measure. Of course, in both situations, a number of extraneous factors existed (i.e. both Brazil and Canada's failure to impose retaliatory measures against each other in the parallel disputes concerning subsidies to regional aircraft).

Other scholars have a slightly different take and believe that compliance with international judgments and decisions is positively affected by a nation's concern for its respect for international obligation and its resulting reputation. In the WTO context, these scholars claim that these factors must be taken into consideration given that there is widespread compliance but a perceived lack of incentives to comply (Kovenock and Thursby, 1992; Guzman, 2002). Other scholars,

---

[20] Statistics in this section have been compiled using thewww.worldtradelaw.net database.

[21] The disputes are *EC–Bananas*, *EC–Hormones*, *Brazil–Aircraft*, *US–FSC*, *Canada–Aircraft II*, *US–1916 Act*, *US–Offset Act* and *US– Gambling Services*.

[22] See Charnovitz, supra note 13, 5.

[23] Ecuador received authorization to retaliate but chose not to, while Guatemala, Honduras and Mexico did not even seek authorization to retaliate. See also *Mexico–HFCS* where the US did not seek the right to retaliate. In both disputes, other factors may have been more influential in the decision not to seek retaliatory measures.

however, have cast doubt on the claims.[24] There have also been many attempts to calculate the costs and benefits of compliance through the use of several (mainly economic) variables,[25] and although these are useful, they are usually theoretical or forward-looking in nature and thus do not aid in resolving the question of why compliance has to date been very high.

Looking at the issue from a different perspective, while the system has proven itself to be both unbiased and effective, it can be said that developed country Members have thus far had a more positive experience. This begins with the fact that Members with larger economies utilize the DSU much more than Members with smaller economies.[26] This is understandable, given the larger economic interests, but can become problematic when the imbalance is related to other factors.[27] In this regard, scholars have come up with a number of influencing factors, including the length, cost and technical complexity of the DSU process, lack of capacity to enforce the decision through trade retaliation, reliance on bilateral assistance or trade preferences and the threat of non-WTO retaliation.[28] There may be some evidence to support these claims. For

---

[24] See, for example, Colin B. Picker, 'Reputational Fallacies in International Law: A Comparative Review of United States and Canadian Trade Actions' (2004) 30 *Brooklyn Journal of International Law 68*; Chad P. Bown, On the Economic Success of GATT/WTO Dispute Settlement, 86 Review of Economics and Statistics 811 (2004) 818–820, 822 (finding only limited evidence that reputation or obligation affects behaviour).

[25] See, for example, Trachtman, supra note 4; Andrew T. Guzman, 'The Cost of Credibility: Explaining Resistance to Interstate Dispute Resolution Mechanisms,' 31 Journal of Legal Studies 303 (2002).

[26] See, for example, Chad P. Bown and Bernard M. Hoekman, "WTO Dispute Settlement and the Missing Developing Country Cases: Engaging the Private Sector" (2005) 8 Journal of International Economic Law 861–890; Henrik Horn, Petros Mavroidis and Håkan Nordström, "Is the Use of the WTO Dispute Settlement System Biased?" in The WTO and International Trade Law/Dispute Settlement (eds) Petros Mavroidis and Alan Sykes (Cheltenham: Edward Elgar, 2005). This is true even though developing countries have initiated over 35% of total cases (approximately 40% of which are against other developing countries), as a handful of countries account for the vast majority of the complainants. No LDC compliant has made it to the panel stage, and only eight LDCs have participated in any dispute as a third party.

[27] See Bown and Hoekman, supra note 26.

[28] See, for example, Chad P. Bown, "Participation in WTO Dispute Settlement: Complainants, Interested Parties and Free Riders," (2005) 19(2) World Bank Economic Review 287; Joost Pauwelyn, "Enforcement and Countermeasures in the WTO: Rules are Rules – Toward a More Collective Approach" (2000) 94 American Journal of International Law 335, 338; Mark Busch and Eric Reinhardt "Developing Countries and GATT/WTO Dispute Settlement" (2003) 37(4) Journal of World Trade 719–735; Bernard M. Hoekman and Petros C. Mavroidis, "WTO Dispute Settlement, Transparency and Surveillance" (2000) 23 World Economy 527. The proposals of developing countries throughout the DSU Review tend to focus on similar areas. See, for example, TN/DS/W/42, TN/DS/W/15, TN/DS/W/17, TN/DS/W/18 and TN/DS/W/19.

instance, Eleso makes a valid observation that even though cotton accounts for a large percentage of exports for several sub-Saharan African countries such as Benin, Burkina Faso, Chad and Mali, these countries did not bring a case to the WTO against the United States for its cotton subsidies, which were subsequently found to be inconsistent with the WTO agreements in *United States–Cotton* (Chad and Benin joined the case as third parties, Eleso, 2006). In a related point, many of the most active developing countries in the DSU Review have not utilized the dispute settlement mechanism but have been active participants in the DSU Review.

Furthermore, Bagwell, Mavroidis and Staiger note that richer country Members who have "won" at the panel/Appellate Body level almost always request authorization to suspend concessions against poorer nations, but developing nations are reluctant to request authorization to suspend concessions from developed nations (Bagwell *et al.*, 2004). Thus, while larger, richer countries substantiate their threat of retaliatory measures (due in large part to their ability to both improve their own welfare and decrease the welfare of a smaller nation through the use of targeted measures) (see Bown, 2002; Busch and Reinhardt, 2000), smaller nations may feel powerless to either retaliate or even credibly threaten retaliation against a larger Member.[29]

At this point, it is prudent to undertake a more detailed preliminary evaluation of the arguments against the current system of retaliatory measures. The first such argument is that the imposition of retaliatory trade measures is economically inefficient for both nations in that it causes consumers in the importing country (or businesses in the case of inputs) in the importing nation to pay more for the imported goods (whether they be from the non-compliant country or substitute products from less efficient producers).[30] Moreover, any significant rise in tariff levels to a segment of imports has the potential to increase

---

[29] Pauwelyn calls the legalization of the system without a more compliance inducing enforcement mechanism a "reactivation of power politics". Pauwelyn, supra note 28, 338. Bagwell, Mavroidis and Staiger succinctly state "…countermeasures in case of non-compliance is not a big hit for developing countries". Bagwell *et al.* (2004).

[30] Charnovitz considers the fact that the arbitrator in the first Article 22.6 arbitration in *EC–Bananas* encouraged the two parties to negotiate "as the suspension of concessions is not in the economic interest of either of them" to be a "a sober assessment of what some analysts consider the most impressive feature of the DSU". See Charnovitz, supra note 13, 11 (citing WT/DS27/ARB, para. 2.13). Robert Hudec, however, was of the view that even though trade retaliation may hurt the country imposing the measure, the very act of imposing retaliatory measures sends out a powerful message to recalcitrant governments. Hudec further argued that by selecting the appropriate sensitive industries of the non-compliant government, a complaining contracting Party could compel compliance. Robert E. Hudec, The GATT Legal System and World Trade Diplomacy (Saint Paul. Butterworth, 1990).

political considerations such as increased lobbying efforts and rent-seeking.

The problem of increased tariff levels as retaliation is particularly troublesome for smaller developing country Members, who more often not depend on one (larger developed) country for a large percentage of their total trade and rely upon imports for both consumer goods and necessary imports. In such a circumstance, implementing traditional retaliatory measures is counterproductive as there may not be an alternative supplier or the additional costs associated with a new supplier may make the goods inaccessible to the local market.[31]

Additionally, as both partners understand that retaliation will likely harm the small partner more than it harms the larger partner, the threat of retaliatory measures will lack credibility.[32] Without credibility, a threat of retaliation loses any potential coercive effect. Without a credible threat of retaliation to perhaps persuade a non-compliant Member to withdraw its offending practices, most developing country Members are limited in their capacity to retaliate (Steinberg, 2002). In a proposal to the DSU Review, India states:

> [T]he tremendous imbalance in the trade relations between developed and developing countries places severe constraints on the ability of developing countries to exercise their rights under Article 22. The economic cost of withdrawal of concessions in the goods sector would have a greater adverse impact on the complaining developing-country Member than on the defaulting developed-country Member and would only further deepen the imbalance in their trade relations already seriously injured by the nullification and impairment of benefits.[33]

Even if a small-sized Member does decide to implement retaliatory measures (regardless of whether it is economically inefficient), it will likely lack the economic strength to exercise any real pressure on the Member

[31] See, for example, Bown and Hoekman, supra note 26.

[32] In many cases, the threat of retaliation may be enough to coerce a Member to withdraw its inconsistent measures, without the implementation of retaliatory measures. Although, as a threat has to be credible to be effective, a Member must be prepared to carry out its threat of retaliation. For example, the ECs threat of retaliatory tariffs is purported to have influenced the Bush administrations repeal of the US Steel safeguards in 2003. See 'Steel: Bush Ends Steel Safeguard Tariffs in Face of Threat by EU to Retaliate' (2003) 20 BNA International Trade Reporter 2021; Jide Nzelibe, 'The Credibility Imperative: The Political Dynamics of Retaliation in the World Trade Organization's Dispute Resolution Mechanism' (Public Law and Legal Theory Working Paper No 55, The Law School, The University of Chicago, 2004), 11; Fritz Breuss, 'Economic Integration, EU-US Trade Conflicts and WTO Dispute Settlement' (2005) 9(12) European Integration Online Papers 1, 14, available at http://eiop.or.at/eiop/texte/2005-012a.htm

[33] WTO Doc TN/DS/W/19 (2002), 1.

concerned.[34] This is not only true for smaller developing countries but is also equally applicable to smaller developed country Members. In fact, the economic strength argument could even extend to trading relationships between larger, developed countries.[35]

Furthermore, as an institution based on the principle that the expansion of trade through reduced barriers leads to growth, development and poverty reduction, the sanctioning of the imposition of higher trade barriers in an attempt to remedy another Member's transgression (or perhaps to punish the offending Member) seems contradictory as the higher trade barriers resulting from the retaliatory measures will inevitably lead to a reduction of trade between the parties concerned.[36] In this regard, reduced trade resulting from retaliatory measures could have the effect of contracting trade, limiting or reducing growth and stymieing poverty reduction.[37]

Additionally, retaliatory measures do not benefit the aggrieved party but instead damage the innocent.[38] As explained above, the imposition of retaliatory measures does not necessarily offer any relief to the aggrieved industry. In fact, in most instances, the suspended concessions (or retaliation targets) bear no relationship to the industry subject to the dispute. To illustrate using the example from above, the banana industry in the United States would not have been positively affected, or made whole, as a result of US retaliatory measures against European sweet biscuits and cheese. Instead, Europe continued to discriminate in favour of certain banana growing countries, US biscuit manufacturers and cheese makers benefit from greater protection while those industries in Europe suffer. For most developing countries, the effect of the system could be even more detrimental as the non-compliant measures could harm one of the only competitive industries in the nation while the retaliatory measures could be structured to provide little to no benefit to the aggrieved industry and at the same time only nominally assisting other national industries due to their lack of international competitiveness.

---

[34] This problem is at its most severe when the complaining Member relies upon the responding Member for a substantial amount of its trade. In such a circumstance, the non-compliant measure not only might affect a large percentage of the complaining Member's exports, and thus a large number of industries and/or workers, but it is also very difficult for the complaining Member to select industries or goods to subject to retaliatory measures without harming its own industries (particularly necessary inputs) or consumers.

[35] See, for example, *US–FSC*, where the EU has not exercised its DSB sanctioned right to impose retaliatory measures in the amount of US$4 billion against US imports, at least in part because of the economic and competitive effect the increased tariff barriers will have on European industries.

[36] See, for example, Anderson, supra note 12, 129 (stating "the idea of legitimizing retaliation is contrary to the objective of reducing impediments to trade").

[37] The EC wrote in a submission to the DSU Review: "the authorization to suspend concessions runs against a basic principle of the WTO, i.e., predictability of the trading system". TN/DS/W/1 (13 March 2002) p 5.

[38] Anderson, supra note 12, 133.

Finally, prospective remedies discourage immediate or timely compliance. Under the current system, Members are not punished for past discretions but are only subject to the suspension of concessions (in the equivalent amount of harm caused) for continuing to apply the measure found to violate the covered agreement. Thus, remedies in the WTO are (almost) without exception only prospective in nature.[39] Such a system emphasizes that the intent, aim and objective of the dispute settlement mechanism is to resolve the dispute, rather than "punish" a Member for failing to abide by its WTO obligations; however, such a system also fails to discipline Members who fail to uphold their obligations and then delay compliance.

4. *Alternatives to retaliatory measures*

With so many perceived flaws in the DSU, it is not surprising that there has been an abundance of commentary and suggestions on how to improve the system. This section analyses and evaluates several of the more interesting proposals: amendments to provide for increased and more targeted compensation, suspension of rights/concessions and increased retaliatory rights. Given that most commentators believe the system is not in need of a major overhaul, the intention should be to improve the system without "depart(ing) from the general principles already contained in the instrument".[40] The proposals will be assessed with this in mind.

---

[39] Although this was not entirely clearly spelled out in the GATT, the fact that there existed an "understanding" among contracting parties on this point cannot be doubted. See Robert Hudec, Enforcing International Trade Law: The Evolution of the Modern GATT System (1993). The practice has been followed in the WTO. See Report of the Panel, *EC–Bananas*, Recourse to Article 21.5 by Ecuador, WT/DS27/RW/ECU, para. 6.105 (April 12, 1999). See contra, the controversial decision in Article 21.5 Panel Report, *Australia–Leather*, which held that Article 19.1 of the DSU does not limit remedies under Article 4.7 of the SCM Agreement to prospective action only. WT/DS126/RW, 11 February 2000, para. 6.27ff. This decision was criticized by many Members, including the complainant in the dispute, the US. It should be noted, however, that the US nevertheless pressed for and received a repayment schedule mandating the recipient of Australian government subsidies to repay the grants and preferential loans. See Minutes of Meeting, Held in Centre William Rappard on 11 February 2000, WT/DSB/M/75. It should also be noted that throughout the GATT period, panels did sometimes recommend that antidumping duties and countervailing duties found to violate the GATT be reimbursed. See, eg, United States–Measures Affecting Imports of Softwood Lumber from Canada, 41 B.I.S.D. 413–415 (1993); New Zealand–Imports of Electrical Transformers from Finland, 32 B.I.S.D. 55 (1985). Most of these reports, however, were not adopted. See Report of the Panel, United States – Imposition of Anti-dumping Duties on Imports of Seamless Stainless Steel Hollow products from Sweden, ADP/47, circulated 20 August 1990, un-adopted; Report of the Panel, United States – Anti-Dumping Duties on Gray Portland Cement and Cement Clinker from Mexico, ADP/82, circulated 7 September 1992, unadopted.

[40] Plasai, supra note 3, 4.

4.1. Compensation

As briefly noted, the DSU allows for "voluntary compensation" as an alternative to retaliatory measures. Article 22.1, however, places limits on the use of compensation:

> Compensation and the suspension of concessions or other obligations are temporary measures available in the event that the recommendations and rulings are not implemented within a reasonable period of time. However, neither compensation nor the suspension of concessions or other obligations is preferred to full implementation of a recommendation to bring a measure into conformity with the covered agreements. Compensation is voluntary and, if granted, shall be consistent with the covered agreements.

Regardless, trade compensation is not the preferred retaliatory method.[41] This is the case even though trade retaliation almost always involves the complainant Member raising its import barriers on certain products exported by the respondent Member and thereby harming the economic welfare in *both* countries (and likely globally), whereas trade compensation is the more efficient form of rebalancing in that it increases liberalization and increases economic welfare in the complaining country, the respondent country and even in third countries (due to the fact that trade compensation must be offered in accordance with the MFN principle).[42] While there may be numerous reasons for the preference towards retaliatory trade measures, two of the more persuasive reasons are as follows. First, a complaining Member does not prefer trade compensation as its exporters are not necessarily the exporters that benefit – exporters in third countries also benefit from responding Members' tariff reductions and, if they are more efficient exporters, they will take the majority of the benefit. Thus, to ensure the complaining Member benefits, tariff concessions would have to be set at a deeper level than if the concession only applied to the complaining Member. Second, Members prefer trade retaliation over compensation because while in the former the complaining Member retains control over both the level of the suspension of concessions and the targeted products, the latter hands over control to the responding Member, who can unilaterally end the trade compensation when it believes it has complied with the rulings of the DSB (or otherwise

[41] The only example of trade compensation given in the WTO is *Japan–Taxes on Alcoholic Beverages* (WT/DS8/AB/R; WT/DS10/AB/R; WT/DS11/AB/R), where the Japan agreed to apply reduced tariff rates on specific items pending full implementation of the Appellate Body report.

[42] See Anderson, supra note 12, 5. This theory holds even though some third countries that import those or like products may lose from a terms of trade deterioration due to the fact that the world as a whole will be better off economically. See Id.

decides it no longer wants to offer trade compensation).[43] Thus, while the current system allows for compensation as an alternative to retaliatory measures, it has not proven to be an attractive option or viable alternative to Members. For this reason, there have been numerous proposals for the extension of compensation. The remaining part of this section will evaluate two such proposals: mandatory trade compensation and financial compensation.

4.1.1. Mandatory trade compensation

In contrast to the current voluntary regime, several developing and least developed countries (LDC) countries have proposed the introduction of mandatory compensation as part of the DSU Review.[44] One immediate benefit mandatory trade compensation has over the suspension of concessions is that it would create rather than contract trade. Trade compensation therefore does not aggravate injury to the complaining Member nor does it injure innocent industries in that state (Davies, 2006). Under most of these proposals, a complaining Member who has prevailed in the dispute but faced with non-compliance could nominate which sectors the offending Member should offer compensation. In the alternative, the DSB (through panel and Appellate Body reports) would be the party that indicates which sector the Member concerned should offer compensation. Another proposal suggests that Members nominate, or pre-establish, the sectors and forms of trade compensation to be triggered if and when the Member fails to comply with a ruling of the DSB (this has been referred to as "contingent liberalization commitments").[45] In all proposals, compensation would continue until the Member concerned modifies its inconsistent measures and is deemed to be in compliance with its WTO obligations.

There are several hurdles to the introduction of mandatory compensation, with the most significant being the enforceability of mandatory compensation. The WTO is a member-driven organization, with tariff schedules and all other commitments contained in the covered agreements being the product of countless hours of complicated negotiations. In most if not all countries, these decisions are taken after much consultation with business and other interests and made only after a careful balancing of all competing interests. Allowing another Member or the panel/Appellate Body to dictate the sector in which compensation must be offered raises a number of practical concerns and does not appear to be politically viable in most Member countries (whether they be democratically elected or an authoritarian dictatorship). More generally, trade compensation, by its very nature, harms an innocent industry in the non-compliant Member. The decision to expose an innocent industries to more foreign competition (by a reduction in tariff rates) is an

---

[43] See Id, 5–6.

[44] See, for example, TN/DS/W/15. Mandatory compensation is also discussed in Pauwelyn, supra note 28, 344–346.

[45] See Lawrence, supra note 13, chapter 5.

important one that should be taken only after careful analysis of the trade policy aims, objectives and the economic positions of all affected innocent industries at issue. Placing such a decision in the hands of the complaining party or a panel/Appellate Body may be seen as a too intrusive step that infringes upon the sovereignty and potentially the economic welfare of a nation. The pre-establishment of contingent liberalization commitments also raises a number of political issues, not least of which is the lobbying, horse-trading and infighting that the process will inevitably foster.

Moreover, as any form of compensation is, by its nature, an act that must be performed by a non-complying Member, it will always essentially be a voluntary act. Neither a harmed Member nor the WTO can force another Member to provide compensation. The consequences of this being that "mandatory" compensation depends on the good faith compliance of the Member concerned. But of course, the fact that mandatory compensation is sought is solely due to the fact that the offending Member failed to abide by the rulings and recommendations of the DSB and remained in violation of its WTO obligations. Given this, the question must be asked whether a non-compliant Member would feel any obligation to comply with this requirement.

Therefore, regardless of whether there is an obligation to comply with the rulings and recommendations of the DSB, without an effective enforcement mechanism, all methods of compensation remain voluntary in nature in that they are dependent on compliance by the non-compliant Member. Furthermore, in the longer term, as an international tribunal, the legitimacy of the DSU depends on the value Members place upon it. To date, both the usage of the system and a high compliance rate demonstrate that Members place a high value on the institution. DSB rulings regarding mandatory compensation, however, would likely face increased enforceability issues and decrease the overall rate of Member compliance. As such, mandatory compensation orders have the potential to threaten the long-term viability of an effective dispute settlement mechanism.

Moreover, requiring the DSB to recommend compensatory sectors would fundamentally alter the nature of WTO adjudicative tribunals. To date, panel and Appellate Body reports have been limited to making rulings as to the consistency of the measures at issue with the WTO agreements and, if applicable, making recommendations that "may suggest ways [to] ... implement the recommendations".[46] In practice, this means generally upon the Member concerned to bring its measures into conformity with its WTO obligations. Under a system of mandatory compensation, however, both the panel and the Appellate Body reports would need to prescribe remedies (which would become binding on the parties to the dispute after the reports were adopted by the DSB). Again, this intrusion into the trade policy determinations of a Member government may be an unwelcome step too far.

[46] DSU Article 19.1.

Another significant detraction to having panels or the Appellate Body recommending or selecting compensatory sectors is that such a system fails to remedy the perceived problem of retaliatory measures not aiding the aggrieved party while at the same time harming innocent parties. For that matter, even when the complaining Member nominates the sector subject to mandatory compensation, there is no guarantee that the aggrieved industry will be assisted. As mentioned earlier, retaliatory measures and trade compensation almost always target a different sector to that subject of the dispute.

Mandatory compensation will not necessarily assist the aggrieved industry or reduce the harm retaliatory measures cause on innocent parties. Furthermore, allowing either the complaining party or the panel/ Appellate Body to recommend or prescribe which sectors compensation should be offered is an unwelcome, intrusive step into domestic trade policy. Remembering that compensation is by its very nature necessarily a voluntary act, the issuance of mandatory compensation orders would likely result in a decrease in the DSU's overall compliance rate. Therefore, based on the above reasoning, mandatory compliance cannot replace the role of traditional trade retaliation in the implementation phase of the dispute settlement process.

4.1.2. Financial compensation

As detailed above, the traditional form of compensation is "trade compensation" whereby the non-compliant Member reduces tariff barriers equivalent to the amount of harm suffered through its measures. Some commentators, however, now view financial compensation as an alternative form of compensation, which could more directly address the grievance and harm of complaining Members and/or increase both the speed and the overall rate of compliance with panel/Appellate Body reports. Financial compensation, as the name suggests, entails the responding Member providing a financial benefit (i.e. a direct payment) to either the complaining Member's government or an industry, group or association within that Member's territory.

While not a novel idea,[47] the legality of financial compensation under the DSU is questionable; however, its use in *US–Copyright* reveals its

[47] The concept of financial compensation has long been a part of public international law and, in fact, was first proposed in the GATT in 1964. See GATT Document L/2195/Rev.1, Annex 4 (1964); COM.TD/F/W.1 (April 27 1965); COM.TD/F/W.4 (October 11 1965). See also, Report of the Ad Hoc Group on Legal Amendments to the General Agreement, COM.TD/F/4, (4 March 1966). See generally, Robert E. Hudec, "Broadening the Scope of Remedies in WTO Dispute Settlement", available at http://www.worldtradelaw.net/articles/hudecremedies.pdf. Proposals of this nature were also made during the Uruguay Round. See 'Negotiating Group on Dispute Settlement: Communication from Nicaragua' MTN.GNG/NG13/W/15 (November 6 1987); MTN.GNG/NG13/W/19, p. 6, para. 3b; "Negotiating Group on Dispute Settlement Differential and More Favourable Treatment of Developing Countries in the GATT Dispute Settlement System"-MTN.GNG/NG13/W/27 (30 June 1988).

salient features. In *US–Copyright*, a panel found that US laws exempting certain small businesses from paying music copyright licence fees contravened Article 9.1 of the TRIPS Agreement.[48] The case, initiated by the EC at the request of the Irish Music Rights Organisation (IMRO), did not involve a substantial amount of monetary damage to the IMRO or any other European collecting society or artist but did form an integral part of the overall US copyright laws. Thus, the dispute was ripe for a mutually agreed solution. Such a solution was reached when the United States agreed to financially compensate the EC in exchange for allowing the continuation of the infringing practices. Both parties agreed the value of financial compensation would be based on the determination of an arbitrator (under Article 25 of the DSU). The arbitrator determined the equivalent level of nullification and impairment to be $1.1 million per year.[49] Interestingly, the United States did not provide financial compensation to the EC directly but instead paid the money into a fund set up by the Groupment Europeen Des Societes D'Auteurs et Compositurs (GESAC).

Financial compensation as an alternative to traditional retaliatory measures has significant support among developing country Members and LDCs as well as from a handful of prominent scholars.[50] The most attractive feature of financial compensation is that, like trade compensation, it is not trade restrictive and thus does not conflict with WTO principles. Moreover, financial compensation is also likely to have a compliance-inducing effect. Faced with a large monetary compensation claim (such as the $4 billion authorization in *US–FSC*), a Member may decide to expedite compliance in order to avoid monetary compensation, it may neither be able to afford or could not pay for political reasons (this compliance-inducing effect would be even stronger if some form of retroactive compensation was also implemented). Moreover, monetary compensation would likely be more attractive to developing countries and smaller developed country Members who may not be able to practically or

[48] United States – Section 110(5) of the US Copyright Act, WTO Doc WT/DS160/R (2000) (Panel Report).

[49] United States – Section 110(5) of the US Copyright Act – Recourse to Arbitration Under Article 25 of the DSU, WTO Doc WT/DS160/ARB25/1 (2001) (Award of the Arbitrators). For more information and analysis of the dispute and compensation package, see Davies (2006).

[50] See, for example, 'Preparations for the 1999 Ministerial Conference – The Dispute Settlement Understanding (DSU), Communication from Pakistan to the General Council', WT/GC/W/162 (1 April 1999); Least Developed Countries' proposal, TN/DS/W/17, of 9 October 2002, at 13 (LDC Proposal). Proposal of Ecuador, TN/DS/W/33, of 23 January 2003, at 4. See Bronckers and van den Broek, supra note 13, 109–126; Marco Bronckers, 'More Power to the WTO?', 4 Journal of International Economic Law (2001) at 41, 62–63; Pauwelyn, supra note 28, 345–46. Other scholars have at times also supported financial compensation, see, for example, S. Esserman and R. Howse, 'The WTO on Trial', 82(1) Foreign Affairs (2003), 130, at 135.

effectively retaliate against the Member concerned. Finally, financial compensation imposes the burden – or costs – of compliance on the Member government, which seems "fair" as it is the Member government and not the industry (except in the case of dumping) who is failing to abide by its WTO obligations.[51]

There are numerous potential problems, however, with compensation as an alternative to retaliatory measures. First, whereas trade sanctions are a quasi form of self-help, any form of monetary compensation relies upon the willingness of the non-complying Member government. If that Member government refuses to financially compensate the complaining Member, there must be an additional enforcement mechanism that is not dependant on the cooperation of the recalcitrant Member (likely trade retaliation).[52] Therefore, and without a doubt, mandatory financial compensation could never replace trade compensation.[53] While some attempt to avoid this problem by recommending a system whereby each Member posts a bond (based on percentage of world trade, much like contribution fees), which remains in escrow, which is used to pay the financial compensation (presumably if the Member refuses to pay the compensation),[54] this too appears to have limitations. For instance, what happens if the compensation is higher than the bond or if the amount in escrow is depleted? Eleso suggests adding the additional amount to the Member's contribution fees, but this recommendation is not without problems.[55]

A second argument against compensation as an alternative to retaliatory measures is that it allows the continuation of the WTO

---

[51] Of course, in reality the industry, through its lobbying efforts, may have been partially responsible for the implementation of the offending activity.

[52] See, for example, Nuno Limao and Kamal Saggi, "Tariff Retaliation versus Financial Compensation in the Enforcement of International Trade Agreements", (2006) available at http://faculty.smu.edu/ksaggi/LIMAO-SAGGI.pdf. Even proponents of financial compensation readily admit that financial compensation could not entirely replace trade compensation. See, for example, Bronckers and van den Broek, supra note 13, 116 ("... financial compensation (sh)ould be an additional choice for injured Members, not a replacement for trade compensation or retaliation. If worse comes to worst, and the violating Member does not live up to its obligation to pay monetary compensation, the aggrieved Member could still be given the option to go back to retaliation".). This is not to suggest that financial compensation could not form a part of other implementation procedures. In fact, recent US FTAs have increased the usage of financial compensation, such as by adopting a format whereby the non-compliant country can prevent the imposition of retaliatory trade measures by agreeing to pay the complaining government an annual "monetary assessment" set at one-half of the level of trade suspension (or set by agreement). See, for example, United States–Singapore Free Trade Agreement, Art 20.6.5-7; United States–Chile Free Trade Agreement, Art 22.15.5-7; United States–Australia Free Trade Agreement, Art 21.11.5-7.

[53] This is true even if some form of penalty, such as suspension of WTO Rights or concessions, was imposed on the recalcitrant Member. Suspension of WTO rights and concessions is discussed at length later in this chapter.

[54] Eleso (2006, pp. 35–36); Limao and Saggi, supra note 53, 4, 14–16.

[55] Eleso (2006, pp. 35–36).

inconsistent measure, and in doing so conflicts with Articles 3 and 22 of the DSU. To illustrate, the United States and EC mutually agreed to resolve the *UC–Copyright* dispute with the United States paying 1.1 million to the GESAC per year for three years (which also raises the question of whether payments to a private entity are legal or should be legal). The agreement did not require the United States to amend the act found to be a violation of US obligations under the relevant WTO agreement (the TRIPS Agreement). To the contrary, the relevant US legislation at issue remains unchanged, meaning the copyright infringements found to be violating WTO obligations continue to be permitted under US law. If the agreement between the United States and EC is viewed as a permanent solution to the dispute, the requirement that mutually agreed solutions be consistent with covered agreements has not been met.[56] While Articles 3 and 22 could be amended to allow for an efficient breach, such a systemic change should be fully studied before its implementation for its effect not only on the system but also on other Members.

This leads us to third potential problem with financial compensation, its consistency with the MFN principle. The fact that MFN applies to compensation has been confirmed by the Appellate Body in *EC–Poultry*.[57] This principle, however, creates a practical problem for financial compensation: while trade compensation can easily be extended to all Members (say, in the form of a reduced tariff rate), financial compensation offered on an MFN basis would be both extremely expensive and nearly impossible to administer. Therefore, and much to the consternation of some other WTO Members (most notably Australia),[58] the United States in *US–Copyright* offered compensation only to the EU. While some commentators dismiss this issue by merely stating that other Members could either have joined in the original dispute or subsequently bring their own claim based upon the same facts, the issue warrants a more serious response. In dismissing interested WTO Members' objections to the payment of financial compensation only to the complaining party commentators fail to realize that in the former the same argument has never been made in the case of trade compensation (and that, being a major shift in the implementation of disputes, serious thought should be given to the wider ramifications of such an argument) and that the latter reason could result in a colossal waste of financial and human resources. Other commentators have summarily dismissed the MFN argument

---

[56] DSU Article 3.7.

[57] Report of the Appellate Body, *EC–Poultry*, WT/DS69/AB/R (1998). For discussion, see Bernard O'Connor and Margareta Djordjevic, 'Practical Aspects of Monetary Compensation: The US - Copyright Case' (2005) 8(1) Journal of International Economic Law 127.

[58] A report of the 14 March 2002 meeting in which Australia tabled its submission can be found at http://www.twnside.org.sg/title/twe276b.htm.

by merely stating that "providing monetary compensation is not 'an advantage, favour or immunity' [sic] which must be immediately and unconditionally granted to every Member ... Therefore, [financial compensation] does not thereby imply that it is to be provided on an MFN basis".[59] While this may ultimately prove to be correct, attempts to avoid the MFN principle are ill-advised and, at the very least, there should be more engagement with and serious consideration of both the text of the DSU and the negotiating history.

The fourth potential problem with financial compensation is that none of the proponents of financial compensation have seriously grappled with the issue of whether distribution (or redistribution) of the compensation to the affected industry would be an illegal subsidy under the SCM Agreement.[60] To illustrate, if a government provides compensation to another government, and the receiving government distributes the compensation to affected (harmed) industries, the receiving government's payout may be deemed to be an actionable subsidy under the SCM Agreement. While the payment of compensation from one government directly to a private entity in another country (rather than to the other government) may avoid the issue, the question would be if the receiving government provided a contribution and whether the affected industry received a benefit. It is beyond the scope of this chapter to analyze the issue in detail, but if such a direct payment does avoid the problem, several important implications arise, not least of which would be the asymmetrical treatment resulting from a direct payment to industry rather than government.

Next, while it has been argued that financial compensation can help redress injury on the part of the aggrieved industry, such a result only occurs when and if the Member government decides to distribute any of the compensation. While proponents of this purported benefit admit it is entirely up to the compensated Member government whether (and if so, how) to distribute the compensation,[61] they have as of yet failed to persuasively argue that the compensation would reach the injured industry. By contrast, when financial compensation is paid to the

[59] Eleso (2006, p. 29). For slightly more analysis, see Davies (2006, pp. 44, 45). See contra, O'Connor and Djordjevic supra note 58, 131–136. In support, O'Connor and Djordjevic point to, among other things, the text and negotiating history of the DSU. See Negotiating Group on Dispute Settlement, Dispute Settlement Proposal, 10 October 1998, MTN.GNG/NG13/W/30; Negotiating Group on Dispute Settlement, Compensation in the context of GATT Dispute Settlement Rules and Procedures, Note by the Secretariat, 14 July 1989, MTN.GNG/NG13/W/32.

[60] For background, see *US–FSC* (DS 108).

[61] For instance, Bronckers and van den Broek mention on at least four occasions that there is not any obligation (nor, in their minds, should there be any obligation) for distribution of financial compensation to an affected industry. Bronckers and van den Broek, supra note 13. See also, Patricio Grané, Remedies under WTO Law, (2001) 4 Journal of International Economic Law 755.

complaining Member government, it seems likely that the aggrieved industry could be in the same position as with retaliatory measures.

The fifth problem with financial compensation is that it has the potential to create division within the institution as only the richer nations would be able to afford to pay financial compensation. If financial compensation is paid, but the measure found to be inconsistent with the WTO agreements is never modified or removed, financial compensation could merely be a proxy for allowing rich nations to "buy-out" of their obligations. While, in theory at least, the non-compliant Member will still have an obligation to remove the offending measure, it may decide that paying financial compensation is a more attractive alternative (for reasons that include but are not limited to political and economic efficiency). Moreover, and perhaps more importantly, this could lead to a situation where traders can no longer rely on the WTO to provide predictable and secure market access. The Sutherland Report expressed reservations regarding financial compensation for this reason, stating that "some experimentation in this regard could be useful, but great care must be exercised to be sure that monetary compensation is only a temporary fallback approach pending full compliance, otherwise the 'buy-out' problems will occur".[62]

Finally, questions remain as to which Members should be eligible to receive financial compensation, how it would be calculated and when it would become payable. On the first matter, most commentators suggest limiting those eligible to receive financial compensation to developing nations or LDCs. Others suggest a milder form of financial compensation whereby countries could opt-in, and thus be able to use the system as well as have the system used against them, or opt-out and not be able to receive or be liable for financial compensation. Such a splintered system raises questions about its long-term viability as well as memories of the problems of rampant "code conditionality" under the GATT. Most proponents of financial compensation would calculate the sum on trade effects and also include a punitive element in that financial compensation would be retroactive to the date of the offending measure,[63] but both of these issues are, no doubt, subject to much debate. It is beyond the scope of this chapter to finalize a workable platform for financial compensation, but the point is that proponents of this system have yet to work out or agree upon all of the important details that are necessary to allow a full and complete evaluation of the proposal.

4.2. Suspension of WTO rights or concessions

Another proposed alternative to the present retaliatory measures is the suspension of a Member's WTO rights or concessions. Two of the more

[62] Sutherland Report, para. 243.
[63] See, for example, Eleso (2006, p. 19).

popular forms of suspension of a Member's rights that have been put forward are (1) the suspension of WTO voting rights and (2) the suspension of the right to bring a dispute to a panel or to the Appellate Body.[64] Proponents of these alternatives believe that each would be able to put enough pressure on the Member concerned to force, coerce or expedite compliance. And while it is true that both the suspension of voting rights and the suspension of the right to file or pursue a dispute severely curtail the "rights" of the Member concerned to a point where non-compliance would be very costly, both proposals raise several troublesome issues and are unlikely to gain large-scale support from the WTO Membership.

For example, while the suspension of voting rights and/or from bringing a dispute to the DSB at first sight appear more attractive than other proposed alternatives or retaliatory trade measures, in that they do not create concerns about trade contraction, a closer look reveals some fundamental problems with these alternatives. First, while compliance with a ruling or recommendation of the DSB is important, it has not been a major problem, and given the severity of the suspension of voting and/or enforcement rights, these proposals represent a disproportionate countermeasure given the importance Members place on the WTO being a "Member driven organisation". Moreover, such an extreme response also risks isolating the non-compliant Member to the point where it may subsequently lose interest in the day-to-day business of the WTO (thereby reducing its incentive to comply with the DSB). Second, if a Member's WTO voting rights were suspended, that Member could find itself bound by a decision that was agreed upon during its suspension. Members have already demonstrated their objection to such situations by rejecting proposals to modify voting procedures to more easily facilitate decisions by majority vote (Zimmermann, 2005). Therefore, any alternative that allows for the possibility of enforcing decisions upon dissenting Members will invariably be extremely controversial and are unlikely to gain the support of the membership. Even more, while such an alternative may in fact reduce instances of continued non-compliance, it radically changes the nature of membership in the organization. Thus, the suspension of voting rights is a disproportionate solution, which would create many more problems than it solves.

The suspension of a Member's right to bring a claim to the DSB is likewise disproportionate as it would leave a Member unprotected in the face of discriminatory treatment by other Members. Even if such a suspension was limited in some way – that is, to measures that were in effect at the time of the Member's suspension – the suspension would essentially amount to the authorization of unilateral reprisals against the

[64] See, for example, TN/DS/W/19 (2002) (Proposals on DSU by Cuba, Honduras, India, Indonesia, Malaysia, Pakistan, Sri Lanka, Tanzania and Zimbabwe).

suspended Member. Such a situation could, in addition to contravening Article 23.2(c) of the DSU, undermine the entire dispute resolution process. In addition, any attempt to limit reprisals (such as to the amount of the non-compliance) again conflicts with the role of the DSU in that it allows Members to unilaterally attempt to enforce the rulings and recommendations of the DSB. Perhaps more importantly, any attempt to limit reprisals would be ungainly, administratively difficult and controversial. Again, suspension of dispute settlement rights seems to be a disproportionate solution, which would create many more problems than it solves.

Given the relatively low levels of non-compliance, both the suspension of voting rights and the suspension of dispute settlement rights represent a "disproportionate response to non-compliance".[65] Both alternatives are punitive in nature and, more importantly, would result in several systemic issues that could potentially be much more problematic than the occurrence of non-compliance. For these reasons, many commentators agree that the suspension of voting and/or dispute settlement rights is "simply not credible".[66]

4.3. Increased retaliatory rights

4.3.1. Retrospective reparation

In order to remedy the perceived problems of prospective remedies, many (mainly developing) countries support the introduction of retrospective reparation. Under the most prominent proposal for retrospective reparations, Mexico points out that the DSU process can and often does last for three years or longer and, to compensate for the delay, requests that complaining Members be compensated (whether monetarily or through the suspension of concessions) for the harm caused by the inconsistent measures "from the date of imposition of the measure, request for consultations or establishment of the panel to the date on which the authorization by the DSB to suspend was granted".[67] Reparations would, presumably, be set at such a level to which would "secure, full compensation for the injury".[68] Furthermore, Mexico also proposed that retaliatory measures be allowed to remain in force after a solution to a dispute has been reached, meaning the suspension of concessions would continue until their accumulated effect had become equivalent to the level of nullification or impairment caused by the harmful measures before DSB authorization for retaliation.[69]

[65] Bronckers and van den Broek, supra note 13, 108.
[66] Nzelibe, supra note 33, 4.
[67] TN/DS/W/40 (2003) (Communication from Mexico) ('Mexican Proposal'), 5.
[68] TN/DS/W/42 (2003) (Communication from Kenya) ('Kenyan Proposal'), 4.
[69] TN/DS/W/40, 6.

Advocates of retrospective reparation firmly believe that retaliatory measures should encourage compliance, rather than rebalance rights of Members. For instance, Trachtman states his preference for a welfare-based approach that encourages compliance through a level of sanctions equivalent to that caused by the inconsistent measure:

> It seems clear that in order to equate retaliation with a welfare-based calculation of damage, it would be necessary to calculate damage on both a retrospective and prospective basis. Thus, first of all, a state that violates WTO law should be required to make a payment even if it ceases its violation after a DSB decision, or within the expiry of the "reasonable period of time" given for compliance. This is necessary in order to make WTO law incentive-compatible, and in order to compensate complainant states for their losses. In fact, unless it were shown that the present approach systematically overstated retaliation, or some other reason were shown to give offending states a "free ride" until adjudication and expiry of time for compliance, this modification should be made in the present system. As stated above, nothing in the text of the DSU limits retaliation to calculation based on prospective nullification or impairment ...[70]

Despite the above, and as with many of the proposals detailed in this chapter, the implementation of retrospective reparations would significantly shift the nature of dispute settlement in the WTO as well as significantly alter the (undefined) objectives and aims of the system. This is true regardless of whether the DSU would have to be amended in order to operationalize retrospective reparations. Neither the drafters of the GATT nor the WTO negotiations intended for retaliatory measures to be equivalent to harm caused by an inconsistent measure before the authorization stage. If the opposite were true, the text would have explicitly allowed for such reparations (and, of course, Members would not see the need to propose the inclusion of retrospective reparations!). It is (or at least was, until recent scholarship) almost without question or controversy that the system is set up to resolve disputes and not to punish Members for past or present transgressions.

Since the issues involving retrospective trade or financial compensation are very similar to those discussed in section 4.1, the remaining portion of this section will focus only on retrospective reparations taking the form of the suspension of concessions. One notable consequence and somewhat perverse effect of retrospective reparations may be a decrease in the coercive effect of retaliation. As Members may be encouraged to comply in order to avoid sanctions, the knowledge that sanctions will begin or continue beyond compliance may cause some Members to consider more

---

[70] Trachtman, supra note 4, 140.

options (such as an efficient breach). This will almost certainly be the case when the level of nullification or impairment has been set, perhaps arbitrarily in the opinion of a number of commentators,[71] at a high level. Moreover, while retrospective reparations may be suitable (or at least feasible) in some situations, such as where the inconsistent measure is a tariff duty or internal tax, its suitability for other situations (such as non-tariff barriers or quantitative restrictions) is questionable.[72] More systemically, allowing retrospective reparations would make Article 21.1, which states that "prompt compliance" is "essential to ensure effective resolution of the dispute to the benefit of all Members", redundant because if past reparations are to be paid, it is not necessarily essential that the dispute be settled promptly. In fact, continuing sanctions will inevitably delay the final resolution of a dispute, which under the current system also seems contrary to the objective of the prompt resolution of disputes.[73]

As designed, the system allows the costs to the aggrieved Member to continue throughout the dispute settlement process. This is far from ideal, but presumably the negotiators of the DSU had the foresight to realize the consequences and yet chose not to include any form of retrospective or greater compliance-inducing mechanism. Commentators should not discount this history or the complex and inter-connected workings of the system. Retrospective reparations would represent a dramatic change to the system and thus should only be undertaken after fully understanding all potential consequences and effects. While the implementation of retrospective reparations is designed to remedy the perceived problem of delayed compliance, it may actually lead to an increase in non-compliance. Furthermore, the goal of reduced instances of non-compliance may be better achieved by differing strategies.

4.3.2. Collective retaliation

A number of developing countries have proposed a system of collective retaliation whereby a group of Members would be authorized to collectively retaliate against the non-compliant Member,[74] thereby

---

[71] See footnote 12, and especially Spamann, supra note 12. Another complaint is that retaliation measures only the gross value of trade between Members but fails to measure the welfare effect of the measures. See, for example, Trachtman, supra note 4, 159–161.

[72] See Plasai, supra note 3, 6.

[73] DSU Article 3.3.

[74] TN/DS/W/15, 3; TN/DS/W/17, 4; TN/DS/W/37, TN/DS/W/42, 3. See also, Pauwelyn, supra note 28, 342–344 (suggesting collective retaliation as a compliance inducing mechanism). Interestingly, Pauwelyn proposes that each Member be allowed to suspend concessions equivalent "to the damage it has suffered", with each Member determining the equivalent level by a set formula. See Id at 345 and footnote 51. Given the lack of agreement on a standard "formula", such a system would undoubtedly prove contentious and unworkable.

allowing a group of Members to wield significantly more retaliatory power than that of a single, isolated Member. The proposals for collective retaliation tend to call for either equivalence-based retaliation or MFN-based retaliation. Under the equivalence-based approach, the Members of a retaliatory group would share the value of suspensions and, as a whole, could suspend concessions up to the equivalence-determined value of suspensions authorized by the DSB. By contrast, the MFN-based retaliatory approach would allow every Member to apply suspensions to a non-complying Member up to the level of harm inflicted upon the complaining Member and authorized by the DSB. Interestingly, Haiti's proposal incorporates both approaches to collective retaliation:

> Where the DSB grants authorization to all Members to suspend concessions or other obligations, the level of suspension for each Member shall be an appropriate percentage of the nullification and impairment determined under arbitration. In a case brought by a least-developed country Member, the level of suspension for each Member shall be the level determined under arbitration to have been suffered by the least-developed country Member.[75]

The main arguments against equivalence-based retaliation are economic in nature. First, as retaliatory measures can economically harm the country imposing the measures more than the responding Member, it may be difficult for the complaining Member to find other Members willing to take on the retaliation for fear that it may lead to economic harm.[76] Second, if the right to impose of sanctions is seen to be a benefit (from a protectionist perspective, in that it is seen to assist a domestic producer or industry), then a complaining Member may not wish to give away part of its retaliatory rights to other Members.

The main objection to the MFN-based collective retaliation proposal is that it is a punitive remedy. This type of retaliation potentially subjects the responding to suspensions from numerous Members, the retaliation from each Member being equivalent to the level of harm caused to the complaining Member. The resultant sanctions applied could amount to many times the level nullification or impairment caused and, as discussed above, would represent a major departure from the equivalence principle that runs throughout the WTO. Punitive damages have never been a part of the GATT/WTO, nor have they been favoured in public international law, therefore such a departure from traditional norms would require a persuasive justification and Members would have to consider both the economic and the political ramifications of the change before its implementation.

---

[75] TN/DS/W/37, 3.

[76] Bronckers and van den Broek, supra note 13, 107.

4.3.3. Tradable rights

Section 4.3.2 leads to a related point – if the right to suspend concessions has value, then it may have tradable value and the complaining Member may be able to sell this right to other Members. Thus, a Member could potentially increase its economic welfare not by instituting retaliatory measures against an offending Member but by transferring its retaliation rights to another Member (who presumably would have a greater capacity and/or desire to suspend concessions against the offending Member) in return for some form of compensation/remuneration.

The concept of the transfer of retaliatory rights (also referred to as auctioning rights) between Members was first seriously posed by Mexico as part of the DSU Review.[77] The Mexican proposal stated:

> The suspension of concessions phase poses a practical problem for the Member seeking to apply such suspension. That Member may not be able to find a trade sector or agreement in respect of which the suspension of concessions would bring about compliance without affecting its own interests ... There may be other Members, however, with the capacity to effectively suspend concessions to the infringing Member.[78]

Therefore, Mexico proposed the addition of Article 22.7*bis*, which provides

> The right to suspend concessions or other obligations may be transferred to one or more Member(s). In that case, the Member(s) transferring the right to suspend concessions or other obligations and the Member(s) acquiring such right shall jointly request the DSB that it authorize the latter to suspend concessions or other obligations. In that case, the DSB shall grant each acquiring Member authorization to suspend concessions or other obligations within 30 days of such request, unless the DSB decides by consensus to reject the request. In no case shall the transfer(s) exceed the level of suspension authorized by the DSB.[79]

The proposal garnered initial support from some leading scholars, including Bagwell, Mavroidis and Staiger.[80] However, further review of the proposal may prove the benefits of the system illusory. For instance, the entire foundation of the idea of tradable retaliatory rights depends on whether retaliatory rights actually have any economic value.[81] This is

---

[77] TN/DS/W/23.

[78] Ibid at 5.

[79] TN/DS/W/40, p 6.

[80] See Bagwell *et al.* (2004).

[81] For discussion on why it might be in third countries interests to bid for the retaliatory rights, see Ibid at 14–19.

questionable given the economic realities of imposing retaliatory measures, as discussed above, as well as the potential political and inter-governmental ramifications entering bids at auction (could such an action lead to a trade war?). The Member most interested in buying the retaliation rights might actually be the offending Member, but should they be allowed to bid? If not, what happens if there are no bidders? Bagwell, Mavroidis and Staiger studied several scenarios and found that in some scenarios the success of the system depended on the participation of the non-compliant Member. Allowing the participation of the non-compliant Member, however, results in a quasi form of financial compensation. More worrying, allowing the non-compliant Member to bid could be seen as allowing recalcitrant (rich) nations to "buy-out" of their WTO obligations. In this regard, allowing a non-compliant Member to buy the retaliation rights of the complaining Member is the perfect example of an "efficient breach", as the non-compliant Member decides that winning an auction is a more efficient allocation of resources than complying with its WTO obligations. The result would be the continuation of the breach, regardless of whether the obligation to comply continues.

While a system of tradable rights may have certain advantages for the complaining Member, this is only true if a number of variables come together and result in a successful auction. Of course, the "success" of the auction depends on the aims and objectives of the system – is it a rebalance of rights, compliance or an efficient allocation of resources?[82] For these reasons, even Bagwell, Mavroidis and Staiger hesitate to fully support or recommend the adoption of tradable remedies, instead merely stating the issue should be "studied seriously".[83] Therefore, while the auction of retaliatory rights is an interesting proposal, there is not enough evidence to conclude that it is a viable method of increasing the retaliatory power of complaining Members. The probability of attracting Members into a spirited auction is low and the uncertainties inherent in an auction could lead to unpredictable levels of compensation. In this regard, it is even uncertain whether the auction would be mandatory or whether the seller could choose to walk away if not happy with the price – and if the latter, then what is the next step? Without more evidence and clearer directives, this proposal remains fraught with uncertainty.

4.3.4. Cross–retaliation

Another possible alternative to the present system is the greater use of cross-retaliation. Article 22.3 of the DSU limits retaliatory measures to the same sector and covered agreement as the original violation, unless it

---

[82] Ibid 24–27.
[83] Ibid 27.

would not be "practicable or effective" for the complaining Member to retaliate within the sector at issue. Article 22.3 reads

> [T]he complaining country should first seek to retaliate in the same sector where the violation has occurred. If that is not practicable or effective it can seek to retaliate in another sector but under the same agreement where the violation has occurred. And if that is also impracticable or ineffective it can seek to retaliate under another agreement.

Cross-retaliation has been requested and, at least in part, granted in *EC—Bananas (Ecuador)*,[84] *Canada–Aircraft*[85] and *US–Gambling*.[86]

In every case, the complainants argued that it would not be practicable or effective in the meaning of Article 22.3(b) and (c) of the DSU to suspend concessions in the same sector or agreement for a number of reasons, most of which relate to insufficient trade quantity in the sector at issue or a dependence on the respondent for necessary inputs. The complainants then made their case why circumstances in the appropriate sector and the economy on the whole were serious enough to justify suspension under another agreement.[87]

As part of the DSU, Members have proposed amendments to the DSU to allow complaining Members to make greater use of cross-retaliation. For instance, Mexico proposed that the precedent set in *EU–Bananas* be extended and codified through the elimination of Article 22.3 of the DSU.[88] In essence, the Mexican proposal would allow for retaliation to be authorized in any sector and under any agreement automatically. In this regard, a complaining Member would not have to justify and prove the impractically of retaliating in the same sector or agreement as the original nullification or impairment before seeking to suspend concessions under a different sector or agreement.

The theory behind these proposals is that the ability to cross-retaliate will somehow increase the coercive power of complaining Members by removing limitations on retaliation across sectors and covered agreements. The ability to cross-retaliate is said to be particularly important to smaller

[84] *EC–Bananas* - Recourse to Arbitration by the European Communities under Article 22.6 of the DSU (WT/DS27/ARB/ECU).

[85] *Canada–Export Credits and Loan Guarantees for Regional Aircraft* (WT/DS222).

[86] US–Gambling and Betting Services WT/DS285/ARB (21 December 2007) 4.1-119.

[87] See, for example, *EC–Bananas*, where the Arbitrators stated: "Given the difficulties and the specific circumstances of this case which involves a developing country Member, it could be that Ecuador may find itself in a situation where it is not realistic or possible for it to implement the suspension authorized by the DSB for the full amount of the level of nullification and impairment estimated by us in all of the sector and/or under all agreements mentioned above combined". EC–Bananas - Recourse to Arbitration by the European Communities under Article 22.6 of the DSU (WT/DS27/ARB/ECU).

[88] N/DS/W/40, 5.

and developing countries due to (1) the fact that imports in a specific sector or agreement may not be large enough to have much impact; (2) the asymmetrical relationship that many smaller and developing countries have with larger trading nations and (3) the fact that many smaller and developing countries rely upon certain imports from larger nations and raising barriers will decrease supply and/or increase the price of the product to its domestic producers and consumers.[89] For most developing countries, the ability to suspend concessions under the TRIPS Agreement is particularly attractive, as most developing countries are net intellectual property (IP) importers and most large-scale IP owners in developed countries have a strong lobbyist presence. For this reason, the mere threat of the suspension of concessions in this area can be used to exert considerable pressure upon developed country Member governments to abide by the rulings and recommendations of the DSB and amend the measures deemed to conflict with their WTO obligations and commitments. In fact, in *EC–Bananas*, the mere threat of suspending European IP rights (IPRs) in Ecuador appears to have been sufficient to coerce the EU into quickly negotiating and a mutually agreeable solution to the dispute. Thus, the creative and bold legal maneuvering by Ecuador in acquiring authorization to suspend concessions under the TRIPS Agreement enhanced Ecuador's bargaining leverage far beyond what it would normally have had if it could only threaten to suspend concessions on imported goods from the EC.[90]

The DSU Review is not the first time the Members have discussed the issue of cross-retaliation. The issue was discussed at length during the negotiations of the TRIPS Agreement. In fact, in a submission as part of the DSU Review, several developing countries recall that "the 'cross retaliation' provision seemed to have been incorporated in the DSU at the instance of developed-country Members, who felt that in the case of non-compliance by developing-country Members in the IPRs area, they would not be able to effectively retaliate against developing-country Members, who would have limited, if any, trade marked or patented products of their own".[91] However, in order to reduce the potential for cross-retaliation by developed countries in the enforcement of their TRIPS and GATS obligations, developing country Members insisted on the

---

[89] See TN/DS/W/47, p. 2. See contra, TN/DS/W/40, pp. 4–5.

[90] See, for example, James McCall Smith, Compliance Bargaining in the WTO: Ecuador and the Bananas Dispute (2005) 21 USC Research Computing Facility Personal Web Pages http://www-rcf.usc.edu/~enn/text/Ecuador%20revised%2005.doc at 18 Jul 07. It has been suggested that Ecuador may have foregone its right to retaliate in exchange for material assistance with its financial crisis, which may have included the EU's support for the reduction of Ecuador's external debt in the Club of Paris and help in securing an international financial support package from IMF, World Bank and others. Id.

[91] TN/DS/W/19, 1.

limitations imposed by Article 22.3 of the DSU (Arvind Subramanian and Watal, 2000).

Given this history and fear on the part of developing countries in the original TRIPS negotiations, the deletion of Article 22.3 and subsequent freedom of every member to cross-retaliate without limitation could well prove harmful to developing countries. To counteract the prospects of the large, IP owning developed countries from taking retaliatory measures in goods or services for a breech of the TRIPS Agreement, India's proposals seek to limit the privilege of unfettered cross-retaliation to developing country Members only.[92]

Leaving aside the potential negative effects of cross-retaliation to developing countries if utilized by the larger, developed countries, the option appears to offer the potential for developing country Members to retaliate, or credibly threaten retaliation, against developed country Members. There are, however, some negative aspects that must also be considered. First, unless a system of collective retaliation is implemented, any retaliatory measures taken against the responding Members IPRs will be restricted to the territory of the complaining Member. This means that the economic effect of the suspension will be limited by the size of the complaining Members constituency (with restrictions on parallel importing and other factors curtailing or prohibiting exports). Thus, while a suspension of either the US or EU's IPRs in Brazil or India would be economically significant, it is less certain if Antigua or Rwanda (or even Ecuador) could effectively make use of the suspension of concessions.[93] In this regard, the mere threat of a suspension of concessions in the IP area would only appear to have a real coercive effect if made by an economically significant Member. Moreover, quantifying the retaliatory amount of each suspension of IPRs seems inherently more difficult than doing so for goods. This will, almost inevitably, lead to disagreements relating to the overall value of the suspension.

Second, while the suspension of trade concessions is most often implemented through an additional tariff on selected products imported from the responding Member, the process of implementing and capitalizing on a suspension of IPRs is more complicated. More specifically, while the levying of an additional tariff is implemented by governmental action

---

[92] TN/DS/W/19, 1; TN/DS/W/47 (2003) (Communication from India on behalf of Cuba, Dominican Republic, Egypt, Honduras, Jamaica and Malaysia) 2.

[93] Ecuador raised this point in *EC–Bananas*, and the arbitrators in the dispute seemed to agree when they stated: "Given the difficulties and the specific circumstances of this case which involves a developing country Member, it could be that Ecuador may find itself in a situation where it is not realistic or possible for it to implement the suspension authorized by the DSB for the full amount of the level of nullification and impairment estimated by us in all of the sectors and/or under all agreements mentioned above combined". *EC–Bananas* - Recourse to arbitration by the EC under Article 22.6 DSU, Decision by the Arbitrators, WT/DS27/ARB/ECU, of 24 March 2000, para. 177.

or executive order, the private sector is needed to take advantage of the suspension of IPRs.

This need for the private sector reveals two main problems. First, any potential gains arising from the suspension of IPRs would need to be economically significant in order to attract investment from the private sector. While an analysis of costs, benefits and risks are usually not very difficult for a company to determine, the analysis cannot be fully undertaken if all of the gains are based upon the suspension of IPRs. As the cultivation of any business opportunity requires the investment of capital and time, a private company wishing to take advantage of the suspension of IPRs is exposed to significant risks because of the temporary nature of suspensions; any potential gains (or even sales) are based upon the responding Members' continued violation of its WTO obligations and the entire business opportunity is lost as soon as the Member comes into compliance.[94] Moreover, the onerous task of restoring the IPRs to the responding Member will likely fall upon the government of the complaining Member (who suspended IPRs), who could eventually become liable to the original responding Member for its failure to (re)enforce IPRs.

Second, this proposal does not alter the alleged problem of the current system in that the harmed industry in the complaining country is not helped in any way (i.e. the banana exporters in *EC–Bananas*), and innocent industries in the non-compliant Member "pay" for the continuation of the WTO inconsistent measure (i.e. the EC sectors targeted for retaliatory measures). Thus, while cross-retaliation makes the countries whole, it does nothing to affect the individual industries. In this regard, it is not an improvement on the current system.

Finally, Charnovitz points out that the non-tariff retaliatory measures "may cause even more unpredictability than the prohibitive tariff" and adds a systemically based argument that claims they have the potential to "undermine[] the normative value of the WTO discipline being suspended. For example, if intellectual property rights (for aliens) warrant societal protection, then how can the WTO be so cavalier in permitting Ecuador to flout them? The WTO cannot pretend to be a rulebased trading system when every rule is potentially erasable through a [suspension of concession or other obligation".[95]

5. *Concluding analysis*

One clear aim of the WTO dispute settlement mechanism is to resolve the dispute at issue. In this regard, the statistics reveal the dispute mechanism

---

[94] The Mexican proposal to allow suspension to remain in place until equivalence is reached would partially address this concern.

[95] Charnovitz, supra note 13, 14.

to be an almost unqualified success. But of course, the reality of the situation is not so clear, and while the system has been very effective at managing and resolving disputes, it is far from perfect. Generally speaking, the developing country Member proposals throughout the course of the DSU Review identify several impediments relating to a few distinct areas: initiating and litigating a dispute, the lack of meaningful special and differential treatment measures in the DSU and the nature of the retaliation measure in order to enforce a decision.[96] Most Member and commentator proposals treat each of these as distinct areas, but this is an incorrect approach. These concerns all revolve around the issue of equality of Members, and a collection of small but important changes to the DSU could accomplish many of the goals of developing countries and create a system that is perceived to be more user-friendly and fairer while possessing a greater ability to enforce decisions more expediently.

Of course, it is important to recognize at the outset that a number of developing country concerns cannot be addressed by any proposed amendments. For instance, numerous developing countries have expressed the fear that they are hesitant or even fearful to initiate a dispute against a larger developed country Member for fear of negative political consequences. As many developing countries rely on aid and trade preferences from the richer countries, these concerns seem entirely reasonable; unfortunately, no amendment to the DSU can placate these concerns. As long as the system allows for complainants and respondents, the threat of reprisal (and vindictive) action on the part of the respondent country will exist. Another concern that cannot be addressed is the fact that there will be situations where a Member will refuse to comply with a panel/ Appellate Body report. This has, of course, already happened in a few disputes and will no doubt happen again. The reality is that for political reasons, economic reasons or no reason whatsoever, a 100% success rate cannot be achieved regardless of the retaliatory measures at the disposal of the complainants.

Another point that needs to be stressed is that the system, as written and interpreted, does not have clear aims and objectives (beyond simply resolving the dispute). The question of whether the retaliatory phase of the process is designed to rebalance concessions, coerce compliance or punish recalcitrant respondents is simply not clearly addressed in the text of the DSU. While every interested commentator holds an opinion on the subject, such diverse views leads to a situation where the DSU is being judged by various competing, and sometimes contradictory, standards. It would be helpful if the aims and objectives of the DSU were clearly set out,

---

[96] See, in particular, TN/DS/W/42, TN/DS/W/15), TN/DS/W/17, TN/DS/W/18 and TN/DS/ W/19. The DSU contains several provisions that call for special treatment for developing country Members, but these are largely minor or discretionary in nature. See Articles 3.12, 4.10, 8.10, 12.10, 12.11, 21.2, 21.7, 21.8, 24, 27.2.

but it is indeed wishful thinking to expect (or even hope) this to occur as part of the DSU Review. Regardless, it is nevertheless important to address developing country concerns of equality.

With this in mind, this chapter concludes with some recommended changes that attempt to remedy the imbalance between developed and developing countries while at the same time maintaining the traditions and (implicit but longstanding) objectives of the current system. The changes will reduce the costs of litigating a complaint and put pressure on respondents to comply with the DSB rulings in a timely manner.[97] In this regard, the system should be fairer and more "equal" for all Members.

Although not related to directly compliance, the first of the proposed changes relate to special and differential treatment to developing countries. Bringing a dispute to the DSU is expensive, time-consuming and technically complex. Thus, despite the assistance rendered through legal and technical capacity building programs as well as the Advisory Centre on WTO Law,[98] more is needed to help defray the costs of the WTO dispute settlement process. While this assistance is no doubt appreciated, developing countries have suggested a more permanent source of assistance in the form of a trust to directly fund the costs of litigating a WTO dispute. Such a trust would be funded by Member contributions and operate similarly to the trust fund established by the UN and managed by the Secretary-General to meet the costs of developing countries litigating in the ICJ. This suggestion was not included in the Balas Draft,[99] but the permanent fund should be implemented as a matter of encouraging participation from all Members in the DSU process. Moreover, the DSU should be amended to allow for a panel or the Appellate Body to award an amount for litigation costs to a developing country Member that "wins" a dispute (whether it be as complainant or

[97] For more on the costs of filing a WTO claim, see Håkan Nordström and Gregory Shaffer, *Access to Justice in the World Trade Organization: The Case for a Small Claims Procedure* (ICTSD, June 2007).

[98] The ACWL is an independent international organization that acts as a law firm and provides high quality, low cost legal services. See Agreement Establishing the Advisory Centre on WTO Law, available at http://www.acwl.ch/e/pdf/agreement_estab_e.pdf. The ACWL website states that the Centre operates to, "level the playing field . . . by enabling [developing countries] to have a full understanding of their rights and obligations under the WTO Agreement". The website continues, "The proper balance of rights and obligations for all WTO Members can only be maintained if all Members have effective and affordable access to, and an equal opportunity to participate in WTO dispute settlement proceedings. The Centre aims to contribute to the rule of law in international relations, to the accessibility of the WTO dispute settlement system for all Members, and to the overall credibility of the rules-based multilateral trading system".

[99] See Special Session of the Dispute Settlement Body, Report by the Chairman, Ambassador Peter Balas, to the Trade Negotiations Committee, TN/DS/9 (6 June 2003). The Chairman's Text of 28 May 2003, doc. Job (03)/91/Rev.1, is contained as in annex to doc. TN/DS/9 (hereinafter Balas Draft).

respondent). This proposal was included in the Balas Draft as bracketed Article 28 (entitled "Litigation Costs"). This measure, if properly implemented, could go a long way in defusing one impediment developing countries currently have in using the system.[100]

The remaining proposals directly relate to measures increasing the rate of compliance with panel and Appellate Body reports. The first suggestion is for the compliance timeline to be shortened at the initial implementation phase of the process. More specifically, the "reasonable period of time" to comply with panel should be shortened to require compliance within the "shortest possible implementation period, adjusted to the particular circumstances of the case". Article 21(3)(c) currently provides a guideline that a losing party should be given, "reasonable period of time ... not exceed(ing) 15 months" to comply with the adopted decision, but then goes on to state that the implementation time may be "shorter or longer, depending upon the particular circumstances".[101] While the problem of arbitrators extending the period to unreasonable lengths is no longer a problem,[102] the reasonable time standard should be reduced on a case-by-case basis taking into account one legislative cycle in the respondent Member country. As most governments do not have the power or authority to automatically implement the recommendations of a panel/Appellate Body report, the reasonable period should not be abandoned altogether. For this reason, Mexico's proposal to eliminate the reasonable period altogether cannot be supported.[103]

The second proposal is for more stringent rules regarding effective surveillance/monitoring during the reasonable period given to a Member to comply with the rulings and recommendations of the DSB and for expedited compliance review so as to allow for authorization to suspend concessions as quickly as possible following the expiration of the reasonable period.

Currently, Article 21(3) of the DSU requires the losing member "inform the DSB of its intentions in respect of implementation of

---

[100] Related proposals addressing increased timelines for developing countries should also be addressed. Several such proposals were incorporated into the Balas Draft. For instance, under the surveillance rules of Article 21.6, where the Member concerned (implementing party) is a developing country, it must report on the status of its implementation at least at every second scheduled DSB meeting, whereas developed country Members must report at every scheduled DSB meeting. See Balas Draft, Article 21.6. Another example of special and differential treatment accorded in the Balas Draft can be seen in Article 4.10, which provides that during consultations, "Members shall give special attention to the particular problems and interests of developing country Members" and "when the party complained against is an least developed country Member, the possibility of holding consultations in the capital of that Member shall always be considered".

[101] See contra, Article 4.7 of the SCM Agreement, which allows a panel to recommend that the subsidy at issue is withdrawn without delay.

[102] Mercurio, supra note 5, 126–129.

[103] TN/DS/W/40, p 4–5.

the recommendations and rulings of the DSB" at a DSB meeting held within 30 days after the date of adoption of the panel or Appellate Body report. But the rules do not require any affirmative action or even good faith on the part of the respondent, who can simply do very little until the expiration of the reasonable period of time without penalty. More specifically, the only obligation placed upon the Member concerned that it must comply with during the implementation period is providing a "status report" six months into the reasonable period and continuing at regular intervals. There is no requirement, however, as to how specific or vague the losing member must be in reporting. All the DSB can insist upon for purposes of fulfilling its obligation under Article 21(6) to "keep under surveillance the implementation of adopted recommendations or rulings" is the report itself. Thus, the Member concerned is not required to identify the changes such as the offending measures it will remove or implementing legislation that will bring it into compliance with the ruling. Members are not even required to specify any sort of implementation schedule or consult with the winning party over implementation.

Misuse of the implementation period was rare in the early years of the WTO,[104] but instances of misuse have both increased and received more attention. Two high profile cases against the EC best illustrate the permissiveness of the current DSU rules in this area.[105] In *EC–Bananas*, the EC repeatedly refused to specifically address its implementation intentions and continuously exhibited a reluctance to correct the violations identified in the ruling. Four months into the reasonable period, after refusing to consult with the complaining parties, the EC issued a new banana proposal. The complaining parties repeatedly claimed the new proposal would not constitute compliance, but the EC insisted that no substantive changes could be made to its proposal. Six months before its reasonable period expired and over strong objection from the original complaining parties (Ecuador, Guatemala, Honduras, Mexico and the US), the European Commission adopted the proposal. All the while, the EC's status reports to the DSB merely noted that "significant progress" was being

---

[104] See, for example, US–Standards for Reformulated and Conventional Gasoline, Status Report by the United States, WT/DS2/10/Add.1 (14 February 1997); US–Standards for Reformulated and Conventional Gasoline, Status Report by the United States, WT/DS2/10/Add.2 (10 March 1997); US–Standards for Reformulated and Conventional Gasoline, Status Report by the United States, WT/DS2/10/Add.3 (18 April 1997); US–Standards for Reformulated and Conventional Gasoline, Status Report by the United States, WT/DS2/10/Add.4 (13 May 1997); US–Standards for Reformulated and Conventional Gasoline, Status Report by the United States, WT/DS2/10/Add.5 (12 June 1997); US–Standards for Reformulated and Conventional Gasoline, Status Report by the United States, WT/DS2/10/Add.6 (18 July 1997); US–Standards for Reformulated and Conventional Gasoline, Status Report by the US, WT/DS2/10/ Add.7 (16 August 1997).

[105] See also, EC–GMOs, US–FSC, US–1910 Act.

made towards implementation.[106] Similarly, in *EC–Beef Hormones*, the EC showed a similar unambiguous reluctance to lift its ban on certain hormones from the beginning of the reasonable period. Interestingly, the reasonable period arbitrator warned "it would not be in keeping with the requirement of prompt compliance to include in the reasonable period of time, time to conduct studies or to consult experts to demonstrate the consistency of a measure already judged to be inconsistent".[107] The EC did not heed the warning, as its first status report noted only that the EC decided to launch numerous scientific studies "with a view to assessing the implications thereof for the Community's import prohibition".[108] The report did not mention anything about lifting the ban, and future official status reports continued to state only that the scientific studies were under way and progressing. Perhaps more importantly, EC officials informally stated that its ban would be maintained. When the reasonable period ended, the EC announced it would not lift its ban and would continue to study its scientific results in more depth "to consider what steps may be necessary".[109]

Resolution of the problem of inadequate checks and recourse during the reasonable period, the lack of incentives or sanctions to encourage the prompt compliance and no good-faith implementation standard are crucial to the both the legitimacy and the credibility of the DSU, and more generally of the WTO. The system currently allows Members, irrespective of good or bad faith, use the implementation period in any way they choose with little oversight from the DSB. Both *EC–Bananas* and *EC–Hormones* demonstrate the problems associated with a losing party receiving a long implementation period even when it is certain from the start that it do not intend to comply with the ruling. Additionally, because Article 22 suspension rights are only granted following the expiration of the reasonable period (or in the highly unlikely event that a Member fails to inform the DSB of its intent to implement the rulings and recommendations of the DSB), a losing party has every incentive to seek the longest period possible. During the "reasonable period", a winning party has no right to

[106] See, for example, EC–Bananas, Status Report by the European Communities, WT/DS27/17, para. 1 (13 July 1998).

[107] EC–Measures Concerning Meat and Meat Products, Status Report by the European Communities - Arbitration under Article 21.3(c) of the Understanding on Rules and Procedures Governing the Settlement of Disputes, WT/DS26/15, WT/DS48/13, para. 39 (29 May 1998). The EC requested a reasonable period of approximately four years, comprising two years for risk assessment and two years for any necessary legislative action. The EC subsequently reduced the period to two years for risk assessment and 15 months for any legislative action. Ibid, at para. 5. The arbitrator awarded a reasonable period of 15 months from the date of the adoption of the Appellate Body and panel reports by the DSB. Ibid, at para. 48.

[108] EC–Measures Concerning Meat and Meat Products, Status Report by the European Communities, WT/DS26/17, WT/DS48/15, p. 4 (14 January 1999).

[109] EC–Measures Concerning Meat and Meat Products, Status Report by the European Communities, WT/DS26/17/Add.4, WT/DS48/15/Add.4 (11 May 1999).

initiate a compliance review, even if it is obvious from the start that the losing party will not be in compliance by the expiration of the reasonable period (i.e. its progress reports do not report any implementation issues, only that it is conducting tests to challenge the ruling; or the party publicly states it does not intend to comply). Moreover, there is no penalty for bad-faith application of the reasonable period, even though that period is to be used exclusively to ensure full implementation. Thus, the system fundamentally conflicts with Article 21.1 requirement of "prompt compliance" in that it facilitates prolonged periods of non-compliance.

The DSU should be amended to prevent, or at least minimize, abuse of the reasonable period for implementation and also to allow for authorization for the suspension of concessions at an earlier time in the process. In furtherance of these goals, complaining Members should be given the right to initiate compliance review at any time following the non-compliant Member's admission that it will not comply with the decision; when it becomes obvious that the Member concerned has taken steps that, in that Members' mind, have removed the inconsistent measures; or upon the expiration of the implementation period. In order to discourage the use of the reasonable period for purposes other than full implementation, non-complaint Members who abuse or misuse the period should be subject to penalties or further retaliation (such as immediate authorization of suspension of concessions). Of course, a standard would need to be pre-set and a special panel would need to be convened in order to decide the matter. In a related point, it should be a condition for any Member seeking an implementation period to set out a schedule for implementation. While Members would not be subject to sanction for simply failing to meet the schedule (as governments are usually at the mercy of a legislative branch), this schedule could be used as evidence of abuse or misuse of the process, or lack thereof. In addition, the compliance review should be accelerated in order to prevent further delay; however, it must be stressed that the accelerated review should not be structured in such a way that favours the non-compliant Member to the detriment of the complaining Member.

Article 21bis of the Balas Draft allows for the complaining party to request consultations or the establishment of a compliance panel at any time after the other Member concerned has indicated that it does not need a reasonable period of time to implement (under Article 21.3), has submitted a notice of compliance under Article 21.6(c)(i) or 20 days before the expiration of the reasonable period of time (whichever comes first). If consultations fail to resolve the dispute, a panel will be established.[110] While this amendment attempts to resolve the issues similar to those in *EC–Bananas*, where the EC approved new measures six months before the expiration of its period, but repeatedly blocked compliance review until the

---

[110] Balas Draft, Articles 21bis(2)-(8).

expiration of the reasonable period, they fail for two main reasons. First, while the proposed amendments allow consultation during the implementation period, they do not specifically grant the complaining Member the right to initiate compliance review or the authorization of the suspension of concessions before the expiration of the implementation period. Second, the draft amendments fail to back the requirements with sanctions.[111] Thus, there is nothing to prevent the Member concerned from delaying implementation until the end of the reasonable period or even from failing to notify the DSB of the measures it has taken to comply. The draft amendments also fail to adequately address the situation of the losing party failing to use the implementation period for purposes of full implementation or compensation.

The Balas draft amendments also create a new Article 22.9 that would allow the non-compliant Member to request the withdrawal of authorization to suspend concessions if that Member feels it has now complied with the rulings and recommendations of the DSB. If the complaining Member disagrees as to the compliance of the new measures, an Article 21bis compliance panel (and if appealed, the Appellate Body) determines if the measures are now compliant. In the case of compliance, the panel/Appellate Body recommends the complaining party to withdraw the suspension of concessions. If the panel determines that the new measures remain inconsistent with WTO obligations, the affected Member can request arbitration under Article 22.6 to determine the new level of nullification or impairment. The complaining party must then modify its retaliatory measures to match the new amount.

While well meaning, the Balas draft amendments require the winning party to wait up to an additional five months to withdraw concessions in cases of non-compliance (as opposed to the current Article 22 period), prolonging the process with no benefit to the winning party.[112] This result is due to the fact that where the parties disagree as to the compliance of the concerned Member and procedures under Article 2bis have been initiated,

---

[111] Bracketed (and thus, disputed) Article 21.6 subsections (ii) and (iii) only state that if the Member concerned has not submitted a notification under Article 21.6(i) by the expiry of the reasonable period of time for implementation, "the Member concerned shall submit, at that date, a written notification of any measures it has taken to comply" and that if the Member concerned has not submitted a notification under Article 21.6(c)(i) or a final status report 45 days before the date of expiry of the reasonable period of time, "it shall, at the latest 15 days after that date, notify any measures that the Member concerned has taken to comply and any measures that it expects to have taken by the expiry of the reasonable period of time".

[112] The proposed DSU amendments to the "normal" panel procedures (i.e. a shortened consultation period, the establishment of a panel upon request, the consolidation of the Panel's "descriptive portion" with the interim report and the elimination of the panel hearing on the interim report) are only anticipated to save on average about 30 days, and thus are not likely to offset the timeline extensions to the implementation procedures that are called for under these amendments.

the complaining party may request such arbitration only "after the adoption of the compliance Panel report and, as relevant, the Appellate Body report on compliance". If necessary, the arbitral decision on damages would then be rendered within 45 days of referral. It is only after this entire process has completed that the complaining party can request authorization to suspend concessions under Article 22(2)(a). The compromise guarantees that the compliance review will not lead to never-ending litigation on minor revisions while also assuring that the winning party, before seeking Article 22 recourse, will not make a "unilateral" determination of non-compliance. However, the draft amendment stretches the present Article 22 timetable that currently requires an arbitral decision on damages within two months after the date of expiry of the reasonable period to a decision within approximately five months following the conclusion of the reasonable period. Moreover, the draft amendments leniently allow losing parties subject to WTO-sanctioned retaliation an accelerated compliance review with the opportunity for an appeal. While this may be appropriate in theory, it allows the losing party, who has resisted compliance to the point of retaliation, to continue to circumvent its compliance obligations even longer.

Furthermore, the accelerated review creates the opportunity for losing parties to implement new, subtle non-compliant measures to further delay the imposition of sanctions and may prejudice the winning party, who may not have time to acquire the detailed evidence needed to demonstrate that the measures continue to be inconsistent with WTO obligations.[113] This may allow the losing party to win the case, even though time would eventually prove the measure is non-compliant. The process would then have to repeat itself before the imposition of sanctions could take effect. In addition, Article 22 recourse would continue to apply prospectively upon the conclusion of this period; therefore, the losing party would have no incentive to comply quicker than required by the extended timeline. Moreover, while the losing party would need to specifically state its intention to implement the DSB rulings to avoid immediate recourse to Article 22, it could easily renege on that intention at the end of its implementation period and not be subject to penalty. Simply redrafting the existing Balas draft amendments to provide an automatic right of compliance review and, if appropriate, an authorization to suspend concessions, coupled with sanctions for abusing or misusing the compliance period, and the creation of a fair expedited review process

---

[113] Paragraph 4 requires the complaining party's request for the establishment of a compliance review Panel to "identify the specific measures at issue and provide a brief summary of the legal basis of the complaint, sufficient to present the problem clearly". While ordinarily such a requirement is not overly burdensome, and in fact expected, the compressed timetable of an Article 21bis compliance review does not provide sufficient time for the complaining party to adequately study the revised measure of the Member concerned.

following the expiration of the implementation period would go a long way in minimizing compliance delays and hastening compliance.

The next recommendation is for increased retaliatory measures to play a larger part in the process. More specifically, the use of cross-retaliation should be available to any complainant in every case and not only in special circumstances. The reason for this proposal is that cross-retaliation, or even the threat thereof, may increase the coercive effect of retaliatory measures. There are downsides and limitations to the use of cross-retaliation, but if fairness and compliance are the aim of any amendments, these are far outweighed by the potential benefits its use can offer.[114] Another increased retaliatory measure that should be explicitly available to Members is the use of carousel retaliation. It is well known that complaining Members carefully select which goods to target for retaliatory measures, often taking into consideration more political considerations than economic or trade considerations. In fact, Members often publicize a list of potential retaliatory targets throughout the implementation phase as a strategic attempt to increase pressure upon the non-compliant Member. Thus, a significant part of the strategy of publishing potential retaliatory targets is to mobilize lobbyist efforts within the non-compliant Member's country in an attempt to convince the government to comply with the rulings and recommendations of the DSB. It is therefore unsurprising that complaining Members usually select a range of industries that both carry some national significance in the exporting country and can yield considerable lobbyist efforts/power.

The use of so-called carousel retaliation extends the "game" and allows for the political targeting and potential targeting of a multitude of industries in the non-compliant Member. Carousel retaliation is the process of rotating the products subject to retaliatory measures following the imposition of the suspension of concessions. By changing targeted industries, the complaining government may be able to keep the pressure on the non-complying government by utilizing multiple domestic lobby groups in a similar way to that used in the list process. Thus, carousel retaliation utilizes the uncertainty among industries that fear being targeted by retaliatory measures to increase the potency of its threat.[115]

---

[114] As cross-retaliation was discussed at length above, there is no need to discuss it at length here.

[115] While the usage of carousel retaliation has the ability to provide pressure onto the responding Member, any enhancement of the retaliation through carousel sanctions assumes that a complaining Member has sufficient trade capacity with the non-complying Member to effectively retaliate. That being said, if developing countries are allowed to increase the range of potential retaliatory targets, carousel retaliation may yet prove to be a more useful tool than the present system.

The use (or mere threat) of carousel retaliation has proven to be extremely controversial. Many Members have objected to its use (including the EC when the United States threatened its use in *EC–Bananas*);[116] that is, these Members argue that once the list of items to be retaliated against has been finalized and implemented it cannot be changed. Such a view, however, does not have textual support. In fact, the WTO Secretariat has stated that the DSU "does not contain any obligation on the retaliating country to submit a list of products targeted for sanctions. Nor does the agreement contain any mention of whether or not the retaliating country can change its selection of targeted products".[117] However, with the Secretariat's publication not having legal effect, and in the absence of either a panel or Appellate Body determination on the matter, it remains unclear whether carousel retaliation is an acceptable part of retaliation.

At this point, only the United States, which enacted domestic legislation to enable the unilateral rotation of the targets of suspensions of concessions,[118] wholeheartedly supports the use of carousel retaliation (see Zimmermann, 2005). On the contrary, the Philippines and Thailand proposed to amend Article 22.7 of the DSU to prevent unilateral changes to suspension of concessions or obligations.[119]

For the most part, these suggestions are not radical, in that they do not conflict with years of precedent or the ideas and intentions of the DSU negotiators. Nor do these suggestions come with unknown consequences. They do, however, provide additional support to the system as a whole and to Members who feel the compliance is a problem in the DSU. Amendments that effectively monitor the implementation period and allow for prompt authorization for the suspension of concessions address complaints that the process takes too long to complete (and thus prolonging the harm to the complaining Member). Increased use of cross-retaliation and use of explicitly legal carousel retaliation could also serve to increase compliance.

On the contrary, all of the proposals analyzed in the previous sections have unknown but potentially large-scale consequences. Even more, while all would address some of the Member and/or commentator concerns, none of the proposals addressed all of the concerns. For instance, while collective retaliation would reduce costs and alleviate the

---

[116] Nzelibe, supra note 33, 12.

[117] "Hong Kong WTO Ministerial 2005: Briefing Notes: Dispute Settlement: Force of Argument, Not Argument of Force", http://www.wto.org/english/thewto_e/minist_e/min05_e/brief_e/brief10_e.htm at 3 August 2007

[118] Part of African and Caribbean Trade Act of 2000, Pub. L. No. 106–200, 114 Stat. 251 (2000), codified in various sections of 19 USC (2000) ('Carousel Retaliation Act').

[119] TN/DS/W/1, 5; TN/DS/W/3, 2. See also, TN/DS/W/49 (Communication from Australia), 6.

inability of developing countries to effectively retaliate against larger Members, it does not eliminate or even slightly reduce the costs of retaliation. Likewise, proponents of monetary compensation argue that it does not reduce trade volume as traditional trade retaliation, yet it is a clear break from GATT/WTO tradition, places compliance in the hands of the non-compliant Member and may have the effect of reducing the overall compliance rate.

The DSU is not in need of a complete overall, and the statistics bear witness to the fact that compliance with DSB rulings have been, in the main, very high. However, all Members, including developing countries and LDCs, must feel that the system will not only give them the opportunity to utilize the system and "win" a dispute but also that the system gives them the means to enforce the rulings. The recommendations made in this chapter should assist in all facets of the process without dramatically parting from the ideals, tenets and traditions and without leaping into the unknown without substantial justification and solid reasoning.

References

Bagwell, K., Mavroidis, P., Staiger, R. (2004), The case for tradable remedies in WTO dispute settlement. World Bank Policy Research Working Paper No. 3314, pp. 8–12.

Bown, C.P. (2002), The economics of trade disputes, the GATT's Article XXIII, and the WTO's dispute settlement understanding. *Economics and Politics* 14, 283.

Busch, M., Reinhardt, E. (2000), Bargaining in the shadow of the law: early settlement in GATT/WTO disputes. *Fordham International Law Journal* 24, 158.

Davey, W.J. (2005), The WTO dispute settlement: how have developing countries fared?" Illinois Public Law and Legal Theory Research Papers Series Research Paper No. 05-17, (November 30), available at http://papers.ssrn.com/sol3/papers.cfm?abstract_id = 862804

Davies, A. (2006), Reviewing dispute settlement at the World Trade Organization: a time to reconsider the role/s of compensation? *World Trade Review* 5, 31, 38.

Eleso, A. (2006), WTO dispute settlement remedies: monetary compensation as an alternative for developing countries. American University Working Paper Series, pp. 24–25.

Guzman, A. (2002), International law: a compliance based theory. *California Law Review* 90, 1823.

Kovenock, D., Thursby, M. (1992), GATT, dispute settlement and cooperation. *Economics and Politics* 4, 151.

Steinberg, R. (2002), In the shadow of law or power? Consensus-based bargaining and outcomes in the GATT/WTO. *International Organization* 56, 339, 347.

Subramanian, A., Watal, J. (2000), Can trips serve as an enforcement device for developing countries in the WTO? *Journal of International Economic Law* 3, 403, 410.

Zimmermann, T. (2005), WTO dispute settlement at ten: evolution, experiences, and evaluation. *Aussenwirtschaft* 60, 27, 53.

CHAPTER 17

Enforcing WTO Compliance through Public Opinion and Direct Effect: Two New Proposals to Enhance the Compliance Perspectives for Least Developed WTO Members

Naboth van den Broek[☆]

International Trade Attorney, Washington, DC/Brussels
E-mail address: naboth.vandenbroek@wilmerhale.com

Abstract
Limited participation of least developed countries (LDCs) in the WTO's dispute settlement system has been the focus of intensive debate among WTO scholars, diplomats and, in particular, WTO lawyers. Central to this debate are the major hurdles (financial and political) that LDCs are generally perceived to face in using the existing system of remedies in the WTO system to enforce compliance. Of the two existing compliance enforcement mechanisms, the first – compensation – is often unrealistic because the WTO Member whose measures have been found to be WTO inconsistent has to agree with it; while the second – retaliation (i.e., the suspension of concessions with regard to the non-complying Member) – is a costly and in many ways counter-productive "shooting oneself in the foot" remedy that LDCs in particular can usually ill afford.

This chapter briefly discusses proposals for reform that have been proposed to alleviate these problems. The chapter then reviews two additional instruments that LDCs could pursue to improve their ability to enforce compliance and make the WTO dispute settlement system a more viable instrument: limited use of direct effect; and increased use of the instrument of publicity and public relations, including through civil society. These instruments, whether independently, or in combination with existing mechanisms and other new compliance enforcement measures, could provide useful tools for the WTO's poorest Members to increase the chances for pay-off from WTO litigation and for compliance with WTO law by larger and more powerful trading partners.

[☆] The author is an attorney at WilmerHale in Washington, DC, and Brussels. The opinions voiced are the author's only and cannot be attributed to WilmerHale or any of its clients.

Frontiers of Economics and Globalization
Volume 6 ISSN: 1574-8715
DOI: 10.1108/S1574-8715(2009)0000006020

Keywords: Direct effect, public opinion, WTO, enforcing compliance, compensation, collective retaliation, suspension of voting rights, tradable retaliation, mandatory compensation, retrospective damages, least developed countries, retroactive effect, Appellate Body, political realism, dispute settlement, state power, rule oriented system, verification, monitoring, cross retaliation, remedies, suspension of right to dispute, financial compensation

JEL classifications: F13, K33, K42, O19

1. Introduction

One of the issues that has kept WTO scholars, diplomats and, in particular, WTO lawyers talking for a number of years now is the limited participation of least developed countries in WTO dispute settlement, their "competitive disadvantage" in bringing cases and – perhaps most importantly – the difficulties they face in using the existing system of remedies in the WTO system (compensation and retaliation) to enforce compliance with WTO law. Compensation is often unrealistic because the WTO Member whose measures have been found to be WTO inconsistent has to agree with it, while retaliation – i.e., the suspension of concessions with regard to the non-complying Member – is costly and in many ways counter-productive. "Shooting oneself in the foot" – as such trade retaliation is often described as – while according to some not necessarily a negative in enforcing compliance when done by a larger, more developed WTO Member, quickly becomes a real impediment to enforcing compliance and a drag on the effectiveness of the WTO dispute settlement to poorer and smaller countries.

Numerous solutions have been suggested, including collective retaliation by more than one WTO Member; tradeable retaliation rights; suspension of voting rights or the right to use the WTO dispute settlement system; mandatory compensation and broader use of monetary and retrospective damages.

Looking at legal, political and political-economic aspects of compliance and enforcement, this chapter reviews two additional instruments that least developed countries could pursue to improve their ability to enforce compliance and thus to make enforcement of WTO law a more viable and attractive option: limited use of direct effect in favour of the world's least developed countries and increased use of the instrument of publicity and public relations, including through civil society, to induce compliance. These instruments, whether independently or in combination with DSU reform efforts, could provide useful tools for the WTO's poorest Members to increase the chances for pay-off from WTO litigation and for compliance with WTO law by large trading nations.

Below, we discuss, first, the general outline and characteristics of the WTO's system of compliance enforcement as laid down in the WTO's dispute settlement understanding ("DSU") (Section 2 below). We then briefly discuss the problems that the WTO's poorest Members experience in using the WTO dispute settlement system in general and its compliance mechanisms in particular (Section 3). Subsequently, we discuss existing proposals for reform of the DSU's compliance enforcement instruments and how most of them remain ineffective from the perspective of least developed WTO Members (Section 4), followed by a discussion of two additional suggestions: limited direct effect to the benefit of the WTO's poorest Members and increased use of public opinion to induce compliance (Section 5). We end with some concluding remarks.

2. *The WTO system of compliance enforcement*

The dispute settlement understanding (DSU) of the WTO generally receives acclaim for its powerful and relatively uncompromising compliance mechanism.[1] When a Member is (temporarily) unable or unwilling to comply with an adverse ruling of a WTO panel or the Appellate Body, the complainant has a right to try to negotiate compensation, in the form of alternative trade concessions. The responding Member – that is, the Member who is alleged not to be acting in compliance with WTO law – has to agree to the compensation sought in order for it to come into place.

When the parties do not reach agreement on compensation, the complainant can ask the WTO's dispute settlement body to authorize it to suspend concessions towards the non-complying party.[2] Suspension of concessions – or, "retaliation" – usually takes the form of higher import duties imposed on certain products imported into the market of the complaining Member by the Member who has been found not to be in compliance. However, it can take certain other forms as well, including, for example, temporary revocation of intellectual property rights.

Whereas these measures were at least originally seen only as temporary compensation for nullified or impaired benefits,[3] they have come to be regarded more and more as instruments of enforcement,[4] in line with the preference for compliance and what has been branded the "growing

[1] Jackson (1997, p. 60); see also, however, Bello (1996, p. 416), who argue that defendants have the option of non-compliance and can opt for payment of compensation or the endurance of suspension of obligations. For more recent discussions of the topic, see, for example, van den Broek (2003, pp. 127–162, 139) and Sykes (2000, pp. 347–357).

[2] Article 22(3) DSU.

[3] On this subject, see also Pauwelyn (2000, pp. 335–447, 335–347).

[4] Horn and Mavroidis (1999, p. 18). The authors discuss three possible purposes of suspension of concessions: compensate – which does not work for economical reasons because the suspension of concessions also negatively influences one's own consumer prices – change behaviour and deter future behaviour.

tension within the WTO legal system between protecting bilateral – contractual balances and enforcing multilateral treaties".[5] The "relative infrequency" (Hudec, 1990) of these measures, their "acknowledged pointlessness from a commercial point of view" (Hudec, 1990, pp. 199–200), the lack of retroactive effect to achieve any form of restitutio in integrum and the fact that other Members can still complain that the measures are WTO inconsistent all show that the point is not remedying, it is compliance.

This system has proven quite effective. The pressure to induce compliance is exercised on the very government institution (the trade ministry) that can be expected to be the driving force behind compliance, the measures induce private parties that are affected by retaliation (or trade compensation) to pressure their government to comply with WTO obligations and the self-inflicted pain suffered by the complainant (who bears at least as much of the pain of trade restrictive sanctions as the responding Member whose exports are curtailed).

Thus, in the period 1995 through 2006, 356 complaints were filed with the WTO (Leitner and Lester, 2007). Over that same period, 108 appeals were brought to the WTO Appellate Body (Leitner and Lester, 2007, p. 172), and 34 so-called compliance disputes – disputes in situations where there is disagreement as to the existence or consistency with a covered agreement of measures taken to comply with recommendations and rulings of the WTO dispute settlement body (Leitner and Lester, 2007, p. 175), roughly 65% of which were then also appealed (Leitner and Lester, 2007, p. 177). Disputes range from relatively limited commercial issues to politically sensitive and large economic matters (e.g., *US–Helms Burton Cuba Sanctions Act*; *US–FSC*; *EC–GMO*, *EC–Hormones* and *EC–Asbestos* cases).

Other statistics indicate that by early 2007, 109 panel/Appellate Body reports were adopted by the WTO dispute settlement body without compliance disputes ensuing, with WTO violations found in nearly 90% of them

[5] Idem; see also Trachtman (1999, p. 671), who argues that "the goal of dispute settlement is not punishment, but tightening the balance of concessions" (referring to the arbitrators' report in the Bananas case: *European Communities – Regime for the Importation, Sale and Distribution of Bananas – Recourse to Arbitration by the European Communities under Article 22.6 of the DSU*, Decisions by the Arbitrators, 9 April 1999, WT/DS27//ARB, at para. 6.3. However, see in this respect also, for example, the US Statement of Administrative Action (SAA) accompanying the transmittal of the Uruguay Round Agreements Act (URAA) to the US Congress:

> (C)ountries that bring successful challenges will be authorized to withdraw Uruguay Round trade benefits from the offending country if, after a reasonable period following the adoption of the panel or Appellate Body report, the matter cannot be settled in a mutually satisfactory manner. These changes mean that when the United States brings a successful challenge against another government under the DSU, the United States will have improved leverage to insist that the defending government remedy its violation.

(Uruguay Round Trade Agreements, H.R.DOC No. 103–316 (1994, p. 1034), see also Grané (2001, pp. 755–772)).

(Wilson, 2007). Only 22 panel reports and 12 Appellate Body reports were subject to compliance proceedings under Article 21.5 of the DSU (Wilson, 2007). While compliance issues certainly remain, the overall record has been quite good.[6]

3. Dispute settlement and compliance enforcement for the WTO's poorest members

The picture is different, however, when one looks more specifically at the poorest, least developed WTO Members. Data shows that, in general, this group does not bring complaints under the WTO's dispute settlement system. Of the 356 complaints brought between 1995 and 2006, 227 were brought by high income WTO Members (and high income Members were respondents in 216 cases) (Leitner and Lester, 2007, p. 169). Low income Members were responsible for only 25 complaints (they were respondents in 22 complaints) (Leitner and Lester, 2007, p. 169) while only one least developed country features as a complainant (Leitner and Lester, 2007, p. 167) and no cases were brought against least developed countries. (Leitner and Lester, 2007, p. 168). Indeed, the EU and the United States clearly the most active litigators, and large emerging economies such as Brazil, India and Korea certainly present in the space, the complete absence of the smaller and poorer African, Asian and Latin American countries is telling.

Even more telling is the almost complete lack of use by developing countries (indeed, by non-OECD countries generally) of countermeasures (retaliation, compensation). Bagwell, Mavroidis and Staiger demonstrate this quite clearly based on the existing empirical data in a publication in 2004 (Bagwell *et al.*, 2004).

In other words, while the WTO's dispute settlement system is actively used to enforce compliance with WTO rules, and its compliance record overall is not at all bad, low income and least developed country WTO Members rarely use the system and rarely enforce their rights vis-à-vis other WTO Members – they are not able to fully use and reap the benefits of the WTO legal system of which they are a part.

Multiple factors likely explain this situation, including the cost of engaging in WTO dispute settlement; political realism; available resources (a country with a small trade department will not easily be able to spare one or more officials to litigate a WTO case) and the complexity of verifying WTO consistency of foreign measures and of bringing a WTO case.

At least in some part, however, developing countries' relative absence from WTO dispute settlement may also be explained by the fact that many of the world's least developed countries feel that for them the

[6] See also Wilson (2007, pp. 397–398) and Hudec (1991, p. 305). See also van den Broek (2003, pp. 127–162, 142–148), for a general overview of early WTO compliance.

system does not offer effective mechanisms to enforce compliance. In very simple economic terms, the cost-benefit analysis simply does not add up.

A core cause of this compliance enforcement problem is that, on the one hand, the WTO's system of compliance enforcement aims to overcome pure power-based international relations, while, on the other hand, relying on (economic) state power to do so. The WTO system in general and the dispute settlement system in particular are often said to aim at, or at least be very supportive in overcoming pure power-based international relations. The system imposes a rule-oriented system, thus creating mutual expectations about other countries' behaviour and incentives to solve disputes legally rather than by means of state power. Indeed, the WTO's compliance enforcement system has often been praised in particular for overcoming traditional power politics in international trade disputes and for offering a more fully legalistic mechanism. This, it was often said, would especially benefit developing countries who would now be able to enforce their WTO rights more effectively and smaller countries who previously were at a disadvantage against larger countries. In reality, the WTO's system of compliance enforcement remains heavily power-based and relies on Members individually (the parties to a dispute) to use their own power and leverage to enforce compliance (van den Broek, 2003). This causes problems for developing countries in particular.

First, compensation is theoretical as it can only be brought about with the agreement of the losing party in a dispute; trade retaliation amounts to trade contraction and therefore goes against the very trade liberalizing principles that the GATT/WTO system stands for and hurts the retaliating country as well as the Member whose compliance is being sought; neither remedy offers relief to the private parties whose interests have been damaged and, instead, "innocent bystanders" (those at whom retaliation is eventually aimed) are damaged because they are either paying the compensation or suffering the consequences or retaliation.[7]

Second, whatever instrument one uses, as long as the level of retaliation, compensation or monetary compensation is calculated the way it currently is (e.g., based on the level of trade concerned in the case of GATT violations), a small (developing) economy is at a disadvantage compared to a large (developed) country in terms of the pressure it can exercise on a non-complying Member. To put it differently, it will be hard for a small, lesser developed country to put sufficient pressure on a (large) trading partner to comply because its trading volumes are so low.

Finally, lack of monitoring abilities, the inability to put effective pressure on larger Members to comply rapidly and – consequently – the fact that more powerful, larger or developed countries may be encouraged to play for time,

---

[7] For a more complete overview of remaining problems with the existing system of remedies, see Bronckers and van den Broek (2005, pp. 101–126).

limits the effectiveness of the current system of remedies even more. Again, this is a problem in particular when the complaining party is a developing country.

As a result, access to dispute settlement in reality is unequal. For many of the smaller and poorer developing countries, the costs (financial and political) of WTO litigation far outweigh any potential benefits.[8] We call compensation and retaliation "remedies", but for some countries, it is questionable whether they really are.

The problems encountered by developing countries are illustrated by the case Ecuador brought against the EC's *Bananas* régime. Ecuador did not see any realistic way to retaliate in the areas (GATT and GATS) where the WTO violations of the EU were found to have taken place. There was simply not enough trade in non-essential goods and services between the EU and Ecuador. Ultimately, Ecuador was given the authority to cross-retaliate in the area of TRIPS. It could allow local wine producers to sell their red wine as "Bordeaux", and it could permit local music pirates to sell unauthorized copies of some European hit recordings, though only for the Ecuadorian domestic market. At most, such retaliation created annoyance amongst French wine producers and certain European hit artists particularly popular in Ecuador. It resulted only in limited political pressure on the EC.

In addition, whatever Ecuador did, WTO remedies offered no relief to Ecuador's exporters of bananas. Their damages could not be repaired, and there was no incentive for the EC to bring its Bananas régime into compliance with WTO rules promptly, as any remedies Ecuador would have imposed could only have been prospective in nature.[9] Antigua is in a similar situation with regard to the United States in the *US – Gambling* dispute (Lester, 2008).

In other words, though certainly not the only reason behind relatively infrequent use of WTO dispute settlement by developing countries, and particularly least developed countries, finding a better way to ensure compliance would make WTO dispute settlement significantly more attractive to developing countries, particularly if such a solution would include a way to ensure some form of compensation for damages suffered.

---

[8] Smaller developed countries of course may face this problem too. See the only case in the history of GATT 1947, where retaliation was authorized yet never exercised by The Netherlands against the US for maintaining GATT-illegal restrictions on Dutch dairy imports. See GATT, 1st Supp. BISD 62 (1953). While larger and more advanced developing countries (e.g., Brazil, China, India and South Africa) are not normally in the same position as either small developing countries or least developed countries, say, Cameroon or Costa Rica.

[9] See further *EC – Regime for the importation, sale and distribution of bananas – recourse to arbitration by the EC under Article 22.6 DSU*, Decision by the Arbitrators, WT/DS27/ARB/ECU, of 24 March 2000, para. 177. We note that in mid-2004, Brazil was also considering "cross-retaliation" in the *US – Cotton Subsidies* case (WT/DS267/R, of 18 June 2004) based on the same concern that traditional retaliation – even by Brazil, despite being so much larger an economy than Ecuador – would not exercise sufficient pressure on the US to comply. BNA, Daily Report for Executives, 17 June 2004, "Brazilian Farmers Eye Retaliatory Options if US Fails to Comply with Cotton Ruling."

It could, as such, ensure greater compliance – and therefore greater trade liberalization, i.e., economic gains – across the board. It could provide both tangible economic benefits – greater liberalization, increased market access and the economic benefits derived from it – and political and developmental gains.

4. None of the existing proposals fully remedy the situation for the world's poorest

Over the past few years, a wide range of proposals for improving the WTO's system of remedies has already been put forward.[10] Many of these have focused particularly on the position of developing country Members and their ability to use and benefit from the system. Under a system of *collective retaliation*, developing countries could be permitted to join forces and jointly exercise pressure on a non-complying developed WTO member. Creation of *tradeable retaliation rights* would allow a developing country to sell its right to retaliate to a developed country. *Mandatory compensation* would imply an obligation on the non-complying country to offer additional trade concessions (e.g., a tariff reduction), normally in another product category, for as long as non-compliance continues. Others have proposed expanding the use of cross-retaliation.[11] Some other solutions have looked beyond the existing WTO remedies: for example, "suspension of voting rights, or suspension of the right to use the dispute settlement system" would penalize non-complying Members by (temporarily) removing some of the procedural and decision-making rights they have under the WTO system.

---

[10] For a fairly complete overview of proposals made by members in the context of the DSU Review, see the website of the Institution of International Economic Law, at http://www.law.georgetown.edu/iiel/research/projects/dsureview/synopsis.html. See also on current remedies and the need for reform: Pauwelyn (2001, pp. 335–447), Reif and Florestal (1998), Subramanian and Watal (2000, pp. 403–416), Mavroidis (2000, pp. 763–814), Charnovitz (2001, pp. 792–832), Grané (2001, pp. 755–772), Anderson (2002, pp. 123–134), Mosoti (2001, p. 231), van den Broek (2003, pp. 127–162) and Bronckers and van den Broek (2005, pp. 101–126). Particularly interesting is also Bagwell *et al.* (2004). Bagwell, Mavroidis and Staiger discuss many of the pros and cons of a Mexican proposal for tradeable retaliation rights. In this author's opinion, however, they do no give sufficient weight to the continued trade restrictive nature of such a remedy (unless the violating member purchases the retaliation right himself and retires it – in which case, however, the retaliation right effectively is transformed into monetary compensation). As will be discussed more generally below, a system of tradeable retaliation rights, like many of the other existing proposals, also does not remedy the inherent asymmetry that exists as a result of the smaller market size of poorer, smaller nations and the immediate effect this has on their ability to induce compliance.

[11] See, for a recent example, Spadano (2008, pp. 511–545). Of course, while cross-retaliation may solve some problems and may be quite effective for a country like Brazil (*cf.* the ongoing *US–Cotton* retaliation debate), the matter is quite different for a small least developed country.

Yet none of these proposals solves the core problems of the current remedy system. They still raise either the same or similar objections – they still contract trade and require the retaliating countries to shoot themselves in the foot (e.g., tradeable retaliation rights; collective retaliation); they create costs for innocent bystanders (e.g., tradeable retaliation rights; collective retaliation; mandatory compensation and in a way also suspension of voting rights or the right to use the dispute settlement system); they rely on the cooperation of the non-complying party and its industry (e.g., any not fully mandatory form of compensation); or they create a whole new set of problems, ranging from sovereignty concerns, incentives for foot-dragging (e.g., mandatory compensation), to systemic questions about the viability of the WTO (suspension of voting rights, suspension of DSU rights, etc.).[12] Moreover, most of these proposals, while arguably resulting in some form of pressure on the non-complying Member to comply, do not do anything to effectively compensate the affected Member and the industry and consumers for the damages of a violation of WTO law (even mandatory compensation would normally benefit the complaining government and other industry sectors only).

Financial compensation – as an instrument that would be broadly available to least developed country WTO Members – would solve at least some of these problems and would be worth considering seriously as part of any future DSU reform.[13]

Financial compensation has several compelling advantages:

1. *Financial compensation is not trade restrictive.* The obligation to pay financial compensation is not trade restrictive, which is attractive both systemically (no further disturbance of optimal allocation of production) and from the point of view of the country imposing the measures (no need to shoot oneself in the foot).
2. *Financial compensation helps redress injury.* Financial compensation also helps to redress the injury of the country and/or the private interests who actually suffer from the WTO illegal measure, because it means at least partial reparation of damages caused by the WTO illegal act. In this

[12] We set out these concerns in more detail in a recent article in JIEL: Bronckers and van den Broek (2005, pp. 106–109, 101–126).

[13] Id. See also, Bronckers (2001, pp. 41, 62–63) and Esserman and Howse (2003, pp. 130, 135). See also, for some remaining question marks and further thoughts, van den Broek (2003, p. 156). Note again that this paper only explicitly deals with financial compensation under GATT and GATS. Under some of the other agreements, for example, TRIPS, SCM, the issues are sometimes somewhat different, though in our view the financial compensation could take roughly the same form.

respect, we submit that it can be left to the individual WTO Members to decide whether and how to redistribute the compensation received.[14]

3. *In most cases, financial compensation will work as well, and sometimes even better to induce compliance.* Partly as a result of these two principal characteristics (not trade restrictive and redressing injury), the deterrent or persuasive effect of monetary compensation will often be no less than that of traditional trade retaliation. In the hands of developing countries, financial compensation is in fact likely to be more effective against non-complying (larger) developed countries than the current instruments of compensation and retaliation. Yet, countries could still be given a choice between classic trade retaliation and the new instrument of financial compensation.
4. *Financial compensation does not lead to a disproportionate burden on innocent bystanders.* The obligation to pay financial compensation would be equally distributed as a charge on the non-complying country's budget and not constitute a disproportionate burden on particular groups of innocent bystanders.
5. *Financial compensation can be a disincentive to foot-dragging.* Financial compensation can be a disincentive to foot-dragging, particularly if some retroactivity would be introduced in the WTO dispute settlement system.[15] This is an advantage from a bilateral perspective both for the country faced with the WTO illegal measures and for the WTO system as such by lowering the overall cost of WTO dispute settlement and the pressure on the system caused by long-term non-compliance.
6. *Financial compensation is in line with general public international law.* Providing instruments both for compensation or reparation and for compliance inducement is fully in line with general public international law. The International Law Commission's Draft Articles on State Responsibility[16] and public international law in general[17] recognize both instruments of compliance inducement and instruments aimed at full reparation. In public international law, an unlawful act calls for two

[14] Reference is also made to the various ways in which this is arranged in other areas of public international law and where compensation is due to either a foreign government or a private party, and where it is up to a government receiving compensatory payments to decide for itself whether or not it redistributes to private parties.

[15] See, for example, Grané (2001).

[16] See *Draft Articles on Responsibility of States for internationally wrongful acts*, adopted by the International Law Commission at its 53rd session (September 2001), Supplement No. 10 (A/56/10), chp.IV.E.1, at http://www.un.org/ilc/texts/instruments/english/draft%20articles/9_6_2001.pdf, particularly Articles 29–31.

[17] Umpire Parker in the "Lusitania" cases (US/Germany) 7 RIAA 32, 39 (1923), at 100–101; PCIJ, *Chorzow Factory* case (jurisdiction) (1927), PCIJ, Series A, No. 9, at 21; PCIJ, *Chorzow Factory* case (indemnity) (1928), PCIJ, Series A, No. 17, at 29, 47. For a further comparison between the rules on remedies on public international law and WTO law, see Mavroidis (2000, p. 766 *et seq.*) and Grané (2001).

reactions: (i) compliance, which is an obligation both towards the injured state and to the international community and the legal system as a whole, and (ii) reparation for remedial purposes, to make good the damages caused to the injured state.

7. *Financial compensation adds an element of fairness*. Providing for more general availability of reparation, especially for developing countries, can also add an element of "fairness" to the WTO legal system. It has been shown quite convincingly that such "fairness" plays an important role in explaining compliance with domestic and international law (Chayes and Chayes, 1995; Frank, 1998) and in the governance of the international system in general.[18]

Both systemic and practical counterarguments against monetary damages tend to fail. In particular, there is no real basis for the argument that financial compensation would run counter to the objective of GATT dispute settlement because the system's objective is only to restore a balance of concessions between governments. Today's rule-based WTO system has moved beyond a reciprocal exchange of concessions (consider, e.g., the SPS, TBT and TRIPS agreements). Rule compliance has become the norm. Moreover, private initiative is the key to achieve the WTO's objectives. As one WTO panel noted:

> Many of the benefits to [WTO] Members which are meant to flow as a result of the acceptance of various disciplines under the GATT/WTO depend on the activity of individual economic operators in the national and global market places. The purpose of many of these disciplines, indeed one of the primary objects of the GATT/WTO as a whole, is to produce certain market conditions which would allow this individual activity to flourish.[19]

Indeed, the success of the WTO, increasing the world's economic welfare, depends to a considerable extent on private initiative.[20]

---

[18] *Cf.*, for example, Nye (2004).

[19] WTO Panel Report, *US – Sections 301–310 of the Trade Act of 1974*, WT/DS152/R, of 22 December 1999, at paras 7.72ff. Note that this view contrasts sharply with the European Court of First Instance (CFI), Joined Cases T-174/00 and T-210/00, Biret International SA, of 11 January 2002, [2002] ECR II-17, at para. 62 ("The purpose of the WTO agreements is to govern relations between States or regional organizations for economic integration and not to protect individuals"). We suggest, with respect, that this contrary view recently expressed by the European Court of First Instance is outmoded. It should also be noted that this judgment was overturned on appeal, albeit on other grounds, by the European Court of Justice (ECJ), Joined Cases C-93/02 and 94/02, Biret International SA, of 30 September 2003, [2003] ECR 1-10565.

[20] Some have even gone as far as distinguishing the WTO from other treaties, arguing that the success of other treaties (such as nuclear disarmament and human rights treaties) depends primarily on state actions. This distinction between treaties was drawn by Davies (2004).

Concerns about such practical aspects of monetary damages as the difficulty of calculating damages and their unenforceability also do not hold when one compares the system, for example, with investment arbitration or general public international law dispute settlement. Finally, there is of course a potential concern that a system of financial compensation would lead (richer) countries to "buy" their way out of compliance, although such "efficient breach" would arguably still run counter to the preference for compliance that is central to the WTO dispute settlement system and could be responded to by engaging in retaliation after all (be it direct or cross-retaliation).[21]

However, despite its merits, even financial compensation alone would not fully solve the problem for the smallest and poorest developing nations. It does not change the fundamental asymmetry that exists between large and small developed and developing countries.[22] Whatever instrument one uses, as long as the level of retaliation, compensation or monetary compensation is calculated the way it currently is (e.g., based on the level of trade concerned in the case of GATT violations), a small (developing) economy is at a disadvantage compared to a large (developed) country in terms of the pressure it can exercise on a non-complying Member.[23] While financial compensation will enable those countries that are now simply unable to take on the burden of withdrawing concessions and shooting themselves in the foot to send a signal, and provides them with at least some form of reparation for the damages caused by non-compliance, it may not do much – when used in isolation – to move the country whose laws or actions have been found to be inconsistent with WTO law towards compliance.

5. *Two additional proposals*

It is for this precise reason that it may be worth floating two additional suggestions that merit further review: the provision of limited forms of direct effect (e.g., limited to enforcement by least developed countries) and increased use of publicity, P.R. and the role of civil society by poorer Members to enforce WTO law against larger, richer Members.

5.1. Limited direct effect

Direct effect of WTO law, like enforcement and compliance, is another hotly debated issue among WTO law scholars. "Direct effect" essentially refers to the way in which rights and obligations incorporated in an international

---

[21] See for a more complete overview of arguments and counter arguments, Broncker and van den Broek (2005, pp. 113–114).

[22] See the discussion of counterarguments against financial compensation in Bronckers and van den Broek (2005, p. 118).

[23] Ibid.

agreement – here the WTO agreements – apply within the domestic legal order of a particular country, that is, whether they are automatically (directly) applicable or require further acts of transformation and whether they can be invoked directly by individuals or other private parties before the courts, including against the government if its actions violate WTO rules.

Most major WTO Members do not provide for direct effect of WTO law in their legal, although some will recognize certain limited forms of such effect, for example, following domestic congressional or executive action making treaty provisions directly effective. In the EU, there has been a particularly extensive debate on the direct effect of WTO law. At least in part, this may have to do with the fact that although the EU itself also does not recognize direct effect of WTO law, it does recognize such effect for certain other treaties, as well as many of its own EU-level treaty provisions (i.e., certain provisions of the EU treaty and of EU laws that would otherwise only create legal obligations between EU Member States apply and can be invoked directly by EU citizens and companies against their governments and the EU itself), based, inter alia, on the language of the EC treaty relating to international agreements that the EC is a party to and that at least in certain interpretations could be read to provide for some form of direct effect.[24]

The European Court of Justice has so far denied private parties the right to invoke violations of WTO law directly. According to the Court, granting direct effect would deprive the EU institutions of the room for manoeuvre that they need in their international trade relations.[25] In particular, says the Court, this is the case because the EU's major trading partners do not provide for direct effect either, and allowing it in the EU would therefore lead to a potential disturbance of the WTO equilibrium that is based on "reciprocity and mutual advantages".[26] It is thus a combination of the special nature of the WTO system – which in the Court's view is based on reciprocity and mutual advantages[27] – and the realpolitik of international trade relations – the absence of direct effect in the EU's major trading partners – that lead the EU's highest court to its denial of the right to challenge violations of WTO law within the EU's domestic legal order.[28]

Such arguments are hardly convincing – from a legal perspective, but even more so from a political-economic perspective – with regard to the

---

[24] See, for example, Kuijper (2005), Lavranos (2005, p. 449), Antoniadis (2005, p. 460), van den Broek (2001, pp. 411, 417), Griller (2000, p. 441) and Eeckhout (1997).

[25] See, for example, Case C-149/96 *Portugal v Council* [1999] ECR I-8395; Case C-377/02 *Van Parys* [2005] ECR I-1465.

[26] Ibid.

[27] Indeed, these are the words used in the Preamble of the WTO Agreement.

[28] Although it should be noted that EU law does allow for forms of "indirect" effect in certain specific circumstances. Thus, individuals can rely on WTO law before the EU courts in order to challenge EU legislation (i) that is intended to implement a particular obligation assumed in the context of the WTO or (ii) that refers expressly to precise provisions of the WTO agreements.

WTO's poorest Members.[29] Even if it were true that a particular least developed country does not recognize direct effect of the WTO Agreements (and thus would not fulfil a reciprocity requirement), it is hard to see how allowing direct effect within the European domestic legal order would be harmful to the EU's broader political interests in such a way as to make this a politically impossible option. Instead, from a developmental perspective – and of course, in any event, from a trade liberalization perspective – doing so would make sense. It would also increase the perception of fairness of the WTO system, as developing countries would be given an easier instrument to enforce compliance with WTO rules that they themselves have been asked to sign up to, and a significant way of giving real meaning to the commitments that LDCs have received and have themselves been asked to undertake in subsequent rounds of trade negotiations, in the Doha Round, and beyond. It would increase the WTO's inclusiveness, its fairness and legitimacy and – last but not least – would help achieve further liberalization.

It is certainly worth considering for least developed countries whether this is a bargaining chip they would want to put on the table. Be it in multilateral trade negotiations (Doha and beyond), or in negotiations on bilateral or regional trade agreements with the EU, the US and others. Having the option for one's companies or their importers (or the government itself), to challenge WTO inconsistent behaviour before the domestic courts of a large trading partner[30] would provide a very powerful tool and significantly better prospects of swift and more complete compliance than WTO litigation. It would also, presumably, make it easier to obtain damage payments (including retrospectively), interim relief or court orders pursuant to which WTO inconsistent behaviour has to be ceased.

From the perspective of the developed, major trading nations, this option would not be very costly as in most cases least developed countries represent only a minimal percentage of trade in any one particular product.[31] The policy, moreover, would be a long-term investment and

---

[29] As to why these arguments are not convincing from a legal point of view, but politically understandable vis-à-vis other major trading partner, see van den Broek (2001).

[30] Such a challenge could either pivot off a prior successful WTO challenge of the measure(s) at issue, or could be a separate, independent challenge before the domestic courts of the country allegedly violating WTO law. While the possibility of subsequent or parallel WTO and domestic court challenges of course poses a number of challenges of its own (e.g., how to deal with a situation where the WTO DSB has not yet ruled on a measure, but private parties have already brought a case before a domestic court?), such challenges are not unique. They exist with regard to other international treaty rules, between international treaty systems (e.g., NAFTA and WTO) and in situations where only limited forms of (in)direct effect are recognized (as is now the case in the EU in particular).

[31] Of course, there may be domestic political objections, but it would be important to emphasize that real current competitive threat does not come from the world's least developed countries but rather from larger, emerging economies.

sound policy towards the economic development and further liberalization of these least developed trading partners and would result – as trade liberalization in general does – in further economic gains for consumers alike. At the same time, a limited form of direct effect – provided only to least developed countries – would not affect trade relations with major trading partners (e.g., United States–EU relations) and would therefore not lead to the risks that the European Court of Justice identified. Indeed, as far as the EU is concerned, this means that, arguably, such a limited form of direct effect could even be implemented consistently with the existing case law of the European Court.

5.2. The force of public opinion

A further additional tool that least developed countries could use to enhance their ability to enforce WTO law is the force of public opinion. A brief venture into political science theory will help explain the value of such an approach.

Regime theory shows how monitoring and transparency induce greater compliance by spotlighting non-compliance and making it easier for countries to know when to sanction in their iterative game, and because the effect of non-compliance on an actor's reputation would be greater (Aceves, 1997). The more transparent the game, the more difficult it is to cheat.

Though often overlooked, norm internalization, public opinion and the role civil society plays in both are also critical elements in explaining compliance with international rules. Thus, in addition to pure powerplay and game theoretical scenarios – the traditional explanations for compliance with international norms[32] – endogenous preferences for legal compliance and a general sense of legitimacy, fairness and justice lead domestic institutions and individuals in leadership roles and in bureaucracies in a general direction of compliance.[33] Franck has described this as the concept of "compliance pull", where compliance is not so much the result of rational cost-benefit calculations, but rather a natural consequence of the "communitarian peer pressure" that results from the legitimacy and distributive justice of rules themselves.[34] Other theories have held that a "fundamental instrument for maintaining compliance with treaties" is not (the threat of) sanctioning, but "an iterative process of discourse among the parties, the treaty organization, and the wider public"

[32] See, for example, Krasner (1976, p. 323), Setear (1996, pp. 139–229), Bates and Bianco (1985, pp. 133–147) and Snidal (1985, pp. 579–614). See also, for a general overview van den Broek (2003, pp. 134–135).

[33] van den Broek (2003, p. 136).

[34] Franck (1995, p. 481). See also, Franck (1990).

(Chayes and Chayes, 1995, p. 25). Indeed, these authors say "instruments of active management" of compliance include things such as transparency, reporting and data collection, verification, monitoring, dispute settlement, capacity building and assistance, strategic review and assessment. They also recognize the role that non-governmental and governmental institutions can play in inducing and increasing compliance.[35]

One can only imagine the public outcry if a small least developed country can effectively show the developmental consequences that a WTO violation has on its industry and enlists the support of non-governmental organizations, the media and public opinion to its cause. Indeed, examples of WTO disputes involving environmental issues (Asbestos in Europe; Tuna-Dolphin in the United States and Shrimp-Turtle in the United States), as well as, for example, the debate about access to medicine (particularly AIDS medicine) that led to the adoption of the *Public Health amendment of the TRIPS Agreement* of December 6, 2005, demonstrate how effective such public pressure can be.

In short, both existing and new NGOs, as well as private business, the media and other opinion makers can play important roles in strengthening the "mobilization of shame" and to increase transparency in the "iterative game" that WTO dispute settlement and compliance are, to induce compliance. The WTO Secretariat, the WTO Advisory Centre or other such institutions could play similar roles, and, indeed, more active monitoring and information gathering on their part could be one way of creating greater transparency and a "mobilization of shame". NGOs could monitor compliance by large traders in cases won by smaller and poorer countries who do not have sufficient means for compliance monitoring and enforcement of their own. Finally, commercial players could be more vigilant themselves and could do more to identify and expose trade barriers, issues of market access and the costs they incur as a result of non-compliance by the larger WTO Members with WTO law.

Whether those instruments alone are sufficient to enforce compliance in all instances or not – I would venture that there may still be situations where compliance inducement simply necessitates power-based realpolitik – such public opinion-based strategies will certainly be very helpful in many instances, as is the realization that WTO law and policy, and enforcement of and compliance with WTO rules and WTO dispute settlement rulings can be significantly enhanced by effective use of the public policy instrument.

---

[35] This was also put forward by Weiss (1997, p. 58).

6. Conclusion

In sum, the WTO's system of compliance enforcement, overall, has proven quite effective. However, it remains heavily power- and "size-based" and as a result disfavours smaller and least developed country WTO Members. While some of the current proposals for DSU reform – monetary compensation in particular – would offer some relief, none would fully deal with the fundamental power asymmetry that underlies the problem.

Two new suggestions merit further attention and review: limited forms of direct effect, focused on least developed country Members (or at least demands for such direct effect in bilateral, regional and multilateral fora), and broader use of public opinion, transparency and plain old publicity to support enforcement action. Such instruments could offer least developed country Members additional means to fully benefit from WTO-imposed liberalization commitments and, as such, could play an important role in making the WTO system more inclusive, and increasing least developed country participation and their economic and commercial gains.

References

Aceves, W.J. (1997), Institutionalist theory and international legal scholarship. *American University Journal of International Law and Policy*, 12 (2), 251.

Anderson, K. (2002), Peculiarities of retaliation in WTO dispute settlement. *World Trade Review* 1 (2), 123–134.

Antoniadis, A. (2005), The Chiquita and Van Parys Judgments: rules, exceptions and the law. *Legal Issues of Economic Integration* 32, 460.

Bagwell, K., Mavroidis, P., Staiger, R. (2004), The case for tradable retaliation rights in WTO dispute settlement. World Bank Policy Research Working Paper 3314, May 2004 (available at http://ssrn.com/abstract = 610359).

Bates, R.H., Bianco, W.T. (1985), Co-operation by design: leadership, structure and collective dilemmas. *American Political Science Review* 84 (1), 133–147.

Bello, J.H. (1996), The WTO dispute settlement understanding: less is more. *American Journal of International Law* 90, 416.

Bronckers, M. (2001), More power to the WTO? *Journal of International Economic Law* 4, 41, 62–63.

Bronckers, M., van den Broek, N. (2005), Financial compensation in the WTO: improving the remedies of WTO dispute settlement. *Journal of International Economic Law* 8, 101–126.

Charnovitz, S. (2001), Rethinking WTO trade sanctions. *American Journal of International Law* 95 (4), 792–832.

Chayes, A., Chayes, A. (1995), *The New Sovereignty: Compliance with International Regulatory Agreements*. Harvard University Press, Cambridge, MA.

Davies, A. (2004), *Reviewing Dispute Settlement at the World Trade Organization: A Time to Reconsider the Role of Compensation*, September. Mimeo, Swansea University, UK.

Eeckhout, P. (1997), The domestic legal status of the WTO agreement: interconnecting legal systems. *Common Market Law Review* 3, 11.

Esserman, S., Howse, R. (2003), The WTO on trial. *Foreign Affairs* 82 (1), 130, 135.

Franck, T. (1990), *The Power of Legitimacy Among Nations*. Oxford University Press, New York.

Franck, T. (1995), *Fairness in International Law and Institutions*. Clarendon, Oxford, p. 481.

Frank, Th. (1998), Fairness in International Law. Clarendon Press, London.

Grané, P. (2001), Remedies under WTO Law. *Journal of International Economic Law* 4, 755–772.

Griller, S. (2000), Judicial enforceability of WTO law in the European Union: annotation to Case C-149/96, *Portugal v. Council. Journal of International Economic Law* 3, 441.

Horn, H., Mavroidis, P. (1999). Remedies in the WTO dispute settlement system and developing countries interests. http://www.econ-law.se/Papers/Remedies%20990611-1.pdf, p. 18.

Hudec, R.E. (1990), *The GATT Legal System and World Trade Diplomacy*, second ed. Butterworth, Salem, NH, pp. 199–200.

Hudec, R. (1991), *Enforcing International Trade Law*. Butterworth, Salem, NH, p. 305.

Jackson, J.H. (1997), The WTO dispute settlement understanding – misunderstanding on the nature of legal obligation. *American Journal of International Law* 91, 60.

Krasner, S.D. (1976), State power and the structure of international trade. *World Politics* 28 (April), 323.

Kuijper, P.J. (2005), WTO law in the European Court of Justice. *Common Market Law Review* 42, 1313.

Lavranos, N. (2005), The Chiquita and Van Parys Judgments: an exception to the rule of law. *Legal Issues of Economic Integration* 32, 449.

Leitner, K., Lester, S. (2007), WTO dispute settlement 1995–2006, a statistical analysis. *Journal of International Economic Law*, 10(1), 165–179, 168.

Lester, S. (2008), The WTO gambling dispute: antigua mulls retaliation as the U.S. negotiates withdrawal of its GATS commitments. *ASIL Insight* 12 (5), available at http://www.asil.org/insights/2008/04/insights080408.html

Mavroidis, P.C. (2000), Remedies in the WTO Legal System: between a rock and a hard place. *European Journal of International Law* 11 (4), 763–814.

Mosoti, V. (2001), In our own image, not theirs: damages as an antidote to the remedial deficiencies in the WTO dispute settlement process: a view from Sub-Saharan Africa. *Boston University International Law Journal* 19, 231.

Nye, J.S. (2004), *Soft Power, The Means to Success in World Politics.* Public Affairs, Inc., New York.

Pauwelyn, J.H.B. (2000), Enforcement and countermeasures in the WTO: rules are rules – towards a more collective approach. *American Journal of International Law* 94, 335–447, 335–347.

Pauwelyn, J.H.B. (2001), Enforcement and countermeasures in the WTO: rules are rules – toward a more collective approach. *American Journal of International Law* 97, 335–447.

Reif, T.M., Florestal, M. (1998), Revenge of the push-me, pull-you: the implementation process under the WTO dispute settlement understanding. *International Lawyer* 32, 755–788.

Setear, J.K. (1996), An iterative perspective on treaties: a synthesis of international relations theory and international law. *Harvard Journal International Law* 37, 139–229.

Snidal, D. (1985), The limits of hegemonic stability theory. *International Organization* 39, 579–614.

Spadano, L.E.F.A. (2008), Cross-agreement retaliation in the WTO dispute settlement system: an enforcement mechanism for developing countries? *World Trade Review* 7 (3), 511–545.

Subramanian, A., Watal, J. (2000), Can TRIPS serve as an enforcement mechanism for developing countries in the WTO? *Journal of International Economic Law* 3, 403–416.

Sykes, A.O. (2000), The remedy for breach of obligations under the WTO dispute settlement understanding: damages or specific performance. In: Bronckers, M.C.E.J., Quick, R. (Eds.), *New Directions in International Economic Law: Essays in Honour of John H. Jackson*. Kluwer, The Hague, pp. 347–357.

Trachtman, J.P. (1999), Direct effect and compliance. *European Journal of International Law* 10, 671.

van den Broek, N. (2001), Legal persuasion, political realism, and legitimacy: the European Court's recent treatment of the effect of WTO agreements in the EC legal order. *Journal of International Economic Law* 4, 411, 417.

van den Broek, N. (2003), Power paradoxes in enforcement and implementation of WTO dispute settlement reports. *Journal of World Trade* 37 (1), 127–162.

Weiss, E.B. (1997), Implementation, compliance and effectiveness. *American Society of International Law Proceedings* at the Theme Plenary Session, p. 58.

Wilson, B. (2007), Compliance by WTO members with adverse WTO dispute settlement rulings: the record to date. *Journal of International Economic Law* 10, 397–403, 398.

CHAPTER 18

Unintentional Breach in the DSU of the WTO: Consultation in the Shadow of Remedies

Indranil Chakraborty[a] and James C. Hartigan[b]

[a]*Department of Economics, National University of Singapore, Singapore 117570*
E-mail address: indro@nus.edu.sg
[b]*Department of Economics, University of Oklahoma, Norman, OK 73019-2103, USA*
E-mail address: hartigan@ou.edu

Abstract

Among the primary suggestions for reform of the Dispute Settlement Understanding (DSU) of the WTO has been remedies for noncompliance. Prior literature has considered remedies in the context of deliberate breach of commitments. The WTO increasingly has, however, been negotiating commitments in subjective areas of policy. Thus, we provide a model of the DSU under which members' interpretations of concessions differ. This induces disputes regarding violation of commitments.

The Dispute Settlement Body (DSB) has promoted compliance primarily through authorization of retaliation (prospective punishment) after expiration of a reasonable period of time for the implementation of a verdict. As has been noted, this does not compensate a complainant for a violation of obligations and enables the respondent to circumvent punishment for imposing a cost upon a member of the WTO by reforming its offending policy reasonably promptly. We consider retrospective penalties (compensation for a loss) with and without reinforcement by retaliation as alternative enforcement mechanisms and find that a simple retaliatory punishment scheme is preferable. A penalty is unenforceable, as a member that is unwilling to reform its policy after an adverse judgment can decline to provide compensation. A penalty reinforced by retaliation can reduce compliance relative to a simple prospective punishment by raising the cost of abiding by the judgement.

Remedies also affect the negotiation of commitments. Members are more willing to make and less willing to accept unenforceable commitments. In this regard, the simple prospective punishment scheme is preferable.

Keywords: WTO, DSB, DSU, trade disputes, retaliation, compensation, penalty, retrospective, prospective, punishment, concessions, obligations, commitments, treaty

Frontiers of Economics and Globalization
Volume 6 ISSN: 1574-8715
DOI: 10.1108/S1574-8715(2009)0000006021

JEL classifications: F13, K33, K42

1. Introduction

The General Agreements on Tariffs and Trade (GATT) ultimately could not succeed as an institution because it was never intended to serve that function. It was a multilateral treaty designed to be implemented under the auspices of the International Trade Organization (ITO). For various reasons, the GATT came into force before the ratification of the ITO through the Protocol of Provisional Application (PPA).[1] Because the ITO was never ratified, the GATT filled the void to the extent that it could. When it became apparent that the GATT entailed too many flaws to effectively serve the interests of its contracting parties and that reform was not viable, the Uruguay Round assumed the mandate of negotiating the establishment of a new institution to address the objectives of its prospective membership. The Uruguay Round concluded in 1994 with the creation of the World Trade Organization (WTO), which came into being in 1995.

One of the most important structural flaws of the GATT was its dispute settlement mechanism.[2] This was addressed by Article XXIII. It allowed for the establishment of a panel of experts, who acted in their own capacities, rather than as governmental representatives. They had the power to investigate and make rulings. As remedies, they could authorize contracting parties to suspend obligations to other contracting parties. The fundamental problem with this procedure was its reliance upon consensus, under which the losing contracting party could block approval of a panel report.

The Dispute Settlement Understanding (DSU) of the WTO has corrected or ameliorated several structural flaws of that under the GATT. First, it is unified, encompassing nearly all parts of the GATT/WTO system. Second, each complainant has the right of consultation with the member that is the subject of a complaint. Third, each complainant has the right to have the process initiated. Fourth, there is an appellate procedure. A fundamental difference from the GATT is that the DSU has been interpreted as requiring the consensus to block, rather than a consensus to adopt, a panel report.[3]

Compliance with commitments to lower trade barriers upon manufactured goods has been consistently high. However, this is likely because

---

[1] For further discussion, see Jackson (1997).

[2] The ITO was to have had an extensive dispute settlement procedure, so there was no need for the GATT to have included rigorous language pertaining to this matter. See Jackson (1997).

[3] See Jackson (1997) and www.wto.org. With a consensus to adopt, a single objection (including by the loser) could preclude implementation of the panel report. Under a consensus to block, the losing member has to persuade all members of the panel (including its adversary) to oppose implementation.

these commitments are objective and unambiguous. As the WTO embraces other negotiating fora such as Trade Related Intellectual Property Rights (TRIPS), Trade Related Investment Measures (TRIMS), the General Agreement on Trade in Services (GATS), the Sanitary and Phytosanitary (SPS) Agreement, and the Technical Barriers to Trade (TBT) Agreement, such objectivity and clarity becomes much more elusive. Improvements in dispute settlement implemented through the DSU, and the expansions of the negotiating agenda of the WTO into more subjective arenas may make serving as a referee for the resolution of disputes as important as trade liberalization in its future role.[4] As a concomitant to disputes, remedies have become a matter of increasing importance.[5]

What is important for our purposes is the remedies for noncompliance under the WTO. Mitchell (1997) has noted that the GATT has relied rarely on punishments to enforce compliance. She notes two aspects of WTO punishments that she regards as rendering them ineffectual. One is the length of time which consultation, investigation, and possible appeal consume.[6] The second, and more important for our purposes, is that punishment must terminate when noncompliance ceases. If a noncompliant signatory agrees to come into compliance within a reasonable period of time, retaliatory actions by the aggrieved member are not sanctioned by the WTO. Sanctions are authorized only if the noncompliant signatory, when adjudicated as noncompliant, continues in its offending policy. This characteristic is what we shall term "forward-looking punishments" or "prospective punishments." If a signatory can benefit by being out of compliance until apprehended, and then can avoid punishment by bringing the offending policy into compliance, it creates an incentive for what we term "strategic noncompliance."[7,8] Kovenock and Thursby (1992) have contended that limiting retaliation to what may occur within the GATT/WTO is unduly narrow, as retaliation may occur through the invocation of policies for which the GATT/WTO has not achieved agreement.[9] Ethier (Chapter 14, this volume), in modeling a treaty as an

[4] In the 47 years of the GATT, 101 panel reports were adopted. From the initiation of the DSU in 1995 until June 20, 2008, 378 disputes have been filed. See www.wto.org

[5] Epstein *et al.* (Chapter 5, this volume) disclose that overall compliance rates under the DSU are about 80 percent. However, full compliance is 66 percent and partial compliance is 13 percent. Hence noncompliance is 21 percent.

[6] Klimenko *et al.* (2008), on the contrary, demonstrate that delay in the restoration of cooperation that the DSU proceedings entail imposes a cost upon the defector that supports compliance and enforcement. This is in the absence of any monitoring ability or coercive power on the part of the Dispute Settlement Body (DSB).

[7] Examples include free riding and Prisoners' Dilemmas.

[8] As another example of a perverse incentive of a GATT rule, consider Hartigan (1996). He demonstrates that the requirement that a subsidy be currently in effect to be actionable creates an incentive to subsidize in the context of consumer switching costs when evidence of material injury is not immediately manifest.

[9] The example they invoke is Section 301 of US trade law.

incomplete contract, has identified the problem of reciprocal conflict in the negotiation of treaties, in that a signatory does not know *ex ante* if it will be an accuser or be accused. This results in constraints being imposed upon the ability to punish or to escape punishment.[10]

The contributions of these authors all assume implicitly that noncompliance is deliberate. That noncompliance with treaties may not be intentional has received considerable discussion amongst legal scholars. This is manifest through the contrasting of enforcement approaches to compliance based on the use or threat of sanctions, with management approaches based on the reduction of ambiguity regarding obligations and the provision of positive incentives for compliance.[11] A primary justification for the management approach is to allow for the adjustment of commitment levels to changing circumstances. Within the GATT/WTO, there has been an emphasis on a management approach. This is manifest through a nearly exclusive reliance upon prospective (retaliation contingent upon noncessation), rather than "retrospective" or "backward looking," penalties (compensation for the cost imposed) for noncompliance.[12,13] Jackson (1997) gives the primary justifications for this reliance as being a matter of national sovereignty, and the perception that the DSU was more of a political institution than a judicial one.[14] Schwartz and Sykes (2002) also have considered the possibility that noncompliance in

---

[10] Of course, there is scholarship that contrasts treaties with private contracts. See, for example, Setear (1996). Trachtman (2007) and Pelzman and Shoham (Chapter 15, this volume) on the contrary are sympathetic to the view that the WTO is a contract with "substantial incompleteness."

[11] Examples include Abbott and Snidal (1998), Frischmann (2003, 2005), Guzman (2002), and Koh (1997).

[12] As Frischmann (2003) discusses, there is a legal distinction between compensation and retaliation under the GATT/WTO. Retaliation refers to measures imposed by the aggrieved signatory. Compensation refers to measures imposed by the accused signatory. The most favored nation principle (MFN) may impose a constraint on compensation in that the offer of a lower trade barrier may have to extend to other members. Thus, the value of compensation offered by the accused and the remedy received by the complainant may not be equivalent. Retaliation through suspension of concessions to the accused does not violate MFN. Grossman and Mavroidis (2003) disclose that the DSU does not restrict compensation to a rebalancing requirement in contrast to authorization of suspension of concessions. See Trachtman (2007) for additional discussion.

[13] Note that retaliation, in principle, can be either forward looking or backward looking. In the forward looking case, retaliation by the complainant is authorized only if the respondent is informed that it is out of compliance and it does not revise the offending policy. In the backward looking case, retaliation by the complainant is sanctioned in substantially equivalent amount for the cost that has been imposed by the defendant. Similarly, the penalty could be forward or backward looking. It appears to be GATT/WTO practice to invoke retaliation prospectively and penalties retrospectively.

[14] Grane (2001) has noted a few exceptions in countervailing duty cases where a panel recommended retrospective compensation.

the GATT/WTO may be unintentional. However, they portray a treaty through analogy with a private contract.

This paper provides a formal model of treaty interpretation as a game of infinite horizon in three stages. In the initial stage, two countries negotiate and sign a treaty and form interpretations of the treaty's obligations.[15] In the second stage, they take actions based on those interpretations with an infinite horizon. The third stage arises if the interpretations of the signatories differ sufficiently for them to bring a dispute to the WTO.[16] The WTO makes an interpretation and authorizes a penalty (retrospective punishment) or a retaliatory action (prospective punishment). We also consider, as one of the possible reforms to the DSU, the possibility of retrospective penalties that are reinforced through retaliation. So as to focus on interpretation, we assume that all disagreements arise unintentionally. One of our results is that the choice of punishment schemes is dispositive. It affects the set of possible disputes that are brought to the WTO for adjudication. Through backward induction, this choice affects the set of treaties (the set of possible states of nature encompassed by the treaty) that are signed. We contend that the basic payoff structure in the treaty creating the WTO makes retrospective penalties ineffectual when disputes arise from a misconstrual of obligations.[17]A respondent that receives an adverse judgement and chooses to remain noncompliant will

---

[15] It should not be surprising that signatories could have differing interpretations of a treaty. For one thing, imprecise text may facilitate agreement. For another, it may enhance prospects for ratification by legislatures. States (circumstances) in which it is difficult to achieve enforcement, verify compliance, or are deemed to be *ex ante* of low probability may induce negotiators to make vague commitments. These may subsequently become the focus of disagreement.

[16] Although there is a substantial legal literature pertaining to disputes in treaties, the contributions by economists are still fairly limited. In addition to the papers by Ethier; Kovenock and Thursby; Klimenko, Ramey, and Watson; and Mitchell, Ludema (2001) modeled the DSU as a set of conditions imposed on the punishment equilibria of a repeated game, with the conditions consistent with the WTO principles of conciliation and reciprocity. Maggi (1999) demonstrates that a DSU can verify violations of a treaty and facilitate enforcement through the informing of nonparties to a dispute. Hungerford (1991) suggested that dispute settlement under the GATT was costly and unproductive. Bown (2002) distinguishes between legal (escape clause) and illegal responses to an exogenous shock between negotiating rounds of the WTO. If a signatory is apprehended after violating the treaty, a trade dispute arises as a form of renegotiation of the agreement. Bown (2004a) provides an empirical assessment of trade disputes and escape under the GATT. Bown (2004b) assesses the potential costs imposed by the GATT/WTO DSU that permit defendant signatories to commit to trade liberalization. Bown (2005), discussing the finding that antidumping (AD) remedies have been frequently inconsistent with GATT/TO obligations, analyzes the determinants of the decision to challenge US invocation of such remedies through the DSU. Butler and Hauser (2000) disclose that weak implementation procedures reinforce the incentives to violate the WTO agreement.

[17] This contrasts with critics of the remedies of the DSU of the WTO. Examples include Guzman (2002), Jackson (2004), Mitchell (1997), Spamann (2006), and Trachtman (2007).

also ignore the penalty. This is because the WTO is not a strong supranational authority and lacks independent enforcement power. Enforcement can be achieved only through authorized retaliation by the complainant. When a penalty is imposed with the authorization to retaliate if compensation is not provided and the offending policy is not reformed, compliance can be undermined relative to a simple retaliatory punishment. This is because the cost to the respondent of a misconstrual of obligations is potentially greater than under simple prospective punishment. The respondent may prefer to incur a retaliatory act than to reform its policy and incur the cost of compensation. Thus, we conclude that simple prospective punishment is the preferable enforcement scheme. This preference for prospective punishment extends to the incentives to make and accept commitments. Signatories are more willing to make and less willing to accept unenforceable commitments. To show this very simply, we consider a symmetric information framework and examine the effect of penalties and retaliatory actions on the incentives to sign a treaty and take a dispute to the WTO and a country's degree of compliance with adverse ruling by the WTO.

In the Section 2, we describe a basic model that allows us to analyze very generally the precise nature of the effects that the fundamental elements of a treaty have on the decisions as to whether or not to comply, whether or not to file a dispute, and whether or not to abide by the outcome of the dispute. We do so in a manner that we hope is accessible to legal scholars and political scientists, as well as economists.

2. *A simple model of a treaty*

We begin with some definitions, notation, and assumptions. A *treaty* between countries *A* and *B* is a broad description of actions to be taken by the two countries in different situations. The precise action that the treaty prescribes for a given situation is open to interpretation/perception of the action as well as the situation itself. In this paper, our objective is to focus on the relative efficacies of prospective punishment, retrospective punishment, and retrospective punishment reinforced by prospective punishment. We provide insights in the simplest possible manner. So we abstract from all strategic issues associated with arriving at an interpretation and assume that countries do not/cannot act strategically to arrive at a certain interpretation. Thus, after a treaty is written, each country arrives at an interpretation of the treaty through some publicly observed process (e.g., public debates or parliamentary proceedings).[18]

---

[18] We still admit that a country arrives at an interpretation to maximize its gain from the treaty, but we assume that it does so in a publicly observable manner. So the country cannot misrepresent its true interpretation at the WTO or other international organization.

We denote by σ_x the interpretation of the treaty by country $X(=A, B)$. Formally, a *dispute* arises whenever $\sigma_A \neq \sigma_B$, each country's payoff under its own interpretation is higher than that under the other country's interpretation, and the countries adhere to the actions under their own interpretations. Whenever a dispute arises, the countries can resolve it through consultation. If this fails, the aggrieved signatory can file under the DSU of the WTO and get a ruling on the "correct" interpretation s of the treaty, or choose to not act on the dispute. To keep the analysis tractable, we assume that the WTO rules either $s = \sigma_A$ or $s = \sigma_B$. We denote by $p(\sigma_A, \sigma_B) \equiv P(s = \sigma_A | \sigma_A, \sigma_B)$ the probability that the WTO rules in country A's favor. We assume, to avoid trivial cases, that $0 < p(\sigma_A, \sigma_B) < 1$ for all $\sigma_A \neq \sigma_B$.

A country can change the action taken under its own interpretation to that under the interpretation of the other country during the consultation phase. In this stage, there is no punishment. The country that agrees to revise its interpretation simply changes its offending policy. The *forward-looking punishment* takes effect when the action of a country is ruled to be incorrect by a panel of the WTO. In that case, the aggrieved country can be authorized by the DSB to undertake retaliatory action to inflict losses on the noncompliant country. It is the practice of the WTO to authorize the latter when a signatory has received an adverse ruling and does not comply after consultations regarding implementation of that ruling within a reasonable period of time. With a *backward-looking punishment*, a signatory that complies upon receiving a ruling that its policy is inconsistent with its obligations under the WTO incurs $\tau_i(\sigma_A, \sigma_B)$. Finally, if the respondent country does not comply with the ruling, and retaliation is not authorized or does not transpire, the payoffs are unaffected by the dispute.[19]

2.1. The timeline

The timeline of the game is of infinite horizon with the following stages observed:

Period 0:

1. A and B agree to a treaty without observing σ_A, σ_B, and s. At this point each country views σ_A, σ_B, and s as random variables on a support S.
2. Next, the countries observe σ_A and σ_B as common knowledge.

[19] We allow for the possibility that certain interpretations are such that they involve the action(s) of only one of the countries. In that case, it will not make sense if this country can take the other country to the WTO over its own action. Therefore, we assume that there are sets $\Delta_A, \Delta_B \subset \Sigma$ such that only country X can approach the WTO if $(\sigma_A, \sigma_B) \in \Delta_X$.

Period 1:

3. A and B take actions $\alpha_A(\sigma_A)$ and $\alpha_B(\sigma_B)$ based on their interpretations.
4. A country has the opportunity to change its action, possibly upon paying compensation or making substitute concessions to the other country. This can arise through consultation.

At the end of period 1 before period 2 begins:

5. If the dispute continues, the countries decide whether or not to request that a panel be convened by the DSB of the WTO.
6. The DSB (through the panel) rules s to be the correct interpretation of the treaty.
7. If the respondent's interpretation is affirmed by the WTO, no policy changes are mandated. If the complainant's interpretation is affirmed, consultations ensue regarding a reasonable period for implementation by the respondent. These consultations can entail further efforts at settlement.

In period 2 and every period that follows:

8. The countries comply, retaliate, or fail to comply with the treaty depending on what is relevant and appropriate in a given situation.[20]

2.2. Payoffs and penalties

We denote by $\Pi_X(\alpha|\sigma_X)$ the expected payoff (per period) to country X if action α is taken. When the panel of the WTO rules against a signatory, the country X may be directed to (i) comply and possibly pay the penalty $\tau_X(\sigma_A, \sigma_B)$, or it may choose to (ii) remain noncompliant and (possibly) face retaliatory action with associated payoffs $\Pi_X^{R_Y}(\sigma_A, \sigma_B)$, $(X, Y = A, B, X \neq Y)$. The superscript R_Y in the payoff is written to indicate that in this case the payoff is possibly the result of Y's (sanctioned) retaliatory action.[21]

A country X files under the DSU of the WTO if and only if $\Pi_X(\alpha|\sigma_X)$ is less than its expected payoff[22] from going to the DSB.[23] When the panel of

---

[20] Again, to keep the insight simple, we do not consider an appeal that is possible in reality.

[21] Our concept of a penalty or retaliation is general. In GATT/WTO jurisprudence, remedies are almost always measured in terms of trade flows. That is, a punishment embodying some metric of equivalence to the distortion in trade flows induced by a policy that is not in compliance with treaty obligations is authorized by the WTO. This remedy is introduced as a rebalancing of trade flows. Monetary penalties have been discussed recently. See Trachtman (2007) and Pelzman and Shoham (Chapter 15, this volume).

[22] We use expectation here in the sense that present actions have consequences that arise in the future. It is not a formal probabilistic specification, as we do not introduce a density function.

[23] In reality, there may be some costs associated with taking a dispute to the WTO, as well as in defending a signatory's interpretation. We ignore such costs for the purpose of our analysis here.

the WTO rules $s = \sigma_A$, country B can comply so that the future discounted payoff to A will be $[\delta/(1-\delta)]\ \Pi_A\ (\sigma_A|\sigma_A)$ with a discounting rate δ. If B is noncompliant, the future payoff under retaliation will be $[\delta/(1-\delta)]\Pi_A^{R_A}(\sigma_A, \sigma_B)$.

Upon complying B has an expected payoff of $[\delta/(1-\delta)]\ \Pi_B\ (\sigma_A|\sigma_B)$ and has an expected payoff of $[\delta/(1-\delta)]\Pi_B^{R_A}(\sigma_A,\sigma_B)$ upon being noncompliant under retaliation. If the WTO rules $s = \sigma_B$, then similarly A has the choice of complying, or not complying with the treaty.

If A complies, its expected payoff is given by $[\delta/(1-\delta)]\ \Pi_A\ (\sigma_B|\sigma_A)$. It is $[\delta/(1-\delta)]\Pi_A^{R_B}(\sigma_A, \sigma_B)$ if A is noncompliant and B retaliates. If A complies, then the expected payoff to B is given by $[\delta/(1-\delta)]\ \Pi_B\ (\sigma_B|\sigma_B)$, and it is given by $[\delta/(1-\delta)]\Pi_B^{R_B}(\sigma_A, \sigma_B)$ if A is noncompliant with retaliation by B.[24]

3. *The process of dispute resolution*

As the WTO has exhibited a preference for prospective punishments, rather than retrospective penalties, and complete compliance not always has transpired, we contrast these inducements for compliance. We also consider a retrospective penalty that is reinforced by retaliation. Because our solution invokes subgame perfection, we begin with the consultation subsequent to a ruling.[25] Our discussion is of interest only if the DSB affirms the complainant, in this case country A.[26]

3.1. Consultation regarding implementation of a ruling

3.1.1. Prospective penalties

If complainant signatory A receives an affirmative verdict, respondent country B can change its policy to comply with the ruling and receive a discounted future payoff of $[\delta/(1-\delta)]\ \Pi_B\ (\sigma_A|\sigma_B)$. Under noncompliance, there are two possible outcomes. It may receive $[\delta/(1-\delta)]\Pi_B^{R_A}(\sigma_A, \sigma_B)$ if A applies for and receives authority to retaliate from the DSB. As the complainant does not always pursue this authority and may not implement

[24] Since a signatory has never renounced the treaty establishing the WTO, we do not consider the payoff from abrogation.

[25] Consultations (negotiations) pertaining to a settlement can occur at any point in the dispute. However, we focus upon the two points in the process for which consultations are a formal step in the process.

[26] At this point, for simplicity, we suppose that disputes are unilateral, with country A being the complainant and B being the respondent. Almost all disputes are unilateral. An exception is the aircraft subsidy dispute between the EU and the United States. Since each disputant is utilizing a different form of subsidy, this could be viewed as a pair of unilateral disputes. The counterargument is that they are being considered together. As the preceding discussion indicates, our method is general, and can be adapted to bilateral disputes.

retaliation even if authorized, respondent B may receive $[\delta/(1-\delta)]\ \Pi_B(\sigma_B|\sigma_B)$.[27] For retaliation to be effective, we require $[\delta/(1-\delta)]\ \Pi_B^{R_A}(\sigma_A,\sigma_B)<[\delta/(1-\delta)]\Pi_B(\sigma_A|\sigma_B)<[\delta/(1-\delta)]\Pi_B(\sigma_B|\sigma_B)$. That is, the first inequality states that B must receive a lower payoff under retaliation than under compliance. The second inequality discloses that a country receives a lower payoff under the complainant's interpretation than under its own, an assumption that we made above. The latter is a necessary condition for a dispute. Recall that the DSU emphasizes a rebalancing of concessions in the authorization to retaliate. Thus, $\max[\delta/(1-\delta)\ \Pi_B^{R_A}(\sigma_A,\sigma_B),\delta/(1-\delta)\Pi_B(\sigma_A|\sigma_B)]$ determines the outcome of this authorization. If the rebalancing of concessions results in retaliation providing a lower payoff than revision of the offending policy, compliance will occur. If it does not, then noncompliance will transpire even under retaliation.[28] The question then is will retaliation be implemented? Recall that the payoff to A under retaliation is $[\delta/(1-\delta)]\Pi_B^{R_A}(\sigma_A,\sigma_B)$. Imposing a retaliatory act may increase or decrease a complainant's payoff.[29] Thus, whether or not retaliation is implemented by A is determined by $\max\{[\delta/(1-\delta)]\ \Pi_A^{R_A}(\sigma_A,\sigma_B),[\delta/(1-\delta)]\Pi_A(\sigma_A,\sigma_B)\}$. The second term in the maximand indicates that each country persists in its own interpretation if A does not retaliate under a unilateral dispute. The policy under dispute is that of B. Thus, the possible stage game payoff relationships are as follows:

1. $$\frac{\delta}{1-\delta}\Pi_A(\sigma_A,\sigma_B)>\frac{\delta}{1-\delta}\Pi_A^{R_A}(\sigma_A,\sigma_B),$$
$$\frac{\delta}{1-\delta}\Pi_B(\sigma_A|\sigma_B)>\frac{\delta}{1-\delta}\Pi_B^{R_A}(\sigma_A,\sigma_B)$$

   The complainant will not retaliate. Hence the respondent will not comply.

2. $$\frac{\delta}{1-\delta}\Pi_A(\sigma_A,\sigma_B)>\frac{\delta}{1-\delta}\Pi_A^{R_A}(\sigma_A,\sigma_B),$$
$$\frac{\delta}{1-\delta}\Pi_B(\sigma_A|\sigma_B)<\frac{\delta}{1-\delta}\Pi_B^{R_A}(\sigma_A,\sigma_B)$$

   The complainant will not retaliate. Hence the respondent will not comply.

3. $$\frac{\delta}{1-\delta}\Pi_A(\sigma_A,\sigma_B)<\frac{\delta}{1-\delta}\Pi_A^{R_A}(\sigma_A,\sigma_B),$$
$$\frac{\delta}{1-\delta}\Pi_B(\sigma_A|\sigma_B)>\frac{\delta}{1-\delta}\Pi_B^{R_A}(\sigma_A,\sigma_B)$$

---

[27] Instances of authorized retaliation are not common, and instances of actual retaliation are even less so. See, for example, Pelzman and Shoham (Chapter 15, this volume).

[28] There is no obligation to withdraw a measure that results in nonviolation nullification and impairment (N&I). See Trachtman (2007).

[29] Retaliatory tariffs impose deadweight losses that may not be completely counterbalanced in terms of trade improvement. On the contrary, retaliatory nonenforcement of the intellectual rights of the respondent may increase the complainant's payoff.

The complainant will retaliate. Hence the respondent complies and retaliation does not occur.

4.
$$\frac{\delta}{1-\delta}\Pi_A(\sigma_A,\sigma_B)<\frac{\delta}{1-\delta}\Pi_A^{R_A}(\sigma_A,\sigma_B),$$
$$\frac{\delta}{1-\delta}\Pi_B(\sigma_A|\sigma_B)<\frac{\delta}{1-\delta}\Pi_B^{R_A}(\sigma_A,\sigma_B)$$

The complainant will retaliate. The respondent does not comply and retaliation occurs.

Thus, the equilibrium for case (1) is $\{[\delta/(1-\delta)]\Pi_A(\sigma_A,\sigma_B),\ [\delta/(1-\delta)]\ \Pi_B(\sigma_B|\sigma_B)\}$. Case (2) also yields $\{[\delta/(1-\delta)]\Pi_A(\sigma_A,\sigma_B),\ [\delta/(1-\delta)]\ \Pi_B(\sigma_B|\sigma_B)\}$. The equilibrium for case (3) is $\{[\delta/(1-\delta)]\Pi_A(\sigma_A|\sigma_A),\ \delta/(1-\delta)\Pi_B(\sigma_A|\sigma_B)\}$. Case (4) generates $\{[\delta/(1-\delta)]\Pi_A^{R_A}(\sigma_A,\sigma_B),\ [\delta/(1-\delta)]\Pi_B^{R_A}(\sigma_A,\sigma_B)\}$. Hence the preferred prospective punishment scheme of the DSB can induce compliance, but it is not assured of doing so. However, negotiation will not affect the outcome, once a verdict has been rendered.

3.1.2. Retrospective penalties

Under retrospective penalties, respondent B will incur a penalty $\tau_B\,(\sigma_A,\sigma_B)$ that may restore complainant A to whole at the time of the judgement.[30] The respondent B incurs the penalty whether or not it revises its offending policy. Since $\Pi_B(\sigma_A|\sigma_B)-\tau_B(\sigma_A,\sigma_B)<\Pi_B(\sigma_B|\sigma_B)-\tau_B(\sigma_A,\sigma_B)$, compliance never occurs. What's more, the penalty is not paid. This is because the WTO is not a strong supranational authority and lacks enforcement powers other than the authorization of retaliation. Hence the retrospective penalty is not viable in the absence of the support of retaliation. This, in combination with a loss in authority of the WTO if its judgements were ignored, explains the rarity of retrospective penalties.[31]

3.1.3. Retrospective penalties enforced by retaliation[32]

The penalty $\tau_B\,(\sigma_A,\sigma_B)$ assessed against the respondent and awarded to the complainant provides restitution to signatory A for the loss induced by B's improper interpretation of its concessions under the WTO. When retaliation enforces the retrospective penalty, the respondent incurs the retaliatory action if it does not reform its policy *and* it does not pay

[30] Recall that Grossman and Mavroidis (2003) disclose that compensation is not subject to a rebalancing requirement.

[31] We believe that the loss of authority would be greater if a judgment and a penalty were ignored than when just the verdict is not implemented.

[32] The GATT/WTO has never combined prospective and retrospective remedies. However, Lawrence (2003) and Trachtman (2007) have contended that a calculation of damages that is based upon welfare must do so. See also Goh and Ziegler (2003) and Nzelibe (2005).

the penalty. If $[\delta/(1-\delta)]\Pi_A^{R_A}(\sigma_A,\sigma_B)+\tau_B(\sigma_A,\sigma_B)>[\delta/(1-\delta)]\Pi_A(\sigma_A,\sigma_B)$, the complainant is willing to retaliate. However, if $[\delta/(1-\delta)]\Pi_A(\sigma_A,\sigma_B)> [\delta/(1-\delta)]\Pi_A^{R_A}(\sigma_A,\sigma_B)$, it will not do so if compliance by B is not induced. If signatory B refuses to reform its policy, it will also decline to pay the penalty. Whether or not the prospect of enforcement by the complainant induces compliance by the respondent depends on $\max\{[\delta/(1-\delta)]\Pi_B^{R_A}(\sigma_A,\sigma_B),[\delta/(1-\delta)]\Pi_B(\sigma_A|\sigma_B)-\tau_B(\sigma_A,\sigma_B)\}$. If the first term in brackets is the larger, the respondent B does not comply with the assessment of the penalty and does not revise its invalid interpretation of its commitments. If the second term is larger, it both reforms its policy and mitigates the loss to the complainant A.[33] The introduction of the penalty may result in $[\delta/(1-\delta)]\Pi_B(\sigma_A|\sigma_B)>[\delta/(1-\delta)]\Pi_B^{R_A}(\sigma_A,\sigma_B)> [\delta/(1-\delta)]\Pi_B(\sigma_A|\sigma_B)-[\tau_B(\sigma_A,\sigma_B)]$. The effort to restore the complainant to whole undermines compliance in this instance. This can provide an opportunity for negotiation to facilitate compliance. The respondent can offer to comply if the retrospective penalty were at least incompletely reduced. If $[\delta/(1-\delta)]\Pi_B^{R_A}(\sigma_A,\sigma_B)<[(\delta/(1-\delta)]\Pi_B(\sigma_A|\sigma_B)-[\tau_B(\sigma_A,\sigma_B)]$, compliance is unaffected by the reinforcement of the penalty by retaliation. Compliance is enhanced by the retrospective penalty cum prospective retaliation if $[\delta/(1-\delta)]\Pi_A^{R_A}(\sigma_A,\sigma_B)<[\delta/(1-\delta)]\Pi_A(\sigma_A,\sigma_B)< [\delta/(1-\delta)]\Pi_A^{R_A}(\sigma_A,\sigma_B)+[\tau_B(\sigma_A,\sigma_B)]$ and $[\delta/(1-\delta)]\Pi_B^{R_A}(\sigma_A,\sigma_B)<[\delta/(1-\delta)]\Pi_B(\sigma_A|\sigma_B)-[\tau_B(\sigma_A,\sigma_B)]$. In this instance, the receipt of the penalty induces the aggrieved country A to retaliate when it would not in the absence of retrospective compensation for a violation of commitments. Since the respondent B will comply when faced with retaliation, compliance is enhanced. Thus, we have the following possibilities:

5.

$$\frac{\delta}{1-\delta}\Pi_A(\sigma_A,\sigma_B)>\frac{\delta}{1-\delta}\Pi_A^{R_A}(\sigma_A,\sigma_B)+\tau_B(\sigma_A,\sigma_B),$$
$$\frac{\delta}{1-\delta}\Pi_B^{R_A}(\sigma_A,\sigma_B)>\frac{\delta}{1-\delta}\Pi_B(\sigma_A|\sigma_B)-\tau_B(\sigma_A,\sigma_B)$$

The complainant will not retaliate. The respondent will not comply.

6.

$$\frac{\delta}{1-\delta}\Pi_A(\sigma_A,\sigma_B)>\frac{\delta}{1-\delta}\Pi_A^{R_A}(\sigma_A,\sigma_B)+\tau_B(\sigma_A,\sigma_B),$$
$$\frac{\delta}{1-\delta}\Pi_B^{R_A}(\sigma_A,\sigma_B)<\frac{\delta}{1-\delta}\Pi_B(\sigma_A|\sigma_B)-\tau_B(\sigma_A,\sigma_B)$$

[33] Whether or not the complainant is restored to whole depends on the magnitude (extent of rebalancing) of the penalty.

The complainant will not retaliate. Hence, the respondent will not comply.

7.
$$\frac{\delta}{1-\delta}\Pi_A(\sigma_A,\sigma_B)<\frac{\delta}{1-\delta}\Pi_A^{R_A}(\sigma_A,\sigma_B)<\frac{\delta}{1-\delta}\Pi_A^{R_A}(\sigma_A,\sigma_B)+\tau_B(\sigma_A,\sigma_B),$$
$$\frac{\delta}{1-\delta}\Pi_B^{R_A}(\sigma_A,\sigma_B)>\frac{\delta}{1-\delta}\Pi_B(\sigma_A|\sigma_B)-\tau_B(\sigma_A,\sigma_B)$$

The complainant will retaliate. The respondent will not comply.

8.
$$\frac{\delta}{1-\delta}\Pi_A(\sigma_A,\sigma_B)<\frac{\delta}{1-\delta}\Pi_A^{R_A}(\sigma_A,\sigma_B)<\frac{\delta}{1-\delta}\Pi_A^{R_A}(\sigma_A,\sigma_B)+\tau_B(\sigma_A,\sigma_B),$$
$$\frac{\delta}{1-\delta}\Pi_B^{R_A}(\sigma_A,\sigma_B)<\frac{\delta}{1-\delta}\Pi_B(\sigma_A|\sigma_B)-\tau_B(\sigma_A,\sigma_B)$$

The complainant will retaliate. Since the respondent complies, retaliation does not transpire.

9.
$$\frac{\delta}{1-\delta}\Pi_A^{R_A}(\sigma_A,\sigma_B)<\frac{\delta}{1-\delta}\Pi_A(\sigma_A,\sigma_B)<\frac{\delta}{1-\delta}\Pi_A^{R_A}(\sigma_A,\sigma_B)+\tau_B(\sigma_A,\sigma_B),$$
$$\frac{\delta}{1-\delta}\Pi_B^{R_A}(\sigma_A,\sigma_B)>\frac{\delta}{1-\delta}\Pi_B(\sigma_A|\sigma_B)-\tau_B(\sigma_A,\sigma_B)$$

The complainant willing to retaliate, but the respondent will not comply. Hence retaliation will not take place.

10.
$$\frac{\delta}{1-\delta}\Pi_A^{R_A}(\sigma_A,\sigma_B)<\frac{\delta}{1-\delta}\Pi_A(\sigma_A,\sigma_B)<\frac{\delta}{1-\delta}\Pi_A^{R_A}(\sigma_A,\sigma_B)+\tau_B(\sigma_A,\sigma_B),$$
$$\frac{\delta}{1-\delta}\Pi_B^{R_A}(\sigma_A,\sigma_B)<\frac{\delta}{1-\delta}\Pi_B(\sigma_A|\sigma_B)-\tau_B(\sigma_A,\sigma_B).$$

The complainant will retaliate. The respondent will comply. Hence, retaliation will not occur.

The equilibrium for case (5) is $[\delta/(1-\delta)]\Pi_A(\sigma_A,\sigma_B),[\delta/(1-\delta)]\Pi_B(\sigma_B|\sigma_B)$. Case (6) also generates $[\delta/(1-\delta)]\Pi_A(\sigma_A,\sigma_B),[\delta/(1-\delta)]\Pi_B(\sigma_B|\sigma_B)$. Case (7) yields an equilibrium of $[\delta/(1-\delta)]\Pi_A^{R_A}(\sigma_A,\sigma_B)$, $[\delta/(1-\delta)]\Pi_B^{R_A}(\sigma_A,\sigma_B)$. The equilibrium for case (8) is $[\delta/(1-\delta)]\Pi_A(\sigma_A|\sigma_A)+\tau_B(\sigma_A,\sigma_B),[\delta/(1-\delta)]\Pi_B(\sigma_A|\sigma_B)-\tau_B(\sigma_A,\sigma_B)$. Case (9) induces $[\delta(1-\delta)]\Pi_A(\sigma_A,\sigma_B),[\delta(1-\delta)]\Pi_B(\sigma_B|\sigma_B)$. Case (10) generates $[(\delta/(1-\delta)]\Pi_A(\sigma_A|\sigma_A)+\tau_B(\sigma_A,\sigma_B),[\delta/(1-\delta)]\Pi_B(\sigma_A|\sigma_B)-\tau_B(\sigma_A,\sigma_B)$. Note that possibilities for negotiation exist in case (7).

The mutually reinforcing use of prospective and retrospective punishment schemes can improve compliance, can leave compliance unaffected, or can undermine compliance relative to prospective retaliation in isolation. The latter conclusion is tempered by the possibility of a negotiated settlement.

3.2. The interpretation of the DSB

A complainant will seek formation of a panel when the expected benefit from doing so exceeds the presented discounted value of expected payoffs when each signatory persists in their differing interpretations of the treaty. Recall that the dispute is unilateral. That is, it pertains to a policy implemented by one of the members, in this case country B. The policy is discrete, and there are two possible interpretations by the panel: σ_A and σ_B. When the DSB receives a request for the formation of a panel, that panel either affirms the complaint by giving interpretation σ_A or endorses the interpretation of the respondent σ_B. There are no other possible interpretations given by the panel. That is, the panel must agree with one or the other disputant. We have, for simplicity, assumed that the filing of a complaint is costless. Thus, the complainant will request that a panel be convened if there are interpretations of the treaty under which enforcement of its construal of its commitments is enhanced. Thus, there are no panels under retrospective penalties because judgements by the DSB are not enforceable, and the expected benefit from the request for a panel is exactly zero.

With prospective punishment or retaliation, compliance by the respondent is not diminished and may increase relative to the absence of a remedy or to the retrospective punishment. Retaliation may also enhance A's payoff. Since $0 < p(\sigma_A, \sigma_B) < 1$, there is a net positive expected gain from the convening of a panel. Therefore, the formation of a panel is requested by the complainant. The complainant can do no worse than $[\delta/(1-\delta)]\Pi_A(\sigma_A, \sigma_B)$, which is what it would receive if it did not request a panel, and may do better.

When the rebalancing of concessions includes compensation for the loss accruing from an invalid interpretation by the respondent that preceded the filing of the complaint, together with enforcement through authorized retaliation, the equilibrium for this stage is not quite so transparent. Recall, in this regard, that compliance can be enhanced, be unaffected, or be undermined relative to simple retaliation. The payoff to A from requesting a panel when the DSB rules $s = \sigma_B$ is $[\delta/(1-\delta)]\Pi_A(\sigma_A, \sigma_B)$. In this circumstance, each country persists in its interpretation. Let Σ de-note the set of possible interpretations of commitments under the WTO. Thus, $\sigma_A, \sigma_B \in \Sigma$. These interpretations determine whether the outcome of a successful filing by A yields $[\delta/(1-\delta)]\Pi_A(\sigma_A, \sigma_B)$, $[\delta/(1-\delta)]\Pi_A(\sigma_A|\sigma_A)$, $[\delta/(1-\delta)]\Pi_A^{R_A}(\sigma_A, \sigma_B)$ or $\Pi_A(\sigma_A|\sigma_A) + \tau_B(\sigma_A, \sigma_B)$. Note that once again, the complainant cannot do worse than $[\delta/(1-\delta)]\Pi_A(\sigma_A, \sigma_B)$ and may do better. Invoking $p(\sigma_A, \sigma_B)$ together with these possible payoffs permits the determination of the expectation to A conditional on the DSB ruling $s = \sigma_A$. Combining this with the payoff when $s = \sigma_B$ and $1 - p(\sigma_A, \sigma_B)$ yields an expected payoff from requesting formation of a panel. This expectation is at least as great as the payoff when a panel is not requested. Hence, the equilibrium to this stage entails the request for the convening of a panel.[34]

3.3. The request for consultations

The initial stage of a dispute under the DSU is the request for consultations. As Epstein *et al.* disclose in Chapter 5, more than half of disputes with a recognized initiation date are settled before a panel ruling. When negotiation, rather than jurisprudence, determines the outcome, a conflict between compliance and settlement arises.[35] As Busch and Reinhardt (2000) consider, the DSU enhanced the rules orientation of settlement at the consultation stage, imparting a legal shadow over negotiations. We consider the shadow cast by the enforcement mechanisms that may be invoked by the DSB.

Analysis of the retrospective penalty is straightforward. Since restitution is unenforceable, a ruling $s = \sigma_A$ is not implemented. Thus, a request to convene a panel is not made by the complainant. Therefore, consultation will be unproductive. Hence, the aggrieved party will not request consultations.

Consultations pertaining to the implementation of a DSB decision may be productive under prospective penalties or retaliation. In contrast to retrospective penalties, a request for the convening of a panel will occur if consultation is not successful. There are two possible interpretations which are common knowledge at this stage. Thus, $p(\sigma_A, \sigma_B)$ permits the calculation of an expected benefit to each disputant from advancing to a formal dispute. These expectations are $E_A(\sigma_A, \sigma_B)$ and $E_B(\sigma_A, \sigma_B)$, respectively. If there is an interpretation $\hat{\sigma}_B \neq \sigma_B$ for the respondent's policy that yields $[\delta/(1-\delta)]\Pi_A(\hat{\sigma}_B|\sigma_A) > [\delta/(1-\delta)]E_A(\sigma_A, \sigma_B)$ and $[\delta/(1-\delta)]\Pi_B(\hat{\sigma}_B|\sigma_B) > [\delta/(1-\delta)]E_B(\sigma_A, \sigma_B)$, then the request for consultations can provide a successful negotiation and settlement.[36] It does, however, introduce the potential tension between settlement and compliance, as $\hat{\sigma}_B$ would not be the verdict of the DSB. It is consistent

[34] Because the cost of filing a complaint is assumed to be zero for simplicity, the choice between the simple prospective punishment scheme and a penalty reinforced by prospective punishment is trivial. However, this is not an innocuous assumption. With a sufficiently high cost of filing, the request for the formation of a panel may occur for simple retaliation, but not for retaliation cum the penalty.

[35] This is addressed by Pelzman and Shoham (Chapter 15, this volume).

[36] Note that $\hat{\sigma}_B$ may not be unique.

with casual observation that many disputes are settled at this stage under the shadow of prospective punishment.

Consultations regarding the implementation of a DSB decision may be fruitful when retrospective penalties are reinforced by prospective retaliation. As was noted earlier, success in the negotiation for the implementation makes compliance more likely, and the request for the formation of a panel will be made if consultation is not successful. This augments success of negotiation in the predecessor stage of consultation. Reasoning analogous to that for prospective retaliation yields $\tilde{\sigma}_B : \hat{\sigma}_B \neq \sigma_B \neq \hat{\sigma}_B$ as the settlement for the interpretation of *B*'s commitment under the WTO. Once again, the possibility of conflict between compliance and settlement may exist.

4. The negotiation of commitments

To the best of our knowledge, the literature has not addressed the connection between the negotiation of the agreement establishing the WTO and subsequent negotiating rounds under its auspices, and the remedies enforcing of the DSU. Through subgame perfection, the consultation regarding implementation of DSB jurisprudence affects the decision of a complainant to request the convening of a panel. The expected outcome of a formal dispute affects the decision to request consultations. The anticipated outcome of consultation affects the willingness to make and accept commitments at the various negotiating rounds of the WTO.

With retrospective penalties, a signatory is most willing to incur obligations and make commitments. This is because it can adhere to its own interpretation of its commitments without the risk of having to acquiesce to the construal of another member or a panel. However, as the negotiation of a round of trade agreements entails an exchange of commitments, the offers of concessions have the least value.

The cost of a mistaken interpretation cannot be avoided necessarily under prospective punishment. Hence a signatory is less willing to make concessions than under retrospective penalties. However, those commitments have greater value because they may not be circumscribed.

When retaliation is combined with a retrospective penalty, the cost of a misinterpretation cannot be increased. A respondent cannot be forced to incur more than the retaliatory punishment. Thus, the willingness to accept obligations is unaffected. Because compliance may be adversely affected, however, relative to the simple retaliatory scheme, these commitments are less valuable. Thus, while criticized for not producing a higher rate of compliance, simple prospective punishments appear to be the most rational enforcement mechanism.

5. Conclusions

The DSU of the WTO has been the subject of considerable criticism in the legal and economics literature. A substantial part of that criticism concerns the incentives for compliance with a signatory's commitments and the remedies for noncompliance with those obligations. We demonstrate that discussion of remedies must consider whether or not noncompliance is deliberate. Our analysis supposes that noncompliance arises as a misinterpretation of obligations, which we contend is quite plausible. It is inherent in the negotiation and ratification of treaties and is something to which the WTO becomes more vulnerable as it addresses nonobjective issues in trade policy. This is, in fact, what has been occurring in the last dozen years.

The GATT/WTO has relied on prospective (forward-looking) punishments that are not invoked if a defendant comes into compliance in a reasonable period of time. It has been contended that this provides an incentive for breach of commitments and precludes compensation of the complainant state for its losses. A system of liability rules under a unilateral decision to defect mandates retrospective (backward looking) penalties. In fact, one of the suggested reforms to the remedies permitted under the DSU is to validate efficient breach of commitments.[37] We disclose that when noncompliance is unintentional, prospective punishments are more conducive to compliance that retrospective penalties. Because the DSB is not a strong supranational authority, the penalty is as difficult to enforce as a judgement that a policy is not in compliance with the obligations of a respondent. What's more, reinforcing a liability rule with authorization to retaliate may be detrimental to compliance, as it may increase the cost of a requisite policy modification attendant to a misinterpretation of commitments relative to simple prospective punishments.

We also disclose that compliance and remedies affect the willingness to accept and make commitments. Because commitments that are not enforceable have no value, retrospective (compensatory) punishments are not conducive to acceptance of commitments. Confidence in commitments can be undermined by the reinforcement of retrospective punishment by retaliation. Hence, the prospective punishment scheme provides the strongest incentives to engage in an exchange in obligations.

[37] It is instructive to provide some perspective as to the potential use of penalties in the context of the WTO. In order to promote a system of efficient breach (benefits to the promisor exceed costs to the promissee), under which a state may unilaterally suspend its commitments and incur liability, it is necessary to utilize retrospective penalties. That permits compensation for a loss under a liability rule. However, this presumes that breach is deliberate. A possible reason that the WTO's invocation of retrospective remedies is rare may be that many disputes arise through the misinterpretation of obligations. A signatory may be unwilling to compensate when it did not violate with intent.

Acknowledgement

The authors thank without implicating participants at the Midwest International Economics Group Meetings.

References

Abbott, K., Snidal, D. (1998), Why states act through formal international organizations. *Journal of Conflict Resolution* 42, 3–32.

Bown, C.P. (2002), The economics of trade disputes, the GATT's article XXIII and the WTO's dispute settlement understanding. *Economics and Politics* 14, 283–323.

Bown, C.P. (2004a), Trade disputes and the implementation of protection under the GATT: an empirical assessment. *Journal of International Economics* 62, 263–294.

Bown, C.P. (2004b), On the economic success of GATT/WTO dispute settlement. *Review of Economics and Statistics* 86, 811–823.

Bown, C.P. (2005), Trade remedies and world trade organization dispute settlement: why so few are challenged. *Journal of Legal Studies* 34, 515–555.

Busch, M.L., Reinhardt, E. (2000), Bargaining in the shadow of the law: early settlement in GATT/WTO disputes. *Fordham International Law Journal* 24, 158–172.

Butler, M., Hauser, H. (2000), The WTO dispute settlement system: first assessment from an economic perspective. *Journal of Law, Economics and Organization* 16, 503–533.

Frischmann, B. (2003), A dynamic institutional theory of international law. *Buffalo Law Review* 51, 679–808.

Frischmann, B. (2005), A comparative analysis of compliance institutions in international trade law and international environmental law. In: Choi, E.K., Hartigan, J.C. (Eds.), *Handbook of International Trade Vol. II: Economic and Legal Analysis of Trade Policy and Institutions*. Blackwell, Oxford.

Goh, G., Ziegler, A.R. (2003), Retrospective remedies in the WTO after automotive leather. *Journal of International Economic Law* 6, 545–564.

Grane, P. (2001), Remedies under WTO Law. *Journal of International Economic Law* 4, 755–772.

Grossman, G.M., Mavroidis, P.C. (2003), Would've or should've? Impaired benefits due to copyright infringement. In: Horn, H-R., Mavroidis, P.C. (Eds.), *The WTO Case Law of 2001: The American Law Institute Reporters' Studies*. Cambridge University Press, Cambridge, pp. 281–299.

Guzman, A. (2002), A compliance based theory of international law. *California Law Review* 90, 1823–1888.

Hartigan, J.C. (1996), Perverse consequences of the GATT: export subsidies and switching costs. *Economica* 63, 53–61.

Hungerford, T.L. (1991), GATT: a cooperative equilibrium in a noncooperative trading regime? *Journal of International Economics* 31, 357–369.

Jackson, J.H. (1997), *The World Trading System: Law and Policy of International Economic Relations*, second ed. MIT Press, Cambridge.

Jackson, J.H. (2004), International law status of WTO dispute settlement reports: obligation to comply or option to "buy out". *American Journal of International Law* 109, 109–125.

Klimenko, M., Ramey, G., Watson, J. (2008), Recurrent trade agreements and the value of external enforcement. *Journal of International Economics* 74, 475–499.

Koh, H.H. (1997), Why do nations obey international law? *Yale Law Journal* 106, 2599–2659.

Kovenock, D., Thursby, M. (1992), GATT, dispute settlement, and cooperation. *Economics and Politics* 4, 51–70.

Lawrence, R.Z. (2003), *Crimes & Punishments? Retaliation Under the WTO*. Institute for International Economics, Washington, DC.

Ludema, R.D. (2001), Optimal international trade agreements and dispute procedures. *European Journal of Political Economy* 17, 355–376.

Maggi, G. (1999), The role of multilateral institutions in international trade cooperation. *American Economic Review* 89, 190–214.

Mitchell, S.K. (1997), Dispute settlement and cooperation: a note. *Economics and Politics* 9, 87–93.

Nzelibe, J. (2005), The credibility imperative: the political dynamics of retaliation in the World Trade Organization's dispute resolution mechanism. *Theoretical Inquiries in Law* 6, 215–254.

Schwartz, W.F., Sykes, A.O. (2002), The economic structure of renegotiation and dispute resolution in the World Trade Organization. *Journal of Legal Studies* 31, 179–204.

Setear, J. (1996), An iterative perspective on treaties: a synthesis of international relations theory and international law. *Harvard International Law Journal* 37, 139–229.

Spamann, H. (2006), The myth of "rebalancing" retaliation in WTO dispute settlement practice. *Journal of International Economic Law* 9, 31–79.

Trachtman, J.P. (2007), Building the WTO cathedral. *Stanford Journal of International Law* 43, 127–167.

World Trade Organization, www.wto.org

SUBJECT INDEX

www.ingramcontent.com/pod-product-compliance
Ingram Content Group UK Ltd.
Pitfield, Milton Keynes, MK11 3LW, UK
UKHW021033041026
15470UKWH00014B/1579

9 781848 552067